Health Psychology
Through the Life Span

Health Psychology Through the Life Span

Practice and Research Opportunities

Edited By

Robert J. Resnick
Ronald H. Rozensky

AMERICAN PSYCHOLOGICAL ASSOCIATION

WASHINGTON, DC

First printing November 1996
Second printing May 1997

Published by the
American Psychological Association
750 First Street, NE
Washington, DC

Copies may be ordered from
APA Order Department
P.O. Box 92984
Washington, DC 20090-2984

In the United Kingdom and Europe, copies may be ordered from
American Psychological Association
3 Henrietta Street
Covent Garden
London WC2E 8LU
England

Typeset in Goudy by Innodata Corporation, Publishing Services Division, Hanover, MD

Printer: Automated Graphic Systems, Inc., White Plains, MD
Cover designer: Minker Design, Bethesda, MD
Technical/production editors: Liliana Riahi and Valerie Montenegro

Library of Congress Cataloging-in-Publication Data
Health psychology through the life span : practice and research
   opportunities / edited by Robert J. Resnick and Ronald H. Rozensky.
          p.   cm.
      Includes bibliographical references and index.
      ISBN 1-55798-378-X (cb : acid-free paper). — ISBN 1-55798-391-7 (pb :
   acid-free paper)
      1. Clinical health psychology.   I. Resnick, Robert J.
   II. Rozensky, Ronald H.
      [DNLM: 1. Preventive Psychiatry.   2. Health Promotion.   WM 31.5
   H434   1996]
   R726.7.H439   1996
   616.89—dc20
   DNLM/DLC
   for Library of Congress   96-41438
                                                                                  CIP

British Library Cataloguing-in-Publication Data
A CIP record is available from the British Library.

Printed in the United States of America

CONTENTS

PART IV: PSYCHOLOGISTS IN DISEASE PREVENTION AND HEALTH PROMOTION

PART V: PSYCHOLOGISTS AS HEALTH CARE PROVIDERS

CONTRIBUTORS

Michael Antoni, *University of Miami*
David H. Barlow, *Center for Anxiety and Related Disorders at Boston University*
Cynthia D. Belar, *University of Florida Health Science Center*
Bruce G. Bender, *National Jewish Center for Immunology and Respiratory Medicine*
James H. Bray, *Baylor College of Medicine*
Anita B. Brown, *U.S. Army*
Lavonda Clarington, *University of Miami*
Jan L. Culbertson, *University of Oklahoma Health Sciences Center*
Nicholas A. Cummings, *Foundation for Behavioral Health, Scottsdale, Arizona*
Patrick H. DeLeon, *U.S. Senate Staff*
Garland Y. (Gary) DeNelsky, *Cleveland Clinic Foundation, Cleveland, Ohio*
Jacqueline Dunbar-Jacob, *University of Pittsburgh*
Jeanne Lawton Esler, *Center for Anxiety and Related Disorders at Boston University*
Tiffany M. Field, *University of Miami School of Medicine*
Ronald Friend, *State University of New York at Stony Brook*
Debra Greenwood, *University of Miami*
William C. Howell, *American Psychological Association*
Gail Ironson, *University of Miami*

James S. Jackson, *University of Michigan*
John B. Jemmott III, *Princeton University*
Loretta Sweet Jemmott, *University of Pennsylvania*
Alfred W. Kaszniak, *University of Arizona–Tucson*
Gwendolyn Puryear Keita, *American Psychological Association*
Daniel S. Kirschenbaum, *Center for Behavioral Medicine,
    Chicago, Illinois, and Northwestern University Medical School*
Gerald P. Koocher, *Harvard Medical School*
Jonathan A. Lerner, *Center for Anxiety and Related Disorders at
    Boston University*
Bruce S. Liese, *University of Kansas Medical Center*
G. Alan Marlatt, *University of Washington*
Scott McIntosh, *University of Miami*
Russ Newman, *American Psychological Association*
Denise C. Park, *University of Michigan*
James O. Prochaska, *University of Rhode Island*
Geoffrey M. Reed, *American Psychological Association*
Lynn P. Rehm, *University of Houston*
Robert J. Resnick, *Randolph-Macon College (formerly of the
    Health Sciences Center, Virginia Commonwealth University)*
Ronald H. Rozensky, *Evanston Hospital and Northwestern University
    Medical School*
Deanne Samuels, *University of Miami*
Elizabeth A. Schlenk, *University of Pittsburgh*
Carolyn S. Schroeder, *Chapel Hill Pediatrics, Chapel Hill, North Carolina*
Kimberly A. Seaton, *University of Kansas Medical Center*
John L. Sexton, *U.S. Navy*
Linda Sorhaindo, *University of Miami*
Petra Symister, *State University of New York at Stony Brook*
José Szapocznik, *University of Miami*
Manuel Tejeda, *University of Miami*
Steven M. Tovian, *Evanston Hospital and Northwestern University
    Medical School*
Belinda A. Vail, *University of Kansas Medical Center*

FOREWORD

As any intelligent person can see from the changes that have already occurred in our health care system and the even more profound changes likely to occur in the not-too-distant future, every American will be increasingly obliged to take care of his or her own health. Medical care is likely to become harder and costlier to obtain, particularly for illnesses that are deemed to be self-inflicted.

It is likely that in the future there will be more and more triaging done in deciding who should—and who should not—undergo costly, heroic medical treatments in a desperate attempt to prolong life. Triaging may not be limited just to catastrophic measures like transplants or bypass surgery. It is possible that more commonplace treatments, such as drugs to lower cholesterol or to control asthma, will also be decided on the basis of who most deserves them. Chances are, people with self-inflicted ailments are going to find themselves increasingly out on a limb, medically speaking, while those who work the hardest to stay healthy get the most help from the medical profession. What would you do with an asthmatic who smokes two packs of cigarettes a day? Supply her with inhalants, hospitalize her for every breathing crisis, or insist that she first quit smoking?

It should be obvious to anyone involved directly or indirectly with medical care that most of the costly, chronic diseases that afflict Americans today are largely a consequence of how they live their lives: what and how much they eat, how they move their bodies, how they manage stress, whether they abuse alcohol or drugs or smoke cigarettes, and even whether they use seat belts. If you take an honest look at how Americans live, you might be forced to conclude that most have a death wish. Far worse, though, than dying is living longer while ill. Chronic, debilitating, and fun-robbing diseases tarnish far too many Americans' so-called golden years.

This, now, is the challenge facing psychologists in the late twentieth century and beyond: How to help people adopt and stick with lifestyle changes that foster continuing good health. We all can, if we choose to, achieve the goal established for humanity by the ancient Greeks: to die young—as late in life as possible.

We are unlikely to get much help from physicians, most of whom are not schooled in behavior modification. Psychologists have the largest role to play in improving the nation's health because psychologists are specialists in understanding behavior and how to change it. Psychologists probably know better than any health professional how to get inside a person's mind, how to change attitudes from helpless and hopeless to the determined optimism of *The Little Engine That Could*. Self-belief is the essential foundation for action.

Cigarette smoking is a good example. Nicotine is an addictive drug, and smoking is an addictive behavior. The use of tobacco is the single most health-damaging and costly habit in America today. But it is more than just health robbing, life shortening, and expensive. Many people find it to be disgusting and antisocial. If you walk the streets of any metropolitan area during working hours, you would think there's been an explosion of prostitution in America. In nearly every doorway, there are young women standing around puffing on cigarettes.

We will make little or no progress in curbing this noxious behavior without the input of psychological principles and techniques, first, to help convince people that they can quit; next, to inspire them to want to quit; then, to help them actually quit; and, finally, to help them repeat the process if they should backslide.

Smokers persist in their habit because it makes them feel better immediately. To quit, it helps to focus on the immediate benefits of becoming a former smoker. These include loss of odor from hair, clothes, house, car, and breath; increased stamina and reduced fatigue; relief from that nagging, chronic cough and coughed-up phlegm; greater resistance to respiratory infections like colds and flu (not just for the smoker who quits but also for the smoker's family and coworkers); and money saved. I know one former smoker who put the money she used to spend on cigarettes into a piggy bank. Before she knew it, she had saved enough to take a trip to Europe!

The same applies to other health-promoting habits: eating properly, exercising regularly, and controlling stress. I think the secret to progress in these areas is to dwell not on long-term benefits, but on the immediate rewards of a healthier lifestyle. These rewards include looking better, feeling better, having more energy, becoming more productive, and being a nicer person to live with and work with.

Of course, before one can help others achieve these goals, he or she would do well to set a good example by adopting a healthier lifestyle. I hear two common complaints about living healthfully. One is, "I don't have time"; the other is, "A healthy life really isn't any longer, it just seems that way." I submit that neither of these excuses has any real validity. I and millions of others like me have proved that a healthy life is not a life of deprivation and self-denial. Rather, it is a full, satisfying, and enjoyable life, filled with delicious, belly-filling foods, pleasurable activities, and rewarding work, with ample time left for rest and relaxation.

I never say "never." The hallmarks of a successful, healthful diet are moderation, not deprivation; variety, not limitation; and gradual, evolutionary change, not revolution. Revolutions only inspire counter-revolutions. I advise people to change just 1 meal a week. Assuming that most people eat 15 to 21 meals a week, within just 4 months, they will be eating significantly better. And they will be far less likely to miss eating the old way and less apt to fall back into their former, disease-promoting habits.

The best way to convince people that exercise is worth the effort is to focus on the immediate rewards of becoming physically active: more energy, greater productivity, improved appearance, higher self-esteem, less stress, and less depression. Exercise doesn't take time, it makes time, by making one a more efficient person, able to accomplish more in less time with less fatigue. Plus, a person can then eat more! Not only does exercise use extra calories while one exercises, but it also increases caloric burn after one stops exercising. Exercise helps a person shed body fat and put on lean muscle tissue. Pound for pound, muscle uses far more calories than fat does. So one can eat more without gaining or can lose weight without going on a diet. Also, pound for pound, muscle tissue takes up less room than fat tissue does, so even if a person does not lose an ounce, she or he will lose inches and sizes by becoming well-muscled instead of well-fatted.

Of course, psychologists do not have to be told about the value of physical activity in countering depression, the emotional epidemic of the late twentieth century. I know a number of therapists who decline to treat depression unless the patient agrees to participate in a regular exercise program. Physical activity helped my husband not only in quitting smoking, and, I might add, quitting without gaining a significant amount of weight, but also in overcoming depression. If more people reached for their running shoes instead of the cookie jar when they felt in need of a lift, there would be far fewer overweight, unhappy people in this country.

Perhaps from the perspective of a psychologist, the most critical aspect of a healthful life is stress management. Regular physical activity has helped me change from a Type A person to a Type A minus! I might like to be a Type B, but it's just not my style. However, Type A minus is a lot better than Type A. Whereas I used to allow 15 minutes to get someplace that took 20 minutes to get to—always trying to do one more thing before I left and being late and anxious even before I started out—I now allow 30 minutes instead. That way, if anything occurs en route to delay me, I will still most likely arrive on time. And if the delay is great enough to make me late, I can say to myself, "It's not my fault. I did everything reasonable to get there when I was supposed to." And that little message to myself can almost always avert a health-damaging stress reaction.

People also must learn to put distressing matters into perspective. Medical evidence strongly indicates that it is not so much the major stressors like death and divorce that are health robbing. It is, rather, how people react to nitty-gritty everyday annoyances that wears down their body's ability to resist disease. I have, for the most part, learned that when things go wrong, I try to fix what I can fix, and if it is something out of my control, I seek a way around it or try to ignore it. Currently, far too many Americans use cigarettes, alcohol, and drugs to help control stress and, in the process, undermine their health even more than the damage caused by the stress itself.

A final thought: Many people are very fatalistic about their health. In former times, they might have said, "It's all in the cards," suggesting that their medical fate is predetermined. Today they say, "It's all in my genes, and there's nothing I can do about it." At this point, at least, changing one's potentially health-robbing genes is not a readily available option, although in the not-too-distant future, it may become a reality for more and more people. For now, it is important to remember that the vast majority of unhealthy genes do not predict certain doom. Rather, they establish a predisposition. Predispositions need a conducive environment in which to express themselves. If you do not give your unhealthy genes a chance to act, they may never do their dirty work, at least not before you are good and ready to depart this world. A "bad" family medical history should not be considered a portent of doom. Rather, it should be welcomed as an opportunity to do whatever you can to keep those nasty genes from ever expressing themselves.

Psychologists have the tools to help people realize that opportunity. Now, go to it!

JANE E. BRODY
Personal Health columnist
The New York Times

ACKNOWLEDGMENTS

We would like to thank the following people, whose hard work helped to make this volume possible: Drs. Norman B. Anderson, Thomas J. Boll, James H. Bray, Sandra Haber, Jean Kristeller, Alan I. Leshner, Ruby Takanishi, and Diane J. Willis, as well as Jane E. Brody, William Coltellaro, Joanne Zaslow, Judy Strassburger, Mayella Valero, and Liz Kaplinski.

1

INTRODUCTION

ROBERT J. RESNICK and RONALD H. ROZENSKY

Disease is not the accident of the individual, nor even of the generation, but of life itself. In some form, and to some degree or other,
it is one of the permanent conditions of life.

Henry David Thoreau

Across the life span, in all developmental stages, we must face
challenges to our health and our well-being. These personal challenges
can include ensuring a healthy lifestyle or can be a direct reaction to
the demands of coping with illness. As a profession, psychology has long
been in the forefront of the scientific inquiry into the understanding of
health and heath care, as well as the treatment of those suffering from
acute illnesses and chronic or terminal disease.

The decade of the 1990s began with a call to psychologists to
become involved in both psychological health care practice and scientific
investigation beyond our traditional role as experts in mental health.
VandenBos, DeLeon, and Belar (1991) stated that psychology "must be
viewed, at a minimum, as a physical health *and* mental health profession—or in short, as a health profession" (p. 444). From a health policy
standpoint, DeLeon (1991) highlighted the importance of psychology
becoming clearly seen as a health care profession with his reminder that
health and well-being are still equated with medicine and physicians
and, thus, allocation of funding for clinical training, research, and even
direct services will tend to go in the direction of those professions
identified with health. Reviewing the trends in the field, DeLeon (1991)

noted that "psychology's survival (and astonishing growth) within medical settings has very significant ramifications for all elements of the profession and shows very good promise for our probable future" (p. 616).

COLLABORATIVE PRACTICE AND HEALTH PSYCHOLOGY

In answer to this challenge of professional redefinition and identity, Newman and Rozensky (1995) pointed out that "psychologists have functioned as *de facto* primary care providers during a sizable part of our discipline's history" (p. 3). Supporting this point, Bray and Rogers (1995) detailed a collaborative practice model for psychologists and physicians in primary care medicine, whereas Morris and Barron (1996) pointed out that for decades, in rural America, psychologists have been involved with primary health care. Psychologists have come to increasingly see primary care physicians as allies. Pace, Chaney, Mullins, and Olson (1995) described how "primary care physicians have access to patients in need of psychological services and are concerned for the health and welfare of these patients" (p. 129). By maintaining appropriate communications, educating physicians about psychological services, and focusing on a problem-oriented method of consultation (Pace et al., 1995), the psychologist can enhance coordination of services in the primary care medical setting. This certainly benefits the patient and his or her family, as well as enhancing the viability of, and visibility of, psychology as a health care profession.

McDaniel (1995) reminded us that much can be done to heal the mind–body split in the day-to-day practice of health care, even though the Cartesian view of the separate mind and body "remains dominant in our society today" (p. 117), both philosophically and in clinical practice. Melamed (1995) looked to researchers, as well, to help heal this duality by asking the "biomedical and psychological research communities to gather indices of each other's spheres of interest so that causal relationships can be examined" (p. 230). Carr (1996) challenged psychologists to not perpetuate the mind–body segregation and to help physicians, through their medical education, bridge the gap between biological and psychological functioning.

Matarazzo (1994) pointed to this bridge, noting that "after a century of benign neglect, physicians and psychologists have rediscovered a common ground in the arena labeled health and behavior" (p. 7). Illustrating this growth in collaborative practice between medicine and psychology, Siegel (1995) reported that "psychologists in medical settings are no longer housed exclusively within departments of psychiatry or psychiatric units. Instead, they are associated with almost every medical subspecialty that is present in health care settings" (p. 342). Furthermore, Holloway

(1995) and Liese, Shepherd, Cameron, and Ojeleye (1995) described how psychologists actually have shaped the practice of clinical medicine as faculty members in formal educational programming for physicians in medical schools and residencies. Reflecting this foothold in health care settings, in 1993, almost 35% of psychologists who paid the American Psychological Association special assessment identified themselves as engaged in full- or part-time practice in hospitals, clinics, or medical–psychological group practices (American Psychological Association Office of Demographic, Employment, and Educational Research, 1993).

In 1995, there were 65 identified doctoral training programs in health psychology (American Psychological Association Division of Health Psychology, 1995). In 1995, 327 of the 525 accredited internship sites had a rotation in behavioral medicine or health psychology (J. Kahout, personal communication, January 18, 1996). Additionally, the number of postdoctoral training opportunities in health psychology is approaching 600 (A. Wiens, personal communication, January 18, 1996). Relevant divisions within the American Psychological Association—for example, Health Psychology, Neuropsychology, and Rehabilitation Psychology—have enjoyed substantial growth in the 1990s, again reflecting broad interest in psychological health care. Dorken, Stapp, and VandenBos (1986) reported that in the decade prior to their report, there was a 125% increase in the number of psychologists who practice in health care settings. Clearly, the integration of mind–body, of psychology and health, has been occurring and is continuing to occur not only in training sites but in employment settings as well.

ORGANIZATION OF THIS TEXT

Frank and Ross (1995) reminded us that "emerging health care delivery systems require a professional psychologist who has broad skills to treat health problems" (p. 524). Toward that end, the 1995 Presidential Miniconvention, "To Your Health: Psychology Through the Life Span," held as part of the 103rd Annual Convention of the American Psychological Association, brought together over 60 psychologists with expertise in various aspects of life span development, health, illness, and behavior. Discussion ranged from prevention of illness to health care solutions, from psychologists working alongside primary care physicians to the broad scope of practice of psychologists found in tertiary care facilities, from psychologists treating medically ill children to the practice of geriatric psychology. The excellent attendance and active participation of attendees during this 3-day event again speak to the interest and importance of psychologists' roles in all areas of health care.

This book was inspired by the exciting discussions that took place during the Miniconvention. The major purpose of this book is to provide the reader with a survey of clinical and scientific issues across a wide range of practice and research topics in health care. It offers a variety of approaches and perspectives from research-based clinical programs to scientific challenges, to help clarify basic and applied health care problems; from clinically based health care programs and strong opinions on present-day issues of care to future trends in health care and the evolution of psychology from a mental health field to a profession that addresses the full spectrum of health care concerns.

The practicing health psychologist should find a useful review of primary and tertiary care treatment and research areas within the context of a developmental or life span approach to health. The practicing clinical psychologist who wishes to begin to explore expanding practice opportunities into health care will find a survey of topics that highlights the depth of knowledge necessary to successfully and ethically expand her or his scope of practice with medically ill patients and their families. The student, intern, or postdoctoral fellow will be able to explore a wide range of practice and research opportunities that will help shape their educational goals and training experiences, as well as help clarify issues related to career choices and direction. Readers of this text who work exclusively in the realm of research will have the opportunity to read about those clinical challenges in search of research answers as well as research topics in need of further study.

Beyond this introduction, the book is divided into five sections. Part I: Overview presents a discussion of the evolution and future directions of the field of psychology as a health care discipline, not just a mental health profession. This section of the book focuses on a life-course perspective while attending to the realities of the changes in health care financing. Part II: Psychologists in Primary Care Settings provides eight chapters that first describe the concepts of collaborative practice and the practical issues psychologists should address when practicing with physicians in medical settings. Prevalent health care issues in primary care—such as anxiety, depression, weight control, substance abuse, and attention deficit hyperactivity disorder—are discussed by experts in those fields, who offer the reader both clinical and scientific reviews of those topics, along with practical, clinical programming suggestions. Part III: Psychologists in Tertiary Care Settings highlights seven of the areas of clinical care in which psychologists are making substantial contributions to the scientific and clinical understanding, as well as treatment, of long-term illnesses. Experts in such clinical areas as pediatric oncology, respiratory medicine, Alzheimer's disease, renal disease, urological diseases, pain and stress management, and compliance to treatment offer a picture of both the wide range of services provided by psychologists and the scientific knowledge supporting that practice. In the four chapters in Part IV: Psychologists in Disease Prevention and Health Promotion, the clinical and research activities of psychologists in enhancing healthy lifestyles are presented. Experts in smoking cessation, reduction of binge drinking, teen pregnancy prevention, and HIV/AIDS and sexually transmitted disease reduction present the reader with answers to present-day problems. Finally, in Part V: Psychologists as Health Care Providers, the reader is challenged to approach psychology from a public policy vantage point, for the betterment of both society and our profession. Leaders in practice, science, and education offer comments to help direct psychology's continued evolution as a health care profession.

REFERENCES

American Psychological Association, Division of Health Psychology. (1995). *Doctoral training programs in health psychology* (3rd ed.). Washington, DC: Author.

Bray, J. H., & Rogers, J. C. (1995). Linking psychologists and family physicians for collaborative practice. *Professional Psychology: Research and Practice, 26*, 132–138.

Carr, J. E. (1996). Psychology and mind–body segregation: Are we part of the problem? *Journal of Clinical Psychology in Medical Settings*, 141–144.

DeLeon, P. H. (1991). Afterword. In J. J. Sweet, R. H. Rozensky, & S. M. Tovian (Eds.), *Handbook of clinical psychology in medical settings* (pp. 615–618). New York: Plenum.

Dorken, H., Stapp, J., & VandenBos, G. (1986). Licensed psychologists: A decade of major growth. In H. Dorken & associates (Eds.), *Professional psychology in transition: Meeting today's challenges* (pp. 3–19). San Francisco: Jossey-Bass.

Frank, R. G., & Ross, M. J. (1995). The changing workforce: The role of health psychology. *Health Psychology, 14*, 519–525.

Holloway, R. L. (1995). Building a primary care discipline: Notes from a psychologist in family medicine. *Journal of Clinical Psychology in Medical Settings, 2*, 7–20.

Liese, B. S., Shepherd, D. D., Cameron, C. L., & Ojeleye, A. E. (1995). Teaching psychological knowledge and skills to family physicians. *Journal of Clinical Psychology in Medical Settings, 2*, 21–38.

Matarazzo, J. D. (1994). Health and behavior: The coming together of science and practice in psychology and medicine after a century of benign neglect. *Journal of Clinical Psychology in Medical Settings, 1*, 7–40.

McDaniel, S. H. (1995). Collaboration between psychologists and family physicians: Implementing the biopsychosocial model. *Professional Psychology: Research and Practice, 26*, 117–122.

Melamed, B. G. (1995). The interface between physical and mental disorders: The need to dismantle the biopsychosocialneuroimmunological model of disease. *Journal of Clinical Psychology in Medical Settings, 2*, 225–231.

Morris, J. A., & Barron, J. (Eds.). (1996). *Rural hospital primer for psychologists.* Washington, DC: American Psychological Association.

Newman, R., & Rozensky, R. (1995). Psychology and primary care: Evolving traditions. *Journal of Clinical Psychology in Medical Settings, 2*, 2–6.

Pace, T. M., Chaney, J. M., Mullins, L. L., & Olson, R. A. (1995). Psychology consultation with primary care physicians: Obstacles and opportunities in the medical setting. *Professional Psychology: Research and Practice, 26*, 123–131.

Siegel, L. J. (1995). What will be the role of psychology in health care settings of the future? *Professional Psychology: Research and Practice, 26*, 341–365.

VandenBos, G. R., DeLeon, P. H., & Belar, C. D. (1991). How many psychologists are needed? It's too early to know! *Professional Psychology: Research and Practice, 22*, 441–448.

I

OVERVIEW

INTRODUCTION

Health care is changing, driven by improved clinical techniques that are based on a growth in scientific inquiry into health and wellness as well as spurred on by dramatic shifts in health care financing. Psychology, as a major health care field, is being influenced greatly by, as well as helping to shape, these changes. The overview section of this book is designed to set the stage for the following chapters, which focus on specific clinical or research topics that relate to psychology's place in the overall health care enterprise.

Four major themes are set forth in this section. The first is that the profession of psychology is evolving into a true health care profession, and the Cartesian mind–body split will have limited utility in any comprehensive understanding of health or health care. The second theme is that, in regard to both wellness and illness, a life-course perspective that focuses on all developmental stages of human growth and health is a key in building that comprehensive understanding. The third theme is that the balanced approach to building that comprehensive knowledge base should be founded on the interplay between scientific and clinical practice. This interaction not only defines psychology but also makes it a powerful profession in shaping the health care field. The final theme is that no matter how sound the clinical practice or scientific knowledge base, there are both political and financial realities that any psychologist must attend to in order to keep the field and his or her practice or research opportunities viable.

In chapter 2, "Psychology as a Health Care Profession: Its Evolution and Future Directions," Russ Newman and Geoffrey M. Reed look briefly at our field's evolution as a health care profession and the economic forces influencing clinical practice. They then provide an optimistic, visionary depiction of the strong future role psychologists will being taking as primary care professionals. On the basis of the profession's successful history of advocating for mental health care, Newman and Reed describe psychology's transition in defining itself as a (primary) health care discipline, a task that will be difficult, necessary, and ultimately successful.

From a more somber, business-oriented, vantage point, Nicholas A. Cummings, a pioneer in managed behavioral health care, details his view that psychology lost its opportunity to control managed care in the 1980s, in chapter 3, "The New Structure of Health Care and a Role for Psychology." However, he believes that in the near future, through the building of megaprovider organizations, those practitioners who are most adaptable to changes in both financial incentives and practice patterns will regain control of health care.

In chapter 4, "A Life-Course Perspective on Physical and Psychological Health," James S. Jackson presents a new perspective on health, which takes the patient's life course and development into consideration. The author uses minority life-course issues to illustrate his overall appeal for a scientific understanding of how the economic, social, and psychological lives of all individuals are understood and explained in the context of a historical context, structural disadvantages in the environment, and blocked mobility opportunities.

In chapter 5, "Aging, Health, and Behavior: The Interplay Between Basic and Applied Science," Denise C. Park clearly illustrates how basic and applied science evolve together with significant utility for both the scientist and practitioner. This chapter heightens the reader's awareness of some of the issues surrounding our aging population. The author focuses on her own scientific work on the psychosocial and cognitive components of medication adherence in older adults, emphasizing how behavioral science can maintain health and vitality into later life.

Cynthia D. Belar, in chapter 6, "A Proposal for an Expanded View of Health and Psychology: The Integration of Behavior and Health," completes the overview by reiterating and expanding on data, perspectives, and information presented in earlier chapters. She challenges the reader to look at the integration of mind and body and avoid any separation of behavioral health from health in general. This then prepares the reader to take an expanded view of the role of both psychological principles and the roles of psychologists in all areas of health care. This chapter forms a natural stepping-off point to look at the role of psychology in primary care, tertiary care, and prevention and wellness.

2

PSYCHOLOGY AS A HEALTH CARE PROFESSION: ITS EVOLUTION AND FUTURE DIRECTIONS

RUSS NEWMAN and GEOFFREY M. REED

In this chapter, we examine the ways in which health care and health care policy in the United States have changed over time. We look at how psychology has responded, in turn, shaping the system. We consider the implications of this history for the current and future direction of psychology as a field and for individual practitioners. This chapter is not intended as a history of how our body of knowledge and clinical skills have evolved over time and now apply to various aspects of health care, topics well covered in other chapters of this book. Rather, our intention is to illuminate the current status of psychology as an evolving health care profession, by examining some of the forces acting on it, and to consider the implications for the future path of our profession.

PSYCHOLOGY AND MENTAL HEALTH POLICY

As has been both pragmatic and appropriate, policy development, to date, in the field of psychology has focused primarily on mental health.

Before the mid-twentieth century, mental health policy had been seen as a state issue and a welfare issue (Kiesler, 1992). Federal policy focusing on mental health began to develop with the establishment of the National Institute of Mental Health (NIMH) in the late 1940s and the Joint Commission on Mental Health and Illness in the 1950s. It was not until the passage of the Community Mental Health Centers Act of 1963, however, that mental health policy was separated from state mental hospitals. This legislation was intended to make mental health care readily available to all Americans through community-based clinics. It made the community mental health system and NIMH the primary players in mental health policy. This lasted until 1981, when the Omnibus Budget Reconciliation Act effectively eliminated both the federal government's commitment to a formal community mental health system and the NIMH role in mental health service delivery.

Perhaps the ultimate achievement of mental health advocacy was the inclusion of mental health in both Medicare and Medicaid legislation passed in 1965. Largely based on this precedent, efforts to gain recognition and reimbursement for mental health services from private insurance carriers were quite successful during the 1960s and 1970s (Cummings & VandenBos, 1983). Mental health services were also included in the Health Maintenance Organization (HMO) Act of 1973. To qualify for federal subsidies, HMOs were required to offer outpatient mental health services, crisis intervention services, and drug and alcohol abuse treatment (DeLeon, VandenBos, & Bulatao, 1991). This has become increasingly important for psychology as progressively larger proportions of the private insurance market and the Medicare and Medicaid populations have been shifted to HMO-based care.

Pursuing the strategy of advocating for, and attempting to exercise influence in, the area of mental health policy has made sense for psychology. As a young and developing profession, psychology's strongest case for inclusion in service delivery could be made in the area of mental health; and we were able to make it quite successfully. However, in this chapter, we argue that to view our development and influence as a mental health care profession as the end goal for psychology will ultimately be unnecessarily limiting. For example, although the inclusion of psychologists in mental health services is well established under Medicare, only 3% of Medicare funding is spent for mental health services (Kiesler, 1992). Although the diagnosis and treatment of mental illness is a centrally important undertaking that must remain an integral component of psychology, we suggest that our self-conception as a mental health profession should be viewed as but a step on the way to much broader involvement and influence.

The next step is to develop patterns of practice, marketplace activity, and supporting policy that position psychology as a true health care profession. This will, no doubt, be a difficult transition, both within and outside the profession. Yet, this step is critical to the continued growth—if not survival—of psychology at a time when health care is becoming increasingly integrated and a past emphasis on specialty care is being replaced with an emphasis on primary care. This step will challenge psychologists "to look beyond diagnostic categories and disciplinary boundaries, beyond the dysfunctional distinction between mind and body, and beyond traditional psychotherapeutic interventions" (Friedman, Sobel, Myers, Caudill, & Benson, 1995, p. 509). Only by doing so will psychology be able to have a voice in how to most effectively and efficiently provide services in the presently evolving health care system.

A BRIEF HISTORY OF HEALTH CARE

VandenBos (1993) provided a history of the health care system in the United States. As he indicated, health care was considered a personal responsibility before about 1920, although those without the ability to pay for it could receive charity care (VandenBos, Cummings, & DeLeon, 1992). Voluntary health insurance began to grow rapidly after the Great Depression (Falk, 1964) and shifted rapidly to employer-paid health plans during World War II, when such benefits were considered exempt from anti-inflationary restrictions on wage increases. By 1960, 69.2% of the U.S. population was covered by some form of health insurance. During the 1960s, health policy was characterized by attempts to expand access to health care, and this decade saw the passage of Medicare, Medicaid, and other legislation designed to extend coverage to those without resources.

These efforts to increase access to and expand consumption of health care were quite effective. Health care spending rose from $27.1 billion in 1960 to $675 billion in 1990. In 1990, health care represented 12.2% of the gross national product, more than double the percentage in 1960. In constant dollars, this represents an increase of over 400% (see VandenBos, 1993). According to cross-national comparisons, the United States spends more on health care than any other nation in the world. Yet, we know that our health care system covers a smaller proportion of our population and does not provide demonstrably better care to those it does cover than those of many other industrialized nations who spend less.

During this period of rapid growth in expense, health insurance was characterized by a fee-for-service indemnity system. Clinical or treatment aspects of care received nearly exclusive focus. Providers and patients alike concerned themselves with the care that they believed necessary, and insurance companies paid the bill as long as services were generally covered. Neither providers nor consumers had much incentive to pay attention to the financial aspects of care. This was a key contributor to the explosion in health care costs.

In addition, health care policy during this period emphasized coverage for acute care, short-term general hospital care, and surgery. Thus, Kiesler (1992) argued that national health policy has represented general hospital policy, not health policy. This pattern has distorted the balance between inpatient and outpatient care, favoring hospitalization and expensive inpatient procedures. Providers have actually had economic disincentives to emphasize prevention, early intervention, and treatment in less restrictive environments and, in general, to mount serious initiatives to maintain health, as opposed to providing medical interventions focused on existing symptoms or illness. At a systemic level, this has been described as another major contributing factor to escalating costs.

Managed Care and Cost Containment

It was against this backdrop that an entire industry, the managed care or health care cost-containment industry, developed, to focus on the costs of health care, which were quickly spreading out of control. Although certain forms of managed care, in particular, HMOs, have historical roots in the early 1900s, these were populist in flavor and minor players by comparison (see DeLeon et al., 1991). The managed care movement changed in character and expanded rapidly after Congress passed the HMO Act of 1973. The HMO Act provided $325 million over a 5-year period to support the development of new HMOs and required that employers with more than 25 employees offering health benefits had to offer an HMO option if a federally qualified HMO was available in their area and requested inclusion in the benefits plan. This law also allowed the participation of profit-making corporations, which had not been part of the movement up to this time, in the development and operation of HMOs. In effect, this law and subsequent regulatory changes created the infrastructure that enabled HMOs and other managed care plans to expand rapidly during the late 1970s and 1980s (see DeLeon et al., 1991, for a detailed discussion), in the hope of slowing the country's rapidly escalating health care costs. The pendulum seemed to have radically shifted away from an almost exclusive emphasis on treatment and services to a comparable singular focus on costs, financial issues, and economic resources in the provision of health care.

Managed Care and Mental Health

From the late 1960s to the mid-1980s, the costs of mental health care also skyrocketed. The media had popularized mental health services, reducing stigma and increasing demand. More important, fee-for-service medical benefit structures that favored more expensive inpatient treatment had been applied to the mental health area as well. For-profit specialty psychiatry and chemical-dependency inpatient facilities had mushroomed as a result. As pressure to cut costs began to grow, the need for more comprehensive-care management of mental health benefits became apparent. One response to this situation was simply to begin eliminating mental health benefits. Professional associations and patient advocates objected vigorously and further argued that managing care for patients with mental health and substance abuse disorders required specialized knowledge and skills different from those needed to manage general medical care (Freeman & Trabin, 1994). There was a concern that if mental health benefits were not separated from medical benefits, mental health benefits would be sharply reduced. Medical systems under pressure to operate in more efficient and cost-effective ways might divert dollars from programs for patients with mental health needs to the medical–surgical side of care.

In response to these forces, a new subsection of the managed care industry was born. Separate companies that focused exclusively on what came to be called *managed behavioral health care* began to form (see Freeman & Trabin, 1994). Under these systems, mental health services are offered by administratively and functionally separate entities that contract directly with payors or subcontract with medical provider systems and assume responsibility for the management and delivery of services defined as belonging to the mental health side of care. This model gained significant momentum between 1986 and 1993, and the percentage of large employers offering separate "carve-out" insurance products for mental health and substance abuse has continued to rise. In 1994, 44% of companies with 20,000 or more employees offered such programs (Foster Iiggins, 1995). Carve-out systems have been successful, in that they have permitted larger companies to see that behavioral health care costs can indeed be managed and have, thus, allowed some form of mental health benefits to remain.

INTEGRATED DELIVERY SYSTEMS

Throughout the 1980s and until quite recently, managed care has focused almost exclusively on supply-side strategies such as altering access, managing utilization, decreasing practice variation, and limiting technology. The demand side has been largely unaddressed (Friedman et al., 1995). However, a number of market forces are beginning to change the structure and nature of managed care delivery systems and have important implications for the direction and future opportunities for psychology. These forces are most obvious in more mature, competitive health care markets in which managed care currently dominates. The first is the need for managed care companies to begin competing with one another, now that they can no longer gain market share at the expense of indemnity plans. It is no longer sufficient to offer a health plan at a lower price; companies are being forced to demonstrate that they offer a better product as well. Thus, the bottom line is shifting from cost to value, as managed care companies compete with one another on price and service. Shortell, Gillies, and Anderson (1994) defined value as "being able to provide additional quality-enhancing features that purchasers desire for a given price, or, conversely, being able to provide a given set of quality attributes or outcomes for a lower price" (p. 48).

The second force, and perhaps the most important trend in the current health care marketplace, is the increasing dominance of *capitated* systems. Capitation-based health care provides care to a defined number of enrollees at a capitated, or fixed, rate per member per month. All of a provider's or a system's revenue is earned up front, when contracts are negotiated. All of a system's components (e.g., hospitals, physician groups, and clinics) become cost centers to be managed. In a marketplace that emphasizes value, capitation creates incentives for keeping people well by emphasizing prevention and health promotion. When people do become ill, there are incentives for treating them at the most cost-effective location (in contrast to earlier policies favoring hospital-based acute care).

These forces are driving what is now the dominant characteristic of health care systems: increasing levels of integration. Assuming health care continues in this direction, the best way to control health care value, that is, cost and service, is to control all of the organization, financing, and delivery of health care as closely as possible, in ways that are responsive to regional demographics and economics. Thus, the traditional lines separating hospitals, providers, and insurers have begun to blur. This is also in keeping with the strong consumer demand for what might be termed *one-stop shopping*. Only integrated delivery systems can offer a seamless, coordinated continuum of health care.

Shortell et al. (1994) defined an integrated delivery system as "a network of organizations that provides or arranges to provide a coordinated continuum of services to a defined population and is willing to be held clinically and fiscally responsible for the outcomes and the health status of the population served" (p. 47). Such systems encompass primary care providers, specialists, ambulatory-care centers, home health care agencies, hospitals, and so on. These networks may be formed in a variety of ways. Sometimes they are owned by or closely associated with an insurance product. Some may grow out of established HMOs. Provider service networks (e.g., alliances of physicians, hospitals, and home health care agencies) are a more recent basis for integrated delivery systems.

These systems have arisen primarily in response to local market forces, not in response to legislative reform. More mature markets are characterized by a greater degree of capitated payment and tend to be further along in the development of integrated delivery systems. On the basis of a systematic study of these markets, Shortell et al. (1994) concluded that more integrated systems perform better on a variety of measures of business performance than do their competitors. Current legislative proposals, such as more flexible application of antitrust laws, are likely to extend the incentives to form such systems to areas that are currently less far along. In spite of the need for more comprehensive measures of clinical performance and more research comparing different models of delivery, neither the market nor legislative policy is likely to wait until all the evidence is in before moving forward.

As systems move toward integration, it has become clear that many existing delivery systems have far more than the required number of specialty physicians and hospital beds and far fewer than the needed number of primary care providers. Shortell et al. (1994) described a variety of signposts of increasing integration:

> Present research suggests that the types of behavior that one should observe in more integrated health systems include significant downsizing of acute care capacity; consolidation of programs and services; development of cross-institutional clinical service lines such as in cardiovascular care, oncology care, behavioral medicine, and women's health; expansion of the number of primary care physicians; growth in both primary care and multispecialty group practices; development of clinical protocols, pathways, and care management systems; acceleration of the clinical applications of continuous quality improvement and expansion to the entire continuum of care; development of outcome measures; and . . . (a) balanced scorecard approach to assessing system performance. One should also observe much closer ties between such systems and local public health and social welfare agencies, schools, prisons, police departments, and related organizations. (pp. 62–63)

Psychologists have much to contribute to health care delivery systems that undertake responsibility for the health of populations and emphasize value as the bottom line. We have known for a long time that the provision of psychological services results in the reduction of overall health care costs (e.g., Cummings & Follette, 1968; Pallak, Cummings, Dorken, & Henke, 1995), yet until now, this message has fallen largely on deaf ears where policymakers are concerned. In addition, psychologists have developed treatment protocols for a variety of physical conditions that are at least as effective and far less costly than surgical interventions (e.g., for chronic back pain; see Turk & Stacey, in press) and even compare favorably to long-term medication use aimed at the same conditions (e.g., for hypertension; see Fahrion, Norris, Green, Green, & Schnar, 1987). Psychological research can provide a basis for behavior-change technologies and education methodologies that will significantly enhance health-promotion efforts. Integrated systems create incentives for liaison and treatment-coordination activities that psychologists are well positioned to provide. If integrated delivery systems are to be held responsible for the health status of populations, they will need to do a better job of assessing the needs, demands, and preferences of their populations. Such assessments will need to focus on community wellness and health promotion, and not exclusively on perceived or diagnosed illness (Shortell et al., 1994). The expertise of psychologists in clinical assessment can be brought to bear on the outcome assessments and quality-assurance systems that health care systems will need, to assess quality of care and cost-effectiveness.

HEALTH PSYCHOLOGY

Although the scope of the emerging opportunities for psychology is new, health care does not represent a new area of expertise for professional psychology. In fact, the marketplace developments described above have occurred simultaneously with the rise of health psychology as a research and clinical discipline. This has occurred within a remarkably short period of time. Although its foundations extend much further back, Division 38 (Health Psychology) of the American Psychological Association (APA) was founded in 1978. By 1990, health psychology had become the most popular area of clinical research in APA-accredited clinical psychology doctoral programs, with nearly twice as many schools, faculties, and grants devoted to this area as any other (Sayette & Mayne, 1990).

Psychologists have directed their efforts toward understanding the psychosocial contributors to and consequences of physical disease. We have focused on health promotion and disease prevention, as well as on the development of psychological and behavioral technologies for the treatment of various medical problems. These efforts have made it clear that our clinical and research expertise has relevance for far more than treating individuals with diagnosed mental health disorders:

> As health professionals, . . . psychologists are involved in research, assessment, intervention, consultation, teaching, and administration related to management of pain, coping with stressful medical procedures, control of pharmacological side effects, training in self-examination and health monitoring, recovery from illness and surgery,

cognitive rehabilitation, behavioral health, adherence to health care regimens, organ transplant decisions, health care staff stress and burnout, physician–patient relationships, and work-site prevention programs. (VandenBos, DeLeon, & Belar, 1991, p. 443)

Moreover, a large body of work has focused on behavioral contributors to health and disease. Indeed, U.S. Department of Health and Human Services officials have pointed out that all of the seven top health-risk factors in the United States—tobacco use, diet, alcohol, unintentional injuries, suicidal behavior, violence, and unsafe sex—are behavioral (cf. VandenBos et al., 1991). Behavioral factors make significant contributions to the development of chronic diseases (e.g., heart disease, cancer, and diabetes), currently the most serious and most costly threat to the nation's health. In addition to being actively involved in prevention efforts, psychologists have developed and presented empirical data on the efficacy of behavioral interventions aimed at a wide range of medical problems, such as coronary artery disease, stress disorders, essential hypertension, migraine headaches, and chronic back pain (Cummings & VandenBos, 1983).

Even more recently, the field of psychoneuroimmunology (PNI) has developed and expanded. Psychoneuroimmunology is concerned with the anatomical and chemical pathways through which the nervous system (especially the brain) and the immune system communicate with one another and with the implications of this communication for the pathogenesis and course of physical disease (Kemeny, Solomon, Morley, & Herbert, 1992). As part of this study, PNI focuses on the impact of psychosocial factors on the immune system. The rapidly growing literature in this area has established that exposure to stressful events can have adverse effects on the immune system and that specific psychological states, such as depression, can also be associated with changes in immunity (see Herbert & Cohen, 1993). Furthermore, research suggests that such immune-system changes may have an impact on the course of immunologically mediated or resisted diseases, including viral and bacterial infections, autoimmune diseases, certain forms of cancer, and HIV-related illness (see Kemeny, 1994). Thus, there is substantial evidence that psychological factors can have an impact on health and disease in ways that are not mediated by behavior. Whether such processes can be influenced through psychological interventions is currently being explored. Currently available data suggest that specific psychological interventions may have an impact on the course of certain types of cancer (Fawzy et al., 1993; Spiegel, Bloom, Kraemer, & Gottheil, 1989) and the course of HIV progression (e.g., Antoni et al., 1991; Esterling et al., 1992), although the mechanisms of these effects are still unclear.

PSYCHOLOGY AS A HEALTH CARE PROFESSION

None of this is to say that all psychologists will need to become health psychologists and immunologists or that there will cease to be a demand for psychologists who provide services directed at the amelioration of psychological distress and psychological disorders. However, one implication of the broader trends we have described is that technologies developed by health psychologists will need to be more fully integrated into professional education. Another is that many professional psychologists may need to become more flexible regarding the settings in which they practice and more collaborative with other health care disciplines.

The potential role of psychology in primary care settings provides an important illustration. Much of the research in this area has examined symptom presentation in primary medical-care settings, rather than focusing on populations with specific diagnoses. For example, one recent study involved the analysis of records for over 1,000 patients followed over 3 years in an internal medicine clinic (Kroenke & Mangelsdorff, 1989). For the 14 most commonly presented complaints, a clear organic etiology was established in less than 16% of the cases. Significant psychological distress was present in over 80%. A large and growing body of literature indicates that both the presence of psychologists as members of the primary care team and a variety of specific psychological interventions reduce unnecessary medical visits, reduce overall health care costs, and enhance patient care (see Friedman et al., 1995; Kenkel, 1995, for recent reviews).

Yet, if psychology is to be taken seriously as a health care profession, there are major challenges that must be met. One of the most important is the development of more sophisticated models and better technologies for health-related behavior change and maintenance. As behavioral risk factors for a variety of diseases have been identified, psychologists have developed and tested theoretically based interventions for modifying those behaviors. Although such interventions have often produced initial change, they have been less successful in maintaining behavior change. Models are needed that acknowledge the complex determinants of behavior, including sociocultural influences and irrational processes, and new interventions that are based on those models must be developed. This is particularly critical in areas like HIV prevention, where the best predictor of safer sexual behavior—whether following interventions, education campaigns, or antibody testing—is consistently found to be past sexual behavior (e.g., Aspinwall, Kemeny, Taylor, Schneider, & Dudley, 1991; McCusker et al., 1990). Although we may argue successfully that psychologists are the experts in behavior, the health care system will demand increasing accountability. We must begin to deliver programs that foster lasting behavior change in areas such as primary prevention, behavioral risk factors for the incidence of progression of disease, and treatment adherence.

A second, overlapping, priority is the management of chronic disease. Two major trends contribute to this priority (Chesney, 1993). The first trend consists of rapidly developing technologies for testing and screening and for identification of genetic risk. With early identification come opportunities for intervention to reduce or eliminate the risk of illness, as well as the need for treatments that address the psychological sequelae of risk identification. The second trend is related to the rapid growth of the aging population. By the year 2020, it is expected that over 50 million U.S. citizens will be age 65 or older. The great majority of these people are likely to have at least one chronic illness such as hypertension, heart disease, arthritis, or diabetes (U.S. Bureau of the Census, 1996). Psychologists will need to form partnerships with medical scientists and practitioners to develop programs for supporting healthy living, managing chronic conditions, and sustaining quality of life (Chesney, 1993). Increasingly, such programs will need to incorporate individual, community, and public health levels of intervention.

POLICY RECOMMENDATIONS

There are a number of general policy recommendations that are important in supporting the development of psychology in the directions described. First and foremost, psychologists must work toward general recognition of psychology as a health-care profession and psychologists as health-service providers. The involvement of psychological practice in health care—in health promotion and disease prevention, as team members in primary care settings, or in interventions directed toward conditions generally considered medical in nature—is not well known to policymakers, either at the local market or legislative level. For the most part, when policymakers think about health, they think about medical interventions provided by physicians (see, e.g., Kerrey & Holfschire, 1993). Advocacy materials and public messages should highlight psychological services related to the prevention, treatment, and rehabilitation of both psychological and physical health problems. Although the tremendous need for psychological expertise in the planning and delivery of health services may be clear to us, we must approach these efforts with a "deep appreciation both for the truly interdisciplinary nature of health care and the very tenuous nature of psychology's participation in its ... planning" (DeLeon, O'Keefe, VandenBos, & Kraut, 1982, p. 480).

A central part of this effort will be to support and participate in the creation of clinically integrated health care delivery systems.

Psychologists can be key advocates for the elimination of mind–body dualism in health policy. Legislation, insurance, and health-plan-benefits language and the administrative structures of health care systems should be scrutinized for instances in which such dualism impedes the creation of integrated health systems. For example, behavioral health carve-outs may pose obstacles to the integration of psychology into health care service delivery, to the ability of systems to realize and track medical-cost offsets as a function of psychological services, and to the application of psychological and behavioral technologies to health promotion and treatment (see Belar, 1995).

To ensure that our opportunities within the health care system are as broad and varied as possible, it is important that common economic incentives be created for various levels of care (e.g., hospitals, primary care settings, and home health) to work together. As mentioned, this involves more flexible application of antitrust laws as they relate to health care systems and the dismantling of policies and benefit structures that favor hospitalization and acute care. For psychologists, restrictions on licensure and certification requirements and other legal barriers to participation in interdisciplinary groups must be removed. Legislative advocacy also can be used to promote cross-training and the use of clinical outcomes and patient satisfaction data in decisions regarding what services psychologists provide. It is important that our ability to provide services not depend on a diagnosis of psychopathology.

We can also encourage more integrated provision of care through promoting greater and more informed consumer choice of health plans and treatment options. For example, the APA has been quite active in supporting requirements for individual choice of plans and out-of-network service options at a legislative level. Similar efforts at a state and local level are at least as important.

The movement toward increasingly integrated systems will require policies and procedures that increase the supply of needed professionals (e.g., primary care providers). Within our own educational system, we must begin to address the disjuncture between the current "product" of our universities and professional schools and the needs of the delivery system. In parallel to our potential collaborators, our own education should include greater emphasis on learning and working in teams, systems thinking, quality improvement and outcomes assessment, the use of protocols and critical pathways, the analysis of cost-effectiveness, clinical epidemiology, program evaluation, and population-based health-status assessment.

THE CHALLENGE TO PSYCHOLOGY

The forces we have described present professional psychology with both great opportunity and great risk. The opportunity is for psychology to take its place as a health care profession, with mental health as a subset of expertise rather than its defining characteristic. The next several years will be a critical period in which to do so. Patterns of health care delivery and supporting policy are more open to reconceptualization, redesign, and renegotiation than at any point in recent history. Current systems are shifting away from previous policies that have favored hospital-based and acute care and have limited the participation of professional psychology. The management of health care delivery systems will become far more interdisciplinary, incorporating medical, nursing, public health, business, legal, and psychological perspectives.

In making this shift, psychology has a strong ally in the public. In preparation for its public education campaign, the APA recently sponsored a random survey of over 1,200 American men and women. More than 8 in 10 people surveyed endorsed the belief that good psychological health plays an important role in maintaining good physical health. Over 80% indicated that they would be more inclined to use a physician who worked with a psychologist over one who did not. Nearly half reported that they would be "much more inclined." A separate series of consumer focus groups revealed that the public believes strongly in a connection between the mind and the body and saw psychological services as an important part of treatment for physical illness and disease, enhancing both the ability to cope with the disease and recovery from it.

We can begin by taking practical and incremental steps toward changing the way we practice our profession. For example, an early step might be to develop group practices of psychologists. This will help to render the diversity within our profession an advantage, rather than a liability, and will relieve us of feeling overwhelmed and burdened by the sense of having to know everything. A second step might be to establish links with other health care providers, particularly with primary care physicians. A third step might be the development of multidisciplinary group practices with psychologists as integral members.

Building these relationships can strengthen referral bases, educate us about the needs for our services that exist on the front lines of health care, and prepare us to participate in integrated health care delivery systems. For most of us, this will involve shifting our frame sufficiently that we are able to conceptualize and incorporate a much wider range of needs and outcomes. Under fee-for-service models, the expanded application of psychological technologies to medical problems pitted psychologists against all of organized medicine (Cummings & VandenBos, 1983). Integrated delivery systems offer far greater opportunities for collaboration, but such collaboration will require more systematic training in health promotion and in the detection and treatment of more medically based problems and the ability to work closely in more flexible ways with other specialists.

The risks of this transition are also great. Perhaps the greatest risk to our profession is that by failing to resolve our internal struggles and anxiety related to this professional role transition, we may fail to develop coherent and well-coordinated models and messages that will carry us into the next century. In addition, the effective communication of these more complex messages to policymakers and payors will be a difficult task for a profession that has not historically articulated its knowledge base to outsiders (Newman & Vincent, 1996). Along with our message that the provision of psychological services as a routine part of medical care can reduce overall medical costs, we need to define what specific services are cost-effective for which individuals under what circumstances (Friedman et al., 1995). By clinging exclusively to traditional models of practice, we may fail to demonstrate our competence to do anything beyond the capabilities of less well trained—and cheaper—mental health providers.

Seizing the opportunity requires that two critical challenges be met simultaneously: differentiation and integration. By differentiation, we mean that psychology must demonstrate clearly the uniqueness of our training and experience and of the contribution we can make to health care delivery. By integration, we mean that providers acting alone or in loose affiliation, without strong interdisciplinary collaborative ties, will have great difficulty participating in the delivery of the full continuum of health care. The model of health care delivery will be the team. We must learn to become team players while maintaining our unique identity. Throughout this shift in our patterns of practice and our definition of ourselves, we must not lose sight of the ultimate purpose of all health care interventions. This is a principle for which psychologists have long been passionate advocates: to improve the quality of human life.

REFERENCES

Antoni, M. H., Baggett, L., Ironson, G., LaPerriere, A., August, S., Klimas, N., Schneiderman, N., & Fletcher, M. A. (1991). Cognitive-behavioral stress management intervention buffers distress responses and immunological changes following notification of HIV-1 seropositivity. *Journal of Consulting and Clinical Psychology, 59,* 906–915.

Aspinwall, L. G., Kemeny, M. E., Taylor, S. E., Schneider, S. G., & Dudley, J. P. (1991). Psychosocial predictors of gay men's AIDS risk-reduction behavior. *Health Psychology, 10,* 434–444.

Belar, C. D. (1995). Collaboration in capitated care: Challenges for psychology. *Professional Psychology: Research and Practice, 26,* 139–146.

Chesney, M. A. (1993). Health psychology in the 21st century: Acquired immunodeficiency syndrome as a harbinger of things to come. *Health Psychology, 12,* 259–268.

Cummings, N. A., & Follette, W. T. (1968). Psychiatric services and medical utilization in a prepaid health setting: Part II. *Medical Care, 6*, 31–41.

Cummings, N. A., & VandenBos, G. R. (1983). Relations with other professions. In C. E. Walker (Ed.), *Handbook of clinical psychology: Theory, research, and practice* (Vol. 2, pp. 1301–1327). Homewood, IL: Dow Jones–Irwin.

DeLeon, P. H., O'Keefe, A. M., VandenBos, G. R., & Kraut, A. G. (1982). How to influence public policy: A blueprint for activism. *American Psychologist, 37*, 476–485.

DeLeon, P. H., VandenBos, G. R., & Bulatao, E. Q. (1991). Managed mental health care: A history of the federal policy initiative. *Professional Psychology: Research and Practice, 22*, 15–25.

Esterling, B. A., Antoni, M. H., Schneiderman, N., Carver, C. S., LaPerriere, A., Ironson, G., Klimas, N. G., & Fletcher, M. A. (1992). Psychosocial modulation of antibody to Epstein–Barr viral capsid antigen and human herpesvirus type-6 in HIV-1 infected and at-risk gay men. *Psychosomatic Medicine, 54*, 354–371.

Fahrion, S., Norris, P., Green, E., Green, A., & Schnar, R. (1987). Biobehavioral treatment of essential hypertension: A group outcome study. *Biofeedback and Self-Regulation, 11*, 257–278.

Falk, I. S. (1964). Medical care: Its social and organizational aspects. Labor unions and medical care. *The New England Journal of Medicine, 270*, 22–28.

Fawzy, F. I., Fawzy, N. W., Hyun, S. C., Elashoff, R., Guthrie, D., Fahey, J. L., & Morton, D. L. (1993). Malignant melanoma: Effects of an early structured psychiatric intervention, coping, and affective state on recurrence and survival 6 years later. *Archives of General Psychiatry, 50*, 681–689.

Foster Higgins, A. (1995). *National survey of employer-sponsored health plans*. New York: Author.

Freeman, M. A., & Trabin, T. (1994). *Managed behavioral healthcare: History, models, key issues, and future course* (CMHS, SAMHSA Report No. #4692). Rockville, MD: U.S. Department of Health and Human Services.

Friedman, R., Sobel, D., Myers, P., Caudill, M., & Benson, H. (1995). Behavioral medicine, clinical health psychology, and cost offset. *Health Psychology, 14*, 509–518.

Herbert, T. B., & Cohen, S. (1993). Stress and immunity in humans: A meta-analytic review. *Psychosomatic Medicine, 55*, 364–379.

Kemeny, M. E. (1994). Stressful events, psychological responses, and progression of HIV infection. In R. Glaser & J. Kiecolt-Glaser (Eds.), *Handbook of human stress and immunity* (pp. 245–266). New York: Academic Press.

Kemeny, M. E., Solomon, G. F., Morley, J. E., & Herbert, T. L. (1992). Psychoneuroimmunology. In C. B. Nemeroff (Ed.), *Neuroendocrinology* (pp. 563–591). Boca Raton, FL: CRC Press.

Kenkel, M. B. (Ed.). (1995). Psychology and primary care/family practice medicine [Special section]. *Professional Psychology: Research and Practice, 26*, 117–146.

Kerrey, B., & Holfschire, P. J. (1993). Hidden problems in current health care financing and potential changes. *American Psychologist, 48,* 261–264.

Kiesler, C. A. (1992). U. S. mental health policy: Doomed to fail. *American Psychologist, 47,* 1077–1082.

Kroenke, K., & Mangelsdorff, D. (1989). Common symptoms in ambulatory care: Incidence, evaluation, therapy, and outcome. *American Journal of Medicine, 86,* 262–266.

McCusker, J., Westenhouse, J., Stoddard, A. M., Zapka, J. G., Zorn, M. W., & Mayer, K. H. (1990). Use of drugs and alcohol by homosexually active men in relation to sexual practices. *Journal of Acquired Immune Deficiency Syndromes, 3,* 729–737.

Newman, R., & Vincent, T. (1996). Balancing expertise with practical realities. In R. P. Lorion, I. Iscoe, P. H. DeLeon, & G. R. VandenBos (Eds.), *Psychology and public policy: Balancing public service and professional need* (pp. 203–206). Washington, DC: American Psychological Association.

Pallak, M. S., Cummings, N. A., Dorken, H., & Henke, C. J. (1995). Effect of mental health treatment on medical costs. *Mind/Body Medicine, 1,* 7–12.

Sayette, M. A., & Mayne, T. J. (1990). Survey of current clinical and research trends in clinical psychology. *American Psychologist, 45,* 1263–1266.

Shortell, S. M., Gillies, R. R., & Anderson, D. A. (1994). The new world of managed care: Creating organized delivery systems. *Health Affairs, 13,* 46–64.

Spiegel, D., Bloom, J. R., Kraemer, H. C., & Gottheil, E. (1989). Effect of psychosocial treatment on survival of patients with metastatic breast cancer. *Lancet,* 888–891.

Turk, D. C., & Stacey, B. R. (in press). Multidisciplinary pain centers in the treatment of chronic back pain. In J. W. Frymoyer, T. B. Ducker, N. M. Hadler, J. P. Kostiuk, J. N. Weinstein, & T. S. Whitecloud (Eds.), *The adult spine: Principles and practices* (2nd ed.). New York: Raven Press.

U.S. Bureau of the Census. (1996). 65+ in the United States. In *Current Population Reports,* (Special Studies Report No. P23-190). Washington, DC: U.S. Government Printing Office.

VandenBos, G. R. (1993). U. S. mental health policy: Proactive evolution in the midst of health care reform. *American Psychologist, 48,* 283–290.

VandenBos, G. R., Cummings, N. A., & DeLeon, P. H. (1992). A century of psychotherapy: Economics and environmental influences. In D. K. Freedheim (Ed.), *History of psychotherapy: A century of change* (pp. 65–102). Washington, DC: American Psychological Association.

VandenBos, G. R., DeLeon, P. H., & Belar, C. D. (1991). How many psychologists are needed? It's too early to know! *Professional Psychology: Research and Practice, 22,* 441–448.

3

THE NEW STRUCTURE OF HEALTH CARE AND A ROLE FOR PSYCHOLOGY

NICHOLAS A. CUMMINGS

Psychotherapists have had more than one occasion to counsel a patient who was lamenting a lost opportunity and expressing no insight into his or her responsibility in missing that opportunity. Still in denial, the patient is full of rage and self-pity, crying that never again will such favorable circumstances repeat themselves. It is incumbent on the psychotherapist to point out that a wonderful feature of life is that it presents repeated opportunities. But if, when the next opportunity occurs, the patient is still in denial, some time in the future the patient and psychotherapist will be repeating this conversation.

Psychology clearly missed the opportunity to own or control the behavior managed care industry. But as the first decade of managed behavioral health care draws to a close, there are megatrends emerging that signal that the second decade will see the restoration of the provider as paramount, albeit in a manner different than anything that has previously existed. Given the determination to respond appropriately, psychology is faced with a new frontier and yet another opportunity (N. A. Cummings, 1995a).

THE FIRST DECADE OF MANAGED BEHAVIORAL HEALTH CARE

In spite of wishful thinking to the contrary on the part of most practitioners, managed care has succeeded in reducing costs (Rich, 1995). In most cases, the cost containment has been in the form of deceleration of the inflationary spiral by as much as 30%, whereas in a few instances, there is an active reduction in the cost of providing health care. The marketplace, which is the final arbiter of the controversy, clearly perceived a significant cost saving, and the number of persons covered by managed care soared in 10 years from under 5% of insured Americans to 67%. This is more than just growth: It is a stampede. In the process, much got trampled, and among the casualties were some quality, much of solo practice, and all of psychoanalysis.

The question now remains of whether managed care companies have outlived their usefulness (Oss, 1995). With most of the fat wrung out of behavioral health care, they may maintain only a layer of bureaucracy that is no longer needed. This does not mean the end of managed care, for now that the industrialization of health care has occurred, for all time, when someone else pays the bill, care will be managed.

WHY CARVE-OUTS ARE OUT

Ten years ago, when I heralded the emergence of the managed behavior health care industry (N. A. Cummings, 1986), it was because existing structures and mechanisms lacked the expertise to control spiraling costs. The federal government in its promulgation of diagnosis-related groups (DRGs) had managed to tether medical–surgical hospital costs, but it did not know how to write DRGs for mental health and chemical-dependency (MH–CD) hospitalization. As DRGs emptied medical–surgical beds, hospitals converted the space to MH–CD, touted these services on radio and television, and MH–CD hospitalization soared out of control and became the new driving force in the inflationary spiral.

Clearly what was needed was expertise outside the then-current health industry, and companies such as American Biodyne (now MedCo. Behavioral Care Corporation) sprang up and flourished. In just 7 years, Biodyne went from 0 to 14.5 million eligible by carving out MH–CD from existing health plans, and a host of competitors also experienced phenomenal growth. It was not long before similar companies followed

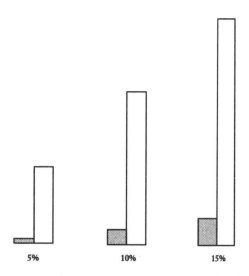

Figure 1. Potential savings in billions of dollars for mental health and chemical-dependency treatment at the 5%, 10%, and 15% levels (shaded columns) and for corresponding savings in all health expenditures (unshaded columns).

American Biodyne's lead, and because of the outside expertise or separate organizal structure of these contractors, they came to be known as "behavioral care carve-outs," or just plain "carve-outs." The carve-out was a necessary first step in tethering MH–CD costs, but now that all the carve-outs are doing essentially the same thing with similar degrees of success, their time may be passing, inasmuch as everyone has learned the technology, which is now also available to practitioner groups. Along with solo practice, long-term therapy, and psychoanalysis, it, too, may have become a dinosaur. But carve-outs have become a gigantic industry, and paleontology has taught us that not all the dinosaurs died at once. A probable scenario is the following, which will usher in the second decade of managed behavioral health care: the era of the *megaprovider*.

WHY CARVE-INS ARE IN

The cost containment that can be realized in MH–CD pales by comparison with the cost containment that lies potentially in medicine and surgery. Dollar amounts tend to obscure the importance of the comparison inasmuch as practitioners have become inured to large monetary sums being bandied about. Figure 1 is startling in that it dramatically shows the difference for 5%, 10%, and 15% cost savings in MH–CD (shaded columns) versus the same percentages in total health care (unshaded columns). All are in billions of dollars, and a 10% savings in total health care is equivalent to all MH–CD expenditures in the United States.

Medical-cost offset is the reduction in overuse or inappropriate use of medicine and surgery by introduction of behavioral health care to address somatization by those 60% of physician visits that are either translating emotional distress into physical symptoms or have a real physical illness that is either complicated by psychological factors or brought on by lifestyle. The figures 5%, 10%, and 15% were chosen because most medical-cost-offset studies report those kinds of savings (Pallak, Cummings, Dörken, & Henke, 1993). A 10% medical-cost offset is modal and readily achieved in settings organized to facilitate such savings (N. A. Cummings, 1994).

Carve-outs are antithetical to conducting medical-cost offset because, by definition, they are not part of the delivery system in which the overuse of medicine and surgery is occurring. The best medical cost offset takes place when the research and the delivery system are so integrated that it is totally unobtrusive (N. A. Cummings, 1994).

THE EMERGENCE OF THE MEGAPROVIDER

One of the few surviving ideas of Ira Magaziner, the architect of the defunct Rodham–Clinton health care proposal, is that of the purchasing alliance. In large metropolitan areas, communities are forming consortia of insurers, employers, consumers, providers, and other volunteers. These consortia have the authority not only to purchase health care delivery but also to bypass the managed care companies and contract directly with regional provider groups. Without the onerousness of government sanctions, these community groups are availing themselves of expertise in outcomes research and quality measures. Contracts will be awarded either to managed care companies or directly to provider groups, whichever has the best value (quality plus price) as demonstrated by real outcomes research. This is schematically shown in Figure 2, where independently conducted outcomes research is fed back to the purchasing alliance, which then makes purchasing decisions accordingly.

The groups of providers who are forming nationally and contracting directly with purchasers cover the entire spectrum of health care, not just MH–CD. They are variously called regional group practices (RGPs; N. A. Cummings, 1995b) or community-accountable health care networks (CAHNs; Neer, 1994). They are organized and owned by providers, and although they demonstrate business organization and acumen, they are clinically driven. The managed care companies, on the other hand, have essentially become isolated from their clinical roots and have become largely business driven.

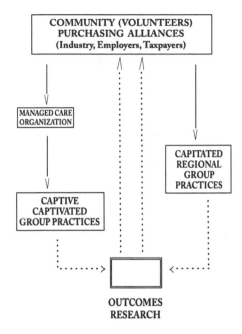

Figure 2. Flowchart illustrating the ability of the purchasing alliances to contract with managed care organizations (MCOs) or directly with regional group practices, with the employment of outcomes research to determine renewals or future contracts.

The salient feature of these emerging provider groups is the physician equity model, in which the practitioners are participant owners in their own delivery systems. Physician equity has been the cornerstone of the world's most successful health maintenance organization (HMO) the Kaiser-Permanente system. The Mullikin Group has extended the physician equity concept to include all health care professionals (De Lafuente, 1993) and has become the prototype of the new practitioner groups.

The health care landscape was replete in the 1980s with physician-owned managed care companies that went bankrupt. Formed as the physician's answer to the encroachment of managed care, they lacked the sophistication and expertise to compete in the business world, and they did not survive. These new groups, whether RGPs or CAHNs, are successful businesses that, nonetheless, retain their ability to be clinically driven. These features, added to the physician equity component, render them a real threat to the existing managed care companies. Forrester (1994) refers to the physician equity model as the "dark horse contender to dominate healthcare delivery in the future" (p. 1). For-profit practitioner groups can "forge an entrepreneurial trail with zeal and speed"

(Forrester, 1994, p. 1) not possible in nonequity systems. It is important that psychologists begin now to assure equity in these systems of the future. Those psychologists who succeed will very likely be those who are involved in the initial formations of CAHNs.

The managed care companies, recognizing the threat from provider groups, are rapidly buying group practices, hoping to capture the field. It is now a race between the emerging provider groups, who have trouble raising capital, and the managed care companies, who have access to expansion dollars. Consequently, the provider groups can no longer be content to remain relatively small entities. Mergers, acquisitions, and consolidations, the steps the fledgling managed care companies had to traverse years ago, now must be the *modis operandi* of the provider groups, eventually forging megaproviders to counter the *megameds*, the name I gave (N. A. Cummings, 1995b) to the giant managed care entities.

The first megaprovider was formed with the acquisition of the Mullikin Group by MedPartners ("Physician Management," 1995). It is the prediction of several observers of the health care industry that the megaproviders will, over the next 10 years, overtake the managed care companies whose overlay of bureaucracy has outlived its usefulness (N. A. Cummings, 1995a; Neer, 1994; Oss, 1995). The health care delivery systems for the year 2000 will be the CAHNs and the HMOs, which are in actual practice their own kind of CAHN.

THE FUTURE IS IN BEHAVIORAL HEALTH

Psychologists, accustomed to pressure from above (psychiatry), are ill prepared to accept pressure from below (master's level practitioners). The fact that master's level psychotherapists will replace doctor's level psychotherapists is in keeping with this megatrend in all health care, involving midwives, nurse practitioners, and physician assistants. In addition, specialization will be curtailed in favor of more general practitioners in the trenches.

More than 15 years ago, with VandenBos (Cummings & VandenBos, 1979), I saw the psychologist as the behavioral primary care physician of the future. In enunciating the "General Practice of Psychology," we anticipated the current era and delineated the parameters, one of which was the psychologist as embodiment of the extinct, caring general practitioner of old, who never refused a house call, related to all the family as a concerned counselor, and coordinated and oversaw the family's health and well-being. Since the disappearance of the "family doctor" in the age of overspecialization, there has been a void, and who is better able to fill this role than the psychologist as primary care giver?

The most powerful economic argument for mental health benefits is the evidence that they reduce inappropriate medical care utilization (N. A. Cummings, 1991; Goldman & Feldman, 1993). In the 130 million Americans now covered by managed behavioral health care, most of the economic "fat" has been effectively wrung from the mental health system. There remains the far greater economic drain in the medical–surgical sectors resulting from the use of services by the millions of physician visits by somaticizing patients (N. A. Cummings, 1993). Thirty years of research have demonstrated the medical-cost-offset effect in organized settings: The reduction of inappropriate medical–surgical care by the use of psychological interventions. The current rediscovery of the medical-cost-offset phenomenon indicates that the future of the doctoral-level psychologist will be found in health psychology.

The doctorally trained psychologist is in a unique position to plan, research, and implement intervention programs for both the somaticizers and the noncompliant chronically physically ill (N. A. Cummings, 1995b; Pallak et al., 1993), as well as behavioral programs for the millions who demonstrate faulty living habits. But in the fact that the interventions of the future will be derived from empirical-outcomes research, resulting in treatment protocols, there is an even broader role for the doctoral-level psychologist.

Somatization

The translation of psychological conflict and stress into physical symptoms takes a heavy economic toll on our health system. Beyond that, there is the fact that when 60% of all visits to a physician are somaticized complaints, the patients are not receiving the appropriate behavioral treatment to ameliorate their pain and suffering. Repeated visits to a physician who attempts to reassure the patient by repeating medical test only strengthen the patient's conviction that a physical illness exists and will be found during the next round of tests.

Psychologists functioning in behavior health have the expertise to design systems and interventions that bring relief to the patient and reduce the strain of overutilization on the medical and surgical system. Somatization not only can mimic any physical condition, it can exacerbate an existing illness. Primarily, however, it challenges the frontiers of medicine. The less certainty regarding a syndrome, the greater the incidence of somatization.

Thirty years ago, the most frequent form of somaticized response was what physicians called "neurotic heart." As cardiology became more sophisticated, this gave way to lower back pain. With increased knowledge in back centers, there was a surge in the little-understood conditions of hypoglycemia and yeast infection. Now, carpal tunnel syndrome is exploding in frequency. Carpal tunnel syndrome demonstrates the critical features of somatization: (a) It challenges the frontiers of medicine, and (b) the extensive use of computer keyboards (i.e., repetitive movement) provides a social rationalization for the "disease." Consider, however, that the old typewriter required much more pressure and the type of repetitive movement that ostensibly contributes to the current wave of carpal tunnel syndrome complaints. The critical feature remains that medicine lacks certainty regarding the syndrome, inasmuch as the state of medical knowledge does not readily allow a differentiation between the somaticized symptom and the genuine physical disorder.

Similarly, patients challenge the frontiers of psychology, and the profession has not adequately addressed this "psychotizing." Thirty years ago, Joanne Woodward won the Academy Award for her performance in *The Three Faces of Eve*, a movie about a woman with multiple personality disorder. Woodward also married Paul Newman. There followed an epidemic in America of female patients manifesting multiple personality disorder. In due time the "epidemic" died out, and multiple personality disorder remained rare for many years, until the popularization of the case of Sybil, after which multiple personality disorder became epidemic again.

It is even as if psychotherapists contribute to the proliferation of multiple personality disorder. I recall how a small rural center of my managed care company was treating more multiple personalities in that center than the entire national delivery system combined. I was baffled until the center director, receiving a significant promotion, was moved to a larger center several states away. Within 60 days, his new location became the multiple personality center of the system.

Unfortunately, iatrogenic "neuroses" are not rare. Borderline personalities can mimic any condition in which a well-meaning therapist shows undue interest. Furthermore, those with personality disorders may plunge into "psychosis" when it suits their purpose, only to emerge when they have gotten their way, somewhat as a diver who emerges from the swimming pool. The unfortunate schizophrenic does not have this capacity, but unwitting therapists fall prey to borderline patients for whom hospitalization is a way out of the consequences of their lifestyle. Other therapists are easily blackmailed by severe personality disorders who will use the threat of suicide as a manipulation device.

We have failed to address scientifically the real parameters of posttraumatic stress disorder, repressed memories, false memories, and a number of other phenomena that challenge the frontiers of psychology, to say nothing of our professional embarrassment with colleagues who seriously treat the trauma resulting from ostensible abduction by space aliens. While helping medicine cope with the somatization, let us not neglect the challenges to the frontiers of psychology. Our future and credibility depend on it.

The Psychotherapy of the Future

When VandenBos and I (1979) described our general practice of psychology, we advocated multimodal group practices whose psychotherapists had combined dynamic and behavioral therapies into interventions designed to ameliorate the presenting life program. We postulated that throughout the life span, the client has available brief, effective interventions designed to meet specific conditions as these may or may not arise. Later termed *brief, intermittent psychotherapy throughout the life cycle* (N. A. Cummings & Sayama, 1995), this approach currently has over 30 years of clinical experience and empirical treatment of choice in the present U.S. health care environment.

As previously stated, most of the hands-on behavioral treatment will be conducted by master's level therapists working with empirically derived treatment protocols of targeted, focused interventions. Research, experience, and the nature of human diversity have shown that protocols serve only about 30% to 35% of the persons suffering from each condition being addressed. The master's level therapists will need the clinical acumen of the doctorally trained therapists for the remaining 65% to 70% of patients.

Outcomes research is beginning to demonstrate that many psychological conditions respond more effectively to group therapy than to individual therapy. In addition, a growing body of evidence indicates that preventive services in the form of psychoeducational groups reduce the demand for both psychotherapy and inappropriate medical–surgical utilization. These psychoeducational groups range from stress management, parenting programs, and smoking cessation to programs designed to improve compliance with medical regimens in hypertensives, diabetics, and other chronic diseases in which noncompliance is rampant. Outcomes research has identified well over 100 potentially useful psychoeducational approaches.

It is very likely, as the result of empirical findings, that only 25% of the psychotherapy of the future will be individual. It is anticipated that another 25% will be group therapy, whereas half of the psychological interventions will be preventive services in the form of structured psychoeducational programs involving small-group participation. The doctoral psychologist will be conducting the empirical research on which the eventual design and implementation of these therapies will rest. Note that the 25:25:50 ratio, or something resembling it, will be the result of tested effectiveness and not primarily a drive for further cost containment.

The Psychologist as Health Economist

The single most important characteristic that will define the successful psychologist of the future will be the ability to predict one's costs, not only for MH–CD and all behavioral care services but also for medicine and surgery. This will make the group to which he or she is a participant owner eligible for capitation or other forms of prospective reimbursement. Without the ability to predict and control costs, no provider group will be in a position to assume risk. It also follows from ongoing outcomes research that the psychologist will be pivotal in a system that constantly evolves toward ever-increasing efficiency (cost containment) and improved effectiveness (treatment and prevention).

Managed care companies have achieved cost containment by addressing the supply side of health care. Precertification, utilization review, case management, and other such techniques are intended to save money by shrinking the supply, a straightforward business approach that serves most industries well. However, this does not address demand, and therein lies the dilemma for the business-driven, as opposed to the clinically driven, system. The following example will illustrate.

In a given month, 23 patients presenting for psychiatric hospitalization manifest suicidal thoughts. None of these demonstrate severity of symptoms sufficient to warrant hospitalization other than possibly for a suicidal aspect. Yet, experience has shown that only 2 or 3 of these are actually lethal. The dilemma becomes who to hospitalize. To deny hospitalization to someone who then goes home and commits suicide is likely to result in a malpractice suit. To play it safe by hospitalizing most, if not all, 23 is costly and inefficient. These are all supply-side questions and dilemmas.

In a clinically driven system, the approach is one of *prevention*, which is another word for the demand side of the equation. By increasing the amount of brief psychotherapy, psychoeducational groups, outreach with early detection and treatment, the demand for hospitalization markedly decreases (J. L. Cummings, 1996; Pallak & Cummings, 1992). Furthermore, a great deal of ambulatory care can be provided for far less than the cost of one day of hospitalization. If prevention is appropriately and intensively provided, it is likely that 5 persons will present for hospitalization in that month, instead of 23. With this reduced demand, all 5 could be hospitalized without an overutilization of inpatient care and without concern for an error in diagnostic judgment.

SUMMARY AND CONCLUSION

Psychologists possess the skills, knowledge, and expertise to create and participate as owners in the provider groups that are likely to replace the current managed care carve-outs that have outlived their usefulness. These provider groups will consolidate into megaproviders and dominate the industry during the second decade of this health care industrial revolution.

Psychologists who participate in this megatrend will do so as participant–provider–owner. It will not be lack of knowledge or skills that stand in the way of the 50% of the psychologists who will not survive this century (N. A. Cummings, 1988) but, rather, outmoded attitudes. Important paradigm shifts are required to transcend the old order into the new, and the reader would do well to review these (N. A. Cummings, 1995b). In the words of Alvin Toffler, "The illiterate of the future are not those who cannot read or write, but those who cannot learn, unlearn and relearn" (cited in N. A. Cummings, 1995a, p. 10).

REFERENCES

Cummings, J. L. (1996). Managing suicidal patients: The ultimate test in overcoming outmoded attitudes. In N. A. Cummings, M. S. Pallak, & J. L. Cummings (Eds.), *Surviving the demise of solo practice: Mental health professionals prospering in the era of managed care* (pp. 253–267). Madison, CT: Psychosocial Press.

Cummings, N. A. (1986). The dismantling of our health system: Strategies for survival of psychological practice. *American Psychologist, 41,* 426–431.

Cummings, N. A. (1988, September). *The future of inpatient and outpatient mental health practice: A series of predictions.* Keynote address to the First Annual *Behavioral Healthcare Tomorrow* conference, San Francisco.

Cummings, N. A. (1991). Arguments for the financial efficacy of psychological services in health care settings. In J. J. Sweet, R. H. Rozensky, & S. M. Tovian (Eds.), *Handbook of clinical psychology in medical settings* (pp. 113–126). New York: Plenum.

Cummings, N. A. (1993). Somatization: When physical symptoms have no medical cause. In D. Goleman & J. Gurin, (Eds.), *Mind–body medicine* (pp. 221–230). Yonkers, NY: Consumer Reports Books.

Cummings, N. A. (1994). The successful application of medical offset in program planning and clinical delivery. *Managed Care Quarterly, 2*(2), 1–6.

Cummings, N. A. (1995a). Behavioral health after managed care: The next golden opportunity for professional psychology. *Register Report, 20*(3), 1, 30–33.

Cummings, N. A. (1995b). Impact of managed care on employment and training: A primer for survival. *Professional Psychology: Research and Practice, 26,* 10–15.

Cummings, N. A., & Sayama, M. (1995). *Focused psychotherapy: A casebook of brief, intermittent psychotherapy throughout the life cycle.* New York: Brunner/Mazel.

Cummings, N. A., & VandenBos, G. R. (1979). The general practice of psychology. *Professional Psychology, 10,* 430–440.

De Lafuente, D. (1993, June). California groups join for survival: Mullikin Healthcare Partners exemplify trend. *Modern Healthcare*, pp. 24–26.

Forrester, D. (1994, March). The "physician equity model." *Integrated Healthcare Report*, pp. 1–4.

Goldman, W., & Feldman, S. (Eds.). (1993). Managed mental health care. *New Directions for Mental Health Services, 59*, 1–112.

Neer, H. M. (1994, July). *The future of occupational medicine*. Address to the National Workers' Compensation and Occupational Medicine Seminar, Hyannis, MA.

Oss, M. (1995). As quoted by Saeman, H., An interview with Monica Oss. *National Psychologist, 4*(3), 2–3.

Pallak, M. S., & Cummings, N. A. (1992). Inpatient and outpatient psychiatric treatment: The effect of matching patients to appropriate level of treatment on psychiatric and medical–surgical hospital days. *Applied and Preventive Psychology, 1*, 83–87.

Pallak, M. S., Cummings, N. A., Dörken, H., & Henke, C. J. (1993, Fall). Managed mental health, Medicaid, and medical cost offset. *New Directions for Mental Health Services*, pp. 27–40.

Physician management merger deal: Medpartners–Mullikin would lead industry. (1995, August 18). *New York Times*, Section D, pp. 1, 8.

Rich, S. (1995, March 19). Study finds savings in some HMOs. *The Washington Post*, p. A20.

4

A LIFE-COURSE PERSPECTIVE ON PHYSICAL AND PSYCHOLOGICAL HEALTH

JAMES S. JACKSON

The purpose of this chapter is to outline a general theoretical and research framework for studying health over the individual life course. A life-course perspective is conducive to psychological research and practice, as well as the implementation of health relevant public policy. This framework encompasses consideration of the continuities and discontinuities over the individual life course and focuses on important developmental and aging related processes, cohort influences, and period events needed to understand physical and psychological health at different points in the individual life span.

Human development, aging, and the life course are the central concepts in any approach to truly comprehending physical and psychological health. A life-course approach is relevant not only in the developmental sciences, but in all areas of cognitive, social, personality, organizational, clinical, and physiological study. Individual, structural, and societal change transform the phenomena of interests in all these areas of psychological science and practice. Age divisions in the study of psychologically meaningful material are no longer tenable, if they ever were (Baltes, 1987).

The life-course framework assumes that individuals have divergent life experiences, beginning at conception, due to genetic, biological, sociostructural, socioeconomic, and cultural factors (Driedger & Chappell, 1988). These differing experiences will have significant positive and negative influences on individual, family, and group well-being at all stages of the life course, ultimately influencing the adjustment to successive major life transitions (e.g. puberty, loss of spouse, retirement, and disability) in adolescence and early, middle, and late adulthood.

A life-course framework is imperative in exploring how environmental factors influence and interact with group and personal resources to both impede and facilitate the health and quality of life of successive cohorts of individuals over their individual life spans and in the nature of their individual human development and aging experiences (Baltes, 1987; Burton, Dilworth-Anderson, & Bengtson, 1991). It is the premise of a life-course perspective that already-born and aging cohorts have been exposed to the conditions that will profoundly influence their social, psychological, and health statuses as they reach middle and older ages in the years and decades to come (Baltes, 1987; Barresi, 1987).

Some recent work on emotional selectivity (Carstensen, 1993) and successful aging (e.g. Mariske, Lang, Baltes, & Baltes, 1995) is beginning to provide testable hypotheses of life-course-related processes in human development and aging. Building on decades of work by interdisciplinary scholars (e.g., Rigle, Hagestad, Brim, Riley, Overton, Neugarten, Havinghurst, Birren, Troll, & Schaie), these new models help to organize what has been more a world view and testament of faith rather than organized theory with the power to generate testable predictions.

THE SIGNIFICANCE OF BIRTH-COHORT AND STRUCTURAL CHANGES

> The health of the Negro today is both an expression and the result of the social and economic burdens imposed upon him. His health is inseparably connected with poor housing, unemployment, and inadequate education. . . . Yet there is insufficient data, as well as a paucity of studies, designed to answer many of the questions confronting us. (Cornerly, 1967, p. 653)

This quotation is taken from the first Nationwide Conference on the Health Status of the Negro in 1967 at Howard University. Its content is still applicable today, to both Blacks and the larger population. During the conference, reports on the widening health gap between Blacks and Whites pointed specifically to fetal death rates, life expectancy, childhood health risks, and disease specific causes of death, all indicating significant increased risks in the Black population (Cornerly, 1967). Since this notable conference, there have been both improvements in Black health status over the early and middle stages of the life course and continued deficits to that found among the general population.

In this chapter, as an illustrative example, consider the health status in 1996 of those middle-aged and young Black people of 1967, and speculate on where they and subsequent birth cohorts might be in the twenty-first century, the millennium right around the corner. This birth cohort perspective highlights the importance of life-span continuity in the aging experiences in America. This experience is reflected in (a) cumulative individual and social deficits; (b) the strength of birth-cohort experiences for all Americans, especially certain racial–ethnic groups; and, (c) the important effects that the processes of human development and aging, and period events (e.g. The Older Americans Act and Medicare) may have in reshaping the future of existing cohorts of middle- and upper-middle-aged people. This characterization of today's older cohorts as the middle aged of 1967 also illuminates the vast heterogeneity in lifestyles; attitudes; and physical, social, and economic preparation for older age among individuals who are now 55 years of age and older. This chapter also addresses the context of the changing demography of older populations and the changing age structure. Both of these structural changes will have profound effects on the physical and psychological health of all Americans. Assuming the middle projection series of the United States Census Bureau (1.9 ultimate lifetime births per woman, mortality life expectancy of 79.6 years in 2050 and annual net immigration of 450,000), it is projected that sustained growth will occur in the over-65-year age group until 2010. From 2010 through 2030, the postwar baby boom cohorts will increase the over-65-year age group from 39 million to 65 million. By the year 2030, every fifth American will be over 65 years of age (Seigel & Taeuber, 1986).

It is quite clear to us who work in this area that life circumstances at younger years have significant influences on the quality (and quantity) of life in the latter stages of the life course. Environmental, social, and economic conditions early in the life course have significant influences on later social, psychological, and biological growth (J. J. Jackson, 1981). These accumulate over the individual life span and, when combined with the concomitants of older age itself, eventuate in higher levels of morbidity and mortality at earlier years in old age.

For example, and as a way of highlighting life-course influences, Blacks have greater disability and morbidity at every point of their individual life spans (J. J. Jackson, 1981). In infancy, this is marked by higher mortality figures as well as accident and disease rates. In adolescence, young adulthood and thereafter, Blacks are characterized by comparatively higher homicide deaths than Whites. Middle age and early old age show increased disability, earlier retirement, and, ultimately, higher death rates in the Black community as compared with the general population. It is only after the ages of 75 to 80 that Blacks tend to show increased longevity in comparison with whites (Manton, 1982; Manton, Poss, & Wing, 1979; Markides, 1983). In support of the substance of this observed crossover, it has been suggested that genetic and environmental factors act in tandem on a heterogeneous Black population to produce hardier older Blacks (Gibson & Jackson, 1987; Manton et al., 1979). One direct implication of this explanation is the existence of the differential aging processes within Black and White populations (Manton, 1982).

More generally, socioeconomic status (SES) has been proposed as a major risk factor and implicated in the effects of other risk factors as well in physical and psychological health (e.g., Haan & Kaplan, 1985). Impressive evidence exists that SES plays a major role in a wide variety of diseases, such that higher SES is associated with better health and lowered morbidity. This effect has been shown at both the individual and the ecological levels on blood pressure, general mortality, cancer, cardiovascular heart disease and cerebrovascular disease, diabetes, and obesity. What has not been shown is how SES status from point of origin in the life course affects these health outcomes (James, 1985).

Work in illness behavior and behavioral medicine, for example, also points to the independent role of cultural and lifestyle differences in accounting for behavioral, physical, and psychological health outcomes (Cooper, 1984, 1991; Dressler, 1985, 1991; Driedger & Chappel, 1988; Richardson, 1990).

Riley and her colleagues (J.W. Riley & Riley, 1994; M.W. Riley, 1994a, 1994b; M.W. Riley & Loscocco, 1994; M.W. Riley & Riley, 1994) have for a number of years proposed that cohort succession and structural lag must be considered in any model of aging and human development, including psychological ones. Their main argument has been that as people age, they encounter changing role opportunities and circumstances in society. At the intersections of lives and structures, lives influence structures, and structures influence lives. This interplay between individual lives and role opportunities for individuals can never be in synchrony; there must always be asynchronies. Thus, there must always be structural lags, that is "changes in social structures that provide role opportunities and norms [that] do not keep pace with the 20th century metamorphoses in people lives" (J. W. Riley & Riley, 1994, p. 17).

This notion of structural lag highlights the problem of allocating education, work, and leisure time over peoples' lives. As one example, the rapid technological advances in medicine and related scientific fields may quickly outstrip the original training of physicians, making them unqualified for continual practice over a long career without extensive re-education and training. Similar examples can be pointed to in highly sophisticated fields, like computer technology. Models of age integration that effectively intersperse work, education, and leisure at every point of the adult life course are needed.

Although the exact shape of the future is difficult to dictate, what is clear is that structural change will continue to be asynchronous with the course of peoples' lives. Thus, there must be developed flexible structures and processes for changes in opportunity and norms that are responsive to structural lags and the course of individual lives.

One of the areas briefly touched on in the Rileys' work on structural lag and age integration is the role of the family as an important mediator in the relationship between individuals and social structure. For many individuals in this country and, in fact, many countries around the world, age integration is accomplished not so much by individuals and their direct relationship in complex social structures, but instead through family systems that provide productive relationships and connections across the age span. Some of these functions have been formal, such as the assumption of leadership positions with age in complex tribal and family economic systems. Many of these role functions have been informal, involving important work within the family, as counselors, helpers for the youngest and most dependent, or sources of informal work, contributing to the economic and social well-being of the family. This has certainly been true among many American racial–ethnic groups.

Now, because of some of the structural changes that Riley and her colleagues have discussed, these formal and informal familial arrangements are in danger. These changes thus threaten to remove one important buffer and facilitator in the lives of many Americans—a buffer that has shielded them from some of the negative consequences of the structural changes that Riley and Riley discuss.

Among African Americans, the family has been an important, stable asset in a hostile and uncompromising world, insulating against the continuing, pernicious effects of racism, especially in its institutional forms (e.g., Jim Crow), that transcend the types of structural changes that have occurred. In fact, the continuing oppression of prejudice, racism, and discrimination interacts with structural changes to make it even more difficult to cope. For example, the technological revolution and its impact on aging individuals are bad enough. But imagine a situation in which systematic barriers to education existed for some groups (e.g., racial–ethnic groups)—barriers that affect not only the aging cohort members but also their offspring. This is exactly the situation that we have in the United States. In fact, it is much more widespread than just education. M. W. Riley (1994b) suggested the following:

> However, other segments of older people in future cohorts may be less advantaged than their predecessors, as, for example their lives will reflect their earlier experience with the deteriorating economic conditions of today, the rise of disadvantaged minorities, the loosening family structure, the spreading use of drugs, and the increasing proportions of younger people who are failing to meet acceptable standards of academic achievement. (p. 1216)

What is notable about this quotation is that in every example, racial and ethnic groups are disadvantaged: deteriorating economic conditions, the weakening of family strengths, spreading use of drugs, increasing poor educational and technical training. Significant improvements in the life situations of many groups (Farley, 1987), particularly health, have occurred over the last 40 years (J. J. Jackson, 1981). On the other hand, recent literature (e.g. Farley, 1987; Gibson, 1986; Jaynes & Williams, 1989) documents the negative life events and structural barriers, especially for impoverished groups, that still exist. These problems include the difficulties of single-parent households, high infant mortality and morbidity, childhood diseases, poor diets, lack of preventive health care, deteriorating neighborhoods, poverty, adolescent violence, unemployment and underemployment, teen pregnancy, drug and alcohol abuse, and broken marriages. Although the exact causal relationships are not known (Williams, 1990), clearly these are predisposing factors for poor physical and psychological health across the entire individual life span (Dressler, 1991; Haan & Kaplan, 1985).

PHYSICAL AND PSYCHOLOGICAL HEALTH OVER THE LIFE COURSE

Cohort succession, aging processes, and the life course are the central concerns in any approach to understanding physical and psychological health patterns over the individual life span. Our overall framework has assumed that different groups have divergent life experiences because of SES and cultural reasons (Driedger & Chappel, 1988). These different experiences will have profound influences, both positive and negative, on the individual, family, and group well-being at all stages of the life course, ultimately influencing the adjustment to major life transitions in older age (e.g., loss of spouse, retirement, and disability). We have tried to understand and empirically demonstrate how these variables provide important coping and adaptive mechanisms in alleviating the distinct socioeconomic and psychological disadvantages of categorical ethnic and racial membership (Stanford, 1990).

We are attempting to develop a coherent life-course framework within which the nature of the economic, social, and psychological lives of all Americans can be understood and explained in the context of historical and current structural disadvantage and blocked mobility opportunities (J. S. Jackson, 1991; J. S. Jackson, Antonucci, & Gibson, 1990a, 1990b). Our research has addressed the question of how structural disadvantages in the environment are translated into physical, social, and psychological aspects of group and self at different points in the individual and group life course. This work has focused on such things as self-esteem, personal efficacy, close personal and social relationships, neighborhood and family integration, physical and mental health, group solidarity, and political participation.

Our theoretical lens has been focused on understanding the interaction and intersection of age-related processes, period events, and cohort-related phenomena, as they influence the family and individual experiences. Thus, we have oriented our studies to examine how the adaptation and quality of life of individuals, families, and larger groups of Americans are influenced by (a) the age cohort into which individuals are born; (b) the social, political, and economic events that occur to cohorts born together; and (c) the individual aging process at different points in a person's life course. For example, African Americans born before the 1940s faced very different environmental constraints and have experienced a very different set of life tasks, events, opportunities, and disappointments than those born in the 1970s (Baker, 1987). Health care advances, family changes, urban migration, and macroeconomic influences, in addition to significant changes in the legal structure, all differed dramatically for these very different birth cohorts, as they will for future cohorts (Richardson, 1990).

Genetic and biological differences also play significant roles in disease, morbidity, and mortality in older ages. In general, members of different ethnic–racial groups evidence varying patterns of disease and limiting health conditions in older ages. These are differentiated due to subpopulation differences, gender as well as heredity, and are influenced by cultural patterns and socioeconomic differences. Although the exact mechanisms of how SES and gender may play a role are not known, the negative effects of low SES are unequivocal. Also, an important overlooked factor has been the patterning and co-occurrence of disease and chronic conditions, especially among racial–ethnic groups. For example, it has been reported that for Native Americans, diabetes is a risk factor, along with malnutrition, fatigue, and crowded living conditions, in the incidence and mortality effects of tuberculosis (McCabe & Cuellar,

1994). Alcohol abuse among Native Americans is a well-known phenomenon, although research on elders in this group is not extensive. McCabe and Cuellar (1994) reported significant differences among tribes. Whereas hypertension has been long recognized as a prevalent disorder among Blacks, recent work shows a dramatic increase among the current generation of Native Americans, especially Navajos, suggesting that the next generation over 65 may show an increase in its prevalence (McCabe & Cuellar, 1994).

Genetic and biological differences may also play a significant role in disease, morbidity, and mortality in older ages. Differential bone mass between Black and White elderly, for example, may play a significant role in predisposition to breaks in older ages (Richardson, 1990). Morioka-Douglas and Yeo (1990) indicated racial–ethnic group differences in drug sensitivity and tolerance among Asian Americans in comparison with other groups. Differential rates of diabetes, cerebrovascular problems, heart problems, and alcoholism may all have significant genetic and physiologic components in accounting for observed differences among groups.

On the other hand, culturally determined differences in beliefs and behaviors related to health may also account for large differences. For example, Yu, Liu, and Kyrzeja (1985) reported that on some measures of preventive health-promoting activities (e.g., well-baby examinations and early physician visits), Asian and Pacific Islander rates exceed those of the general population. Kuo (1984) noted, however, that Asian Americans tend to underutilize services and that the negative consequences of such underutilization differ among specific Asian American groups. Yu et al. (1985) reported that cultural factors related to family ties and health beliefs (e.g., use of herbal prescriptions or balance of hot and cold elements of the body) play a significant role in the health status of the elderly in these groups. Among Native Americans, several indicators of health prevention and promotion approximate those of the general population. The lack of sensitivity to cultural differences, however, lowers the quality of service delivery and utilization by Native American Indians (National Indian Council on Aging, 1984).

How different birth cohorts, historical and current environmental events, and individual differences in aging processes interact with one another must form the overall context of our psychological research, interventions, and public policy. Thus, whereas one focus is on scientific aspects of phenomena, such as political behavior, mental disorder, or service provision, the overarching framework is one that contextualizes these individual and group experiences by birth cohort, period events, and individual aging processes. The following are examples of selected areas of research.

Socially Supportive Processes

Descriptive studies of social support suggest that a life-course perspective is particularly useful for understanding specific events or behaviors. To understand current social participation and supportive exchanges, it is best to view the present within the context of past experiences and exchanges. In addition, research has shown that demographic factors, such as socioeconomic status, sex, marital status, and age, also affect supportive behaviors. For example, a lifetime of limited economic resources does not provide the same capability of building a tangible support reserve, that is, a history of having provided tangible resources to others so that they might provide the same or similar to you in some future time of need (Antonucci, 1985). However, the research does suggest that exchanges do occur among disadvantaged groups (e.g., Stack, 1974) using the more limited tangible and perhaps more bountiful emotional and affective resources that are available, creating special, mutually supportive, intergenerational, though not necessarily linear, exchanges (Mutran, 1985; Stevens, 1988).

Similarly, because structural position affects socially supportive arrangements, people of lower SES are more likely to have exclusively family-linked networks and to have multiple relations with fewer people. Because spouses are important support resources, especially for men, the decreased availability of a spouse, for example, among older Filipino men or older Black women, has negative effects on support relationships. Sex differences in social support (women have more complex and qualitatively superior relations) seem to hold across ethnic and racial groups. Thus, both minority and nonminority women without spouses are better able than men without spouses to develop substitute or compensatory support relationships.

On the other hand, many racial–ethnic groups, while showing deficits in comparisons to majority groups in some areas, have developed alternative sources of support. For example, for many Blacks, the church is an important alternative source of support to that of family and friends (Ortega, Crutchfield, & Rushing, 1983). (Religion as social support should not be confused with religiosity—the intrinsic value of religion.)

Another major area of investigation has been the function of social network and social support in alleviating the effects of stress, promoting effective health behaviors, and influencing health outcomes (Berkman, 1988). Some work (e.g., Krause, 1987) shows that the causal effects among stress, social support, and a variety of health and effective function outcomes in the elderly are highly complex and differ among groups. Other studies (e.g., James, 1985) suggest the following: (a) Social disorganization is related to elevated stroke mortality rates, (b) individuals within strong families are at reduced risk for elevated blood pressure, and (c) there is a positive role of social ties and support in reducing elevated blood pressure. In summary, it seems indisputable that social networks and social support have etiologic and buffering roles in health and well-being over the individual life course (Berkman, 1988).

Intellectual Functioning and Cognitive Potential

A great deal of research has been conducted on intellectual functioning. Theorizing by Perlmutter (1988) suggests that a belief in an inevitable decline in cognitive potential in late life is even less defensible than a view of inevitable decline with increased age in intellectual abilities (Baltes, 1987; Schaie, 1983). As has been suggested by an impressive body of empirical work (e.g., Baltes, 1987; Schaie, 1983), some abilities decline, some remain the same, and some improve with chronological age. The direction of change depends on the specific ability under investigation and the prevalence of risk factors, such as educational level and decline in the ability of the spouse. The fact that some groups (e.g., ethnic and racial cultural groups) show such marked differences on standardized measures of cognitive ability among the young may make for an interesting comparison with patterns of lifelong changes in these abilities found in other groups. It remains to be seen if there is lifelong continuity or a crossover effect, as compared with Whites, in the intellectual functioning among racial–ethnic groups.

The work of Labouvie-Vief (1985) stresses the importance of cultural evolution in considering adult cognitive development, suggesting a critical role of the opportunity structure and the definition of adaptive roles by elders within these structures. This view of adult cognitive development seems compatible with perspectives on behaviors that emphasize coping capacities and adaptive skills in the face of real systemic constraints (J. S. Jackson, 1988, 1991). One of the most fruitful areas of study is the role of how opportunity-structure variables interact with individual difference factors (e.g., capacity and motivation) and with family and formal support systems, to influence health and effective functioning over the life course. Recent advances in experimental work designed to explicate the role of retrieval, encoding, and decoding processes in the learning of meaningful material (Perlmutter, 1988) also shows promise. The investigation of cultural and ethnic factors (contextual factors) related to changes in learning and memory over the life span could be a very fruitful area of study, a point also made in a recent Institute of Medicine report (Lonergan, 1991).

Personality and Motivation

The construct of control has assumed an important role as an organizing framework in aging research (Lachman, 1995; Rodin, 1989).

Rodin (1989) suggested that the relations between health and control may strengthen with increased age. She speculated that this may occur because: (a) control experiences increase with age, (b) the association between control and health may be altered by aging, or (c) age may influence the association between control and health-related behaviors. Recent research by Krause (1987) and Lachman (1995), for example, on the pivotal role of control beliefs and self-conceptions as important mediators in social support effects is in keeping with these observations. My own work with Toni Antonucci on personal efficacy and social support also gives control beliefs a central theoretical position in understanding the mechanisms that may underlie the influence of socially supportive behaviors (Antonucci & Jackson, 1987). More empirical research, however, is needed on the distribution of control perceptions, and their etiology and relationship to health and mental health outcomes among different groups over the life course.

Personality and motivational research has shown that a distinction between personal and general control beliefs is necessary and leads to different behavioral predictions. In particular, externality, defined in terms of sensitivity to social system determinants, predicts greater rather than less effectiveness (Gurin, Gurin, Lao, & Beattie, 1969; J. S. Jackson, Tucker, & Bowman, 1982). Enhanced control, shown experimentally under certain conditions to have positive relationships to health and well-being in White elderly persons (Rodin, 1989), may not be as effective for—in fact, may be detrimental to—the adjustment of some groups of ethnic and racial group adults.

Another related area that appears fruitful for understanding how race and ethnic statuses serve as contextual variables is age-related changes in self-conceptions, particularly self-esteem (Bengtson, Reedy & Gordon, 1985). Self-esteem has been found often to be positively correlated with age. Similarly, positive racial ethnic group identity is also positively correlated with age, though we find that a complex interaction with region and education is also present (e.g. Broman, Neighbors, & J. S. Jackson, 1988).

Psychopathology, Social Pathology, and Mental Health

Epidemiological research reveals few differences in the distribution of the major mental disorders among the full age populations of groups (Roberts, 1987). A great deal of research on Americans of racial and ethnic background points to important cultural distinctions that make the assessment and treatment of mental disorders difficult (J. S. Jackson, Chatters, & Neighbors, 1982). Differences in cultural expression, distribution of disorders, differential reactions to environmental factors, and differential responsiveness to treatment modality all have been found to be related to ethnic and racial background.

Some race and ethnic differences in paranoia, suicide, and depression may exist. Alcoholism, neuroses and schizophrenia decrease, for example, while depressive and organically based psychiatric disorders increase in successively older age groups (LaRue, Dessonville, & Jarvik, 1985). A given disease, in fact, can manifest itself differently among the young and old (Minaker & Rowe, 1985), and individuals at midlife, in contrast to those at older ages, may be at higher risk for stress reactions and perhaps depression due to major life losses, such as divorce and death of loved ones.

Stress events, responses, consequent adaptation, and ways in which these factors are interrelated also differ across age (Schaie, 1981). The personal resources of the elderly, for example, appear to insulate against or buffer stress in ways that may be different from the young (e.g., Kasl & Berkman, 1981). Age also changes relationships between mental health status and selected variables. For example, risks for nervous and mental disorders are greater for Black than White men age 24 to 64, but less for Black than White women age 65 to 69—young black men are at greater risk for certain mental disorders than older Black women (Manton, Patrick, & Johnson, 1987). These findings suggest complex interactions among age, race, gender, and the risk for developing mental disorders. Heterogeneity in physical and mental health and functioning increases in successively older age groups (Rowe & Kahn, 1987). For example, Manton et al. (1987) found that the relationship between age and mental illness diagnoses and mental status, is nonlinear in older age groups of Black women. Thus, caution must be taken in extrapolating the psychiatric epidemiology of one age group to another.

Age group, aging processes, and cohort membership have special effects on mental health status; aging is clearly pivotal in the interpretation of any model of stress and adaptation (Gibson, 1986). Adaptation to stressors and stress, in fact, could vary at different ages or points in the life span, among different cohorts, and in different sociohistorical periods. This makes it clear that the mental status and functioning must be examined within a theoretical model that takes a life-course perspective (Barresi, 1987).

The examination of physical and psychological health status and functioning has been conducted in a relative life-course vacuum. Although several authors have indicated the necessity of considering life-course models (e.g., Baltes, 1987; Barresi, 1987; Manton & Soldo, 1985) and history, cohort, and period effects in the nature of physical and psychological health status and functioning, few have actually collected the type of data or conducted the types of analyses that would shed any light on this process. (Schaie's and the Baltes' work on intellectual and cognitive functioning and successful aging are exceptions.) This has been as much the fault of a lack of good conceptual life-course models of physical and psychological health status and functioning as it has been the lack of quality data over time on sizable numbers of representative samples.

SUMMARY AND CONCLUSIONS

Older age among the general population is not a time of inevitable decline (J. S. Jackson et al., 1990a; Rowe, 1985). Changes in lifestyles, environmental risk reductions, and medical interventions can have positive influences on the quantity and quality of physical and psychological health in late life among older adults, even given the negative life-course experiences I have outlined. Some data (e.g., Gibson & Jackson, 1987) show that many historically disadvantaged older groups are free from functional disability and limitations of activity due to chronic illness and disease. For example, after the age of 65, Blacks and Whites, within sex groups, differ very little in years of expected remaining life. Health care has improved significantly for older adults, and consecutive cohorts have been better educated and better able to take advantage of available opportunities. On the other hand, without extensive environmental interventions, it is highly likely that a significant, and undoubtedly growing, proportion of older adults of the year 2051, those being born in 1996, are at severe risk for impoverished conditions, and poor social, physical, and psychological health in old age.

A convergence of theory and research derived from resource-based, life-course models of health and effective functioning is emerging (e.g., Baltes & Baltes, 1990). The data briefly reviewed in this chapter suggest directions that new psychological theory and research on physical and psychological health over the life course might take (Barresi 1987; Carstensen, 1993; Fry, 1988; Holzberg, 1982; Mariske et al., 1995; Rosenthal, 1986).

The life-course framework holds great promise. There is a need, however, for a greater infusion of cultural considerations in life-course theorizing and research in human development and aging (Fry, 1988; Gelfand & Barresi, 1987). Theories, research paradigms, service delivery models, and public policies continue to be developed that are not sensitive to the ever-increasing, large, ethnically and culturally diverse segments of our population. Culture and lifestyle differences are of fundamental importance in psychological constructs, theories, and interventions (Holzberg, 1982; J. J. Jackson, 1985; Rosenthal, 1986). Some studies have shown how recognition and sensitivity to cultural and racial factors in service delivery programs can increase the effectiveness and reduce the cost of delivering services to some populations (J. S. Jackson, Burns, & Gibson, 1992). It also has been suggested that the infusion of cultural content has positive effects on the health of the nation more broadly, regardless of whether the direct focus of that work is on specific racial–ethnic groups (Cooper, Steinhauer, Schatzkin, & Miller, 1981)

A positive future for psychological, life-course research, practice, and policy related to aging and age related changes in physical and psychological health, lies in the increased emphasis on the important contextual variables of race, culture, ethnicity, gender, and social and economic statuses (J. S. Jackson et al., 1990a). A recent Institute of Medicine and National Institute on Aging report on aging research in the behavioral and social sciences (Lonergan, 1991) concluded that during the last 40 years an impressive acquisition of knowledge on the nature of aging in sensory, behavioral, and cognitive systems has occurred, indicating that: (a) People do not age the same way—Individuals differ greatly in age-related declines (and increments) in physical, behavioral, and cognitive functioning; (b) some aging processes and the probability of aging well are modifiable; and (c) observed functional differences across individuals are greatly influenced by societal, environmental, and health-related statuses, and, most important, by the background and makeup of the individual. Thus, we now know the following: (a) Cognitive declines are not universal with age, some intellectual abilities are actually maintained or improve with age; (b) positive social and psychological change is possible through interventions among older adults and, in fact, at every point of the life span; (c) intergenerational models of aging and human development are of critical importance in understanding individual aging trajectories; (d) there is a causal role of period events and cohort membership on aging-related physical and psychological health processes; and (e) we must conceptualize aging-related changes in physical and psychological health processes within individual, family, cultural, and societal life-course frameworks.

Our work, and the work of many others, is attempting to extend the life-course framework to encompass an integrated model that includes historical, cohort, and cultural influences on successful social, physical, and psychological development and aging. The relevance, power, and importance of comprehensive life-course models in psychological research, practice, and public policy cannot be overstated. It is the key to the evolution of comprehensive theory, appropriate research, and successful interventions and programs to ameliorate poor physical and psychological health conditions at every point in the life course.

REFERENCES

Antonucci, T. C. (1985). Personal characteristics, social networks, and social behavior. In R. H. Binstock, & E. Shanas (Eds.), *Handbook of aging and the social sciences* (pp. 94–128). New York: Van Nostrand Reinhold.

Antonucci, T. C., & Jackson, J. S. (1987). Social support, interpersonal efficacy and health. In L. Carsstensen & B. A. Edelstein (Eds.), *Handbook of clinical gerontology* (pp. 291–311). New York: Pergamon Press.

Baker, F. M. (1987). The Afro-American life cycle: Success, failure, and mental health. *Journal of the National Medical, 7,* 625–633.

Baltes, P. B. (1987). Theoretical propositions of life-span developmental psychology: On the dynamics between growth and decline. *Developmental Psychology, 23,* 611–626.

Baltes, P. B., & Baltes, M. M. (Eds.) (1990). *Successful aging: Perspectives from the behavioral sciences.* Cambridge, England: Cambridge University Press.

Barresi, C. M. (1987). Ethnic aging and the life course. In D. E. Gelfand & C. M. Barresi (Eds.), *Ethnic dimensions of aging* (pp. 18–34). New York: Springer.

Bengtson, V. L., Reedy, M. N., & Gordon, C. (1985). Aging and self-conceptions: Personality processes and social contexts. In J. E. Birren & K. W. Schaie (Eds.), *Handbook of the psychology of aging* (pp. 544–593). New York: Van Nostrand Reinhold.

Berkman, L. F. (1988). *The changing and heterogenous nature of aging and longevity: A social and biomedical perspective.* Unpublished manuscript, Yale University, School of Medicine, New Haven, CT.

Broman, C. L., Neighbors, H. W., & Jackson, J. S. (1988). Racial group identification among Black adults. *Social Forces, 67,* 146–158.

Burton, L. M., & Dilworth-Anderson, P., & Bengtson, V. L. (1991). Creating culturally relevant ways of thinking about diversity. *Generations, 15,* 67–72.

Carstensen, L. L. (1993). Motivation for social contact across the life span: A theory of socioemotional selectivity. In J. Jacobs (Ed.), *Nebraska symposium on motivation: Vol. 40. Developmental perspectives on motivation* (pp. 209–254). Lincoln: University of Nebraska Press.

Cooper, R. (1984). A note on the biological concept of race and its application in epidemiological research. *American Heart Journal, 108,* 715–723.

Cooper, R. (1991). Celebrate diversity—Or should we? *Ethnicity and Disease, 1,* 3–7.

Cooper, R., Steinhauer, M., Schatzkin, A. & Miller, A. (1981). Improved mortality among U.S. Blacks, 1968–1978: The role of antiracist struggle. *International Journal of Health Services, 11,* 511–522.

Cornerly, P. B. (1968). The health status of the Negro today and in the future. *American Journal of Public Health, 58,* 647–654.

Dressler, W. (1985). Extended family relationships, social support, and mental health in a Southern Black community. *Journal of Health and Social Behavior, 26,* 39–48.

Dressler, W. W. (1991). Social class, skin color, and arterial blood pressure in two societies. *Ethnicity and Disease, 1,* 60–77.

Driedger, L., & Chappell, N. (1988). *Aging and ethnicity: Toward an interface.* Toronto, Ontario, Canada: Butterworths.

Farley, R. (1987). Who are Black Americans?: The quality of life for Black Americans twenty years after the civil rights revolution. *Milbank Memorial Fund Quarterly, 65* (Suppl. 1), 9–34.

Fry, C. (1988). Theories of aging and culture. In J. E. Birren & V. L. Bengston (Eds.), *Emergent theories of aging* (pp. 447–481). New York: Springer.

Gelfand, D. E. & Barresi, C. M. (Eds.). (1987). *Ethnic dimensions of aging.* New York: Springer.

Gibson, R. (1986). Blacks in an aging society. *Daedalus, 115,* 349–372.

Gibson, R. C., & Jackson, J. S. (1987). Health, physical functioning, and informal supports of the Black elderly. *Milbank Memorial Fund Quarterly, 65* (Suppl 1), 1–34.

Gurin, P., Gurin, G., Lao, R. C., & Beattie, M. (1969). Internal–external control in the motivational dynamics of Negro youth. *Journal of Social Issues, 25,* 29–53.

Haan, M. N., & Kaplan, G. A. (1985). *The contribution of socioeconomic position to minority health.* In *Report of the Secretary's Task Force on Black and Minority Health: Volume II. Crosscutting issues in minority health.* Washington, DC: U.S. Department of Health and Human Services.

Holzberg, C. S. (1982). Ethnicity and aging: Anthropological perspectives on more than just the minority elderly. *Gerontologist, 22,* 249–257.

Jackson, J. J. (1981). Urban Black Americans. In A. Harwood (Ed.), *Ethnicity and medical care.* Cambridge, MA: Harvard University Press.

Jackson, J. J. (1985). Race, national origin, ethnicity, and aging. In R. B. Binstock & E. Shanas (Eds.), *Handbook of aging and the social sciences* (pp. 264–303). New York: Van Nostrand Reinhold.

Jackson, J. S. (1988). *The Black American elderly: Research on physical and psychological health.* New York: Springer.

Jackson, J. S. (Ed.). (1991). *Life in Black America.* Newbury Park, CA: Sage.

Jackson, J. S., Antonucci, T. C., & Gibson, R. C. (1990a). Cultural, racial, and ethnic minority influences on aging. In J. E. Birren & K. W. Schaie (Eds.), *Handbook of the psychology of aging* (3rd ed., 103–123). San Diego, CA: Academic Press.

Jackson, J. S., Antonucci, T. C., & Gibson, R. C. (1990b). Social relations, productive activities, and coping with stress in late life. In M. A. P. Stephens, J. H. Crowther, S. E. Hobfoll, & D. L. Tennenbaum (Eds.), *Stress and coping in later life families* (pp. 193–212). Washington, DC: Hemisphere.

Jackson, J. S., Burns, C., & Gibson, R. C. (1992). An overview of geriatric care in ethnic and racial minority groups. In E. Calkins, A. B. Ford, & P. R. Katz (Eds.), *Practice of geriatrics* (2nd ed., pp. 57–64). Philadelphia: W. B. Saunders.

Jackson, J. S., Chatters, L. M., & Neighbors, H. W. (1982). The mental health status of older Black Americans: A national study. *Black Scholar, 13,* 21–35.

Jackson, J. S., Tucker, M. B., & Bowman, P. J. (1982). Conceptual and methodological problems in survey research on Black Americans. In W. T. Liu (Eds.), *Methodological problems in minority research* (pp. 11–39). Chicago: Pacific/Asian American Mental Health Research Center.

James, S. A. (1985). Coronary heart disease in black Americans: Suggestions for future research on psychosocial factors. In A. M. Ostfield (Ed.), *Measuring psychosocial variables in epidemiologic studies of cardiovascular disease* (pp. 499–508). Bethesda, MD: National Institutes of Health.

Jaynes, G. D. & Williams, R. M. (Eds.). (1989). *A Common Destiny: Blacks and American society.* Washington, DC: National Academy Press.

Kasl, S. V., & Berkman, L. F. (1981). Some psychosocial influences on the health status of the elderly: The perspective of social epidemiology. In J. L. McGaugh & S. B. Kiesler (Eds.), *Aging, biology and behavior* (pp. 345–385). San Diego, CA: Academic Press.

Krause, N. (1987). Life, stress, social support, and self-esteem in an elderly population. *Psychology and Aging, 2,* 349–356.

Kuo, W. H. (1984). Prevalence of depression among Asian Americans. *Journal of Nervous and Mental Disease, 172,* 449–457.

Labouvie-Vief, G. (1985). Intelligence and cognition. In J. E. Birren & K. W. Shaie (Eds.), *Handbook of the psychology of aging* (pp. 500–530). New York: Van Nostrand Reinhold.

Lachman, M. E. (1995, August). *Maintaining a sense of control over physical and mental function.* Presentation at the 103rd Annual Convention of the American Psychological Association, New York.

LaRue, A., Dessonville, C., & Jarvik, I. (1985). Aging and mental disorders. In J. Birren & K. Schaie (Eds.), *Handbook of the psychology of aging* (pp. 664–702). New York: Van Nostrand Reinhold.

Lonergran, E. T. (Ed.). (1991). *Extending life, enhancing life.* Washington, DC: National Academy Press.

Manton, K. G. (1982). Differential life expectancy: Possible explanations during the later years. In R. C. Manual (Ed.), *Minority aging: Sociological and psychological issues* (63–70). Westport, CT: Greenwood Press.

Manton, K. G., Patrick, C. H., & Johnson, K. W. (1987). Health differentials between Blacks and Whites: Recent trends in mortality and morbidity. *Milbank Memorial Fund Quarterly, 65,* 129–199.

Manton, K. G., Poss, S. S., & Wing, S. (1979). The Black/White mortality crossover: Investigation from the perspective of the components of aging. *Gerontologist, 63,* 177–186.

Manton, K. G., & Soldo, B. J. (1985). Dynamics of health changes in the oldest old: New perspectives and evidence. *Milbank Memorial Fund Quarterly, 63*, 206–285.

Mariske, M., Lang, F. R., Baltes, P. B., & Baltes, M. M. (1995). Selective optimization with compensation: Life-span perspectives on successful human development. In R. A. Dixon & L. Backman (Eds.), *Psychological compensation: Mananging losses and promoting gains*. Hillsdale, NJ: Erlbaum.

Markides, K. S. (1983). Aging, religiosity and adjustment: A longitudinal analysis. *Journal of Gerontology, 38*, 621–625.

McCabe, M., & Cuellar, J. (1994). *Aging and health: American Indian/Alaska natives* (Working Paper No. 6). Stanford, CA: Stanford University, Stanford Geriatric Education Center, Division of Family & Community Medicine.

Minaker, K. L., & Rowe, J. W. (1985). Health and disease among the oldest old: A clinical perspective. *Milbank Memorial Fund Quarterly, 63*, 324–349.

Morioka-Douglas, N., & Yeo, G. (1990). *Aging and health: Asian/Pacific Island elders* (Working Paper No. 6). Stanford CA: Stanford University, Stanford Geriatric Education Center, Division of Family & Community Medicine.

Mutran, E. (1985). Intergeneratinal family support among Blacks and Whites: Response to culture or to socioeconomic differences. *Journal of Gerontology, 40*, 382–389.

National Indian Council on Aging. (1984). Indian and Alaskan natives. In E. B. Palmore (Ed.), *Handbook on the aged in the United States* (pp. 269–278). Westport, CT: Greenwood Press.

Ortega, S. T., Crutchfield, R. D., & Rushing, W. A. (1983). Race differences in elderly personal well-being. *Research on Aging, 5*, 101–118.

Perlmutter, M. (1988). Cognitive potential throughout life. In J. E. Birren & V. L. Bengtson (Eds.), *Emergent theories of aging* (pp. 247–268). New York: Springer.

Richardson, J. (1990). *Aging and health: Black elders* (Working Paper No. 4). Stanford, CA: Stanford University, Stanford Geriatric Education Center, Division of Family & Community Medicine.

Riley, J. W., & Riley, M. W. (1994, June). Beyond productive aging: Changing lives and social structure. *Aging International*, pp. 15–19.

Riley, M. W. (1994a). Aging and society: Past, present, and future. *Gerontologist, 34*, 436–446.

Riley, M. W. (1994b). Changing lives and changing social structures: Common concerns of social science and public health. *American Journal of Public Health, 84*, 1214–1217.

Riley, M. W., & Loscocco, K. A. (1994). The changing structure of work opportunities: Toward an age integrated society. In R. P. Abeles, H. C. Gift, & M. C. Orey (Eds.), *Aging and the quality of life* (pp. 235–252). New York: Springer.

Riley, M. W., & Riley, J. W. Jr. (1994). Age integration and the lives of older people. *Gerontologist, 34*, 110–115.

Roberts, R. E. (1987, December). *Depression among Black and Hispanic Americans*. Paper present at the National Institutes of Mental Health Workshop on Depression and Suicide in Minorities, Bethesda, MD.

Rodin, J. (1989). Sense of control: Potentials for intervention. *Annals of the American Academy of Political and Social Science, 503,* 29–42.

Rosenthal, C. J. (1986). Family supports in later life: Does ethnicity make a difference? *Gerontologist, 26,* 19–24.

Rowe, J. W. (1985). Health care of the elderly. *New England Journal of Medicine, 312,* 827–835.

Rowe, J. W., & Kahn, R. L. (1987). Human aging: Usual and successful. *Science, 237,* 143–149.

Schaie, K. W. (1981). Psychological changes from midlife to early old age: Implications for the maintenance of mental health. *American Journal of Orthopsychiatry, 51,* 199–218.

Schaie, K. W. (Ed.). (1983). *Longitudinal studies of adult psychological development.* New York: Guilford Press.

Seigel, J. S., & Taeuber, T. C. (1986). Demographic dimensions of an aging population. In A. Pifer & L. Bronte (Eds.), *Our aging society: Paradox and promise* (pp. 79–110). New York: Norton.

Stack, C. B. (1974). *All our kin.* New York: Harper & Row.

Stanford, E. P. (1990). Diverse Black aged. In Z. Harel, E. A. McKinney, & M. Williams (Eds.), *Black aged: Understanding diversity and service needs* (pp. 33–49). Newbury Park, CA: Sage.

Stevens, J. H. (1988). Social support, locus of control, and parenting in three low-income groups of mothers: Black teenagers, Black adults, and White mothers. *Child Development, 59,* 635–642.

Williams, D. R. (1990). Socioeconomic differentials in health: A review and redirection. *Social Psychology Quarterly, 53,* 81–99.

Yu, E. S. H., Liu, W. T., & Kyrzeja, P. (1985). Physical and mental health status indicators for Asian-American communities. In Department of Health and Human Services (Ed.), *Black and minority health: Vol. II. Cross-cutting issues in minority health* (pp. 255–286). Washington, DC: U.S. Department of Health and Human Services.

5

AGING, HEALTH, AND BEHAVIOR: THE INTERPLAY BETWEEN BASIC AND APPLIED SCIENCE

DENISE C. PARK

The composition of American society is changing. Besides a dramatic increase in racial and ethnic heterogeneity, perhaps an even more striking change is the massive shift in the age distribution of the population. Americans are getting old. The baby boomers are on the crest of late adulthood. By the year 2030, it appears that there will be as many elderly people in this country as there are children. To fully appreciate the magnitude of the demographic shift, consider that in the year 1900, only 4% of the U.S. population was over 65, whereas children constituted 40% of the population (Task Force on Aging Research, 1995). Thus, in 1900, there were 10 children for every elderly adult, and by 2030, that will have shifted to a 1:1 ratio of adult to child. It may chill you to recognize that the shift I am describing will happen in the lifetimes of most of you who are reading this book.

Preparation of this chapter was supported by National Institute on Aging Grants AGO6265-08, AGO9868-02, and P5011715-01. I thank Natalie Davidson and Maria Brinks for their assistance.

On the basis of just these few statistics, it should be apparent that at the least, the graying of America represents an amazing social and economic challenge for our society. What needs to be emphasized is that this problem is certain, and virtually on us, and that Social Security and Medicare were predicated on a large number of young adults to maintain the system. As government resources become more scarce, it seems likely that the successful adaptation of any given individual to the aging process will be tremendously influenced by his or her health behavior. It has become increasingly evident that health is not just a result of genetic and environmental contributions, but the behavior of the person plays a critical role in disease prevention as well as health outcomes once a disease process has begun. The focus of this chapter is twofold: First, I discuss the critical role that development of the behavioral sciences can play in maintaining health and vitality into late adulthood, with an emphasis on the importance of fostering both basic and applied behavioral research and the interplay between the two. Second, I follow this discussion with a concrete example of how my own research program on the psychosocial and cognitive components of medication adherence in older adults evolved from a long-term basic research program on mechanisms associated with age-related changes in memory function.

THE LINKAGE OF BEHAVIORAL RESEARCH TO HEALTH OUTCOMES

Behavior is the fundamental link between medical knowledge, services, and technology and successful health outcomes. Behavioral issues permeate all aspects of medical care and treatment. For example, it seems self-evident that health can be maintained only if people engage in preventive behaviors. What is less recognized is that successful treatment of illness requires that individuals both understand and follow relevant medical advice, once treatment is initiated. Moreover, effective treatments can be administered only to the extent that health care professionals understand the needs, attitudes, and goals of their clients. Finally, the individual cannot adjust his or her health behaviors in a direction that leads to adaptation and to successful aging if he or she does not know what behaviors prevent disease. It is only through behavioral research that we can address the issues raised thus far and then isolate and disseminate information to the general public and health care professionals that will lead to the maintenance of health in late adulthood.

The ominous developments in the recent past with respect to changes in Medicare and gatekeeping of access to health care make it eminently clear that baby boomers should be particularly concerned that they maintain their health. When the baby boomers are old, there

TABLE 1
Behavioral Recommendations Associated With Each Research Domain in the Report of the Task Force on Aging Research

Research domain	No. goals	No. goals with a behavioral component	Proportion
Biological processes	25	5	.20
Diseases and disabilities	42	24	.57
Mental disorders	12	12	1.00
Health care	27	22	.81
Social & behavioral functioning	16	16	1.00
An aging society	13	10	.77
Economic security	9	3	.33
Social & supportive services	12	11	.92
Special populations	18	17	.94
Research & data resources	18	11	.61
Total	192	131	.68

will be increasing competition for scarce medical resources, and many boomers also will have limited pension resources. Thus, health and vitality are likely to become even more important predictors of well-being in late adulthood than is the case at present. We need to know what behaviors lead to good health. Until the very recent past, the focus of most research within the National Institutes of Health has been on basic disease mechanisms and treatment, with much less attention being paid to behavioral factors. This is changing, especially with respect to health issues associated with the aging process.

Behavioral research and targeted behavioral objectives are permeating the goals of the National Institute on Aging. The National Institute on Aging has released a document prioritizing research objects for the future with respect to aging (Task Force on Aging Research, 1995). Categories of emphasis are divided into 10 research domains, as shown in Table 1. Within each domain, there are a series of research objectives and goals. There are a total of 192 goals specified across the 10 domains. What is particularly exciting is that 131 of them (68%) have a behavioral component or objective. Of course, one would expect categories such as social and behavioral functioning to have behavioral objectives. But what is most telling is that behavioral goals permeate every category, even basic medical objectives. For example, in the category of "diseases and disabilities," there are numerous goals that are primarily behavioral, including "frailty prevention"; "exercise, strength training, and metabolism"; "cancer prevention and early detection in older persons"; and "the effect of aging on biomechanical efficiency." Under the category of "health care," behavioral objectives include "compliance with health promotion and disease prevention measures"; "prevention of falls";

"smoking cessation"; and "autonomy in health-care decision making." There are many other goals that mandate the assessment of preferences and decision-making processes on the part of older adults with respect to health services, housing, and caregiving—these are all goals that have primarily behavioral science objectives. This report demonstrates conclusively that there is at last recognition that understanding disease mechanisms is entirely insufficient without understanding both the psychological mechanisms underlying the use of and adherence to treatments and the prevention behaviors individuals can engage in so that they will not need to be treated at all—they will stay healthy!

It is essential never to lose sight of the role that basic research plays as the foundation for applied, outcome-based research. It is our understanding of basic cognitive functioning and psychosocial processes that is the foundation for all of the prevention and intervention research that permits us to determine how to maintain sustained vitality into late adulthood. There are innumerable important questions about health and aging that psychologists are poised to answer, and some important developments have already occurred. The Human Capital Initiative is a scientific advocacy effort undertaken by the American Psychological Society. Under the auspices of this initiative, psychological scientists have prepared a series of reports based on their consensual opinions. The reports prioritize the important scientific questions that will have significant impact on society that psychologists are able to address now. One of these reports focused on aging and was developed in collaboration with the American Psychological Association. It is entitled "Vitality for Life: Psychological Research for Productive Aging" (Cavanaugh & Park, 1993). The report presents four major research objectives: (a) understanding relationships about health and behavior, (b) securing more information, much of it with health objectives, about the oldest old, (c) addressing issues associated with aging and the workplace, and (d) developing a better understanding of well-being in late adulthood and treatment for mental disorders in older adults. These priorities are very similar to many research objectives identified in the Task Force on Aging Research report (1995). It is very encouraging to see that there is considerable agreement about research priorities on aging for the future among both research scientists and representatives of federal agencies. Both reports emphasize areas where breakthroughs are possible due to the assembled corpus of basic knowledge and the fact that there are already beginnings of applications of that information to real-world problems.

FROM BASIC TO APPLIED RESEARCH: COGNITIVE FUNCTION AND MEDICATION ADHERENCE

One of the most highly researched basic areas in the psychology of aging that has tremendous implications for adaptation to aging is the understanding of aging and cognitive function. The knowledge base in cognitive aging is sufficiently developed that there are beginning to be substantial applications of basic behavioral work to areas of health and aging. In an effort to illustrate the link between basic laboratory research and effecting changes in health behavior, I devote the remainder of this chapter to presenting an overview of how basic research in the laboratory on aging and memory has led to the development of a substantial research program on aging and medication adherence, including intervention-based work. I close with a summary of important areas for future development in the area of health, behavior, and aging.

Cognition and Aging

I have spent the past 16 years studying memory function across the life span—from young adulthood to very late adulthood. In this work, my colleagues and I, along with many other researchers, have found convincing evidence that older adults perform more poorly on cognitive tasks that are measures of processing speed or processing resource. By this I mean that we have evidence that older adults process information more slowly than young adults (Park et al., 1994), that they have less *working memory* capacity (working memory is the ability to simultaneously process new incoming information while storing and retrieving old information), and that they have poorer recall abilities (Park & Shaw, 1992; Park, Smith, Morrell, Puglisi, & Dudley, 1990).

At the same time, we have demonstrated a number of cases in which older adults perform comparably to young adults on some types of memory tasks. For example, as Figure 1 illustrates, we have found that older adults have comparable picture-recognition abilities to young adults across a range of conditions (Park, Puglisi, & Smith, 1986), whereas Figure 2 demonstrates that age deficits observed in *direct, explicit recall* (recall items that one has studied) are not observed when indirect or implicit measures of recall are used (Park & Shaw, 1992). We have also found evidence for age invariance on some types of spatial memory and vocabulary abilities (Park et al., 1994). We believe that memory deficits occur when a memory task is high in its demands for mental effort (e.g., recall of information from memory, speeded measures of cognitive function, measures of maximal working memory capacity). In contrast, age deficits are minimized when a task requires less mental effort (e.g., recognition of pictures, implicit memory, and other processes requiring less direct, effortful memory search) or when it relies on world knowledge, which grows rather than decreases with age (e.g., vocabulary). On the basis of these premises, we have attempted to develop conditions where we can facilitate cognitive function of older adults by minimizing the processing resources required in a task. Figure 3 demonstrates that age differences for recall of pictures are markedly attenuated in a cued-recall

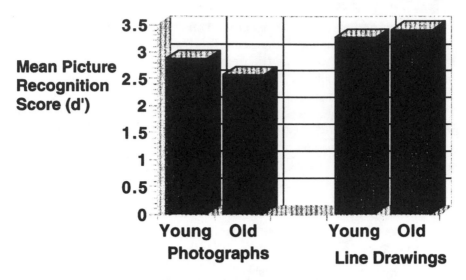

Figure 1. Picture-recognition scores (*d'* values) for old and young adults for photographs and line drawings of real-world scenes. Data derived from "Picture Memory in Older Adults: Does an Age-Related Decline Exist?" by D. C. Park, J. T. Puglisi, and A. D. Smith, 1986, *Psychology and Aging, 1*, 11–17.

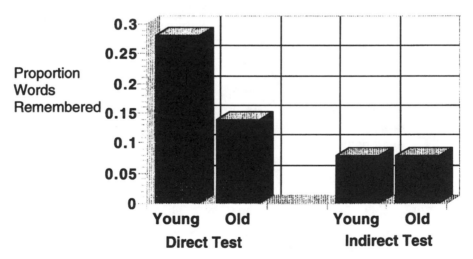

Figure 2. Proportion of words recalled in a stem-completion task as a function of age and type of memory test (direct or indirect). Data derived from "Effect of Environmental Support on Implicit and Explicit Memory in Young and Old Adults" by D. C. Park and R. Shaw, 1992, *Psychology and Aging, 7*, 632–642.

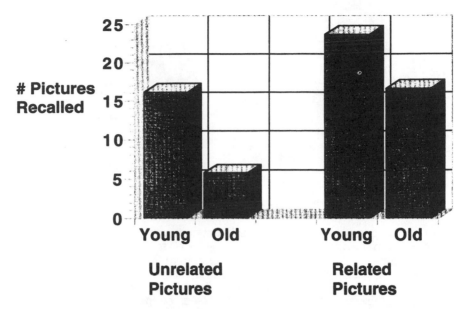

Figure 3. Number of items recalled in a cued-recall task when subjects were presented with unrelated compared with weakly related pictures. Data derived from "Effects of Contextual Integration on Recall of Pictures in Older Adults" by D. C. Park, A. D. Smith, R. W. Morrell, J. T. Puglisi, and W. N. Dudley, 1990, *Journal of Gerontology: Psychological Sciences, 45*, 52–58.

task when the cue is weakly related to the target word (e.g., spider–ant), compared with unrelated pictures (cherry–ant), because subjects can use their intact world knowledge to help them recall the words (Park et al., 1990). We also found that providing subjects with pictorial illustrations of an action represented in a sentence that they were to remember resulted in disproportionately greater improvement for older adults compared with younger adults, as shown in Figure 4 (Cherry, Park, Frieske, & Smith, in press).

The findings reported thus far probably appear to have little to do with health behaviors. However, as this basic laboratory work on memory and aging progressed, I became increasingly interested in understanding the meaning of these findings for a memory problem of practical significance to older adults.

Remembering to take medications correctly seemed to be a practical problem of great significance to older adults, as they consume more prescription medications than any other age group and are frequently placed in a situation where they must manage a complex regimen consisting of multiple medications. It has been estimated that medication nonadherence results in costs of $100 billion a year in the United States in terms of direct medical costs as well as lost time (Robbins, 1990). Thus, based on the importance of the problem and the significant role that memory and cognitive function appeared to play in this health

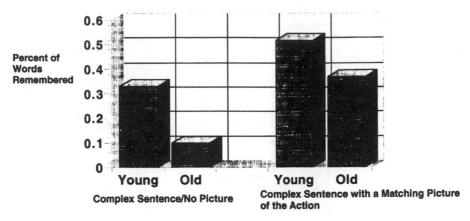

Figure 4. The percentage of target words remembered in a complex sentence when it was presented alone or with a matching picture of the action described in the sentence. Data derived from "Verbal and Pictorial Elaborations Enhance Memory in Younger and Older Adults" by K. E. Cherry, D. C. Park, D. A. Frieske, and A. D. Smith, 1996, *Aging, Neuropsychology, and Cognition, 3*, 15–29. Used with permission.

behavior, I embarked on a program of research on medication adherence, along with my colleague, Roger Morrell. *Medication adherence* can be defined as taking medication correctly, in the right amount, at the right time, and according to any special instructions, such as "take with food" (Park & Jones, in press). We hypothesized that there were four major cognitive components involved in the accurate use of medications: (a) comprehension of the individual instructions for each medication, (b) integration of the instructions across multiple medications to form a temporal plan—a working memory task; (c) remembering (or writing down) the plan—a long-term memory task; and (d) remembering to carry out the plan, that is, to take the medication—a prospective memory task (Park, 1992).

Laboratory Work on Medication Adherence

The initial work we conducted on this topic was a straightforward translation of our basic work in the laboratory into paradigms that examined age differences in comprehension and memory for medication information. We found evidence for significant age differences in both comprehension and memory for medication information (Morrell, Park, & Poon, 1989), with older adults remembering less information than young adults. This pattern of findings occurred even under conditions of unlimited study time. On the basis of the finding of age invariance for picture recognition presented in Figure 1, we attempted to design more memorable prescription labels for older adults by designing medication labels where information was presented pictorially. We then tested how memorable young and old adults found these redesigned pictorial labels compared with verbal labels (Morrell, Park, & Poon, 1990). We found that the pictorial labels were superior to verbal labels for young but not old adults, whereas old adults functioned better with the more familiar verbal labels.

As this work progressed, we became more interested in learning how older adults functioned with their own medications rather than with unfamiliar medication information designed for laboratory studies. Thus, for our next study, we focused on understanding how existing memory aids for organizing and taking medications were used with patients' actual medications. In this study, we presented patients with three types of medication organizers, commercial memory aids sold over-the-counter, designed to help facilitate the individual's medication-adherence behavior (Park, Morrell, Frieske, Blackburn, & Birchmore, 1991). We tested 45 arthritis patients taking multiple medications and asked them to load their own medications into three different types of organizers: one had merely 7 compartments, 1 for each day of the week; another was a medication wheel with 12 slots for 12 hours of the day; and a third had 28 compartments in which to place pills, created by crossing the 7 days of the week with 4 times during the day (morning, noon, dinner, and evening). We found that more errors were made in loading the first two organizers than with the third (the 28-compartment organizer). These findings, at the least, suggested that patients who loaded their organizers incorrectly were unlikely to be helped by these alleged memory supports.

Medication Adherence Outside the Laboratory

Although we were concerned that two of the organizers were loaded incorrectly, we were also intrigued by the finding that the error rate for the 28-compartment organizer (the 7-day organizer with 4 times per day) was below 5%. We were becoming increasingly interested in measuring what older adults actually did with their medications in the real world and in assessing the effect of a cognitive intervention, such as the use of a medication organizer, on adherence. We were concerned that verbal reports or diaries might not be accurate measures of adherence behavior, so we located a system based on bar-coding technology that we could use to monitor medication-taking behaviors outside of the laboratory. To implement the bar-coding measurement system, we provided 64 older adults with unique bar-coding stickers for each of the medications they were taking and put the stickers in a wallet. We also gave subjects a credit-card-sized bar code scanner with the wallet. The subjects were instructed to keep the wallet with their medications and scan the bar code, which was clearly labeled with the medication name, whenever they took that medication. The date and time of the scan were recorded

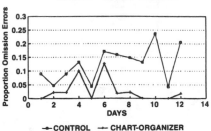

Figure 5. Mean adherence rates for young-old and old-old adults in a control condition compared with subjects receiving a chart and medication organizer. Reprinted from "Medication Adherence Behaviors in Older Adults: Effects of External Cognitive Supports" by D. C. Park, R. W. Morrell, D. Frieske, and D. Kincaid, 1992, *Psychology and Aging, 7*, 252–256. Copyright 1992 by the American Psychological Association.

in the tiny bar-coding device, and when the subject returned the device to us, we downloaded a complete record of their adherence behaviors for a 2-week period. The 64 older adults we studied were all taking multiple medications for various disorders, and they were randomly assigned to one of four groups. The first set of subjects was assigned to a control group where no intervention occurred. A second group of subjects was assigned to a chart condition, where they were provided with a chart in the form of a poster or booklet that provided them with an hour-by-hour, day-by-day account of which medications they should take for a 2-week period. There was a check-off space for them to record when they did take the medication. We hypothesized that this type of intervention would reduce the comprehension, working memory, and long-term memory components of medication adherence. A third group received the 28-compartment organizer, with their medications loaded in it by the experimenter. The organizer also facilitated the same cognitive components of medication adherence as the chart, but the medications were actually physically organized for the subject in the device, unlike the chart, where the medications remained in their original bottles. A final group received both aids: the medication chart and organizer. Results are displayed in Figure 5 for the control group and the group receiving the two interventions (Park, Morrell, Frieske, & Kincaid, 1992). The results indicate that young-old adults, those age 60–77, evidenced nearly perfect adherence, as shown in the left panel of Figure 5. An intervention was not effective for these subjects because they were making so few errors that there was no need to intervene. For old-old adults, however, the subjects receiving the two interventions made fewer medication errors than subjects in control conditions. The findings suggest that very old community-dwelling adults' medication adherence could be facilitated by cognitive aids.

In a subsequent study, we followed 48 adult hypertensives age 35 to 75 (Park, Morrell, Lautenschlager, & Firth, 1993) and found once again that the oldest old were most nonadherent and, as in Park et al. (1992), that young-old adults were the least nonadherent. Intermediate levels of nonadherence were evidenced by middle-aged adults. The poor adherence of the middle-aged subjects combined with the good adherence of the young-old adults caused us to reconceptualize medication-adherence behavior as involving more than merely remembering to take medications. We believe the nonadherence of the oldest old is a function of declines in working memory and long-term memory function that we have seen in the laboratory. In contrast, we hypothesize that the middle-aged show nonadherence due to the contextual press and high engagement of their lives. The high degree of obligations characteristic of middle age results in prospective forgetting, that is, subjects know what to do with their medications but cannot remember to take them. We also believe that young and middle-aged subjects may have had beliefs that were incompatible with adherence. In other words, they might have thought that they were not ill or that the medication was not useful, or they simply may have felt invulnerable and did not prioritize taking hypertension medication very highly. In contrast to these two groups, the young-old had both intact cognitive function and appropriate belief systems about medication and illness that led to high rates of adherence.

Psychosocial Aspects of Medication Adherence

On the basis of this work, we became very interested in understanding the joint contributions of cognitive function and psychosocial constructs to medication adherence (see Park & Mayhorn, in press, for a detailed discussion of the psychosocial aspects of medication adherence, and Park & Kidder, 1996, for an extended discussion of the role of prospective memory in medication adherence). We focused on the social psychological underpinnings of medication-adherence behavior and the self-regulatory framework of illness management and medication adherence espoused by Leventhal and Cameron (1987). Leventhal and Cameron argued that it is an individual's representation of her or his illness that drives illness behavior, rather than objective measures of illness status and function. In a sense, the Leventhal and Cameron view contrasts with our view of adherence, in which we view nonadherence simply as a cognitive–memory problem. At the same time, we recognized the views to be complementary rather than contradictory, because both health representations and cognitive function can contribute jointly to nonadherence. Based on the work described thus far, we reached three conclusions. These conclusions are quite likely generalizable to many aspects of aging, health, and behavior research:

1. The statistical techniques and methodologies we had used to date were inadequate to determine causality as well as to evaluate simultaneously the contributions of multiple constructs to adherence behaviors. The limitations imposed by collecting actual medication behaviors of patients at home over prolonged periods of time added to the complexity of the problem, because the dependent measures of the behavior of interest were also complex. Finally, we were unable to assess in a causal fashion the consequences of adherence. For example, do people who take medication for hypertension have measurably lower blood pressure, or do individuals with arthritis who take nonsteroidal anti-inflammatory drugs (which have numerous side effects of some consequence) actually function better and feel better? We concluded that to better address complex issues of this sort, we needed to use structural equation modeling techniques in our work, to permit the determination of complex causal relationships and the development of complex models that allow for the simultaneous and relative contributions of multiple constructs to a behavior (Jöreskog, 1993). Structural equation modeling techniques would allow us to examine the joint roles of cognitive function and illness representation, as well as other constructs to medication-adherence behaviors. Although the measurement requirements of constructs can be formidable for structural equation models (e.g., it is desirable to have three measures or indicators of every construct used in the model), these techniques are much better suited to addressing complex real-world problems than analysis of variance and even regression approaches.

2. We concluded that disease-specific approaches are necessary to understand medication-adherence behaviors. In other words, we believe that the adherence behaviors for individuals who have a silent disease like hypertension, where there are no obvious consequences of nonadherence except over the very long term, might be quite different from those of an individual with osteoarthritis, who has difficulty moving about without the use of pain-relieving medications.

3. We hypothesized that basic cognitive function was a factor in forgetting to take medications only for the very old and that belief systems, contextual press, and emotional states were more important for younger adults in determining

medication adherence. From this view, forgetting in younger adults would be caused by prospective memory failure, whereas in older adults, the focus would be on basic comprehension, working memory, and long-term memory function.

To address these issues in a systematic fashion, Roger Morrell and I developed a multidisciplinary research team that had the expertise to design a research program congruent with the conclusions described above. We now have a research team that consists of Howard Leventhal, a social psychologist who has been a key figure in the development of both theoretical and empirical tests of self-regulatory models of health behavior; Christopher Hertzog, a noted methodologist with expertise in both cognitive aging and structural equation modeling; Elaine Leventhal, a geriatric physician whose primary research interests are in aging, health, and behavior; and Daniel Birchmore, a practicing rheumatologist at the Wilmington, Delaware, Veterans Administration Hospital.

We have developed a model of medication adherence, portrayed in Figure 6, that integrates the roles of beliefs about illness and medications and cognitive function, as well as the role of external supports, as determinants of medication adherence. We are also interested in the relationship between medication adherence and well-being and physical function. We have elected to study two related populations across the adult life span: rheumatoid arthritis patients and osteoarthritis patients. In the case of rheumatoid arthritis, which is a serious, systemic autoimmune disorder, adherence to medications quite likely can prevent disease progression and the associated severe disability. In contrast, osteoarthritis is a local disorder specific to individual joints, and medications can only relieve pain, have relatively serious side effects, and in no way can prevent disease progression. Thus, we have somewhat similar disorders where in one case, it is in the patient's best interest to be highly adherent but in another case, it is in the patient's best interest to use as little medication as possible to avoid stomach ulcers and renal disease.

We have developed a complex psychosocial and cognitive battery for rheumatoid and osteoarthritis patients and are administering this, as well as measuring adherence behaviors for more than a month, using accurate microelectronic monitors. We are testing the role of cognitive interventions on nonadherent subjects, including devices such as beeping bottle caps on the medication and programmable reminder watches. We also are examining beliefs and adherence behaviors in a sample of Black hypertensives in a health clinic for low-income individuals. Our data are preliminary, and it is well beyond the scope of the present work to present a detailed description of it. Nevertheless, from the corpus of this work to date, we are able to conclude that it is a myth that older adults

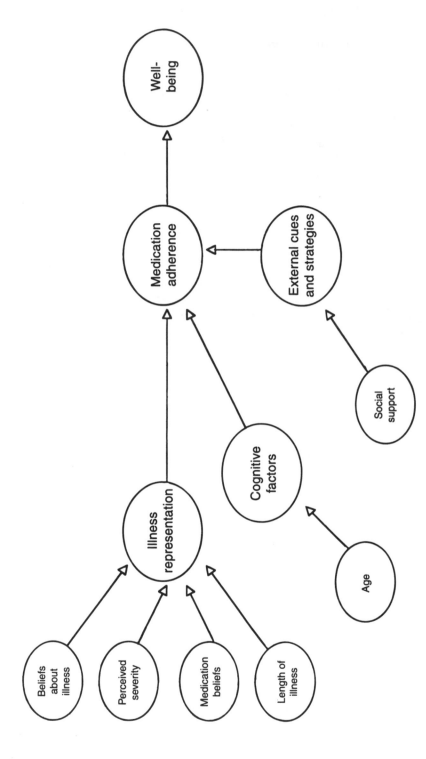

Figure 6. A conceptual model for medication adherence that integrates the role of beliefs and cognitive functions. From "Medication Adherence and Aging" by D. C. Park and T. R. Jones, in *Handbook of Human Factorss and the Older Adult*, edited by A. D. Fiske and W. A. Rogerss, in press, San Diego, CA: Academic Press. Copyright 1966 by Academic Press. Reprinted with permission.

are highly nonadherent with their medications. We consistently find evidence that the most adherent group is young-old adults, those age 60–75. It is also a myth that low-SES Black samples are highly nonadherent. We find evidence that our subjects, all of whom have hypertension, are highly adherent, recognizing at the same time that they are in a clinic situation where they receive structured, supportive information from a caring physician. We have not found strong evidence at this point that cognitive function plays a critical role in determining medication adherence. Rather, we find evidence that subjects' beliefs about their medications, strategies for coping with illness, and strategies for remembering to take medications are strong predictors of nonadherence. Finally, the most nonadherent group of subjects are the very elderly: those age 75 and above. We expect that as our sample increases, we will find evidence for cognitive function being related to nonadherence behavior.

CONCLUSION

The work presented is a long way from basic laboratory research on memory function. At the same time, the fundamental ways the basic work has informed, and continues to impact on, the applied work on medication adherence should be evident. The problem of medication adherence is one example of many dozens of issues that have tremendous implications for the effectiveness of treatment of older adults and judicious use of increasingly limited medical resources. How older adults make treatment decisions, what information they take away from an encounter with a physician, and how information can be structured to be maximally comprehended by older adults are just a few examples of critically important behavioral questions related to work on cognitive function and aging. Despite the threats to funding of research efforts, this is a very promising time to conduct socially important research that will result in sustained health and vitality for older adults and improve the overall productivity and well-being of our older population, resulting in increased gains of human resources to the social fabric of the lives of our citizens.

REFERENCES

Cavanaugh, J. & Park, D. C. (1993). *Vitality for life: Psychology research for productive aging* [A component of the Human Capital Initiative of the American Psychological Society]. Washington, DC: American Psychological Society.

Cherry, K. E., Park, D. C., Frieske, D., & Smith, A. D. (in press). Verbal and pictorial elaborations enhance memory in younger and older adults. *Memory & Cognition*.

Jöreskog, K. G. (1993). Testing structural equation models. In K. A. Bollen & J. S. Long (Eds.), *Testing structural equation models* (pp. 294–316). Newbury Park, CA: Sage.

Leventhal, H., & Cameron, L. (1987). Behavioral theories and the problem of compliance. *Patient Education and Counseling, 10*, 117–138.

Morrell, R. W., Park, D. C., & Poon, L. W. (1989). Effects of the quality of instructions on memory and comprehension of prescription information in young and old adults. *The Gerontologist, 29*, 345–353.

Morrell, R. W., Park, D. C., & Poon, L. W. (1990). Effects of labeling techniques on memory and comprehension of prescription information in young and old adults. *Journal of Gerontology: Psychological Sciences, 45*, 166–172.

Park, D. C. (1992). Applied cognitive aging research. In F. I. M. Craik & T. A. Salthouse (Eds.), *The handbook of aging and cognition* (pp. 449–493). Hillsdale, NJ: Erlbaum.

Park, D. C., & Jones, T. R. (in press). Medication adherence and aging. In A. D. Fiske & W. A. Rogers (Eds.), *Handbook of human factors and the older adult*. San Diego, CA: Academic Press.

Park, D. C., & Kidder, D. P. (1996). Prospective memory and medication adherence. In M. Brandimonte, G. Einstein, & M. McDaniel (Eds.), *Prospective memory: Theory and applications* (pp. 369–390). Hillsdale, NJ: Erlbaum.

Park, D. C., & Mayhorn, C. B. (in press). Remembering to take medications: The importance of nonmemory variables. In D. Herrman, M. Johnson, C. McEvoy, C. Hertzog, & P. Hertel (Eds.), *Research on practical aspects of memory* (Vol. 2) Hillsdale, NJ: Erlbaum.

Park, D. C., Morrell, R. W., Frieske, D., Blackburn, B., & Birchmore, D. (1991). Cognitive factors and the use of over-the-counter medication organizers by arthritis patients. *Human Factors, 33*, 57–67.

Park, D. C., Morrell, R. W., Frieske, D., & Kincaid, D. (1992). Medication adherence behaviors in older adults: Effects of external cognitive supports. *Psychology and Aging, 7*, 252–256.

Park, D. C., Morrell, R. W., Lautenschlager, G., & Firth, M. (1993, March). *Electronic monitoring of medication adherence hypertensives: Nonadherence is predicted by advanced age*. Paper presented at the meeting of the Society of Behavioral Medicine, San Francisco.

Park, D. C., Puglisi, J. T., & Smith, A. D. (1986). Picture memory in older adults: Does an age-related decline exist? *Psychology and Aging, 1*, 11–17.

Park, D. C., & Shaw, R. (1992). Effect of environmental support on implicit and explicit memory in young and old adults. *Psychology and Aging, 7*, 632–642.

Park, D. C., Smith, A. D., Lautenschlager, G., Earles, J., Frieske, D., Zwahr, M., & Gaines, C. (1994). Mediators of long-term memory across the life span. *Psychology and Aging.*

Park, D. C., Smith, A. D., Morrell, R. W., Puglisi, J. T., & Dudley, W. N. (1990). Effects of contextual integration on recall of pictures in older adults. *Journal of Gerontology: Psychological Sciences, 45,* 52–58.

Robbins, J. (1990). Schering report SVI—"OBRA '90' ": *Pharmacists not only count, but they also make a difference.* Kenilworth, NJ: Shering Laboratories.

Task Force on Aging Research. (1995). *The threshold of discovery: Future directions for research on aging.* Washington, DC: U.S. Government Printing Office.

6

A PROPOSAL FOR AN EXPANDED VIEW OF HEALTH AND PSYCHOLOGY: THE INTEGRATION OF BEHAVIOR AND HEALTH

CYNTHIA D. BELAR

Various chapters in this text describe the prevalence of psychological and behavioral problems (e.g., anxiety, depression, attention deficit hyperactivity disorder, substance abuse, obesity, and domestic violence) in persons seeking treatment by physicians. There is little doubt that biomedical treatments alone are not sufficient in the management of these well-known mental health and behavioral problems and that psychological services must be available if treatment is to be successful.

Overall, it has been estimated that some 25% of all visits in primary care are for mental health problems (Kamerow, Pincus, & MacDonald, 1986; Magill & Garrett, 1988). In addition, we have known for nearly 3 decades that 60% of all physician office visits fail to result in a confirmed biological diagnosis (Cummings & Follette, 1968; Follette & Cummings, 1967). It has been repeatedly stated that 60% of ambulatory-care visits involve problems with psychosocial components, and research reviews note that up to 80% of medical patients have evidence of significant psychological distress (Barskey, 1981).

However, the point of my discussion is that in actuality, it is not 25%, or 60%, or 80% of medical visits that should be considered psychological in nature. I am asserting that 100% of all medical visits are psychological and that Cartesian mind–body dualism simply does not belong in any conceptualization or implementation of the health care system. Behavior and health are inextricably intertwined, and psychology as the science of behavior has much to offer in both research and practice.

For example, we know that medical illness per se may precipitate emotional distress. Research has demonstrated that emotional distress can complicate medical treatment and thus elevate medical cost and that psychological interventions targeted to those with chronic diseases (e.g., diabetes, respiratory disorders, or hypertension) can actually reduce medical costs (Levenson, 1992; Schlesinger et al., 1983). In fact, there is an extensive body of knowledge concerning the medical cost offset of psychological services that in and of itself has been used to argue for the availability of psychological services in health care (e.g., Mumford et al., 1984).

However, the need for appropriate treatments of mental health problems and the potential for cost savings if psychological interventions are provided for chronic illness are only part of the total health care picture. In this discussion, I provide some sketchy outlines within a larger portrait, some of which will be more carefully drawn within other chapters of this text.

Over the last 2 decades, the body of knowledge in health psychology and its clinical applications has mushroomed. For example, psychological interventions have been developed to facilitate the management of a wide variety of health problems. Take coronary heart disease—the major cause of death and disability in the Western world. One of the most comprehensive studies of behavioral interventions in severe heart disease patients demonstrated significant and clinically meaningful decreases in low-density lipoprotein cholesterol (37%), systolic blood pressure (134 to 127 mmHg), angina pain (90%), and vessel blockage on angiogram in 18 of 22 patients. Over the same year, the control group receiving standard medical treatment experienced a 165% increase in angina pain, and angiograms revealed increased artery blockage in nearly half the patients (Ornish et al., 1990).

Research also demonstrates that psychological interventions have improved a number of troublesome physical symptoms, including but not limited to the following:

1. asthmatic episodes
2. pain during dressing change in burn patients

3. fecal and urinary incontinence
4. cramping and diarrhea in irritable bowel syndrome
5. anticipatory nausea with chemotherapy
6. vasospasms associated with Raynaud's disease
7. dyspnea with chronic obstructive pulmonary disease
8. headache severity, frequency, and duration
9. muscle spasms
10. insomnia and other sleep disorders
11. itching in neurodermatitis

Psychological support groups have helped patients and families deal with cancer, arthritis, disability, and bereavement. In addition to decreases in subjective distress and improved quality of life, there are some data to suggest health benefits in terms of reduced mortality and morbidity, especially for postmastectomy and heart attack patients (e.g., Spiegel, Gottheil, Kraemer, & Bloom, 1989).

With respect to even such overtly technical medical procedures as surgery, a meta-analysis of 191 studies involving both major and minor surgery revealed that brief presurgical psychological intervention has been consistently associated with fewer postsurgical complications, less medical usage, and an average of 1.5 fewer hospital days (Devine, 1992).

Traumatic injuries are major causes of morbidity and mortality and account for utilization of enormous amounts of some of our most expensive health care resources. Almost all injuries have behavioral risk factors: reckless driving, poor body mechanics, falls, substance abuse, failure to wear seatbelts or helmets, access to firearms, unsafe storage of toxic substances, interpersonal violence, and child and elder abuse.

Adherence to health care regimens is integral to virtually every service area. Noncompliance, a behavior, is a major issue throughout health care. In fact, it is estimated that half of the 1.6 billion prescriptions dispensed annually are taken incorrectly (Levy, 1989). Compliance is also especially important in smoking cessation, safe sex practices, exercise, dietary management, control of HIV and other infectious diseases, immunization programs, dental hygiene, and clinical trial research. As an example, some have noted that the incidence of polio can be directly related to a behavioral variable: failure to obtain vaccination.

In examining psychological and behavioral issues in a medical visit, it is also important not to focus too narrowly on the patient him- or herself. Health care outcomes can also be affected by family members' and service providers' behavior, on which there is also a substantial literature. The literature on physician–patient communication is especially illustrative of the latter.

Other provider determinants are infection-control procedures, which are essentially behavioral in nature. Although important, they are not always followed. For example, one author found a 50% failure rate in hand washing before seeing patients in a pediatric ambulatory-care setting (Lohr, Ingram, Dudley, Lawton, & Donowitz, 1991). Health systems are most concerned about the development of effective behavior-change programs for staff in areas such as promotion of hand washing and prevention of needle sticks.

At a more macro level, as public "report cards" for hospitals and health care plans become increasingly common and the health care industry becomes increasingly competitive, the interest in consumer behavior (e.g., satisfaction and appointment keeping) will increase, and there will be more focus on developing user-friendly systems marked by congenial staff behavior. The increased corporatization of health care also brings with it more focus on leadership behavior, personnel management (including concerns re staff burnout), and practice patterns.

In my opinion, one of the most positive features about health psychology in our discipline is that it is an area of research and practice to which virtually every area of psychology can contribute:

- From the behavioral epidemiologist to the behavioral geneticist
- From the experimental psychologists conducting basic pain research to the clinical health psychologist providing services
- From the human-factors engineer designing surgical-suite safety systems to the environmental psychologist designing user-friendly, and health-enhancing, spaces
- From the industrial psychologist providing executive management consultation and consumer studies to social and community psychologists developing community-based interventions
- From the basic scientist to the service provider to the policy advocate for health-promoting legislation and health care reform

So, back to my original perspective of the medical visit. Is there really any medical visit that is not psychological or that is impervious to behavioral influences? I cannot think of any. As stated before, behavior and health are inextricably intertwined, and psychology as the science of behavior has already demonstrated its potential for contributions to knowledge and practice.

REFERENCES

Barsky, A. J. (1981). Hidden reasons some patients visit doctors. *Annals of Internal Medicine*, 94, 492–498.

Cummings, N. A., & Follette, W. T. (1968). Psychiatric services and medical utilization in a prepaid health plan setting: Part II. *Medical Care, 6*, 31–41.

Devine, E. C. (1992). Effects of psychoeducational care for adult surgical patients: A meta-analysis of 191 studies. *Patient Education and Counseling, 19*, 129–142.

Follette, W. T., & Cummings, N. A. (1967). Psychiatric services and medical utilization in a prepaid health plan setting. *Medical Care, 5*, 25–35.

Kamerow, D. B., Pincus, H. A., & MacDonald, D. I. (1986). Alcohol abuse, other drug abuse and mental disorders in medical practice. *Journal of the American Medical Association, 255*, 2054–2057.

Levenson, J. L. (1992). Psychosocial interventions in chronic medical illness: An overview of outcome research. *General Hospital Psychiatry, 14S*, 43S–49S.

Levy, R. A. (1989, March). Improving compliance with prescription medications: An important strategy for containing health care costs. *Medical Interface*, pp. 34–41.

Lohr, J. A., Ingram, D. L., Dudley, S. M., Lawton, E. L., & Donowitz, L. (1991). Handwashing in pediatric ambulatory care settings: An inconsistent practice. *American Journal of Disease of Children, 145*, 1198–1199.

Magill, M. K., & Garrett, R. W. (1988). Behavioral and psychiatric problems. In R. B. Taylor (Ed.), *Family medicine* (3rd ed.), pp. 534–562). New York: Springer-Verlag.

Mumford, E., Schlesinger, H. J., Glass, G., Patrick, C., & Cuerdon, B. A. (1984). A new look at evidence about reduced cost of medical utilization following mental health treatment. *American Journal of Psychiatry, 141*, 1145–1158.

Ornish, D., Brown, S. E., Scherwitz, L. W, Billings, J. H., Armstrong, W. T., Ports, T. A., McLanahan, S. M., Kirkeeide, R. L., Brand, R. J., & Gould, K. L. (1990). Can lifestyle changes reverse coronary heart disease? *Lancet, 336*, 129–133.

Schlesinger, H. J., Mumford, E., Glass, G., Patrick, C., & Sharfstein, S. (1983). Mental health treatment and medical care utilization in a fee-for-service system: Outpatient mental health treatment following the onset of a chronic disease. *American Journal of Public Health, 73*, 422–429.

Spiegel, D., Bloom, J. R., Kraemer, H. C., & Gottheil, E. (1989). Effect of psychosocial treatment on survival of patients with metastatic breast cancer. *Lancet, 2*(8668), 888–891.

II

PSYCHOLOGISTS IN PRIMARY CARE SETTINGS

INTRODUCTION

As we pointed out in the introductory chapter to this book, psychologists have been practicing in primary health care settings for a significant portion of our field's history. Similarly, as primary care providers, psychologists have been involved in the comprehensive health care of patients and their families as well as serving as experts in practice areas such as internal medicine, family medicine, and pediatrics. In this section, again we see psychology defined by the interplay of the scientific study of clinical topics and the application of those research findings in the provision of health care services. We first learn about several collaborative-practice models in which psychologists and physicians work closely together to enhance the health care system. The section then goes on to elucidate the scientific and clinical understanding and treatment of various disorders found in primary care practice.

James H. Bray, in chapter 7, "Psychologists as Primary Care Practitioners," offers a description of a training program, detailing how psychologist–practitioners and physicians can, and do, work together successfully. This chapter offers a practical definition of primary care and elaborates on some of the findings of the American Psychological Association's Committee for the Advancement of Professional Practice's Primary Care Task Force. The collaborative-practice model discussed is based on defining the psychologist provider in primary care as a generalist.

In chapter 8, "Collaborative Practice: Psychologists and Internists," Garland Y. (Gary) DeNelsky offers general guidelines on how the practicing psychologist can produce and sustain a quality relationship with an internist. On the basis of DeNelsky's successful clinical practice experience and discussions with physicians, he also suggests that there are research and administrative opportunities that will enhance practice-based relationships.

In chapter 9, "Psychologists and Pediatricians in Collaborative Practice," Carolyn S. Schroeder offers a practical practice model for interfacing with pediatricians who are the primary gatekeepers for children's behavioral health care needs. On the basis of her successful pediatric psychology practice, Schroeder details the extent of problems seen in practice and clinical activities ranging from assessment and community consultation to parent "Call-In Hour" and from various treatment interventions to training models and research opportunities in pediatric practice.

David H. Barlow and colleagues describe the prevalence of the most common behavioral disorder that might be encountered in a primary care setting. In chapter 10, "Behavioral Health Care in Primary Care Settings: Recognition and Treatment of Anxiety Disorders," they offer information on the efficacy of psychological treatments of, and a model for intervention with, anxiety disorders that is applicable for psychologists working in or wishing to work in primary health care settings.

In chapter 11, "Catching Depression in Primary Care Physicians' Offices," Lynn P. Rehm focuses on the high incidence of depressive disorders found in primary care physicians' offices. He suggests that much can be done by psychologists to aid in the appropriate diagnosis of depression, given its high base rate but low and inaccurate detection rate in primary care settings. With health care moving to a "one-stop shopping" orientation with the growth of capitated care, Rehm encourages the psychologist to become involved in primary care settings in order to provide both accurate diagnosis of and effective psychotherapeutic intervention for depression.

Daniel S. Kirschenbaum, in chapter 12, "Helping Physicians Make Useful Recommendations About Losing Weight," provides valuable information for what psychologists can teach physicians about how to help patients who suffer from obesity. Rates of obesity are steadily climbing. Kirschenbaum uses both his research findings and clinical experience to detail a treatment strategy based on a six-step approach in counseling patients in successful weight loss.

In chapter 13, "Substance Use Problems in Primary Care Medical Settings: Is There a Psychologist in the House?" Bruce S. Liese and colleagues describe how substance abuse problems evidence themselves in primary care settings. The etiology of various drug problems are detailed by the authors, as are various diagnostic and treatment approaches.

The reader is offered useful suggestions on how to establish practice relationships with primary care physicians by marketing psychological services to physicians who will encounter substance abuse problems on a daily basis in their practices.

Jan L. Culbertson details the prevalence of attention deficit hyperactivity disorder and learning disabilities, two of the most common neurodevelopmental disorders of childhood. She discusses, in chapter 14, "Attention Deficit Hyperactivity Disorder and Learning Disabilities in the Pediatrician's Office," the need for a broad-based assessment of these problems, which often are first presented in the pediatrician's office. There is often less stigma if these problems are seen by parents within the context of a medical approach than when directly diagnosed or treated by a psychologist. Thus, with a strong working relationship with the pediatrician, the psychologist can establish alliances that facilitate information sharing in the community, cross-referral, and assistance in diagnosis and management of these disorders.

7

PSYCHOLOGISTS AS PRIMARY CARE PRACTITIONERS

JAMES H. BRAY

Psychologists are expanding their roles in the delivery of behavioral health services in a variety of health care settings. With the implementation of health care reform and the expansion of managed health care, psychologists are being forced to change their practices from providing only mental health services to offering a broad array of behavioral health services (Gaus & DeLeon, 1995). Psychologists have practiced in general medical settings for some time and have offered psychosocial interventions for both mental disorders and medical problems. With the new emphasis on primary health care, psychologists have additional opportunities to expand their role in the diagnosis and treatment of patients. However, this shift in practice will require an expanded knowledge base of primary care medicine and new skills in caring for primary care patients. This chapter reviews the definition of primary care and the role of psychologists in this setting and outlines the components of a training

Work on this chapter was supported partially by National Institute of Alcoholism and Alcohol Abuse Grant RO1 AA08864.

model intended to teach psychologists and physicians how to work in collaborative practice.

DEFINITION OF PRIMARY CARE

What is primary care, and who provides it? This has become a very controversial and "hot" topic because of the recent moves toward emphasizing primary care as the entry point and major provider of health care services. Primary care was defined by the Institute of Medicine as follows:

> the provision of integrated, accessible health care services by clinicians who are accountable for addressing a large majority of personal health care needs, developing a sustained partnership with patients, and practicing in the context of family and community. (Donaldson, Yordy, & Vanselow, 1994, p. 15)

The American Academy of Family Physicians defined primary care as follows:

> a form of medical care delivery that emphasizes first-contact and assumes ongoing responsibility for the patient in both health maintenance and therapy of illness. It is personal care involving a unique interaction and communication between the patient and the physician. It is comprehensive in scope and includes the overall coordination of the care of the patient's health problems, be they biological, behavioral, or social. The appropriate use of consultants and community resources is an important part of effective primary care. (American Academy of Family Physicians, 1994, p. 1)

Primary care is a form of delivery of medical care which encompasses the following functions:

1. It is "first-contact" care, serving as a point-of-entry for the patient into the health care system;
2. It includes continuity by virtue of caring for patients over a period of time, both in sickness and in health;
3. It is comprehensive care, drawing from all the traditional major disciplines for its functional content;
4. It serves a coordinative function for all the healthcare needs of the patient;
5. It assumes continuing responsibility for individual patient follow-up and community health problems; and
6. It is a highly personalized type of care. (American Academy of Family Physicians, 1975, p. 14)

A more common determination of a primary care provider is whether the provider takes care of routine health problems—such as checking patients' blood pressure and caring for common illnesses, such as colds, infections, depression, or hypertension. There are three medical specialties that are the core providers of primary care: family physicians, general internal medicine physicians, and pediatricians. Other specialties that are sometimes included are obstetrics/gynecologists and family nurse practitioners.

PSYCHOLOGISTS IN PRIMARY CARE

Where do psychologists fit within primary care? Are psychologists primary care providers? According to Rakel, one of the originators of the family physician movement,

> Primary care, to be done well, requires extensive training specifically tailored to problems frequently seen in primary care. These include the early detection, diagnosis, and treatment of depression, . . . and the care of those with chronic and terminal illnesses. (Rakel, 1995, p. 7)

These are clearly areas in which psychologists can provide services.

Although psychologists are usually not trained to take blood pressure or treat the common cold, they are trained to treat the most common behavioral health problems, such as depression and anxiety, and to provide behavioral interventions to prevent or intervene with major health problems, for example, cardiovascular disease or cancer, through lifestyle modification, weight management, smoking cessation, or stress management (Million, Green, & Meagher, 1982). In addition, many of the chronic diseases, such as diabetes, hypertension, or chronic back pain, can be helped or treated effectively through behavioral interventions (Holland & Rowland, 1989; Routh, 1988; Stager & Fordyce, 1982). Thus, psychologists are able to provide primary care behavioral health services and to diagnose or manage a number of health problems seen in primary care settings.

The American Psychological Association Committee for the Advancement of Professional Practice convened a Primary Care Task Force to examine the role of psychologists in primary medical care (1995). The core assumption of the task force is that psychology is defined as a health profession and not just a mental health profession. The task force believes that psychologists and psychological services are essential to the primary health care team to deliver cost-effective and clinically effective comprehensive care.

The task force discussed several models of psychology in primary care. One concept that gained support was that psychologists should provide comprehensive care. This type of care is provided over time, is coordinated with other members of the health care team, and uses specialists and subspecialists as needed. Comprehensive care makes use of community resources and recognizes the role of systems such as families and contextual factors in health and illness. Primary comprehensive health care teams emphasize prevention, education, consultation, and treatment. Furthermore, this care rests on a growing fund of knowledge and the science that underlies collaboration and the biopsychosocial, or systemic, model.

What kinds of characteristics do psychologists that work in primary care have? The Primary Care Task Force identified three major characteristics: First, the psychologist works in a primary care setting. This could be a clinic, group practice, or with an individual medical practitioner. This could also include both clinical and educational services, such as teaching in a family medicine residency.

Second, the psychologist is capable of working with all patients seen in the setting. This means that the psychologist can work with the broad range of behavioral and mental health problems found in primary care settings. In addition, the psychologist may serve as a consultant to the other primary care providers, such as family physicians or nurse practitioners, regarding patient-care issues, doctor–patient issues, or system issues. Furthermore, the psychologist is able to provide interventions for behavioral components of medical problems, such as facilitating compliance to medical regimes, lifestyle changes, or reducing complications due to surgery.

Third, the psychologist contributes to the patient's total health care, both in sickness and in health. Psychologists in primary care are not limited solely to the assessment and treatment of mental disorders. In essence, this model of psychology requires that the psychologist provider be a generalist and be able to treat the full range of problems, from birth to death, with individuals and families, that present in these settings.

COLLABORATIVE-PRACTICE MODEL

There is a critical need for the appropriate diagnosis and treatment of common types of behavioral health problems seen in primary care settings. Despite the high prevalence of certain mental disorders, such as anxiety and depression, in primary care settings (Katon & Sullivan, 1990), primary care physicians often overlook these types of problems and focus on diagnosis and treatment of physical health symptoms (Eisenberg, 1992). The expense of not diagnosing and treating these types of problems can be staggering. For example, the costs associated with depression have been recently estimated as high as $43.7 billion a year (Greenberg, Stiglin, Finkelstein, & Berndt, 1993). In addition, anxiety and depression result in higher medical utilization rates and costs (Simon, Ormel,

VonKorff, & Barlow, 1995). Furthermore, Kroenke and Mangelsdorff (1989) found that of patients from an internal medicine clinic, only 16% had clear organic causes of their problems, 10% had clear psychological problems, but nearly 80% of patients had significant psychological distress. These facts point to the need for psychological services in primary care settings.

With the increase in managed health care and integrated health care systems, primary care physicians have added pressures to diagnose and treat a broad spectrum of biomedical and psychosocial problems. Thus, they could benefit from greater access to behavioral health practitioners (Coleman, Patrick, Eagle, & Hermalin, 1979; MacDonald, Baloun, & McKenna, 1995). Collaborative practice between psychologists and physicians is one method to meet the multiple needs of primary care patients (Bray & Rogers, 1995; Clinical psychology, 1991; McDaniel, Hepworth, & Doherty, 1992). However, psychologists are not regularly trained to work with primary care physicians and often do not have access to the general health care system (Bray & Rogers, 1995).

Primary care physicians are the front-line medical providers and are frequently the first health care professionals to encounter patients with mental health or psychosocial problems ("Mental Health," 1995; Higgins, 1994). Unfortunately, psychologists are often isolated from the primary care medical system. Thus, the professionals best trained to assess and treat psychosocial problems may not be available to medical professionals and their patients who need these services. The change from psychologists as mental health providers to health care providers will require special training on how to work closely with primary care physicians.

Collaboration between psychologists and physicians is hampered by factors such as differences in theoretical orientations (biomedical vs. psychosocial), lack of a common language (medical jargon vs. psychological jargon), different practice styles, lack of accessibility to the different providers, and varying expectations for assessment and treatment (Bray & Rogers, 1995; McDaniel et al., 1992). Even with these cultural and practice difficulties, there are excellent examples of fruitful collaboration between psychologists and other medical professionals (Abraham et al., 1991; Biaggio & Bittner, 1990; Coleman, Patrick, Eagle, & Hermalin, 1979; Dym & Berman, 1986; Glenn, 1985; Hepworth & Jackson, 1985; McDaniel et al., 1992; McDowell, Burgio, Dombrowski, Locher, & Rodriguez, 1992; Natvig, 1991; Sargent, 1985). Most of these examples occurred in traditional medical settings, such as hospitals, group practices, or in educational settings.

A demonstration project that trained psychologists and family physicians for collaborative practice was recently reported by Bray and Rogers (1995). The Linkages Project developed a training model for psychologists and family physicians to facilitate collaborative practice that focused on treatment of alcohol and other drug abuse problems in rural areas. This section reviews the training program and general principles that were learned from this demonstration project (Bray & Rogers, 1995, in press).

The training included two 1-day workshops for pairs of psychologists and family physicians. The first day of training provided updated material on current information on the diagnosis and treatment of alcohol and other drug abuse problems, models of collaborative practice, and methods for developing linkages between professionals. This session included both didactic and experiential training.

Psychologists and physicians met in small groups to discuss training and "cultural" differences between psychologists and physicians. The psychologist trainer provided information to the physician group regarding training and educational backgrounds of psychologists, differences between psychologists and other mental health professionals, practice styles and issues, differences between psychological and medical practices, collaboration and referral recommendations, and financial issues. In addition, issues concerning differences in methods of handling confidentiality and sharing patient records between the professions were discussed. At the same time, the physician trainer discussed similar issues with the psychologist group concerning physicians and medical practice. The trainers discussed stereotypes of each profession and factors that might obstruct collaborative practice. The trainers switched groups to answer questions from their professional group and to discuss experiences and concerns that were raised in the other group. Also, the trainers initiated group discussion to develop possible solutions to concerns about collaboration raised by the participants.

Training was also provided on how to make successful referrals. This discussion included information about how to prepare a patient for a referral to a psychologist, how to include the psychologist in the evaluation of the referral, and how to communicate expectations concerning the referral to the psychologist. Differences in expectations about referral by the two provider groups were discussed. This part of the training focused on the etiquette of collaboration and the potential forms of collaboration.

Experiential exercises and role plays on cases were provided to demonstrate how the different professionals approach patient care and to practice diagnosing and referring patients. Questions about the cases were raised to reveal differences in assessment strategies between psychologists and physicians. In addition, participants explored in greater depth the differences between the two professions with regard to language, theoretical models, confidentiality, time constraints, and turf issues.

The last part of this training was for the participants to develop a linkage plan for establishing and maintaining collaborative practices between the professionals. The trainers provided several options: having regular meetings or phone contacts, establishing referral routines, and clarifying referral and treatment expectations. Regular contact between the professionals was strongly recommended, as was the development of expectations and methods for communicating about referrals. This part of the training emphasized the need for accessibility and the etiquette of collaboration for fostering collaborative relationships. This ended the first day of training.

The second day of training occurred about 6 months after the initial training session. The first part of the day reviewed the collaboration that developed after the initial training. The participants evaluated the initial training and provided feedback on areas that needed to be changed. Participants gave specific case examples of how their linkage plan worked or did not work and examples of successful and unsuccessful collaboration. Problems and concerns that hindered successful collaboration were also reviewed.

The participants were trained to use the process and stages of change model (Prochaska, DiClemente, & Norcross, 1992) and the motivational enhancement therapy model (Miller, Zweben, DiClemente, & Rychtarik, 1992) for treating alcohol and other drug abuse problems. The model seemed particularly relevant for family physicians because they often encounter patients who have behavioral and addictive problems. However, the patients are not necessarily seeking treatment for those specific problems and may not be ready to change their behavior. The model was expanded to be applicable to a wide range of medical and psychosocial problems. The trainers presented videotape examples of these models and discussed specific application of the models in primary care settings.

The training program was successful in linking providers and in enhancing the level and quality of collaborative practice between these professionals. The predominant changes in the collaborative relationship was from self-contained, independent practitioners to independent practices with mutually exclusive skills and from no relationship to limited referral and some consultation between professionals. In most cases, this type of arrangement was a step forward, but the training did not result in fully integrated forms of practice.

The participants indicated that collaboration enhanced the effectiveness of each professional and resulted in better diagnosis and treatment of medical and psychosocial problems. Participants reported that the linkage improved their own sense of efficacy and satisfaction in working with patients. In addition, through the collaboration, patients were provided enhanced treatment options for their problems. Although this project focused on rural practitioners, it appears that most of the training is applicable to both rural and urban practitioners. We are currently undertaking another demonstration project on linking psychologists and primary care physicians in an urban area.

There were several factors that facilitated or hindered the development of a collaborative practice between providers (Bray & Rogers, 1995). Developing a specific collaboration plan was a key factor in the development of a working relationship. Professionals who had regular contact with each other were most likely to consult and refer patients to each other. Practicing in close proximity also enhanced the linkage between providers. Participants who had regular meetings with each other or practiced in the same building were the most successful in establishing a collaborative relationship. Regular meetings included scheduled telephone contacts, lunch or breakfast appointments, use of faxes to make referrals, or shared hospital rounds.

Several factors can interfere with collaboration. Lack of proximity and regular settings for contact were major components that hindered referrals. In many cases it takes a special effort to develop the relationship, and it is necessary to have a regular setting or routine for continuing the collaboration. Psychologists may need to take the lead in developing and maintaining this relationship. Managed care and reimbursement issues are ongoing problems that interfere with collaborative practice. Not being on the hospital staffs where physicians practice further interferes with collaboration. Because many psychologists do not practice in general hospital settings, a convenient place for informal and formal consultations between providers, the opportunities for collaboration are decreased.

CONCLUSION

With the move from specialized medical care to primary medical care and the increase in integrated, managed health care services, it is essential that psychologists expand their practices into the general health care area. Psychologists can provide important diagnostic and intervention services, which enhance treatment options to patients in primary care settings. In addition, psychologists can provide valuable systems consultation to primary health care teams and providers (McDaniel et al., 1992).

Psychologists need to gain additional training and experience in working in primary care settings to be effective providers in these areas (Bray & Rogers, in press). This type of training needs to be offered in both graduate psychology programs and in continuing education programs, to familiarize psychologists with primary health care and psychological interventions for primary care patients. Finally, psychologists will need to shift their focus from an exclusively psychosocial orientation to a biopsychosocial orientation, to fully integrate into the general health care system. The movement from mental health to health care provider is an exciting opportunity to expand the roles and areas of practice for psychologists.

REFERENCES

Abraham, I. L., Thompson-Heisterman, A. A., Harrington, D. P., Smullen, D. E., Onega, L. L., Droney, E. G., Westerman, P. S., Manning, C. A., & Lichtenberg, P. A. (1991). Outpatient psychogeriatric nursing services: An integrative model. *Archives of Psychiatric Nursing, 5,* 151–164.

American Academy of Family Physicians. (1975). *Official AAFP definition of family practice and family physician* (AAFP Publication No. 303). Kansas City, MO: Author.

American Academy of Family Physicians. (1994, February). AAFP revises primary care definition and exhibit. *AAFP Reporter,* p. 1.

American Psychological Association, Committee for the Advancement of Professional Psychology. (1995, July). *Primary Care Task Force working recommendations.* Washington, DC: Author.

Biaggio, M. K., & Bittner, E. (1990). Psychology and optometry: Interaction and collaboration. *American Psychologist, 45,* 1313–1315.

Bray, J. H., & Rogers, J. C. (1995). Linking psychologists and family physicians for collaborative practice. *Professional Psychology: Research and Practice, 26,* 132–138.

Bray, J. H., & Rogers, J. C. (in press). Training mental health professionals for collaborative practice with primary care physicians. *Families, Systems, and Health.*

Clinical psychology and general practice. (1991). *Drug and Therapeutics Bulletin, 29,* 9–11.

Coleman, J. V., Patrick, D. L., Eagle, J., & Hermalin, J. A. (1979). Collaboration, consultation, and referral in an integrated health–mental health program at an HMO. *Social Work in Health Care, 5,* 83–96.

Donaldson, M., Yordy, K., & Vanselow, N. (Eds.) (1994). *Defining primary care: An interim report. Committee on the Future of Primary Care* (Part 3, pp. 15–33). Washington, DC: National Academy Press.

Dym, B., & Berman, S. (1986). The primary health care team: Family physician and family therapist in joint practice. *Family Systems Medicine, 4,* 9–21.

Eisenberg, L. (1992). Treating depression and anxiety in primary care: Closing the gap between knowledge and practice. *New England Journal of Medicine, 326,* 1080–1084.

Gaus, C. R., & DeLeon, P. H. (1995). Thinking beyond the limitations of mental health care. *Professional Psychology, 26,* 339–340.

Glenn, M. L. (1985). Toward collaborative family-oriented health care. *Family Systems Medicine, 3,* 466–475.

Greenberg, P. E., Stiglin, L. E., Finkelstein, S. N., & Berndt, E. R. (1993). The economic burden of depression in 1990. *Journal of Clinical Psychiatry, 54,* 405–418.

Hepworth, J., & Jackson, M. (1985). Health care for families: Models of collaboration between family therapists and family physicians. *Family Relations, 34,* 123–127.

Higgins, E. S. (1994). A review of unrecognized mental illness in primary care. *Archives of Family Medicine, 3,* 908–917.

Holland, J. C., & Rowland, J. H. (Eds.). (1989). *Handbook of psycho-oncology: Psychological care of the patient with cancer.* New York: Oxford University Press.

Katon, W., & Sullivan, M. D. (1990). Depression and chronic medical illness. *Journal of Clinical Psychiatry, 51,* 3–11.

Kroenke, K., & Mangelsdorff, D. (1989). Common symptoms in ambulatory care: Incidence, evaluation, therapy, and outcome. *The American Journal of Medicine, 86,* 262–266.

MacDonald, A. S., Baloun, E. T., & McKenna, Q. L. (1995). Emerging models of integrated health systems. *GFP Notes, 8,* 1–5.

McDaniel, S. H., Hepworth, J., & Doherty, W. J. (1992). *Medical family therapy.* New York: Basic Books.

McDowell, J., Burgio, K. L., Dombrowski, M., Locher, J. L., & Rodriguez, E. (1992). An interdisciplinary approach to the assessment and behavioral treatment of urinary incontinence in geriatric outpatients. *Journal of the American Geriatric Society, 40,* 370–374.

Miller, W. R., Zweben, A., DiClemente, C. C., & Rychtarik, R. G. (1992). *Motivational enhancement therapy manual: A clinical research guide for therapists treating individuals with alcohol abuse and dependence* (DHHS Publication No. ADM 92-1894). Rockville, MD: National Institute of Alcohol Abuse and Alcoholism.

Million, T., Green, C., & Meagher, R. (Eds.). (1982). *Handbook of clinical health psychology.* New York: Plenum.

Natvig, D. (1991). The role of the interdisciplinary team in using psychotropic drugs. *Journal of Psychosocial Nursing and Mental Health Services, 29,* 3–8.

Mental health: Does therapy help? (1995, November). *Consumer Reports,* pp. 734–739.

Prochaska, J. O., DiClemente, C. C., & Norcross, J. C. (1992). In search of how people change: Applications to addictive behaviors. *American Psychologist, 47,* 1102–1114.

Rakel, R. E. (1995). The family physician. In R. E. Rakel (Ed.), *Textbook of family practice* (5th ed., pp. 3–19). Philadelphia: W. B. Saunders.

Routh, D. K. (Ed.). (1988). *Handbook of pediatric psychology.* New York: Guilford Press.

Sargent, J. (1985). Physician–family therapist collaboration: Children with medical problems. *Family Systems Medicine, 3,* 454–465.

Simon, G., Ormel, J., VonKorff, M., & Barlow, W. (1995). Health care costs associated with depressive and anxiety disorders in primary care. *American Journal of Psychiatry, 152,* 352–357.

Stager, J., & Fordyce, W. (1982). Behavioral health care in the management of chronic pain. In T. Million, C. Green, & R. Meagher (Eds.), *Handbook of clinical health psychology* (pp. 467–498). New York: Plenum.

8

COLLABORATIVE PRACTICE: PSYCHOLOGISTS AND INTERNISTS

GARLAND Y. DENELSKY

It has been estimated that a large percentage of the patient visits to internists and primary care physicians are driven by primarily psychological problems. A number of estimates have been made that more that 50% of patients seen by primary care physicians arc somatizers (Wickramasekera, 1989). Because proper psychological interventions may result in substantial improvement in patients' physical health, it becomes mutually advantageous for psychologists and internists to form close working relationships as a means of enhancing patient care.

The purpose of this chapter is to consider some of the factors that can contribute to smooth, harmonious working relationships between psychologists and internists. Much of what will be discussed is based on my own experiences of nearly 25 years at the Cleveland Clinic, a large, tertiary (and primary) care hospital and outpatient clinic. In addition, several internists and primary care physicians at the Cleveland Clinic were interviewed to capture their views of what they are expecting when they refer a patient to a psychologist, what criteria they use to decide whether to refer to a psychologist or a psychiatrist, and what type of communication process between psychologist and physician is most valued by them. This chapter outlines important areas that psychologists should focus on to create a positive collaboration with internists, including communication, the referral process, briefing, and the ongoing relationship.

COMMUNICATION

Several factors can facilitate smooth working relationships between psychologists and internists. Perhaps the most important, and certainly one of the most basic, is a friendly, collegial relationship between the two individual professionals. Quite frequently, some of the most valuable communication takes place informally: at a lunch table, in the corridors, on the phone. This type of contact is particularly helpful in discussing patient progress, talking over whether a particular patient would be an appropriate referral, and similar issues. But this type of informal contact also helps build an atmosphere of trust and cooperation, critically important ingredients in a sound, collaborative relationship between internist and psychologist. Put another way, the physician comes to view the psychologist as a reasonable person who does sensible and useful things to help his or her patients. The psychologist comes to appreciate the challenges to the internist who is trying to manage the patient's physical health, precisely what the physician is trained to do. Not infrequently, management of the patient's health is seriously complicated by psychological and emotional difficulties, something the internist may be neither trained nor interested in handling!

The actual process of collaboration between psychologist and internist begins with discussion and agreement on the types of patients most likely to benefit from psychological interventions. It has been noted that this collaboration is even more effective if the psychologist's office is on site, with an office on or near the service where patients are seen; such an arrangement can also permit a better understanding of the stressors and other situational factors in a patient's life (Cummings, 1992). But solid working relationships can be developed even when psychologist and physician are geographically separated. The communication process is the crucial ingredient; it is important at this stage for the psychologist to create realistic expectations as to the benefits (and limitations) of psychological interventions.

THE REFERRAL PROCESS

Each internist that I interviewed for this chapter described slightly different criteria for referral to a psychologist. One common denominator was that the patient had significant emotional or psychological issues that were either not responding or were not expected to respond to the internist's interventions. Antidepressant and anxiolitic medications were the most commonly used interventions of the internists. Brief counseling was the second most used tool, although the internists varied considerably with regard to how much counseling they typically employ.

The matter of whether to refer to a psychologist or a psychiatrist elicited some interesting comments. The common thread in several internists' comments was that they refer to a psychiatrist when they feel that medication is necessary and they feel that their knowledge of medications may be insufficient, either because it has not worked thus far or there are reasons to suspect that it will not work. Some internists mentioned that if the patient is clearly suicidal and is suspected to "need medications," then the referral is more likely to go to a psychiatrist. This is particularly interesting in view of the finding that suicidal patients not infrequently use their medications as a means of attempting suicide (Antonuccio, Danton, & DeNelsky, 1995). But the internists interviewed indicated a clear preference for psychologists when the primary problem seemed to involve interpersonal problems, inadequate coping skills, situational adjustment issues, chronic internal conflicts, or one of a variety of other primarily psychological problems. One internist confided that he refers to a psychiatrist when he suspects that a patient may be unworkable psychologically and that only medications or some other somatic therapy has any chance of making a dent!

When the internist refers a patient to a psychologist, that physician is pretty certain that psychological and emotional factors are relevant. Perhaps the most common exception here is when a physical condition exists that is suspected to be functional (e.g., a conversion, psychophysiologic, or somatization disorder) for which no physiopathology can be established. In these cases, internists often turn to other ways of verifying their suspicions before actually making a referral; psychological testing can be a particularly useful step here. When the internist orders psychological testing on the patient, the message begins to be conveyed to the patient that psychological factors are suspected to be playing some role in the patient's physical complaints. When the internist next orders a psychological consult, that message is strengthened. If the psychologist's conclusions are in keeping with the internist's hypothesis, the message is strengthened further. One internist specifically mentioned that the psychologist may need to help convince the patient of the role of psychological factors, if in fact psychological factors are felt to be fundamental. If this process has developed correctly, and if the patient feels that indeed a comprehensive medical evaluation of the patient's physical condition has been performed, the patient is much more likely—though not necessarily certain—to accept a psychological formulation of the problem.

BRIEFING THE INTERNIST

After the psychologist receives the referral, meets the patient, and performs a consultation, the findings must be communicated. Timeliness is a most important factor here; it is important for the psychologist to be able to respond reasonably promptly to requests from the physician and to communicate her or his findings fairly quickly. Excessive delay anywhere in this process can lead to a rapid diminution of referrals. The communication process is quite vital; the physician frequently is not as interested in a lengthy, comprehensive report so much as a succinct statement of the problem and the psychologist's plan for managing it. Brief phone or face-to-face discussions of the patient are frequently more satisfying and relevant for both parties than more formal reporting. But a more formal report is necessary as well.

The internists interviewed varied a good deal with regard to what they like to see in reports. One stated quite clearly, "I want a brief, concise report—the fewer words, the better!" Another indicated a preference for lengthier reports, "I like a more detailed report, one that teaches me something about the patient. I like to learn something new." Still another confessed, "I like it when there's a little 'gossip' about the patient—it lets me know that the psychologist has really come to know my patient!" Different preferences regarding reporting style may to some degree reflect gender differences. It has been noted that women physicians talk more with patients and ask more questions about psychosocial issues than male physicians (Hall, Irish, Roter, Ehrlich, & Miller, 1994). But even the internists who preferred longer reports agreed that they strongly desire a brief, succinct summary as well. That summary should include a formulation, a diagnosis (which may or may not be a product of the *Diagnostic and Statistical Manual of Mental Disorders* [American Psychiatric Association, 1994]), and a set of recommendations, which in many cases will include a treatment plan. If that plan is to include follow-up psychological interventions, the specifics of who, when, and where need to be delineated as well. Several internists expressed dismay about getting the patient back from a mental health professional's consultation with the conclusion "no psychiatric illness," and no additional comments or plan offered. On the other hand, one internist emphasized the value of honesty, "If psychological issues are not suspected to be playing a role, the psychologist should say so!"

THE ONGOING RELATIONSHIP

In most cases where the internist requests psychological involvement, the physician's expectations are that the psychologist will provide ongoing treatment as required, or arrange for such treatment to be delivered by someone else. Internists not infrequently voice frustration when they refer a patient to a mental health professional only to find that the patient has been given an initial evaluation with no provision made for further involvement. In these times when patients have complex (and frequently limiting) arrangements with third-party payers, however, the issue of who will be reimbursed for treatment can, of course, become quite complicated.

Note that there is the potential for complexities and conflicts whenever psychologists collaborate with physicians. Medical centers, both outpatient clinics and hospitals, are now and historically have been controlled by physicians. Psychologists may find themselves disadvantaged in medically dominated health care systems because they do not have the knowledge of disease that physicians have (Miller & Swartz, 1990). Psychologists may be tempted to permit devaluation of their expertise for the sake of harmonious working relationships and may find themselves at a decided disadvantage in terms of power issues between the two professions (Miller & Swartz, 1990). Yet these and other similar problems need not develop if the environment supports true teamwork, characterized by open communication and shared leadership (Lowe & Herranen, 1981). Although such teamwork is the ideal, the reality is that especially in the inpatient setting, most commonly the physician is the captain of the team, who is viewed as ultimately responsible for patient care (Shaw, 1986). In facing these complexities, psychologists need to be appropriately assertive with regard to patient management and treatment recommendations, but should avoid the extremes of passivity or aggressiveness, to maximize their contributions to patient care.

THE BENEFITS OF COLLABORATION WITH INTERNISTS

In addition to providing direct clinical services with physicians in primary care and internal medicine settings, there are numerous opportunities for research and teaching, as well as administration (Belar, 1989). Collaboration between psychologist and internist in such endeavors further enhances the working relationship between the two professionals.

Another benefit of such collaboration is personal but potentially quite significant; truly satisfying relationships can and often do develop between psychologists and physicians. Psychologists report "doubling their efforts to make their reports and opinions meaningful and helpful because of the fine level of professional acceptance they experienced" (Cummings, 1992, p. 78).

A strong case can be made that graduate education and training programs need to do much more than they are now doing to help prepare psychologists to develop and maintain solid working relationships with internists in medical settings, much as research psychologists are prepared for "grantsmanship" in their graduate education (Belar, 1989). As health care is increasingly restructured toward cost containment and prevention, the role of the psychologist can and should become increasingly prominent. It is well known that appropriate psychological care for patients with psychological and emotional problems can reduce medical utilization and that psychologically based health interventions (e.g., smoking cessation programs) can have a dramatic impact on reducing future morbidity and mortality.

CONCLUSION

Facilitating a solid working relationship with internists requires the psychologist to provide reasonable access; thorough evaluations, which include specific treatment recommendations; appropriate and timely reporting; and the willingness to continue working with difficult patients when appropriate. When a smooth, harmonious working relationship is established, the patient, the psychologist, and the physician all benefit. The patient gets enhanced health care, the psychologist gets interesting (and frequently challenging) cases, and the physician gets assistance in dealing with some of his or her most difficult and time-consuming patients. Such collaboration benefits psychology, it benefits medicine, and most important, it benefits the patient and the patient's physical health and psychological well-being.

REFERENCES

American Psychiatric Association. (1994). *Diagnostic and statiscal manual of mental disorders* (4th ed.). Washington, DC: Author.

Antonuccio, D. O., Danton, W. G., & DeNelsky, G. Y. (1995). Psychotherapy vs. medication for depression: Challenging the conventional wisdom with data. *Professional Psychology: Research and Practice, 26,* 574–585.

Belar, C. D. (1989). Opportunities for psychologists in health maintenance organizations: Implications for graduate education and training. *Professional Psychology: Research and Practice, 20,* 390–394.

Cummings, J. W. (1992). Psychologists in the medical surgical setting: Some reflections. *Professional Psychology: Research and Practice, 23,* 76–79.

Hall, J. A., Irish, J. T., Roter, D. L., Ehrlich, C. M., & Miller, L. H. (1994). Gender in medical encounters: An analysis of physician and patient communication in a primary care setting. *Health Psychology, 13,* 384–392.

Lowe, J. I., & Herranen, M. (1981). Understanding teamwork: Another look at basic concepts. *Social Work in Health Care, 7,* 1–11.

Miller, T., & Swartz, L. (1990). Clinical psychology in general hospital settings: Issues in interprofessional relationships. *Professional Psychology: Research and Practice, 21,* 48–53.

Shaw, B. (1986). Improving the management of illness behavior by changing roles within multidisciplinary treatment teams. In S. McHugh & T. M. Vallis (Eds.), *Illness behavior: A multidisciplinary model* (pp. 59–70). New York: Plenum.

Wickramasekera, I. (1989). Somatizers, the health care system, and collapsing the psychological distance the somatizer has to travel for help. *Professional Psychology: Research and Practice, 20,* 105–111.

9

PSYCHOLOGISTS AND PEDIATRICIANS IN COLLABORATIVE PRACTICE

CAROLYN S. SCHROEDER

Most parents are likely to talk initially to a pediatrician when they have concerns about their children's behavior or development (Clarke-Stewart, 1978; Schroeder & Wool, 1979). Thus, pediatricians are the first professionals most likely to encounter children's behavior problems. It has been estimated that 20% of pediatric primary care patients have biosocial or developmental problems, which, for the pediatrician seeing a total of 27 patients a day, translates into 4 patients per day (American Academy of Pediatrics, 1978). Clearly, the primary care setting offers unique opportunities for clinical psychologists.

The idea of psychologists and pediatricians working together is not new. Drotar (1995), in his recent book, *Consulting with Pediatricians: Psychological Perspectives*, gave a nice review of the evolution of collabora-

Parts of this chapter appear in Schroeder, C. S. (in press). Mental health services in pediatric primary care. In M. Roberts (Ed.), *Model programs in service delivery in child and family mental health*. Hillsdale, NJ: Erlbaum. Used with permission.

tion among psychologists and pediatricians. As early as 1964 (in his presidential address to the American Academy of Pediatrics), Wilson stated that "one of the things that I would do if I could control the practice of pediatrics would be to encourage groups of pediatricians to employ their own clinical psychologists" (p. 988). Indeed, Haggerty (1986), an influential leader in pediatrics who directed the William T. Grant Foundation from 1980 to 1992, referred to childhood behavioral and school problems as the new morbidity, requiring pediatricians to collaborate with mental health professionals. Work in a primary health care setting does, however, require a shift in the way that mental health services have traditionally been offered: (a) More clients are seen; (b) less time is spent with each client; (c) clients generally present with less debilitating disorders (Wright & Burns, 1986). The focus is thus on prevention and early intervention rather than on treatment of severe psychopathology. Although this approach is especially reasonable for parents and children, it is not widely practiced and has not received a great deal of attention in the literature or in the training of child mental health workers.

One of the earliest reports on a clinical collaboration in primary pediatrics appeared in a 1967 issue of *Journal of Pediatrics* in an article by two pediatricians and a psychologist (Smith, Rome, & Freedheim, 1967). They described the psychologist providing services in the pediatric office for half a day each week with a monthly meeting of the psychologists and pediatricians. They felt that the more visible pediatrician–psychologist collaboration reduced parent resistance to referral to a psychologist.

The practice model to be described in this chapter is based on work in a primary pediatric practice in Chapel Hill, North Carolina, that has evolved over a period of 22 years. In addition to developing a variety of preventative programs and clinical services, we have been able to coordinate our work with other community agencies that serve children, as well as to engage in professional training and research. These activities have been described, in part, in other publications (e.g., Hawk, Schroeder, & Martin, 1987; Kanoy & Schroeder, 1985; Mesibov, Schroeder, & Wesson, 1977; Routh, Schroeder, & Koocher, 1983; Schroeder, 1979; Schroeder & Gordon, 1991; Schroeder, Gordon, Kanoy, & Routh, 1983). This chapter will provide an overview of the population served, the clinical services offered, and the research opportunities in this setting. The chapter ends with a discussion of the issues surrounding collaborative practice.

POPULATION SERVED

Chapel Hill Pediatrics is a private group practice with 8 pediatricians serving approximately 20,000 patients in a small university town. Mental health professionals have been involved with the practice since 1973, offering services that have evolved out of the needs of the children and their parents. Although our clients are primarily from the pediatric practice, anyone in the community may use our services, and no referral from a pediatrician is necessary. The population served is primarily well educated, middle class, and White. Contracts with the Department of Social Services and other community agencies have given us an opportunity also to work with a more diverse cultural, ethnic, and economic population.

From 1973 to 1982, the services offered focused on prevention and early intervention (parent groups, brief face-to-face contacts, and telephone consultation), so the population served was primarily a well-child one, with about 17% of the clients referred for more in-depth assessment and treatment (Schroeder et al., 1983). In 1982, when a wider range of services was offered, the population served expanded to include children presenting with the full range of behavioral and emotional problems. In a descriptive study of a random sample of new clients (304 out of 681 referrals) seen over a 5-year period, from 1982 to 1987, Hawk et al. (1987) reported that 48% were girls and 52% were boys. The percentages of referrals by age were as follows: birth to 5 years, 34%; 6 to 11 years, 45%; and 12 to 20 years, 20%. The ages with the highest number of referrals were 7 years (11.4%) and 5 years (10.8%). The most frequent problems were negative-behavior and child management issues (24.4%); learning problems (18.4%); divorce, stepparenting, and adoption issues (11.5%); and developmental or medical problems (11.4%). There were also a substantial number of children who had suffered a sudden loss of a parent or sibling through death or disappearance.

Hawk et al. (1987) found that the number of sessions (1 hour per session) spent with families varied rather significantly, depending on the problem. Developmental issues such as sleep, toilet training, enuresis, and encopresis took an average of 2.19 sessions; negative behaviors required an average of 5.35 sessions; and specific fears and anxieties took an average of 6.75 sessions. Children with multiple problems required more sessions. For example, a child who had sleep problems as well as negative behavior was seen for an average of 7 sessions. A child who exhibited problems that were more pervasive and occurred across a number of settings required an average of 54 hours spent with child, parents, school, and other community agencies.

Schroeder (1992), in a review of all new referrals (714) for the years 1989 and 1990, reported that 54% were boys and 46% were girls. The percentage of referrals by age were as follows: birth to 5 years, 22%; 6 to 10 years, 44%; 11 to 15 years, 21%; and 16 years and older, 13%. Compared with the Hawk et al. (1987) data for the 5-year period (1982 to 1987), this represented a significant decrease in children seen from birth to 5 years (22% vs. 34%) and an increase in the children seen who were 11 or more years old (34% vs. 20%). The age distributions for the older group differed for the two studies (10 years and older; 11 years or older), which could account for part of the discrepancy for that age group. The increased number of services for the older age group (groups and family therapy) and the parents' greater awareness of the range of psychological services being offered in the practice could also account for the increase in the number of initial referrals at these ages. Certainly, the number of new referrals, 714 in a 2-year period versus 681 in a 5-year period, attests to the increased use of the psychological services over time. Currently, new referrals average 37 per month, or approximately 444 in a year. The addition of more preventive and early-intervention services (e.g., prenatal classes, free ongoing support and information groups for parents with infants and toddlers, more anticipatory guidance handouts, a daily on-call nurse) could account, in part, for the decrease in referrals for the birth to 5-year-old age range. The pediatricians also have indicated that through their close collaboration with the psychology staff, they have become more adept at handling developmental and behavioral issues in this age range and, therefore, could be decreasing the number of younger children who are either referred by them or their parents.

The most frequent problems seen in 1989 and 1990 were negative behavior (18%); anxiety (15%); attention deficit hyperactivity disorder (ADHD; 12%); learning problems and school problems (17%); divorce and separation (9%); peer- and self-esteem (7%); depression (6%); child abuse (6%); and developmental or medical problems (3%). This represents a shift to an increase in the number of internalizing problems and a decrease in the developmental or medical problems being referred to the psychology clinic. It is not clear if the rate at which the children with developmental or medical problems are referred has decreased or if the primary referral question for these children is now a behavioral or emotional problem versus the chronic illness or disability. When we began our work in the pediatric office, we anticipated that we would be seeing a significant number of children with chronic diseases or developmental disabilities. We, however, have learned over the years that most of the children seen in outpatient pediatric practices do not have major medical or developmental problems. This is especially true in our demographic area, given that there are two major medical schools within 10 miles of each other. The care provided by specialized clinics in the medical centers (often with their own pediatric or medical psychologists) decreases the number of children with significant medical or developmental problems followed in the primary care setting. Thus, while we call ourselves pediatric psychologists, the role is reflected more by the setting than the types of problems that are being addressed. Our goal as pediatric psychologists in the primary care setting is to enhance the development of all children and to reduce the number of children with significant emotional and behavioral problems through early identification and intervention.

The length of time clients are seen has remained fairly stable over the years, with five sessions being the mean for 1989–1990 and 13% of the clients seen for one session. Given the sheer number of referrals, our goal has been to provide short-term treatment with a quick turnover of clients. We have thus been faced with the dilemma of deciding what types of problems are best suited to the primary care setting as opposed to a setting geared to handling longer term clients. Although we could try to focus only on short-term clients, the reality is that in a population of 20,000 pediatric patients, there are probably 200 children at any one time who have serious emotional or behavioral problems. We have discovered that neither the parents nor the pediatricians want us to refer these children out of the practice. They argue for continuity of care and working with people with whom they have come to trust. Thus, there are an increasing number of children and families that require more extensive and extended treatment.

In addition to new referrals, we have discovered that a number of children and parents return for help at different points in the children's development. Initially, we felt that perhaps we had not done a thorough enough assessment and treatment the first time around, but the clinical and consumer satisfaction data have indicated that the initial treatment goals were accomplished. Indeed, these children appear to be more vulnerable to the occurrence of stressful events, and their parents periodically seek help in managing a developmental stage or particular event in their life. The stresses can be developmental problems; traumatic experiences, such as sexual abuse or the death of a parent; environmental instability; parental psychopathology; or behavioral or emotional problems that persist at a subclinical level but are exacerbated by a certain developmental stage. We have come to accept that successful treatment at one point in time does not automatically mean a "cure" for these children, nor does it mean that continuous long-term treatment is necessary. As in the moving-risk model described by Gordon and Jens (1988), these children appear to need help at different points in their life; with this periodic help, they are able to learn the necessary skills to cope with the stresses of life.

STAFF AND PERSONNEL

The mental health staff include 5.5 full-time–equivalent PhD clinical child psychologists, 1 full-time person with an MS degree in child development as well as training in marriage and family therapy; a part-time adult and child psychiatrist, and a part-time social worker. In addition, there are 3 full-time office staff and a group administrator. At various times, there are also research students, psychology practicum students, interns and postdoctoral fellows from universities and medical schools.

I began the practice alone and, within a year, began training other psychologists who already had their doctorates or were finishing graduate school, to help with the preventative services, diagnostic testing, school consultation, parent–child training, and treatment of behavior problems. The training necessary for psychologists to work in this type of setting and with this client population includes a strong background in clinical child psychology with an emphasis on a developmental perspective and the opportunity to work with preschoolers, children, and youth developing along a normal continuum; an internship or postdoctoral fellowship in a multidisciplinary clinic or hospital setting; and a strong background in behavioral approaches to treatment. Given the range of problems and issues, the quick pace, and the number of contacts the psychologist confronts on a daily basis, experience in an ambulatory pediatric setting is imperative. If a person is lacking this experience, then they must be prepared to spend some time in training and have supervision readily accessible. It is also important to understand and know the services available to children and families in the community and establish a network with the professionals in those service agencies. In addition, in our clinic, each psychologist brings a unique expertise to the practice (e.g., family therapy, substance abuse, assessment of learning disabilities and ADHD, school consultation, assessment and treatment of sexual abuse, public relations skills, or supervisory skills).

Professional staff have been selected to join the practice on the basis of patient-identified needs for services. For example, with an increased number of parents being referred for individual work, we added the clinical social worker. The child development specialist was added for her expertise in parent education, and the psychiatrist was added in response to the increased number of children and parents presenting with severe psychopathology and the need for a physician knowledgeable in psychotropic drugs.

The office staff is an integral part of the practice. They must not only perform the routine office tasks but also route a myriad of calls to the proper staff member or community agency, score questionnaires, manage the parent library and requests for parent handouts, interface with the pediatric staff and personnel, keep the individual and various clinic appointments straight, deal with the increasing number of managed care groups, and handle the consumer satisfaction questionnaires. A friendly, composed, and efficient person is a prerequisite, and time for proper training is also a necessary part of the job. We added the group administrator, who manages the business and office staff of both the pediatric and the psychology practices, to help streamline the business aspects of the practices and to determine more accurately the financial issues involved in providing a full array of free and fee-based services. This role is increasingly important as we enter the era of health care reform.

PEDIATRIC PSYCHOLOGY SERVICES

The work in the private pediatric office was initially developed in 1973 as an opportunity for graduate and postgraduate students in psychology, social work, nursing, pediatrics, and psychiatry to do preventive and early-intervention work with parents whose children were developing along a normal continuum. The primary placement for these students was in a developmental disabilities clinic at the University of North Carolina Medical School. A randomly selected group of parents from the pediatric office was surveyed by telephone, to assess the need for mental health services and the types of services desired to meet these needs. As a result of that survey, three services were developed: (a) a "Call-In Hour" twice a week, when parents could ask questions about child development and behavior; (b) weekly evening parent groups, which focused on different ages and stages of development; and (c) a "Come-In" time 2–4 hr a week, to give parents an opportunity to discuss their child-related concerns in greater depth. These services, 6 to 8 hr a week, were provided free by the psychologists, social workers, and nurses and their students from the hospital-based clinic.

In 1982, as a result of requests for more in-depth assessment and short-term treatment as well as the need to demonstrate the viability of a practice in this setting on a fee-for-service basis, I joined the pediatric practice on a full-time basis. Clinical services, community consultation, training, and research have always been integral parts of the psychological practice, with each part stimulating the activities of the other parts. Each of these aspects of the practice will be described separately.

Clinical Services

We use a behavior theory orientation with a transactional–developmental perspective in our clinical work. The clinical services cover a range of preventive work, screening, assessment, and short- and long-term treatment.

Preventive Services

Preventive services offered include the evening parent groups, a parent library, the Call-In Hour, and parent handouts. The evening parent groups, which have been ongoing since 1973, are 1.5-hr sessions that focus on different ages and stages in development. For example, a month of sessions might focus on toddlers, with the following topics: Ages and Stages, Toilet Training, Preventing Power Struggles, and Survival Tactics: Dinner Through Bedtime. For adolescents, the topics might be Adolescence: What to Expect, Balancing Their Needs: Independence and Rules, and Tips for Parenting During the Adolescent Years. The sessions are limited to 20 parents each and are organized to include a didactic presentation of material, an opportunity for questions and answers, and the use of handouts that focus on the presented materials. These sessions are advertised in the community as well as in the pediatric examination rooms; parents must register in advance for individual sessions, and there is a charge. We have not formally evaluated the effectiveness of the groups, but consumer satisfaction questionnaires have high ratings. Their popularity often results in two separate sessions on the same topic in order to accommodate the number of parents who wish to attend. The pediatricians offer prenatal parent groups, and there are ongoing groups for parents of newborns to 6-month-olds and parents of 7-month-olds to 24-month-olds. These latter groups are free for the parents, with the pediatricians paying the psychology practice to run them.

A parent library is another preventive service offered free of charge to the parents. Parents' first choice of an information source is books or reading material (Clarke-Stewart, 1978), although there is little empirical evidence on the usefulness of books (Bernal & North, 1978). Our parent library was developed in response to the continual requests of parents for reading material on child-related issues. The parent library is located in the receptionist's office, and an annotated list of books (organized by topic) in a three-ring notebook is kept in the waiting area. The books can be checked out for 2 weeks at no charge. The books that are included in the library have been selected from the "Books for Parents and Children" section of the *Journal of Clinical Child Psychology* (see, e.g., Schroeder, Gordon, & McConnell, 1987). This section was published several times a year from 1984 to 1990 and included reviews of books on divorce, sexuality education, sexual abuse prevention, learning disabilities, developmental disabilities, general parenting, behavior management, stepparenting, single parenting, death, and medical problems. These books are widely used by the general pediatric clientele, in addition to being used as adjuncts to treatment. The psychology practice buys and maintains the books.

The Call-In Hour, offered free twice a week, is a time when parents can ask psychologists about common child development and management concerns. From the inception of this program in 1973, a log has been kept of the phone calls received, the nature of the parents' concerns, and the advice given to them. Reports on the types and frequency of problems, as well as the effectiveness of the advice given, have been published in a number of sources (Kanoy & Schroeder, 1985; Mesibov et al., 1977; Schroeder et al., 1983). In general, the suggestions given to parents usually focus on environmental changes, punishing (using time-out by isolation or removing privileges) or ignoring inappropriate behavior, and rewarding and encouraging appropriate behavior. An important part of the program is to share information on appropriate developmental expectations and behaviors, so that the parents can put their children's behavior in perspective.

Telephone follow-up indicated that in general, the Call-In Hour and specific suggestions were rated highly by parents (Kanoy & Schroeder, 1985). Suggestions for socialization problems (e.g., negative behavior, sibling or peer difficulties, or personality or emotional problems) were rated more effective than those for developmental problems (e.g., toileting, sleep, or developmental delays). Only about 25% of the suggestions for sleep and toileting difficulties were rated between 4 and 5 on a 5-point scale (1 = *not helpful*, and 5 = *very helpful*), whereas about 75% of those for socialization problems were rated between 4 and 5. None of the scores for any behavior category, however, were rated below 3.

Kanoy and Schroeder (1985) found that parents were much more likely to use both the Come-In service and the Call-In Hour when they had concerns about socialization (about 50% used both services), as compared with developmental problems (fewer that 30% used both services). The increased contact with professionals could account for the parents' finding the suggestions for socialization concerns more helpful. With developmental problems, the parents were concerned about a skill or ability their children had failed to acquire by the age the parents believed was normal. We found that providing only support and developmental information did not decrease parents' concerns but that when this information was combined with suggestions for specific actions, the ratings for both developmental information and suggestions increased. The effectiveness of giving specific suggestions was evident for socialization problems (most often behaviors children had acquired that were undesirable). Suggestions such as time-out and rewarding appropriate behaviors with stars gave parents specific strategies to use. These findings led to the development of a series of handouts that are sent to parents who use the Call-In Hour, to reinforce specific suggestions. Further follow-up studies will have to be done to determine parents' perceptions of the effectiveness of the handouts.

One concern that we had with the Call-In Hour was determining when a parent should be referred for more in-depth assessment or treatment. If a problems or concern did not remit after two or three contacts, the parents and child were referred elsewhere. In addition, referrals were made when any of the following constellations of problems was evident:

1. a parent had serious personal problems (e.g., depression or marital problems);
2. a child had multiple emotional and behavioral problems that occurred across settings (e.g., home, school, and neighborhood);
3. a family had multiple psychological problems or stress events (e.g., several children with problems);
4. a child exhibited behavior that had caused (or could cause) significant harm to self or others or serious property damage;
5. there was evidence or suspicion of child abuse, which was reported to appropriate authorities for further investigation;
6. an infant or preschool child showed delayed development, which had been targeted through standardized developmental screening tests and had not responded to stimulation recommendations within a 3–6-month period;
7. a child's general development or academic achievement was below the child's, parent's, or teacher's expectations.

As previously stated, over the years, about 17% of the parents using the Call-In Hour have been referred for further assessment or treatment. Those parents who did follow through with the referral rated the suggestion very highly, but 33% of the parents who had been referred did not use the referral suggestion. Now that more clinical services are being offered in the pediatric setting, it is rare that a parent does not follow through with the recommendation for referral.

The number of parents who called in with concerns regarding developmental delays led to the routine use of the Denver Developmental Screening Test (Frankenburg & Dodds, 1967) for all children at their 3-year checkup. In this way, parents could get direct feedback on how their children were developing, and the number of calls regarding this concern has accordingly dropped.

It had been planned that the handouts developed for the Call-In Hour also would be used in conjunction with well-child physical examinations. For example, the toilet training handout was to be included in the 18-month physical examination. We have discovered, however, that unless the nurses remember to include it with the chart, the pediatricians do not routinely give these to the parents. It is usually a parent's request for information that results in a handout being given. Although this has been rather disappointing, particularly given this group of pediatricians' interest in and support for anticipatory guidance, it is not an atypical problem. One observational study (Reisinger & Bires, 1980) of 23 pediatricians found that the time spent on anticipatory guidance averaged a high of 97 seconds for children under 5 months and a low of 7 seconds for adolescents! One way to ensure that certain areas are discussed with parents both before and after the birth of a baby is to include forms in the patient's medical chart that include the physical and psychosocial areas to be covered at the well-child visit (Christopherson & Rapoff, 1979). Without such a system, it is not likely that this information will be shared with parents at the proper anticipatory time. It would also be important to study the effect of such an anticipatory guidance system on parents' behavior versus just giving the handouts to them or giving the handouts only when they request them.

Direct Clinical Services

In 1982, when the services offered were expanded to include more in-depth assessment and short-term treatment, we were not quite certain about the types of problems that would be referred for these services. The number of referrals made from the Call-In Hour was small and primarily focused on developmental delays, learning problems, and negative behavior. The earlier Population Served section reviewed the number and types of problems that have been referred over the years. Although the number and types of problems are probably not significantly different from those referred to mental health centers, given the number of clients seen for only one session (13%) and a mean of five sessions for assessment and treatment, the presenting problems appear to be less severe than those referred to more traditional mental health settings. Parents appear to be more willing to talk to mental health workers in the pediatric setting and, consequently, more willing to seek help before the problem becomes clinically significant. This, however, is an empirical question that has to be answered by comparing the data from our clinic on numbers, types, and severity of referred problems to other mental health care settings with comparable socioeconomic populations.

Our group offers a full array of clinical child psychology assessment and treatment services. This section gives a brief overview, with a focus on services or methods developed primarily by virtue of our working in the pediatric primary care setting.

Assessment. Assessment is recognized as an integral part of every contact, whether it be talking to a parent who has called for a suggestion on how to handle a specific problem, determining the need for treatment, or gathering and integrating information from multiple sources and with multiple methods to answer specific questions about a child or family. We use a behaviorally oriented system for assessment that is based on

Rutter's (1975) work, which we call the comprehensive assessment-to-intervention system (CAIS). The CAIS is described in detail in Schroeder and Gordon (1991). It focuses on the specifics of the behavior of concern, as well as taking into account other characteristics of the child, family, and environment that influence the behavior. It also provides a framework for choosing instruments or techniques for gathering information and for summarizing the assessment data. This leads to a judgment about the significance of the behavior problem for the child, family, or wider community and, if necessary, the appropriate areas to be considered for further assessment or treatment. The CAIS was developed initially as a systematic way to quickly assess and offer suggestions to parents who used the Call-In Hour, and it allows us to get an understanding of the dimension of the problem without needing to attach a label or initially categorize the problem with a system such as the fourth edition of the *Diagnostic and Statistical Manual of Mental Disorders* (American Psychiatric Association, 1994). This is particularly important in our setting because many of the referral problems would not be considered clinically significant or pathological, although they may be significantly impacting on the child or family's life.

An issue frequently presented to pediatricians by parents is the diagnosis of ADHD and the appropriateness of treating the disorder with stimulant medication. In the light of the controversies surrounding the use of stimulant medication, as well as the limited contact they have with the patient to make such determinations, the pediatricians in our practice felt ill equipped to make assessments regarding diagnosis and treatment. In fact, they refused to prescribe medication without some formal assessment of the problem. Thus, if a child is suspected of having ADHD, we work not only with the child but also with the child's pediatrician, the school, and the parents to assess the behavior through formal psychometric testing, direct behavioral observations, parent and teacher questionnaires, and daily observational data. If the child is determined to have ADHD or attention problems, a behavioral program is developed with the parents and teachers. After this work has commenced, it may be determined that a trial of medication is indicated. At this point, a double-blind, placebo-controlled multimethod assessment of the effects of high and low doses of medication, which includes teacher and parent questionnaires, laboratory measures of attention, and academic analogue tasks, is carried out over a 3-week period. This practice-based clinical protocol is based on a research protocol developed by Barkley (1990). The clinical data of over a 100 children receiving the protocol in our practice have been analyzed with a focus on its effectiveness and ways to streamline the protocol to make it more cost-effective (Riddle, 1993). For example, we initially included a baseline session (insisted on by a parent of a child who had ADHD who also happened to be a clinical researcher for a drug company!) but learned that it essentially duplicated the results from the placebo trial. We have also been able to reduce the time for an evaluation session from 60 minutes to 30 minutes, by selecting the tests most sensitive to treatment. This approach not only has proven to be clinically effective in determining the child's response to medication but also has been very positively received by the children and parents, who feel it has given them a better understanding of the effects of the medication. It also presents the opportunity for long-term follow-up on the cognitive functioning of children on stimulant medication. We are now considering the use of similar protocols for assessing the feasibility of other medications or the effect of medications used for conditions such as seizure disorders.

The pediatric clinic serves as the county medical evaluation center for children who have been neglected or abused. One of the pediatricians in the practice (Charles Sheaffer) is responsible for much of the work on behalf of physically and sexually abused children in North Carolina, and after we joined the pediatric practice, he was instrumental in getting the state to fund psychological evaluations for children for whom abuse or neglect is suspected or has been substantiated. We now are part of the statewide Child Mental Health Evaluation Program, which involves answering a wide range of referral questions. We may be asked, for example, "Has the child been abused?" "What are the effects of the abuse?" "Is the mother or father capable of protecting the child?" "Does the child need treatment?" "How will the child be affected by going to court?"

Our clinical work in the area of sexual abuse led us to engage in research on memory issues with colleagues from the university. This work, done in the pediatric office, has been extensively published (e.g., See Baker-Ward, Gordon, Ornstein, & Clubb, 1993; Gordon et al., 1993; Ornstein, Larus, & Clubb, 1991). Furthermore, the clinical implications of this empirical work resulted in the development of guidelines for clinicians to use when interviewing children suspected of being sexually abused (Gordon, Schroeder, Ornstein, & Baker-Ward, 1995).

Treatment. We have found ourselves involved in a number of roles in the process of providing intervention services to children and families, including the following:

1. Educator: giving specific information, sharing books and other written material, offering parent groups, or helping parents or teachers to develop more realistic expectations;
2. Advocate: speaking for the child in court, helping the parents negotiate with the educational system, or advocating for the child's needs within the family system;

3. Treatment provider: giving direct treatment to the child or family or providing indirect treatment (e.g., intervention in the environment);
4. Case manager: accessing and networking services to meet the needs of the child and family.

The role of case manager is particularly pertinent to the primary care setting. This involves networking the often fragmented and specialized services of the community, to meet the individual needs of the child and family. This approach, as described by Hobbs (1975), involves looking for unique ways to use the available services, as well as for creative ways to develop services that are needed but unavailable. Children with developmental disabilities are most often thought of as in need of case managers, but this is an important role in work with most children and parents. It requires the clinician to be very familiar with the resources in the community and to become skilled in negotiating cooperation between agencies.

The practice offers individual treatment for children and parents as well as couple and family therapy. The treatment protocols for common childhood problems—such as enuresis, encopresis, sleep, negative behavior, bad habits, and anxiety—and for stressful events—such as death, divorce, and sexual abuse—have been published in a book by Schroeder and Gordon (1991), *Assessment and Treatment of Childhood Problems: A Clinician's Guide*. The empirical literature indicates that we should be able to meet the needs of parents and children in a more cost-effective and efficient manner through groups, and this would appear to be particularly true in the primary care setting. Although we have offered group treatment for both parents and children, which has focused on specific problem areas or life events, such as ADHD, divorce, social skills, sexual abuse, and stepparenting, it has actually been very difficult to provide a variety of group treatments on an ongoing basis. We have had difficulties with scheduling and finding the right mix and number of children or parents at the right time. The treatment group for parents of ADHD children has been successful, given the number of children who are evaluated for this problem and for the use of medication. The parents in this group meet for four consecutive sessions and then may attend a once-a-month support group. The staff is also very involved in the local parent groups focusing on these children.

In cooperation with the local department of social services, we developed a group-treatment program for children who had been sexually abused and their parents. The goal was to help the children and families deal with the complex emotional sequelae of the abuse and to find ways to cope effectively with the aftermath of the abuse. The children's groups were divided into preschool, elementary school, and adolescent ages.

They met for 10 weekly sessions, focusing on the issues of traumatic sexualization, stigmatization, betrayal of trust, and powerlessness (Finkelhor & Browne, 1986; Walker, Bonner, & Kaufman, 1988). The parents met separately and focused on the effects of abuse, the role of the legal system in abuse cases, problem solving for ways to meet their individual needs, and learning about ways to prevent the abuse from recurring. At the end of these sessions, a determination was made for each child and family regarding the need for further treatment. Although the predata and postdata, plus the consumer satisfaction questionnaires, indicated that the program was effective in treating these children and their families, the funding for the program was cut.

Community Consultation

Being in a primary care setting gives the professional a great deal of visibility in the community and also a great deal of responsibility to advocate for children. We have discovered that when the newspaper wants information about a particular issue (e.g., "Is it morally right to tell children there is a Santa Claus?") or the court system wants information on a particular problem, they are just as likely to call the pediatric office as are parents. We have, thus, increasingly found ourselves in the position of having to interface with the community on a number of levels.

As noted earlier, in the late 1960s and early 1970s, a pediatrician in the practice became the coordinator for all of the community agencies involved with children who were physically or sexually abused. Regular meetings were held with representatives from the pediatric office, the police department, the schools, and the department of social services, together with mental health professionals from the community. The focus of the meetings was initially educational, but it quickly moved to case management issues. Problems of roles and responsibilities were worked out (sometimes hammered out!), and the result has been an ongoing coordinated community effort on behalf of these children. At times the system falters, especially when new people are added to one of the agencies or new regulations change the nature of the services. However, the short- and long-term benefits of this work cannot be underestimated, as is demonstrated by the statewide Child Mental Health Evaluation Program and the contract with the local department of social services to provide group treatment for children in our county who have been sexually abused.

Another example of community involvement is that we first convinced and then consulted with the school system to include sex education and sexual abuse prevention at all grade levels. In addition, both pediatricians and psychologists have been asked to provide training for the North Carolina Guardian Ad Litem program, district judges, district attorneys, the department of social services, the rape crisis center, the Young Men's Christian Association, day care centers, and many other community groups that are involved in the lives of children. We have discovered, however, that all of this work is made possible by the community interaction concerning a particular child or family, which identifies problems and solutions that can then be applied to the benefit of other children in the community. In the real world, where one must juggle time, economic issues, and altruism, this is as it should be.

Training

Training has always been part of the work in the pediatric office. From 1973 to 1982, graduate students, interns, and postdoctoral fellows in psychology; graduate students in social work; and medical students and residents participated in all aspects of the program. In 1982, the Division of Community Pediatrics at the University of North Carolina at Chapel Hill Medical School began a training program for all 1st-year pediatric residents and 4th-year medical students taking an ambulatory pediatrics elective (Sharp & Lorch, 1988). The goals of the program were to introduce the pediatric trainees to community resources for children and to increase their knowledge of the factors affecting a child's development. The pediatric psychology practice was one of 25 community agencies involved in this training. This is a unique approach to training pediatricians in the biosocial aspects of development, and in 1984 the program won the prestigious American Academy of Ambulatory Pediatrics Excellence in Teaching Award. The residents and medical students each spent 1 day a week for a month in our office; they learned about the types of developmental and behavioral problems parents bring to the pediatric office, how to interview parents and to develop intervention strategies for common problems, and what a psychologist has to offer in a primary health care setting and when children should be referred to them. It was hoped that we would alert these residents at an early stage in their careers to the value of psychologists! We plan to do a survey of graduates of this program to determine how they now interface with psychologists; however, we already know that a number of them (three in our area alone) have psychologists in their practices. Unfortunately, in 1992, the funds for this training program were cut, and we have not had the opportunity to train residents since that time.

Clinical psychology graduate students have continued to participate in the Call-In Hour and to provide treatment one afternoon a week. We have also had a 2-year postdoctoral fellow in psychology, who was jointly sponsored by our practice and the University of North Carolina Medical School Department of Pediatrics. Interns from the University of North Carolina Psychiatry Department spend a day a week for a 3-month rotation in the ADHD clinic, doing the drug protocol evaluations.

Training in a busy private clinic takes time and effort, which in part can be recouped by the trainees' work in the community or with families who cannot afford the full fee for service. The ultimate benefit is having more mental health professionals trained to work in primary care settings and pediatricians who are more aware of mental health issues and the desirability of having psychologists in their practices.

Research

The primary health care setting is a fertile ground for psychological research. The sheer number of available children who are developing along a normal continuum offers opportunities for interesting developmental research, and the smaller number of children who have chronic physical and behavioral or emotional disorders encourages research on treatment effectiveness as well as longitudinal research on these problems. The primary health care setting also offers the opportunity to evaluate the effectiveness of primary and secondary prevention programs. To do this work, one has to demonstrate credibility within the system by offering a range of high-quality services.

The first 5 years of the expanded practice (1982–1987) were devoted to developing the clinical services, and as we entered another 5-year era, we began to look at the research issues that were raised by the clinical practice. One study, done as a doctoral dissertation in the University of North Carolina School of Public Health Department of Epidemiology, compared a group of 2- to 7-year-old children who had received treatment for noncompliance with a control group matched for age and level of noncompliance (Martin, 1988). In view of the number of children identified with this potentially persistent problem, and the desire to provide early intervention to change the course of the behavior, the research questions were whether the treatment would be effective and (given the age of the children) whether the behavior of the untreated control group would improve without intervention. The parent-training program for the negative behavior was based on the work by Eyberg and Boggs (1989) and Forehand and McMahon (1981). Martin found that at a 3-month follow-up, the 31 children in the treatment group showed clinically and statistically significant decreases in both the number and frequency of behavior problems. The behavior of the 22 untreated control children did not improve over the same time period. Further follow-up of these children will provide more information about the course of this behavior.

Current work involves the collaboration of developmental and clinical psychologists in the study of the questions raised by our work with sexually abused children. We quickly discovered that questions asked by the legal system exceeded our knowledge in this area. We were asked, for example, "Can we believe what young children tell us about what has happened to them?" "Can children remember and report events as completely and as accurately as adults, especially when events may have been traumatic?" "Are children particularly vulnerable to suggestive and leading questions?" "What are the effects of repeated questioning on children's abilities to remember particular events?"

To begin answering these questions, we first looked at the role of prior knowledge. A common belief among professionals who testify in court on behalf of preschoolers who have been abused is that young children's knowledge of sexuality is limited and, therefore, that these children cannot describe sexual acts unless they have actually experienced them. To provide empirical evidence for this belief, we studied 192 nonabused children (age 2–7 years) to determine their knowledge of gender identity, body parts and functioning, pregnancy and birth, adult sexual behavior, private parts, and personal safety skills (Gordon, Schroeder, & Abrams, 1990a). There were significant age differences in children's knowledge of all areas of sexuality, but under the age of 6 or 7 years, children had little knowledge of adult sexual behavior. The children's sexual knowledge was directly related to their parents' attitudes about sexuality: Parents with more restrictive attitudes had children who knew less about sexuality than parents who had more liberal attitudes. A second study examined sexual knowledge of children for whom sexual abuse had been substantiated and an age-matched control group of non-abused children (Gordon, Schroeder, & Abrams, 1990b). This study indicated that sexually abused children do not necessarily have greater knowledge of sexuality than nonabused children of the same age. The children who were sexually abused, however, gave qualitatively unusual responses to the stimulus materials. For example, a 3-year-old withdrew in fright when presented with a picture of a child being put to bed by an adult.

A second line of research focused on factors that influence the accuracy of children's testimony. This research initially was supported by a National Institute of Mental Health grant. It examined children's memory for a personally experienced event, a physical examination (an analogue to sexual abuse). The purpose of this research was to establish baseline data for children's memory over varying periods of time and to examine factors that influence children's memory (e.g., repeated interviews, use of props in interviews, reinstatement, prior knowledge of visits to the doctor, painful procedures, and traumatic injuries). This research has been presented and published extensively (e.g., Baker-Ward et al., 1993; Baker-Ward, Hess, & Flanagan, 1990; Gordon et al., 1993;

Ornstein, Gordon, & Larus, 1992). Gordon et al. (1995) documented the clinical implications of this work for testimony of young children with guidelines for interviewing young children and evaluating their responses. This basic research, born out of our clinical work and carried out by necessity in the primary care setting, is an excellent example of the type of research that can be done in natural settings.

IMPLEMENTATION ISSUES

In recent years, pediatric practices have advertised for psychologists, but usually, it is the psychologist who must approach the pediatricians to set up a collaborative relationship. The published description of the psychologist's role in the Chapel Hill Pediatrics practice and other publications (e.g., Drotar, 1993; Wright & Burns, 1986) have served to present the positive benefits of such a relationship. More psychologists and pediatricians in private practice are developing collaborative relationships, as evidenced by the Society of Pediatric Psychology's Special Interest Group on Psychologists Working in Primary Care Settings (Division 12, Section V, American Psychological Association). As more psychologists doing this work are identified, we will, hopefully, be able to provide more information on the nature of these relationships and the variety of services offered in these settings.

Setting up a pediatric psychology practice in a primary health care setting is not dissimiliar to establishing a private practice, but the options available to the psychologist in a primary health care setting will depend on the particular health care setting and the relationship the psychologist wants with the other professionals in that setting. It is usually not possible for a psychologist to be a partner in another professional group (e.g., pediatrics); thus, other options for association must be considered. A psychologist may be employed by a pediatric practice, and may have a fixed salary or a salary based on a percentage of the collected receipts or may pay a fixed percentage of collected receipts to the pediatric practice. Another option is for the psychologist to establish an independent practice within the health care setting, with overhead paid by the psychologist. The administrative functions may be contracted to the pediatric practice or handled independently by the psychologist. Establishing an independent practice within the health care setting gives the psychologist the options of sole proprietorship, a partnership (if more than one psychologist is involved), or a corporation. The pediatric psychology practice described in this chapter was established as an independent corporation. For the first 2 years, I paid the pediatric practice for overhead costs. As the pediatric psychology staff grew, we hired a secretary, obtained separate phone numbers, did our own billing, paid a fixed rent, and so forth, while still being physically located within the pediatric setting. Due to space constraints, the mental health part of the practice moved to a building directly behind the pediatricians, keeping one office in the pediatrician's space. This decision was a difficult one for all involved, but we felt that our long-term collaboration would survive the short physical distance separating us. Only time will tell how well this arrangement works. We have agreed, however, that if we all survive managed care, we will eventually move to a building that will house both the pediatricians and the mental health professionals. The parents have actually appreciated the physical separation; they state that it provides them greater privacy and that the atmosphere is more conducive to mental health work.

The space available in the primary health care setting is geared to medical rather than psychological needs; it is therefore important to negotiate for space that will permit privacy, as well as flexibility to serve small children and families for diagnosis and treatment. It has been our experience that private pediatric offices are under renovation every 5 to 8 years, so although the clinician may have to start with less-than-optimal space, a goal to improve the space options as the value of the practice is demonstrated is usually realistic.

As described in previous sections, the types of services offered and the staffing patterns were the direct result of identified client needs and the interests of the psychologists and pediatricians in the practice. Keeping careful records of our work and doing follow-ups to determine consumer satisfaction have always been a part of our practice. Also, by taking the time to share the importance of certain research topics with the pediatricians, staff, parents, and children, we have had the opportunity to research some interesting questions. My association with a university and the availability of university students and staff to help carry out the research are key to being able to do this work. Doing any type of research in the primary setting presents obstacles: lack of sufficient time on the part of the doctors, nurses, and patients to collect extensive data; getting representative subject samples, which usually requires gathering data from several offices in several communities; lack of instruments that focus on the kinds of concerns reflected in a primary care setting; developing collaborative relationships with the physicians, which takes time; and lack of time and money on the psychologist's part to carry out the work. The importance of doing this work, however, is reflected in National Institute of Mental Health and the Agency for Health Care Prevention and Research funding research on mental health services in primary health care settings. With the increased interest in providing mental health services for children and parents in this area, new approaches should be forthcoming. The work by the American Academy of Pediatrics

Task Force on the Coding of Mental Health in children should help to better identify mental health disorders in primary care settings and generate further training, clinical services, and research in the primary care setting.

CONCLUSION

The collaboration of psychologists and pediatricians provides a unique opportunity to enhance children's and parents' lives over the trajectory of the child's development. The focus is on promoting the child's healthy development through services that focus on prevention and early intervention rather than the treatment of severe psychopathology. The collaborative practice described in this chapter has also included training opportunities for both pediatricians and psychologists as well as opportunities for research. Although special training to work in a pediatric primary care setting is necessary, psychologists working with children and adolescents have a great deal to offer in this setting.

REFERENCES

American Academy of Pediatrics, Task Force on Pediatric Education. (1978). *The future of pediatric education*. Evanston, IL: Author.

American Psychiatric Association. (1994). *Diagnostic and statistical manual of mental disorders* (4th ed.). Washington, DC: Author.

Baker-Ward, L. E., Gordon, B. N., Ornstein, P. A., & Clubb, P. A. (1993). Young children's long-term retention of a pediatric examination. *Child Development, 64*, 1519–1533.

Baker-Ward, L. E., Hess, T. M., & Flanagan, D. A. (1990). The effects of children's involvement on children's memory for events. *Cognitive Development, 4*, 393–407.

Barkley, R. A. (1990). *Attention deficit hyperactivity disorder: A handbook for diagnosis and treatment*. New York: Guilford Press.

Bernal, M. E., & North, J. A. (1978). A survey of parent training manuals. *Journal of Applied Behavior Analysis, 11*, 533–544.

Christopherson, E. R., & Rapoff, M. A. (1979). Behavioral pediatrics. In O. F. Pomerleau & J. P. Brady (Eds.), *Behavioral medicine: Theory and practice* (pp. 99–123). Baltimore: Williams & Wilkins.

Clarke-Stewart, K. A. (1978). Popular primers for parents. *American Psychologist, 33*, 359–369.

Drotar, D. (1993). Influences on collaborative activities among psychologists and pediatricians: Implications for practice, training, and research. *Journal of Pediatric Psychology, 18*, 159–172.

Drotar, D. (1995). *Consulting with pediatricians: Psychological perspectives.* New York: Plenum.

Eyberg, S. M., & Boggs, S. R. (1989). Parent training for oppositional–defiant preschoolers. In C. E. Schaefer & J. M. Briesmeister (Eds.), *Handbook of parent training: Parents as cotherapists for children's behavior problems* (pp. 105–132). New York: Wiley.

Finkelhor, D., & Browne, A. (1986). Initial and long-term effects: A conceptual framework. In D. Finkelhor & associates (Eds.), *A sourcebook on child sexual abuse* (pp. 180–198). Beverly Hills, CA: Sage.

Forehand, R. L., & McMahon, R. J. (1981). *Helping the noncompliant child: A clinician's guide to parent training.* New York: Guilford Press.

Frankenburg, W. K., & Dodds, J. B. (1967). The Denver Developmental Screening Test. *Journal of Pediatrics, 71,* 181–191.

Gordon, B. N., & Jens, K. G. (1988). A conceptual model for tracking high-risk infants and making services decisions. *Developmental and Behavioral Pediatrics, 9,* 279–286.

Gordon, B. N., Ornstein, P. A., Nida, R. E., Follmer, A., Crenshaw, M. C., & Albert, G. (1993). Does the use of dolls facilitate children's memory of visits to the doctor? *Applied Cognitive Psychology, 7,* 1–16.

Gordon, B. N., Schroeder, C. S., & Abrams, J. M. (1990a). Children's knowledge of sexuality: Age and social class differences. *Journal of Clinical Child Psychology, 19,* 33–43.

Gordon, B. N., Schroeder, C. S., & Abrams, J. M. (1990b). Children's knowledge of sexuality: A comparison of sexually abused and nonabused children. *American Journal of Orthopsychiatry, 60,* 250–257.

Gordon, B. N., Schroeder, C. S., Ornstein, P. A., & Baker-Ward, L. E. (1995). Clinical implications of research in memory development. In T. Ney (Ed.), *Child sexual abuse cases: Allegations, assessment and management* (pp. 99–124). New York: Brunner/Mazel.

Haggerty, R. J. (1986). The changing nature of pediatrics. In N. A. Krasnegor, J. D. Arasteh, & M. F. Calaldo (Eds.), *Child health behavior: A behavioral pediatric perspective* (pp. 9–16). New York: Wiley.

Hawk, B. A., Schroeder, C. A., & Martin, S. (1987). Pediatric psychology in a primary care setting. *Newsletter of the Society of Pediatric Psychology, 11,* 13–18.

Hobbs, N. (1975). *The futures of children.* San Francisco: Jossey-Bass.

Kanoy, K., & Schroeder, C. S. (1985). Suggestions to parents about common behavior problems in a pediatric primary care office: Five years of follow-up. *Journal of Pediatric Psychology, 10,* 15–30.

Martin, S. L. (1988). *The effectiveness of a multidisciplinary primary health care model in the prevention of children's mental health problems.* Unpublished doctoral dissertation, University of North Carolina, Chapel Hill.

Mesibov, G. B., Schroeder, C. S., & Wesson, L. (1977). Parental concerns about their children. *Journal of Pediatric Psychology, 2,* 13–17.

Ornstein, P. A., Gordon, B. N., & Larus, D. M. (1992). Children's memory for a personally experienced event: Implications for testimony. *Applied Cognitive Psychology, 6,* 49–60.

Ornstein, P. A., Larus, D. M., & Clubb, P. A. (1991). Understanding children's testimony: Implications of research on the development of memory. In R. Vasta (Ed.), *Annals of child development* (Vol. 8, pp. 145–176). London: Jessica Kingsley.

Reisinger, K. S., & Bires, J. A. (1980). Anticipatory guidance in pediatric practice. *Pediatrics, 66,* 889–892.

Riddle, D. B. (1993, August). *Double blind protocol research within a pediatric practice.* Paper presented at the 101st Annual Convention of the American Psychological Association, Toronto, Ontario, Canada.

Routh, D. K., Schroeder, C. S., & Koocher, G. P. (1983). Psychology and primary health care for children. *American Psychologist, 38,* 95–98.

Rutter, M. (1975). *Helping troubled children.* New York: Plenum.

Schroeder, C. S. (1979). The psychologist in a private pediatrics office. *Journal of Pediatric Psychology, 1,* 5–18.

Schroeder, C. S. (1992, August). *Psychologists working with pediatricians.* Paper presented at the 100th Annual Convention of the American Psychological Association, Washington, DC.

Schroeder, C. S., & Gordon, B. N. (1991). *Assessment and treatment of childhood problems: A clinician's guide.* New York: Guilford Press.

Schroeder, C. S., Gordon, B. N., Kanoy, K., & Routh, D. K. (1983). Managing children's behavior problems in pediatric practice. In M. Wolraich & D. K. Routh (Eds.), *Advances in developmental and behavioral pediatrics* (Vol. 4, pp. 25–86). Greenwich, CT: JAI Press.

Schroeder, C. S., Gordon, B. N., & McConnell, P. (1987). Books for parents and children on behavior management. *Journal of Clinical Child Psychology, 16,* 89–94.

Schroeder, C. S., & Wool, R. (1979, March). *Parental concerns for children one month to 10 years and the informational sources desired to answer these concerns.* Paper presented at the annual meeting of the Southeastern Psychological Association, New Orleans, LA.

Sharp, M. C., & Lorch, S. C. (1988). A community outreach training program for pediatrics residents and medical students. *Journal of Medical Education, 63,* 316–322.

Smith, E. E., Rome, L. P., & Freedheim, D. K. (1967). The clinical psychologist in the pediatric office. *Journal of Pediatrics, 21,* 48–51.

Walker, C. E., Bonner, B. L., & Kaufman, K. L. (1988). *The physically and sexually abused child: Evaluation and treatment.* Elmsford, NY: Pergamon Press.

Wilson, J. L. (1964). Growth and development in pediatrics. *Journal of Pediatrics, 65,* 984–991.

Wright, L., & Burns, B. J. (1986). Primary mental health care: A "find" for psychology. *Professional Psychology: Research and Practice, 17,* 560–564.

10

BEHAVIORAL HEALTH CARE IN PRIMARY CARE SETTINGS: RECOGNITION AND TREATMENT OF ANXIETY DISORDERS

DAVID H. BARLOW, JONATHAN A. LERNER, and
JEANNE LAWTON ESLER

Community surveys indicate that anxiety disorders are the single most prevalent class of mental disorders in the population at large, with 1-year estimates ranging from 13% to 17% (Kessler et al., 1994; Regier et al., 1984). This makes the prevalence of anxiety disorders greater than other major classes of disorders, including addictive disorders or mood disorders.

DO PATIENTS WITH ANXIETY DISORDERS SEEK TREATMENT IN PRIMARY CARE SETTINGS?

For many years, we had difficulty estimating the number of individuals with anxiety disorders presenting to primary care settings. More recently, information gleaned from various surveys indicates that these numbers are substantial, although the objectives of these surveys have typically varied widely. For example, Regier et al. (1993) reported that individuals with anxiety disorders seek out treatment in primary care settings and other medical facilities as often as they present to mental health providers. Barrett, Barrett, Oxman, and Gerber (1988), while examining more specifically the types of patients found in rural primary care settings, found that fully 21.3% of all patients met research diagnostic criteria (Spitzer, Endicott, & Robins, 1978) for anxiety disorders, depressive disorders, or mixed anxiety–depressive syndromes, including masked (suspected) depression and mixed anxiety–depression.

More recently, the fourth edition of the *Diagnostic and Statistical Manual of Mental Disorders* (*DSM–IV*; American Psychiatric Association, 1994) Task Force examined the distribution of anxiety disorders, as well as anxious symptoms sufficient to be impairing but not reaching definitional threshold for one or more of the anxiety disorders, in five primary care settings. Three of the five primary care settings were in the United States, one in Australia, and one in Paris. All patients filled out a brief screening instrument designed to detect the possible presence of anxiety and related symptomatology. Two thirds of the sample were chosen from patients falling above a cutoff point, indicating the possible presence of anxious or dysphoric symptoms, whereas one third were chosen from patients falling below the cutoff point. For this reason, the numbers in this study do not reflect absolute prevalence of anxiety disorders in primary care settings but do give a good idea of the distribution of specific problems. Patients were then carefully assessed with semistructured interviews to determine the presence and nature of a disorder, if any. Results showed that very high percentages of patients received diagnoses of generalized anxiety disorder (11.9%), social phobia (13%), and specific phobia. In addition, 8% of patients fell under a category labeled *not otherwise specified* (NOS) consisting of patients presenting with mostly anxious symptoms or symptoms of negative affect that did not meet definitional criteria for one disorder or another. Patients met criteria less frequently for panic disorder (4.3%), obsessive–compulsive disorder (1.2%), posttraumatic stress disorder (4.5%), and dysthymia (1.1%). Major depressive episode was diagnosed in 7.9% of patients, and fully 34.7% of patients were given a diagnosis of no mental disorder (see Zinbarg et al., 1994). The symptoms of negative affect, which are present in most anxiety disorders as well as depressive disorders, form the basis for a proposed new category in *DSM–IV*, termed mixed anxiety–depressive disorder (Zinbarg et al., 1994). This group would most likely encompass Barrett et al.'s (1988) categories of masked (suspected) depression, mixed anxiety–depression, and other depressive content.

More recent estimates indicate that the presence of anxiety-related symptoms and disorders in primary care settings may even be higher than previous numbers. For example, Fifer et al. (1994) discovered that 33% of over 6,000 eligible patients completing an up-to-date screening instrument in the offices of 75 physicians in a large mixed-model health maintenance organization reported elevated symptoms or disorders of anxiety. Shear, Schulberg, and Madonia (1994) also found high prevalence rates of anxiety disorders in primary care centers when primary care patients were assessed by semistructured interviews. Specifically, fully 11% of unselected patients in primary care settings met criteria for panic disorder and 10% for generalized anxiety disorder.

Approaching the issue from another direction, Katerndahl and Realini (1995) conducted a community survey to identify patients who had experienced panic attacks, to ascertain whether they had sought treatment for their attacks and, if so, where they went for treatment. Only 59% of the participants had ever sought care from the health care system for their panic attacks. Information on the specific health and mental health sites from which these patients sought help is presented in Table 1. These data are broken down by the percentage of patients seeking out various sites the first time that they presented for help with panic attacks and any time they presented for help, including subsequent episodes of panic. As one can see, medical settings are used far more frequently than mental health settings to care for panic attacks, even after the initial contact, where presumably the problem is identified as anxiety or panic related. Specifically, 49% of these patients sought out, and continue to seek out, medical settings, compared with 26% receiving help from mental health practitioners. The breakdown of type of medical setting or type of mental health practitioner or setting is also provided. In addition, fully 13% of this sample, located in south Texas, sought help from alternative sources of care such as telephone help lines or clergy. Of course, many participants used more than one site, so the percentages are not mutually exclusive.

From these surveys, it would seem that symptoms of anxiety and anxiety disorders are highly prevalent in primary care settings. Furthermore, because these disorders are chronic in nature, typically displaying patterns of exacerbation and remission often associated with life stress, the observation that these patients form a substantial core of the practices of primary health care practitioners gains credence (Barlow, 1988; Brown & Barlow, 1995).

ARE PATIENTS WITH ANXIETY DISORDERS RECOGNIZED IN PRIMARY CARE SETTINGS?

Although only 32.2% of patients with anxiety disorder seek treatment, approximately half of these patients seek treatment in primary

TABLE 1
Sites Selected by Patients Seeking Treatment for Panic Attack

Treatment site	% of patients presenting at any time ($N = 97$)	% of patients presenting for episode of initial contact ($N = 53$)[a]
Medical health care settings	49	85
Emergency department	32	43
Minor emergency center	11	7
Clinic	9	7
Physician's office		
General/family physician	35	35
General internist	3	6
Cardiologist	9	6
Otolaryngologist	3	6
Ambulance	19	15
Mental health care settings	26	35
Psychiatrist	24	22
Psychologist	10	13
Social worker	5	4
Mental health clinic	11	7
Alternative care settings	13	19
Telephone help line	10	6
Clergy	8	7
Folk healer/*curandero*	8	7
Chiropractor	6	6

Note: Subjects may have presented to >1 site, so percentages may not total 100.
[a]Only the 57 patients who presented to at least one site were included. Four of these subjects did not respond to this question.
Data are from "Where Do Panic Attacks Sufferers Seek Care?" by D. A. Katerndahl and J. P. Realini, 1995, *Journal of Family Practice, 40,* 237–243. Copyright 1995 by Appleton & Lange, Inc. Used with permission.

care settings. Because anxiety disorders are the most prevalent class of mental disorders, the number of individuals seeking treatment in primary care settings is enormous, with estimates in the range of 6 million (Regier et al., 1993).

It is now well recognized that approximately half of patients presenting with emotional disorders, such as anxiety or mood disorders, are not recognized or diagnosed by primary care physicians (e.g., Broadhead, 1994; Fifer et al., 1994; Shear & Schulberg, 1995). Because, as Ford (1994) pointed out, at least 50% of patients with psychological disorders receive all or part of their care from primary care physicians, lack of recognition is a source of major concern. In the Fifer et al. (1994) study, as noted above, 33% of the patients screened positive for anxiety symptoms and possible anxiety disorders. As represented in Figure 1, fully 56% of these patients were unrecognized and untreated, and only 44% were recognized as presenting with anxiety and were treated in

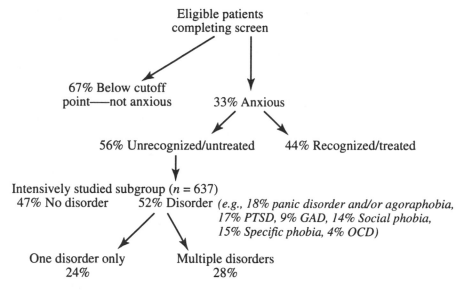

Eligible patients
completing screen

67% Below cutoff
point——not anxious   33% Anxious

56% Unrecognized/untreated   44% Recognized/treated

Intensively studied subgroup (*n* = 637)
47% No disorder   52% Disorder *(e.g., 18% panic disorder and/or agoraphobia,*
                                      17% PTSD, 9% GAD, 14% Social phobia,
                                      15% Specific phobia, 4% OCD)

One disorder only   Multiple disorders
24%   28%

Figure 1. Anxiety in primary care settings. PTSD = posttraumatic stress disorder, GAD = generalized anxiety disorder, OCD = obsessive–compulsive disorder. From "Untreated Anxiety Among Adult Primary Care Patients in a Health Maintenance Organization," by S. K. Fifer et al., 1994, *Archives of General Psychiatry, 51,* p. 743. Copyright 1994 by the American Medical Association. Adapted with permission.

some fashion or other. The figure of 44% recognized and treated is somewhat higher than estimates from community samples, in which data suggest that only 25% of individuals diagnosed with anxiety disorders are receiving any kind of treatment, and many of these treatments would also not necessarily be efficacious. Data on recognition of anxiety disorders in the Fifer et al. study may actually be an overestimate, because practitioners in this mixed-model health maintenance organization were provided some specific training in recognizing and treating these disorders. Katon, Vitaliano, Russo, Jones, and Anderson (1987) found that over 30% of patients in a primary care practice had experienced at least one panic attack during the previous year, and because somatic symptoms are such a heavy component of panic attacks, panic and anxiety were not recognized in the large majority of these patients. Returning to the Fifer et al. study, approximately half (*n* = 637) of the individuals unrecognized and untreated for anxiety symptoms or disorders were available for more intensive study. As reflected in Figure 1, 52% of these patients presented with a recognizable anxiety disorder upon semistructured interviewing. Approximately half of the individuals constituting this 52% (24%) presented with only one disorder, whereas the remainder presented with more than one anxiety disorder. Percentages of specific disorders were very similar to other surveys (e.g., Shear & Schulberg, 1995): Large percentages of patients presented with panic disorder with or without agoraphobia, posttraumatic stress disorder, generalized anxiety disorder, social phobia, and so on. On the other hand, 47% of these intensively studied individuals did not meet definitional criteria for a disorder but clearly presented with substantial anxious symptomatology. As we have seen above in the Zinbarg et al. (1994) study, many of these patients probably presented with generalized symptoms of negative affect that might meet criteria for the newly proposed diagnostic category of mixed anxiety–depressive disorder. Most of these patients also presented with substantial functional impairment that was as great as those meeting all criteria for one or more anxiety disorders. These patients are very much in need of treatment due to the chronic and recurring nature of this symptomatology (Zinbarg et al., 1994).

IMPAIRMENT

Several studies have addressed the issue of functional impairment associated with anxious or depressive symptoms in primary care settings. For example, Wells et al. (1989) reported on the functional status and well-being of patients with depressive disorders or depressive symptoms. They found that these patients were at least as impaired, and in some cases more impaired, than patients with chronic medical conditions. For example, individuals with symptoms of depression, or more generalized negative affect, were more impaired than patients with chronic pulmonary disease, diabetes, arthritis, back problems, and gastrointestinal disorders. Only coronary artery disease produced as much impairment. Although anxiety symptoms and disorders were not specifically identified in this study, more recent efforts, which included symptoms and disorders of anxiety, have essentially replicated these findings (K. B. Wells, January 12, 1994, personal communication).

COMPLAINTS OF ANXIOUS PATIENTS IN PRIMARY CARE SETTINGS

Patients presenting to primary care settings who are ultimately diagnosed with severe anxiety often somatize their complaints in some characteristic ways. Most often, the pattern of symptoms is not well explained by identifiable physical illnesses. For example, Van Hemert, Hengeveld, Boek, Rooijmans, and Vandenbroucke (1993) compared patients whose symptoms were explained by a known physical illness to those presenting with vague symptoms that were not well explained. Fully 38% to 45% of those patients presenting with symptoms that were not well explained by a known physical illness were later identified to have a psychological disorder, as compared with 15% of those whose symptoms were well explained. The majority of these disorders were anxiety or mood disorders.

Other common presentations include chest pain in the absence of clinical evidence of cardiac disease. For example, Yingling, Wulsin, Arnold, and Rovan (1993) found that 17% of 229 patients seeking treatment for chest pain at an emergency department met criteria for panic disorder. These individuals were significantly more likely than individuals without panic disorder to have visited an emergency department for chest pain at least once in the past year. Of individuals identified with panic disorder, fully 27% had made at least three emergency department visits for chest pain in the previous year.

Finally, Ford (1987) found that those patients presenting with atypical chest pain were four times as likely to have panic disorder than those without chest pain. Katon (1984) found that 89% of 55 primary care patients with panic disorder had initially presented to their general practitioners with somatic complaints and had been misdiagnosed with physical problems. The most common somatic complaints reported by individuals in this sample included cardiac symptoms, gastrointestinal symptoms, and neurological symptoms. In a 1986 study of panic in primary care settings, Katon et al. found that panic disorder patients had an average of 14.1 somatic symptoms, as compared with 7.3 symptoms in a control group. Katon et al. (1987) pointed out that the somatic focus of many individuals with panic disorder often leads to misdiagnosis. Other symptomatic presentations associated with anxiety include dizziness, joint pain, and breathlessness (e.g., Shear & Schulberg, 1995).

Of course, correctly identifying anxiety and mood disorders or anxiety and depressive symptoms not meeting definitional criteria for disorders in the context of the enormous complexity of the presentation of the variety of physical disorders is a very difficult task indeed. Broadhead (1994) noted that the presentation of psychological symptoms may be somewhat different in primary care settings compared with more traditional mental health settings and that cultural variations in the expression of anxiety symptoms often confuse the picture further for the primary care health practitioner. Indeed, expressions of anxiety are often tightly integrated with specific cultural idioms that may vary greatly from one culture to another, requiring some knowledge of these cultural expressions (Barlow, 1988).

ARE PATIENTS WITH ANXIETY DISORDERS APPROPRIATELY TREATED?

Recent studies have suggested that patients with anxiety disorders are seldom treated and, when they are treated, often receive ineffective

TABLE 2
Utilization of Effective Psychological Treatments in Cases of Panic and Phobic Disorders

Study	N	Total % receiving effective psychological treatment
Breier (1986)	60	16%
Goisman et al. (1993)	231	38% (93% of these receiving medication)
Taylor et al. (1989)	794	15% (50% of these receiving counseling and hospitalization)

Note: Data are from Barlow (1994).

treatments. As noted above, findings from the epidemiologic catchment area study (Regier et al., 1993) suggested that only approximately 1 in 3 patients with a diagnosed anxiety disorder was receiving any treatment at all, let alone an effective treatment. More recent studies suggest that little has changed. Three studies, summarized in Table 2, surveyed patients presenting to emergency rooms or other primary care facilities with panic and phobic disorders, regarding their experiences with psychosocial treatments. Although it has been recognized since the time of Freud that some sort of exposure-based treatment is essential for phobic disorders, only between 15% and 38% of the patients had ever experienced an exposure-based treatment. A somewhat greater percentage had received counseling or relaxation treatments, and an even larger percentage had received some sort of medication. Although effective medications exist for some anxiety disorders (Liebowitz & Barlow, 1995), a number of studies suggest that medication is often prescribed inappropriately or at an incorrect dosage (Shear & Schulberg, 1995).

The status of treatment of psychological disorders in primary care settings was recently dramatically demonstrated by Schulberg et al. (in press), who identified 276 primary care patients meeting criteria for a current major depressive episode. These patients were then randomized to either usual care on the part of the primary care physician or one of two treatments delivered by a mental health professional: pharmacotherapy (nortriptyline) or interpersonal psychotherapy. Because all therapists, including the primary care physician, were informed that the patient was suffering from a major depressive episode, the fact of recognizing the disorder did not play a role in subsequent treatment strategies. After 8 months of treatment, the results indicated that approximately 70% of the patients receiving one of the treatments from a mental health professional were essentially asymptomatic on the Hamilton Rating Scale for Depression (Hamilton, 1960). In comparison, only 20% of the patients receiving usual care from the primary care physician were asymptomatic, a highly significant difference. Further inquiry revealed that most primary care physicians did not intervene actively or in a structured way to treat the depressive episode, even with an effective pharmacological agent, despite being aware of the diagnosis. This study and other similar findings (e.g., Sturm & Wells, 1995) would suggest that patients with psychological disorders, particularly emotional disorders such as anxiety and mood disorders, are not being well treated at the present time in primary care settings.

MODELS OF PSYCHOLOGICAL TREATMENT IN PRIMARY CARE SETTINGS

Highly effective psychological treatments have been developed for most psychological disorders. In most cases, clinical trials have demonstrated that these treatments are not only more effective than no-treatment or waiting list controls but also more effective than credible alternative psychological treatments or drug placebos (Barlow, 1994). A recent review indicates that we now have effective psychological treatments meeting the above criteria for all of the anxiety disorders (Barlow & Lehman, in press). In view of the enormous numbers of patients presenting with psychological disorders in primary care settings, one of the major problems facing psychologists and other mental health practitioners today is the dissemination of effective psychological treatments to those who need them.

In the United States, health care policy and the delivery of health care are undergoing revolutionary changes (e.g., Cummings, 1995). Although few agree at the present time on the end result of these changes, it is clear to all that mental health practitioners will have to adapt to remain important players in the delivery of mental health care (Barlow, 1994; Barlow & Barlow, 1995). There is also wide agreement that primary care settings will become an increasingly important arena for the delivery of behavioral health care and that psychologists and other mental health professionals need to come to grips with changes and practice patterns that would allow effective participation in primary care settings (DiBartolo, Hofmann, & Barlow, 1995; Liebowitz & Barlow, 1995).

Evidence has already been reviewed on the clinical and cost-effectiveness of mental health practitioners such as psychologists working in primary care settings (Schulberg et al., in press; Sturm & Wells, 1995). Various models are also under development for the delivery of effective psychological treatments in these settings. Because there is wide agreement that the number of people presenting with anxiety disorders in these settings far exceeds the capabilities of psychologists and other mental health professionals using traditional one-on-one models of treatment delivery, alternative, more efficient models are being developed. Within the anxiety disorders, one recent report by Swinson, Solios,

Cox, and Kuch (1992) examined the effects of treatment for patients presenting to emergency room settings with panic attacks. In this study, 33 patients presenting to the emergency room with panic attacks were identified, and they agreed to random assignment to two treatment conditions as well as follow-up. Seventeen patients ultimately received exposure instructions, in which patients were told that the most effective way to reduce fear and phobic behavior was to confront the situation in which the attack had occurred. These instructions were delivered in the course of one session. The other group of 16 patients were simply provided with reassurance that what they had suffered was a panic attack and that no serious physical or psychological consequences were anticipated. This also occurred in one session. Patients were then followed up at 3 months (midpoint) and 6 months (end point). Those people who had received exposure instructions had significantly less avoidance, as well as fewer panic attacks in the previous week, than the group receiving reassurance only. Clearly, this is a very cost-effective intervention, which takes advantage of the fact that most of these patients were in the very early stages of what might have become a more severe case of panic disorder with agoraphobia if left unchecked. Thus, it seems that structured psychological interventions, even minimal interventions, may be effective if delivered early enough to less severe patients in primary care settings.

As noted above, effective psychological treatments now exist for all anxiety disorders. Most of these treatments are available in manual or workbook form, so that they can be handed directly to the patient working under the supervision of a psychologist (e.g., Barlow & Craske, 1994). Thus, these treatments can be prescribed much like a medication, in the context of good general psychological care and attention to idiosyncratic problems that arise during the course of this treatment (Craske & Barlow, 1989). Evidence is accumulating that supports the viability of this type of approach to specific psychological disorders, even with minimal therapist contact (e.g., Cote, Gauthier, Laberge, Cormier, & Plamondon, 1994). Other studies have indicated that structured psychological interventions can be delivered in briefer format than has been customary, with beneficial results for a number of patients (e.g., Craske, Maidenberg, & Bystritsky, 1995). However, it is very likely that individuals presenting with severe levels of interference and symptomatology may require more substantial degrees of therapist involvement than afforded by brief treatments. In one study conducted in the Center for Stress and Anxiety Disorder, University at Albany, people suffering from panic disorder with agoraphobia did not benefit from self-administered manualized treatment but did benefit once a therapist was introduced into the process (Holden, O'Brien, Barlow, Stetson, & Fantino, 1983).

In another notable effort in a primary care setting, White, Brooks, and Keenan (1995) randomized 62 patients meeting criteria for an anxiety disorder to one of three conditions. The first condition was no intervention, in which patients were placed on a waiting list for a 3-month period. The second condition was advice only, in which patients met with a therapist once and were offered advice on ways of coping with anxiety. In the third condition, patients were given a self-help information package, containing a brief manual explaining the nature of stress and anxiety and ways of developing appropriate coping mechanisms. Patients were then placed on a 3-month waiting list for brief individual treatment. During this 3-month period, they were assessed monthly by mail. Results from the General Severity Index of the Symptom Distress Checklist (Derogatis & Melisaratos, 1983) are presented in Figure 2.

As one can see, patients receiving the manual (stress pack) had improved significantly more in 3 months than patients receiving advice only or patients on the waiting list. Furthermore, on entering individual treatment, patients receiving the manual required fewer appointments (approximately four) than patients receiving alternative interventions, who required approximately six sessions. Eight patients who had received the manual felt that they did not require additional therapy, whereas almost all patients in the other two conditions entered treatment. Finally, it seems that receiving the manual provided a "boost" to individual treatment, because patients at the end of individual therapy who had received the manual had done significantly better than the other groups.

White et al. (1995) carried out this evaluation in Scotland in the context of the National Health Service, where the number of patients suffering from these problems is substantial and the waiting list for treatment by psychologists is very long indeed. Thus, any psychological program that improves the efficiency of the therapist, as well as the clinical outcome, a very positive development. Furthermore, these results were maintained at a 12-month follow-up.

SUMMARY AND IMPLICATIONS

All indications point to an important and increasing role for psychologists in primary care settings. First, the number of patients suffering from psychological disorders in primary care settings or in the behavioral health care system as a whole, for that matter, is enormous and far outstrips current capacities to provide treatment. Second, the majority of patients suffering from anxiety and other psychological disorders in primary care settings are not recognized, and even fewer are treated effectively. Evidence exists that behavioral health care providers, particularly psychologists, are more clinically effective and more cost-effective

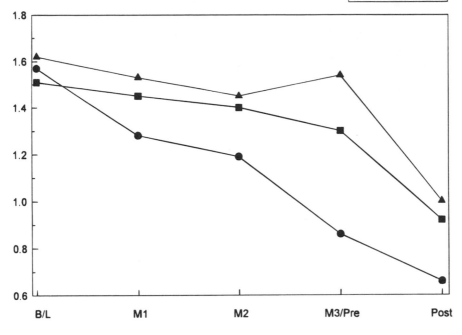

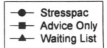

SCL-90R: GSI

Figure 2. Results of study by White (1995), as measured by General Severity Index (GSI) of the revised Symptom Checklist–90 (SCL-90-R). B/L = baseline; M1 = first month of manual; M2 = second month of manual; M3 = third month of manual; Pre = pre individual treatment; Post = post individual treatment.

From "Stresspac: A Controlled Trial of a Self-Help Package for the Anxiety Disorders," by J. White, 1995, *Behavioural and Cognitive Psychotherapy, 23,* 89–107. Copyright 1995 by the British Association for Behavioural and Cognitive Psychotherapies. Adapted with permission.

in the provision of behavioral health care in these settings than overburdened primary care physicians. Because the large number of these patients will preclude individual assessment and intervention, more efficient models for the delivery of behavioral health care must be developed, and some preliminary evidence suggests what these models may look like. One possible model is presented in Figure 3. In this model, psychologists and other behavioral health care professionals will supervise appropriate but cost-effective screening and assessment of all patients coming into primary care settings. These professionals will then triage patients with less severe psychological disorders or symptoms of anxiety into cost-effective self-help programs or programs administered largely by parapro-

A) Development and Supervision of Screening and
   Assessment Strategies

   ↓

B) Supervision of Psychological Programs for Less Severe
   Psychopathology (Manuals - Paraprofessionals)

   ↓

C) Administration and Individual or Group Treatment
   Approaches for More Severe or Treatment-Resistant
   Psychopathology

Figure 3. The role of psychologists in primary care settings.

fessionals working under the supervision of psychologists. Patients will continue to be assessed by means of cost-effective screening instruments, and those individuals not benefiting from the less costly interventions because of severity, or some other treatment-resistant feature, will be candidates for individual therapeutic approaches with doctoral-level psychologists having expertise in these areas.

It is very likely, as these models develop, that we will discover fairly sensitive predictors of response to the various stepped levels of care that will allow early identification of patients and more immediate assignment to appropriate treatment methods. Much of the necessary data to develop this model more fully have yet to be collected, and when they are collected, it is likely that psychologists will be in the best position to develop this information.

REFERENCES

American Psychiatric Association. (1994). *Diagnostic and statistical manual of mental disorders* (4th ed.). Washington, DC: Author.

Barlow, D. H. (1988). *Anxiety and its disorders: The nature and treatment of anxiety and panic.* New York: Guilford Press.

Barlow, D. H. (1994). Psychological interventions in the era of managed competition. *Clinical Psychology: Science and Practice, 1,* 109–122.

Barlow, D. H., & Barlow, D. G. (1995 May/June). Practice guidelines and empirically validated psychosocial treatments: Ships passing in the night? *Behavioral Healthcare Tomorrow,* pp. 25–76.

Barlow, D. H., & Craske, M. G. (1994). *Mastery of your anxiety and panic: II.* Albany, NY: Graywind Publications.

Barlow, D. H., & Lehman, C. (in press). Advances in the psychosocial treatment of anxiety disorders: Implications for national health care. *Archives of General Psychiatry.*

Barrett, J. E., Barrett, J. A., Oxman, T. E., & Gerber, P. D. (1988). The prevalence of psychiatric disorders in a primary care practice. *Archives of General Psychiatry, 45,* 1100–1106.

Breier, A., Charney, D. S., & Heninger, G. R. (1986). Agoraphobia with panic attacks: Development, diagnostic stability, and course of illness. *Archives of General Psychiatry, 43,* 1029–1036.

Broadhead, W. F. (1994). Presentation of psychiatric symptomatology in primary care. In J. Mirandra, A. A. Hohmann, C. C. Attkisson, & D. B. Larson (Eds.), *Mental disorders in primary care* (pp. 139–162). San Francisco: Jossey-Bass.

Brown, T. A., & Barlow, D. H. (1995). Long-term outcome in cognitive–behavioral treatment of panic disorder: Clinical predictors and alternative strategies for assessment. *Journal of Consulting and Clinical Psychology, 63,* 754–765.

Cote, G., Gauthier, J. G., Laberge, B., Cormier, H. J., & Plamondon, J. (1994). Reduced therapist contact in the cognitive–behavioral treatment of panic disorder. *Behavior Therapy, 25,* 123–145.

Craske, M. G., & Barlow, D. H. (1989). *Mastery of your anxiety and panic.* Albany, NY: Graywind Publications.

Craske, M. G., Maidenberg, E., & Bystritsky, A. (1995). Brief cognitive–behavioral vs. non-directive therapy for panic disorder. *Journal of Behavior Therapy and Experimental Psychiatry, 26,* 113–120.

Cummings, N. A. (1995). Impact of managed care on employment and training: A primer for survival. *Professional Psychology: Research and Practice, 26,* 10–15.

Derogatis, L. R., & Melisaratos, N. (1983). The Brief Symptom Inventory: An intoductory report. *Psychological Medicine, 13,* 595–605.

DiBartolo, P. M., Hofmann, S. G., & Barlow, D. H. (1995). Psychosocial approaches to panic disorder and agoraphobia: Assessment and treatment issues for the primary care physician. *Mind/Body and Medicine, 1,* 1–12.

Fifer, S. K., Mathias, S. D., Patrick, D. L., Majonson, P. D., Lubeck, D. P., & Buesching, D. P. (1994). Untreated anxiety among adult primary care patients in a health maintenance organization. *Archives of General Psychiatry, 51,* 740–750.

Ford, D. (1987). *The relationship of psychiatric illness to medically unexplained chest pain.* Paper presented at the research conference, Mental Disorders in General Health Care Settings, Seattle, WA.

Ford, D. E. (1994). Recognition and underrecognition of mental disorders in adult primary care. In J. Miranda, A. A. Hohmann, C. C. Attkisson, & D. B. Larson (Eds.), *Mental disorders in primary care* (pp. 186–205). San Francisco: Jossey-Bass.

Goisman, R. M., Rogers, M. P., Steketee, G. S., Warshaw, M. G., Cuneo, P., & Keller, M. B. (1993). Utilization of behavioral methods in a multi-center anxiety disorders study. *Journal of Clinical Psychiatry, 54,* 213–218.

Hamilton, M. (1960). A rating scale for depression. *Journal of Neurology, Neurosurgery, and Psychiatry, 23,* 56–62.

Holden, A. E., O'Brien, G. T., Barlow, D. H., Stetson, D., & Fantino, A. (1983). Self-help manual for agoraphobia: A preliminary report of effectiveness. *Behavior Research and Therapy, 14,* 545–556.

Katerndahl, D. A., & Realini, J. P. (1995). Where do panic attacks sufferers seek care? *Journal of Family Practice, 40,* 237–243.

Katon, W. (1984). Panic disorder and somatization: Review of 55 cases. *American Journal of Medicine, 77,* 101–106.

Katon, W., Vitaliano, P. P., Russo, J., Cormier, L., Anderson, K., & Jones, M. (1986). Panic disorder: Epidemiology in primary care. *The Journal of Family Practice, 23,* 233–239.

Katon, W., Vitaliano, P. P., Russo, J., Jones, M., & Anderson, K. (1987). Panic disorder: Spectrum of severity and somatization. *The Journal of Nervous and Mental Disease, 175,* 12–19.

Kessler, R. C., McGonagle, K. A., Shanyang, Z., Nelson, C. B., Hughes, M., Eshleman, S., Wittchen, H.-U., & Kendler, K. (1994). Lifetime and 12-month prevalence of DSM–III–R psychiatric disorders in the United States: Results from the National Comorbidity Survey. *Archives of General Psychiatry, 51,* 8–19.

Liebowitz, M., & Barlow, D. H. (1995). Panic disorder: The latest on diagnosis and treatment. *Journal of Practical Psychiatry and Behavioral Health, 1,* 10–19.

Ormel, J., VandenBrink, W., Koeter, M. W. J., Giel, R., Vander Meer, K., VandeWillige, G., & Wilmink, I. W. (1990). Recognition, management and outcome of psychological disorders in primary care: A naturalistic follow-up study. *Psychological Medicine, 20,* 909–923.

Regier, D. A., Myers, J. K., Kramer, M., Robins, L. N., Blazer, D. G., Hough, R. L., Eaton, W. W., & Locke, B. Z. (1984). The NIMH Epidemiologic Catchment Area: Historical context, major objectives, and study population characteristics. *Archives of General Psychiatry, 41,* 934–941.

Regier, D. A., Narrow, W. E., Rae, D. S., Manderscheid, R. W., Locke, B. Z., & Goodwin, F. K. (1993). The deFacto US mental and addictive disorders service system: Epidemiologic catchment area prospective 1-year prevalence rates of disorders and services. *Archives of General Psychiatry, 50,* 85–94.

Schulberg, H. C., Block, M., Madonia, M., Scott, C., Rodriguez, E., Imbero, S., Perel, J., Laze, J., Houck, P., & Coulehan, J. (in press). Treating major depression in primary care practice: Eight-month clinical outcomes. *Archives of General Psychiatry.*

Shear, M. K., & Schulberg, H. C. (1995). Anxiety disorders in primary care. *Bulletin of the Menninger Clinic, 59,* A73–A85.

Shear, M. K., Schulberg, H. C. & Madonia, M. (1994, September). *Panic and generalized anxiety disorder in primary care.* Paper presented at a meeting of the Association for Primary Care, Washington, DC.

Spitzer, R. L., Endicott, J., & Robins, E. (1978). *Research diagnostic criteria: Rationale and reliability. Archives of General Psychiatry, 35,* 773–782.

Sturm, R., & Wells, K. B. (1995). How can care for depression become more cost-effective? *Journal of American Medical Association, 273,* 51–58.

Swinson, R. P., Solios, C., Cox, B. J., & Kuch, K. (1992). Brief treatment of emergency room patients with panic attacks. *American Journal of Psychiatry, 149,* 944–946.

Taylor, C. B., King, R., Margraf, J., Ehlers, A., et al. (1989). Use of medication and in vivo exposure in volunteers for panic disorder research. *American Journal of Psychiatry, 146,* 1423–1426.

Van Hemert, A. M., Hengeveld, M. W., Boek, J. H., Rooijmans, H. G. M., & Vandenbroucke, J. P. (1993). Psychiatric disorders in relation to medical illness among patients of a general medical out-patient clinic. *Psychological Medicine, 23,* 167–173.

Wells, K. B., Stewart, A., Hays, R. D., Burnam, M. A., Rogers, W., Daniels, M., Berry, S., Greenfield, S., & Ware, J. (1989). The functioning and well-being of depressed patients: Results from the Medical Outcomes Study. *Journal of American Medical Association, 262,* 914–919.

White, J. (1995). Stresspac: A controlled trial of a self-help package for the anxiety disorders. *Behavioural and Cognitive Psychotherapy, 23,* 89–107.

Yingling, K. W., Wulsin, L. R., Arnold, L. M., & Rouan, G. W. (1993). Estimated prevalences of panic disorder and depression among consecutive patients seen in an emergency department with acute chest pain. *Journal of General Internal Medicine, 8,* 231–235.

Zinbarg, R. E., Barlow, D. H., Liebowitz, M., Street, L., Broadhead, E., Katon, W., Roy-Byrne, P., Lepine, J.-P., Teherani, M., Richards, J., Brantley, P. J., & Kraemer, H. (1994). The *DSM–IV* field trial for mixed anxiety–depression. *American Journal of Psychiatry, 151,* 1153–1162.

11

CATCHING DEPRESSION IN PRIMARY CARE PHYSICIANS' OFFICES

LYNN P. REHM

The scenario for this topic is fairly clear. Depression is presented in primary care medical settings at a high frequency with substantial disability to the patient. Detection is poor, and many patients are not treated or are treated inappropriately. If detection and treatment in primary care settings can be improved, patient well-being can be improved and medical costs can be reduced. Psychology and psychologists should be inserted into the system, to develop efficient means of detection and screening, to provide treatment for depression, and to offer prevention services to head off depression at its earliest signs. Psychology has developed efficient assessment, effective treatment, and promising prevention programs. Its value to the primary care system should be obvious, and its participation should be welcome. It sounds like a simple and straightforward proposal, but let me examine the individual components of the argument and point out some of the problems and complications.

PREVALENCE OF DEPRESSION

Depression is presented in primary care medical settings in substantial proportions. For example, in a report of the Agency for Health Care

Policy and Research (AHCPR; Depression Guideline Panel, 1993), John Rush and his colleagues reviewed 11 studies in primary care settings in which major depression was diagnosed by means of structured diagnostic interviews, usually after paper-and-pencil screening. Estimates of the point prevalence of major depression ranged from 4.8% to 8.6%, with a median of around 6.5%. Other mood disorders such as dysthymia, minor depression, or intermittent depression brought totals up to around 10%. A new study (Coyne, Fechner-Bates, & Schwenk, 1994) found an estimated prevalence of 13.5% for major depression and 22.6% for all depressive disorders. Patients who are frequent users of primary health care have a particularly high rate of psychiatric comorbidity (54% in one study). Mood disorders, identified in 24% of cases, and anxiety disorders, identified in another 24% of cases, are the most prevalent among these diagnoses (Karlsson, Lehtinen, & Joukamaa, 1995).

Substantial disability is associated with untreated depression. Figures from the medical outcomes studies (Depression Guideline Panel, 1993; Sturm & Wells, 1995) indicate that patients with depression have substantial problems in life functioning. For example, in one study, 23% of depressed patients reported that their health kept them in bed all or most of the day at least once in the past 2 weeks, as compared with 5% of the general population. Patients with major depression report 11 days of disability per 90 days, as compared with 2.2 days for the general population. Their decrements in functioning equal or exceed those of patients with chronic medical illnesses (Hays, Wells, Sherbourne, Rogers, & Spritzer, 1995). Depressed patients also report poorer intimate relations, less satisfying social interactions and poorer general health. Health care use is increased for these patients.

Depressed patients represent a disproportionate cost to the health system. In a major study of computerized records in a large-staff-model health maintenance organization (Simon, VonKorff, & Barlow, 1995), patients were identified as depressed either by a depression diagnosis recorded at an index visit or by a pharmacy record of a prescription for an antidepressant medication. A sample of 6,257 such patients was compared with an individually matched sample of 6,257 controls. For the 12 months after the index visit, depressed patients cost the health maintenance organization an average of $4,246, in comparison with $2,371 for the control sample. Costs for depressed patients were elevated in every category (primary care, specialty care, medical inpatient, pharmacy, and laboratory). Mean pharmacy costs were nearly three times greater for the depressed sample ($632 vs. $231), and only $194 of this was attributable to antidepressants. The depressed sample was found to have a higher index of chronic medical illness, but even when this was statistically controlled, their medical costs were higher. Depressed patients were a greater economic burden to the system at every level of chronic medical illness severity. In summary, the problem is of large proportion, the disability is considerable, and the economic impact on the medical system is substantial.

PROBLEMS OF DETECTION IN PRIMARY CARE

Depression is often poorly detected and treated in primary care settings. A number of studies suggest that physicians underdetect and undertreat depression in primary care settings. A general estimate is that one third to one half of depressed patients are diagnosed with the disorder (Depression Guideline Panel, 1993). Coyne, Fechner-Bates, and Schwenk (1995) identified a sample of depressed patients in a primary care setting by screening with the Center for Epidemiological Studies Depression Scale (CES–D; Radloff, 1977) and structured clinical interviews. Of the sample they diagnosed, family physicians had detected 35% of cases of major depression and 28% of cases of any mood disorder.

Coyne et al. (1995) highlighted another problematic dimension to the detection issue. They pointed out that the undetected patients tended to be mildly depressed and highly functioning. Such patients may not actively seek treatment and may not accept treatment recommendations and referral. When these mildly depressed patients are treated, they may benefit from relatively minimal interventions. Level of depression may be an important variable for differential treatment recommendations. Severe depression may require hospitalization, and medication may be required with severe outpatients, who may not be amenable to the effort involved in psychotherapy. Psychotherapy appears to be useful across most ranges of depression, but mild depression may well benefit from minimal interventions such as bibliotherapy.

High base rates and low detection rates lead to an assumption that appropriate assessment and treatment will improve effective treatment outcomes and produce a cost offset in medical utilization. Improved detection and treatment in primary care is the purpose of the AHCPR guidelines (Depression Guideline Panel, 1993), which were written to guide physicians in making appropriate decisions in treating depression. Within the guidelines, the panel recommended an interview when history or other vulnerability factors indicated risk. Self-report depression scales were also recommended for screening, with a note that they may be lacking in specificity and that some authorities suggest increased cutoff scores in primary care to decrease false positives. Fechner-Bates, Coyne, and Schwenk (1994) examined the power of the CES–D to detect depression in primary care. Most distressed patients did not meet criteria for mood diagnoses, and the scale was as predictive of anxiety disorders as it is of depression. Fechner-Bates et al. concluded that the CES–D measured general distress rather than depression per se. Any screening program in a primary care setting must look not only at depression but at other common psychological problems that may accompany or complicate medical visits. Differentiating among problems and making accurate diagnoses require a second step after a paper-and-pencil measure such as the CES–D. Brief physician interviews, as recommended by the AHCPR guidelines, may not be sufficient. Differential diagnosis is important not only between depression and anxiety disorders, but also among these disorders. Differentiations between unipolar and bipolar depression have important treatment implications, as does differentiation between panic disorder and obsessive–compulsive disorder. Psychological treatment modalities also vary considerably in their appropriateness for depression or anxiety diagnoses.

In part, the issue is one of the reliability of detection and of the criterion for depression. Diagnosis by the fourth edition of the *Diagnostic and Statistical Manual of Mental Disorders* (American Psychiatric Association, 1994) is but one criterion, and it, too, has a reliability of less than one. Detection by one instrument may not be perfectly correlated with detection by another instrument or method. Both false negatives and false positives will occur if instruments are compared. To detect clinically meaningful depression in efficient ways in primary care settings, alternative criteria and how specific criteria might be related to intervention strategies must be recognized. Self-report scales such as the CES–D may not be specific to *DSM–IV* Major Depression, but distress should be examined seriously, and appropriate interventions should be evaluated. It might be more effective to ask patients about the nature of the problems that are producing distress, how they are coping, and whether they are coping effectively. Psychological interventions might be matched more exactly to the patient by the nature of the coping problems than by *DSM–IV* diagnosis. The review, later in this chapter, of treatment strategies for depression illustrates the different treatment foci of each approach.

Adding to the problems of lack of detection are the problems of inaccurate detection or misdiagnosis. Patients who are detected may not receive proper treatment. Sturm and Wells (1995), in examining the data from the large RAND study of medical outcomes (Tarlov et al., 1989), found that in general medical settings, the probability of severe depression being detected was 49%, but the probability that it was treated with minor tranquilizers, rather that antidepressants or counseling, was 36%. Treatment with minor tranquilizers was associated with a poorer, more deteriorating outcome in terms of ability to function 1 year later than was no treatment at all. A fairly extensive and sophisticated evaluation, preferably by a mental health expert, may be required to make these distinctions accurately.

Referral to a mental health practitioner raises other issues. The AHCPR guidelines encourage the primary care practitioner to be the first line of treatment. Referral for psychotherapy is recommended as a secondary alternative. Patients often do not follow through on referrals, and it has been suggested that primary care physicians thus may become discouraged in making referrals of depressed patients to mental health professionals (Munoz & Ying, 1993).

In their 1995 study, Sturm and Wells addressed the question of whether treatment outcomes in current settings with current resources could be improved. Sturm and Wells looked at actual outcome in primary care and in mental health settings for patients in multiple types of practices, in three cities. They found that three treatment factors were associated with improved functioning of depressed patients. *Functioning* was defined as serious limitations in daily life (i.e., not able to work at a paying job; not able to do housework; not able to do strenuous exercise, such as lawn mowing; or not able to do moderate exercise, such as climbing stairs). The three factors that improved outcomes were increased use of counseling, increased use of appropriate antidepressants, and avoidance of regular minor tranquilizer use. Counseling and antidepressants were found to add to total costs, but they improve the value of care because each dollar spent provided more benefit in terms of health and functioning improvements. Sturm and Wells (1995) also concluded that "in contrast with the effects of more appropriate care for depression, the trend away from mental heath specialty care and toward general medical provider care under current treatment patterns reduces cost, worsens outcomes, and does not increase the value of health care spending in terms of health improvement per dollar" (p. 51). That is, the direction taken by the AHCPR guidelines may save money, but at the expense of better outcomes.

Where Sturm and Wells (1995) found the combination of antidepressants and counseling to be the most effective treatment strategy, an article by Wexler and Cicchetti (1992) addresses the larger issue of the relative efficacy of pharmacotherapy, psychotherapy, and their combination for the treatment of depression. They question the often-made recommendation that the combination of treatments is best. Their review of the literature on treatment success and failure rates and on dropout rates indicates that the combined treatment offers no advantage over psychotherapy alone and only minimal advantage over medication alone. The difference in the two conclusions may have to do with the fact that Sturm and Wells had a very minimal definition of counseling— essentially, any record of some time spent discussing the patient's problems—whereas, Wexler and Cicchetti were reviewing studies of carefully administered forms of psychotherapy compared with trials of medication.

When a full course of an effective psychotherapy is administered, medications appear to add little to outcomes.

If effective intervention is to be instituted in primary care settings, it appears that a mental health component would best be integrated into the health system. Initial screening might lead to better diagnosis if the psychologist or other mental health worker was involved at the point of diagnosis. Treatment recommendations might be more acceptable to the patient if they were made by the appropriate expert, and patients might be more likely to follow up on referral if it did not require contacting another professional in another setting. Patients would be more likely to comply with treatment if a range of treatments were available to match severity and problem type.

MODELS OF TREATMENT

Much needs to be done if we are to actualize the scenario for improved detection and treatment of depression in primary care settings. In an article critiquing the AHCPR guidelines, Munoz, Hollon, McGrath, Rehm, and VandenBos (1994) pointed out some serious limitations to the guidelines. To begin with, they underestimate the problems in detection and diagnosis, some of which I mention above. The AHCPR guidelines acknowledge, but underestimate, the problems of generalization of studies in research mental health settings to primary care settings and systems. Treatments that are effective in trials in mental health settings may not be as effective in primary care settings where acceptability of psychiatric diagnosis may be less and where patients may not be persuaded of the necessity or utility of treatment. Research needs to be done in primary care settings or with primary care patients in collaborating settings. We need to find out what treatments are effective in these settings. Psychotherapy, for example, may need to be offered in formats acceptable and affordable to patients in primary care. We may need to adapt treatments to match patients' beliefs about their problems and about what they think they need to do to make changes. We need to take into account issues of diversity and the efficacy and acceptability of treatment to different groups.

It is clear that severity level has to be taken into account. Differential diagnosis is very important at moderate-to-severe levels of depression. At milder levels, the differentiation of distress into depression or anxiety may be difficult, and treatment options may need to be different than those for more severe levels of disorder. Intervention at milder levels may also be effective as a prevention strategy to ward off more severe depression. Munoz and Ying (1993) provided an example of a treatment program for patients with mild depressive symptoms in a preventative treatment program. They argued that treating mild symptoms of depression may prevent more serious disorder and disability later on. Their San Francisco Depression Prevention Project screened 700 primary care patients at two hospitals and identified 150 who showed symptoms of depression but did not meet diagnostic criteria for a clinical disorder. The research sample of adults was diverse with regard to ethnicity, age, and socioeconomic status. Participants were randomly assigned to either a prevention class, an informational-videotape minimal-intervention comparison group, and a no-treatment control. Classes were available in Spanish- and English-language versions. The classes consisted of eight weekly sessions aimed at an eclectic set of topics drawn from the cognitive–behavioral treatment literature. Topics included the effect of thoughts and behavior on feeling, ways to change thinking and increase positive thoughts, ways to increase pleasurable activities, and ways to improve interpersonal relationships. Outcome was assessed on a number of variables, including symptoms and diagnosis of depression, sense of well-being, life stress, cognitive and behavioral mediators of depression, and medical utilization. The group sessions were found to have a greater effect on symptoms, well-being, mediators, and life stress. Prevention of depression diagnosis was not demonstrated, largely because in the 1-year follow-up, few patients in any of the conditions developed the full syndromal disorder. Similarly, the study was not able to detect differences in subsequent medical utilization, largely due to small numbers in gross utilization indices. This study is exemplary in many ways. It is one of the few intervention studies in a primary care setting. It identified a diverse sample and provided a short-term, state-of-the-art intervention. Results were measured on a variety of relevant variables. On the other hand, the study also illustrates that it is difficult to demonstrate prevention and reduction of medical utilization in an intervention study. Such effects require very large numbers, like those in the naturalistic, retrospective studies of treatment outcomes cited above.

A number of treatment strategies have been shown to be useful in treating depression in efficacy studies. These are primarily cognitive–behavioral therapies that have been tested in controlled clinical trials. These treatments are based on therapist manuals that increase the replicability and portability of the therapies, although, of course, they do not ensure therapist skill or competence with the treatment. I will provide a brief overview of the major treatment models for those readers unfamiliar with this area.

Behavioral Model

The behavioral model of depression is primarily identified with the work of Lewinsohn. Lewinsohn (1974) posited that depression was the result of a loss or lack of response-contingent positive reinforcement. Loss of a loved one or loss of a job is seen as removing a source of reinforcement that maintains multiple chains of behavior. It is the resulting reduction in behavior that constitutes depression. Early approaches to depression treatment by Lewinsohn's group focused on developing therapy modules aimed at ameliorating specific forms of reinforcement loss. Modules focused on increasing previously enjoyable activities, on increasing skills to elicit positive reinforcement from the environment, and on decreasing social anxiety that might interfere with experiencing social reinforcement. Later versions of the therapy program have combined the various modules into a psychoeducational therapy program. The program takes participants through a series of lessons and homework assignments, related to components of depression, organized around the general theme of increasing contingent positive reinforcement. Munoz and Ying's (1993) intervention relied heavily on the basics of the Lewinsohn behavioral model.

The current program is well suited to use in primary care health care settings. It has evolved for use in an economical group format. A therapist manual is available for group leaders (Lewinsohn, Antonuccio, Breckenridge, & Teri, 1987). A participant's textbook has been developed for the course (Brown & Lewinsohn, 1984a), and a self-help version of the program has been published as well (Lewinsohn, Munoz, Youngren, & Zeiss, 1978). This is one of the few programs for which an evaluation has been done of the effectiveness of the program in bibliotherapy format (Brown & Lewinsohn, 1984b) and in group versus individual formats (Brown & Lewinsohn, 1984b). A version of the program has also been developed for use with adolescents (Clarke, Lewinsohn, & Hops, 1991) and their parents (Lewinsohn, Rohde, Hops, & Clarke, 1991). A number of assessment instruments have been developed by Lewinsohn's group to evaluate sources of reinforcement and their availability and frequency in the patient's environment. These instruments could be helpful in determining whether this strategy would be a fit with a particular patient's deficits as well as being appropriate measures of treatment progress. In general, depressions that seem to be typified by a withdrawal from previously pleasurable activities might best be targeted by this approach.

Social Skills Model

A number of approaches, including Lewinsohn's behavioral program, have viewed depression as a result of certain skill deficits or of insufficient skill level to deal with specific types of interpersonal stressors (cf. Gotlib & Colby, 1987). A number of different strategies arise from this basic approach. Hersen, Bellack, Himmelhoch, and Thase (1984) evaluated a traditional assertiveness-oriented approach with a depressed population. Nezu, Nezu, and Perri (1989) argued for a problem-solving approach to depression that sees depression as a series of deficits in interpersonal problem-solving deficits. They demonstrated in one study (Nezu, 1986) that a treatment strategy based on this approach was superior to placebo therapy and waiting list controls. This approach is best suited to depressed patients who perceive their interpersonal circumstances as uncontrollable when faced with a situation that could be defined as a problem to be solved.

Beach and O'Leary (1986) and Jacobson (1984) have made a case for depression as an interpersonal problem in the context of marriage and have illustrated marital therapy interventions as appropriate treatments for depression. Dysfunctional marriages may be detected in primary care as a focus for treatment of depression.

From a more psychodynamic perspective, Klerman, Weissman, Rounceville, and Chevron (1984) provide a manual for interpersonal therapy. Interpersonal therapy is based on the idea that current interpersonal problems, whether they be relational or due to a loss of relationship, should be the priority targets for therapy for depression. Interpersonal therapy was one of the psychotherapies evaluated in the National Institute of Mental Health Collaborative Treatment of Depression study (Elkin et al., 1989), where it was found to be equivalent to a tricyclic antidepressant medication and to cognitive therapy.

Cognitive Therapy Model

At present, the best researched model of therapy for depression is Beck's cognitive therapy. Cognitive therapy is based on the assumption that depression is based in a systematic, negative cognitive distortion of the person's experience. Depressive cognitive schema filter experience to create depressive inferences and interpretations of everyday experiences. These distortions are relatively automatic and are based on unspoken and unexamined assumptions that underlie views of self, world, and future. Cognitive therapy was also evaluated in the National Institute of Mental Health national collaborative study (Elkin et al., 1989). Cognitive therapy appears to be widely suited to depression and other problems. It can be seen as an approach to viewing problems as much as a particular set of therapy strategies.

Two additional cognitive conceptions of depression deserve note, although they have not led to specific forms of therapy. Seligman's learned helplessness theory has evolved through several forms (Abramson, Seligman, & Teasdale, 1978; Alloy, Abramson, Metalsky, & Hartlage, 1988; Seligman, 1975). The essential feature of the theory is the assumption that one path to depression is a negative interpretive style whereby depression-prone people attribute negative events to internal, stable, and global causes. Thus, "an aversive event happened because of me, because of something constant about me, and because of something about me that applies to everything I do." As a vulnerability theory, learned helplessness may be particularly applicable to prevention programs.

Nolen-Hoeksema (1987) focuses on sex differences between women and men and presents a case that higher rates of depression in women may be due to women's greater likelihood of having a cognitive style of ruminating about negative events, in contrast to men's tendency to distract themselves from rumination. Again, the vulnerability aspect of the theory suggests an application to prevention, especially with women.

Self-Management Model

My own work on psychotherapy for depression (Rehm, 1984) has been based primarily on a self-control or self-management model of depression (Rehm, 1977). The model began as an attempt to integrate elements of prior theories under a self-control framework but has, as a defining feature, a focus on how people organize their thinking and behavior around long-term goals. Resistance to depression is seen as an ability to sustain efforts toward long-term goals in the face of current negative events and contrary reinforcement contingencies. This is accomplished by providing oneself with overt or covert rewards contingent on progress toward goals. The behavior of the depressed person deteriorates because of a loss of organization of behavior by immediate external contingencies that do not occur regularly for long-term goals. The approach has empirical support for the theory (Rehm, 1988) and for the psychoeducational, group-format therapy that has been derived from the model (Rehm, 1984). Adaptations of the program have been developed for children (Stark, 1990). In application to primary care settings, the program is applicable to prevention and to cost-effective treatment because of the group-therapy format.

RESEARCH NEEDS AND FUTURE DIRECTIONS

Today we can feel confidant that efficacy of several treatments for depression have been empirically demonstrated (Task Force on the Promotion and Dissemination of Psychological Procedures, 1995). That is, several approaches or strategies have been demonstrated to be more effective than placebo therapy or no treatment. This does not, however, answer the question as to whether these programs are going to be effective in nonresearch settings, such as primary care. Many conditions differentiate research studies from clinical practice (Seligman, 1995). More diverse patient populations with multiple problems may not respond as well as the carefully defined and delimited samples in research studies. We badly need effectiveness research in practical settings such as primary care.

We also need to disseminate these valid treatments. Although consumer surveys tend to show public satisfaction with the unspecified forms of treatment that are in use in the practice world, utilization and training in the better validated treatment methods is sparse (Task Force on the Promotion and Dissemination of Psychological Procedures, 1995). It is one thing to say that empirically validated treatments are available for application or testing in primary care settings, but it is quite another to say that psychologists or other mental health practitioners are ready to offer these programs.

We need to study and validate our treatments in primary care and our screening and detection methodologies as well. In the long run, the inclusion and integration of psychological assessment and intervention in primary care will depend on our ability to demonstrate valid outcomes that benefit patients. To be persuasive to primary care systems, we need to show that instituting screening and intervention not only improves the health, both mental and physical, of patients but also improves their functioning and reduces unnecessary use of medical services.

With the changes that are taking place in our health care system, it is important to consider the economics of the delivery of treatments for depression in primary care settings. This consideration, however, needs to take into account not only the costs of treatments but also the costs of lack of treatment and the value of treatment. Value can be measured in terms of medical cost offset, in terms of improved health, and in terms of improved life functioning.

Psychology needs to be better integrated into primary care settings. As health care change moves us toward capitated, integrated health care systems with "one-stop shopping," psychology needs to be in place in primary care settings, to set up programs of detection and treatment of patients with depression and other debilitating psychological disorders. Psychology will be able to do so to the degree that its value can be demonstrated in improving health in dollars and cents.

REFERENCES

Abramson, L. Y., Seligman, M. E. P., & Teasdale, J. (1978). Learned helplessness in humans: Critique and reformulation. *Journal of Abnormal Psychology, 87*, 49–74.

Alloy, L. B., Abramson, L. Y., Metalsky, G. I., & Hartlage, S. (1988). The hopelessness theory of depression: Attributional aspects. *British Journal of Clinical Psychology, 27*, 5–21.

American Psychiatric Association. (1994). *Diagnostic and statistical manual of mental disorders* (4th ed.). Washington, DC: Author.

Beach, S. R. H., & O'Leary, K. D. (1986). The treatment of depression occurring in the context of marital discord. *Behavior Therapy, 17,* 43–49.

Brown, R. A., & Lewinsohn, P. M. (1984a). *Participant workbook for the coping with depression course.* Eugene, OR: Castalia.

Brown, R. A., & Lewinsohn, P. M. (1984b). A psychoeducational approach to the group treatment of depression: Comparison of group, individual, and minimal contact procedures. *Journal of Consulting and Clinical Psychology, 52,* 774–783.

Clarke, G., Lewinsohn, P. M., & Hops, H., (1991). *Adolescent coping with depression course: Leader's manual for adolescent groups.* Eugene, OR: Castalia.

Coyne, J. C., Fechner-Bates, S., & Schwenk, T. L. (1994). The prevalence, nature, and comorbidity of depressive disorders in primary care. *General Hospital Psychiatry, 16,* 267–276.

Coyne, J. C., Fechner-Bates, S., & Schwenk, T. L. (1995). Nondetection of depression by primary care physicians reconsidered. *General Hospital Psychiatry, 17,* 3–12.

Depression Guideline Panel. (1993). *Depression in primary care: Volume 1. Detection and diagnosis, clinical practice guideline, number 5.* (AHCPR Publication No. 93-0550) Rockville, MD: U.S. Department of Health and Human Services, Public Health Service, Agency for Health Care Policy and Research.

Elkin, I., Shea, T., Watkins, J., Imber, S., Sotsky, S., Collins, J. F., Glass, D. R., Pilkonis, P., Leber, W. R., Docherty, J. P., Fiester, S. J., & Parloff, M. B. (1989). National Institute of Mental Health treatment of depression collaborative research program: General effectiveness of treatments. *Archives of General Psychiatry, 46,* 971–982.

Fechner-Bates, S., Coyne, J. C., & Schwenk, T. L. (1994). The relationship of self-reported distress to depressive disorders and other psychopathology. *Journal of Consulting and Clinical Psychology, 62,* 550–559

Gotlib, I. H., & Colby, C. A. (1987). *Treatment of depression and interpersonal systems approach.* New York: Pergamon, Press.

Hays, R. D., Wells, K. B., Sherbourne, C. D., Rogers, W., & Spritzer, K. (1995). Functioning and well-being outcomes of patients with depression compared with chronic general medical illnesses. *Archives of General Psychiatry, 52,* 11–19.

Hersen, M., Bellack, A. S., Himmelhoch, J. M., & Thase, M. E. (1984). Effects of social skills training, amitriptyline, and psychotherapy on unipolar depressed women. *Behavior Therapy, 15,* 21–40.

Jacobson, N. S. (1984). Marital therapy and the cognitive–behavioral treatment of depression. *The Behavior Therapist, 7,* 143–147.

Karlsson, H., Lehtinen, V., & Joukamaa, M. (1995.) Psychiatric morbidity among frequent attender patients in primary care. *General Hospital Psychiatry, 17*, 19–25.

Klerman, G. L., Weissman, M. M., Rounceville, B. J., & Chevron, E. S. (1984). *Interpersonal psychotherapy for depression.* New York: Basic Books.

Lewinsohn, P. M. (1974). A behavioral approach to depression. In R. M. Friedman & M. M. Katz (Eds.), *The psychology of depression: Contemporary theory and research.* New York: Wiley.

Lewinsohn, P. M., Antonuccio, D. O., Breckenridge, J. L., & Teri, L. (1987). *The coping with depression course.* Eugene, OR: Castalia.

Lewinsohn, P. M., Munoz, R. F., Youngren, M. A., & Zeiss, A. M. (1978). *Control your depression.* Englewood Cliffs, NJ: Prentice Hall.

Lewinsohn, P. M., Rohde, P., Hops, H., & Clarke, G. (1991). *Adolescent coping with depression course: Leader's manual for parent groups.* Eugene, OR: Castalia.

Munoz, R. F., Hollon, S. D., McGrath, E., Rehm, L. P., & VandenBos, G. R. (1994). On the AHCPR depression in primary care guidelines: Further considerations for practitioners. *American Psychologist, 49*, 42–61.

Munoz, R. F., & Ying, Y. (1993). *The prevention of depression: Research and practice.* Baltimore: Johns Hopkins University Press.

Nezu, A. M. (1986). Efficacy of a social problem-solving therapy approach for unipolar depression. *Journal of Consulting and Clinical Psychology, 54*, 196–202.

Nezu, A. M., Nezu, C. M., & Perri, M. G. (1989). *Problem-solving therapy for depression: Theory, research and clinical guidelines.* New York: Wiley.

Nolen-Hoeksema, S. (1987). Sex differences in unipolar depression: Evidence and theory. *Psychological Bulletin, 101*, 259–282.

Radloff, L. S. (1977). The CES-D scale: A self-report depression scale for research in the general population. *Applied Psychological Measurement, 1*, 385–401.

Rehm, L. P. (1977). A self-control model of depression. *Behavior Therapy, 8*, 787–804.

Rehm, L. P. (1984). Self-management therapy for depression. *Advances in Behavior Therapy and Research, 6*, 83–98.

Rehm, L. P. (1988). Self-management and cognitive processes in depression. In L. B. Alloy (Ed.), *Cognitive processes in depression* (pp. 143–176). New York: Guilford Press.

Seligman, M. E. P. (1975). *Helplessness: On depression, development, and death.* San Francisco: W. H. Freeman.

Seligman, M. E. P. (1995). The effectiveness of psychotherapy: The *Consumer Reports* study. *American Psychologist, 50*, 965–974.

Simon, G. E., VonKorff, M., & Barlow, W. (1995). Health care costs of primary care patients with recognized depression. *Archives of General Psychiatry, 52*, 850–856.

Stark, K. D. (1990). *Childhood depression: School-based intervention*. New York: Guilford Press.

Sturm, R., & Wells, K. B. (1995). How can care for depression become more cost-effective? *Journal of the American Medical Association, 273,* 51–58.

Tarlov, A., Ware, J. E., Greenfield, S., Nelson, E. C., Perrin, E., & Zubkoff, M. (1989). The Medical Outcomes Study: An application of methods for monitoring the results of medical care. *Journal of the American Medical Association, 262,* 925–930.

Task Force on the Promotion and Dissemination of Psychological Procedures. (1995). Training in and dissemination of empirically-validated psychological treatments: Report and recommendations. *The Clinical Psychologist, 48(1),* 3–23.

Wexler, B. E., & Cicchetti, D. V. (1992). The outpatient treatment of depression: Implications of outcome research for clinical practice. *The Journal of Nervous and Mental Disease, 180,* 277–286.

12

HELPING PHYSICIANS MAKE USEFUL RECOMMENDATIONS ABOUT LOSING WEIGHT

DANIEL S. KIRSCHENBAUM

Imagine that you are a successful San Francisco internist in 1992. Rock icon Jerry Garcia walks into your office for a checkup. After telling the Grateful Dead guitarist that you love his music and you even love his ties, you begin to scold him.

"Look, Mr. Garcia—"

"Hey, Doc, no one calls me Mr. Garcia! Call me Jerry."

"OK, Jerry. Between your smoking, drug use, and excess poundage, you are going to kill yourself. If you don't make some big changes soon, your 'long, strange trip' might get a lot shorter than you'd like."

Jerry Garcia died in the summer of 1995. He was 53 years old.

Physicians generally receive inadequate training regarding the nature and treatment of obesity. Inadequate knowledge often combines with the notoriously refractory nature of the problem, to produce frustration. Frustration, in turn, can become manifested in negative doctor-to-patient communications. Such communications have little chance of helping people lose weight. The present article provides alternatives to guilt-inducing negative communication, through several specific suggestions. Physicians can learn, quite readily, how to confront denial, acknowledge efforts toward change, and construct a practical treatment plan with their overweight patients. This approach should increase commitment, improve the alliance between physician and patient, and promote more effective change. Psychologists can also provide physicians with information that they can then offer to patients, to help them achieve their weight-loss goals. This chapter reviews both communica-

163

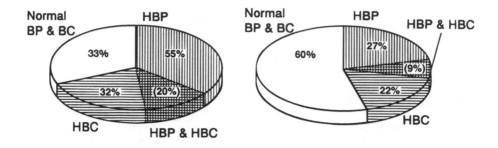

Normal BP & BC   HBP   HBP & HBC

OVERWEIGHT MEN   NON-OVERWEIGHT MEN

Figure 1. The prevalence of high blood pressure (HBP; ≥140/90 mmHg or on hypertensive medication) and high blood cholesterol (HBC; ≥240 mg/dL) among overweight men compared with nonoverweight men (according to the 1976 to 1980 National Health and Nutrition Examination Survey; National Heart, Lung, and Blood Institute, 1992).

tion strategies and behavioral interventions that psychologists can teach physicians who work with overweight patients. This information can, in turn, help patients find weight-loss programs that may exist outside the physician's office.

PREVALENCE AND HEALTH RISKS OF OBESITY

Rates of obesity in the United States are climbing steadily, currently affecting approximately 1 in 3 adult Americans (Williamson, 1995). Obesity is generally defined as 20%+ over ideal weight based on health data (see Andres, 1989; Blackburn & Rosofsky, 1992). Some estimates suggest that the total costs of obesity include approximately $45 billion for direct costs associated with such diseases as diabetes, cardiovascular disease, musculoskeletal disease, and cancer; indirect costs have been estimated at $23 billion (Wolf & Colditz, 1994). These extraordinary costs coincide with a proponderance of scientific evidence that indicates that obesity often has widespread and serious adverse consequences on physical health (e.g., Berg, 1993; Bray, 1985; Pi-Sunyer, 1993). For example, Figures 1 and 2 show that according to data from the 1976 to 1980 National Health and Nutrition Examination Survey, obesity is associated with very clear differences in two key health-risk factors (high blood pressure, defined as greater than or equal to 140/90 mmHg or on antihypertensive medication; and high blood cholesterol, defined as total cholesterol levels greater than or equal to 240 mg/dL; Berg, 1993; National Heart, Lung, and Blood Institute, 1992).

Research also suggests that even modest weight losses (e.g., 5% to 10% of initial weight) can result in substantial improvements in a variety

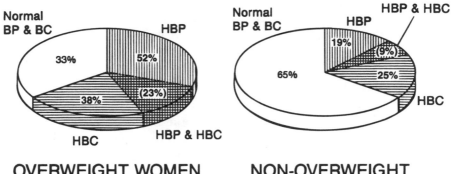

OVERWEIGHT WOMEN   **NON-OVERWEIGHT WOMEN**

Figure 2. The prevalence of high blood pressure (HBP; ≥140/90 mmHg or on hypertensive medication) and high blood cholesterol (HBC; ≥240 mg/dL) among overweight women compared with nonoverweight women (according to the 1976 to 1980 National Health and Nutrition Examination Survey; National Heart, Lung, and Blood Institute, 1992).

of health-risk factors (see, for review, Kirschenbaum & Fitzgibbon, 1995). Because physicians are on the front line of combating this very serious epidemic, their patients and society at large would benefit tremendously if they could adopt communication strategies that would help overweight people improve their commitments to change.

APPROACHES TO WEIGHT LOSS

The research evidence clearly indicates that complex, chronic, multifaceted difficulties, such as obesity, change in slow, refractory, and sometimes imperceptible ways for most people most of the time (Meichenbaum & Turk, 1987). This scenario frustrates physicians, particularly in an economic climate in which increasing demands are made of them to see increasing numbers of patients for limited amounts of time. The inevitable frustration this situation produces often leads to ineffective and rather negative communication by physicians with their overweight clients (e.g., Shapiro, Boggs, Melamed, & Graham-Pole, 1992). This negativity, sometimes emerging as scolding or guilt-inducing diatribes, tends to increase patients' anxiety and distress (e.g., Shapiro et al., 1992); decrease the accuracy of their memory for information conveyed (Shapiro et al., 1992); and decrease the probability of effective change (e.g., Hall, Roter, & Katz, 1988; Korsch & Francis-Negrete, 1972). Alternative approaches to communication, by physicians, particularly as it pertains to this very common and substantial health problem, may increase the probability of healthful change by their patients (Sweet, Rozensky, & Tovian, 1991).

I have worked closely with physicians in medical centers and in private practice for more than 20 years, focused on the treatment of obesity. This experience, coupled with guidance from the empirical literature (e.g., Kirschenbaum & Flanery, 1984; Putnam, Finney, Barkley, & Bonner, 1994), has resulted in some specific suggestions to offer physicians. These suggestions should enable physicians to decrease their frustrations and potential negativity when communicating with their obese clients about how to make changes in their life. Before I describe these suggestions, three key assumptions are worth reviewing.

First, most physicians know very little about nutrition or weight loss. Relatively little information is provided in their medical school curriculum, and they are usually too busy to focus on this issue when they begin their practice. Second, most physicians also seem quite responsive to information about this problem. They see many patients who are overweight and often seem frustrated and lost when directing them toward effective solutions. Third, physicians seem to respond best to relatively brief and well-encapsulated words of advice that they can use in a practical way immediately.

EFFECTIVE WEIGHT CONTROL

Brownell (1993) summarized the results of a survey involving more than 20,000 readers of Consumer Reports who have attempted to lose weight. He noted that of those who reported losing a significant amount of weight (M = 34 lb) and maintaining those losses, "72% had done so on their own compared to 20% in commercial programs, 3% with diet pills and only 5% in a hospital or university based program" (Brownell, 1993, p. 339). Population surveys indicate that of that 72% who attempt to lose weight on their own (or perhaps more in the wider population of people who do not read Consumer Reports) approximately 15%–25% may achieve very good results (Jeffery & Wing, 1983; Orne & Binik, 1987; Schachter, 1982).

These findings suggest that physicians could play a role in pointing the many individuals who attempt to lose weight on their own in the direction of effective approaches. Perhaps with a little guidance from a health professional, many of these self-directed weight controllers could do so more efficiently and effectively. On the other hand, studies of self-help materials suggest that only a modest percentage of people are likely to be successful when attempting to lose weight on their own (e.g., Meyers, Cuvillier, Stalgaitis, & Cooke, 1980). In addition, commercially available weight-control programs provide relatively little evidence of long-term effectiveness (e.g., Fatis, Weiner, Hawkins, & Van Dorsten, 1989; Volkmar, Stunkard, Woolston, & Bailey, 1981).

Although some people can lose weight and maintain weight loss remarkably well with relatively little professional guidance (Brownell, 1993), a higher percentage of people achieve good outcomes when they participate in long-term intensive cognitive–behavioral treatments (Kirschenbaum & Fitzgibbon, 1995; Perri, Nezu, & Viegener, 1992). Such programs are usually directed by psychologists. They include the following elements: (a) a thorough initial assessment of psychological issues, (b) a complete cognitive–behavioral therapy component, (c) a complete nutritional component, (d) a clear emphasis on increasing exercise, (e) staff who are well trained in cognitive–behavioral therapy, (f) at least weekly sessions for at least 1 year, (g) assistance provided for promoting support and otherwise managing social environments, and (h) use of protein-sparing modified fasting when appropriate. Some recent evidence also indicates that the impact of programs with these eight elements could be augmented by the appropriate use of modern appetite-suppressant drugs (see, for reviews, Bray 1993; Silverstone, 1993).

Relatively few programs have included all of these eight (or nine) elements, and fewer still have evaluated their combined impact (Kirschenbaum & Fitzgibbon, 1995). Nonetheless, some programs that have included many of these elements have demonstrated some remarkable outcomes. Brownell and Jeffery (1987) noted that average weight losses in the outcome studies they reviewed in the 1980s almost doubled those obtained in studies in the 1970s. This trend seems to be continuing into the 1990s. For example, participants in programs that combined protein-sparing modified fasting and behavior therapy lost more than 40 pounds (on average) and maintained more than 20-pound weight losses 1.5 years posttreatment; these numbers are based on a review that included all 11 studies published before 1990 of such interventions that included at least 1.5-year follow-ups (Conviser, Kirschenbaum, & Fitzgibbon, 1990). Several recent reports of long-term cognitive–behavioral interventions also presented evidence suggesting that most people can lose and maintain substantial weight losses (e.g., Beliard, Kirschenbaum, & Fitzgibbon, 1992; Perri et al., 1988; Perri, Nezu, Patti, & McCann, 1989; Wadden, Foster, Letizia, & Stunkard, 1992).

Length of treatment deserves special emphasis; the evidence that supports treating obese people for years, instead of weeks, includes experimental research (e.g., Baum, Clark, & Sandler, 1991; Perri et al., 1989) and meta-analytic results (e.g., Bennett, 1986). Another argument for length and intensity of cognitive–behavioral treatments is provided in the clinically derived stages-of-change model that my colleagues and I developed recently (Kirschenbaum et al., 1992). Figure 3 shows the three primary stages, or those posited as experienced by most weight controllers during their first 2 years in intensive treatment, and the three secondary

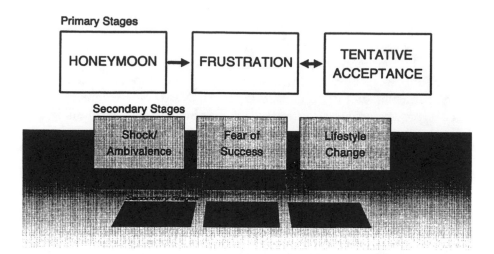

Figure 3. A model of the primary and secondary stages of change in long-term weight control. From *Weight Loss Through Persistence: Making Science Work for You* (p. 36), by D. S. Kirschenbaum, 1994, Oakland, CA: New Harbinger Publications. Copyright 1994 by D. S. Kirschenbaum.

stages, those that seem to occur regularly, but for a minority of participants. The behaviors, thoughts, and feelings that Kirschenbaum et al. (1992) viewed as characterizing the stages make it clear that participants usually struggle for long periods of time to persist at this highly challenging process of life change. First, the relatively easy honeymoon stage passes into the much more difficult, but ostensibly inevitable, frustration stage. Fortunately, many people, with the help of the relationship with a professional therapist, cognitive–behavioral techniques, and the other weight-loss-treatment elements listed earlier in this section, find their way to the peaceful sense of resolve and behavioral consistencies of supernormal eating and exercising that characterize tentative acceptance. Some weight controllers even develop the aggressive self-protectiveness of lifestyle change ("unwilling, and adamantly so, to place [themselves] in a position to become 'mindless' . . . again about eating, exercise, and weight"; Kirschenbaum et al., 1992, p. 627). Another way of describing this transition through stages of change is to suggest that long-term, intensive cognitive–behavioral treatments may help people reach the often elusive but potentially critical goal of obsessive–compulsive self-regulation (Kirschenbaum, 1987; Kirschenbaum & Tomarken, 1982).

A HIERARCHICAL WEIGHT-CONTROL PLAN DIRECTED BY PHYSICIANS

Exhibit 1 shows an example of a handout for physicians that outlines six hierarchical steps for weight control. The steps are ordered from least

EXHIBIT 1
Weight-Loss Recommendations

1. Self-directed attempts?	5. Weight Watchers: [telephone number]
2. Increase exercise (Join club? Walk?)	6. Professional weight-control program: [telephone number]
3. Spouse or friend involvement	
4. Take Off Pounds Sensibly (TOPS): [telephone number]	

intrusive interventions to most elaborate. In accord with the preceding information about effectiveness of various approaches to weight control, some people can lose weight effectively with relatively minimal guidance. For these individuals, the first two to three steps may provide all the encouragement they need. On the other hand, many other individuals may benefit from more structured interventions, including assistance from widely available self-help or commercial programs. The most intensive level of intervention (and the most effective), the sixth step, pertains to professional programs. These programs are generally directed by psychologists. They incorporate the 8–9 elements noted above for state-of-the-art/science treatments of obesity. In other words, the best of the professional programs (the sixth step) will meet the definition for long-term, intensive cognitive–behavioral treatment.

Psychologists who are consulting to physicians can give them a version of Exhibit 1 as a handout when accompanying an educational talk about the treatment of obesity (e.g., a workshop used to generate referrals). The psychologist can then review each of the hierarchical steps and provide suggestions for using each step. More specifically, physicians would be encouraged to talk with their patients about what they have tried in the past as the first step. Generally, people who have attempted to lose weight many times, and have used a variety of approaches without notable success, could proceed directly to Step 6. Patients who have not made many serious attempts to lose weight could be advised to attempt Steps 1, 2, or 3 and then return for a follow-up visit to the physician 2 or 3 months later. If they have not made progress on weight control (e.g., approximately 1/2 to 1 pound weight-loss per week for individuals starting at least 20% over ideal body weight), then Steps 4 through 6 would be recommended. It would be most helpful and appropriate for psychologists to identify the best professional programs in their area for physicians to use in their Step 6 referrals.

It seems worthwhile to know a few more details about the six steps in this plan before providing a lecture or workshop advocating its adoption:

1. Self-directed attempts? Physicians can ask their patients what approaches they have used to lose weight. They can discuss each major weight-loss effort and determine if the patient may be willing to try one of them again or if the patient is looking for something new. If the patient wishes additional direction, the physician can proceed to Step 2.

2. Increase exercise. It is sometimes useful for physicians to recommend dramatic increases in exercise. Many patients do not realize that a daily brisk 30-minute walk might do them a world of good. A knowledgeable physician can help them understand that such efforts might increase their metabolic rates (e.g., Donahoe, Lin, Kirschenbaum, & Keesey, 1984) and greatly facilitate weight-loss attempts (Hill, 1995; Wadden, 1995). This brief education could be followed by discussion about the feasibility and usefulness of joining health clubs or going for regular walks in the morning. For weight-loss purposes, it is helpful to recommend that patients attempt to exercise at least once per day, every day. This is in keeping with recent recommendations from the American College of Sports Medicine (1991), the *U.S. Department of Agriculture* (1995), and Kirschenbaum (1994). As the physician discusses this and other options with his or her patient, it is also useful to recommend some self-help reading about nutrition, exercise, and weight loss. Exhibit 1 includes some recommended books that are readily available.

3. Spouse or friend involvement. Physicians can make the point that weight controllers tend to maintain exercise better if they exercise with a friend or their spouse (e.g., Dishman, 1988).

4. and 5. Take Off Pounds Sensibly (TOPS) and Weight Watchers. Physicians can provide specific recommendations as to the type of nonprofessional programs that he or she believes will be the most effective and reasonable. The two programs that I recommend are the self-help program, Take Off Pounds Sensibly (TOPS), and Weight Watchers. Both of these programs are very well established (among the oldest self-help programs in the country), and both provide responsible information at reasonable costs. They're also widely available. On the other hand, patients should be warned that most people have great difficulty sustaining their involvement in nonprofessional programs. Most patients drop out of these programs within several weeks

or months (Volkmar et al., 1981). However, they can work for some people some of the time (Stuart & Guire, 1979).

6. Professional weight-control program. A professional approach to losing weight is offered in many major metropolitan areas, usually at hospitals or universities. As noted previously, the best examples of these programs are the ones that provide appropriate intensive cognitive–behavioral treatment and long-term care (Kirschenbaum & Fitzgibbon, 1995; Perri, Nezu, & Viegener, 1992; Wadden, 1995).

SUPPORTING WEIGHT LOSS EFFORTS

In addition to implementing a hierarchical weight-control plan, the second major issue about which some physicians could use some assistance pertains to acknowledging and supporting their patients' weight-loss efforts (cf. Hall et al., 1988; Shapiro et al., 1992). My colleagues and I believe that it is important to help physicians understand the distinction between double messages and encouragement. More specifically, double messages include comments such as, "You look much better!" Although this is intended to provide encouragement, it is concurrently critical. The critical aspect is the underlying message that the person looked much worse previously. An alternative method of encouragement would be to say something like, "Congratulations! What have you been doing?" This approach engages the patient in a dialogue about the effort, thereby suggesting its importance. It may also prove very helpful for physicians to make notes in their charts about the patient's specific efforts to lose weight. Periodic comments from authority figures like physicians can be very supportive if provided in a consistently positive fashion (Putnam et al., 1994; Sweet et al., 1991). This support, in turn, can increase the probability of meaningful behavior change (Hall et al., 1988).

THERAPEUTICALLY CONFRONTING DENIAL

A third issue, one with which many physicians seem to struggle, is denial. Many overweight people have become masters at denying the magnitude and importance of their weight status (Kirschenbaum et al., 1992). The natural tendency, and the one that seems to be followed by many physicians, is to criticize, rather directly, patients' ostensible lack of concern regarding their health. These parentally styled remarks tend to produce denigration and avoidance of the physician (cf. Hall et al., 1988; Shapiro et al., 1992). Negative feedback tends to be avoided rather than embraced (Stockton & Morran, 1981). Physicians, like most nonpsychologists, seem generally unaware of this perspective.

Instead of the parentally styled critical approach, a more informative approach often produces better outcomes (e.g., DiMatteo et al., 1993). For example, the physician could express concern about the patient's health status and the way it may affect her or him in the years to come. This concern, coupled with an appropriate referral, may lead to an increased readiness of the patient to change. In fact, the results of several studies suggest that when people devise specific plans to manage challenging behavioral regimens, they adhere more closely to those plans (e.g., Kirschenbaum & Flanery, 1984; Putnam et al., 1994).

CONCLUSIONS AND FUTURE DIRECTIONS

In summary, physicians often find it rather useful to have specific recommendations that they can provide to their patients about appropriate ways to lose weight. They also seem to benefit from education about how to acknowledge their patients' efforts at weight loss and how to confront, therapeutically, denial of obesity. The research evidence suggests that supportive, informative interactions, accompanied by specific plans for change, should enhance commitment and change.

It would, of course, be most helpful to have additional research investigating the actual usefulness of the strategy outlined in this chapter. For example, workshops could be conducted with groups of physicians. In the experimental workshops, these specific recommendations could be provided. In the comparison workshop, similar information could be provided without including the hierarchical plan and handout. It would be helpful to include some follow-up sessions to check on the implementation of these recommendations in the experimental condition.

Research could focus on the extent to which the patients to whom physicians made these specific recommendations actually changed behavior over time. This could include investigating changes in weight, percentage fat, and other health-risk factors over long periods of time (at least 1 year, ideally 3–5 years).

The evidence presented in this chapter would suggest that the experimental workshops would produce better outcomes for at least some of the patients to whom they were applied. Because this would be a relatively minimal type of intervention, however, these recommendations alone would not be expected to lead to dramatic weight losses for most of the people to whom they were offered (cf. Meyers et al., 1980). Additional research on weight-loss recommendations that could be used by primary care physicians would be quite useful (e.g., Williams & Duncan, 1976). Perhaps physicians could use some elements that are incorporated in state-of-the-art/science treatments offered in professional programs to the advantage of at least some of their patients.

RECOMMENDED READING

References marked with an asterisk indicate books that are technically oriented and recommended for health care professionals.

Bennion, L. H., Bierman, E. L., & Ferguson, J. M. (1991). *Straight talk about weight control*. Fairfield, OH: Consumer Report Books.

Brody, J. (1987). *Jane Brody's nutrition book*. New York: Bantam Books.

*Brownell, K. D., & Foreyt, J. P. (Eds.). (1986). *Handbook of eating disorders*. New York: Basic Books.

Fletcher, A. M. (1994). *Thin for life*. Shelburne, VT: Chapters.

Kirschenbaum, D. S. (1994). *Weight loss through persistence: Making science work for you*. Oakland, CA: New Harbinger Publications.

*Kirschenbaum, D. S., Johnson, W. G., & Stalonas, P. M. (1987). *Treating childhood and adolescent obesity*. New York: Wiley.

Perri, M. G., Nezu, A. M., & Viegener, B. J. (1992). *Improving the long-term management of obesity*. New York: Wiley.

Stunkard, A. J., & Wadden, T. A. (1993). *Obesity: Theory and therapy*. New York: Raven Press.

REFERENCES

American College of Sports Medicine. (1991). *Guidelines for exercise testing and prescription* (4th ed.). Philadelphia: Lea & Febiger.

Andres, R. (1989). Does the "best" body weight change with age? In A. J. Stunkard & A. Baum (Eds.), *Perspectives in behavioral medicine: Eating, sleeping, and sex* (pp. 100–108). Hillsdale, NJ: Erlbaum.

Baum, J. G., Clark, H. B., & Sandler, J. (1991). Preventing relapse in obesity through posttreatment maintenance systems: Comparing the relative efficacy of two levels of therapists support. *Journal of Behavioral Medicine, 14*, 287–302.

Beliard, B., Kirschenbaum, D. S., & Fitzgibbon, M. L. (1992). Evaluation of an intensive weight control program using *a priori* criteria to determine outcome. *International Journal of Obesity, 16*, 505–517.

Bennett, G. A. (1986). Behavior therapy for obesity: A quantitative review of the effects of selected treatment characteristics on outcome. *Behavior Therapy, 17*, 554–562.

Berg, F. (1993). *Health risks of obesity*. Hettinger, ND: Healthy Living Institute.

Blackburn, G. L., & Rosofsky, W. (1992). Making the connection between weight loss, dieting, and health: The 10% solution. *Weight Control Digest* [Professional ed.], *2*, 124–127.

Bray, G. A. (1985). Complications of obesity. *Annals of Internal Medicine, 103*, 1052–1062.

Bray, G. A. (1993). Use and abuse of appetite-suppressant drugs in the treatment of obesity. *Annals of Internal Medicine, 119*, 707–713.

Brownell, K. D. (1993). Whether obesity should be treated. *Health Psychology, 12*, 339–341.

Brownell, K. D., & Jeffery, R. W. (1987). Improving long-term weight loss: Pushing the limits of treatment. *Behavior Therapy, 18*, 353–374.

Conviser, J. H., Kirschenbaum, D. S., & Fitzgibbon, M. L. (1990, April). *Toward clinically effective weight control programs: Efficient long-term evaluation of an intensive program.* Paper presented at the meeting of the Society of Behavioral Medicine, Chicago.

DiMatteo, M. R., Sherbourne, C. D., Hays, R. D., Ordway, L., Kravitz, R. L., McGlynn, E. A., Kaplan, S., & Rogers, W. H. (1993). Physicians' characteristics influence patients' adherence to medical treatment: Results from the Medical Outcomes Study. *Health Psychology, 12*, 93–102.

Dishman, R. K. (Ed.), (1988). *Exercise adherence: Its impact on public health.* Champaign, IL: Human Kinetics Books.

Donahoe, C. P., Lin, D. H., Kirschenbaum, D. S., & Keesey, R. E. (1984). Metabolic consequences of dieting and exercising in the treatment of obesity. *Journal of Consulting and Clinical Psychology, 48*, 869–877.

Fatis, M., Weiner, A., Hawkins, J., & Van Dorsten, B. (1989). Following-up on a commercial weight loss program: Do the pounds stay off after your picture has been in the newspaper? *Journal of the American Dietetic Association, 89*, 547–548.

Hall, J. A., Roter, D. L., & Katz, N. R. (1988). Meta-analysis of correlates of provider behavior in medical encounters. *Medical Care, 26*, 1–19.

Hill, J. O. (1995). The role of exercise in weight maintenance. In D. B. Allison & F. X. Pi-Snunyer (Eds.), *Obesity treatment: Establishing goals, improving outcomes, and reviewing the research agenda* (pp. 127–132). New York: Plenum.

Jeffery, R. W., & Wing, R. R. (1983). Recidivism and self-cure of smoking and obesity: Data from population studies. *American Psychologist, 38*, 852.

Kirschenbaum, D. S. (1987). Self-regulatory failure: A review with clinical implications. *Clinical Psychology Review, 7*, 77–104.

Kirschenbaum, D. S. (1994). *Weight loss through persistence: Making science work for you.* Oakland, CA: New Harbinger Publications.

Kirschenbaum, D. S., & Fitzgibbon, M. L. (1995). Controversy about the treatment of obesity: Criticisms or challenges? *Behavior Therapy, 26*, 43–68.

Kirschenbaum, D. S., Fitzgibbon, M. L., Martino, S., Conviser, J. H., Rosendahl, E. H., & Laatsch, L. (1992). Stages of change in successful weight control: A clinically derived model. *Behavior Therapy, 23*, 623–635.

Kirschenbaum, D. S., & Flanery, R. C. (1984). Toward a psychology of behavioral contracting. *Clinical Psychology Review, 4*, 597–618.

Kirschenbaum, D. S., & Tomarken, A. J. (1982). On facing the generalization problem: The study of self-regulatory failure. In P. C. Kendall (Ed.), *Advances in cognitive behavioral research and therapy* (Vol. 1, pp. 121–200). San Diego, CA: Academic Press.

Korsch, B. M., & Francis-Negrete, V. (1972). Doctor–patient communication. *Scientific American, 227*, 66–74.

Meichenbaum, D., & Turk, D. C. (1987). *Facilitating treatment adherence: A practitioner's guidebook*. New York: Plenum.

Meyers, A. W., Cuvillier, C., Stalgaitis, S., & Cooke, C. J. (1980). An evaluation of self-help treatment programs for weight loss. *The Behavior Therapist, 3*, 25–26.

National Heart, Lung, and Blood Institute. (1992). Obesity education initiative takes a high risk in a population approach. *Infomemo, 1*, 16–17.

Orne, C. M., & Binik, Y. M. (1987). Recidivism and self-cure of obesity: A test of Schacter's hypothesis in diabetic patients. *Health Psychology, 6*, 467–475.

Perri, M. G., McAllister, D. A., Gange, J. J., Jordan, R. C., McAdoo, W. G., & Nezu, A. M. (1988). Effects of four maintenance programs on the long-term management of obesity. *Journal of Consulting and Clinical Psychology, 56*, 529–534.

Perri, M. G., Nezu, A. M., Patti, E. P., & McCann, K. L. (1989). Effect of length of treatment on weight loss. *Journal of Consulting and Clinical Psychology, 57*, 450–452.

Perri, M. G., Nezu, A. M., & Viegener, B. J. (1992). *Improving the long-term management of obesity: Theory, research, and clinical guidelines*. New York: Wiley.

Pi-Sunyer, F. X. (1993). Medical hazards of obesity. *Annals of Internal Medicine, 119*, 655–660.

Putnam, D. E., Finney, J. W., Barkley, P. L., & Bonner, M. J. (1994). Enhancing commitment improves adherence to a medical regimen. *Journal of Consulting and Clinical Psychology, 62*, 191–194.

Schachter, S. (1982). Recidivism and self-cure of smoking and obesity. *American Psychologist, 37*, 436–444.

Shapiro, D. E., Boggs, S. R., Melamed, B. G., & Graham-Pole, J. (1992). The effect of varied physician affect on recall, anxiety, and perceptions in women at risk for breast cancer: An analogue study. *Health Psychology, 11*, 61–66.

Silverstone, T. (1993). The place of appetite-suppressant drugs in the treatment of obesity. In A. J. Stunkard & T. A. Wadden (Eds.), *Obesity: Theory and therapy* (2nd ed., pp. 275–286). New York: Raven Press.

Stockton, R., & Morran, D. K. (1981). Feedback exchange, in personal growth groups: Received acceptance as a function of valence, session, and order of delivery. *Journal of Counseling Psychology, 28*, 490–497.

Stuart, R. B., & Guire, K. (1979). Some correlates of weight loss through behavior modification. *International Journal of Obesity, 3,* 87–96.

Sweet, J. J., Rozensky, R. H., & Tovian, S. M. (Eds.). (1991). *Handbook of clinical psychology in medical settings.* New York: Plenum.

U.S. Department of Agriculture. (1995). *Nutrition and your health: Dietary guidelines for Americans* (Publication No. 96-402-519). Washington, DC: U.S. Government Printing Office.

Volkmar, F. R., Stunkard, A. J., Woolston, J., & Bailey, B. A. (1981). High attrition rates in commercial weight reduction programs. *Archives of Internal Medicine, 141,* 426–428.

Wadden, T. A. (1995). What characterizes successful weight maintainers? In D. B. Allison & F. X. Pi-Snunyer (Eds.), *Obesity treatment: Establishing goals, improving outcomes, and reviewing the research agenda* (pp. 103–112). New York: Plenum.

Wadden, T. A., Foster, G. D., Letizia, K. A., & Stunkard, A. J. (1992). A multicenter evaluation of a proprietary weight reduction program for the treatment of marked obesity. *Archives of Internal Medicine, 152,* 961–966.

Williams, A. E., & Duncan, B. (1976). A commercial weight-reducing organization: A critical analysis. *Medical Journal of Australia, 1,* 781–785.

Williamson, D. F. (1995). Prevalence and demographics of obesity. In K. D. Brownell & C. G. Fairburn (Eds.), *Eating disorders and obesity: A comprehensive handbook* (pp. 391–395). New York: Guilford Press.

Wolf, A. M., & Colditz, G. A. (1994). The cost of obesity: The U.S. perspective.

13

SUBSTANCE USE PROBLEMS IN PRIMARY CARE MEDICAL SETTINGS: IS THERE A PSYCHOLOGIST IN THE HOUSE?

BRUCE S. LIESE, BELINDA A. VAIL, and KIMBERLY A. SEATON

The use of alcohol, tobacco, and illicit drugs is pervasive in the United States, and excessive use of these psychoactive substances contributes to the health problems of millions of men, women, and children. The physical sequelae of these health problems have traditionally been treated in primary care medical settings. However, most primary care physicians feel unprepared to deal with the psychological and behavioral manifestations of substance use.

In this chapter, it is argued that health psychologists should be actively involved in the treatment of substance use problems because these problems involve psychological (cognitive, behavioral, and affective) processes that directly influence health and physical well-being. It is further argued that primary care physicians will welcome health psychologists offering to help in the management of their patients with substance use problems.

PREVALENCE OF SUBSTANCE USE AND ASSOCIATED PROBLEMS

Millions of Americans use psychoactive substances every day. According to a recent National Household Survey on Drug Abuse conducted by the Substance Abuse and Mental Health Services Administration (1993), 68% of Americans over the age of 12 drank alcohol in the past year, 32.1% smoked cigarettes, 12.7% used illicit drugs, 4.7% used smokeless tobacco, and 4.5% used prescription drugs for nonmedical use. Furthermore, 84.6% of respondents said they had used alcohol *at some time in their lives*, 72.7% had smoked cigarettes, 37% had used illicit drugs, 14.1% had used smokeless tobacco, and 12.5% had used prescription drugs for nonmedical purposes. Although these data do not specifically reflect problematic use, they certainly reflect the pervasiveness of drug and alcohol use in the United States.

In another important study, Regier et al. (1993) examined the prevalence of psychopathology and substance use disorders. These investigators reported results of the National Institute of Mental Health's Epidemiologic Catchment Area study, a collaborative project involving five research groups and over 20,000 respondents. Regier et al. (1993) found that 28.1% of their sample had some alcohol, drug, or mental disorder within the preceding year. Approximately 10% reported substance use disorders; 7.4% specifically reported alcohol use disorders, and 3.1% reported drug use disorders.

Regier et al. (1993) also compared service utilization in the treatment of mental disorders with that of substance use disorders. They found that more than 50% of individuals with schizophrenia, bipolar disorder, somatization disorder, and panic disorder received formal treatment, whereas only 23% of individuals with substance use disorders received formal treatment for their disorders. Approximately 11% of individuals with substance use disorders received services from drug or alcohol treatment facilities, and 9.9% received treatment in general medical settings. This study established that most Americans with substance use disorders do not receive formal treatment.

HEALTH PROBLEMS ASSOCIATED WITH EXCESSIVE SUBSTANCE USE

Excessive psychoactive substance use may result in profound health problems. It is important for health psychologists to be knowledgeable about the health problems associated with excessive substance use.

Alcohol

Alcohol is a psychoactive drug that has a variety of effects, depending on the drinker's physiology, expectations, circumstances, and environment. Small amounts of alcohol can produce the desired effects of sedation, relaxation, and disinhibition. But substantially larger doses may produce cognitive impairment, poor judgment, labile mood, slurred speech, *ataxia* (difficulty walking), coma, respiratory failure, and death (Barker & Whitfield, 1991). Chronic or heavy use may impair peripheral nerve function and destroy brain cells, potentially resulting in memory loss and reduced learning capability (Schuckit, 1991).

Alcohol is a major contributor to heart disease, the leading cause of death in the United States (Friedman, 1990; Schuckit, 1991). Alcohol appears to be a direct cardiac toxin that contributes to fat deposition on the heart muscle and a subsequent decrease in the ability of the heart to beat effectively. Acutely, alcohol increases heart rate and the volume of blood pumped by the heart. It causes skin vessels to dilate, leading to loss of body heat (despite the warm sensation experienced by the drinker). Over time, alcohol may cause an increase in the drinker's blood pressure and cholesterol and hasten the development of cholesterol plaques in the coronary arteries. When a coronary artery is occluded by pieces of these plaques, a myocardial infarction may result.

Alcohol is a direct gastric irritant that induces a highly acidic state in the stomach. With chronic use, alcohol may lead to inflammation and ulcer formation in the esophagus and stomach. Even young drinkers may experience vague or chronic unexplained abdominal pain. Because teenagers are seen infrequently by physicians and rarely disclose their alcohol consumption, this abdominal pain is typically undiagnosed.

Acute inflammation of the liver (*hepatitis*) and fatty liver infiltrates are often seen in heavy drinkers. Contrary to popular belief, even social drinkers may develop these liver problems, which may lead to *cirrhosis* and liver cancer. Cirrhosis is the replacement of normal liver cells by fibrous tissue, with the eventual loss of liver function. Because a large percentage of blood passes through the liver before returning to the heart, cirrhosis causes an accumulation of fluid in the abdomen (*ascites*) and dilation of other large vessels that return blood to the heart. Some of the vessels may become enlarged, rupture, and produce massive hemorrhage into the throat and stomach. Alcohol is also one of the leading causes of *pancreatitis*, a dangerous inflammation of the pancreas that causes severe abdominal pain (Schuckit, 1991).

Other organ systems may also be adversely affected by heavy alcohol consumption (Schuckit, 1991). Production of red and white blood cells may be decreased. *Gout*, a condition characterized by painful inflammation of the joints, results from decreased uric acid secretion. Testosterone levels may also decrease, leading to sexual dysfunction in males. The acid–base balance of the body may be disrupted, leading to an array of vitamin and mineral deficiencies. Alcohol-dependent individuals have cancer rates 10 times greater than those of the general public, with an increased risk of mouth, throat, esophagus, stomach, liver, pancreas, and breast cancers.

Alcohol harms more than just those individuals who drink excessively. At least 50% of fatal automobile accidents are alcohol related, and a majority of victims are innocent passengers, pedestrians, and other drivers who have not been drinking. Women who drink during early pregnancy may place their babies at risk for *fetal alcohol syndrome*, characterized by mental retardation, cardiac anomalies, abnormal facial features, and genital malformation (McKenzie & Kipke, 1992).

Cigarettes

Nicotine, the addictive ingredient in cigarettes, is a powerful central nervous system stimulant and depressant. The acute physiological effects of nicotine include increased heart rate, blood pressure, and an increased demand for oxygen by the heart. Peripheral vessels vasoconstrict, and skeletal muscles relax. Some additional effects of nicotine are decreased appetite and the release of endogenous opiates (Holbrook, 1991).

The risks of smoking are well documented; the mortality rate for smokers is 70% higher than for nonsmokers. Adverse effects are primarily seen in the respiratory and cardiovascular systems, but other systems are affected as well. The most publicized adverse effect in smokers is the development of lung cancer. However, smoking is also implicated in cancers of the mouth, larynx, esophagus, stomach, pancreas, kidney, bladder, and cervix (Newcomb & Carbone, 1992).

Chronic obstructive pulmonary disease, chronic bronchitis, emphysema, and respiratory infections are closely associated with smoking (Sherman, 1992). Mild pulmonary function abnormalities may be seen even in teenagers who smoke (Holbrook, 1991). Cigarette smoke paralyzes the *cilia* (tiny hairlike structures) lining the respiratory tract while it simultaneously increases mucous production. Without the effective action of the cilia, clearance of the bronchial tracts is impaired. Cigarette smoke also interferes with the immune mechanism of the respiratory tract, potentially resulting in direct damage and an inability to protect against disease. Over time, the *alveoli* (tiny air sacs in the lungs) may rupture, leading to emphysema (McKenzie & Kipke, 1992).

The effects of cigarette smoke on the heart and blood vessels are equally dangerous (McBride, 1992). Smoking increases heart rate and blood pressure while constricting peripheral arteries. It also increases cholesterol circulating in the bloodstream, potentially leading to a rapid increase in arteriosclerosis. Tobacco and diabetes account for the majority of leg amputations from peripheral vascular disease. Tobacco and hypertension are the leading contributors to coronary artery disease and myocardial infarction (Holbrook, 1991; McBride, 1992). Tobacco smoke also decreases skin elasticity, which leads to premature wrinkling. In heavy smokers, the risk of developing impotence is heightened (McKenzie & Kipke, 1992).

As with alcohol, the dangers of smoking extend beyond the risks to the smoker. Substantial evidence has demonstrated that environmental smoke is dangerous to nonsmokers (Byrd, 1992). For example, children living with smokers are more likely than those living with nonsmokers to develop ear and nasal infections, pneumonia, and eczema. The heart rate of a pregnant woman's fetus increases when she smokes. Pregnant women smokers are more likely to miscarry and have underweight infants, and their babies are more likely to die from sudden infant death syndrome (Byrd, 1992).

Illicit Drugs

Marijuana. The acute (short-term) effects of marijuana primarily involve the central nervous system. Marijuana produces mild elation and relaxation, distortion of time, increased sensitivity to auditory and visual cues, and impairment of learning and cognitive functioning. A user's appetite often increases (McKenzie & Kipke, 1992), and mild increases in heart rate and blood pressure are likely, as well as marked redness of the eyes and increased body temperature (Mendelson, 1991). Chronic use may lead to decreased motivation levels (*amotivational syndrome*) and depression. Mood swings, anxiety, delusions, and paranoia may develop with extremely heavy use (D'Lugoff & Hawthorne, 1991).

Over time, the most severe effect of marijuana is probably damage to the lungs. The irritation from the smoke leads to cellular changes in the bronchial wall, bronchospasms, and bronchitis. Definite decreases in lung capacity and function occur with regular use (Mendelson, 1991). Other organ systems are less affected, but there is a decrease in fertility and sex drive with chronic use (D'Lugoff & Hawthorne, 1991).

Cocaine. Cocaine is a particularly dangerous and powerful central nervous system stimulant. Its effects include hyperalertness, anxiety, anorexia, labile affect, insomnia, paranoia, agitation, and heightened sensual awareness. Initially, cocaine causes an increase in blood pressure and heart rate that may advance to potentially fatal cardiac arrhythmias. Cocaine is a potent vasoconstrictor and may also lead to coronary artery spasm and sudden death by myocardial infarction. Users will occasionally develop seizures and stroke. When ingested nasally, cocaine causes membrane drying and atrophy that may lead to septal perforation. Cocaine also may cause reflex congestion and chronic sinusitis. Deeper in the respiratory tract, it produces more severe symptoms of fluid or blood accumulation in the lungs (Mendelson, 1991). Many of the side effects of cocaine are idiosyncratic and not dose related, making even occasional use dangerous. For some individuals, cocaine becomes highly addictive.

The recent development of "crack" cocaine has resulted in a dramatic increase in cocaine use in the United States (Schulz, 1993). Crack is a smokable cocaine derivative that is far less expensive than powder cocaine. The term *crack* comes from the crackling sound made by this drug when it is smoked (D'Lugoff & Hawthorne, 1991). In addition to the risks associated with powder cocaine use, crack seems to be more addictive and may lead to life-threatening lung symptoms with heavy use.

Opioids. Opioids such as heroin, codeine, and Demerol are used medically to manage pain and produce mild sedation. The physical effects of opioids include increased body temperature, heart rate, respiratory rate, and blood pressure. These drugs are abused primarily for their euphoric effects, but their use presents several risks: decreased digestive-tract motility, anorexia, constipation, and respiratory depression. Overdose can result in the fatal failure to initiate breathing. Withdrawal symptoms may be intense and influenza-like, including nausea, vomiting, cough, rhinorrhea, sweating, and twitching (Mendelson, 1991; Schuckit & Segal, 1991).

Phencyclidine. Phencyclidine (PCP) is a drug developed for veterinary medicine that produces variable responses. In low doses, it produces excitement, agitation, and analgesia. However, the toxic dose is very close to the dose producing desired effects, so overdose is common. Individuals who overdose may manifest psychological and physical effects. Psychological effects include disorganized thinking, body-image distortions, and feelings of estrangement. Physical side effects include vomiting, hypersalivation, muscle rigidity, convulsions, fever, coma, and death (Mendelson, 1991).

Hallucinogens. Hallucinogens, or psychedelics, like LSD and psilocybin are drugs that produce visual, auditory, tactile, and olfactory hallucinations (Schulz, 1993). Like PCP, hallucinogens may produce time distortions, confusion, and paranoia. When their judgment becomes impaired, users become endangered because they mistake illusions for reality. Thus, users may experience panic attacks and "bad trips" (McKenzie & Kipke, 1992; Mendelson, 1991).

Inhalants. Because they are inexpensive and easily acquired, inhalants, such as glue, paint, gasoline, lighter fluid, and paint thinner are most commonly used by young people. The acute symptoms of inhalant intoxication are similar to alcohol intoxication (D'Lugoff & Hawthorne, 1991). Impulsive behavior, confusion, and a general loss of inhibition are common. When the user is too confused to quit inhaling, oxygen depletion may occur, with resulting seizures or cardiorespiratory arrest (McKenzie & Kipke, 1992). Chronic use is believed to produce multiple organ damage.

PSYCHOLOGICAL PROBLEMS ASSOCIATED WITH SUBSTANCE USE DISORDERS

Recent evidence has demonstrated that individuals with substance use disorders are likely to have significant coexisting psychological problems. Regier et al. (1990) surveyed individuals with lifetime mental disorders and found that 28.9% had coexisting drug and alcohol disorders, 22.3% had coexisting alcohol disorders, and 14.7% had other drug disorders. These investigators found that individuals with alcohol use disorders had a 36.6% prevalence rate of other mental disorders. This figure was much higher (53.1%) in individuals with other drug use disorders.

Regier et al. (1990) found that the risk of substance use disorders varies with specific psychiatric diagnoses. Compared with the general public, the risk of a substance use disorder increases 4.6 times with schizophrenia, 29.6 times with antisocial personality disorder, 1.7 times with anxiety disorders, and 2.5 times with obsessive–compulsive disorder. In their study, Regier et al. (1990) also investigated the risk of psychiatric problems among particular drug users. They found that mental disorders increased by 2.3 times with alcohol use disorders, 3.8 times with marijuana, 11.3 times with cocaine, 6.7 times with opiates, 10.8 times with barbiturates, 6.2 times with amphetamines, and 8.0 times with hallucinogens. These data were consistent with other findings that cocaine addicts have a higher prevalence of depression, bipolar disorder, and attention deficit disorder than the general public (Group for the Advancement of Psychiatry, 1991). Rounsaville, Weissman, Kleber, and Wilber (1982) reported that opiate addicts have a heightened lifetime risk of psychiatric disorders (86.9%), with depression the most common disorder (53.9%). Ross, Glaser, and Germanson (1988) found high lifetime rates of antisocial personality disorder (46.9%), anxiety disorders (61.9%), affective disorders (33.7%), and psychosexual disorders (34.5%) among individuals with substance use problems. Given these data, indicating widespread psychological problems associated with substance use disorders, it becomes even more important that psychologists attend to substance use problems.

SUBSTANCE USE PROBLEMS IN PRIMARY CARE MEDICAL SETTINGS

It is well established that substance use disorders are common in primary care medical settings. For example, Bradley (1994) reported that between 11% and 20% of patients in general medical clinics have alcohol use disorders. In family practice clinics, these figures range from 8% to 16%, and in obstetrics and gynecology clinics, 12% to 16% of patients have alcohol use disorders (Bradley, 1994).

Unfortunately, it is also well established that physicians tend to focus on physical symptoms and problems rather than on underlying substance use problems (Chappel, 1992). In a study by Pursch (1978), 75% of physicians were unable to deal effectively with alcohol-troubled patients. Difficulties were attributed to inadequate training, unresolved personal or family substance use problems, negative experiences with addicted patients, rigid personality styles, lack of empathy, and fear of loss of collegial support.

Although brief interventions by primary care physicians have been found to be effective (Bien, Miller, & Tonigan, 1993; Schwartz, 1992), most physicians feel ill-prepared or uncomfortable treating substance use problems. Their training almost exclusively focuses on physical and life sciences (including biology, chemistry, physiology, pathology, pharmacology, and microbiology) and stresses the need to cure or control illness. Consequently, physicians generally prefer not to treat substance use problems that are not immediately curable. Goodwin (1981) characterized the situation poignantly:

> Like the employer, the alcoholic's doctor (if there is one) is in a good position to identify a drinking problem early. Doctors are notoriously slow to take advantage of this. Sometimes the patient has to show up drunk, jaundiced, with his liver down to his pelvis, before it occurs to the physician to ask whether he drinks. Why so unobserving? One reason is that doctors don't know much about alcoholism. The subject isn't brought up much in medical school. Doctors don't like to see alcoholics. They don't know what to do with them when they see them. . . . "Stay away from my door" is the message sent out by many doctors, and alcoholics get the message. (p. 121)

Editorials in the *Journal of the American Medical Association* (Bowen & Sammons, 1988; Delbanco, 1992) and elsewhere concur with Goodwin's claims. Bowen and Sammons (1988) referred to the alcohol-abusing patient as "a challenge to the profession" (p. 2267). Delbanco (1992) asked, "Where are their doctors?" (p. 702). Both editorials highlighted deficiencies in the substance abuse curricula of medical schools. Bowen and Sammons additionally pointed out that inadequate attention has been given to the educational needs of 500,000 physicians already in practice. In an article in *Science* entitled "The Neglected Disease in Medical Education," Holden (1985) described physicians as "notoriously deficient when it comes to early diagnosis and intervention with alcoholic patients. . . . And no wonder: they never learned much about the disease in medical school" (p. 742). And, in summarizing the empirical literature, Maly (1993) estimated that as many as 90% of addicted patients are undiagnosed by primary care physicians.

A physician's lack of training may be only one obstacle preventing him or her from addressing substance use problems. There is evidence suggesting that physicians' negative attitudes toward addicted patients also create substantial obstacles. It seems that physicians succumb to the same negative stereotypes of addicted patients as society at large (e.g., that such patients are "derelicts" or "skid row bums").

Denial and poor motivation are thought by some physicians to be chronic, inherent characteristics of patients with substance use disorders; however, this assumption is not empirically supported. Instead, these perceptions may be a function of poor doctor–patient relationships. Hanna (1991) found that patients who admitted to drinking problems were treated negatively by their doctors. In response, these patients were more likely to resist doctors' suggestions and report less satisfaction with treatment.

Even when their patients reveal overt signs and symptoms of alcohol problems, many physicians ignore the diagnosis, neglect to make appropriate referrals, or are pessimistic about potential behavioral change. Physicians may avoid addicted patients because of lack of training or role models, heavy time demands, the risk of making a socially stigmatized diagnosis, and the frustrations of managing a chronic illness (Delbanco, 1992). This avoidance is especially unfortunate, given that alcohol-dependent individuals who achieve long-term abstinence reduce their mortality rates to those of nondependent individuals (Bullock, Reed, & Grant, 1992). Similar reductions in morbidity and mortality rates have been found for people who abstain from smoking for extended periods of time (U.S. Department of Health and Human Services, 1990).

HEALTH PSYCHOLOGISTS AND THE TREATMENT OF SUBSTANCE USE PROBLEMS

Unfortunately psychologists, like physicians, generally have not become involved in the treatment of substance use problems. In fact, the American Psychological Association (APA) existed for more than 100 years before the creation of its Division on Addictions in 1993. Before the recent establishment of APA's College of Professional Psychology, there had been no mechanism for certifying psychologists to treat addictive behaviors. Furthermore, few doctoral training programs have provided even minimal training regarding substance use problems.

According to Matarazzo (1980), health psychology is primarily concerned with the "promotion and maintenance of health, the prevention and treatment of illness, and the identification of etiologic and diagnostic correlates" (p. 815). Given this definition, health psychologists should be ideally suited to provide services to individuals with substance use problems. Psychologists interested in addressing these problems will find abundant opportunities in primary care medical settings. Such opportunities may provide an important niche for health psychologists competing in an increasingly competitive market.

Liese and Chiauzzi (1995) listed six categories of activities for addressing substance use problems: (a) screening, (b) conceptualization, (c) assessing motivation to change, (d) intervention, (e) consultation and referral, and (f) follow-up and relapse prevention. It is strongly recommended that health psychologists get involved in the full range of substance use treatment activities.

Screening for Substance Use Problems

Substance use problems may be difficult to detect because of their insidious onset and associated social stigma. Screening is essential; substance use problems that are not detected are not likely to be treated. The best strategy for detecting substance use problems is to simply ask, "Have you ever had problems with drug or alcohol use?" followed by questions about recency, quantity, and frequency of substance use (Cyr & Wartman, 1988). Given the profound health consequences of substance use problems, it is imperative that *all* psychologists ask their patients about substance use.

Several standardized screening instruments also exist for the initial evaluation of persons with substance use disorders. The CAGE (Ewing, 1984) is among the most commonly cited screening instruments for alcohol problems. CAGE is an acronym for the following four questions:

1. Have you ever felt the need to Cut down on your drinking?
2. Have people ever Annoyed you by criticism of your drinking?
3. Have you ever felt Guilty about your drinking?
4. Have you ever taken a morning Eye-opener to steady your nerves or get rid of a hangover?

These four questions can be administered in less than a minute and consistently have established high sensitivity (80% range) and specificity

(85% range). Individuals who endorse two or more items are likely to have alcohol use problems.

The Michigan Alcoholism Screening Test (MAST; Selzer, 1971) is another important screening instrument. The MAST consists of 24 questions and has a demonstrated sensitivity of 90% and a specificity of 80% (Selzer, 1971). A shortened version of the MAST (SMAST; Selzer, Vinokur, & van Rooijen, 1975) consists of 13 items. The SMAST has a demonstrated sensitivity of 70% and a specificity of 80%. Regardless of the specific method used, psychologists are strongly encouraged to screen for substance use problems.

Conceptualizing Individuals With Substance Use Problems

The case conceptualization (Beck, Wright, Newman, & Liese, 1993) involves the process of gathering data to establish an accurate and comprehensive understanding of individuals with substance use problems. The case conceptualization should include background information, presenting problem and current functioning, psychiatric diagnoses, developmental profile (including family history of substance use problems), and cognitive–behavioral profile. The case conceptualization is essential for effective treatment planning (Liese, 1994; Liese & Beck, 1996; Liese & Franz, 1996).

The fourth edition of the *Diagnostic and Statistical Manual of Mental Disorders* (DSM–IV; American Psychiatric Association, 1994) provides well-validated diagnostic criteria for diagnosing and conceptualizing psychiatric and substance use problems. The DSM–IV distinguishes between substance abuse and dependence. *Abuse* is defined as a maladaptive pattern of use leading to significant impairment or distress (e.g., failure to fulfill responsibilities and legal, social, or interpersonal problems). *Dependence* is more severe than abuse, often involving tolerance, withdrawal, use of increasing amounts of a substance, and persistent desire for a substance despite significant substance-related problems. These two categories of the DSM–IV, however, may exclude certain individuals with mild or idiosyncratic substance use problems. In addition to these two categories, some authors (e.g., Bradley, 1994) have proposed that substance use problems be conceptualized on a continuum from *none* or *mild* to *severe*.

Numerous methods are available for assessing substance use problems. Most rely on self-report instruments or structured interviews; however, reports of significant others (i.e., *collaterals*) and biochemical tests may also be useful. Sobell, Toneatto, and Sobell (1994) provided an excellent review of the most practical, useful methods for assessing substance use disorders. They outlined six areas for assessment: (a) recent substance use, (b) antecedents and consequences of use, (c) substance use history, (d) psychiatric comorbidity or other life problems, (e) medical problems, and (f) barriers or potential barriers to change. Health psychologists are encouraged to become familiar with these assessment methods.

Assessing Motivation to Change

Despite well-known medical, legal, and psychological consequences, millions of people persist in their cigarette smoking, excessive alcohol consumption, and use of illicit drugs. Prochaska, DiClemente, and Norcross (1992) have made an enormous contribution to the field of addictions with their conceptual model for understanding the complex process of change (i.e., the stages-of-change model). In their model, Prochaska et al. distinguish among five levels of motivation: *precontemplation, contemplation, preparation, action,* and *maintenance.* Individuals who are least motivated to change are understood to be in the precontemplation stage. In the contemplation stage, individuals have begun to admit that they may have problems. Those in preparation have concluded that they have problems and plan to make changes to resolve these problems. In the action stage, individuals have recently begun to modify their undesired behaviors. And in the maintenance stage, individuals have successfully sustained changes for at least 6 months.

Individuals' motivation levels should largely influence the types of interventions selected for them. After determining motivation to change, the psychologist's challenge is to facilitate movement toward the next stage of change. For example, relatively unmotivated individuals (i.e., precontemplators) are likely to benefit most from nonjudgmental, empathic listening that focuses attention on problems associated with substance use. In contrast, individuals who have recently and willingly made changes might benefit from direct advice about how to maintain changes. The work of Miller and Rollnick (1991) has become extremely important as a model for applying the stages of change. Their text, *Motivational Interviewing,* serves as an excellent manual for psychologists assisting individuals at all stages of change.

Intervention

Treatment for substance use problems may be provided on an inpatient or outpatient basis, brief or long-term, individual or group, oriented toward insight or change, structured or unstructured, and focused on the individual or on the family. Theoretical approaches guiding treatment vary widely, and they include concepts and strategies from cognitive, behavioral, psychodynamic, medical, and spiritual models. Rotgers, Keller, and Morganstern (1996) recently edited a text that describes the theories and techniques of five intervention models: 12-step treatment (e.g., Alcoholics Anonymous), psychoanalytic therapy, family therapy, behavioral therapy, and motivational interviewing. Beck and his colleagues (Beck et al., 1993; Liese, 1994; Liese & Beck, 1996; Liese & Franz, 1996) have applied cognitive therapy to the treatment of addictive disorders.

Presently, there is not unequivocal evidence for the efficacy of any one substance use treatment approach over the others. Large-scale clinical trials, sponsored by the National Institute on Alcohol Abuse and Alcoholism and the National Institute on Drug Abuse, are under way to test the efficacy of the most promising approaches. Health psychologists are encouraged to critically evaluate the substance use treatment literature in order to become knowledgeable about the most effective strategies.

Consultation and Referral

Consultation and referral are extraordinarily important activities in managing individuals with substance use problems. Health psychologists addressing these problems may serve as consultants *to* other service providers, or they may request consultation *from* other service providers. For example, a health psychologist might conduct a psychological evaluation on a heavy drinker referred *by* a physician. That psychologist might also refer a patient with a substance use problem *to* the same physician for the medical management of depression.

In order for health psychologists to be effective in addressing substance use disorders, it is essential that they be familiar with treatment options available in the community. For example, the levels of care for substance use treatment can range from relatively brief outpatient treatment to extremely intensive inpatient treatment. The health psychologist wishing to refer a patient with a substance use problem needs to accurately understand these levels of care, as well as the types of clinicians that provide such care.

Support groups (e.g., Alcoholics Anonymous, Rational Recovery, Moderation Management, and S.M.A.R.T. Recovery) provide important services to individuals with substance use problems. These groups are readily available and free of charge. Some offer training in various interpersonal and intrapersonal skills, whereas others provide primarily social support. Again, it is essential for health psychologists to be knowledgeable about these services and to encourage patients with substance use problems to use them.

Follow-Up and Relapse Prevention

Relapse is extremely common in persons recovering from substance use problems (Marlatt & Gordon, 1985). After treatment has been initiated and change has occurred, it is important for health psychologists to follow up and offer relapse-prevention services.

Marlatt and Gordon (1985), in their classic text, provide a comprehensive review of the relapse process. Relapse prevention efforts generally focus on eight major areas: (a) identification of high-risk situations, (b) understanding relapse as a process rather than as an event, (c) development of a supportive network, (d) coping with craving and pressures to use substances, (e) maintaining emotional balance, (f) clarifying maladaptive thinking that may trigger usage, (g) altering or eliminating environmental cues for substance use, and (h) coping with stressful life events.

• SUMMARY AND RECOMMENDATIONS

Millions of Americans use psychoactive substances in ways that cause them substantial harm. Unfortunately, only a small proportion of these individuals receive formal help for their substance use problems. In this chapter, we have described the scope of substance use, and we have argued that health psychologists should be addressing substance use problems, because these problems have profound implications for health. The following are five specific recommendations for health psychologists:

1. Learn as much as possible about the medical and psychological aspects of substance use and keep current with the ever-evolving addiction literature.
2. Learn about the full spectrum of treatments for substance use problems. Become familiar with popular modalities (e.g., 12-step programs) as well as psychologically based treatments (e.g., cognitive–behavioral models).
3. Identify and address substance use problems in "traditional" psychotherapeutic settings (e.g., private practice). At the very least, reliably ask all new patients about their substance use attitudes and behaviors.
4. Market psychological services to primary care physicians who see a large volume of patients with substance use problems. Learn about their needs vis-à-vis the psychological care of their addicted patients. Collaborate with primary care physicians by providing consultation services to their patients. Use primary care physicians as consultants.

5. Participate in professional activities related to substance use problems. Join the APA's Division (50) on Addictions. Attend continuing education programs on substance use sponsored by the APA and other professional organizations. Consider proficiency certification in treating substance use disorders by the recently formed APA College of Professional Psychology.

In 1980, Matarazzo declared that "health psychology and behavioral health appear to be ideas whose time has come" (p. 816). Today it seems that the marriage between health psychology and substance use treatment is an idea whose time has come.

REFERENCES

American Psychiatric Association. (1994). *Diagnostic and statistical manual of mental disorders* (4th ed.). Washington, DC: Author.

Barker, L. R., & Whitfield, C. L. (1991). Alcoholism. In L. R. Barker, J. R. Burton, & P. D. Zieve (Eds.), *Principles of ambulatory medicine* (3rd ed., pp. 245–277). Baltimore: Williams & Wilkins.

Beck, A. T., Wright, F. D., Newman, C. F., & Liese, B. S. (1993). *Cognitive therapy of substance abuse*. New York: Guilford Press.

Bien, T. H., Miller, W. R., & Tonigan, J. S. (1993). Brief interventions for alcohol problems: A review. *Addiction, 88,* 315–336.

Bowen, O. R., & Sammons, J. H. (1988). The alcohol-abusing patient: A challenge to the profession. *Journal of the American Medical Association, 260,* 2267–2270.

Bradley, K. A. (1994). The primary care practitioner's role in the prevention and management of alcohol problems. *Alcohol Health and Research World, 18,* 97–104.

Bullock, K. D., Reed, R. J., & Grant, I. (1992). Reduced mortality risk in alcoholics who achieve long-term abstinence. *Journal of the American Medical Association, 267,* 668–672.

Byrd, J. C. (1992). Environmental tobacco smoke: Medical and legal issues. *Medical Clinics of North America, 76,* 377–378.

Chappel, J. N. (1992). Attitudes toward the treatment of substance abusers. In J. G. Lowinson, P. Ruiz, R. B. Millman, & J. G. Langrod (Eds.), *Substance abuse: A comprehensive textbook* (pp. 983–996). Baltimore: Williams & Wilkins.

Cyr, M. G., & Wartman, S. A. (1988). The effectiveness of routine screening questions in the detection of alcoholism. *Journal of the American Medical Association, 259,* 51–54.

Delbanco, T. L. (1992). Patients who drink too much: Where are their doctors? *Journal of the American Medical Association, 267,* 702–703.

D'Lugoff, B., & Hawthorne, J. (1991). Use and abuse of illicit drugs and substance abuse. In L. R. Barker, J. R. Burton, & P. D. Zieve (Eds.), *Principles of ambulatory medicine* (3rd ed., pp. 278–290). Baltimore: Williams & Wilkins.

Ewing, J. A. (1984). Detecting alcoholism: The CAGE questionnaire. *Journal of the American Medical Association, 252,* 1905–1907.

Friedman, H. S. (1990). Alcohol and hypertension. *Alcohol Health and Research World, 14,* 313–319.

Goodwin, D. W. (1981). *Alcoholism: The facts.* New York: Oxford University Press.

Group for the Advancement of Psychiatry. (1991). Substance abuse disorder: A psychiatric priority. *American Journal of Psychiatry, 148,* 1291–1300.

Hanna, E. Z. (1991). Attitudes toward problem drinkers, revisited: Patient–therapist factors contributing to the differential treatment of patients with alcohol problems. *Alcoholism: Clinical and Experimental Research, 15,* 927–931.

Holbrook, J. H. (1991). Tobacco. In J. D. Wilson, E. Baunwald, K. J. Isselbacher, R. A. Petersdorf, A. S. Fauci, & K. R. Root (Eds.), *Harrison's principles of internal medicine* (12th ed., pp. 2158–2161). New York: McGraw-Hill.

Holden, C. (1985). The neglected disease in medical education. *Science, 229,* 741–742.

Liese, B. S. (1994). Brief therapy, crisis intervention and the cognitive therapy of substance abuse. *Crisis Intervention, 1,* 11–29.

Liese, B. S., & Beck, A. T. (1996). Back to basics: Fundamental cognitive therapy skills for keeping drug-dependent individuals in treatment. In J. J. Boren, L. S. Onken, & J. D. Blaine (Eds.), *Beyond the therapeutic alliance: Keeping drug dependent individuals in treatment* (National Institute on Drug Abuse Research Monograph, pp. 210–235). Rockville, MD: National Institute on Drug Abuse.

Liese, B. S., & Chiauzzi, E. (1995). Alcohol and drug abuse. *Home study self-assessment program* (Monograph No. 189). Kansas City, MO: American Academy of Family Physicians.

Liese, B. S., & Franz, R. A. (1996). Treating substance use disorders with cognitive therapy: Lessons learned and implication for the future. In P. M. Salkovskis (Ed.), *Frontiers of cognitive therapy* (pp. 470–508). New York: Guilford Press.

Maly, R. C. (1993). Early recognition of chemical dependence. *Primary Care, 20,* 33–50.

Marlatt, G. A., & Gordon, J. R. (Eds.). (1985). *Relapse prevention: Maintenance strategies in the treatment of addictive behavior.* New York: Guilford Press.

Matarazzo, J. D. (1980). Behavioral health and behavioral medicine: Frontiers for a new health psychology. *American Psychologist, 35,* 807–817.

McBride, P. E. (1992). The health consequences of smoking: Cardiovascular diseases. *Medical Clinics of North America, 76,* 333–353.

McKenzie, R. G., & Kipke, M. D. (1992). Substance use and abuse. In S. B. Friedman, M. Fisher, & S. K. Schonberg (Eds.), *Comprehensive adolescent health care* (pp. 765–786). St. Louis, MO: Quality Medical Publications.

Mendelson, J. H. (1991). Commonly abused drugs. In J. D. Wilson, E. Baunwald, K. J. Isselbacher, R. A. Petersdorf, A. S. Fauci, & K. R. Root (Eds.), *Harrison's principles of internal medicine* (12th ed., pp. 2155–2158). New York: McGraw-Hill.

Miller, W. R., & Rollnick, S. (1991). *Motivational interviewing: Preparing people to change addictive behavior.* New York: Guilford Press.

Newcomb, P. A., & Carbone, P. P. (1992). The health consequences of smoking: Cancer. *Medical Clinics of North America, 76,* 305–331.

Prochaska, J. O., DiClemente, C. C., & Norcross, J. C. (1992). In search of how people change: Applications to addictive behaviors. *American Psychologist, 47,* 1102–1114.

Pursch, J. A. (1978). Physicians' attitudinal changes in alcoholism. *Alcoholism: Clinical and Experimental Research, 2,* 358–361.

Regier, D. A., Farmer, M. E., Rae, D. S., Locke, B. Z., Keith, S. J., Judd, L. L., & Goodwin, F. K. (1990). Comorbidity of mental disorders with alcohol and other drug abuse: Results of the Epidemiologic Catchment Area (ECA) study. *Journal of the American Medical Association, 264,* 2511–2518.

Regier, D. A., Narrow, W. E., Rae, D. S., Manderscheid, R. W., Locke, B. Z., & Goodwin, F. K. (1993). The de facto US mental and addictive disorders service system: Epidemiologic Catchment Area prospective 1-year prevalence rates of disorders and services. *Archives of General Psychiatry, 50,* 85–94.

Ross, H. E., Glaser, F. B., & Germanson, T. (1988). The prevalence of psychiatric disorders in patients with alcohol and other drug problems. *Archives of General Psychiatry, 45,* 1023–1031.

Rotgers, F., Keller, D. S., & Morganstern, J. (Eds.). (1996). *Treating substance abuse.* New York: Guilford Press.

Rounsaville, B. J., Weissman, M. M., Kleber, H., & Wilber, C. (1982). Heterogeneity of psychiatric diagnosis in treated opiate addicts. *Archives of General Psychiatry, 39,* 161–166.

Schuckit, M. A. (1991). Alcohol and alcoholism. In J. D. Wilson, E. Baunwald, K. J. Isselbacher, R. A. Petersdorf, A. S. Fauci, & K. R. Root (Eds.), *Harrison's principles of internal medicine* (12th ed., pp. 2146–2151). New York: McGraw-Hill.

Schulz, J. E. (1993). Illicit drugs of abuse. *Primary Care: Clinics in Office Practice, 20,* 221–230.

Schwartz, J. L. (1992). Methods of smoking cessation. *Medical Clinics of North America, 76,* 451–476.

Selzer, M. L. (1971). The Michigan Alcoholism Screening Test: The quest for a new diagnostic instrument. *American Journal of Psychiatry, 127,* 1653–1658.

Selzer, M. L., Vinokur, A., & van Rooijen, L. (1975). A self-administered Short Michigan Alcoholism Screening Test (SMAST). *Journal of Studies on Alcohol, 36*, 117–126.

Sherman, C. B. (1992). The health consequences of smoking: Pulmonary diseases. *Medical Clinics of North America, 76*, 355–375.

Sobell, L. C., Toneatto, T., & Sobell, M. B. (1994). Behavioral assessment and treatment planning for alcohol, tobacco, and other drug problems: Current status with an emphasis on clinical applications. *Behavior Therapy, 25*, 533–580.

Substance Abuse and Mental Health Services Administration. (1993). *National household survey on drug abuse: Main findings 1991* (DHHS Publication No. SMA 93-1980). Washington, DC: Government Printing Office.

U.S. Department of Health and Human Services. (1990). *The health benefits of smoking cessation* (DHHS Publication No. CDC 90-8416). Washington, DC: Government Printing Office.

14

ATTENTION DEFICIT HYPERACTIVITY DISORDER AND LEARNING DISABILITIES IN THE PEDIATRICIAN'S OFFICE

JAN L. CULBERTSON

Attention deficit hyperactivity disorder (ADHD) and learning disabilities are two of the most common neurodevelopmental disorders of childhood, and children with these disorders present frequently to the pediatrician for diagnosis and treatment. It is common for specialists in developmental and behavioral pediatrics or child neurology to indicate that referrals for ADHD now total 50% to 75% of their practices (B. A. Shaywitz & Shaywitz, 1991). Physician involvement in the management of more chronic handicapping conditions, such as learning disabilities, has also increased dramatically in conjunction with the decrease in acute, life-threatening illnesses among the pediatric population (S. E. Shaywitz, Shaywitz, Fletcher, & Escobar, 1990).

Not only the specialists, however, are involved in management of ADHD and learning disabilities. Both the growing movement toward managed care and the increased focus on primary care are leading primary care pediatricians to attempt to diagnose and treat ADHD and learning disabilities in their offices rather than refer to specialists. With capitation, there is often a financial disincentive to refer to specialists, such as psychologists, who can provide a more comprehensive and appropriate level of care for ADHD and learning disabilities. The disincentive for referral sets the stage for possible misdiagnosis, failure to diagnose, or inappropriate management, due to the pediatrician's often cursory training with regard to ADHD and learning disabilities. At this time in our history, more than ever before, there is a need to explore ways in which pediatricians and psychologists can work together to provide optimal care for children with these two common childhood disorders.

A pediatrician's office often is the point of entry to the health care system for parents who have questions about their children's behavioral and learning problems as well as their medical problems. There are many possible reasons why questions about ADHD and learning disabilities are so often presented to a medical doctor rather than a psychologist. For instance, the pediatrician is one of the first professionals with whom parents develop a relationship, and this relationship may extend over many years as the pediatrician follows a child's growth and development. The physician–parent relationship often results in a high level of trust that leads parents to bring even nonmedical concerns about their child to the office visit. Second, parents have greater access to pediatricians than to psychologists and, therefore, become accustomed to bringing their concerns to physicians before seeking out other professionals. Pediatricians often are seen as the professionals who coordinate referrals to other professionals when needed. Finally, there may be less stigma associated with having a medical problem than a mental or behavioral problem, leading parents to try to "medicalize" their child's behavioral and learning problems. The implication is that if the child's problem is medical, it may not reflect as negatively on the parents' genetic endowment or their parenting practices.

For these reasons, psychologists are, to a large degree, dependent on pediatricians to screen for ADHD and learning disabilities and to make referrals. This chapter explores the scope of the problem, as to prevalence of ADHD and learning disabilities, review of diagnostic and management approaches that represent the current state of our knowledge about best practice methods, and a discussion that contrasts and compares the roles of pediatricians and psychologists in the diagnosis and treatment of both disorders. Suggestions are made for collaboration between psychologists and pediatricians, with a focus on contributing their respective knowledge and skills to achieve optimal care for children with ADHD and or learning disabilities.

PREVALENCE OF ADHD AND LEARNING DISABILITIES

Both ADHD and learning disabilities are disorders that occur commonly in the general population. Prevalence estimates for ADHD among school-age children range from 3% to 5% (Barkley, 1990), and estimates for learning disabilities range from 4% to 6% (Chalfant, 1989; Hynd & Cohen, 1983). Both disorders are being diagnosed with increasing frequency as public awareness increases and as public agencies (such as schools) provide both recognition and appropriate educational services for these disorders. The number of students identified as having a learning disability tripled between 1976 and 1982 (Reynolds, 1990), and students with learning disabilities now constitute about 50% of the children who are served in special education programs in public schools (U.S. Department of Education, 1991). Attention deficit hyperactivity disorder also is being diagnosed more frequently than a decade ago (Safer & Krager, 1994; B. A. Shaywitz & Shaywitz, 1991), and the concomitant use of psychostimulant medication as the treatment of choice for this disorder is on the rise. A recent survey of Baltimore County, Maryland, schools revealed a dramatic increase in stimulant medication use among public school students, from 1.07% in 1971 to 3.58% in 1993 (Safer & Krager, 1994), with the greatest increase being at the secondary level.

Given the prevalence rates of ADHD and learning disabilities, these disorders quite likely make up a significant percentage of the referrals to pediatricians. This underscores the need to improve pediatricians' awareness of appropriate diagnostic and treatment approaches for these disorders and to highlight the role that psychologists can play in managing patients with ADHD or learning disabilities.

DIAGNOSIS AND MANAGEMENT OF ADHD

Recently published *Diagnostic and Statistical Manual of Mental Disorders* (*DSM–IV*; American Psychiatric Association, 1994) nosology for ADHD recognizes the empirical support for three primary subtypes: predominantly inattentive type, predominantly hyperactive–impulsive type, and combined type. The essential feature of ADHD is a "persistent pattern of inattention and/or hyperactivity–impulsivity that is more frequent and severe than is typically observed in individuals at a comparable level of development" (American Psychiatric Association, 1994, p. 78). Children with ADHD have been characterized as having deficient rule-governed behavior, behavioral disinhibition, and variability in task performance, in addition to the primary symptoms of inattention and excessive motor activity (Barkley, 1990).

The diagnosis of ADHD is made primarily by history and observation rather than by diagnostic tests. This has led many pediatricians to view ADHD as a diagnosis that can be made in a brief office visit merely by questioning the mother and observing the child. In fact, only the most severely hyperactive and impulsive children with ADHD are likely to squirm and fidget in the doctor's presence, perhaps due to illness or fear of a painful medical procedure if they "misbehave." Many children can suppress their overactive and impulsive behavior for a brief period of time or in settings where adults are closely watching their behavior. The constraints inherent in a physician's office visit raise the risk of the pediatrician misdiagnosing or failing to diagnose ADHD when it is present.

Diagnosis of ADHD is made even more complex and time-consuming by developmental influences that can affect the symptom picture and by the possible co-occurrence of other disorders that present in a fashion similar to ADHD. The professional must understand these developmental processes and must conduct an assessment that is detailed enough to rule in or rule out comorbid disorders, to develop an effective treatment plan. Failure to do so results in increased risk for misdiagnosis or underdiagnosis of ADHD. Several factors that complicate the diagnostic picture are discussed in the following sections.

Developmental Influences on Symptom Presentation

The presence of developmental factors can lead to misdiagnosis if care is not taken to obtain a detailed clinical history and chronology of symptom presentation. For instance, about 40% of children up to 4 years of age are considered to have significant symptoms of hyperactivity and inattention for brief periods (3 to 6 months), but few go on to have ADHD (Palfrey, Levine, Walker, & Sullivan, 1985). Young children whose symptoms persist for 12 months or longer are at greater risk to have ADHD than those whose symptoms are of briefer duration (Campbell, 1990; Campbell & Ewing, 1990). To distinguish normal developmental patterns from clinically significant symptoms of ADHD, professionals must consider both the duration and severity of symptoms to obtain an accurate diagnosis. Similar arguments can be made for developmental influences during adolescent years, when milder presentations of symptoms may still interfere significantly with functioning. Adolescents may no longer display the "motor-driven" quality that identifies their younger cohorts with ADHD, but a careful interview may reveal that adolescents continue to experience a subjective feeling of restlessness and significant problems with attentional focus (Brown & Borden, 1986). Both the age and developmental stage of the child must be considered, to make an accurate diagnosis.

Comorbid Disorders That Masquerade as ADHD or Complicate the Presenting Picture

ADHD has been subtyped not only according to the dimensions of inattention, hyperactivity, and impulsivity but also according to the presence or absence of learning and behavioral problems that are often comorbid with ADHD. For instance, the comorbidity between ADHD and learning disabilities has been estimated to range from 15% to 38%, depending on the stringency of diagnostic criteria used to define the learning disability (Semrud-Clikeman et al., 1992). Various researchers have reported that 50% to 65% of clinic-referred children with ADHD also meet diagnostic criteria for oppositional–defiant disorder (Barkley, DuPaul, & McMurray, 1990; Barkley, Fischer, Edelbrock, & Smallish, 1990; Loney & Milich, 1982). Herein lies one of the problems with diagnosis of ADHD in the pediatrician's office. A brief office visit and a screening approach to diagnosis are not conducive to making fine differential diagnoses among the various disorders that may be comorbid with ADHD.

Need for a Broad-Based Assessment

Accurate diagnosis is facilitated by use of multiple assessment methods, gathering information from multiple informants, and demonstrating that symptoms are present across multiple settings, as suggested by Shelton and Barkley (1993). The multimethod component refers to the range of assessment approaches needed to provide the best overview of the child's functioning:

1. Direct observation of the child (e.g., in the classroom, on the playground, on the bus, at home, and during structured and unstructured activities). Direct observations in the clinic setting can be done by using one of the observational paradigms devised for children suspected of having ADHD, such as the Restricted Academic Situation Observation (Barkley, 1990) or the Child Behavior Checklist—Direct Observation Form (Achenbach, 1986).

2. Use of age-normed behavioral checklists, completed by at least two or three informants, such as the parent, teacher, child self-report, or day care teacher. These checklists provide a yardstick for determining if the child's symptom severity is excessive for his or her age or developmental level. If the child's mental functioning is below an IQ of 85, mental age comparisons rather than chronological age comparisons should be used. Use of a clinical cutoff at the

97th percentile (2 standard deviations above the mean) on normed behavioral rating scales will identify children whose symptoms are more deviant from the norm, are likely to persist for several years, and will be more predictive of later adjustment (DuPaul, 1990).

3. Review of primary symptoms of ADHD to determine not only their presence but also their severity. Use of a structured-interview format based on *DSM–IV* diagnostic criteria will be useful.

4. Detailed clinical interview to obtain history and to screen for symptoms of comorbid disorders (e.g., learning disability, oppositional–defiant disorder, conduct disorder, internalizing disorders).

5. Laboratory measures of vigilance and impulsivity, to refine the observations of the primary symptoms of ADHD. Measures such as the continuous performance test paradigm from the Gordon Diagnostic System (Gordon & Mettelman, 1988) or the Conners' Continuous Performance Test computer program (Conners, 1994) might be used. The continuous performance test laboratory measures have been shown empirically to discriminate between children with and without ADHD (Barkley, DuPaul, & McMurray, 1990).

The assessment components just discussed would constitute a basic evaluation for ADHD. If comorbid disorders, such as learning disabilities, were suspected, a more detailed psychoeducational evaluation might be necessary, including intellectual, academic achievement, and perceptual processing measures. Likewise, if oppositional–defiant disorder is suspected, further assessment of the nature and severity of the behavioral disturbance must be done. A psychologist also might opt to provide a brief therapeutic intervention, such as parent–child interaction therapy (Eyberg & Boggs, 1989), to address relational and behavior management issues while observing changes in the ADHD symptoms as a function of treatment of the oppositional behavior problems. Symptoms of an oppositional disorder may include agitation and overactivity that are misconstrued as ADHD; if this is the case, these symptoms often diminish or disappear during and after a treatment program designed to address the behavior disorder, especially in preschool children.

Thus, the multimethod, multi-informant, multisetting assessment will provide the basis for a more accurate diagnosis than assessments based on more narrow parameters, as are often used by pediatricians. However, the pediatrician contributes important medical information as part of the diagnostic workup and management of children with suspected ADHD, as described in the next section.

Medical Consultation With ADHD

Pediatricians provide helpful medical information through reviewing a child's genetic background, pre- and perinatal events, and developmental and medical history, as well as the child's current health, nutritional status, and sensorimotor development (Barkley, 1990). The pediatric exam can rule out medical conditions that present with symptoms similar to ADHD, such as thyroid dysfunction (Weiss, Stein, Trommer, & Refetoff, 1993) and adrenal overactivity. Likewise, the medical examination will assess for associated soft neurological signs, motor incoordination (Barkley, DuPaul, & McMurray 1990; McMahon & Greenberg, 1977; S. E. Shaywitz & Shaywitz, 1988; Szatmari, Offord, & Boyle, 1989b), enuresis or encopresis (Stewart, Pitts, Craig, & Dieruf, 1966), sleep problems (Kaplan, McNichol, Conte, & Moghadam, 1987; Stewart et al., 1966; Trommer, Hoeppner, Rosenberg, Armstrong, & Rothstein, 1988), otitis media (Mitchell, Aman, Turbott, & Manku, 1987), and asthma and allergies (Hartsough & Lambert, 1985; Szatmari, Offord, & Boyle, 1989a), all of which have been reported to occur at a higher rate in children with ADHD. The physician also will obtain a thorough individual and family medical history, to determine the presence of tics or Tourette's syndrome, seizure disorder, and other medical problems that might contraindicate the use of psychostimulant medications. Finally, if a trial of stimulant medication is appropriate, the pediatrician plays an important role in monitoring the dosage level and effectiveness of the medication while remaining alert for side effects (such as appetite suppression, weight loss, or liver dysfunction) that might be harmful. Laboratory studies, such as blood work, urinalysis, chromosome studies, electroencephalograms, evoked potential studies, magnetic resonance imaging, or computerized axial tomograms, are not used routinely in the evaluation of children with ADHD but are used only if the physical exam or medical history suggest that these diagnostic studies are necessary to determine the presence of a treatable medical problem (Barkley, 1990).

DIAGNOSIS AND MANAGEMENT OF LEARNING DISABILITIES

In contrast to the diagnosis of ADHD, which depends largely on history and observations, the diagnosis of learning disability is established on the basis of performance on tests of ability and achievement. This diagnostic process requires specialized knowledge about cognitive, linguistic, and perceptual processing abilities. Learning disabilities have been conceptualized as an inability to learn in children who otherwise have normal or above normal intellectual ability (B. A. Shaywitz & Shaywitz, 1991). The definition of learning disabilities in the Education for All Handicapped Act of 1975 remains the most widely accepted. According to this law, diagnosis of learning disabilities is based on whether a child does not achieve commensurate with his or her own age and ability when provided with appropriate educational experiences and whether the child has a severe discrepancy between achievement and intellectual ability in one of seven areas, including listening, thinking, speaking, reading, writing, spelling, or doing mathematical calculations. Most state guidelines for implementing this law require that the professional demonstrate a child's failure to achieve; demonstrate the presence of psychological processing disorders that are presumed to underlie academic learning; rule out several exclusionary criteria (i.e., mental retardation; educational, economic, or cultural disadvantage; or emotional disturbance); and demonstrate a severe discrepancy between achievement and intellectual ability in one of the seven areas listed earlier (Chalfant, 1984). Although there is much controversy about the definition and diagnostic criteria for learning disabilities, it is basically a psychoeducational rather than a medical diagnosis.

Present-day conceptualization of learning disabilities suggests that it is a heterogeneous set of disorders with different subtypes, based on either the underlying processing deficits (e.g., linguistic, neurocognitive, or visuospatial reasoning deficits) or the clinical presentation of symptoms (e.g., reading, mathematics, written language, or social emotional deficits). To date, over 100 different subtyping classification models have been published based on achievement, neurocognitive, or neurolinguistic variables (Hooper & Willis, 1989). Assessment of children suspected of having a learning disability must include measures that carefully examine the pattern of strengths and deficits in information processing, to determine the subtype of that child's learning deficits. A clear delineation of the learning disability subtype provides a foundation for development of an appropriate educational plan and curriculum for each child.

From the foregoing discussion, it is clear that diagnosis of a learning disability requires detailed evaluation of a child's intellectual, academic, linguistic, perceptual processing, and perceptual–motor abilities to determine whether there is a learning disability, what processes underlie the learning disability, and how to intervene. It is not sufficient merely to establish an IQ–achievement discrepancy; rather, the psychologist must also examine a range of information-processing abilities to determine a profile of the child's strengths and weaknesses. Although pediatricians are an important member of the multidisciplinary team of professionals needed to assess for a learning disability, their assessment methods are not sufficient for making a diagnosis or providing the information necessary to develop an appropriate educational intervention plan.

Pediatricians play an important role in ruling out basic sensory acuity deficits before psychoeducational evaluation and assessing the integrity of the child's motor system. Pediatricians also provide important etiological information about children who have a learning disability, through review of pre- and perinatal risk factors and other medical factors that can have an impact on learning and development. The pediatrician who is aware of the definition and primary symptoms of learning disabilities can facilitate a referral for evaluation and can act as an advocate for the child and family with the school system. The pediatrician provides unique and important information to the diagnostic process, but the primary contributor to this process is the psychologist.

PSYCHOLOGISTS' ROLE IN COLLABORATING WITH PEDIATRICIANS ABOUT ADHD AND LEARNING DISABILITIES

Psychologists who develop a collaborative relationship with pediatricians may offer several types of training or provide information that can facilitate the management of children with ADHD or learning disabilities:

1. Provide a workshop or brief training sessions about normal child development and developmental influences on the symptom presentation of ADHD and learning disabilities.
2. Provide training about the primary symptoms of ADHD and learning disabilities, contrasted with common comorbid disorders. The primary symptoms may be condensed into a brief checklist or questionnaire that can be used readily in the office.
3. Offer training on use of appropriate screening measures for ADHD and learning disabilities and suggest decision rules about when it is appropriate to refer for further evaluation based on the screening results. For instance, screening measures such as the Conners parent and teacher questionnaires (Conners, 1989) are useful for ADHD, and an academic-screening test such as the Wide Range Achievement Test—3 (Wilkinson, 1993) is useful for screening academic progress in reading decoding, mathematics calculation, and spelling. Training may be provided to the pediatrician or to other professionals in the pediatric office (e.g., nurse practitioners) in the use of these measures or symptom checklists. Psychologists should include information about how to order appropriate screening tests for office practice.

4. Provide a roadmap for how to obtain essential information through the school system. For instance, inform the pediatrician about who should be contacted to determine if a child already has had psychometric assessment in the school system or if the child is currently receiving special education services. If the child is receiving special education, explain how the pediatrician can obtain a copy of the child's psychoeducational test results and the individualized educational plan records that detail the special education category and placement decisions regarding the child.

5. Provide suggestions for when it is appropriate to refer a child for further assessment and which professionals would be most helpful to answer specific referral questions (e.g., a speech/language pathologist may provide important information regarding the impact of language deficits on the child's learning disability).

6. Psychologists also can play an active role in forming alliances with pediatricians in the community for informal information sharing, cross-referral, and assistance in management (particularly with learning disabilities and ADHD). For instance, children with ADHD often respond better to a dual intervention that combines psychostimulant medication and behavioral treatment (e.g., parent-training programs or individual or group counseling for the child). The dual intervention approach is best carried out with collaboration between the pediatrician and psychologist.

7. Provide training about the rights and privileges afforded children and parents under the current special education and disability laws, such as the Individuals With Disabilities Education Act of 1990 or the Americans With Disabilities Act of 1990. Encourage the pediatrician to be an advocate for the child and family through providing information about rights to a free and appropriate education and the availability of potential diagnostic and treatment resources.

In addition to these factors, it is helpful for psychologists to remain aware of the contributions that pediatricians make in terms of their knowledge about medical aspects of learning disabilities and ADHD, their longitudinal knowledge about the child and family, and their probable rapport with the child and family. As mentioned earlier, parents often perceive less of a stigma in seeing a medical doctor compared with a psychologist. The pediatrician can be helpful in defusing that stigma associated with a possible mental or behavioral problem and facilitate the family in following through on the referral.

In conclusion, the trend toward greater involvement of primary care pediatricians in managing disorders such as learning disabilities and ADHD in the primary health care arena is of concern due to the increased risk for misdiagnosis or failure to diagnose these complex disorders. However, psychologists can and must make efforts to build the alliances that make such a trend workable and, most of all, provide the most optimal level of care for children and their families.

REFERENCES

Achenbach, T. M. (1986). *Manual for the Child Behavior Checklist—Direct Observation Form*. Burlington: University of Vermont, Department of Psychiatry.

American Psychiatric Association. (1994). *Diagnostic and statistical manual of mental disorders* (4th ed.). Washington, DC: Author.

Americans With Disabilities Act of 1990, 42 U.S.C.A. §12101 *et seq.* (West, 1993).

Barkley, R. A. (1990). *Attention deficit hyperactivity disorder*. New York: Guilford Press.

Barkley, R. A., DuPaul, G. J., & McMurray, M. B. (1990). Comprehensive evaluation of attention deficit disorder with or without hyperactivity as defined by research criteria. *Journal of Consulting and Clinical Psychology, 58,* 775–789.

Barkley, R. A., Fischer, M., Edelbrock, C. S., & Smallish, L. (1990). The adolescent outcome of hyperactive children diagnosed by research criteria: I. An 8 year follow-up study. *Journal of the American Academy of Child and Adolescent Psychiatry, 29,* 546–557.

Brown, R. T., & Borden, K. A. (1986). Hyperactivity at adolescence: Some misconceptions and new directions. *Journal of Clinical Child Psychology, 15,* 194–209.

Campbell, S. B. (1990). *Behavior problems in preschoolers: Clinical and developmental issues*. New York: Guilford Press.

Campbell, S. B., & Ewing, L. J. (1990). Follow-up of hard-to-manage preschoolers: Adjustment at age 9 years and predictors of continuing symptoms. *Journal of Child Psychology and Psychiatry and Allied Disciplines, 36,* 870–889.

Chalfant, J. C. (1984). *Identifying learning disabled students: Guidelines for decision-making*. Burlington, VT: Northeast Regional Resource Center.

Chalfant, J. C. (1989). Learning disabilities: Policy issues and promising approaches. *American Psychologist, 44,* 392–398.

Conners, C. K. (1989). *Manual for Conners' Rating Scales (Conners' Teacher Rating Scales, Conners' Parent Rating Scales)*. North Tonawanda, NY: Multi-Health Systems.

Conners, C. K. (1994). *Conners' Continuous Performance Test computer program*. North Tonawanda, NY: Multi-Health Systems.

DuPaul, G. J. (1990). *The ADHD Rating Scale: Normative data, reliability, and validity.* Unpublished manuscript, University of Massachusetts Medical Center, Worcester.

Education for All Handicapped Children Act of 1975, Pub. L. No. 94-142. 89 Stat. 773. (1975).

Eyberg, S. M., & Boggs, S. R. (1989). Parent training for oppositional–defiant preschoolers. In C. E. Schaefer & J. M. Briesmeister (Eds.), *Handbook of parent training: Parents as cotherapists for children with behavior problems* (pp. 105–132). New York: Wiley.

Gordon, M., & Mettelman, B. B. (1988). The assessment of attention: I. Standardization and reliability of a behavior-based measure. *Journal of Clinical Psychology, 44,* 682–690.

Hartsough, C. S., & Lambert, N. M. (1985). Medical factors in hyperactive and normal children: Prenatal, developmental, and health history findings. *American Journal of Orthopsychiatry, 55,* 190–210.

Hooper, S. R., & Willis, W. G. (1989). *Learning disability subtyping: Neuropsychological foundations, conceptual models, and issues in clinical differentiation.* New York: Springer-Verlag.

Hynd, G. W., & Cohen, M. (1983). *Dyslexia: Neuropsychological theory, research, and clinical practice.* New York: Grune & Stratton.

Individuals With Disabilities Education Act of 1990, Pub. L. No. 101-476. 104 Stat. 1142. (1990).

Kaplan, B. J., McNichol, J., Conte, R. A., & Moghadam, H. K. (1987). Sleep disturbance in preschool age hyperactive and nonhyperactive children. *Pediatrics, 80,* 839–844.

Loney, J., & Milich, R. (1982). Hyperactivity, inattention, and aggression in clinical practice. In D. Routh & P. Wolraich (Eds.), *Advances in developmental and behavioral pediatrics* (Vol. 3, pp. 113–147). Greenwich, CT: JAI Press.

McMahon, S. A., & Greenberg, L. M. (1977). Serial neurologic examination of hyperactive children. *Pediatrics, 59,* 584–587.

Mitchell, E. A., Aman, M. G., Turbott, S. H., & Manku, M. (1987). Clinical characteristics and serum essential fatty acid levels in hyperactive children. *Clinical Pediatrics, 26,* 406–411.

Palfrey, J. S., Levine, M. D., Walker, D. K, & Sullivan, M. (1985). The emergence of attention deficits in early childhood: A prospective study. *Developmental and Behavioral Pediatrics, 6,* 339–348.

Reynolds, C. R. (1990). Conceptual and technical problems in learning disability diagnosis. In C. R. Reynolds & R. W. Kamphaus (Eds.), *Handbook of psychological and educational assessment of children* (pp. 571–592). New York: Guilford Press.

Safer, D. J., & Krager, J. M. (1994). The increased rate of stimulant treatment for hyperactive/inattentive students in secondary schools. *Pediatrics, 94,* 462–464.

Semrud-Clikeman, M., Biederman, J., Sprich-Buckminster, S., Lehman, B. K., Faraone, S. V., & Norman, D. (1992). Comorbidity between ADDH and learning disability: A review and report in a clinically referred sample. *Journal of the American Academy of Child and Adolescent Psychiatry, 31*, 439–448.

Shaywitz, B. A., & Shaywitz, S. E. (1991). Comorbidity: A critical issue in attention deficit disorder. *Journal of Child Neurology, 6*(Suppl. #1), S13–S22.

Shaywitz, S. E., & Shaywitz, B. A. (1988). Attention deficit disorder: Current perspectives. In J. F. Kavanaugh & T. J. Truss, Jr. (Eds.), *Learning disabilities: Proceedings of the national conference* (pp. 369–523). Parkton, MD: York Press.

Shaywitz, S. E., Shaywitz, B. A., Fletcher, J. M., & Escobar, M. D. (1990). *Journal of the American Medical Association, 264*, 998–1002.

Shelton, T. L., & Barkley, R. A. (1993). Assessment of attention deficit hyperactivity disorder in young children. In J. L. Culbertson & D. J. Willis (Eds.), *Testing young children: A reference guide for developmental, psychoeducational, and psychosocial assessments* (pp. 290–318). Austin, TX: PRO-ED.

Stewart, M. A., Pitts, F. N., Craig, A. G., & Dieruf, W. (1966). The hyperactive child syndrome. *American Journal of Orthopsychiatry, 36*, 861–867.

Szatmari, P., Offord, D. R., & Boyle, M. H. (1989a). Correlates, associated impairments, and patterns of service utilization of children with attention deficit disorders: Findings from the Ontario child health study. *Journal of Child Psychology and Psychiatry, 30*, 205–217.

Szatmari, P., Offord, D. R., & Boyle, M. H. (1989b). Ontario child health study: Prevalence of attention deficit disorder with hyperactivity. *Journal of Child Psychology and Psychiatry, 30*, 219–230.

Trommer, B. L., Hoeppner, J. B., Rosenberg, R. S., Armstrong, K. J., & Rothstein, J. A. (1988). Sleep disturbances in children with attention deficit disorder [Abstract]. *Annuls of Neurology, 24*, 322.

U.S. Department of Education. (1991). *Thirteenth annual report to Congress on the implementation of the Individuals With Disabilities Education Act* (OCLC #25000254). Washington, DC: Author.

Weiss, R. E., Stein, M. A., Trommer, B., & Refetoff, S. (1993). Attention-deficit hyperactivity disorder and thyroid function. *Journal of Pediatrics, 123*, 539–545.

Wilkinson, G. S. (1993). *The Wide Range Achievement Test: 1993 edition administration manual.* Wilmington, DE: Wide Range.

III

PSYCHOLOGISTS IN TERTIARY CARE SETTINGS

INTRODUCTION

Often surprising to the public, to referring physicians, and even to psychologists, is the extent to which psychologists practice in tertiary care settings or are involved in trend-setting research into the understanding and treatment of acute or chronic life-threatening diseases. Although we chose to focus on only six clinical specialty areas in this text, psychologists can be found in most medical settings, on many treatment teams, caring for patients suffering from a myriad of illnesses.

In chapter 15, "Pediatric Oncology: Medical Crisis Intervention," Gerald P. Koocher focuses on the acute psychological and physiological distress symptoms experienced by otherwise psychologically well adjusted individuals coping with the diagnosis and treatment of childhood cancer. Reminding the psychologist not to interpret the patient or family responses to illness from the framework of psychopathology, Koocher furnishes guidelines for both providing crisis counseling and helping patient and families adapt to long-term survival.

Bruce G. Bender describes the clinical services of psychologists in chapter 16, "Establishing a Role for Psychology in Respiratory Medicine," and introduces the importance of psychological programming for those suffering from respiratory disorders, by highlighting the prevalence of these illnesses. He describes the treatment program at the National Jewish Center for Immunology and Respiratory Medicine and expands on psychologically based treatment protocols and their clinical efficacy.

Early detection of Alzheimer's disease is often hampered by common behavioral affects of aging and depression. In chapter 17, "The Role of

Clinical Neuropsychology in the Assessment and Care of Persons With Alzheimer's Disease," Alfred W. Kaszniak explores the critical role that psychologists can take in health care and geriatric settings to help with early detection. He outlines important criteria for accurate assessment, as well as interventions that will help patients and their families cope with Alzheimer's long-term affects.

In chapter 18, "Quality of Life and Adjustment in Renal Disease: A Health Psychology Perspective," Petra Symister and Ronald Friend provide a review of the quality-of-life issues for those who suffer from end-stage renal disease. Symister and Friend discuss both kidney transplant patients and those treated by hemodialysis and the process of psychological adjustment to the range of medical and surgical treatments. Research and clinical approaches to adherence to medical treatment regimes also are discussed.

In chapter 19, "Health Psychology and the Field of Urology," Steven M. Tovian covers a range of topics, from research ideas to practitioner interventions to collaborative suggestions for advocacy in a clinical area not often associated with psychologists, urology. Tovian defines types of adult urinary incontinence, the effects of incontinence on quality of life, and psychological treatments for the emotional sequelae of these disorders. Another disorder encountered in urological practice, erectile dysfunction, is also discussed from medical and psychological perspectives. Tovian offers suggestions for psychologists wishing to market their clinical services to urologists.

Tiffany M. Field, in chapter 20, "Touch Therapies for Pain Management and Stress Reduction," describes research studies and clinical interventions using touch therapy, massage, to reduce anxiety and stress in infants who are premature or who have been exposed to cocaine or HIV; children with a range of problems, such as diabetes, burns, or posttraumatic stress disorder; and adults who are HIV-positive. Clinical changes in anxiety were also found in those providing the massages, whether they were volunteer "grandparent therapists" or the parents of ill children. Field discusses proposed underlying biological mechanisms that explain the clinical utility of this approach to stress reduction.

Jacqueline Dunbar-Jacob and Elizabeth A. Schlenk, in chapter 21, "Treatment Adherence and Clinical Outcome: Can We Make a Difference?" describe the research outcomes of the level to which patients fail to comply with both their medication and behavioral treatment regimes and the health problems that ensue when patients do not follow treatment. Although most research has concentrated on the adverse outcomes of noncompliance with medication regimes, Dunbar-Jacob and Schlenk provide evidence that suggests that noncompliance with behavioral regimes (e.g., failure to follow diet plans) also adversely affects patients' health and adds to health care costs. Areas of research in this critical field of health care are suggested.

15

PEDIATRIC ONCOLOGY: MEDICAL CRISIS INTERVENTION

GERALD P. KOOCHER

The adventure begins in a relatively uneventful manner, as childhood medical problems go: a few bruises, a low-grade fever, a bruise or "athletic injury" that seems to worsen, a prolonged nosebleed, and curious minute red lines on the skin, which you will soon learn to identify as *petechiae*. The almost-casual visit to the pediatrician leads to a recommendation for "a few more tests." Then the diagnosis hits full-force: acute lymphoblastic leukemia, osteogenic sarcoma, Hodgkin's disease. The roller coaster ride begins bringing the threat of death, the hope of proven treatments, the necessity of an amputation or invasive surgical procedure, the promise of a "normal life down the road," the rocky course of high-dose chemotherapy. At times, the wait for information seems maddeningly slow. At other points, it seems that changes in medical status and the pace of interventions proceed at breakneck speed. All this in quest of a cure that is a real possibility for more than 70% of the children diagnosed with the most common forms of pediatric cancer.

What are psychologists doing in this setting? These events present especially intense coping challenges to both pediatric patients and their families. The emotional toll taken by these stresses is often sufficient to trigger acute psychological and physiological distress symptoms in individuals who are otherwise well adjusted. Symptoms affecting physically healthy family members may include anxiety, depression, difficulty concentrating, insomnia, sibling school phobia, and the inability to attend to important work- or family-related needs. Behavioral problems also occur among the child and adolescent cancer patients, including anxiety, depression, conditioned reflex vomiting, school refusal, and resistance or nonadherence to recommended medical regimens. The existing health care system is generally oriented to respond reactively, rather than preventively, with respect to emotional distress and is not well equipped to assist patients and families psychologically during these crises. Too often, health and mental care providers tend to function in parallel, rather than synchronous, interaction.

That is to say, mental health care does not make an effort to communicate or coordinate services with the physicians treating the medical condition. Too often, mental health professionals approach such patients in much the same manner as they would a client with entrenched neurotic symptoms. In so doing, the practitioner might attempt to explore early trauma or peel back layers of unconscious material, all the while ignoring the surface issues and illness-related stresses the patient and family must face.

Physicians managing the medical aspects of such cases are dedicated specialists but seldom talk with community-based mental health care providers serving a patient's family, and the psychological clinicians based outside the medical setting frequently lack a meaningful understanding of the illness, course and side effects of treatment, and medical prognosis that constitute their patient's reality. As a result, integrated approaches addressing both health and mental health needs of people in the midst of medical crisis are all too rare. Neither mental health professionals nor their patients can accept a continuation of such patterns of service.

Many mental health clinicians have noted the need for psychologists to prepare to work in health care settings. Perhaps the best known is Cummings (1995), who noted, "The future professional psychologist will be primarily a health psychologist who will require retraining to acquire an enabling attitude for success and a knowledge of the growing body of efficient–effective therapies" (p. 14).

Leading pediatric oncology treatment centers are ahead of the curve on this issue. Perhaps it is the appealing nature of children or the wish to spare them discomfort that has propelled development of psychosocial services in pediatric oncology treatment centers. Whatever the reason, the advent of high-dose-chemotherapy protocols and the resulting increases in both medical side effects and survivorship, which began in the 1970s, have resulted in important roles for psychologists in such centers around the country, as both behavioral scientists and practicing clinicians.

Psychologists and other mental health practitioners have provided an array of important behavioral and psychosocial interventions for children with cancer across at lease five domains: crisis-oriented therapies, psychoeducational interventions, improved relief of symptoms, tolerance of stressful procedures, and programs to improve the adaptation of long-term survivors. Outcome research has consistently demonstrated the enhancements to quality of life provided by psychosocial intervention. So valuable are these contributions, they are now routinely incorporated as integral elements of the medical care system. They have become required services in nearly every comprehensive pediatric oncology treatment center. This chapter summarizes some of the more recent developments in such programs and illustrates in detail what psychologists are doing in such sites as both scientists and practitioners.

CRISIS-ORIENTED PSYCHOTHERAPIES

Although restoring patients to a prior level of functioning may be feasible in some clinical populations, such restoration is an inadequate, if not unrealistic, goal for most patients facing medical crises. The child with cancer will face painful and invasive testing, arduous chemotherapy, daunting medical side effects, and considerable uncertainty. The clinician who approaches these patients with the goal of restoring them to a prior level of functioning denies the very real life-changing nature of medical crises and risks alienating patients and families by minimizing these challenges, communicating unrealistic expectations, or interpreting their responses from the framework of psychopathology (Shapiro & Koocher, 1996).

The psychological landscape of most lives is permanently altered by a brush with cancer, even if in positive ways. However, returning to "the way things were" is simply not possible. This is not to say that restoring a sense of normalcy is impossible, but rather that patients and family members must come to a new personal homeostasis and understanding of what constitutes normality for them. The goal of the medical crisis intervention is to help the patient optimize functioning socially, occupationally, and in management of the medical aspects of the disease (Pollin, 1995).

Four a priori clinical assumptions are critical when working with patients who are struggling with medical crises. First, human responses to medical crises rarely represent psychopathology in the traditional sense. Rather, anyone facing the extreme stress of illness may react with a host of psychological distress symptoms, including those frequently associated with mental illness: dissociation, denial, and the so-called vegetative symptoms often indicative of anxiety disorders and major depression. Such people in medical crisis, however, do not warrant the same treatment approach as the patient experiencing the same symptoms independent of medical distress (Pollin, 1995). A pathologizing model and long-term treatment plan are seldom warranted. Rather, an approach that helps normalize the distress (under the circumstances), focuses on the illness, and emphasizes an intensive short-term or brief, intermittent intervention model is most likely to be helpful and well received.

Second, there is a continuum of social, occupational, and biomedical functioning that demands consideration. Imagine, for example, two adolescents with the same chronic, life-threatening illness. One may stay in touch with peers over the phone, even when bedridden, continue to invest energy in schoolwork, and talk openly about the illness. The other may find changes in her or his appearance (e.g., hair loss or amputation) devastating and retreat into social isolation, seeking home tutoring rather than a return to school and focusing energy on high-violence video games. Functional coping responses to the same illness and symptoms may be radically different, and although the observer might prefer one coping strategy over the other, neither can be described as pathological per se or useful for everyone (Shapiro & Koocher, 1996).

Third, a child's responses to serious medical illness cannot be understood in a vacuum. The patient's relationships at home, school, work, and in the neighborhood are often affected by illness. As in systems theory, we assume that changes in one part of the patient's personal ecology (e.g., the onset of illness) resonate throughout the entire system. Therefore, it is necessary to assess and work toward optimal functioning in every social system with which the patient interacts. The psychotherapist must be prepared to shift between individual and family meetings and must be able to consult with school personnel and members of the medical team as the child's medical treatment progresses. Intervention must be contextual to the site, the coping tasks required, and the developmental level of the child.

Finally, we assume that the duration of a given crisis will vary from disease to disease, symptom to symptom, and person to person. Cancer treatment can be a series of turbulent periods broken up by periods of relative calm. This unfolding natural history or course of the illness has implications for the frequency, duration, and intensity of psychological treatment. Psychotherapeutic intervention may prove to be a one-time course of sessions, or a series of clusters of interventions that are linked to treatment events (e.g., diagnosis, reintegration to school, relapse, survivorship issues, or terminal care).

PSYCHOEDUCATIONAL AND FAMILY INTERVENTIONS

Psychologists have been instrumental in developing psychoeducational programs to enhance the coping of children with cancer. Research focused on understanding developmental stressors and coping processes has led to interventions that facilitate coping by both child patients and their families. These strategies and techniques are often rather simple to implement, although not a part of routine training for most physicians. Hence, they would not be readily available without psychologists working in these settings.

School Reintegration

Maintaining as normal a life as possible is important for medically ill children, just as the ability to continue or resume work is a concern for chronically ill adults. Several investigations by psychologists have shed light on strategies for school reintegration. One example is a 1992 study by Katz, Varni, Rubinstein, and Blew in Southern California, which evaluated the effectiveness of a comprehensive school reintegration intervention. A total of 49 children (age 5–17 years), newly diagnosed with cancer, received a comprehensive school reintegration consisting of supportive counseling, educational presentations, systematic liaison between the hospital and the school, and periodic follow-ups. Children, their parents, and teachers rated their perceptions of the utility and value of the intervention approach. Evaluations were uniformly very positive, providing support for the social validity of the school reintegration approach for children with newly diagnosed cancer.

Social Support

For a child or adolescent who has undergone prolonged hospitalization, has become weakened and lost hair as a result of chemotherapy, or suddenly feels very different from peers, self-esteem loss and a sense of social isolation or stigma can be overwhelming. Varni and his colleagues (Varni, Katz, Colegrove, & Dolgin, 1993, 1994) have focused attention on issues of social support as a key issue in fostering coping of children with cancer. In 1993, they conducted a prospective investigation to determine whether explicit social skills training could enhance the psychological and social adjustment of children with newly diagnosed cancer. A total of 64 children (age 5–13 years) with newly diagnosed cancer were randomized to either a social skills training experimental treatment group or a school reintegration standard treatment group. Children who received explicit training in social skills reported higher perceived classmate and teacher social support at a 9-month follow-up, by comparison with pretreatment levels. At the same time, parents reported a decrease in internalizing and externalizing behavior problems and an increase in school competence among the children.

Another report on this same clinical population (Varni et al., 1994) described 30 children (age 8–13 years) who were evaluated for depressive symptoms, state anxiety, trait anxiety, social anxiety, general self-esteem, and perceived social support from classmates, parents, teachers, and friends. Perceived classmate, parent, and teacher social support correlated with the psychologic adjustment parameters in the direction of greater support predicting lower psychologic distress and higher self-esteem. Perceived classmate social support was the most consistent predictor of the ill child's adaptation.

Children's Understanding of Cancer

How children understand their illness and necessary treatments can be an important factor in their ability to cope. Bearison, Sadow, Granowetter, and Winkel (1993) reported on the kinds of causal attributions that pediatric cancer patients and their parents make about cancer. Their beliefs were systematically examined to determine whether different types of attributions were associated with different coping strategies. A total of 20 pediatric oncology patients (age 4 to 19 years) were interviewed to determine the kinds of attributions they made (if any) about their cancer. The parents also were interviewed, concerning their causal attributions of their child's cancer. The parents then completed the Strategies for Coping With Illness—Parents' Scale to determine their coping strategies. Pediatric oncology nurses rated the children's coping strategies. Findings indicate that both patients and parents who made external types of attributions coped significantly better than did those who made internal types of attributions or simply accepted the physicians' advice that the cause of pediatric cancers was unknown (i.e., who made no attributions).

Springer (1994) evaluated whether preschoolers with cancer are more or less likely than their healthy counterparts to consider illness a form of punishment for misdeeds (i.e., *imminent justice*). Seventeen 4–5-year-olds with cancer rejected imminent justice as a general cause of illness, both in themselves and in others, just as frequently as 17 age-matched healthy controls did. Both groups also rejected imminent justice in cases where misbehavior was prolonged. Children with cancer demonstrated a view of illness causality based on greater differentiation between themselves and other people, in that they were more likely than healthy controls to accept imminent justice as a cause of illness in themselves but not others and vice versa. Nearly all of the children with cancer who accepted imminent justice as a general cause of illness in themselves also attributed their cancer specifically to imminent justice.

These findings are among the latest in a long series of studies that inform both physicians and psychosocial support staff about how to explain these illnesses and their treatments to children of all ages (for detailed discussion in historical perspective, see Koocher, 1986b; Koocher & MacDonald, 1992; Slavin, O'Malley, Koocher, & Foster, 1981).

Family Coping in General

Mental health professionals have been highly successful in getting pediatric oncologists to recognize that when a child has cancer, the family must be considered the psychological unit of treatment. In an excellent article, Kazak and Nachman (1991) discussed select research studies on adjustment to childhood cancer and organized them within a social ecological framework, including consideration of social systems larger than the family. They used childhood cancers as an example and presented family research agendas relevant to cancer and other childhood chronic diseases. Research questions pertained to the ill child, siblings, parents, families, social support networks, education and health care systems, and policy and societal attitudes. Recommendations for research were suggested, and the importance of considering normalcy, family development, and methodology in research on ill children and their families is also discussed.

Horwitz and Kazak (1990) assessed 25 preschool (3–5-year-old) siblings and families of children with cancer and 25 preschool siblings and families of healthy children, by means of standardized measures of child adjustment and family adaptability and cohesion (including the Child Behavior Checklist and the Family Adaptability and Cohesion Evaluation Scale—II). Siblings' behavior, social competence, and self-perceptions in the oncology family group were in keeping with published norms and did not differ significantly from the comparison group. The oncology family group had more extreme levels of adaptability, and mothers were more likely to describe sibling pairs as alike. There was a negative correlation between behavior problems and adaptability and cohesion in the oncology group.

Unfortunately, there are times when surviving family members, including children, must cope with the loss of a loved one from cancer. Coping with a cancer death can be an agonizing experience, but once again this is an area of science and practice where there are many positive contributions by behavioral scientists (Koocher, 1986a).

Coping With the Death of a Child

Many books and papers have been published also on coping with the death of a child. Some recent work, however, has focused on a preventive approach. Koocher (1994) described a preventive-intervention program for families that suffered the loss of a child from cancer and other causes. Using a manualized intervention designed to mobilize mutual support among those who had shared the loss and guide the mourning process, interveners were able to provide significant benefit to families over the course of three sessions lasting 2–2 1/2 hours each. Once again, the model involved a normalizing focus on the loss event from the intervener's perspective.

SYMPTOMATIC RELIEF

Psychologists have been actively involved in the development of biobehavioral models (Andersen, Kiecolt-Glaser, & Glaser, 1994) and intervention protocols designed to assist patients in coping with the rigors of cancer therapies, ranging from control of nausea and vomiting symptoms to improved pain control (Koocher, 1985; Schulz & Masek, 1996). Some of these interventions are described in the next section of this chapter, but many involve simple adaptations of well-known behavioral techniques such as systematic desensitization procedures, applied in a context specific to pediatric oncology.

IMPROVED TOLERANCE OF STRESSFUL PROCEDURES

Before one can successfully intervene to reduce stress during medical procedures, it is important to understand the child's perspective. Bearison and Pacifici (1989) described the schematic organization of children's knowledge of the routine procedures they experience when being treated for cancer (leukemia). A total of 27 leukemia patients (age 4–17 years) participated in the study. The effects of several independent variables, including age, duration of treatment, prognostic condition, and gender, were tested on the participants' cognitive organization and recall of their experiences in oncology clinics relative to their experiences of other common recurrent events in their lives. Interview data showed that the participants demonstrated well-organized knowledge about the events they experienced in oncology clinics, particularly the administration of chemotherapy.

Venipuncture and bone marrow aspirations are two of the most frequent and distressing procedures to which children with cancer are subjected. Dahlquist, Power, Cox, and Fernbach (1994) examined the relationship between children's distress during invasive cancer procedures and parent anxiety, parent disciplinary attitudes, and parent behavior during the medical procedure. Sixty-six 2- to 17-year-olds with cancer and their parents were evaluated during a routine (but nonetheless painful) bone marrow aspiration. Significantly higher levels of distress existed for children under 8 years. Patterns of relationships with parent variables also varied by age. Young children's distress was positively associated with parental reassurance, ignoring, and agitation before the procedure and with information giving during the procedure. Older children's distress was negatively associated with parental distraction during the procedure. The substantial age differences in the correlations between child distress and parenting practices demonstrate the young child's greater dependence on caregivers for emotional regulation and control.

Manne et al. (1995) examined the impact of three coping behaviors (non-procedure-related statements and behaviors, information seeking, and requests for modifications in the procedure) exhibited during stressful medical procedures performed on 45 children (age 3–10 years) undergoing cancer treatment. By means of videotaped recordings of venipuncture, the relationship among the three coping behaviors and between coping and distress were investigated. Because age was associated with both distress and coping, age was partialed out when computing correlations. Coping behaviors were independent (i.e., not correlated). A pattern of consistent, weak-to-moderate associations was noted between non-procedure-related behaviors and reductions in both concurrent and subsequent distress. These results illustrate that studies of children's coping should be sensitive to developmental issues and show the special value of a psychological approach to the problem.

In an 1990 study, Manne, Redd, Jacobsen, and Gorfinkle, at Memorial Sloan Kettering Cancer Institute, reported on a behavioral intervention incorporating parent coaching, attentional distraction, and positive reinforcement to control child distress during invasive cancer treatment. Children who had previously required physical restraint to complete venipuncture were alternately assigned to either a behavioral intervention or an attention-control condition. Child distress behaviors were recorded, and self-reports of parent, child, and nurse distress were obtained. Parents and nurses also rated child distress. Results of planned comparisons indicate that observed child distress, parent-rated child distress, and parent ratings of his or her own distress were significantly reduced by behavioral intervention and were maintained across the course of three intervention trials. The use of physical restraint to manage child behavior was also significantly reduced. Child self-reported pain and nurse ratings of child distress were not significantly affected.

These are but a few illustrations of the contributions that psychologists have made in helping children with cancer to cope with difficult treatments. In so doing, they are also helping to calm anxious parents and relieve the pressures on physicians and nurses as well.

IMPROVED COPING FOR LONG-TERM SURVIVORS

Because the early reports on long-term survivors of childhood cancer focused on the uncertainty of outcome as a stressor (Koocher & O'Malley, 1981), psychological research has had a profound impact on the actual course of medical treatment for children with cancer. For example, psychologists were leaders in emphasizing the importance of honest and direct communication regarding the cancer diagnosis, to promote coping (Koocher & O'Malley, 1981; Spinetta, Rigler, & Karon, 1974). In addition, pediatric neuropsychology has led to important changes in the course of treatment for acute lymphoblastic leukemia (ALL), the most common form of childhood cancer.

Leukemia cells too often find sanctuary from curative chemotherapy in the fluids of the central nervous system, where the blood–brain barrier blocks passage of medications. The result may be a central nervous system relapse of ALL among children who were otherwise effectively treated. Irradiating the brain is one way of killing cancer cells that may escape the chemotherapy, but such treatments can also cause neurological damage. Pediatric psychologists were the first to document such sequelae in detail.

For example, Waber and her colleagues (Waber, Bernstein, Kammerer, & Tarbell, 1992; Waber, Gioia, Paccia, & Sherman, 1990) are among a group of pediatric neuropsychologists who have documented the devastating consequences that cranial irradiation can have on the developing brain. In controlled studies comparing children with ALL and other cancers that did not require brain irradiation, they described severe neuropsychological diagnoses and established dose and age relationships. Their research showed that high does of radiation to the brain were especially damaging in children under 36 months of age. They also documented female sex as a risk factor for cognitive delay in the aftermath of cranial irradiation for ALL. Because of such research, treatment protocols have been modified to minimize the amount of radiation used in treating newly diagnosed children with ALL. Baseline neuropsychological assessment and follow-up for long-term educational and learning problems are now routine components of treatment protocols for pediatric ALL.

Following early reports on the importance of open communication in families confronting childhood cancer (Koocher & O'Malley, 1981; Spinetta et al., 1974), Claflin and Barbarin (1991) examined the effects of parents telling young children less about the diagnosis, treatment, and prognosis of cancer than older children and adolescents. A total of 43 children diagnosed with cancer reported on information disclosed to them at diagnosis, their causal attributions, illness-related stress, and coping strategies. In keeping with parental reports, 18 children age under 9 years were told less than 15 children age 9–13 years and 10 adolescents age 14–18 years. Young children's reports of illness impact differed from those of older children and adolescents only with respect to school and social domains. Younger children reported fewer cognitive strategies than older children and adolescents. Even though young children were told much less than older children, they reported similar levels of distress. Claflin and Barbarin concluded that nondisclosure failed to mask the salient and distressing aspects of the illness.

CONCLUSION

The message to be gleaned from this overview is that psychologists are doing quite a bit in pediatric oncology settings. As both behavioral scientists and practitioners, psychologists are making significant contributions to health status and quality of life. These contributions involve both traditional and crisis-oriented interventions, as well as cognitive, behavioral, and neuropsychological approaches, to resolve the difficulties patients commonly encounter in the course of cancer treatment. The full magnitude of the impact psychology has had in these settings is evident in the fact that psychological components are routine parts of all major pediatric oncology treatment settings and research programs. The National Cancer Institute's research grant reviewers routinely expect that psychological and quality-of-life factors will be addressed in applications for funding. The American Cancer Society added a doctoral level psychologist as a vice president for behavioral science research in 1994, and its board of directors voted in 1995 to increase set-aside funds for psychosocial and behavioral research. The influence of psychology and psychologists in pediatric oncology settings over the past 25 years has been highly significant. So, what are we doing here? Plenty!

REFERENCES

Andersen, B. L., Kiecolt-Glaser, J. K., & Glaser, R. (1994). A biobehavioral model of cancer, stress, and disease course. *American Psychologist, 49,* 389–404.

Armstrong, F. D. (1995). Commentary: Childhood cancer. *Journal of Pediatric Psychology, 20,* 417–421.

Bearison, D. J., & Pacifici, C. (1989). Children's event knowledge of cancer treatment. *Journal of Applied Developmental Psychology, 10,* 469–486.

Bearison, D. J., Sadow, A. J., Granowetter, L., & Winkel, G. (1993). Patients' and parents' causal attributions for childhood cancer. *Journal of Psychosocial Oncology, 11,* 47–61.

Claflin, C. J., & Barbarin, O. A. (1991). Does "telling" less protect more? Relationships among age, information disclosure, and what children with cancer see and feel. *Journal of Pediatric Psychology, 16,* 169–191.

Cummings, N. A. (1995). Impact of managed care on employment and training: A primer for survival. *Professional Psychology: Research and Practice, 26,* 10–15.

Dahlquist, L. M., Power, T. G., Cox, C. N., & Fernbach, D. J. (1994). Parenting and child distress during cancer procedures: A multidimensional assessment. *Children's Health Care, 23,* 149–166.

Horwitz, W. A., & Kazak, A. E. (1990). Family adaptation to childhood cancer: Sibling and family systems variables. *Journal of Clinical Child Psychology, 19,* 221–228.

Katz, E. R., Varni, J. W., Rubenstein, C. L., & Blew, A. (1992). Teacher, parent, and child evaluative ratings of a school reintegration intervention for children with newly diagnosed cancer. *Children's Health Care, 21,* 69–75.

Kazak, A. E., & Nachman, G. S. (1991). Family research on childhood chronic illness: Pediatric oncology as an example. *Journal of Family Psychology, 4,* 462–483.

Koocher, G. P. (1985). Promoting coping with illness in childhood. In J. C. Rosen & L. J. Solomon (Eds.), *Prevention in health psychology* (pp. 217–223). Hanover, NH: University Press of New England.

Koocher, G. P. (1986a). Coping with a death from cancer. *Journal of Consulting and Clinical Psychology, 54,* 623–631.

Koocher, G. P. (1986b). Psychosocial care of the child during acute cancer treatment. *Cancer, 58,* 468–472.

Koocher, G. P. (1994). Preventive interventions following a child's death. *Psychotherapy: Theory, Research, and Practice, 31,* 377–382.

Koocher, G. P., & MacDonald, B. L. (1992). Preventive intervention and family coping with a child's life threatening or terminal illness. In T. J. Akamatsu, M. A. P. Stephens, S. E. Hobfoll, & J. H. Crowther (Eds.), *Family health psychology* (pp. 67–88). Washington, DC: Hemisphere.

Koocher, G. P., & O'Malley, J. E. (1981). *The Damocles syndrome: Psychosocial consequences of surviving childhood cancer.* New York: McGraw-Hill.

Manne, S. L., Bakeman, R., Jacobsen, P. B., & Redd, W. H. (1993). Children's coping during invasive medical procedures. *Behavior Therapy, 24,* 143–158.

Manne, S. L., Lesanics, D., Meyers, P., Wollner, N., Steinherz, P., & Redd, W. (1995). Predictors of depressive symptomatology among parents of newly diagnosed children with cancer. *Journal of Pediatric Psychology, 20,* 491–510.

Manne, S. L., Redd, W. H., Jacobsen, P. B., & Gorfinkle, K. (1990). Behavioral intervention to reduce child and parent distress during venipuncture. *Journal of Consulting and Clinical Psychology, 58*, 565–572.

Pollin, I. (1995). *Medical crisis counseling: Short-term therapy for long-term illness.* New York: Norton.

Schulz, M., & Masek, B. (1996). Medical crisis intervention with children and adolescents with chronic pain. *Professional Psychology: Research and Practice, 27*, 121–129.

Shapiro, D. E., & Koocher, G. P. (1996). Goals and time considerations in outpatient medical crises intervention. *Professional Psychology: Research and Practice, 27*, 109–120.

Slavin L., O'Malley J. E., Koocher, G. P., & Foster D. J. (1981). Communication of the cancer diagnosis to pediatric patients: Impact on long-term adjustment. *American Journal of Psychiatry, 139*, 179–183.

Spinetta, J. J. Rigler, D., & Karon, M. (1974). Personal space as a measure of a dying child's sense of isolation. *Journal of Consulting and Clinical Psychology, 42*, 751–756.

Springer, K. (1994). Beliefs about illness causality among preschoolers with cancer: Evidence against imminent justice. *Journal of Pediatric Psychology, 19*, 91–101.

Varni, J. W., Katz, E. R., Colegrove, R., & Dolgin, M. (1993). The impact of social skills training on the adjustment of children with newly diagnosed cancer. *Journal of Pediatric Psychology, 18*, 751–767.

Varni, J. W., Katz, E. R., Colgrove, R., & Dolgin, M. (1994). Perceived stress and adjustment of long-term survivors of childhood cancer. *Journal of Psychosocial Oncology, 12*, 1–16.

Waber, D. P., Bernstein, J. H., Kammerer, B. L., & Tarbell, N. J. (1992). Neuropsychological diagnostic profiles of children who received CNS treatment for acute lymphoblastic leukemia: The systematic approach to assessment. *Developmental Neurology, 8*, 1–28.

Waber, D. P., Gioia, G., Paccia, J., & Sherman, B. (1990). Sex differences in cognitive processing in children treated with CNS prophylaxis for acute lymphoblastic leukemia. *Journal of Pediatric Psychology, 15*, 105–122.

16

ESTABLISHING A ROLE FOR PSYCHOLOGY IN RESPIRATORY MEDICINE

BRUCE G. BENDER

Asthma is a chronic inflammation of the lung airways characterized by shortness of breath and wheezing. This disease affects about 12 million Americans, including 4 million children. Annually, asthma accounts for approximately 15 million physician visits, 479,000 hospitalizations, 1.2 million emergency room visits, and 10 million missed school days (S. T. Weiss et al., 1992). According to the Centers for Disease Control (1995), the morbidity and mortality associated with asthma have been on the rise in recent years. The number of asthma deaths has progressively increased since 1982 from 3,000 to 5,000 per year, with mortality significantly higher in African Americans.

The incidence of psychological difficulty is increased in asthmatic children. However, the rate of psychological disorder is not increased for all groups of asthmatic children (Kashani, Konig, Shepperd, Wilfley, & Morris, 1988; Klinnert, in press). Rather, there appears to be a generalized increase in problems of adaptation, self-esteem, and social confidence that may affect many asthmatic children, while actual psychological disorder is increased only among children with severe asthma (Bussing, Halfon, Benjamin, & Wells, 1995; Graham, Rutter, Yule, & Pless, 1967; Hamlett, Pelligrini, & Katz, 1992; Klinnert, in press). In one study of 81 asthmatic children, MacLean, Perrin, Gortmaker, and Pierre (1992) stratified the children into groups having mild, moderate, or severe asthma. Comparison of scores from the Child Behavior Checklist (Achenbach & Edelbrock, 1983) among these groups indicated that behavioral problems were increased and social competence decreased only in the group with severe asthma. Graham et al. (1967) similarly concluded almost 30 years ago that psychiatric disturbance is slightly increased among all asthmatic children, but particularly so in those with more severe asthma.

In this chapter, I review the psychologist's role in respiratory medicine. Particular emphasis is given to the currently changing place for psychological services as disease-management models redefine how tertiary care is delivered. I argue that the continued inclusion of psychological services in such settings will depend on several factors, including the ability of psychologists to demonstrate that untreated psychological disorders undermine successful medical treatment, that psychological intervention is cost-effective and improves treatment response, and that psychology's tradition of outcome research offers a means for continued reevaluation of multidisciplinary management of respiratory disease. I review evidence for each of these assertions.

WHY PSYCHOLOGICAL SERVICES ARE NECESSARY IN THE TERTIARY CARE MEDICAL SETTING

National Jewish Center for Immunology and Respiratory Medicine, a Denver-based tertiary care center, typically receives those patients with difficult-to-control asthma, often characterized by repeated emergency room visits and hospitalizations, chronic need for systemic steroids, and annual medical care costs in excess of $15,000. Because psychological disorders are increased in this high-risk asthma group (Todd, 1995) and often interfere with medical management (Bender & Klinnert, in press; Klinnert, in press), psychological assessment and intervention represent a primary service area at National Jewish Center.

The central role of psychosocial staff at National Jewish Center continues because of the high need for direct psychological intervention in this patient population. In response to the health care revolution taking place in the United States, significant changes are occurring in all health care centers. These dramatic changes require that psychology redefine its place in tertiary health care settings. The average length of hospitalization for a patient at National Jewish Center today is less than half of what it was 5 years ago, a change directly resulting from limitations imposed by the health insurance and managed care industries. Consequently, the delivery of health care to severe, chronically asthmatic patients at National Jewish Center is changing. Most immediately apparent is the change of primary treatment setting from inpatient hospitalization to day-treatment program. The highly structured day program provides education and training about chronic disease, medical evaluation and treatment, and psychosocial evaluation and treatment, in a manner that significantly reduces costs as compared with the inpatient program.

The relationship between psychological disorder and chronic disease is complex and interactive. At first glance, it appears fairly obvious that the imposition of chronic disease represents an enormous stressor, which can induce psychological difficulty, most frequently depression (Mrazek, 1985; Yellowless, Haynes, Potts, & Ruffin, 1988). However, the causal relationship is not uni directional. The preexistence of a psychological disorder also can contribute to poorly controlled, and, consequently, more severe disease. Nonadherence to essential medical care, in particular, can result from the patient's, or the patient's family's, psychological difficulties, exacerbating the illness and causing excessive, inappropriate, and expensive overuse of health care services.

Although the pharmacologic means for effective asthma management are readily available, treatment failure and excessive emergency room visits and hospitalizations occur largely because of patient nonadherence. In some cases, treatment nonadherence is directly related to psychological disorder. Studies using new microchip technologies, which allow investigators to document the exact date and time when patients use aerosolized medications, have revealed that much of the necessary anti-inflammatory medication prescribed to the patient is not taken as directed (Milgrom et al., 1995). As physicians increase the frequency of prescribed dosages, to gain better control of the disease, patients actually become less adherent (Coutts, Gibson, & Paton, 1992). Children from dysfunctional families are more nonadherent than other patients in their use of asthma medications (Bender et al., 1995). However, even seemingly stable and cooperative patients can be markedly nonadherent with medications essential to the control of their asthma (Milgrom, Bender, Sarlin, & Leung, 1994). The absence of necessary health care behavior, then, contributes to dangerously out-of-control asthma, a finding that is particularly prevalent among inner-city African Americans (Greineder, Loane, & Parks, 1995), which can result in asthma-related death (Strunk, Mrazek, Fuhrmann, & La Brecque, 1985).

Tertiary care psychological services then are a necessary component of disease management in the tertiary care medical setting. Mental health professionals with developed expertise can most effectively provide such services. Furthermore, when these services are provided within the tertiary care setting in collaboration with medical caregivers, they are more likely to result in an effective change in health care behavior and quality of life than those provided in settings with no connection to the patients' health care (Bender & Klinnert, in press). Such multidisciplinary approaches to asthma treatment at National Jewish Center are characterized by the following examples:

Working with conflicted families with a history of poor management of a child's asthma requires that the psychologist understand the behaviors necessary for optimal self-management and the best approaches for helping families to share responsibility for the various components of disease control.

When a depressed adolescent declines to adhere to a medication regimen as an act of angry rebellion, the psychologist must have an understanding of the function of various medications, assist in removing the sources of resistance, and help the adolescent to plan to take the medication at times and places that avoid embarrassment.

An adult patient with chronic obstructive pulmonary disease complains that a particular medication causes depression. The psychologist may assist in assessing whether the medication or other disease-related factors are contributing to the affective concerns and may discuss alternative medications with the prescribing physician.

When a 4-year-old child becomes highly anxious about a scheduled invasive procedure necessary for evaluation of lung damage, a psychologist knowledgeable about the procedure can help alleviate some of the concern by enabling the child to practice the procedure with a doll and by advising the parents about discussions they may have with their child in the days leading up to the procedure.

A patient appears to lose some memory and motor skills in the period immediately after a severe respiratory arrest. The psychologist may be asked to help evaluate the neurological and functional implications of this event and to help plan a program of remediation.

STUDIES EXAMINING THE INFLUENCE OF PSYCHOLOGICAL INTERVENTIONS ON DISEASE OUTCOME

Not all initiatives targeting health care behavior have been successful. Numerous asthma education programs have been studied to determine the effects of increased patient knowledge on disease morbidity. In many cases, providing patients with better knowledge about asthma has been found to be insufficient to change behavior without the inclusion of additional behavioral or psychological interventions. Although asthma-education programs increase knowledge about asthma and its appropriate care, evidence that education intervention alone significantly alters health care behavior is at best mixed. Some support can be found for the effect of asthma education on reducing health care use (Bolton, Tilley, Kuder, Reeves, & Schultz, 1991; Osman et al., 1994), but a meta-analysis analyzing results across 11 education-intervention studies concluded that such teaching programs do not reduce morbidity outcomes, including rate of school absenteeism and frequency of hospitalization and emergency room visits (Bernard-Bonnin, Stachenko, Bonin, Charette, & Rousseau, 1995). Other investigators have similarly concluded that asthma education alone is ineffective in changing health care behavior and morbidity (Rubin, Bauman, & Lauby, 1989; Tettersell, 1993).

Although asthma-education programs by themselves are generally insufficient to change health care behavior and outcome, they are a necessary component of a multidisciplinary effort to improve asthma self-management. When asthma education is combined with other psychologically based approaches to changing health care behavior, the intervention becomes more effective. Several psychoeducational interventions exemplify this approach, using asthma education within individually tailored and administered programs administered by a health care giver, usually a nurse. The introduction of a new caregiver who is sympathetic to the patient can have a powerful influence on health care behavior. In one study, 53 high-risk asthmatic children with histories of repeated emergency room visits and hospitalizations were enrolled in an intensive self-management program (Greineder et al., 1995). In addition to direct asthma education, these children and their families met individually with, and received regular telephone contact from, an outreach nurse. This intervention, distinct from other education programs in its inclusion of a relationship with a care giver unavailable to patients outside the program, resulted in a 79% reduction in emergency room visits, an 86% reduction in hospitalizations, and an average savings of over $1,600 for each patient. Because all patients received the same health maintenance organization medical care before, during, and after the program, these changes were attributed solely to the psychoeducational intervention. In another study, 47 adult asthmatics with multiple hospitalization histories were randomly assigned to a routine-care control group or an intervention group receiving intensive, individual counseling and education on self-management strategies (Mayo, Richman, & Harris, 1990). The intervention group alone demonstrated a dramatic reduction in hospitalizations. Although both of these programs were presented as primarily educational interventions, they included an educator/counselor who played a central role in advising, encouraging, instructing, and motivating patients. Given the convincing evidence that offering factual information to chronically ill patients does not by itself change behavior (Tettersell, 1993), the importance of this therapeutic figure should not be underestimated.

The psychological component of other psychoeducational intervention programs has been more clearly recognized and labeled. Creer and colleagues at the University of Ohio have used a social learning theory model to design intensive health care behavior interventions for asthmatic patients. These investigators have repeatedly demonstrated that a combination of education, specific instruction, and strategic-problem-solving training can result in decreased frequency and severity of asthma exacerbations, use of the medical care system, and treatment cost. Evaluating a behavioral and educational program for asthmatic adults, Kotses et al. (1995) randomly assigned 76 subjects to either a treatment group or a waiting-list control group. Patients in the treatment group participated in a 7-week program providing education and training that included an emphasis on self-management and problem solving. In a 6-month follow-up, patients were found to experience less frequent asthma attacks, reduced medication use, and improved overall self-management skills. In a second report, the investigators demonstrated a significant cost-benefit from this intervention program: The cost of administering the program to each patient was $208, with an average cost savings of $475.

A similar intervention was equally effective with asthmatic children. Twenty families with asthmatic children were randomly assigned to a control group or an intervention group, receiving 2 months of education and training in self-management and problem solving. A social learning theory model provided the framework within which the patient was helped to select appropriate behavioral options, depending on the nature of symptoms and environment in which they were experienced. An 18-month follow-up indicated both a significant improvement in asthma, relative to the baseline period, and reduced school absenteeism and health-care-related expenditures (Creer et al., 1988).

Other psychological interventions have also been used with chronically ill patients, successfully altering morbidity. Such services become more essential with increasing asthma severity. For high-risk asthmatic patients, the higher frequency of psychopathology and widespread failure to adhere to health-promoting self-management techniques underscore the essential inclusion of direct psychological services. However, psychological services must be tailored specifically to the disease population if they are to efficiently alter health care behavior. Improved asthma symptoms have been demonstrated in response to family therapy (Gustafsson, Kjellman, & Cederblad, 1986; Gustafsson, Kjellman, Ludvigsson, & Cederblad, 1987; Lask & Matthew, 1979); relaxation training (Leher, Isenberg, & Hochron, 1986); biofeedback (Kotses et al., 1991; Mussell & Harley, 1988); and hypnosis (Murphy et al., 1989); but the use of such techniques in isolation from a larger program of intervention is likely to be ineffective in the long run.

In the treatment of children with severe, poorly controlled asthma, psychological interventions must focus on the entire family system and on the full spectrum of behaviors required for effective asthma management (Bender & Klinnert, in press). Adherence in asthma involves not only taking medications with appropriate technique and at the correct times but also working in a partnership with a physician, pursuing environmental controls of asthma triggers, and recognizing and treating asthma symptoms when they occur. For many families of children with out-of-control asthma, overwhelming problems in living take precedence over attending to the specific needs of their asthmatic child. These can include markedly dysfunctional families with a variety of financial, social, and psychological needs. Intervention requires the involvement of mental health providers, who can help to address a range of problems that face these families. With such families, interventions must focus on specific, manageable problems and provide an arena within which to address the family's motivation to change. Discussion of family problems and interactions occur in the context of the behaviors required in the asthmatic child's care, the cost of medication, the shared responsibilities of various family members, and the actions required when an exacerbation of asthma symptoms occurs. When clearer lines of communication and clarification of responsibilities related to the asthmatic child are directly addressed, the intervention is likely to improve the effective and efficient management of the illness.

ENSURING THE FUTURE OF PSYCHOLOGY IN TERTIARY CARE SETTINGS

The future of psychology in tertiary health care centers will depend at least in part on its ability to change health care behavior. To do this, psychologists must (a) be highly knowledgeable about the disease they are helping to treat, (b) be present as a member of the treatment team in the health care setting, and (c) demonstrate that the services they offer are definable, effective, and result in cost savings.

The managed care preference to contract for psychological services with a mental health provider group separate from all medical services conflicts directly with the model of subspecialty psychological services integrated with the medical health care system. The provision of general practice psychological services is unlikely to result in significant changes in health care behavior or to alter the course of chronic illness.

Such an approach may be less costly in the short run but ineffective in the long run. A telephone conversation or two between psychologist and physician, perhaps followed by a letter summarizing the mental health consultation, cannot replace the ongoing collaboration between psychological and medical caregivers in the medical care setting. The mental health practitioner who is located in the treatment facility is much more effectively positioned to develop psychological interventions integrated with other health care. For example, in one hospital-based asthma program, the psychological intervention included identification of the patient's health beliefs, tailoring of prescribed treatment to specific patient characteristics, negotiating a behavioral contract between patient and physician, and, where indicated, problem-focused family therapy (Weinstein, 1995). Such innovative multidisciplinary programs can occur only when the psychological caregiver understands the disease and its treatment and has a direct voice in patient care and treatment planning.

Demonstrating the Cost-Effectiveness of Psychological Services

Cost-effective interventions are those that provide a reasonably effective outcome that is judged to be worth the cost involved, whereas a cost-saving intervention actually results in money saved (Doubilet, Weinstein, & McNeil, 1986). From the perspective of a disease-management planner, then, the judgment of cost-effectiveness may depend on debatable criteria. Nonetheless, the decision as to whether psychological interventions are worth the cost is likely to rest on whether (a) a demonstrable change occurs and (b) the change can be achieved within a reasonable period of time or number of sessions. Open-ended psychotherapy sessions lasting many months with nonspecific goals are less likely to be well received than interventions with specific objectives (e.g., to increase medication adherence, to improve judgment about avoiding environmental triggers of respiratory distress, or to reduce conflict among family members in order to achieve better coordination of an asthmatic child's care) and a session- or time-limited length. It is unreasonable to expect that all psychological interventions should necessarily be cost saving. However, in some instances, this will be so. The interventions described above, which yielded improved symptom control, also resulted in large cost savings. Changing behavior in low-to-moderate-risk asthmatics saved an average of $475 per patient (Kotses et al., 1995), whereas the intervention with high-risk, frequently hospitalized patients saved $1,642 per patient (Greineder et al., 1995). Although economic benefit cannot be allowed to become the sole criteria for behavioral medicine, those instances in which cost savings are achieved become powerful arguments in its favor (Friedman, Sobel, Myers, Caudill, & Benson, 1995).

The Importance of Continued Outcome Research

The inclusion of psychological services in tertiary care settings will depend on the demonstration of their direct impact on health care, including cost-effectiveness. With training and experience in outcome research, many psychologists are well equipped to conduct the research necessary to demonstrate the impact of psychological interventions. Such investigative efforts have several advantages: First, they require the investigator to clearly structure, define, and standardize the intervention, not only allowing for the measurement of the services' impact but also facilitating the "packaging" of interventions, making them more clearly understood, thus appealing to managed care contractors, and more easily duplicated in multiple health care settings. Second, such research establishes that psychological services can change health care behavior, improve the effectiveness of medical interventions, and save money. Finally, systematic investigation of the effect of psychological interventions on chronic illness can, in the best tradition of the science of psychology, result in an ongoing process of refinement and reevaluation of the intervention.

Comparison across studies of the effectiveness of various psychological and psychoeducational interventions is difficult because of large methodological variability. Individual studies have been weakened by failure to include an appropriate control group, to clearly define the patient sample or intervention, to use objective outcome measures, or to extend patient follow-up to a sufficient interval to adequately evaluate outcome (Bender & Klinnert, in press; Bernard-Bonnin et al., 1995). Creer, Wigal, Kotses, and Lewis (1990) argued that if studies of the impact of self-management interventions on treatment of asthma are to include the scientific merit necessary to stand up to peer review, and if the results of these investigations are to receive widespread acceptance, they must meet a number of criteria: (a) participants recruited in an unbiased fashion, with well-defined asthma and in numbers sufficient to allow appropriate statistical analysis; (b) random assignment to treatment and control groups; (c) use of clearly described and standardized treatments; (d) use of well-defined, valid, and reliable outcome measures; (e) collection of sufficient follow-up data; and (f) appropriate interpretation of data, including distinguishing between statistical and clinical significance.

CONCLUSION

Psychologists can continue to own an important role in the treatment of asthma and other chronic diseases, particularly in tertiary care settings, where severe, difficult-to-control illnesses are often accompanied by the presence of psychological problems. However, in today's climate of cost-effectiveness and efficiency, psychologists must demonstrate their ability to directly enhance medical treatment, increase efficiency, and reduce costs. In many regards, psychologists are poised to take a leading role as experts in health care behavior intervention, which can result in more effective and efficient medical treatment. The strong research background that defines much of psychology also equips psychologists with the ability to evaluate treatment outcomes and determine which combination of psychological and medical interventions result in most effective and cost-efficient disease control. To do this effectively in a tertiary care setting, such as National Jewish Center, psychologists must be knowledgeable about the disease and have full faculty membership. With specialized knowledge and skills, and integrated into the treatment setting, psychologists will be able to design, implement, and study innovative programs that can change health care behavior and improve treatment of chronic disease.

REFERENCES

Achenbach, T. M., Edelbrock, C. S. (1983). Manual for the Child Behavior Checklist and Revised Child Behavior Profile. Burlington: University of Vermont, Department of Psychiatry.

Bender, B., & Klinnert, M. (in press). Psychological correlates of asthma severity and treatment outcome. In H. Kotses & A. Harver (Eds.), *Behavioral contributions to the management of asthma*. New York: Dekker.

Bender, B., Milgrom, H., Bowry, P., Gabriels, R., Ackerson, L., & Rand, C. (1995). Asthmatic children's adherence with aerosolized medications. *American Journal of Respiratory and Critical Care Medicine, 151*, A352.

Bernard-Bonnin, A., Stachenko, S., Bonin, D., Charette, C., & Rousseau, E. (1995). Self-management teaching programs and morbidity of pediatric asthma: A meta-analysis. *Journal of Allergy and Clinical Immunology, 95*, 34–41.

Bussing, R., Halfon, N., Benjamin, B., & Wells, K. B. (1995). Prevalence of behavior problems in U.S. children with asthma. *Archives of Pediatric and Adolescent Medicine, 149*, 565–572.

Centers for Disease Control. (1995). Asthma—United States, 1982–1992. *Morbidity and Mortality Weekly Report, 43*, 952.

Coutts, J. A., Gibson, N. A., & Paton, J. Y. (1992). Measuring compliance with inhaled medication in asthma. *Archives of Disease in Childhood, 67*, 332–333.

Creer, T. L., Backial, M., Burns, K. L., Leung, P., Marion, R. J., Miklich, D. R., Morrill, C., Taplin, P. S., & Ullman, S. (1988). Living with asthma:

I. Genesis and development of a self-management program for childhood asthma. *Journal of Asthma, 25*, 335–362.

Creer, T. L., Wigal, J. K., Kotses, H., & Lewis, P. (1990). A critique of 19 self-management programs for childhood asthma: Part II. Comments regarding the scientific merit of the programs. *Pediatric Asthma, Allergy, and Immunology, 4*, 41–55.

Doubilet, P., Weinstein, M. C., & McNeil, B. J. (1986). Use and misuse of the term "cost effective" in medicine. *New England Journal of Medicine, 314*, 23–25.

Friedman, R., Sobel, D., Myers, P., Caudill, M., & Benson, H. (1995). Behavioral medicine, clinical health psychology, and cost offset. *Health Psychology, 14*, 509–518.

Graham, P. J., Rutter, M., Yule, W., & Pless, I. B. (1967). A psychosomatic disorder? *British Journal of Preventive and Social Medicine, 21*, 78–85.

Greineder, D. K., Loane, K. C., & Parks, P. (1995). Reduction in resource utilization by an asthma outreach program. *Archives of Pediatric and Adolescent Medicine, 149*, 415–420.

Gustafsson, P. A., Kjellman, N. M., & Cederblad, M. (1986). Family therapy in the treatment of severe childhood asthma. *Journal of Psychosomatic Research, 30*, 369–374.

Gustafsson, P. A., Kjellman, N. M., Ludvigsson, J., & Cederblad, M. (1987). Asthma and family interaction. *Archives of Disease in Childhood, 62*, 258–263.

Hamlett, K. W., Pelligrini, D. S., & Katz, K. S. (1992). Childhood chronic illness as a family stressor. *Journal of Pediatric Psychology, 17*, 33–47.

Kashani, J. H., Konig, P., Shepperd, J. A., Wilfley, D., & Morris, D. A. (1988). Psychopathology and self-concept in asthmatic children. *Journal of Pediatric Psychology, 13*, 509–520.

Klinnert, M. D. (in press). The psychology of asthma in the school-aged child. In J. Kember & J. Bemporand (Eds.), *Handbook of child and adolescent psychiatry: The grade school child.* New York: Wiley.

Kotses, H., Bernstein, I. L., Bernstein, D. I., Reynolds, R. V. C., Korbee, L., Wigal, J. K., Ganson, E., Stout, C., & Creer, T. L. (1995). A self-management program for adult asthma: Part I. Development and evaluation. *Journal of Allergy and Clinical Immunology, 95*, 529–540.

Kotses, H., Harver, A., Segreto, J., Glaus, K. D., Creer, T. L., & Young, G. A. (1991). Long-term effects of biofeedback-induced facial relaxation on measures of asthma severity in children. *Biofeedback and Self Regulation, 16*, 1–22.

Lask, B., & Matthew, D. (1979). Childhood asthma. A controlled trial of family psychotherapy. *Archives of Disease in Childhood, 54*, 116–119.

Lehrer, P. M., Isenberg, S., & Hochron, S. M. (1986). Asthma and emotion: A review. *Journal of Asthma, 30*, 5–21.

MacLean, W. E., Perrin, J. M., Gortmaker, S., Pierre, C. B. (1992). Psychological adjustment of children with asthma: Effects of illness severity and recent stressful life events. *Journal of Pediatric Psychology, 17,* 159–171.

Mayo, P. H., Richman, J., & Harris, H. W. (1990). Result of a program to reduce admissions for adult asthma. *Annals of Internal Medicine, 112,* 864–871.

Milgrom, H., Bender, B., Ackerson, L., Bowry, P., Smith, B., & Rand, C. (1995). Children's compliance with inhaled asthma medications. *Journal of Allergy and Clinical Immunology, 95,* 217.

Milgrom, H., Bender, B., Sarlin, N., & Leung, D. Y. M. (1994). Difficult to control asthma: The challenge posed by noncompliance. *American Journal of Asthma and Allergy for Pediatricians, 7,* 141–146.

Mrazek, D. A. (1985). Childhood asthma: The interplay of psychiatric and psychological factors. *Advances in Psychosomatic Medicine, 14,* 16–32.

Murphy, A. I., Karlin, R., Hochron, S., Lehrer, P. M., Swartzman, L., & McCann, B. (1989). Hypnotic susceptibility and its relationship to outcome in the behavioral treatment of asthma: Some preliminary data. *Psychological Reports, 65,* 691–698.

Mussell, M. J., & Harley, J. P. (1988). Trachea-noise biofeedback in asthma: A comparison of the effect of trachea-noise biofeedback, a bronchodilator, and no treatment on the rate of recovery from exercise- and eucapnic hyperventilation-induced asthma. *Biofeedback and Self Regulation, 13,* 219–234.

Osman, L. M., Abdalla, M. I., Beattie, J. A. G., Ross, S. J., Russell, I. T., Friend, J. A., Legge, J. S., & Douglas, J. G. (1994). Reducing hospital admission through computer supported education for asthma patients. *British Medical Journal, 308,* 568–571.

Strunk, R. C., Mrazek, D. A., Fuhrmann, G. S., & LaBrecque, J. F. (1985). Physiologic and psychological characteristics associated with deaths due to asthma in childhood: A case controlled study. *Journal of the American Medical Association, 254,* 1193–1198.

Tettersell, M. J. (1993). Asthma patients' knowledge in relation to compliance with drug therapy. *Journal of Advanced Nursing, 18,* 103–113.

Todd, W. E. (1995). New mindsets in asthma: Interventions and disease management. *Journal of Care Management, 1,* 2–8.

Weinstein, A. G. (1995). Clinical management strategies to maintain drug compliance in asthmatic children. *Annals of Allergy, Asthma, and Immunology, 74,* 304–310.

Weiss, S. T., Tosteson, T. D., Segal, M. R., Tager, I. B., Redline, S., & Speizer, F. E. (1992). Effects of asthma on pulmonary function in children: A longitudinal population-based study. *American Review of Respiratory Disease, 145,* 58–64.

Yellowless, P. M., Haynes, S., Potts, N., & Ruffin, R. E. (1988). Psychiatric morbidity in patients with life-threatening asthma: Initial report of a controlled study. *Medical Journal of Australia, 149,* 246–249.

17

THE ROLE OF CLINICAL NEUROPSYCHOLOGY IN THE ASSESSMENT AND CARE OF PERSONS WITH ALZHEIMER'S DISEASE

ALFRED W. KASZNIAK

Clinical neuropsychologists are being employed in increasing numbers within medical settings in which they provide clinical services to neurologic patients and consultation to neurologists. Among the most frequent requests for neuropsychological consultation within such settings are those concerning persons with known or suspected dementia, particularly Alzheimer's disease (AD). The term *dementia* refers to a syndrome, caused by brain dysfunction, of acquired intellectual impairment that is of sufficient severity to interfere with social or occupational functioning. According to most definitions (e.g., Bayles & Kaszniak, 1987; Cummings & Benson, 1992), the syndrome of dementia involves deterioration in two or more of the following domains of psychological functioning: memory, language, visuospatial skills, judgment or abstract thinking, and emotion or personality. In studies of dementia in various countries, prevalence rates have ranged from 2.5% to 24.6% for persons over the age of 65 (see Ineichen, 1987). Differences in dementia definitions, sampling techniques, and sensitivity of instruments used to identify cases may account for the variability in estimates of the prevalence of dementia. Cummings and Benson (1992), calculating the average of prevalence estimates across studies, suggest that approximately 6% of persons over the age of 65 have severe dementia, with an additional 10% to 15% having mild-to-moderate dementia. The prevalence of the syndrome of dementia is age related, doubling approximately every 5 years after age 65 (Jorm, Korten, & Henderson, 1987). Not surprisingly, the prevalence of dementia is higher among hospital and nursing home residents than among those living within the community (for reviews, see Kramer, 1986; Smyer, 1988).

The dementia syndrome can be associated with more than 50 different causes of brain dysfunction (Haase, 1977; Katzman, 1986). Alzheimer's disease accounts for the largest proportion of all causes, with published reports varying from a low of 22% to a high of 70% of all dementia patients receiving diagnoses of AD (for review, see Cummings & Benson, 1992). However, in some community surveys (particularly, although not exclusively, those in Japan and China), dementia associated with cerebrovascular disease is reportedly more common than AD (Folstein, Anthony, Parhad, Duffy, & Gruenberg, 1985; Li, Shen, Chen, Zhao, & Li, 1989; Rorsman, Hagnell, & Lanke, 1986; Shibayama, Kasahara, & Kobayashi, 1986). It is unclear whether differences in reported relative prevalence reflect methodological variation across studies or actual regional and international disparities. Despite differences in the relative prevalence estimates provided by epidemiological investigations, there is agreement that AD and vascular dementia are the most frequent causes of age-associated dementia (Roman, 1991). Alzheimer's disease and vascular dementia are also the most frequent diagnoses made of patients referred for comprehensive assessment because of memory complaints (Thal, Grundman, & Klauber, 1988).

Clinical neuropsychology is the applied science dealing with the cognitive and behavioral manifestations of human brain dysfunction. Its primary concern is with the assessment, diagnosis, management, and rehabilitation of patients with developmental and acquired brain dysfunction. As greater numbers of individuals are surviving into older age (Myers, 1990), the prevalence of dementing illness has increased (Manton, 1990). Accordingly, research and practice in the clinical neuropsychology of dementia has also increased dramatically, particularly over the past 2 decades (La Rue, 1992; Poon, Kaszniak, & Dudley, 1992). Neuropsychological consultation now plays a critical role in identifying the presence of the syndrome of dementia, contributes to differential neurologic diagnosis of the many possible causes of dementia, and aids in the treatment and clinical management of dementing illness. Clinical neuropsychologic consultation with the person having known or suspected dementia may be performed to address any or all of the following aims (see Albert & Moss, 1988; Bayles & Kaszniak, 1987; La Rue, 1992; Zec, 1993): (a) identification of the presence of cognitive impairment and patterns of impairment relevant to differential diagnosis; (b) provision of information to health care providers, patients, and family members, concerning specific strengths and deficits in cognitive functions and their practical implications; (c) assessment of treatment effects or disease progression; and (d) provision of, or recommendations for, treatment and management of cognitive and behavior problems.

IDENTIFICATION OF THE PRESENCE AND PATTERN OF COGNITIVE IMPAIRMENT

The clinical neuropsychologist has available a large number of standardized tests that have known reliability and sensitivity in the detection of cognitive deficits that result from either focal or diffuse brain damage (Kolb & Whishaw, 1995; Lezak, 1995; Spreen & Strauss, 1991). These tests have been designed to assess specific aspects of a wide range of cognitive functioning, including general intellectual ability, memory functions, orientation and attention, language functions, perceptual functions, visual–motor constructional ability, abstract and conceptual reasoning, and so-called executive functions (i.e., goal formulation, planning, and the execution of goal-directed plans). Because many such tests meet psychometric criteria of acceptable reliability and validity, they provide accurate procedures for describing the cognitive strengths and weaknesses of a person. Accurate description is important in detecting the presence of (particularly mild) dementia and in determining whether the pattern of deficits is consistent with that expected in some particular dementia etiology. According to the *Diagnostic and Statistical Manual of Mental Disorders* (American Psychiatric Association, 1994), the diagnosis of Dementia of the Alzheimer's Type requires that the following criteria be met: (a) presence of multiple cognitive deficits, including memory impairment and at least one other impairment (e.g., aphasia, apraxia, agnosia, or disturbed executive functioning); (b) a gradual onset and progressive course of deterioration; and (c) exclusion of all other possible causes of dementia (e.g., cerebrovascular disease, Huntington's disease, Parkinson's disease, or brain tumor) by history, physical examination, and laboratory tests. In addition, the impairment must significantly interfere with social or occupational functioning, must represent a significant decline from a previous level of functioning, and must not occur exclusively during the course of *delirium* (an acute confusional state, most often due to systemic physical illness). An increasingly large body of research (for review, see Zec, 1993) has demonstrated the reliability and validity of neuropsychological assessment procedures in detecting the multiple cognitive deficits of AD in its early stages and in documenting the course of deterioration. Research has also shown that particular patterns of relatively impaired and preserved areas of cognitive functioning are associated with different dementia etiologies, such as AD versus Huntington's disease (for review, see Butters, Salmon, & Butters, 1994).

In neurologic and psychiatric practice, clinical screening for cognitive deficit in older adults is typically done through brief mental status tests, such as the Mini-Mental State Examination (MMSE; Folstein, Folstein, & McHugh, 1975). However, brief mental status tests typically have substantial *false-negative* (identifying a cognitively impaired person as normal) rates in detecting cognitive impairment (Nelson, Fogel, & Faust, 1986), particularly for individuals who are more highly educated (O'Connor, Pollitt, Hyde, Miller & Fellowes, 1989). There is also evidence for low education increasing the probability of *false-positive* errors (misclassifying normal individuals as cognitively impaired), particularly when the individual in question has less than 9 years of education (Anthony, LaResche, Niaz, Voh Koroff, & Folstein, 1982; Murden, McRae, Kaner, & Bucknam, 1991).

Most psychometric tests used in neuropsychological assessment contain a range of item difficulty, so that test scores ideally approximate a normal distribution when administered to individuals in the general population. This can provide for greater sensitivity to mild or subtle cognitive deficits than what is provided by mental status screening tests on which most normal individuals achieve near-perfect scores (e.g., Crum, Anthony, Bassett, & Folstein, 1993). Appropriately selected neuropsychological tests can reveal subtle cognitive impairments in neurologic patients who show no evidence of deficit on mental status screening tests (e.g., Bondi, Kaszniak, Bayles, & Vance, 1993). The ability of neuropsychological test batteries to reliably assess the pattern of performance across different domains of cognitive functioning may be particularly important in evaluating persons with high premorbid intellectual functioning (Naugle, Cullum, & Bigler, 1990). In such persons, performance can be at or above general-population normative expectation on all tests, yet a comparison of performance across different tests may reveal a pattern consistent with deterioration characteristic of a particular dementing illness, such as AD.

GENERAL CONSIDERATIONS IN THE NEUROPSYCHOLOGICAL ASSESSMENT OF OLDER ADULTS

Given the age-associated prevalence of most dementing illnesses, the majority of persons referred for neuropsychological assessment because of suspected or known dementia will be older adults. Clinical and experimental psychologists have been responsible for generating a large body of research concerning the psychological changes of normal aging, which has important implications for the interpretation of neuropsychological assessment results. The competent neuropsychological evaluation of older persons requires particular knowledge of research concerning those aspects of aging that impact on the conduct and interpretation of psychological testing.

Sensory Changes With Aging

One significant aspect of aging, influencing both selection of test materials and their interpretation, concerns sensory changes characteristic of normal aging, as well as age-related sensory disorders. Changes in auditory functioning with age have been well documented (Corso, 1985; Fozard, 1990; Schieber, 1992). Decreased auditory acuity, particularly for high frequencies (termed *presbycusis*), occurs with increasing age and affects the perception of speech. Word comprehension thus becomes increasingly difficult with advancing age. Older individuals can become handicapped in speech comprehension and oral communication due to these deficits (Pickett, Bergman, & Levitt, 1979; Plomp & Mimpen, 1979). In some cases, older adults with hearing loss may be mistakenly presumed to be confused or demented (Becker, 1981).

The prevalence of hearing loss in those over 75 years of age has been estimated to be 50% (Plomp, 1978). Hearing loss occurring early in life can be associated with late-life paranoid psychosis (Cooper, 1976), and the association between hearing loss and emotional disturbance, particularly depression, in the elderly has been documented (e.g., O'Neil & Calhoun, 1975). Hearing loss in an older person can clearly affect the results of verbal tests of cognitive status, leading to inaccurate interpretations of test performance (e.g., Peters, Potter, & Scholer, 1988). Weinstein and Amsel (1986) administered a mental status questionnaire, with and without the tester's voice amplified to compensate for hearing loss, to a group of institutionalized older adults with hearing impairment. They found that 33% of the individuals were reclassified as being less severely demented when amplification was used. Roccaforte, Burke, Bayer, and Wenger (1992) similarly found diminished hearing to be associated with lower scores on a telephone-administered version of a commonly used mental status screening test. Auditory acuity screening is thus an important component of any neuropsychological evaluation of an older individual. Note that screening for auditory impairment can effectively be accomplished, even in institutionalized older adults with dementia (Ciurlia-Guy, Cashman, & Lewsen, 1993).

Older persons are also quite susceptible to auditory masking, making the perception of speech difficult when there is background noise (Storandt, 1994). Finally, the rate of auditory information processing slows with age (Lima, Hale, & Myerson, 1991) and is even further slowed in dementing illness, such as AD (Tomoeda, Bayles, Boone, Kaszniak, & Slauson, 1990). In conducting a neuropsychological examination of an older person, it is therefore important to take precautions to maximize auditory comprehension. These include making sure that the patient is wearing any prescribed hearing aids, securing a quiet examination room, speaking somewhat (although not dramatically) more slowly, maintaining eye contact (so that comprehension may be aided by watching the examiner's lips), and (for examiners with high-pitched voices) possibly using a lower-pitched voice than usual. Patients with dementing illness may experience additional impairment of higher level aspects of auditory perception. For example, persons with AD show impaired recognition of meaningful nonverbal sounds, even when high-frequency hearing is within normal limits for age and verbal comprehension (Rapcsak, Kentros, & Rubens, 1989).

Similarly, there is an age-related decline in visual acuity (Johnson & Choy, 1987; Kosnik, Winslow, Kline, Rasinski, & Sekuler, 1988) and a decline in the amount of light that is transmitted through the lens of the eye (due to cataracts or clouding of the lens; Lerman, 1983). As reviewed by Owsley and Sloane (1990) and Schieber (1992), visual capability begins to decline during the 4th decade of life, with, by 65 years of age, about half of all people showing a visual acuity of 20/70 or less. Blindness or other serious visual problems affect more than 7% of the population between 65 and 75 years of age and 16% of those over age 75. Age-associated visual impairment appears to be greater among aging women, as compared with men, and ability to read, watch television, and engage in other visual activities is reduced. Reduced visual capacity has been reported to contribute to apparent disorientation and behavioral deterioration in older adults (O'Neil & Calhoun, 1975). Given the age-related changes in visual functioning and the age-related prevalence of various visual disorders, it is important to consider the possible impact of visual impairment on any cognitive test that requires processing of visual information. Thus, older adults may require higher levels of illumination and larger printed verbal information than younger adults. Uncorrected visual impairment would appear to have the potential for contributing to errors on any cognitive task involving visual information processing, thus potentially increasing false-positive rates in the identification of cognitive impairment.

In some cases of AD and other dementias, the predominant or presenting symptoms may be visual. Research applying visual psychophysical testing, neuro-ophthalmologic examination, and electrophysiologic testing of the visual system (Rizzo et al., 1992) has suggested that these visual impairments result primarily from cortical disease rather than retinocalcarine dysfunction. The most common visual complaints in AD are problems relating to visuospatial functioning (e.g., not bumping into things when walking, finding door handles or other common objects, finding their way in surroundings, sewing, locating the next word or line of print; for review, see Mendez, Tomsak, & Remler, 1990). Until the later stages of dementia, AD patients and their caregivers less frequently complain of difficulties in visually identifying objects, faces, or scenes (Cogan, 1985).

Physical Disability in Older Age

Clearly, another factor to be considered is the possible contribution of any physical disability (e.g., neuromuscular disorder or severe arthritis) to below-expectation performance on any cognitive task. Mental status examination procedures, for example, have poorer ability to discriminate demented from nondemented subjects with some physical disability versus those without such disability (Jagger, Clarke, & Anderson, 1992). The contribution of physical disability is of particular concern when evaluating the oldest old, as it has been estimated that 29% of all persons over age 85 suffer from severe disability (Kunkel & Applebaum, 1992). In neuropsychologically evaluating the person who has a physical disability, the neuropsychologist must rely on those tests that are not likely to be influenced by the person's particular physical impairments.

Response Slowing and Aging

Both simple and choice reaction time show progressive slowing from early through late adulthood (Lima et al., 1991; Wilkinson & Allison, 1989). One obvious implication of this observation is that older adults will take longer to complete various neuropsychological testing procedures than younger adults (Storandt, 1994). This suggests that it may be necessary to take more frequent breaks during a neuropsychological examination session, when evaluating older, particularly ill or frail adults. Although healthy older people are unlikely to fatigue more rapidly than younger adults during average-length (e.g., 2 1/2 hr) testing sessions

(Cunningham, Sepkoski, & Opel, 1978), older persons in poor health are likely to fatigue quickly. The slowing of response speed with aging has other implications for neuropsychological assessment. For example, response slowing may result in slight underestimations of ability (Storandt, 1977) on tasks such as the Arithmetic and Block Design subtests of the Wechsler Adult Intelligence Scale–Revised (Wechsler, 1981) that assign bonus points for faster performance. Examiners therefore often "test the limits" by allowing an older person to continue working on the task after standard cutoff times have elapsed, to get a more complete picture of that person's cognitive strengths and deficits.

Need for Age-Appropriate Normative Data

Another important factor in the interpretation of neuropsychologic test performance is the fact that for both healthy people and people with cerebral disorders, performance on many tests is negatively correlated with adult age (Albert, 1988; Albert, Heller, & Milberg, 1988; Heaton, Grant, & Mathews, 1986; Kaszniak, 1990; Kaszniak, Garron, Fox, Bergen, & Huckman, 1979; La Rue, 1992; Mittenberg, Seidenberg, O'Leary, & DiGiulio, 1989; Moehle & Long, 1989; Petersen, Smith, Kokmen, Ivnik, & Tangalos, 1992; Reitan & Wolfsen, 1986; Vannieuwhirk & Galbraith, 1985). Age relationships with commonly used neuropsychological measures are particularly strong for tests of abstraction and complex problem-solving performance (Elias, Robbins, Walter, & Schultz, 1993). Such age relationships imply the necessity of using age-appropriate normative data when interpreting neuropsychological test performance. A particular problem has been the relative lack of adequate normative data on most neuropsychological tests for the oldest old (i.e., those over age 85; Albert, 1981; Erickson, Eimon, & Hebben, 1992; Kaszniak, 1987; Zec, 1990). Recently, however, relatively large scale normative studies have been published for some of the more commonly used neuropsychological tests, extending norms to over age 90 (Ivnik et al., 1992a; 1992b; 1992c; Malec, Ivnik, & Smith, 1993; VanGorp, Satz, Kiersch, & Henry, 1986). A comprehensive listing of neuropsychological and other cognitive test norms for older adults can be found in Erickson, Eimon, and Hebben (1994).

Need for Education-Appropriate Normative Data

Another factor to be considered is that performance on various neuropsychological tests is correlated with the person's educational background and other indicators of premorbid intellectual functioning (e.g., Barona, Reynolds, & Chastain, 1984; Heaton et al., 1986; Kaszniak et al., 1979). The availability of normative data for particular tests (Heaton, Grant, & Mathews, 1991; Malek et al., 1992), allowing a comparison of an individual to norms for the persons same age (by half-decade) and number of years of formal education, have helped to reduce the impact of this factor on interpretation of assessment results. However, such age- and education-specific normative data is not available for all neuropsychologic tests used in clinical practice, necessitating considerable caution when interpreting performance of any person who is either much more, or much less, educated than the average for the normative sample with which she or he is being compared.

The relationship between education and neuropsychological test performance is particularly problematic in the assessment of possible mild dementia in older adults. Research applying a neuropsychological paradigm-based criterion for identifying dementia (i.e., defective performance on memory testing and tests of at least two other areas of cognitive functioning) in community-resident older adults has classified as demented a significantly higher percentage of those participants with 8 or less years of education, compared with those with more than 8 years of education (Stern et al., 1992). Although this may indicate a greater false-positive rate for neuropsychological identification of dementia in less educated persons, it is also possible that rates of dementia are truly higher among those with little education (for discussion, see Berkman, 1986). Adding a measure of functioning in activities of daily living to the neuropsychological paradigm-based diagnosis may reduce the likelihood of false-positive identification of dementia in less educated people (Pittman et al., 1992).

EVIDENCE SUPPORTING THE VALIDITY OF NEUROPSYCHOLOGICAL DETECTION OF ALZHEIMER'S DISEASE

Much of the increasingly large body of research in the neuropsychology of dementia has focused on an understanding of the nature of cognitive dysfunction in Alzheimer's disease (for review, see Nebes, 1992). Other research has focused on the diagnostic utility of neuropsychological testing in differentiating dementia from normal aging and in distinguishing among the different causes of dementia (for review, see La Rue, 1992; La Rue, Yang, & Osato, 1992; Parks, Zec, & Wilson, 1993). The majority of diagnostic studies have examined the differentiation between normal aging and dementia. Most of these studies (e.g., Bayles, Boone, Tomoeda, Slauson, & Kaszniak, 1989; Eslinger, Damasio, Benton, & Van Allen, 1985; Huff et al., 1987; Kaszniak, Wilson, Fox, & Stebbins, 1986; Storandt, Botwinick, Danziger, Berg, & Hughes, 1984) have compared healthy older people with those having clinically diagnosed AD (of mild-to-moderate dementia severity) on a battery of neuropsychological tests. Results are consistent in showing AD patients to have deficits in two or more areas of cognitive functioning assessed by the tests, with the largest deficits seen on tests of ability to learn new information and retain this information over time.

Studies concerned with the differentiation of very mildly demented probable AD patients from healthy elderly people (Knopman & Ryberg, 1989; Morris et al., 1991; Welsh, Butters, Hughes, Mohs, & Heyman, 1991) have shown that measures of recent memory, particularly those involving delayed recall of newly learned material, are most discriminating. In one study (Morris et al., 1991), the neuropsychologic differentiation of normal older adults from those with very mild cognitive impairment was supported by subsequent postmortem histopathologic evidence of AD in all of those neuropsychologically classified as mildly impaired and in none of those classified as normal elderly. Also, Flicker, Ferris, and Reisberg (1991) reported that tests of recent memory have high sensitivity and specificity in discriminating mildly impaired individuals who cognitively decline at 2-year reexamination from those who do not. Despite this encouraging data for the application of neuropsychological testing, particularly of memory functioning, in the detection of very mild dementia, high sensitivity can be at the cost of lower specificity. Neuropsychological assessment batteries specifically designed or selected for the detection of mild dementia are correlated with participant educational level (Ganguli et al., 1991) and can clearly be affected by physical disability, visual or auditory impairment, psychiatric illness (including depression), and limited facility with the English language (O'Connor, Pollitt, Hyde, Miller, & Fellowes, 1991). Therefore, caution in the clinical interpretation of neuropsychological test results is necessary when any of these confounding conditions is present.

Overall, the available research indicates that neuropsychological assessment, particularly when measures of delayed recall are included, makes an important contribution to the identification of mild dementia, when interpreted within the context of other clinical data (e.g., informant-based history of cognitive decline, evidence of impairment in instrumental activities of daily living, educational background, assessment for depression, sensory impairment, or other factors than dementing illness to account for impaired performance). Due to the lower sensitivity of mental status screening tests, such as the MMSE, for detecting mild as compared to moderate-to-severe degrees of cognitive impairment (for review, see Tombaugh & McIntyre, 1992), neuropsychological testing may be particularly helpful when there is a history of apparent cognitive decline, but where a brief mental status test is performed within normal limits.

DIFFERENTIAL DIAGNOSIS OF DEMENTIA VERSUS DEPRESSION

A particularly difficult clinical problem involves the differential diagnosis of persons who present with signs of both cognitive impairment and depression. It must be determined whether the person is experiencing cognitive difficulty secondary to a depressive disorder or has developed a depressive syndrome secondary to a dementing illness, such as AD.

On the basis of available research, it has been estimated that between 1% and 31% of patients diagnosed as having a progressive dementing illness may actually be suffering from depression with associated cognitive deficits (Katzman, Lasker, & Bernstein, 1988). It has been estimated that 20% of older depressed patients may have cognitive deficits sufficiently severe as to merit the term *dementia syndrome of depression* (La Rue, D'Elia, Clark, Spar, & Jarvik, 1986). There are significant clinical risks associated with errors in differential diagnosis. Mistakenly diagnosing an irreversible dementing illness in a person actually suffering from depression deprives the person of appropriate treatment (psychologic and pharmacologic) and risks further deterioration of function. There are also risks associated with misdiagnosing a progressive dementing illness as depression. These include inappropriate treatment and the failure to provide prognostic information that would permit the patient and family members the opportunity to prepare for the consequences of progressive dementing illness.

Diagnosis is also complicated by the fact that dementing illnesses and depression often coexist. Teri and Wagner (1992) noted that published prevalence estimates of depressive syndromes in AD range from 0 to 86% with the majority of studies reporting rates in the 17%–29% range. Once a person has been diagnosed as having probable AD, symptoms of depression may go unrecognized. Because patients with coexisting depression and AD can expect to benefit from treatment of their depression (for review of the evidence for this conclusion, see Teri & Wagner, 1992), failure to diagnose and treat depression in an AD patient may result in unnecessary emotional, physical, and social discomfort. Patients with coexistent depression and AD have also been found more likely to exhibit delusions, various behavior problems such as restlessness and agitation, and greater impairment of instrumental activities of daily living than AD patients without depression (see Kaszniak & Christenson, 1994).

Neuropsychological assessment has an important role to play in the differential diagnosis of dementia and depression in older adults, as reviewed in detail by Kaszniak and Christenson (1994). Psychologists have contributed to the development and validation of various interview-based and self-report measures of depressive symptoms that are appropriate for use with older, cognitively impaired individuals (see Kaszniak &

Scogin, 1995). In addition, research has supported the validity of particular patterns of neuropsychological test performance, particularly involving different aspects of memory (e.g., rate of forgetting, free recall vs. recognition, or response to semantic organization of material to be remembered) as important contributors in the effort to differentiate the cognitive effects of dementia and depression. Despite such encouraging data, caution must be exercised in the interpretation of neuropsychological assessment results for persons with signs of both dementia and depression. The long-term prognosis of such patients is quite variable (i.e., some showing remission of both depression and cognitive impairment with effective depression treatment and some showing progressive dementia in long-term follow-up), and neuropsychological assessment may not be helpful in clarifying prognosis (Nussbaum, Kaszniak, Allender, & Rapcsak, 1995). Differential diagnosis in this area remains a necessarily interdisciplinary endeavor, with physicians and other health care providers also playing important roles. Complex interactions exist among biological aspects of illness, medications (both psychotropic and nonpsychotropic), age-related changes in pharmacokinetics and pharmacodynamics, and a variety of psychologic and social factors that influence the occurrence and nature of both cognitive and affective symptoms in older adults (see Cummings & Benson, 1992; Depression Guideline Panel, 1993).

PROVISION OF INFORMATION TO HEALTH CARE PROVIDERS, PATIENTS, AND FAMILY MEMBERS

Neuropsychological assessment can also be helpful to patients and their caregivers (whether personal or professional) in assisting them to understand the patient and in reducing anxiety and confusion (see Lezak, 1995). In my experience, this can be one of the most valuable aspects of neuropsychological consultation. Patients and their family members are often understandably distressed by the cognitive and behavioral changes that have provoked the request for consultation. Even when, as in AD, there is no available treatment to reverse or arrest the disorder, persons can be comforted by gaining an understanding of which specific functions are impaired and which remain fairly intact. It can be particularly important to identify and accurately describe patterns of cognitive strengths and deficits as early as possible in the course of a progressive dementing illness. Persons early in the course of AD may have relatively severe impairment of memory but considerably more intact functioning in language comprehension and expression, conceptual reasoning, and judgment. Therefore, the capacity of such persons to make decisions concerning necessary future plans (e.g., disposition of their estate or wishes concerning future medical and long-term care) may remain intact at this early stage. Providing the patient and family members with accurate assessment information can allow the person to make decisions and plans before the progression of illness renders him or her incompetent to do so.

There is also some evidence (e.g., LaBarge, Rosenman, Leavitt, & Cristiani, 1988) to suggest that mildly demented persons can improve their utilization of coping mechanisms and identify strategies to compensate for memory loss when they are given information concerning their specific cognitive strengths and deficits (derived from neuropsychological testing), within the context of brief supportive counseling. Again, it is important that such information be provided as early as possible to the person with a progressive dementing illness such as AD, because insight and the ability to maintain awareness of cognitive deficits may be lost with illness progression (Kaszniak & Christenson, 1996; McGlynn & Kaszniak, 1991a, 1991b).

ASSESSMENT OF DISEASE PROGRESSION AND TREATMENT EFFECTS

Dementing illnesses are typically progressive in their effects on cognitive functioning. Neuropsychological consultation can play an important role in assessing the severity of dementia and in tracking disease progression (for purposes of guiding caregivers and adjusting goals of clinical management). When mildly demented probable AD patients are compared with moderately demented individuals (Hill, Storandt, & LaBarge, 1992; Welsh, Butters, Hughes, Mohs, & Heyman, 1992), moderately demented patients show more severe memory impairment (often at the "basement" of the measurement range of the memory test) and an increased number and severity of deficits in other areas of cognitive functioning. The severity of recent memory deficits, particularly delayed recall, early in the course of AD, renders memory tests less useful (because of basement effects) for staging the severity of dementia across individuals (Welsh et al., 1992) or for tracking the progression of dementia over time (Kaszniak et al., 1986). Neuropsychological measures of other aspects of cognitive functioning (e.g., recognition memory, verbal fluency, confrontation naming, and praxis) appear better for staging dementia severity or tracking dementia progression (Kaszniak et al., 1986; Welsh et al., 1992).

Information concerning the differential sensitivity and specificity of neuropsychological tests for the initial detection versus the staging or tracking of dementia severity has important implications for the choice of outcome measures to evaluate intervention efficacy (see Berg et al., 1992). Neuropsychological tests, when carefully selected (e.g., according to criteria such as reliability, sensitivity to change, absence of marked basement effects, brevity, and high face validity), can play a very important role in the evaluation of medication or other intervention trials for patients with dementing illness (see Flicker, 1988). Clinical neuropsychologists have therefore been critical collaborators in the design and execution of such clinical trials.

As already noted, most dementing illness involves a progressive deterioration in cognitive functioning. Therefore, the documentation of deterioration is an important task in any clinical evaluation of an individual with possible AD or other dementia. The most direct approach to obtaining such evidence would be to compare performance on neuropsychological tests over time. In most instances, however, prior test scores are unavailable at the time when an initial assessment is made of an individual suspected of having a dementing illness. In such cases, the neuropsychologist has to rely on a history of progressive cognitive deterioration, obtained from a close relative or other informant. Relatives appear able to provide valid reports of progressive deterioration in dementia patients. McGlone et al. (1990) compared older adults with complaints of memory difficulty who later showed evidence of progressive dementia (as determined by 8- to 24-month neuropsychological reassessment) with those with memory complaints but without evidence of progressive dementia. The two groups of patients reported comparable numbers of memory complaints. However, when relatives rated memory change over time, the first group of patients, who did not show evidence of dementia, did not differ significantly from healthy elderly controls (without memory complaints), whereas the second group of patients, who did show evidence of progressive dementia, were rated by their relatives as having become significantly worse. Furthermore, the relatives' assessments of patients' memory were significantly intercorrelated with objective-memory-test scores, and not with patients' depression. This later observation is of importance because other research has shown self-reported memory complaints in healthy older adults to be more closely correlated with depressed mood than with objective-memory-test performance (e.g., Bolla, Lindgren, Bonaccorsy, & Bleecker, 1991). Research concerning the retrospective accounts of dementia symptoms, obtained from relatives of patients referred to a memory-disorders clinic, has also shown that relatives' reports are reasonably reliable over a 4- to 17-month test–retest interval (La Rue, Watson, & Plotkin, 1992). Bayles and Tomoeda (1991), in a study of 99 AD patients and their caregivers, also found that caregiver reports of memory and linguistic communication symptoms were significantly correlated with patients' performance on select corresponding items of a linguistic-communication test battery. Although such results encourage the use of caregiver interview data for assessing the presence of multiple cognitive deficits, it has also been found that relatives' reports are influenced by the nature of the relationship to the patient. For example, La Rue, Watson, and Plotkin (1992) found that spouses of memory-impaired patients reported lower levels of impairment than did younger relatives. Thus, neuropsychologists will often include more than one family informant or a family consensus approach, to increase the accuracy of conclusions about the presence and range of cognitive impairments in persons suspected of dementia. When no reliable informant is available, the clinician may have to rely on a qualitative evaluation of neuropsychological assessment results, to determine whether the pattern of cognitive deficits is more consistent with a dementing illness or with relatively focal or diffuse nonprogressive cerebral disease. Although patients with focal cerebral damage (e.g., left-hemisphere stroke) can show neuropsychological evidence of deficits in more than one area of cognitive functioning (e.g., language, memory, or executive functioning; Beeson, Bayles, Rubens, & Kaszniak, 1993), the pattern of deficits across tests differs from that of AD patients (Bayles et al., 1989).

TREATMENT AND MANAGEMENT OF COGNITIVE AND BEHAVIOR PROBLEMS

Neuropsychological consultation can also make important contributions to the clinical management of patients with AD or other dementing illness. Identification of relatively intact cognitive functioning can assist in developing plans for sharing daily responsibilities between the patient and others in their environment (see La Rue, Yang, & Osato, 1992). Conversely, neuropsychological documentation of particular deficits can direct caregivers to areas where the patient will require additional supervision or assistance. For example, Henderson, Mack, and Williams (1989), in a study of patients with probable AD, found that neuropsychologically documented visuoconstructive deficits (equating patients with vs. without visuospatial deficits for degree of memory impairment) significantly predicted real-world spatial disorientation (i.e., caregiver-reported episodes of getting lost, failing to recognize familiar environments, and wandering). Although research results to date have been mixed, neuropsychological evaluation may also be able to make contributions to decisions regarding whether the patient can safely continue in potentially risky activities such as driving (for review, see Kaszniak, Keyl, & Albert, 1991).

Finally, neuropsychologists and clinical geropsychologists have made important contributions to the design and delivery of interventions to reduce behavioral problems in AD and other dementing illnesses. Fisher and Carstensen (1990) reviewed available empirical studies of various behavior-management procedures that have been successfully applied in reducing behavior problems (e.g., aggressiveness or agitation) in dementia. Although continuing research needs to be directed toward answering questions concerning predictors of who will respond best to behavioral interventions and how treatment gains can be maintained in the face of progressive dementia, results to date have encouraged the application of behavioral interventions with persons having Alzheimer's and other dementing illnesses. Psychologists with training in behavioral treatment methods remain those best qualified to deliver such interventions. As recently reviewed by Teri and McCurry (1994), there exist a small number of studies that have reported effectiveness of cognitive–behavioral therapy in reducing coexistent depression in outpatients with progressive dementias, such as AD. Note that in the ongoing study by Teri and colleagues (described in Teri & McCurry, 1994), cognitive–behavior therapy for depression in AD patients also resulted in an improvement of caregiver's mood, even though treatment did not specifically focus on the caregiver. Teri and McCurry speculated that increased patient-management skill (caregivers were taught behavioral strategies for improving patient mood by increasing pleasant events, decreasing unpleasant events, and using behavioral problem-solving strategies to alter depression-related contingencies), the availability of regular support (eight 60-minute training sessions, once per week), and the reduced depression in their family member with dementia may explain the added caregiver benefits.

Within long-term-care settings, where large numbers of AD patients with more advanced dementia reside, psychologists have also been involved in providing behavioral interventions aimed at increasing sensory stimulation, maintaining social activity, and reducing particular problem behaviors (e.g., incontinence). The few available studies that have evaluated psychotherapeutic interventions with nursing home residents have suggested improvements in depression, social interaction, and patient self-concept (for review, see Terri & McCurry, 1994).

SUMMARY AND CONCLUSION

It is clear that psychologists have much to offer, both in assessment and intervention, to persons with AD or related dementias and their caregivers. Research evidence supports the reliability and validity of neuropsychological assessment in the early detection of dementia, in contributions to differential diagnosis, in the evaluation of disease progression and treatment trials, and in providing accurate descriptive information to patients and their caregivers. Furthermore, although the available body of research is still small, there is also growing research support for the role of psychological, particularly behavioral and cognitive–behavioral, interventions in the treatment and management of mood and behavioral problems of AD patients. The contributions of psychologists within neurological settings serving persons with AD, both in conducting necessary research and in the direct delivery of clinical service, have been substantial. The success of these efforts, to date, argues for an expanding role for psychology within this area of tertiary medical care.

REFERENCES

Albert, M. S. (1981). Geriatric neuropsychology. *Journal of Consulting and Clinical Psychology, 49*, 835–850.

Albert, M. S. (1988). Assessment of cognitive function. In M. S. Albert & M. B. Moss (Eds.), *Geriatric neuropsychology* (pp. 57–81). New York: Guilford Press.

Albert, M. S., Heller, H. S., & Milberg, W. (1988). Changes in naming ability with age. *Psychology and Aging, 3*, 173–178.

Albert, M. S., & Moss, M. B. (Eds.). (1988). *Geriatric neuropsychology.* New York: Guilford Press.

American Psychiatric Association. (1994). *Diagnostic and statistical manual of mental disorders* (4th ed.). Washington, DC: Author.

Anthony, J. C., LaResche, L., Niaz, U., Von Koroff, M. R., & Folstein, M. F. (1982). Limits of the 'Mini-Mental State' as a screening test for dementia and delerium among hospital patients. *Psychological Medicine, 12*, 397–408.

Barona, A., Reynolds, C., & Chastain, R. (1984). A demographically based index of premorbid intelligence for the WAIS–R. *Journal of Consulting and Clinical Psychology, 52*, 885–887.

Bayles, K. A., Boone, D. R., Tomoeda, C. K., Slauson, T. J., & Kaszniak, A. W. (1989). Differentiating Alzheimer's patients from the normal elderly and stroke patients with aphasia. *Journal of Speech and Hearing Disorders, 54*, 74–87.

Bayles, K. A., & Kaszniak, A. W. (1987). *Communication and cognition in normal aging and dementia.* Boston: College-Hill/Little, Brown.

Bayles, K. A., & Tomoeda, C. K. (1991). Caregiver report of prevalence and appearance order of linguistic symptoms in Alzheimer's patients. *The Gerontologist, 31*, 210–216.

Becker, G. (1981). *The disability experience: Educating health professionals about disabling conditions.* Berkeley: University of California Press.

Beeson, P. M., Bayles, K. B., Rubens, A. B., & Kaszniak, A. W. (1993). Memory impairment and executive control in individuals with stroke-induced aphasia. *Brain and Language, 45*, 253–275.

Berg, L., Miller, J. P., Bary, J., Rubin, E. H., Morris, J. C., & Figiel, G. (1992). Mild senile dementia of the Alzheimer type: 4. Evaluation of intervention. *Annals of Neurology, 31,* 242–249.

Berkman, L. F. (1986). The association between educational adjustment and mental status examinations: Of etiologic significance for senile dementia or not? *Journal of Chronic Disease, 39,* 171–174.

Bolla, K. I., Lindgren, K. N., Bonaccorsy, C., & Bleecker, M. L. (1991). Memory complaints in older adults: Fact or fiction? *Archives of Neurology, 48,* 61–64.

Bondi, M. W., Kaszniak, A. W., Bayles, K. A., & Vance, K. T. (1993). The contributions of frontal system dysfunction to memory and perceptual abilities in Parkinson's disease. *Neuropsychology, 7,* 89–102.

Butters, M. A., Salmon, D. P., & Butters, N. (1994). Neuropsychological assessment of dementia. In M. Storandt & G. R. VandenBos (Eds.), *Neuropsychological assessment of dementia and depression in older adults: A clinician's guide* (pp. 33–59). Washington, DC: American Psychological Association.

Ciurlia-Guy, E., Cashman, M., & Lewsen, B. (1993). Identifying hearing loss and hearing handicap among chronic care elderly people. *The Gerontologist, 33,* 644–649.

Cogan, D. G. (1985). Visual disturbances with focal progressive dementing disease. *American Journal of Ophthalmology, 100,* 68–72.

Cooper, A. F. (1976). Deafness and psychiatric illness. *British Journal of Psychiatry, 129,* 215–226.

Corso, J. F. (1985). Communication, presbycusis, and technological aids. In H. K. Ulatowska (Ed.), *The aging brain: Communication in the elderly* (pp. 33–51). San Diego, CA: College-Hill Press.

Crum, R. M., Anthony, J. C., Bassett, S. S., & Folstein, M. F. (1993). Population-based norms for the Mini-Mental State Examination by age and educational level. *Journal of the American Medical Association, 269,* 2386–3291.

Cummings, J. L., & Benson, D. F. (1992). *Dementia: A clinical approach* (2nd ed.). Stoneham, MA: Butterworth-Heinemann.

Cunningham, W. R., Sepkoski, C. M., & Opel, M. P. (1978). Fatigue effects on intelligence test performance in the elderly. *Journal of Gerontology, 33,* 541–545.

Depression Guideline Panel. (1993). *Depression in primary care: Volume 1. Detection and diagnosis: Clinical Practice Guideline, Number 5* (AHCPR Publication No. 93-0550). Rockville, MD: Public Health Service, Agency for Health Care Policy and Research.

Elias, M. F., Robbins, M. A., Walter, L. J., & Schultz, N. R. (1993). The influence of gender and age on Halstead–Reitan Neuropsychological Test performance. *Journal of Gerontology: Psychological Sciences, 48,* P278–P281.

Erickson, R. C., Eimon, P., & Hebben, N. (1992). A bibliography of normative articles on cognitive tests for older adults. *The Clinical Neuropsychologist, 6,* 98–102.

Erickson, R. C., Eimon, P., & Hebben, N. (1994). A listing of references to cognitive test norms for older adults. In M. Storandt & G. R. VandenBos (Eds.), *Neuropsychological assessment of dementia and depression in older adults: A clinician's guide* (pp. 183–197). Washington, DC: American Psychological Association.

Eslinger, P. J., Damasio, A. R., Benton, A. L., & Van Allen, M. (1985). Neuropsychologic detection of abnormal mental decline in older persons. *Journal of the American Medical Association, 253*, 670–674.

Fisher, J. E., & Carstensen, L. L. (1990). Behavior management of the dementias. *Clinical Psychology Review, 10*, 611–629.

Flicker, C. (1988). Neuropsychological evaluation of treatment effects in the elderly: A critique of tests in current use. *Psychopharmacology Bulletin, 4*, 535–556.

Flicker, C., Ferris, S. H., & Reisberg, B. (1991). Mild cognitive impairment in the elderly: Predictors of dementia. *Neurology, 41*, 1006–1009.

Folstein, M. F., Anthony, J. C., Parhad, I., Duffy, B., & Gruenberg, E. M. (1985). The meaning of cognitive impairment in the elderly. *Journal of the American Geriatrics Society, 33*, 228–235.

Folstein, M. F., Folstein, S., & McHugh, P. R. (1975). Mini-mental state: A practical method for grading the cognitive state of patients for the clinician. *Journal of Psychiatric Research, 12*, 189–198.

Fozard, J. L. (1990). Vision and hearing in aging. In J. E. Birren & K. W. Schaie (Eds.), *Handbook of the psychology of aging* (3rd ed., pp. 150–170). New York: Van Nostrand Reinhold.

Ganguli, M., Ratcliff, G., Huff, F. J., Belle, S., Kancel, M. J., Fisher, L., Seaberg, E. C., & Kuller, L. H. (1991). Effects of age, gender, and education on cognitive tests in a rural elderly community sample: Norms from the Monongahela Valley Independent Elders Survey. *Neuroepidemiology, 10*, 42–52.

Haase, G. R. (1977). Diseases presenting as dementia. In C. E. Wells (Ed.), *Dementia* (2nd ed., pp. 27–67). Philadelphia: Davis.

Heaton, R. K., Grant, I., & Mathews, C. G. (1986). Differences in neuropsychological test performance associated with age, education, and sex. In I. Grant & K. M. Adams (Eds.), *Neuropsychological assessment of neuropsychiatric disorders* (pp. 100–120). New York: Oxford University Press.

Heaton, R. K., Grant, I., & Mathews, C. G. (1991). *Comprehensive norms for an expanded Halstead–Reitan Battery: Demographic corrections, research findings, and clinical applications.* Odessa, FL: Psychological Assessment Resources.

Henderson, V. W., Mack, W., & Williams, B. W. (1989). Spatial disorientation in Alzheimer's disease. *Archives of Neurology, 46*, 391–394.

Hill, R. D., Storandt, M., & LaBarge, E. (1992). Psychometric discrimination of moderate senile dementia of the Alzheimer type. *Archives of Neurology, 49*, 377–380.

Huff, F. J., Becker, J. T., Belle, S. H., Nebes, R. D., Holland, A. L., & Boller, F. (1987). Cognitive deficits and clinical diagnosis of Alzheimer's disease. *Neurology, 37,* 1119–1124.

Ineichen, B. (1987). Measuring the rising tide. How many dementia cases will there be by 2001? *British Journal of Psychiatry, 150,* 193–200.

Ivnik, R. J., Malec, J. F., Smith, G. E., Tangalos, E. G., Petersen, R. C., Kokmen, E., & Kurland, L. T. (1992a). Mayo's Older Americans Normative Studies: Updated AVLT norms for ages 56 to 97. *The Clinical Neuropsychologist, 6* (Suppl.), 83–104.

Ivnik, R. J., Malec, J. F., Smith, G. E., Tangalos, E. G., Petersen, R. C., Kokmen, E., & Kurland, L. T. (1992b). Mayo's Older Americans Normative Studies: WAIS–R norms for ages 56 to 97. *The Clinical Neuropsychologist, 6* (Suppl.), 1–30.

Ivnik, R. J., Malec, J. F., Smith, G. E., Tangalos, E. G., Petersen, R. C., Kokmen, E., & Kurland, L. T. (1992c). Mayo's Older Americans Normative Studies: WMS–R norms for ages 56 to 94. *The Clinical Neuropsychologist, 6* (Suppl.), 49–82.

Jagger, C., Clarke, M., & Anderson, J. (1992). Screening for dementia: A comparison of two tests using receiver operating characteristics (ROC) analysis. *International Journal of Geriatric Psychiatry, 7,* 659–665.

Johnson, M. A., & Choy, D. (1987). On the definition of age-related norms for visual function testing. *Applied Optics, 26,* 1449–1454.

Jorm, A. F., Korten, A. E., & Henderson, A. S. (1987). The prevalence of dementia: A quantitative integration of the literature. *Acta Psychiatrica Scandinavica, 76,* 465–479.

Kaszniak, A. W. (1987). Neuropsychological consultation to geriatricians: Issues in the assessment of memory complaints. *The Clinical Neuropsychologist, 1,* 35–46.

Kaszniak, A. W. (1990). Psychological assessment of the aging individual. In J. E. Birren & K. W. Schaie (Eds.), *Handbook of the psychology of aging* (3rd. ed., pp. 427–445). San Diego, CA: Academic Press.

Kaszniak, A. W., & Christenson, G. D. (1994). Differential diagnosis of dementia and depression. In M. Storandt & G. R. VandenBos (Eds.), *Neuropsychological assessment of dementia and depression in older adults: A clinician's guide* (pp. 81–117). Washington, DC: American Psychological Association.

Kaszniak, A. W., & Christenson, G. D. (1996). Self-awareness of deficit in patients with Alzheimer's disease. In S. R. Hameroff, A. W. Kaszniak, & A. C. Scott (Eds.), *Toward a science of consciousness: The first Tucson discussions and debates* (pp. 227–242). Cambridge, MA: MIT Press.

Kaszniak, A. W., Garron, D. C., Fox, J. H., Bergen, D., & Huckman, M. (1979). Cerebral atrophy, EEG slowing, age, education, and cognitive functioning in suspected dementia. *Neurology, 29,* 1273–1279.

Kaszniak, A. W., Keyl, P., & Albert, M. (1991). Dementia and the older driver. *Human Factors, 33,* 527–537.

Kaszniak, A. W., & Scogin, F. R. (1995). Assessing for dementia and depression in older adults. *The Clinical Psychologist, 48*(2), 17–24.

Kaszniak, A. W., Wilson, R. S., Fox, J. H., & Stebbins, G. T. (1986). Cognitive assessment in Alzheimer's disease: Cross-sectional and longitudinal perspectives. *Canadian Journal of Neurological Sciences, 13*, 420–423.

Katzman, R. (1986). Alzheimer's disease. *New England Journal of Medicine, 314*, 964–973.

Katzman, R., Lasker, B., & Bernstein, N. (1988). Advances in the diagnosis of dementia: Accuracy of diagnosis and consequences of misdiagnosis of disorders causing dementia. In R. D. Terry (Ed.), *Aging and the brain* (pp. 17–62). New York: Raven Press.

Knopman, D. S., & Ryberg, S. (1989). A verbal memory test with high predictive accuracy for dementia of the Alzheimer type. *Archives of Neurology, 46*, 141–145.

Kolb, B., & Whishaw, I. Q. (1995). *Fundamentals of human neuropsychology* (4th ed.). New York: Freeman.

Kosnik, W., Winslow, L., Kline, D., Rasinski, K., & Sekuler, R. (1988). Visual changes in daily life throughout adulthood. *Journal of Gerontology, 43*, P53–P70.

Kramer, M. (1986). Trends of institutionalization and prevalence of mental disorders in nursing homes. In M. S. Harper & B. D. Lebowitz (Eds.), *Mental illness in nursing homes: Agenda for research* (DHHS Publication No. ADM 86-1459, pp. 7–26). Rockville, MD: National Institute of Mental Health.

Kunkel, S. R., & Applebaum, R. A. (1992). Estimating the prevalence of long-term disability for an aging society. *Journal of Gerontology: Social Sciences, 47*, S253–S260.

LaBarge, E., Rosenman, L. S., Leavitt, K., & Cristiani, T. (1988). Counseling clients with mild senile dementia of the Alzheimer's type: A pilot study. *Journal of Neurological Rehabilitation, 2*, 167–173.

La Rue, A. (1992). *Aging and neuropsychological assessment.* New York: Plenum.

La Rue, A., D'Elia, L. F., Clark, E. O., Spar, J. E., & Jarvik, L. F. (1986). Clinical tests of memory in dementia, depression, and healthy aging. *Journal of Psychology and Aging, 1*, 69–77.

La Rue, A., Watson, J., & Plotkin, D. A. (1992). Retrospective accounts of dementia symptoms: Are they reliable? *The Gerontologist, 32*, 240–245.

La Rue, A., Yang, J., & Osato, S. (1992). Neuropsychological assessment. In J. E. Birren, R. B. Sloane, & G. D. Cohen (Eds.), *Handbook of mental health and aging* (2nd. ed., pp. 643–670). San Diego, CA: Academic Press.

Lerman, S. (1983). An experimental and clinical evaluation of lens transparency and aging. *Journal of Gerontology, 38*, 293–301.

Lezak, M. D. (1995). *Neuropsychological assessment* (3rd ed.). New York: Oxford University Press.

Li, G., Shen, Y. C., Chen, C. H., Zhao, Y. W., & Li, S. R. (1989). An epidemiological survey of age-related dementia in an urban area of Beijing. *Acta Psychiatrica Scandinavica, 79,* 557–563.

Lima, S. D., Hale, S., & Myerson, J. (1991). How general is general slowing? Evidence from the lexical domain. *Psychology and Aging, 6,* 416–425.

Malec, J. F., Ivnik, R. J., & Smith, G. E. (1993). Neuropsychology and normal aging: The clinician's perspective. In R. W. Parks, R. F. Zec, & R. S. Wilson (Eds.), *Neuropsychology of Alzheimer's disease and other dementias* (pp. 81–111). New York: Oxford University Press.

Malec, J. F., Ivnik, R. J., Smith, G. E., Tangalos, E. G., Petersen, R. C., Kokmen, E., & Kurland, L. T. (1992). Mayo's Older Americans Normative Studies: Utility of corrections for age and education for the WAIS–R. *The Clinical Neuropsychologist, 6* (Suppl.), 31–47.

Manton, K. G. (1990). Mortality and morbidity. In R. H. Binstock & L. K. George (Eds.), *Handbook of aging and the social sciences* (3rd ed., pp. 64–90). San Diego, CA: Academic Press.

McGlone, J., Gupta, S., Humphrey, D., Oppenheimer, S., Mirsen, T., & Evans, D. R. (1990). Screening for early dementia using memory complaints from patients and relatives. *Archives of Neurology, 47,* 1189–1193.

McGlynn, S. M., & Kaszniak, A. W. (1991a). Unawareness of deficits in dementia and schizophrenia. In G. P. Prigatano & D. Schacter (Eds.), *Awareness of deficit after brain injury: Clinical and theoretical issues* (pp. 84–110). New York: Oxford University Press.

McGlynn, S. M., & Kaszniak, A. W. (1991b). When metacognition fails: Impaired awareness of deficit in Alzheimer's disease. *Journal of Cognitive Neuroscience, 3,* 184–189.

Mendez, M. F., Tomsak, R. L., & Remler, B. (1990). Disorders of the visual system in Alzheimer's disease. *Journal of Clinical Neuro-ophthalmology, 10,* 62–69.

Mittenberg, W., Seidenberg, M., O'Leary, D. S., & DiGiulio, D. V. (1989). Changes in cerebral functioning associated with normal aging. *Journal of Clinical and Experimental Neuropsychology, 11,* 918–932.

Moehle, K. A., & Long, C. J. (1989). Models of aging and neuropsychological test performance decline with aging. *Journal of Gerontology: Psychological Sciences, 44,* P176–P177.

Morris, J. C., McKeel, D. W., Storandt, M., Rubin, E. H., Price, J. L., Grant, E. A., Ball, M. J., & Berg, L. (1991). Very mild Alzheimer's disease: Informant-based clinical, psychometric, and pathologic distinction from normal aging. *Neurology, 41,* 469–478.

Murden, R. A., McRae, T. D., Kaner, S., & Bucknam, N. E. (1991). Mini-Mental State Exam scores vary with education in Blacks and Whites. *Journal of the American Geriatric Society, 39,* 149–155.

Myers, G. C. (1990). Demography of aging. In R. H. Binstock & L. K. George (Eds.), *Handbook of aging and the social sciences* (3rd ed., pp. 19–44). San Diego, CA: Academic Press.

Naugle, R. I., Cullum, C. M., & Bigler, E. D. (1990). Evaluation of intellectual and memory function among dementia patients who were intellectually superior. *The Clinical Neuropsychologist, 4*, 355–374.

Nebes, R. D. (1992). Cognitive dysfunction in Alzheimer's disease. In F. I. M. Craik & T. A. Salthouse (Eds.), *The handbook of aging and cognition* (pp. 373–446). Hillsdale, NJ: Erlbaum.

Nelson, A., Fogel, B. S., & Faust, D. (1986). Bedside cognitive screening instruments: A critical assessment. *Journal of Nervous and Mental Disease, 174*, 73–83.

Nussbaum, P. D., Kaszniak, A. W., Allender, J., & Rapcsak, S. (1995). Depression and cognitive decline in the elderly: A follow-up study. *The Clinical Neuropsychologist, 9*, 101–111.

O'Connor, D. W., Pollitt, P. A., Hyde, J. B., Miller, N. D., & Fellowes, J. L. (1989). The reliability and validity of the Mini-Mental State in a British community survey. *Journal of Psychiatric Research, 23*, 87–96.

O'Connor, D. W., Pollitt, P. A., Hyde, J. B., Miller, N. D., & Fellowes, J. L. (1991). Clinical issues relating to the diagnosis of mild dementia in a British community survey. *Archives of Neurology, 48*, 530–534.

O'Neil, P. M., & Calhoun, K. S. (1975). Sensory deficits and behavioral deterioration in senescence. *Journal of Abnormal Psychology, 84*, 579–582.

Owsley, C., & Sloane, M. E. (1990). Vision and aging. In F. Boller & J. Grafman (Eds.), *Handbook of neuropsychology* (Vol. 4, pp. 229–249). Amsterdam: Elsevier.

Parks, R. W., Zec, R. F., & Wilson, R. S. (Eds.). (1993). *Neuropsychology of Alzheimer's disease and other dementias*. New York: Oxford University Press.

Peters, C. A., Potter, J. F., & Scholer, S. G. (1988). Hearing impairment as a predictor of cognitive decline in dementia. *Journal of the American Geriatric Society, 36*, 981–986.

Petersen, R. C., Smith, G., Kokmen, E., Ivnik, R. J., & Tangalos, E. G. (1992). Memory function in normal aging. *Neurology, 42*, 396–401.

Pickett, J. M., Bergman, M., & Levitt, M. (1979). Aging and speech understanding. In J. M. Ordy & K. Brizzee (Eds.), *Aging: Vol. 10. Speech systems and communication in the elderly* (pp. 167–186). New York: Raven Press.

Pittman, J., Andrews, H., Tatemichi, T., Link, B., Struening, E., Stern, Y., & Mayeux, R. (1992). Diagnosis of dementia in a heterogeneous population: A comparison of paradigm-based diagnosis and physician's diagnosis. *Archives of Neurology, 49*, 461–467.

Plomp, R. (1978). Auditory handicap of hearing impairment and the limited benefit of hearing aids. *Journal of the Acoustical Society of America, 63*, 533–549.

Plomp, R., & Mimpen, A. M. (1979). Speech reception threshold for sentences as a function of age and noise level. *Journal of the Acoustical Society of America, 66*, 1333–1342.

Poon, L. W., Kaszniak, A. W., & Dudley, W. N. (1992). Approaches in the experimental neuropsychology of dementia: A methodological and model review. In M. Bergner, K. Hasegawa, S. Finkel, & T. Nishimura (Eds.), *Aging and mental disorders: International perspectives* (pp. 150–173). New York: Springer.

Rapcsak, S. Z., Kentros, M., & Rubens, A. (1989). Impaired recognition of meaningful sounds in Alzheimer's disease. *Archives of Neurology, 46,* 1298–1300.

Reitan, R. M., & Wolfsen, D. (1986). The Halstead–Reitan Neuropsychological Test Battery and aging. *Clinical Gerontologist, 5,* 39–61.

Rizzo, J. F. III, Cronin-Golumb, A., Growdon, J. H., Sorkin, S., Rosen, T. J., Sandberg, M. A., Chiappa, K. H., & Lessell, S. (1992). Retinocalcarine function in Alzheimer's disease: A clinical and electrophysiological study. *Archives of Neurology, 49,* 93–101.

Roccaforte, W. H., Burke, W. J., Bayer, B. L., & Wenger, S. P. (1992). Validation of a telephone version of the Mini-Mental State Examination. *Journal of the American Geriatrics Society, 40,* 697–702.

Roman, G. C. (1991). The epidemiology of vascular dementia. In A Hartman, W. Kuschinsky, & S. Hoyer (Eds.), *Cerebral ischemia and dementia* (pp. 9–15). Berlin: Springer-Verlag.

Rorsman, B., Hagnell, O., & Lanke, J. (1986). Prevalence and incidence of senile and multi-infarct dementia in the Lundby study: A comparison between the time periods 1947–1957 and 1957–1972. *Neuropsychobiology, 15,* 122–129.

Schieber, F. (1992). Aging and the senses. In J. E. Birren, R. B. Sloane, & G. D. Cohen (Eds.), *Handbook of mental health and aging* (pp. 251–306). San Diego, CA: Academic Press.

Shibayama, H., Kasahara, Y., & Kobayashi, H. (1986). Prevalence of dementia in a Japanese elderly population. *Acta Psychiatrica Scandinavica, 74,* 144–151.

Smyer, M. A. (1988). The nursing home community. In M. A. Smyer, M. D. Cohn, & D. Brannon (Eds.), *Mental health consultation in nursing homes* (pp. 1–23). New York: New York University Press.

Spreen, O., & Strauss, E. (1991). *A compendium of neuropsychological tests: Administration, norms, and commentary.* New York: Oxford University Press.

Stern, Y., Andrews, H., Pittman, J., Sano, M., Tatemichi, T., Lantigua, R., & Mayeux, R. (1992). Diagnosis of dementia in a heterogeneous population: Development of a neuropsychological paradigm-based diagnosis of dementia and quantified correction for the effects of education. *Archives of Neurology, 49,* 453–460.

Storandt, M. (1977). Age, ability level, and method of administering and scoring the WAIS. *Journal of Gerontology, 32,* 175–178.

Storandt, M. (1994). General principles of assessment of older adults. In M. Storandt & G. R. VandenBos (Eds.), *Neuropsychological assessment of demen-*

tia and depression in older adults: A clinician's guide (pp. 7–32). Washington, DC: American Psychological Association.

Storandt, M., Botwinick, J., Danziger, W. L., Berg, L., & Hughes, C. P. (1984). Psychometric differentiation of mild senile dementia of the Alzheimer type. *Archives of Neurology, 41,* 497–499.

Strub, R. L., & Black, F. W. (1988). *Neurobehavioral disorders: A clinical approach.* Philadelphia: Davis.

Teri, L., & McCurry, S. M. (1994). Psychosocial therapies. In C. E. Coffey & J. L. Cummings (Eds.), *Textbook of geriatric neuropsychiatry* (pp. 661–682). Washington, DC: American Psychiatric Press.

Teri, L., & Wagner, A. (1992). Alzheimer's disease and depression. *Journal of Consulting and Clinical Psychology, 60,* 379–391.

Thal, L. J., Grundman, M., & Klauber, M. R. (1988). Dementia: Characteristics of a referral population and factors associated with progression. *Neurology, 38,* 1083–1090.

Tombaugh, T. N., & McIntyre, N. J. (1992). The Mini-Mental State Examination: A comprehensive review. *Journal of the American Geriatrics Society, 40,* 922–935.

Tomoeda, C. K., Bayles, K. A., Boone, D. R., Kaszniak, A. W., & Slauson, T. J. (1990). Speech rate and syntactic complexity effects on the auditory comprehension of Alzheimer patients. *Journal of Communication Disorders, 23,* 151–161.

VanGorp, W. G., Satz, P., Kiersch, M. E., & Henry, R. (1986). Normative data on the Boston Naming Test for a group of normal older adults. *Journal of Clinical and Experimental Neuropsychology, 8,* 702–705.

Vannieuwhirk, R. R., & Galbraith, G. G. (1985). The relationship of age to performance on the Luria–Nebraska Neuropsychological Battery. *Journal of Clinical Psychology, 41,* 527–532.

Wechsler, D. (1981). *Manual for the Wechsler Adult Intelligence Scale—Revised.* New York: Psychological Corporation.

Weinstein, B. E., & Amsel, L. (1986). Hearing loss and senile dementia in the institutionalized elderly. *Clinical Gerontologist, 4,* 3–15.

Welsh, K., Butters, N., Hughes, J., Mohs, R., & Heyman, A. (1991). Detection of abnormal memory decline in mild cases of Alzheimer's disease using CERAD neuropsychological measures. *Archives of Neurology, 48,* 278–281.

Welsh, K., Butters, N., Hughes, J., Mohs, R., & Heyman, A. (1992). Detection and staging of dementia in Alzheimer's disease: Use of the neuropsychological measures developed for the consortium to establish a registry for Alzheimer's disease. *Archives of Neurology, 49,* 448–452.

Wilkinson, R. T., & Allison, S. (1989). Age and simple reaction time: Decade differences for 5, 325 subjects. *Journal of Gerontology: Psychological Sciences, 44,* P29–P35.

Zec, R. F. (1990). Neuropsychology: Normal aging versus early AD. In R. E. Becker & E. Giacobini (Eds.), *Alzheimer disease: Current research in early diagnosis* (pp. 105–117). New York: Taylor & Francis.

Zec, R. F. (1993). Neuropsychological functioning in Alzheimer's disease. In R. W. Parks, R. F. Zec, & R. S. Wilson (Eds.), *Neuropsychology of Alzheimer's disease and other dementias* (pp. 3–80). New York: Oxford University Press.

18

QUALITY OF LIFE AND ADJUSTMENT IN RENAL DISEASE: A HEALTH PSYCHOLOGY PERSPECTIVE

PETRA SYMISTER and RONALD FRIEND

Although much research has focused on chronic illnesses such as cancer and cardiovascular disease, there are other chronic illnesses that have not received adequate attention or resources. One of these areas of research concerns end-stage renal disease (ESRD). In 1991, over 230,000 people were treated for this disease (National Institutes of Health [NIH], 1993), and unfortunately, the number of individuals beginning treatment continues to grow. Currently $8.59 billion, a vast sum, is expended on ESRD treatment. With an aging U.S. population, the projected number of patients by the year 2000 is expected to be 300,000 (NIH, 1993). Given the pervasiveness of ESRD treatment, health psychology and behavioral medicine can make an important contribution to the quality of life and rehabilitation of these patients. However, research and grant support in this area are sadly lacking, in relation to what is found for the more "popular" illnesses, such as cardiovascular disease and cancer. In this chapter, we review some current psychosocial research on ESRD patients, focusing on quality of life, adjustment processes, adherence, and survival. Because renal patients suffer a loss of autonomy and become more dependent on family and medical staff, we emphasize the influence of personal control and interpersonal relations in patients' adjustment to treatment and illness.

MISCONCEPTIONS OF THE QUALITY OF LIFE

Before reviewing the quality of life of end-stage renal disease patients and how it can be improved, it might be fruitful to discuss the way in which outside observers view the life of these patients. In a society that fosters individualism, the ideology of individual control and responsibility for one's life is a strong cultural and psychological force. However, the onset of chronic renal disease is characterized by individuals being forced to relinquish control to life-sustaining treatment. It is therefore not surprising that healthy individuals, who in their everyday lives attempt to maintain as much individual personal control as possible, view the prospect of dialysis treatment and resulting loss of control as one of the worse things that can happen to someone. This image of dialysis patients tied daily to their machines was portrayed in the *New York Times* headline, "A Bleak U.S. Report on Kidney-Failure Patients" (1993). The article presented a dismal outlook for these patients due to the fact that treatment effectiveness is not being maximized, because individuals are often already critically ill by the time they receive dialysis. Moreover, the article's image of patients' day-to-day living once dialysis has started was an equally somber depiction. The renal patient's life was described as one that is difficult, owing to the complex dietary regimen, abundant treatment side effects, and emotional stress that accompany renal replacement therapy ("Bleak U.S. report," 1993)

But is the woeful undertone of this article merely a representation of the projections of healthy people, projections of their own fears and uncertainties, or is it an expression of the actual realities and experiences of dialysis patients? How poor is the quality of life of ESRD patients? Is it really as bleak as the headlines of the *New York Times* portray? We have reason to believe that it is not, as we address in our next section.

A glance at the survival statistics may give some insight into the reasons for the bleak portrayal of the lives of these patients. When one looks at the number of years that patients survive after starting treatment, it becomes apparent that White patients survive longer than Black patients, for the 30-year-old and under patients. However, over-30-year-old Black patients survive longer than White patients of this age group. At any rate, for both groups, the expected survival is well below normal. A comparison of the expected survival of ESRD patients to that of the

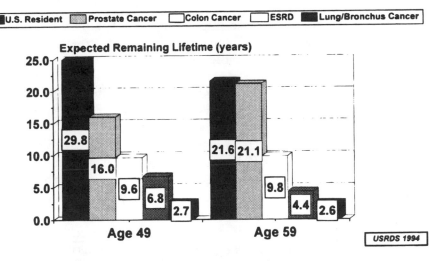

normal population is presented in Figure 1. Generally, a 59-year-old diagnosed with ESRD can only expect to survive an average of 4.4 more years, whereas healthy people will survive an average of 21.6 more years in this age category (United States Renal Data System [USRDS], 1994).

COMPARISONS WITH OTHER ILLNESSES

A comparison of the expected survival at age 59 of ESRD patients with the survival of patients of other chronic illnesses can be used to evaluate the length of time patients live with this disease (see Figure 1). Although ESRD patients survive nearly twice as long as lung cancer patients, the former only live half as long as individuals with colon cancer and one fifth as long as those diagnosed with prostate cancer (USRDS, 1993).

It is perhaps this knowledge of the dramatic cut in life expectancy that accompanies renal failure that accounts for the way these patients are pictured. These survival figures, however, are improving, and dialysis units are presently reporting patients who have survived as long as 25 years while on dialysis. Therefore, the quality of life of patients may not be so bleak as the *New York Times* reports and as the survival statistics suggest.

DEFINING QUALITY OF LIFE

It must be more than the duration of these patients' lives that causes people to see their existence as bleak. The perception of the quality of that existence is also responsible. What is meant by quality of life? The many ways in which quality of life is defined are represented in the literature. Measures of the quality of life of dialysis patients, in particular, usually include either one or more variables, which are sometimes combined to form an overall quality-of-life score (Bihl, Ferrans, & Powers, 1988; Churchill, Wallace, Ludwin, Beecroft, & Taylor, 1991; Simmons, Anderson, & Kamstra, 1984). Some of these variables are considered objective. Objective measures are usually physical measures and refer to areas of the patients' life that can be rated and generally agreed on by persons other than the patient. Measures of illness severity and employment status are examples of objective quality-of-life measures. On the other hand, subjective quality-of-life measures are usually psychological in nature and are often assessed by a questionnaire or interview given to the patient. Measures of depression and anxiety are examples of subjective quality-of-life measures.

QUALITY-OF-LIFE STUDIES OF END-STAGE RENAL DISEASE

The lives of ESRD patients are sustained by one or more treatment modalities. Patients, in fact, have a variety of modalities from which to choose, each with its own unique features. Therefore, patients can tailor their treatment to complement aspects of their life that they value. The modalities vary considerably in the amount of control they allow patients, the time flexibility they provide, and the level of interaction and dependence on medical staff, family, and other patients they require. The four major treatments are in-center hemodialysis, in which patients are dialyzed three times per week for several hours in a hospital setting; home hemodialysis, in which the same procedure is carried out in the patient's home or workplace; continuous ambulatory peritoneal dialysis (CAPD), in which patients are dialyzed daily using a solution inserted into their peritoneal cavity that extracts waste products through an osmotic process; and kidney transplantation. Transplantation is considered a treatment, because medications such as immunosuppressants must be taken after surgery to reduce the likelihood of graft rejection. In fact, the probability of graft failure even after 7 years is still as high as 50%, and it is not unusual for patients to have changed from one treatment modality to another, including those with failed transplants (McGee & Bradley, 1994). With this variety of modalities, an important issue becomes, How different is the quality of life across treatment options?

Although there are several studies that are concerned with the ways in which the quality of life differs as a function of modality, getting an idea of which treatment is best can be difficult because many of the findings are not in agreement. Most do agree, however, that transplant

EXHIBIT 1
Multiple Measures of Quality of Life

Objective	Subjective
Evans et al. (1985)	
Functional impairment	Well-being
Ability to work	Psychological affect
	Life satisfaction
Bremer, McCauley, Wrona, and Johnson (1989)	
Days in hospital	Positive affect
Hours spent seeking health care per week	Negative affect
Hours spent sleeping each night	Affect balance
No. of activities given up	General affect
Income	Well-being
Level of pain	Overall life
Days since intercourse	Hard/easy
Days since orgasm	Tied down/free
% more tired	Helpless/independent
% employed	Satisfactions (e.g., standard of living, friends, health, and religion)

patients have the highest quality of life (Levenson & Glocheski, 1991), but the collective body of research regarding the order in which the remaining treatments fall is equivocal. An inspection of these studies, however, uncovers methodological differences that may account for discrepant findings. So, we turn to the most methodologically sound studies for an accurate comparison of the different treatment groups with each other and with the normal population.

The two important studies addressing the quality-of-life issue are Evans et al. (1985) and Bremer, McCauley, Wrona, and Johnson (1989), and there are several reasons that these studies are important. First, both studies used adequate sample sizes. The Evans et al. study contains 859 patients, whereas the Bremer et al. study contained 489 patients. Second, the samples were diverse; a total of 12 centers in both urban and rural settings, both academic and nonacademic, were surveyed. Third, both studies were careful to control for case mix. This is the most important difference between these studies and others that looked at quality of life across modalities. *Case mix* refers to the varied composition of the treatment groups that is likely to confound comparisons. By taking variables on which treatment groups differ, such as age, race, and sex, into account, lack of homogeneity in composition between groups on these variables is controlled for. Finally, these studies used multiple measures of objective and subjective quality of life (see Table 1). Objective measures included functional ability and labor participation, whereas subjective

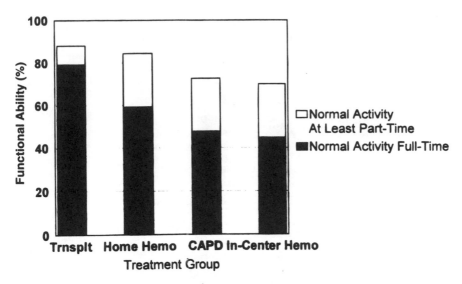

Figure 2. Functional status. Trnsplt = transplant, Home Hemo = home hemodialysis, CAPD = continuous ambulatory peritoneal dialysis, In-Center Hemo = in-center hemodialysis. Data are from Evans et al., (1985).

measures were represented by positive and negative affect and satisfaction with life. National norms were available for some of these scales, making comparisons with ESRD patients possible.

Comparisons With the Healthy Population

Renal patients showed a small-to-moderate reduction in objective quality of life when compared with the healthy population. With 100% on the Karnofsky Index (Mor, Laliberte, Morris, & Wiemann, 1984), designating the average functional status of a healthy sample, the majority of patients in the four modality groups either took part in normal physical activities "sometimes" or retained a level of physical activity that was nearly normal: transplanted, 88.1%; home hemodialysis, 84.4%, CAPD, 72.5%, and in-center hemodialysis 69.9% (see Figure 2). It is in regard to employment that ESRD patients differed. Patients showed a dramatic drop in labor participation, from 67.1% before illness onset (compared with 63.8% in the general population) to 33.5% after becoming ill. As can be seen, transplantation patients had a 53.5% labor participation rate (see Figure 3).

In summary, transplant patients were able to do more activities and were more likely to work, but all groups were able to maintain around 70% of their previous (healthy) activity levels (Bremer et al., 1989; Evans et al., 1985).

A surprising fact is that patients' subjective quality of life was similar to the national standards of healthy populations. On well-being,

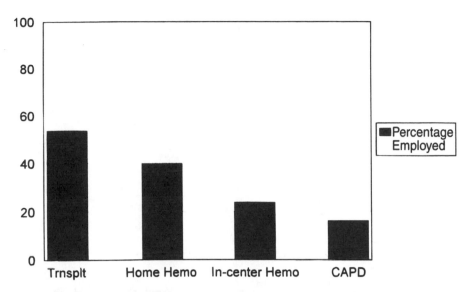

Figure 3. Employment status of renal patients. Trnsplt = transplant, Home-Hemo = home hemodialysis, In-Center Hemo = in-center hemodialysis, CAPD = continuous ambulatory peritoneal dialysis. Data are from Evans et al. (1985).

psychological affect, and life satisfaction, the healthy population averaged within 1 point of the ESRD group (healthy group $M = 11.77$, $SD = 2.21$ vs. ESRD group $M = 11.09$, $SD = 2.72$, on a 15-point scale measuring well-being; healthy group $M = 5.68$, $SD = 1.12$ vs. ESRD group $M = 5.33$, SD 1.25, on a 7-point scale measuring psychological affect; healthy group $M = 5.55$, $SD = 1.25$ vs. ESRD group 5.25, $SD = 1.62$, on a 7-point scale measuring life satisfaction). These differences were small, and individual differences within groups were much larger than were those between ESRD and normal samples.

Comparisons Within the Renal Patient Group

Just as there was very little difference between ESRD patients and the healthy population, there was also very little difference between patients in the various modalities, except on labor participation. With regard to objective quality of life, transplanted patients had the highest percentage of employed members, at 53.5%, followed by 39.6% of home hemodialysis, 23.7% of in-center hemodialysis, and 16.2% of CAPD patients (see Figure 3). When asked about their ability to work, as measured by the question, "Are you now able to work for pay full-time, part-time or not at all?" the groups responded in similar fashion, with transplants showing the greatest ability (62.30%), followed by home hemodialysis (54.80%), in-center hemodialysis (44.80%), and CAPD (27.80%). In general, the transplant group, whether it was a first, second,

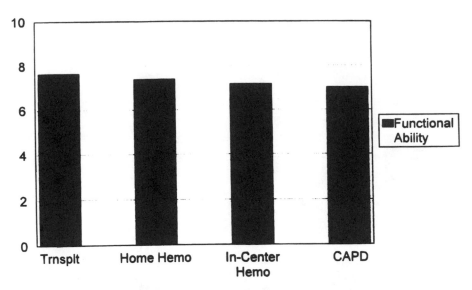

Figure 4. Functional ability of renal patients. Trnsplt = transplant, Home Hemo = home hemodialysis, CAPD = continuous ambulatory peritoneal dialysis, In-Center Hemo = in-center hemodialysis. Data are from Evans et al. (1985).

or later transplant, followed by the home hemodialysis group, showed the most meaningful difference in employment status from the in-center hemodialysis group and the CAPD group.

Regarding functional status, the transplanted group showed the least impairment on a scale of 1 to 10, with 10 representing normal functioning, followed by home hemodialysis, in-center hemodialysis, and CAPD (7.63, 7.37, 7.15, and 7.00, respectively). These were significant differences among groups, but inspection of the scores shows that the magnitude of these differences was small (see Figure 4).

For the remaining objective quality-of-life indicators, patients again displayed significant differences among groups. In the number of hours each night spent sleeping, the number of days since last having sexual intercourse, the number of days since last having an orgasm, fatigue level, time spent pursuing medical attention, amount of activities given up, and income level, there were significant differences among groups. The differences that existed among groups on the variables, hours of sleep per night and number of activities given up, were small. However, the differences among groups on the remaining variables were significantly large. It is easy to understand how the nature of the treatments could contribute to these differences. For example, it is not surprising that transplant patients and home hemodialysis patients would have higher incomes than patients in the other groups, because the former are not required to visit the hospital for treatment as often as patients in the other treatment groups and can therefore find or retain jobs more easily. There were no differences, however, between groups on the number of days hospitalized and the level of pain experienced (Bremer et al., 1989).

On subjective indicators, well-being (possible score range = 2.0–15.0, sample range = 10.4–12.18) and psychological affect (possible score range = 1.0–7.0, sample range = 5.09–5.72), transplant patients scored highest, followed by home hemodialysis, CAPD, and in-center hemodialysis patients, but the differences appear minute. For life satisfaction (possible score range = 1.0–7.0, sample range = 4.99–5.90), transplant patients still scored highest but were followed by CAPD, home hemodialysis, and then in-center hemodialysis groups. As indicated, the scores again were not vastly different. To clarify, the scores were statistically different from each other, but they were not very large.

On negative affect, the groups differed slightly from the U.S. norm but not from each other. Similarly for positive affect, treatment groups did not differ from one another, with the exception of the transplant group and the home hemodialysis group. Analyses showed that patients in all groups scored the same as healthy individuals, with home hemodialysis patients scoring slightly higher than the normal population. However, the most interesting finding concerning this scale was that transplant patients who experienced successful transplants either on the first attempt or a later attempt scored much higher on positive affect than the normal U.S. population.

For the final subjective quality-of-life indicators (see Table 1), all of which were based on 7-point scales, the treatment groups did not differ significantly from each other, except on the adjective pair, tied down/free, and on satisfaction with health (see Figure 5). High scores on the first scale indicated that the patient felt free, and high scores on the second scale indicated that the patient was highly satisfied with her or his health. Transplant patients and self-administered hemodialysis patients, whose treatments provide increased control for them, not surprisingly, experienced the greatest freedom, similar to that of the healthy population. However, the differences were not large among treatment groups, and all groups felt more free than tied down. All groups, with the exception of the transplant group, were significantly less satisfied with their health than were healthy individuals (see Figure 6).

COMPARING QUALITY OF LIFE ACROSS CHRONIC ILLNESSES

Are the responses of these ESRD patients unique, or do they characterize the experiences of all chronically ill patients? When we compare the measurements of psychological variables, such as mental health,

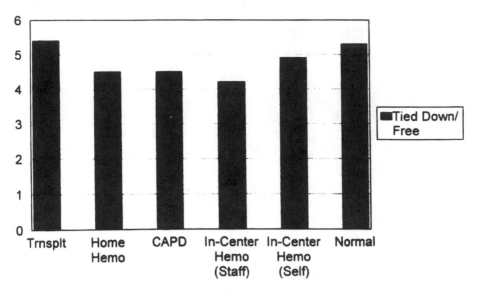

Figure 5. Scores on the tied down/free scale. Trnsplt = transplant, Home-Hemo = home hemodialysis, CAPD = continuous ambulatory peritoneal dialysis, In-Center Hemo (Staff) = staff-administered treatment; In-Center Hemo (Self) = patient-administered treatment; Normal = healthy population. Data are from Bremer, McCauley, Wrona, and Johnson (1989).

emotional ties, depression, loss of control, anxiety, and general positive affect, patients with ESRD are not very different from patients with skin disorders, diabetes, cancer, or arthritis, and like ESRD patients, patients in the other groups show no significant differences on these variables when compared with the healthy population (Cassileth et al., 1984).

In summary, research comparing the quality of life of various treatments shows some advantage of transplantation and home dialysis over in-center hemodialysis and CAPD, with the two former modalities reporting higher objective quality of life and somewhat higher subjective quality of life. Compared with the healthy population, renal patients show a drop in objective quality of life with a matching (lower) satisfaction with health. With regard to subjective quality-of-life measures, renal patients report minimally less quality of life than the healthy population, with little differences among modalities. However, individual variations within each treatment are substantial. This raises the question as to whether different treatments are important and have substantial benefits. Why does transplantation, which provides substantially more control and flexibility than other forms of treatment, not provide substantial improvement in subjective quality of life? One explanation from the nephrology community, which views subjective quality-of-life measures pejoratively, is that these measures lack validity (Nissenson, 1994). On the other hand, social psychologists report that measures of subjective well-being are indeed reliable and valid (Diener, 1995).

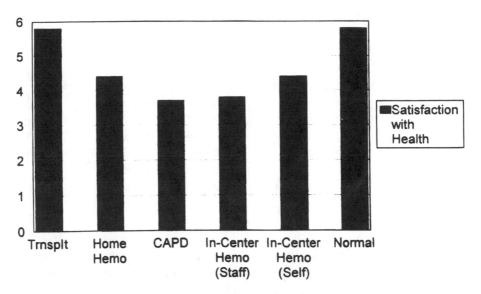

Figure 6. Scores on the satisfaction with health scale. Trnsplt = transplant; CAPD = continuous ambulatory peritoneal dialysis; In-Center Hemo (Staff) = staff-administered treatment. In-Center Hemo (Self) = patient-administered treatment; Normal = health population. Data are from Bremer, McCauley, Wrona, and Johnson (1989).

Perhaps a more fruitful answer to this paradoxical finding can be found by approaching these results from a theoretical perspective. A major problem in quality-of-life research is that it is descriptive and lacks theory to guide its findings and research. Recently, Diener (1995) developed a theory of subjective well-being that explains the low correlations observed between "resources," such as money and status, which may be considered objective measures, and subjective well-being. According to his theory, resources only predict subjective well-being if they help a person achieve their personal goals. To the extent that there is a congruence between a person's resources and the goals for which he or she strives, subjective well-being will be high. If there is a mismatch between resources and personal goals, then poor subjective well-being will occur. This social psychological theory, perhaps, can help explain this paradox. Modes of treatment can be conceived as resources to attain personal goals. Thus, for instance, if continuing to work is an important goal for a patient, then transplantation or home dialysis may be an important resource that contributes to subjective quality of life. If other goals predominate, such as countering isolation or having frequent available health care, then in-center hemodialysis may improve subjective quality of life, by providing patients with the resources of social interaction, social support, and health care, which the dialysis personnel can provide. Thus, two patients with different personal goals and with different treatment may report near equivalent subjective quality of life. Furthermore, a patient who, for medical reasons, needs to transfer to in-hospital treatment may relinquish previously important goals that were compatible with the old treatment and develop new goals compatible with the new treatment, thereby maintaining congruence and their quality-of-life level, even though their options have changed. From this vantage, it is necessary to match the features of treatments that can act as resources for reaching personal goals important to patients. Thus, development of theory to guide and explain quality-of-life research may help to explain apparent paradoxes in quality of life.

In conclusion, although renal patients do experience a loss of objective quality of life, including a lower life expectancy, the belief that renal patients undergoing dialysis are suffering a low subjective quality of life may be a misconception. It, perhaps, stems from the faulty labeling that healthy individuals project onto these patients. Forty years ago, a person who suffered renal failure had little chance of survival, and unfortunately, that image of renal disease has yet to fade. Despite advances in therapies and a decrease in mortality, patients are still perceived as being tied to a life of pain and suffering. This is not to belittle the fact that renal failure is a serious condition with many treatment side effects, but many patients whose lives are sustained by this treatment have learned to cope with the change in health status. Recall the *New York Times* article that portrayed patients as adjusting poorly. A letter from a dialysis patient was printed in response to that article and argued that patients are able to adjust to a life on dialysis. The response agreed that there was a change in lifestyle but maintained that renal patients adjust to what they are able to accomplish as chronically ill individuals. The letter was entitled "Life Can Continue After Kidney Failure," and the respondent stated the following:

> End-stage renal disease is indeed serious and disabling. . . . But a substantial part of the dialysis patient population leads reasonably productive, comfortable and long lives. For example, I am 65 years old and have been on dialysis for almost three years. I use a therapy known as peritoneal dialysis through a cycler machine in my home. . . . I go to work every day—albeit a five-hour workday—and lead a restrained but active social, community and family life. I am substantially free of discomfort and pain almost all the time, although my energy level and appetite are clearly down. (Marqusee, 1993, p. A26)

PROCESS OF PSYCHOLOGICAL ADJUSTMENT

The different modalities (transplantation, home hemodialysis, CAPD, and in-center hemodialysis) reflect a continuum of behavioral control over treatment, which provides a convenient method for observ-

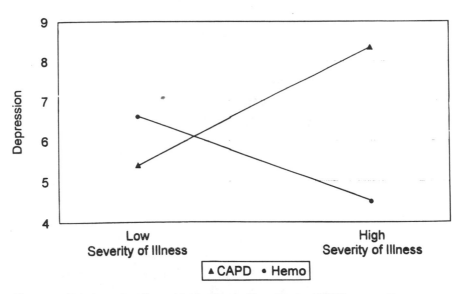

Figure 7. Burden of self-care in seriously ill patients. CAPD = continuous ambulatory peritoneal dialysis, Hemo = in-center hemodialysis. Data are from Eitel, Hatchett, Friend, Griffin, and Wadhwa (1995).

ing how different amounts of control can influence psychological adjustment (Eitel, Friend, Griffin, & Wadhwa, 1995). In one of the first thorough investigations, Devins and colleagues (Devins et al., 1982; Devins, Binik, Hollomby, Barre, & Guttman, 1981) found no relation between treatment control and depression. However, measures of psychological control (internal locus of control, health locus of control, and self-efficacy) strongly predicted depression and helplessness. Several other studies also found no effect of treatment control on psychological adjustment (Christensen, Smith, Holman, & Gregory, 1990; Sacks, Peterson, & Kimmel, 1990). These studies tend to parallel those comparing various treatment modalities and quality of life. Other studies found that control over nontreatment factors is strongly related to psychological adjustment (Devins et al., 1981; Sacks et al., 1990). One possible explanation is that situational or contextual variables interact with treatment control to influence psychological adjustment (Christensen et al., 1990).

Eitel, Hatchett, Friend, Griffin, and Wadhwa (1995) reasoned that as illness severity increases, the burden of controlling one's treatment, as in CAPD, would increase depression (see Figure 7). They predicted that depression would increase for CAPD patients with increasing disease severity, but not for in-center hemodialysis patients whose treatment was administered by hospital personnel.

Their results supported this hypothesis. As the severity of illness increased for CAPD patients, depression also increased. In keeping with Devin's previously reported work, mediational analyses indicated that seriously ill CAPD patients reported that the illness interfered in their social relations. They responded that others did not understand how seriously ill they were and that their illness disrupted their social relations. Interestingly, for in-center hemodialysis patients, depression decreased with increasing severity illness. Seriously ill in-center hemodialysis patients may have received more support and understanding from hospital staff, and fewer demands and expectations may have been placed on them by others because of the severity of their illness.

An additional study showed the relationship between illness severity and psychological well-being. Christensen, Turner, Slaughter, and Holman (1989) found patients with high-illness impairment to be less depressed and anxious when they had supportive families. For patients who had less illness impairment, the relationship between their well-being and perceived family support was not significant.

Most studies on adjustment in the renal area are cross-sectional. In one of the few prospective studies, Hatchett, Friend, Symister, and Wadhwa (1996), expanded on Eitel, Hatchett, Friend, Griffin, and Wadhwa's (1995) finding that patients reported that they were not well understood by others. Hatchett et al. assessed the patients' perceptions of family and medical staff demands and expectations placed on them regarding their responsibilities for everyday routine functions and medical care. Hatchett et al. hypothesized that the inability to meet these expectations regarding their ability to cope and fulfill routine functions would lead to poorer adjustment. Hatchett et al. assessed patients' expectations toward family and medical staff at two time points, separated by 2 months. Additionally, they assessed depression, hopelessness, satisfaction with quality of life, and illness intrusiveness at the same two time points. Results showed that discrepant expectations perceived by the patient predicted subsequent decreases in adjustment. Furthermore, an alternative hypothesis, that the more poorly adjusted patients would come to distort or misperceive the expectations of others, was not supported. Perceptions that family and friends did not understand the patient's illness, as measured by discrepant expectations, were much stronger predictors of adjustment than were social support measures. Many renal patients report a lack of energy. This may contribute to interpersonal conflict in the family regarding the fulfillment of routine functions. Hatchett et al. suggested that modifying interpersonal expectations between patient and families may improve adjustment.

ADHERENCE

Adherence to medical regimens is an area of great concern because of the difficulties that many renal patients experience in following dietary and fluid-intake restrictions. Earlier research focused on predictors; sociodemographic factors such as age, gender, and education; and personality factors such as internal locus of control and denial (Binik et al., 1982; Schneider, Friend, Whitaker, & Wadhwa, 1991). It is now understood that demographic and personality factors are inconsistently related to adherence (Binik et al., 1982; Schneider et al., 1991). More recent studies focus on the cognitive, emotional, and interpersonal processes that underlie compliance (Christensen et al., 1990; Schneider et al., 1991). Note that similar to other illnesses with complex regimens, there is little consistency in adherence from one area to the other; patients who adhere to their fluid regimen, for example, do not necessarily adhere to their dietary or medication regimen (Cummings, Becker, Kirscht, & Levin, 1981; Eitel, Friend, et al., 1995; Lamping & Campbell, 1989). There are generally few "good" or "poor" compliers.

Rosenbaum and Ben-Ari Smira (1986) proposed a self-regulating model in which resourcefulness (self-control skills) combined with various cognition (attributions of effort and success to one's past compliance) to predict future compliance. Resourcefulness assesses the ability to delay gratification and self-efficacy as personal skills. They found that patients with resourcefulness were more likely to label their past adherence as successful and due to their own effort. These attributions led to expectations of self-efficacy, which in turn predicted future fluid intake. Schneider et al. (1991) made the distinction between resourcefulness and locus of internal control. Whereas *resourcefulness* refers primarily to a repertoire of self-control skills, *locus of control* refers to a set of beliefs about whether behavior and consequences are internally or externally controlled. Schneider et al. replicated Rosenbaum and Ben-Ari Smira's model but assessed beliefs about control rather than self-control skills. They also hypothesized that negative emotions, such as anger, depression, and anxiety, would undermine cognitive control and therefore adherence to fluid intake. However, their results indicated that belief about control did not influence perceptions of success and effort. Furthermore, negative emotions did not undermine patients' ability to comply. However, the attribution and self-efficacy aspects of the model strongly supported Rosenbaum and Ben-Ari Smira's model. Attributions of effort and success to past compliant behavior appear to influence feelings of self-efficacy, which in turn are related to fluid control. These studies suggest that fluid intake is a cognitive-control problem and that interventions that encourage patients to make internal attributions to past adherence behavior will increase efficacy expectations. Thus, interventions to change compliance should encourage patients to attach these cognitive labels to their compliant behaviors.

A third study attempted to generalize Rosenbaum and Ben-Ari Smira's (1986) model to dietary and medication compliance. Eitel,

Friend, Griffin, and Wadhwa (1995) once again replicated the results with fluid compliance, but the model did not hold up for dietary and medication compliance. This suggested that different processes may underlie different adherence regimens. It is possible that unlike fluid intake, which is frequently and publicly monitored by the medical staff, dietary and medication compliance may not be well monitored. Also, the need for a nourishing protein diet to maintain body mass (Lindsay, Spanner, & Heidenheim, 1994) while maintaining potassium, sodium, and phosphorous control may be particularly difficult to achieve.

Christensen and his colleagues (1990) also approached adherence from a control perspective. Their person/environment model related preference for control or behavioral involvement with features of the treatment that are in keeping with such preferences. They found that self-care home patients who were high in preference for behavioral involvement in care showed greater dietary compliance, as measured by serum potassium levels, than those low in preference for behavioral compliance. The obverse was found was for patients whose hemodialysis was staff-administered. Among these patients, patients low in behavioral involvement complied better than those high in behavioral involvement. Similar results were obtained with fluid compliance, but they were not as strong.

An additional study by Christensen, Smith, Turner, and Cundick (1994) concerned coping and compliance. In this study, coping was defined by two behaviors, namely, information vigilance and active coping (behavioral involvement). Among in-center patients, higher information vigilance was associated with poorer dietary compliance, whereas self-care home patients showed an association between higher information vigilance and greater dietary compliance. The Information × Modality interaction was not significant for medical compliance.

In many of these studies, the proposed models or hypotheses hold up for some areas of compliance but not others, even for the same sample. Lamping, Campbell, and Churchill (1988); Eitel, Friend, Griffin, and Wadhwa (1995); and Cummings et al. (1981) noted the "crazy quilt" phenomena, in which one patient may comply on fluid levels but not on potassium, or vice versa. There appears to be no consistency in compliance, and very few patients are compliant on everything. The models described above, and their predictive capacities, often occur for some measures of compliance and not for others. For instance, Rosenbaum and Ben-Ari Smira's (1986) self-regulatory model was replicated by Schneider et al. (1991) and Eitel, Friend, Griffin, and Wadhwa (1995) for fluid compliance but not for dietary compliance. The Person × Environment interaction model appeared to be more predictive for potassium than it was for fluid intake. One possible explanation would be that compliance is very much determined by situational factors and that the obstacles to complying for fluid levels may be different than that for dietary compliance or medication. Cummings et al. (1981) reported that thirst was most important for fluid levels, whereas being reminded and obtaining prescription appeared to be important for medication. Very different sets of situational variables may be implicated. Concepts such as resourcefulness, which should have some generality, may not be predictive, unless the specific situations are identified as in the Lewinian model of behavior f(PE). Future research needs to conceive adherence in situational terms and identify characteristics of compliance situations.

THE NEED FOR PSYCHOLOGICAL INTERVENTIONS TO IMPROVE CARE

In one of the earliest studies, Foster, Cohn, and McKegney (1973) observed that poor social relations between the dialysis staff and patients influenced the survival of patients. Friend, Singletary, Mendell, and Nurse (1986), in a study of 126 patients at Harlem Hospital Center in New York City, compared those who participated in a patient-controlled support group with a control group of patients who did not. The two groups did not differ in etiology of renal disease or among demographic factors. Survival was substantially greater among patients participating in the support group than those who did not, even after controlling for 13 psychosocial and medical factors. Furthermore, when patients who expired during the first 6 months of dialysis were excluded from analysis— presumably the sickest patients—the results remained substantially significant. The results of this study are in keeping with experimental studies of cancer patients (Grossarth-Maticek, 1980; Spiegel, Bloom, Kraemer, & Gottheil, 1989) that compared social assistance and support groups with a usual-care control group. Cassileth et al. (1984), however, found no differences in survival rate between cancer patients who had high, medium, or low psychosocial assets, assessed by questionnaire, which included measures of both social ties and personality measures of depression, hopelessness, and life satisfaction. However, as social psychologists have forcefully demonstrated in their discipline, actual group and situational forces are considerably more powerful predictors of behavior than is assessment of individual differences.

Several studies that assessed individual differences in psychosocial assets produced conflicting results. Burton, Kline, Lindsay, and Heidenheim (1986) found that depression predicted survival. Devins et al. (1990), in contrast, found that it did not. Christensen, Wiebe, Smith, and Turner (1994), on the other hand, found that perceived family social support, not depression, predicted survival. Peterson et al. (1991) found that family support, however, did not predict survival but that depression (minus the somatic symptoms) distinguished between a group of survivors and nonsurvivors. However, Kimmel, Weihs, and Peterson (1993) reviewed the literature on depression and survival and concluded that measures of cognitive depression that exclude symptoms might predict depression. Friend et al. (1986) found that psychiatric illness diagnoses (which included depression) before dialysis or while on dialysis predicted poorer survival rates. In summary, strong supportive relations may influence survival rates in chronically ill patients. Peer support groups may influence patient survival by increasing compliance; facilitating coping skills, including optimism; reducing stress; and improving immune function (Boyer, Friend, Chlouverakis, & Kaloyanides, 1990; Kimmel et al., 1993; Plough & Salem, 1982). However, the relation between depression and survival is still equivocal.

CONCLUSION

Psychological and educational interventions to improve patient care and adjustment are few and far between in ESRD. With the exception of mostly case studies to change fluid compliance (Barnes, 1976; Cummings et al., 1981; Hegel, Ayllon, Thiel, & Oulton, 1992), there are few, if any, intervention studies designed to improve patient quality of life and adjustment (Devins et al., 1982). Given the number of ERSD patients and the enormous expenditure of funds, there is a clear need for such interventions. Presently, most research funding is for medical interventions. For example, the recent development and availability of recombinant erythropoietin (EPO) to correct anemia provide an important advance in the physical treatment of ESRD patients. Renal patients suffer substantially from loss of energy and fatigue, resulting from deficiency in endogenous erythropoietin, a hormone responsible for maintaining normal red blood cells. Although the advent of EPO signaled an important new phase in the treatment of anemia, some expectations regarding its influence have not been realized. It was expected that substantially more patients would become active, remain employed, or become reemployed. However, there are many additional reasons why patients continue to feel fatigued. Physical interventions do not always have a direct or desired impact.

The Canadian EPO study, a double-blind EPO trial, indicated that the recombinant drug resulted in improvement in exercise tolerance, increased strength, reduced fatigue, and fewer complaints of severe physical symptoms. There were also moderate improvements in depression and global psychosocial and physical well-being. Other studies showed that patients on EPO are not more likely to return to work, as was initially expected with the introduction of EPO therapy. This suggests that other factors are preventing this from occurring. Furthermore, correlations between changes in hemoglobin and the fatigue and physical functioning were low (.32 and .31, respectively), indicating that additional factors were contributing to fatigue and lack of energy. Although EPO is no doubt important for improving the physical condition of ESRD patients, there is not always a direct or strong relation between improvements in physical or objective conditions and subjective and psychological well-being. Recall also that the variance in well-being among maintenance therapies—transplantation, hemodialysis, and CAPD—is, in fact, far larger than the variance among treatment effects, indicating that many transplanted patients report worse quality of life than hemodialysis patients and that many hemodialysis patients report a better quality of life than do transplanted patients. In the case of EPO, why are the psychological or quality-of-life benefits not always commensurate with the dramatic changes that EPO provides in physically correcting for anemia? Some have suggested that the EPO dose needs to be increased but that physicians are reluctant to do so. Another approach, one that we prefer, argues the need for explicit and systematic psychological interventions to supplement the benefits accruing from medical interventions.

It is interesting to compare the effects of EPO treatment on work with a psychosocial intervention to maintain labor participation (Rasgon et al., 1993). The patients in this study were not receiving EPO. They were blue-collar workers who needed to expend considerable physical energy as a part of their work (see Figure 8). Rasgon et al. (1993) instituted an intensive predialysis program with medical staff that encouraged patients and family to remain working, by teaching them how to integrate their work and personal lives with ESRD treatment. Of the patients who received this psychosocial intervention, 47% continued working while on dialysis, in contrast to 24% of patients of a comparison group who were not provided with the intervention. This result draws attention to the important impact that psychosocial interventions alone can have. If such interventions were coupled with medical interventions, such as EPO treatment, they both could maximize the benefits that accrue from each. Given the multiple causes of fatigue and loss of energy, psychological and physical, patients need to be taught what to realistically expect and what to attribute or not attribute their energy level to as they receive medical treatment. Research reveals that interventions that fully explain the rationale for complex treatments improve patient adjustment (Taylor, 1995). Without parallel systematic psychological intervention, changes from physical intervention may be misperceived or misinterpreted, and benefits may not be maximized. How physical

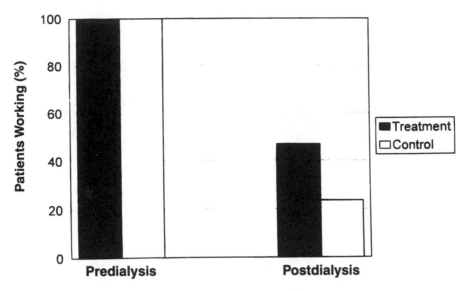

Figure 8. Blue-collar work status of end-stage renal disease patients. Data are from Rasgon et al. (1993).

changes and treatment modalities are subjectively experienced, how they translate psychologically, and what interpretations patients make may be crucially important to realizing the benefits of these changes and modalities. Given the large contribution of psychological factors to the subjective well-being and adjustment of ESRD patients, health psychology and behavioral medicine have an important role to play in the treatment of these patients.

REFERENCES

Barnes, M. R. (1976). Token economy control of fluid overload in a patient receiving hemodialysis. *Journal of Behavior Therapy and Experimental Psychiatry, 7,* 305–306.

Bihl, M. A., Ferrans, C. E., & Powers, M. (1988). Comparing stressors and quality of life of dialysis patients. *American Nephrology Nurses' Association Journal, 5,* 27–36.

Binik, Y. M., Baker, A. G., Kalogeropoulos, D., Devins, G. M., Guttman, R. D., Hollomby, D. J., Barre, P. E., Hutchison, T., Prud'homme, M., & McMullen, L. (1982). Pain, control over treatment, and compliance in dialysis and transplant patients. *Kidney International, 21,* 840–848.

A bleak U.S. report on kidney-failure patients. (1993, November 4). *The New York Times,* p. A17.

Boyer, C. B., Friend, R., Chlouverakis, G., & Kaloyanides, G. (1990). Social support and demographic factors influencing compliance of hemodialysis patients. *Journal of Applied Social Psychology, 20,* 1902–1918.

Bremer, B. A., McCauley, C. R., Wrona, R. M., & Johnson, J. P. (1989). Quality of life in end-stage renal disease: A reexamination. *American Journal of Kidney Diseases, 13,* 200–209.

Burton, H. J., Kline, S. A., Lindsay, R. M., & Heidenheim, A. P. (1986). The relationship of depression to survival in chronic renal failure. *Psychosomatic Medicine, 48,* 261–269.

Cassileth, B. R., Lusk, E. J., Strouse, T. B., Miller, D. S., Brown, L. L., Cross, P. A., & Tenaglia, A. N. (1984). Psychosocial status in chronic illness: A comparative analysis of six diagnostic groups. *The New England Journal of Medicine, 331,* 506–511.

Christensen, A. J., Smith, T. W., Holman, J. M., Gregory, M. C. (1990). Type of hemodialysis and preference for behavioral involvement: Interactive effects on adherence in end-stage renal disease. *Health Psychology, 9,* 225–236.

Christensen, A. J., Smith, T. W., Turner, C. W., & Cundick, K. E. (1994). Patient adherence and adjustment in renal dialysis: A Person × Treatment interactive approach. *Journal of Behavioral Medicine, 17,* 549–566.

Christensen, A. J., Turner, C. W., Slaughter, J. R., & Holman, J. M. (1989). Perceived family support as a moderator psychological well-being in end-stage renal disease. *Journal of Behavioral Medicine, 12,* 249–265.

Christensen, A. J., Wiebe, J. S., Smith, T. W., & Turner, C. W. (1994). Predictors of survival among hemodialysis patients: Effect of perceived support. *Health Psychology, 13,* 521–525.

Churchill, D. N., Wallace, J. E., Ludwin, D., Beecroft, M. L., & Taylor, D. W. (1991). A comparison of evaluative indices of quality of life and cognitive function in hemodialysis patients. *Controlled Clinical Trials, 12,* 159–167.

Cummings, K. M., Becker, M. H., Kirscht, J. P., & Levin, N. W. (1981). Intervention strategies to improve compliance with medical regimens by ambulatory hemodialysis patients. *Journal of Behavioral Medicine, 4,* 111–127.

Devins, G. M., Binik, Y. M., Gorman, P., Dattel, M., McClosky, B., Oscar, G., & Briggs, J. (1982). Perceived self-efficacy, outcome expectancies, and negative mood states in end-stage renal disease. *Journal of Abnormal Psychology, 91,* 241–244.

Devins, G. M., Binik, Y. M., Hollomby, D. J., Barre, P. E., & Guttman, R. D. (1981). Helplessness and depression in end-stage renal disease. *Journal of Abnormal Psychology, 90,* 531–545.

Devins, G. M., Mann, J., Mandin, H., Paul, L. C., Hons, R. B., Burgess, E. D., Taub, K., Schorr, S., Letourneau, P. K., & Buckle, S. (1990). Psychosocial predictors of survival in end-stage renal disease. *Journal of Nervous and Mental Disease, 178,* 127–133.

Diener, E. (1995). Resources, personal strivings, and subjective well-being: A nomothetic and idioic approach. *Journal of Personality and Social Psychology, 68,* 926–935.

Eitel, P., Friend, R., Griffin, K., & Wadhwa, N. K. (1995). *Cognitive control and consistency in compliance*. Manuscript submitted for publication.

Eitel, P., Hatchett, L., Friend, R., Griffin, K. W., & Wadhwa, N. K. (1995). Burden of self-care in seriously ill patients: Impact on adjustment. *Health Psychology, 14*, 457–463.

Evans, R. W., Manninen, D. L., Garrison, L. P., Hart, G., Blagg, C. R., Gutman, R. A., Hull, A. R., & Lowrie, E. G. (1985). The quality of life of patients with end-stage renal disease. *The New England Journal of Medicine, 312*, 553–559.

Foster, F., Cohn, G., & McKegney, F. (1973). Psychobiological factors and individual survival on chronic renal hemodialysis—A two-year follow-up: Part I. *Psychosomatic Medicine, 35*, 64–81.

Friend, R., Singletary, Y., Mendell, N. R., & Nurse, H. (1986). Group participation and survival among patients with end-stage renal disease. *American Journal of Public Health, 76*, 670–672.

Grossarth-Maticek, R. (1980). Social psychotherapy and course of the disease: First experiences with cancer patients. *Psychotherapy and Psychosomatics, 33*, 129–138.

Hatchett, L., Friend, R., Symister, P., & Wadhwa, N. (1996). *Interpersonal expectations and adjustment to chronic illness*. Manuscript submitted for publication.

Hegel, M. T., Ayllon, T., Thiel, G., & Oulton, B. (1992). Improving adherence to fluid restrictions in male hemodialysis patients: A comparison of cognitive and behavioral approaches. *Health Psychology, 11*, 324–330.

Kimmel, P. L., Weihs, K., & Peterson, R. A. (1993). Survival in hemodialysis patients: The role of depression. *Journal of the American Society of Nephrology, 4*, 12–27.

Lamping, D. L., & Campbell, K. A. (1989). A methodological study of hemodialysis compliance criteria. *Journal of Compliance in Health Care, 4*, 117–134.

Lamping, D., Campbell, K., & Churchill, D. (1988, November). *Consistency and stability of hemodialysis compliance criteria*. Paper presented at the meeting of the Association for the Advancement of Behavior Therapy, New York.

Levenson, J. L., & Glocheski, S. (1991). Psychological factors affecting end-stage renal disease: A review. *Psychosomatics, 32*, 382–389.

Lindsay, R. M., Spanner, E., & Heidenheim, P. A. (1994). Dietary requirements of renal patients and their impact on quality of life. In H. McGee & C. Bradley (Eds.), *Quality of life following renal failure: Psychosocial challenges accompanying high technology medicine* (pp. 265–273). Chur, Switzerland: Harwood Academic.

Marqusee, J. E. (1993, November). Life can continue after kidney failure [Letter to the editor]. *The New York Times*, p. A26.

McGee, H., & Bradley, C. (1994). Quality of life following renal failure: An introduction to the issues and challenges. In H. McGee & C. Bradley (Eds.),

Quality of life following renal failure: Psychosocial challenges accompanying high technology medicine (pp. 1–22). Chur, Switzerland: Harwood Academic.

Mor, V., Laliberte, L., Morris, J. N., & Wiemann, M. (1984). The Karnofsky performance status scale: An examination of its reliability and validity in a research setting. *Cancer, 53,* 2002–2007.

National Institutes of Health. (1993). Morbidity and mortality of dialysis. *National Institutes of Health Consensus Statement, 11,* 1–33.

Nissenson, A. R. (1994). Measuring, managing, and improving quality in the end-stage renal disease treatment setting: Peritoneal dialysis. *American Journal of Kidney Disease, 24,* 368–375.

Peterson, R. A., Kimmel, P. L., Sacks, C. R., Mesquita, M. L., Simmens, S. J., & Reiss, D. (1991). Depression, perception of illness and mortality in patients with end-stage renal disease. *International Journal of Psychiatry in Medicine, 21,* 343–354.

Plough, A. L., & Salem, S. (1982). Social and contextual factors in the analyses of mortality in end-stage renal disease: Implications for health policy. *American Journal of Public Health, 72,* 1293–1295.

Rasgon, S., Schwankovsky, L., James-Rogers, A., Widrow, L., Glick, J., & Butts, E. (1993). An intervention for employment maintenance among blue-collar workers with end-stage renal disease. *American Journal of Kidney Diseases, 22,* 403–412.

Rosenbaum, M., & Ben-Ari Smira, K. B. (1986). Cognitive and personality factors in the delay of gratification of hemodialysis patients. *Journal of Personality and Social Psychology, 51,* 357–364.

Sacks, C. R., Peterson, R. A., & Kimmel, P. L. (1990). Perception of illness and depression in chronic renal disease. *American Journal of Kidney Diseases, 15,* 31–39.

Schneider, M. S., Friend, R., Whitaker, P., & Wadhwa, N. K. (1991). Fluid noncompliance and symptomatology in end-stage renal disease: Cognitive and emotional variables. *Health Psychology, 10,* 209–215.

Simmons, R. G., Anderson, B. A., & Kamstra, B. A. (1984). Comparison of quality of life of patients on continuous ambulatory peritoneal dialysis, hemodialysis, and after transplantation. *American Journal of Kidney Diseases, 9,* 253–255.

Spiegel, D., Bloom, J. R., Kraemer, H. C., & Gottheil, E. (1989). Effect of psychosocial treatment on survival of patients with metastatic breast cancer. *The Lancet, 2,* 888–891.

Taylor, S. E. (1995). *Health psychology.* New York: McGraw-Hill.

United States Renal Data System. (1993). Annual data report. *American Journal of Kidney Diseases, 22* (Suppl. 2), S1–S118.

United States Renal Data System. (1994). Annual data report. *American Journal of Kidney Diseases, 24* (Suppl. 2), S1–S181.

19

HEALTH PSYCHOLOGY AND THE FIELD OF UROLOGY

STEVEN M. TOVIAN

The role of clinical psychologists in medical settings is expanding significantly to include a wide range of medical problems (Sweet, Rozensky, & Tovian, 1991). This chapter highlights two problem areas that offer research and practice opportunities for clinical health psychologists working in adult urological medicine. These areas in urology involve urinary incontinence (UI) and erectile dysfunction (ED).

URINARY INCONTINENCE

Urinary incontinence presents concerns for public health professionals, physicians, nurses, and psychologists because of its high incidence, its medical implications, and its psychological sequelae. It also imposes a large financial burden on the patient, his or her family, and society. The number of patients with urinary incontinence who are not successfully treated, either medically or psychologically, remains surprisingly high because of several factors, including the following:

underreporting by patients; underrecognition as a significant clinical problem by health providers; lack of education of health providers regarding new research findings; inadequate staffing in long-term-care settings; and persistent major gaps in understanding the natural history, pathophysiology, and most effective treatments of the common forms of UI. The amount of basic research, as well as research focusing on prevention, is meager (National Institutes of Health Consensus Conference, 1988).

Definition

Incontinence is a symptom, not a disease (Orzeck & Ouslander, 1987), and can result from pathologic, anatomic, or physiologic conditions within the urinary system or elsewhere in the body. Urinary incontinence is a condition in which involuntary loss of urine can be a social or hygienic problem and is objectively demonstrable (Ory, Wyman, & Yu, 1986). Many causes of UI can be reversed, such as infection, atrophic vaginitis, acute confusional states, restrictions in mobility, fecal impaction, and the side effects of drugs. Longer term or permanent causes of UI include diabetes, stroke, cerebral palsy, multiple sclerosis, prostate enlargement, cancer, spinal cord injuries, and birth defects such as spinal bifida (American Association of Retired Persons and Simon Foundation for Continence, 1993). Depending on the underlying cause, the bladder may malfunction in different ways, resulting in several types of UI.

Prevalence

It is estimated that over 10 million Americans suffer from UI (American Association of Retired Persons and Simon Foundation for Continence, 1993). Urinary incontinence may be underreported because of the stigma attached to the disorder and because of the inherent difficulty in measuring its occurrence. Among the population between 15 and 64 years of age, the prevalence of UI in men ranges from 1.5% to 5% and in women ranges from 10%–25% (Thomas, Plymat, Blannin, & Meade, 1980). In one series of randomly selected women (30–59 years old), 26% reported having experienced UI as a social or hygienic problem (Elving, Foldspang, Lain, & Mommens, 1989; Resnick, Welte, Scherr, Branch, & Taylor, 1986).

Among the more than 1.5 million U.S. nursing facility residents, the prevalence of UI is 50% or higher, with episodes generally occurring more than once per day (Urinary Incontinence Guideline Panel, 1992).

Costs

A reportedly conservative estimate (Hu, 1990) of the direct costs of caring for persons of all ages with incontinence is $7 billion annually in the community and $3.3 billion in nursing homes (based on 1987 dollars). If guidelines and protocols for improved treatment of UI were followed, Hu et al. (1992) estimated that there would be a savings of $105 per episode in the outpatient setting and $535 in the inpatient setting, for stress incontinence (to be discussed later) alone. From 1990 hospital discharge figures, Hu et al. (1991) noted that there were 53,000 patients discharged with a primary diagnosis of stress incontinence, of which 38,000 were less than 65 years of age. If existing guidelines and protocols for stress incontinence in individuals under age 65 were followed, the total estimated savings would be approximately $20.3 million per year. If guidelines and protocols for overflow UI among individuals under age 65 discharged from hospitals in 1990 were followed, the total estimated savings would be an additional $21.5 million per year (Hu et al., 1991).

Absorbent pads and undergarments, either disposable or reusable, are widely used by persons with UI, and their widespread use is reflected by growth of the market of disposable pads and adult undergarments from $99 million in 1972 to $496 million in 1987 (Urinary Incontinence Guideline Panel, 1992). These costs contribute to about half of the direct-care costs for incontinence among residents in nursing homes (Sowell, Schnelle, Hu, & Traughbers, 1987).

From a public health and financial viewpoint, when considering the costs of service use, medical supplies, and absorbent paper products, for example, UI clearly presents a far-reaching and costly health care problem.

Medical, Psychological, and Social Impact

Less than half of those individuals with UI living in the community consult health care providers about the problem (American Association of Retired Persons and Simon Foundation for Continence, 1993). Urinary incontinence is rarely detected and reported by hospital personnel, making its true extent and clinical impact difficult to assess. Instead, many people with UI turn prematurely to the use of absorbent materials and supportive aids, without having their condition properly diagnosed and treated. The long-term use of absorbent products should occur only after a basic evaluation of the person's incontinence by a physician. Dependence on caregivers increases as incontinence worsens, and the homebound frequently use indwelling catheters and other supportive devices, which increase the risk of urinary tract infections, morbidity, and mortality (Urinary Incontinence Guideline Panel, 1992).

The psychosocial impact of UI imposes a burden on individuals, their families, and health care providers. Individuals with UI are often depressed and embarrassed about their problem, appearance, and even odor. Consequently, excursions outside the home, social interactions with friends and family, and sexual activity may be restricted or avoided secondary to UI.

Types

Urge incontinence is the sudden and intense desire to urinate, with the inability to suppress the urge long enough to reach a toilet (Orzeck & Ouslander, 1987). Involuntary voiding is preceded by a warning of a few seconds to a few minutes. Leakage is periodic, but frequent, with a moderate-to-large volume (Resnick & Yalla, 1985). *Stress incontinence*, more common in women than in men (Mohr, Rogers, Brown, & Starkweather, 1983; Resnick & Yalla, 1985), occurs when physical stress on the abdomen (e.g., coughing, sneezing, and laughing) causes excess pressure in the bladder, which overrides the bladder's normal restraint (Orzeck & Ouslander, 1987). The volume leaked is small to moderate (Resnick & Yalla, 1985). *Overflow incontinence* is the leakage of small amounts of urine without the urge to void (Orzeck & Ouslander, 1987). This occurs when the weight of the urine in the bladder overcomes the outlet resistance, and the excess amount runs off, but the bladder remains full (Resnick & Yalla, 1985). *Total (reflex) incontinence* is a complete absence of bladder control, with either continuous or periodic leakage. When leakage is periodic, it is frequent, with a moderate volume (Resnick & Yalla, 1985). *Functional incontinence* is the loss of urine resulting from an inability or unwillingness to use the toilet appropriately. Factors that contribute to functional incontinence may include deficits of mobility, mental status, motivation, or environmental barriers (Burgio & Engel, 1987). *Iatrogenic incontinence* occurs after surgery or due to the effects of medication combinations (Resnick & Yalla, 1985). *Complex (mixed) incontinence* occurs when a person experiences simultaneously more than one type of incontinence. An example is the development of urge incontinence in someone with a history of stress incontinence (Resnick & Yalla, 1985).

Causes

Urinary incontinence itself is a symptom, not a disorder (Orzeck & Ouslander, 1987). It has many predisposing factors and is associated with impaired physiological or psychological functioning (Resnick & Yalla, 1985; Trombini, Rossi, Umilta, & Baccarani, 1982; Yarnell et al., 1982).

Urinary incontinence affects individuals of all ages but is most prevalent among the elderly. As a result, UI is commonly and mistakenly attributed to the aging process. The elderly are more likely to have conditions that predispose them to incontinence or contribute to the causes of incontinence. For example, conditions such as decreased bladder capacity, decreased capacity of the urethral muscle to keep the bladder neck closed, increased frequency of bladder contractions, and increased postvoid residuals can contribute to UI and are seen in the elderly (American Association of Retired Persons and Simon Foundation for Continence, 1993; Burgio & Engel, 1987). However, many of these conditions can be controlled or avoided when properly identified. Other risk factors include childbearing, directly related to the delivery experience and number of children delivered vaginally, weakening the muscles of the pelvic floor; prostate surgery, with removal of all or part of the prostate gland secondary to prostate cancer or benign prostatic hyperplasia; and disease processes such as multiple sclerosis, stroke, Parkinson's disease, and cerebral palsy. Additionally, birth defects affecting the bladder or nervous system (i.e., spinal bifida) can be associated with UI (American Association of Retired Persons and Simon Foundation for Continence, 1993).

Urinary incontinence is not a normal aspect of aging, nor is it irreversible. Some transient or temporary causes of UI include delirium; urinary tract infection; vaginitis; use of pharmaceuticals (e.g., sedative hypnotics, diuretics, anticholinergics, alpha-adrenergics, and calcium channel blockers); severe depression; excessive urine production; restricted mobility; and stool impaction. Information about the causes of UI are available from Orzeck and Ouslander (1987) and from the *Clinical Practice Guidelines: Urinary Incontinence in Adults* from the Agency for Health Care Policy and Research (Urinary Incontinence Guideline Panel, 1992).

Assessment

Assessment in the treatment of UI includes characterization of the incontinence, identification of mechanisms of urine loss, and evaluating the emotional and behavioral responses to UI and its causes, as well as a possible psychological treatment regimen, if appropriate. The clinical health psychologist would do well to assess the adaptive tasks that must be accomplished by any medical patient (Moos, 1977). The psychologist should assess how the patient is coping with possible pain, incapacitation, and other symptoms. The patient's coping style in response to special assessment and treatment procedures unique to UI, as well as how the patient is developing and maintaining adequate relationships with the health care staff, is important. In the light of the nature of UI, whether the patient is maintaining a reasonable emotional balance, preserving a satisfactory self-image, and maintaining a sense of competence and mastery should be assessed. Also, whether the patient is preserving relationships with family and friends, and how the patient is preparing for an uncertain future, need to be determined.

Psychological and behavioral assessment for UI should follow a physician's thorough medical examination. An excellent review and summary of the medical assessment, including a discussion of the measurement of urodynamics (physiological measurements of bladder pressure and sphincter activity) are available in the *Clinical Practice Guidelines: Urinary Incontinence in Adults*, from the Agency for Health Care Policy and Research (Urinary Incontinence Guideline Panel, 1992). Again, this review should help the psychologist to be a well-informed member of the health care team.

Burgio and Engel (1987) provided a thorough review of behavioral assessment techniques that can be used by the psychologist when working in collaboration with physicians and nurses in the area of UI. Although the authors limit their discussion to geriatric populations, their methods can be generalized to other populations as well.

Burgio and Engel (1987) used techniques involving interview guidelines, mental status evaluations, bladder records or symptom diaries, and assessment of mobility and toileting skills. According to the Burgio and Engel (1987), interview guidelines need to take into account antecedents of incontinence, descriptions of incontinent episodes, and the consequences of UI. As mentioned previously, there are different types of UI, and each type may have its own unique antecedents and consequences for the patient. Interviews with significant others and other family members are also important.

Voiding habits and continence can be disrupted by depression or cognitive deficits, such as confusion, disorientation, and memory impairment. Burgio and Engel (1987) recommended use of the Mini-Mental State Examination (Folstein, Folstein, & McHugh, 1975) with acutely ill patients, as a brief measure of mental status. Depression may be evaluated by interview and other structured devices, such as the Beck Depression Inventory (Beck, 1972). Referral to a neuropsychologist for a more thorough cognitive evaluation may also be warranted.

Burgio and Engel (1987) also provided examples of bladder records or symptom diaries, which document patterns of UI on a day-to-day basis. Records provide a source of data to diagnose causes of UI and a means to assist in evaluating progress and treatment effectiveness. Finally, observations of mobility and assessment of toileting skills can be used to assess whether environmental barriers or physical handicapping conditions exacerbate or cause UI. As the expert in behavioral and psychological assessments, the psychologist can become a valuable member of the diagnostic team.

Psychological Aspects

Each person who suffers from incontinence feels differently about it and reacts with varying degrees of emotional distress. Tovian, Rozensky, Sloan, and Slotnik (1995) summarized numerous studies identifying the psychological aspects of incontinence.

Depression may be the most commonly reported reaction (Cuhna, 1986; Macaulay, Stern, Holmes, & Stanton, 1987; Ouslander, 1982; Stone & Judd, 1978; Sutherland, 1976; Tovian & Rozensky, 1985). Both agitated and retarded symptoms of depression are common (Yu, 1987), and Macaulay et al. (1987) reported that 25% of patients viewed life as not worth living because of their incontinence. Actual embarrassment and fear of possible public embarrassment from "accidents" or others noticing urine odor are also very pertinent psychological factors in the everyday management of incontinence (Dobson, 1973; Mitteness, 1987; Norton, 1982; Stone & Judd, 1978). Symptom complexes, including shame, humiliation, or damaged self-image are frequently experienced by the incontinent patient (Mitteness, 1987; Norton, 1982; Sadler, 1982; Stone & Judd, 1978). Anxiety, irritability, frustration, and anger have also been identified among incontinent patients (Tovian & Rozensky, 1985). Those patients with catheters, for example, tend to be constantly aware of its presence and are often fearful of others noticing the odor of urine (Roe & Brocklehurst, 1987).

Hafner, Stanton, and Guy (1977) asserted that roughly one third of all incontinence patients would benefit from psychological intervention. Given this estimate, as well as the figure of over 10 million known suffers of UI (Berkman, 1986), there would appear to be a large number of people in need of the health psychologist's clinical and research expertise.

Quality of Life

Work. In some cases, people with incontinence find it difficult to obtain a job and even more difficult to hold one (Dobson, 1973; Norton, 1982). Norton also reported that patients can lose their jobs or have to change employment because of the restriction of activities due to their incontinence. Fear and worry of leakage or odor can impair work concentration.

Social aspects. Many people rearrange their physical and social environments to accommodate their incontinence (Mitteness, 1987). The feelings of isolation often are reinforced due to a self-induced social withdrawal because of fears of being "found out" (Breakwell & Walker, 1988; Mitteness, 1987; Norton, 1982). Ouslander et al. (1987) found that people with incontinence in nursing homes felt that they had fewer close friends or talked with friends less often but that, in actuality, they engaged in activities as frequently as others.

Home life. One often unavoidable artifact of incontinence is dependency, especially for the elderly. This is reflected in their difficulties with activities of daily living, such as shopping, housekeeping, and hygiene (Noelker, 1987; Norton, 1982). More help is then needed from spouses and other family members (Ekelund & Rundgren, 1987). Many incontinent people fear entering a marriage, either because of fear of rejection by the spouse once they are told of the incontinence or because of possible awkwardness of the sexual aspect of the relationship (Dobson, 1973; Norton, 1982).

Reactions of Caregivers

Institutional caregivers. Mitteness (1987) believes that physicians often hold the attitude that UI is inevitable in old age and untreatable and, therefore, relegate the management of the incontinent patients to nurses. In a survey, Yu and Kaltreider (1987) found that the nursing personnel had both positive and negative feelings toward UI, feeling sympathy toward the patients as victims while experiencing stress due to the tedious maintenance of the incontinent patients.

Home caregivers. Living with a person who suffers from incontinence can have negative effects on family relations (Jakovac-Smith, 1988). The tasks involved in caring for the incontinent are tiring, difficult, and upsetting (Noelker, 1987), and there is a reluctance to talk openly about the subject (Dobson, 1973; Tovian & Rozensky, 1985). For this reason, caregivers are often unsure as to whether they are caring properly for their incontinent relative (Noelker, 1987). Because of the many tasks and time requirements, the caregivers' social activities may be restricted (Noelker, 1987). This nonmedical issue, the restriction of the caregiver's social activities, can often lead to a nursing home placement for the incontinent relative. Such a decision may be medically unnecessary for the patient (Jakovac-Smith, 1988). Although many relatives are willing to provide this home care, they may need regular relief and support (Dobson, 1973).

Treatment

The treatment of UI falls within four areas: behavioral, pharmacologic, surgical, and supportive devices (including catheters and absorbent pads and garments). A combination of interventions may be used, depending on the patient's needs and physician's diagnosis. For this chapter, discussion focuses on the behavioral interventions that fall into the scope of practice of clinical health psychologists. Thorough reviews of all treatment options for UI, including their risks, benefits, and outcome, are discussed in the *Clinical Practice Guidelines: Urinary Incontinence in Adults* (Urinary Incontinence Guideline Panel, 1992).

Behavioral Techniques

Behavioral techniques include bladder training, habit training (timed voiding), prompted voiding, pelvic muscle exercises, and biofeedback. Behavioral techniques show improvement ranging from complete dryness to reductions of wetness (Urinary Incontinence Guideline Panel, 1992). Improved bladder control can occur in cognitively impaired individuals (McCormick, Scheve, & Leahy, 1988; Schnelle, 1990). Behavioral techniques have no reported side effects, do not limit future treatment options, and can be used in combination with other therapies for UI.

Some limitations, however, are noteworthy in published results determining the effectiveness of behavioral interventions with UI. These include use of different outcome criteria, variability and frequency of treatment sessions, variability of comprehensiveness in training procedures, absence or variability in follow-up data, use of heterogeneous samples, and lack of standardized terminology for various behavioral techniques. These are important issues when considering future directions for clinical health psychologists in research with UI. Despite these limitations, behavioral interventions appear to be most effective for urge UI and stress UI. Behavioral interventions are not effective for patients with overflow UI (Urinary Incontinence Guideline Panel, 1992).

Bladder training. Bladder training (also termed *bladder retraining*) consists of three primary components: education, scheduled voiding, and positive reinforcement. The education program usually combines written, visual, and verbal instruction that addresses physiology and pathophysiology. The voiding schedule uses a progressively increased interval between mandatory voidings, with concomitant distraction or relaxation techniques. The person is taught to delay voiding consciously. If the patient is unable to delay voiding between schedules, one approach is to adjust this schedule and start the timing from the last void. Another option is to keep the prearranged schedule and disregard the unscheduled void between schedules. Finally, positive reinforcement is provided. More specific details regarding bladder-training programs, such as optional time involving voiding intervals, are available in the *Clinical Practice Guidelines: Urinary Incontinence in Adults* (Urinary Incontinence Guideline Panel, 1992). Fantl et al. (1991), in a randomized controlled study, reported that 12% of the women who underwent bladder training became continent, and 75% improved to at least a 50% reduction in the number of incontinent episodes. This form of training has been used to manage

UI due to bladder instability. However, studies indicate that this training may also control stress incontinence (Burgio, Whitehead, & Engel, 1985; Burton et al., 1988; Fantl et al., 1990; Rose, Baigis-Smith, Smith, & Newman, 1990).

Habit training. Habit training, or timed voiding, is scheduled toileting on a planned basis. The goal is to keep the person dry by telling them to void at regular intervals. Attempts are made to match the voiding intervals to the person's natural voiding schedule. Unlike bladder training, there is no systematic effort to motivate the patient to delay voiding and resist urge. Studies indicate improvement in patients (Colling, Ouslander, Hadley, Campbell, & Eisch, 1991; Engel et al., 1990; Schnelle, Newman, & Fogarty, 1990). In one controlled study on habit training, when 51 nursing home residents who were identified with an electronic monitoring device, Jarvis (1981) found that 86% of the participants improved their UI over baseline levels, when compared with control groups.

Prompted voiding. Prompted voiding is a supplement to habit training and attempts to teach the incontinent person to discriminate their incontinence status and to request toileting assistance from caregivers. There are three elements to prompted voiding: monitoring (the person is checked by caregivers on a regular basis and asked to report if wet or dry), prompting (the person is asked or prompted to try to use the toilet), and reinforcement (the person is praised for maintaining continence and for attempting to toilet). Prompted voiding has been shown to be effective in dependent or cognitively impaired nursing home incontinent patients (Colling et al., 1991; Engel et al., 1990; Hu et al., 1991; Schnelle, 1990).

Pelvic muscle exercises. Pelvic muscle exercises, also called *Kegel exercises*, improve urethral resistance through active exercise of the pubococcygeus muscle. The exercises strengthen the voluntary periurethral and pelvic muscles. The contraction inherent in the exercise exerts a closing force on the urethra and increases muscle support to the pelvic visceral structures (Urinary Incontinence Guideline Panel, 1992).

Pelvic muscle exercises have been shown to be effective with women with stress incontinence (Castleden, Duffin, Asher, & Yeomanson, 1985; Klarskov, Gerstenberg, & Hald, 1986); with men after prostate surgery (Burgio, Stutzman, & Engel, 1989); and after multiple surgical repairs in women (Baigis-Smith, Smith, Rose, & Newman, 1989; Burgio & Engel, 1990). This exercise is often coupled with pharmacologic therapy (Wells et al., 1991; Brody, 1985) and biofeedback (Burgio, Robinson, & Engel, 1986), to maximize results.

Biofeedback. Biofeedback uses electronic or mechanical instruments to relay information to patients about their physiologic activity.

It aims to alter bladder dysfunction by teaching people to change physiologic responses that mediate bladder control (Burgio & Engel, 1990). Display of this information, through auditory or visual displays, forms the core of the biofeedback procedure (Schwartz, 1987).

Biofeedback is often used with other behavioral and medical procedures; such studies report a range of 54%–95% improvement across different patient groups (Urinary Incontinence Guideline Panel, 1992). For women, a biofeedback device, called a *perineometer*, attaches by cable to a sensor that is inserted into the vagina. The sensor comes in contact with the pubococcygeus muscle and shows the strength of the muscle, the ability of the muscle to relax, and the level of control of that muscle (Burns, Marack, Duttmar, & Bullogh, 1985).

Burgio et al. (1986) found that 92% of the biofeedback patients significantly reduced incontinence, but only 55% of the patients without biofeedback achieved a reduction. Similarly, Shepherd, Montgomery, and Anderson (1983) found that 91% of the patients receiving biofeedback improved or were cured, whereas only 55% of those who did not use the perineometer improved.

Smith, Smith, Rose, and Kaschak (1987a) found that patients in an outpatient clinic improved by 75% when using a clinical perineometer for diagnosis and a personal perineometer for home use. Smith, Smith, Rose, and Kaschak (1987b) obtained similar results with homebound senior citizens, using a portable perineometer. Perry, Hullett, and Bollinger (1987) used computerized software (for diagnostic evaluations), home trainers, and patient telephone reports (to assure greater compliance). All 31 of their patients had marked improvement, with 100% symptom reduction and elimination of urinary incontinence. A replication with 56 new patients found 99.95% improved and 98% cured (Perry, Hullett, & Bollinger, 1988).

Biofeedback increases the effectiveness of Kegel exercises, because the patient can observe progress and learn from past attempts at controlling the muscle (Burgio et al., 1986). Henderson and Taylor (1987) found that as pubococcygeal strength increases, the amount and occurrence of urine loss, use of the devices to protect clothing, and patient concern about the problem decrease.

Behavioral techniques in outpatient adults. Combined analyses were conducted on 22 studies that dealt with all behavioral interventions on outpatient basis (Urinary Incontinence Guideline Panel, 1992). The studies were standardized along measures of efficacy, reflecting the percentage of wetness and dryness. Results indicated that the average percentage reduction in incontinence frequency at the end of behavioral treatments was 64.6%, with a 95% confidence interval range of from 58.8% to 70.4%. Additional randomized controlled trials (Burns, Pranikoff, Nochajski, Desotelle, & Harwood, 1990; Fantl et al., 1991) and a randomized but not controlled study (Wells et al., 1991), all with women in outpatient settings, suggested that behavioral techniques result in subjective cure/improvement rates of 70%–77%, with improvements maintained for at least 6 months.

Behavioral techniques in the nursing home. The severity of UI in nursing home residents is often aggravated by the effects of institutionalization, declining medical conditions, and inconsistent nursing care. Nevertheless, a similar combined analysis of 428 persons studied in nursing homes using habit training and prompted voiding (Urinary Incontinence Guideline Panel, 1992) suggested that patients were dry 70% of the time at baseline and rose 81% after behavioral treatments during daytime hours only. These techniques have the potential to reduce the costs and improve the quality of life for long-term-care patients, as well to as serve as an important place of intervention for clinical health psychologists.

Appliances and garments. When incontinence is severe or cannot be reversed, appliances and garments are comfortable ways of managing (Burton, Pearce, Burgio, & Engel, 1988). For those patients using these products for management only, it should be remembered that a concurrent medical problem exists (Ory et al., 1986). Therefore, the clinical health psychologist should insist on concurrent medical therapeutic procedures (Mohr et al., 1983). Alvero and Gartley (1985) provided a thorough list of the various devices that are available (pad and pant systems, absorbent pants, adult undergarments, bed protection pads, drip collectors, condom catheters, intermittent catheterization, and Foley catheters).

Additional Psychological Treatment Issues

Self-help and patient education. Given the proper selection of clients, appropriate goal setting, and patient compliance, self-help programs can be very effective in the treatment of chronic illnesses. Under the self-help paradigm, skills are taught to an active participant who assumes partial responsibility for designing and administering her or his own treatment. By these learning skills, some individuals can assume considerable responsibility necessary for the self-management of their chronic illness (Tobin, Reynolds, Holroyd, & Creer, 1986).

"I Will Manage" is a Simon Foundation program based on the principles of self-help. It is hosted by both lay and professional persons. The program is divided into four sessions: "Incontinence in America Today" (an introduction), "The Urologic System, Fixing It When It Fails," "Managing Incontinence With Products and Devices," and "Dealing Effectively With the Psychological Aspects of Incontinence." The program's format is designed to accomplish two goals: (a) to present practical multidisciplinary information on incontinence and (b) to encourage people to share their experiences and develop the confidence to make changes in their life ("I Will Manage" self-help groups, Simon Foundation for Continence, 1991). This patient-education approach assumes that much of the psychosocial distress accompanying incontinence is largely a result of a lack of knowledge concerning incontinence, its causes and treatment, and the health care system. Empirical evidence of the efficacy of this approach would be useful. Given the large psychosocial component of this self-help program, there is a defined role in which the psychologist may become involved.

Supportive group therapy. The second goal inherent in the self-help paradigm, that of encouraging people to share their experiences, is also important in another treatment modality, supportive group therapy. The effectiveness of supportive group therapy has been reviewed, in the context of such medical problems as cancer (Telsch & Telsch, 1985) and cardiac surgery (Bond et al., 1979). Researchers in group therapy (e.g., Yalom & Greaves, 1977) maintain that the support offered and the opportunity to express needs, concerns, and fears are the salient ingredients in the group therapy experience. Both support and catharsis are therapeutic tools used to diminish mood disturbance, improve relationship distress, and enhance adjustment. A common therapeutic strategy is to enlist patients in becoming active in the group process, where group members are encouraged to express problems, concerns, and feelings and to share personal methods of coping. In this way, it is expected that members will serve as peer models for one another. The therapeutic mechanism of community and mutuality in group therapy would seem especially relevant to the social problems of UI patients. This therapeutic approach may also be useful for the needs of the home caregiver. To date, however, there have been no published studies of the effectiveness of supportive group therapy with UI patients or their families.

Coping skills approach. The coping skills approach involves structured training in specific cognitive, behavioral, and affective competencies for managing the disruptive effects of UI. The coping skills approach assumes that the distress experienced in managing the effects of illness and disability is partially due to a limited or ineffective skills repertoire. Rozensky and Tovian (1985) suggested the use of self-instruction techniques, which help individuals with UI learn constructive self-talk and avoid negativistic thinking. Rozensky and Tovian also proposed assertiveness techniques and progressive relaxation approaches to be used by UI patients in distressing social situations. For example, the use of covert reinforcement and structured exposure to feared situations could be applied to the problems of social withdrawal and social phobia seen among UI patients. Learning both cognitive and behavioral coping strategies may enhance adjustment by expanding coping repertoires, thereby increasing one's perception of control; a problem that is very relevant to the UI patient. Among the coping skills area, Rozensky and Tovian also recommended stress inoculation training and problem-solving strategies. The coping skills techniques may be used in group- or individual-treatment formats. There exist no controlled studies examining the effectiveness of individual or combinations of cognitive–behavioral therapeutic interventions with UI patients.

ERECTILE DYSFUNCTION

Definition and Prevalence

Erectile dysfunction is defined as a persistent or recurrent, partial or complete, failure to attain or maintain sufficient penile erections for satisfactory sexual functioning to occur with subsequent marked distress and interpersonal difficulty (American Psychiatric Association, 1994). It is estimated that more than 10 million American men experience erectile dysfunction, with the prevalence of ED increasing with age as a result of physical and mental illnesses with concomitant prescription drug use that is common during the middle and later years of life. The incidence of ED is estimated to be found in at least 10% of the male population at age 50, 20% by age 60, 30% at age 70, and 40% at age 80 (Ackerman, 1992). Using a biopsychosocial model, ED is not seen as either organic or psychogenic but, rather, is perceived as an interacting set of variables, requiring assessment of cognitive, behavioral, and interpersonal factors as well as physical factors for effective treatment. The psychological consequences of ED include depression, performance anxiety, and relationship distress (Ackerman, 1995; Ackerman & Carey, 1995).

Causes

The clinical health psychologist needs to be aware of the many biological risk factors associated with ED. Diseases of the endocrine, vascular, and neurologic systems should be carefully screened before or after any referral to the psychologist (Ackerman & Carey, 1995). Some common medical conditions that are associated with ED are presented in the Appendix. Like UI, ED is not a result of natural aging.

Many medications prescribed for various physical and mental disorders can impair erectile dysfunctioning as well as sexual desire.

Medications such as antihypertensive agents, anticholinergics, and drugs used in the treatment of psychiatric disorders (i.e., phenothiazines, benzodiazepines, and antidepressants) can be associated with ED (Ackerman, 1995). Some medications associated with ED also are presented in the Appendix.

Assessment

Ackerman (1992; Ackerman & Carey, 1995) provided excellent reviews on the role of the psychologist in establishing a multidisciplinary research-based clinical program for the evaluation and treatment of ED. Ackerman noted that the primary role of the psychologist in the assessment of ED is to provide insights about patient behaviors, thoughts, affect, and the psychosocial data through interview and assessment protocols. Screening for psychological dysfunction, substance abuse, cognitive distortions, personality disorders, or life-stress events known to adversely affect erectile functioning can be accomplished through clinical interviews and self-report questionnaires such as the Minnesota Multiphasic Personality Inventory, Beck Depression Inventory, and the Short Marital Adjustment Test (Lock & Wallace 1959). According to Ackerman, men who are either married or report a significant other should be interviewed individually and conjointly to ascertain corroborative information regarding sexual performance and relationship factors.

The Miami Sexual Dysfunction Protocol (MSDP; Ackerman, Helder, & Antoni, 1989) is a broad, semistructured interview format designed for use in medical settings to help organize information taken from the sexual dysfunctional male and his partner. Another important skill that the psychologist brings to the evaluation of ED is the ability to elicit concise information regarding sexual functioning while creating a relaxed, trusting atmosphere (Ackerman & Carey, 1995). Having an organized protocol, such as the MSDP, helps to facilitate the collection of baseline data for clinical training and research purposes in a relaxed atmosphere.

Ackerman and Carey (1995) recommended a thorough evaluation of past and current erectile functioning (i.e., description of the presenting complaint and its duration, frequency, and nature of onset), once rapport has been established. Other relevant information includes masturbatory fantasies, sexual drive, sexual techniques, and sexual knowledge. Frequency and outcome attempts at intercourse should be reviewed, as well as coping effort for unsuccessful attempts. Questions pertaining to sexual orientation, sexual deviations, and past sexual abuse should be included. Occasionally, special treatment circumstances such as vasoactive injection therapy or penile implant surgery require the psychologist to assess misconceptions, attitude, or unrealistic expectations, to maximize treatment outcome.

Ackerman (1992) highlighted the importance of assessing the absence or presence of morning erections, quality of erections, and ejaculatory ability. Ackerman (1992) noted that the final step in the assessment process involves the patient returning to the urologist for 2 consecutive nights of in-hospital Rigiscan diagnostic monitoring. Rigiscan monitoring involves the assessment of erectile functioning, including rigidity and tumescence at the base and tip of the penis and duration of these events throughout the sleep cycle.

Treatment

Ackerman, Montague, and Morganstern (1994) outlined treatment options for ED. Treatment options will depend on the suspected cause of the ED. If the causes are psychological or behavioral in nature, sex therapy will be a crucial component or sole method of treatment. If relationship problems exist, conjoint therapy is recommended with or before sex therapy. Testosterone replacement therapy is used only when there is clear evidence of hormonal insufficiency. If the ED developed after medications were prescribed, cessation or substitution of those medications may be attempted. Ackerman et al. (1994) also reviewed possible medicinal approaches with Yohimbine HCl and Frental, and they concluded that these drugs provide nothing more than placebo effects at best.

In addition, Ackerman et al. (1994) thoroughly reviewed invasive therapeutic options such as injection methods with Pavaverine HCl, vascular surgery, and implant prosthesis. Although injection methods continue to be the first-line treatment option for ED, Ackerman et al. noted that patients undergoing any of these invasive procedures often will require adjunct psychological support and psychoeducational therapy, with a psychologist experienced with ED, to ensure the technical success of these procedures.

PROGRAM DEVELOPMENT

The general purpose of integrating clinical health psychology into urology programs is to enhance patient care. From the previous discussion, it is clear that the clinical health psychologist can offer a full spectrum of services to multidisciplinary programs treating urological disorders. In addition to direct interventions involving individual assessment and psychotherapy in response to patients' psychological reactions to urological disorders, the clinical health psychologist can provide specialized interventions involving biofeedback and behavioral treatments to individuals, families, and professional caregivers, in medical settings and nursing homes. In addition to individual-treatment modalities, the clinical health psychologist can provide and supervise supportive and self-help group interventions to both patients and their families. As a member of a multidisciplinary health care team or in a specific urology program, the clinical health psychologist can also provide consultation in regular staff meetings to medical staff, regarding particular problems involving adherence to medical treatment or patient reactions to stressful medical procedures, often experienced with urology problems, such as UI and ED.

Psychology and Surgery Interface

Clinical health psychologists working in medical settings will find themselves consulting with surgeons in this tertiary field of urology. In communicating with surgeons, written reports need to be prompt, concise, and free of psychological jargon (Ackerman, 1992; Adams, 1992). Reports should begin with a direct and concise answer to the restated referral question, followed by brief and equally concise data to support that answer. Recommendations for specific interventions need to be stated succinctly and early in the report. Contradictions for specific medical interventions should be clearly noted, with evidence for potential problems delineated (Ackerman, 1992). Lengthy reports discussing test results are too often obscure to the surgeon and answer questions that are not asked but fail to answer those that are obvious (Adams, 1992).

The clinical health psychologist working in urology needs to become familiar also with the surgical procedures used. A request to observe a surgical procedure, or "scrub" for a procedure, is an excellent way to demonstrate a willingness to learn firsthand about a given intervention, as well as to become a "member of the team." A clinical health psychologist working in a surgical specialty such as urology needs to relate to both the nature of a surgeon's work and the patient's surgical experience, expectancies, fears, and consequences (Adams, 1992).

Research Interface

Engaging in psychosocial research with urological problems can provide the clinical health psychologist scholarly recognition in the medical setting and a place on a multidisciplinary medical team. Working with a urologist or gynecologist as a co-investigator, for example, is also an effective means of establishing and maintaining referral sources, as well as a presence in urology programs.

Marketing Issues

In marketing services to relevant medical departments and professionals, the clinical health psychologist must be aware of his or her training and experience with urological problems, as well as those sociopolitical issues that exist in any medical setting (Sweet et al., 1991). Establishing professional relationships with nurse-clinicians and physicians in such tertiary areas as urology, gynecology, surgery, and oncology (especially those involving prostate cancer) may involve the psychologist's offering to present at medical grand rounds or notifying various medical staff about their interest and experience with urology patients. Major medical centers often have broad multidisciplinary programs that cross over various specialties, such as programs in geriatrics or women's health, for example, which can serve as a place for membership for a clinical health psychologist interested in UI, for example.

Finally, as a result of their training and expertise, clinical psychologists in medical settings can be instrumental in the necessary and increased efforts needed to inform and educate the public about urological problems. The public should be aware that a problem such as incontinence, for example, is not inevitable or shameful but is often treatable and always manageable. The psychology profession would appear to be a crucial link in any comprehensive, multidisciplinary attempts to design effective patient-education programs about the prevention, assessment, and treatment of urological problems such as UI and ED. Given the approximately 3,000 psychologists employed as faculty in medical schools (Clayson & Mensh, 1987), contributions from clinical health psychologists would also appear to be crucial in efforts to educate other medical professionals about the psychological evaluation and treatment of those who suffer from urological dysfunctions.

Appendix
Factors Associated With Erectile Dysfunction

Endocrine
Diabetes
Increased estrogen
Decreased testosterone

Neurologic
Epilepsy (including temporal lobe)
Multiple sclerosis
Peripheral neuropathy
Spinal cord injury
Stroke

Penile
Trauma
Peyronie's disease

Prostatic
Prostatitis
Prostate cancer treatment

Lifestyle
Alcohol use
Tobacco use
Recreational and illicit drug use

Psychologic
Anxiety
Depression
Stress
Marital discord

Vascular
Atherosclerosis

Pharmacological agents
Addictive substances
Antihypertensive agents
Endocrine agents
Psychotropic agents
Antihypertensive agents
Chemotherapy agents
Histamine-receptor antagonists

Adapted from Ackerman, Montague, & Morganstern (1994).

REFERENCES

Ackerman, M. D. (1992). Consultation with clinical urology: Expanded roles for health psychologists. *The Health Psychologist, 14*, 3–4.

Ackerman, M. D. (1995). Behavioral approaches to assessing erectile dysfunction. *The Behavior Therapist, 18*, 31–34.

Ackerman, M. D., & Carey, M. P. (1995). Psychology's role in the assessment of erectile dysfunction: Historical precedents, current knowledge, and methods. *Journal of Consulting and Clinical Psychology, 63*, 862–876.

Ackerman, M. D., Helder, L. H., & Antoni, M. H. (1989, March). *The Miami sexual dysfunction protocol.* Poster presented at the Tenth Annual Scientific Session of the Society of Behavioral Medicine, San Francisco.

Ackerman, M. D., Montague, D. K., & Morganstern, S. (1994, March). Impotence: Help for erectile dysfunction. *Patient Care,* pp. 22–56.

Adams, D. B. (1992). Medical and surgical interface: Problems with philosophy and nosology. *Psychotherapy Bulletin, 27(2)*, 23–25.

Alvero, J., & Gartley, W. A. (1985). Products and devices for managing incontinence. In C. B. Gartley (Ed.), *Managing incontinence* (pp. 81–92). Ottawa, IL: Jameson Books.

American Association of Retired Persons and Simon Foundation for Continence (1993). *Promoting continence: Educating older Americans about incontinence.* Washington, DC: American Association of Retired Persons.

American Psychiatric Association (1994). *Diagnostic and statistical manual of mental disorders* (4th ed.). Washington, DC: Author.

Baigis-Smith, J., Smith, D. A., Rose, M., & Newman, D. K. (1989). Managing urinary incontinence in community-residing elderly persons. *The Gerontologist, 29,* 229–233.

Beck, A. (1972). *Depression: Its causes and treatment.* Philadelphia: University of Pennsylvania Press.

Berkman, S. (1986, November). Those embarrassing ailments: Here's help! *Good Housekeeping,* pp. 318–319.

Bond, G. R., Borman, L. D., Bankoff, E. A., Daiter, S., Lieberman, M. A., & Videka, L. M. (1979). The self-help, mutual support group. In M. A. Lieberman & L. D. Borman (Eds.), *Self-help groups for coping with crisis* (pp. 489–526). San Francisco: Jossey-Bass.

Breakwell, S. L., & Walker, S. N. (1988). Differences in physical health, social interaction, and personal adjustment between continent and incontinent homebound aged women. *Journal of Community Health Nursing, 5*(1), 19–31.

Brody, J. E. (1985, June 5). Personal health. *The New York Times,* p. 47.

Burgio, K. L., & Engel, B. T. (1987). Urinary incontinence; Behavioral assessment and treatment. In L. L. Carstensen and B. A. Edelstein (Eds.), *Handbook of clinical gerontology.* New York: Pergamon Press.

Burgio, K. L., & Engel, B. T. (1990). Biofeedback-assisted behavioral training for elderly men and women. *Journal of the American Geriatrics Society, 38,* 338–340.

Burgio, K. L., Robinson, J. C., & Engel, B. T. (1986). The role of biofeedback in Kegel exercise training for stress urinary incontinence. *American Journal of Obstetrician Gynecology, 154,* 58–64.

Burgio, K. L., Stutzman, R. E., & Engel, B. T. (1989). Behavioral training for prostatectomy urinary incontinence. *Journal of Urology, 141,* 303–306.

Burgio, K. L., Whitehead, W. E., & Engel, B. T. (1985). Urinary incontinence in the elderly: Bladder–sphincter biofeedback and toilet skills training. *Annals of Internal Medicine, 103,* 507–515.

Burns, P. A., Mareck, M. A., Duttmar, S. S., & Bullogh, B. (1985). Kegel's exercises with biofeedback therapy for stress incontinence. *Nurse Practitioner, 4,* 28–33.

Burns, P. A., Pranikoff, K., Nochajski, T., Desotelle, P., & Harwood, M. K. (1990). Treatment of stress incontinence with pelvic floor exercises and biofeedback. *Journal of the American Geriatrics Society, 38,* 341–344.

Burton, J. R., Pearce, K. L., Burgio, K. L., Engel, B. T. (1988). Behavioral training for urinary incontinence in elderly ambulatory patients. *Journal of the American Geriatrics Society, 36,* 693–698.

Castleden, C. M., Duffin, H. M., Asher, M. J., & Yeomanson, C. W. (1985). Factors influencing outcome in elderly patients with urinary incontinence and detrusor instability. *Age and Aging, 14,* 303–307.

Clayson, D., & Mensh, I. (1987). Psychologists in medical schools: The trials of emerging political activism. *American Psychologist, 42,* 859–862.

Colling, J. C., Ouslander, J., Hadley, B. J., Campbell, E. B., & Eisch, J. (1991). *Patterned urge-response toileting for incontinence.* Portland: Oregon Health Sciences University.

Cuhna, U. V. (1986). Antidepressants: Their uses in nonpsychiatric disorders of aging. *Geriatrics, 41*(10), 63–71.

Dobson, P. (1973). Urinary incontinence: Social aspects. *Physiotherapy, 59,* 358–359.

Ekelund, P., & Rundgren, A. (1987). Urinary incontinence in the elderly with implications for hospital care consumption and social disability. *Archives of Gerontology and Geriatrics, 6,* 11–18.

Elving, L. B., Foldspang, A., Lain, G. W., & Mommens, S. (1989). Descriptive epidemiology of urinary incontinence in 3,100 women age 30–59. *Scandinavian Journal of Urology and Nephrology, 125,* 37–43.

Engel, B. T., Burgio, L. D., McCormick, K. A., Bergman, S., & Williams, J. P. (1990). Behavioral treatment of incontinence in the long-term care setting. *Journal of the American Geriatrics Society, 38,* 361–363.

Fantl, J. A., Wyman, J. F., Harkins, S. W., & Hadley, E. C. (1990). Bladder training in the management of lower tract urinary dysfunction in women: A review. *Journal of the American Geriatrics Society, 38,* 329–332.

Fantl, J. A., Wyman, J. F., McClish, D. K., Harkins, S. W., Elswick, K. K., Taylor, J. R., Hunt, W. G., Dunn, L. J., & Bump, R. C. (1991). Efficacy of bladder training in older women with urinary incontinence. *Journal of the American Medical Association, 265,* 609–613.

Folstein, M. F., Folstein, S. E., & McHugh, P. R. (1975). Mini-mental state exam: A practical method for grading the cognitive state of patients for clinicians. *Journal of Psychiatric Research, 12,* 189–198.

Hafner, R. J., Stanton, S. L., & Guy, J. (1977). A psychiatric study of women with urgency and urgency incontinence. *British Journal of Urology, 49,* 211–214.

Henderson, J. S., & Taylor, K. H. (1987). Age as a variable in an exercise program for the treatment of simple urinary stress incontinence. *British Journal of Obstetrics and Gynecology, 96,* 266–272.

Hu, T. W. (1990). Impact of urinary incontinence on health-care costs. *Journal of the American Geriatrics Society, 38,* 292–295.

Hu, T. W., Gabelko, K., Weis, K. A., Dionko, A. C., McCormick, K. A., & Fogarty, T. E. (1992). Urinary incontinence: Treatment patterns, costs, and clinical guidelines. *Journal of the American Medical Association, 10,* 184–186.

Hu, T. W., Igou, J. F., Kaltreider, D. L., Yu, L. C., Rohner, T. J., Dennis, P. J., Craighead, W. E., Hadley, E. C., & Ory, M. G. (1991). A clinical trial of behavior therapy to reduce urinary incontinence in nursing homes: Outcome and implications. *Journal of the American Medical Association, 261,* 2656–2662.

The Simon Foundation for Continence (1991). *"I Will Manage" self-help groups.* (Simon Foundation, P.O. Box 815, Wilmette, IL 60091)

Jakovac-Smith, D. A. (1988). Continence restoration in the homebound patient. *Nursing Clinics of North America, 23,* 207–218.

Jarvis, G. J. (1981). A controlled trial of bladder drill and drug therapy in the management of detrusor instability. *British Journal of Urology, 53,* 565–566.

Klarskov, P., Gerstenberg, T. C., & Hald, T. (1986). Bladder training in females with urge incontinence and stable detrusor function. *Scandinavian Journal of Urology and Nephrology, 20,* 41–46.

Locke, H., & Wallace, K. (1959). Short marital adjustment and prediction tests: Their reliability and validity. *Marriage and Family Living, 21,* 251–255.

Macaulay, A. J., Stern, R. S., Holmes, D. M., & Stanton, S. L. (1987). Micturition and the mind: Psychological factors in the aetiology and treatment of urinary symptoms in women. *British Medical Journal, 294,* 540–543.

McCormick, K. A., Scheve, A. S., & Leahy, E. (1988). Nursing management of urinary incontinence in geriatric inpatients. *Nursing Clinics of North America, 23,* 231–264.

Mitteness, L. S. (1987). The management of urinary incontinence by community-living elderly. *The Gerontological Society of America, 27*(2), 285–293.

Mohr, J. A., Rogers, J., Jr., Brown, T. N., & Starkweather, G. (1983). Stress urinary incontinence: A simple and practical approach to diagnosis and treatment. *Journal of the American Geriatrics Society, 31,* 476–478.

Moos, R. H. (1977). *Coping with physical illness.* New York: Plenum.

National Institutes of Health Consensus Development Conference Statement. (1988, October). *Urinary incontinence in adults, 7,* 1–11.

Noelker, L. S. (1987). Incontinence in elderly cared for by family. *The Gerontological Society of America, 27*(7), 194–200.

Norton, C. (1982). The effects of urinary incontinence in women. *International Rehabilitative Medicine, 4*(1), 9–14.

Ory, M. G., Wyman, J. F., & Yu, L. C. (1986). Psychosocial factors in urinary incontinence. *Clinics in Geriatric Medicine, 2,* 657–671.

Orzeck, S., & Ouslander, J. G. (1987). Urinary incontinence: An overview of causes and treatment. *Journal of Enterostomal Therapy, 14*(1), 20–27.

Ouslander, J. G. (1982). Physical illness and depression in the elderly. *Journal of the American Geriatrics Society, 30,* 593–599.

Ouslander, J. G., Morishita, L., Blaustein, J., Orzeck, S., Dunn, S., & Sayre, J. (1987). Clinical, functional, and psychosocial characteristics of an incontinent nursing home population. *Journal of Gerontology, 42,* 631–637.

Perry, J. D., Hullett, L. T., & Bollinger, J. R. (1987, November). Urinary incontinence treated by EMG biofeedback method. *Gerontological Society of America*.

Perry, J. D., Hullett, L. T., & Bollinger, J. R. (1988, March). EMG Biofeedback treatment of incontinence. *Biofeedback Society of America*, 3, 84–89.

Resnick, N. M., Welte, T. T., Scherr, P., Branch, L., & Taylor, J. (1986). Urinary incontinence in community dwelling elderly: Prevalence and correlates. *Proceedings of the International Continence Society*, 1, 76–78.

Resnick, N. M., & Yalla, S. V. (1985). Management of urinary incontinence in the elderly. *The New England Journal of Medicine*, 313, 800–805.

Roe, B. H., & Brocklehurst, J. C. (1987). Study of patients with indwelling catheters. *Journal of Advanced Nursing*, 12, 713–718.

Rose, M. A., Baigis-Smith, J., Smith, D., & Newman, D. (1990). Behavioral management of urinary incontinence in homebound older adults. *Home Healthcare Nurse*, 8, 10–15.

Rozensky, R. H., & Tovian, S. M. (1985). Strategies for a full life. In C. B. Gartley (Ed.), *Managing incontinence* (pp. 58–69). Ottowa, IL: Jameson Books.

Schnelle, J. F. (1990). Treatment of urinary incontinence in nursing home patients by prompted voiding. *Journal of the American Geriatrics Society*, 38, 356–360.

Schnelle, J. F., Newman, D. R., & Fogarty, T. (1990). Management of patient continence in long-term care nursing facilities. *The Gerontologist*, 30, 373–376.

Schwartz, M. S. (1987). *Biofeedback: A practitioner's guide*. New York: Guilford Press.

Shepherd, A. M., Montgomery, E., & Anderson, R. S. (1983). Treatment of genuine stress incontinence with a new perineometer. *Physiotherapy*, 69, 113.

Smith, D., Smith, J., Rose, M., & Kaschak, D. (1987a). Control of urinary incontinence in the acutely ill home patient. *Proceeds of the International Continence Society*, 2, 56–60.

Smith D., Smith J., Rose M., & Kaschak, D. (1987b). Kegel's exercise, biofeedback and relaxation training for the treatment of urinary incontinence in a community setting. *Proceedings of the International Continence Society*, 2, 61–65.

Sowell, V. A., Schnelle, J. F., Hu, T. W., & Traughbers, B. (1987). A cost comparison of five methods of managing urinary incontinence. *QRB. Quality Review Bulletin*, 13, 411–414.

Stone, C. B., & Judd, G. E. (1978). Psychogenic aspects of urinary incontinence in women. *Clinical Obstetrics and Gynecology*, 21, 807–815.

Sutherland, S. S. (1976). The psychology of incontinence. In F. L. Willington (Ed.), *Incontinence in the elderly* (pp. 13–27). London: Academic Press.

Sweet, J. J., Rozensky, R. H., & Tovian, S. M. (1991). *Handbook of clinical psychology in medical settings*. New York: Plenum.

Telsch, C. F., & Telsch, M. J. (1985). Psychological approaches for enhancing coping among cancer patients: A review. *Clinical Psychology Review, 5,* 325–345.

Thomas, T. M., Plymat, K. R., Blannin, J., & Meade, T. W. (1980). Prevalence of urinary incontinence. *British Medical Journal, 21,* 1243–1245.

Tobin, D. L., Reynolds, R. V. C., Holroyd, K. A., & Creer, T. L. (1986). Self-management and social learning theory. In K. A. Holroyd & T. L. Creer (Eds.), *Self-management of chronic disease: Handbook of clinical interventions and research* (pp. 29–58). Orlando, FL: Academic Press.

Tovian, S. M., & Rozensky, R. H. (1985). Building inner confidence. In C. B. Gartley (Ed.), *Managing incontinence* (pp. 48–57). Ottowa, IL: Jameson Books.

Tovian, S. M., Rozensky, R. H., Sloan, T. B., & Slotnik, G. M. (1995). Adult urinary incontinence: Assessment, intervention, and the role of clinical health psychology in program development. *Journal of Clinical Psychology in Medical Settings, 1,* 339–362.

Trombini, G., Rossi, N., Umilta, C., & Baccarani, C. P. (1982). Experimental stress and systomanometric recordings of patients with primary enuresis: A preliminary report. *Perceptual and Motor Skills, 54,* 771–777.

Urinary Incontinence Guideline Panel. (1992, March). *Urinary incontinence in adults: Clinical practice guidelines* (ACHPR Publication No. 92-0038). Rockville, MD: Public Health Service.

Wells, A. J., Rink, C. A., Dionko, A. C., Lawson, A. L., Neal, D. E., & Hoopes, J. M. (1991). Pelvic muscle exercises for stress urinary incontinence in elderly women. *Journal of the American Geriatrics Society, 38,* 296–299.

Yalom, I. D., & Greaves, C. (1977). Group therapy with the terminally ill. *American Journal of Psychiatry, 134,* 396–400.

Yarnell, J. W. G., Voyle, G. J., Sweetnam, P. M., Milbank, J., Richards, C. J., & Stephenson, T. P. (1982). Factors associated with urinary incontinence in women. *Journal of Epidemiology and Community Health, 36,* 58–63.

Yu, L. C. (1987). Incontinence stress index: Measuring psychological impact. *Journal of Gerontological Nursing, 13*(7), 18–24.

Yu, L. C., & Kaltreider, D. L. (1987). Stressed nurses dealing with incontinent patients. *Journal of Gerontological Nursing, 13*(1), 27–30.

20

TOUCH THERAPIES FOR PAIN MANAGEMENT AND STRESS REDUCTION

TIFFANY M. FIELD

Touch therapy is listed in the *Ayur-Veda*, the earliest known medical text from India (around 1800 B.C.), along with diet and exercise, as primary healing practices of that time. Exotic uses of massage in contemporary cultures have been described by Older (1982). He noted that in New Zealand, the pre-European Maori mothers massaged their children's noses to improve their shape, and they massaged their legs to lengthen and straighten them. In Cuba, garlic and oil massages are prepared and applied to the stomach after "a meal lodged in the stomach where it caused pain and fever" (Older, 1982, p. 86). In Samoa, massage is used for every disorder from diarrhea to migraine headache, using a mixture of coconut milk, flowers from trees, plants, and roots of grasses (Older, 1982). Touch therapies such as massage are used in many parts of the

This research was supported by National Institute of Mental Health (NIMH) Research Scientist Award MH00331 and NIMH Research Grant MH46586.

world for managing pain and reducing stress. The United States, though a latecomer to this field, is beginning to use touch therapies for wellness and chronic illness at all ages. This chapter is a review of recent data on the use of touch therapies.

Life's stressors begin as early as the prenatal period. In many countries, such as India, pregnant women are massaged several times daily for relaxation and to reduce their anxiety levels. This therapy is considered beneficial for both the pregnant woman and her fetus. We at the Touch Research Institute have been teaching the significant others of pregnant women to massage the women during pregnancy and labor. Ultrasound images taken after the massages reveal some very happy responses from the fetus. Most of them like the massage, as can be seen by their smiles on ultrasound. When we coded fetal movements, we found a normalization of activity level. This may relate to the reduced anxiety and depression in the mothers. In addition, during labor, the need for medication and for cesarean section by these mothers decreased, and the neonatal outcome was superior.

TOUCH THERAPIES FOR INFANTS

Premature infants. Some pregnancies, unfortunately, end in premature deliveries, and the babies are treated in the neonatal intensive care unit. We found many years ago that one could give babies in the neonatal intensive care unit a 15-minute massage three times a day for 10 days while they were still in the incubator (by putting one's hands through the incubator portholes and massaging them; Field et al., 1986; Scafidi et al., 1990). We were able to document a 47% weight gain for the treatment infants compared with the control infants, and they were hospitalized for 6 days less at a hospital cost savings of $10,000 per infant. If all 450,000 preterm infants born per year received this treatment, $4.5 billion in hospital costs would be saved per year. We also found an elevation in their norepinephrine and epinephrine levels (Kuhn et al., 1991), suggesting that we were able to facilitate the natural increase in these catecholamines at this stage in life.

Our assessments of these infants at 1 year suggested that they were still advantaged in terms of their weight, and they also showed greater gains on the Bayley Scales of Infant Development (Field, Scafidi, & Schanberg, 1987). On the Bayley Mental Scale, their scores averaged 12 points higher; on the Bayley Motor Scale, they averaged 13 points higher. Massaging these infants for 10 days in the first few days after birth seemed to lead to the infants being more responsive. The infants gained more weight as newborns, became more responsive, and apparently elicited more stimulation from their parents. That cycle then led to later growth and developmental gains.

Cocaine-exposed infants. Another infant that is seen very often in the neonatal intensive care unit is the cocaine-exposed baby. In a study on these infants, we were able to show similar weight gain in those who received massage therapy (Wheeden et al., 1993). These infants also showed superior motor behavior. In explaining the mechanism involved in weight gain, we assessed vagal tone. The vagus (1 of the 10 cranial nerves) slows heartbeat during tasks that require attention, and it enhances gastric motility and facilitates the release of food-absorption hormones such as insulin. When we measured vagal activity and insulin levels, we noted increases after the massage. The massaged infants did not eat more food, and they did not sleep more, so they were not conserving calories. Rather, the weight gain seems to have been mediated by an increase in vagal activity, which in turn increased metabolic activity by increasing the release of food-absorption hormones (at least insulin).

HIV-exposed infants. Another infant who is frequently treated on the neonatal intensive care unit is the HIV-exposed infant. In this study, we hypothesized that the mothers of HIV infants would be willing and reliable massage therapists, partly because the mothers might have some feeling of guilt for having transmitted HIV to their infants (Scafidi & Field, 1995).

We often teach parents to massage their infants for two reasons: (a) We find that parents' anxiety levels are highly related to their feeling helpless about their infant's or their child's condition. Helping with their infant's treatment will typically decrease the parents' anxiety levels and make them feel like they are contributing to the treatment. (b) The continuing daily massages are not practically or economically feasible without the parents' providing these.

One surprising result of this study was the 100% compliance from the mothers, most especially because our low-income, low-educated population in Miami is typically noncompliant. The mothers massaged their infants every day for the first 2 months of life. The massaged infants' weight gain was significantly greater than that of the control group, and the massaged group showed significantly fewer stress behaviors.

TOUCH THERAPY FOR HIV-POSITIVE ADULTS

In a related study that we did on HIV-positive adults, we found a significant increase in natural killer cells after 20 days of massage (Ironson et al., 1996). For 1 month, 29 gay men (20 of whom were HIV-positive) were massaged. A subset of 11 of the HIV-positive participants served as a within-participant control group (1 month with and 1 month without massages). Major immune findings for the effect of the month of massage included a significant increase in natural killer cell number, natural killer cell cytotoxity, soluble CD_8, and the cytotoxic subset of CD_8 cells. There was no change in HIV disease progression markers (i.e., CD_4, CD_4/CD_8 ratio, beta-2 microglobulin, and neopterin). Major neuroendocrine findings, measured through urine specimens collected over a 24-hr period, included a significant decrease in cortisol and nonsignificant trends toward decrease of catecholamines. There were also significant decreases in anxiety and increases in relaxation, which were significantly correlated with increases in natural killer cell number. Thus, an increase in cytotoxic capacity apparently is associated with massage. Because natural killer cells are the front line of defense in the immune system, combating the growth and proliferation of viral and cancer cells, the HIV patients who received the massage might be expected to experience fewer opportunistic infections, such as pneumonia, which often are fatal for them.

"GRANDPARENT" VOLUNTEERS MASSAGING INFANTS

The question remained as to how to deliver this intervention cost-effectively, because not too many nursing or medical staff have time to massage infants. So we used volunteer grandparents. We were surprised to find that the grandparents were also benefiting. They reported a better sense of well-being, a significant decrease in depression after the 1-month period of massaging the infants, an increase in their self-esteem, and a decrease in their urinary cortisol levels. We then compared their giving massage with their receiving massage. They gave infant massages for a month and then received massages for a month, or vice versa. We found that the grandparent volunteers benefited more from giving the massage than from receiving the massage. Their affect and self-esteem improved, as did their lifestyle habits (e.g., they reported drinking fewer cups of coffee per day, they made more social phone calls, and they made fewer trips to the doctor's office).

TOUCH THERAPIES FOR CHILDREN

Asthmatic children. In studies where we used parents as therapists, such as with asthmatic children, the parents were asked to give the massages for 15 minutes before bedtime each night for a 1-month period (Field et al., 1996). Typically the parents' anxiety decreased, the child's anxiety decreased, and the child's affect improved. This may have contributed to the significant increase noted in peak air flow (the gold standard measure that physicians use for determining the clinical improvement of asthmatic children).

Diabetic children. In diabetic children, the gold standard is blood-glucose levels. Those levels decreased significantly from a high level of 159 to a level of 118, which is within the normal range for blood-glucose levels in children (Field, Delamater, Shaw, & LaGreca, 1995). The improvement in the diabetic children's clinical condition also may have related to the decrease in their anxiety levels and the associated decrease in cortisol levels.

Burn children. Burn patients are reporting lower anxiety levels at the end of their first and last treatments 5 days later, after a 30-minute treatment each day, and an associated decrease in cortisol levels (Field, Peck, Burman, & Krugman, 1995). Pain has also decreased by Day 5, as reported on a faces scale, showing painful expressions, and depression is decreased, probably because of the decrease in pain. Postburn patients, whose problem is not only pain but also itching, are reporting a decrease in their pain and itching on the McGill Pain Adapted Scale for Children (Melzack, 1987).

Autistic children. Another sample we have been working with are autistic children. They have been described as being extremely sensitive to touch and typically disliking being touched. However, we have noted surprisingly little resistance to their being massaged. Massage may not be aversive to them because it is predictable and does not involve social relations. In our study on autistic children, their off-task behavior in the classroom decreased after a 10-day period of massage, and their relating to their teachers increased (Field et al., 1996).

Children suffering from posttraumatic stress disorder. Many children showed symptoms of posttraumatic stress disorder (PTSD) after Hurricane Andrew. A number of these children had shown acting-out problems in the classroom, which were then exacerbated by Hurricane Andrew. We massaged a group of children two times per week for 5 weeks after the hurricane (Field, Seligman, Scafidi, & Schanberg, 1996). We compared them with a video control group of children, who watched a relaxing video. After the 5-week period, we observed a decrease in depression in the massage therapy group but not in the video control group. We also saw a decrease in their anxiety, and their drawing problems decreased. Drawings often tell the best story. For example, a girl (Ashley) drew a picture of a girl on the first day. The picture was very small, had dark colors, and had no facial features (see Figure 1). By the last day, she drew a birthday party, with bright colors, balloons, sunshine, birds, and all of her friends (see Figure 2). A very clear change in her affect was reflected in the change in her drawings.

Child and adolescent psychiatric patients. In Field et al. (1992) a 30-minute back massage was given daily for a 5-day period to 52 hospitalized depressed and adjustment-disordered children and adolescents. Compared with a control group, who viewed relaxing videotapes,

Ashley

Figure 1. A drawing by Ashley on the first day of massage therapy.

the massaged participants were less depressed and anxious and had lower saliva cortisol levels after the massage sessions. In addition, nurses rated the participants as being less anxious and more cooperative on the last day of the study, and nighttime sleep increased over this period. Finally, urinary cortisol and norepinephrine levels decreased, but only for the depressed participants.

TOUCH THERAPIES FOR ADULTS

Fibromyalgia syndrome. Thirty adults suffering from fibromyalgia syndrome were randomly assigned to a massage therapy group, a transcutaneous electrical stimulation group, or a transcutaneous electrical stimulation–no current group for 30-minute treatment sessions two times per week for 5 weeks (Sunshine et al., in press). The massage therapy participants reported lower anxiety and depression, and their cortisol levels were lower immediately after the therapy sessions on the first and last days of the study. The TENS group showed similar changes, but only after therapy on the last day of the study. The massage therapy group improved on the dolorimeter measure of pain. They also reported less pain last week, less stiffness and fatigue, and fewer nights of difficulty sleeping. Thus, massage therapy was the most effective therapy with these fibromyalgia patients.

Figure 2. A drawing by Ashley after 5 weeks of massage therapy.

Job stress. In the job-stress study, we massaged staff and faculty at the medical school for 15-minute lunch periods, in massage chairs in their offices (Field, Ironson, et al., 1995). These massage sessions involved deep pressure in the back, shoulders, neck, and head. We were somewhat concerned that people might be even more sleepy than usual at the time of day after massage. However, we found instead that they reported heightened alertness, much like a runner's high. This led us to recording electroencephalograms (EEG) before, during, and after the massage sessions. We found that alpha levels significantly decreased during massage, in contrast to what happens during relaxation and, of course, during sleep, when alpha levels significantly increase. This decrease combined with increased theta and decreased beta waves suggested a pattern of heightened alertness. We then assessed whether this EEG pattern of heightened alertness translated into performance, by adding a math computation task. The computation time was almost half, and the computation accuracy almost doubled, after the massages, suggesting that 15-minute massages during the lunch hour can enhance alertness and job performance.

UNDERLYING MECHANISMS

These, then, are the improvements that we have noted after massage therapy. Some of the changes were unique to the clinical condition being studied, such as increased peak air flow in arthritis or decreased glucose levels in diabetes. However, across all of these studies, we observed decreases in anxiety, depression, stress hormones (cortisol), and catecholamines. The underlying mechanism may relate to increased parasympathetic activity. The pressure stimulation associated with touch increases vagal activity, which in turn lowers psychological arousal and stress hormones. The pressure is critical, for if a person is lightly stroked, she or he usually finds it aversive, because it is too much like a tickle stimulus. The decreased stress hormones, in turn, have a positive impact on immune function. The parasympathetic state (enhanced vagal tone) also enhances alertness and performance on cognitive tasks and reduces stress. Given that most diseases are exacerbated by stress and that massage therapy alleviates stress, receiving massages should probably be high on the health priority list, along with diet and exercise, as it was around 1800 B.C. in India.

REFERENCES

Field, T. (in press). Infants of depressed mothers. *Infant Behavior and Development*.

Field, T., Delamater, A. M., Shaw, K. H., & LaGreca, A. (1995). *Massage therapy reduces glucose levels in children with insulin-dependent diabetes*. Manuscript in preparation.

Field, T., Henteleff, T., & Mavunda, K. (1994). [Asthmatic children have less anxiety and respiratory problems after touch therapy]. Unpublished raw data.

Field, T., Ironson, G., Pickens, J., Nawrocki, T., Fox, N., Scafidi, F., Burman, I., & Schanberg, S. (1995). *Massage effects on job stress, EEG, and math computations*. Manuscript submitted for publication.

Field, T., Morrow, C., Valdeon, C., Larson, S., Kuhn, C., & Schanberg, S. (1992). Massage reduces anxiety in child and adolescent psychiatric patients. *Journal of the American Academy of Child and Adolescent Psychiatry, 31*, 124–131.

Field, T., Peck, M., Burman, I., & Krugman, S. (1995). *Massage therapy reduces anxiety in children with burns*. Manuscript in preparation.

Field, T., Scafidi, F., & Schanberg, S. (1987). Massage of preterm newborns to improve growth and development. *Pediatric Nursing, 13*, 385–387.

Field, T., Schanberg, S. M., Scafidi, F., Bauer, C. R., Vega-Lahr, N., Garcia, R., Nystrom, J., & Kuhn, C. M. (1986). Tactile/kinesthetic stimulation effects on preterm neonates. *Pediatrics, 77*, 654–658.

Field, T., Seligman, S., Scafidi, F., & Schanberg, S. (in press). Alleviating posttraumatic stress in children following Hurricane Andrew. *Journal of Applied Developmental Psychology*.

Field, T., Taylor, S., Quintino, O., Kuhn, C., & Schanberg, S. (1995). *Massage reduces anxiety and pain in women during labor*. Manuscript in preparation.

Ironson, G., Field, T., Kumar, A., Price, A., Kumar, M., Hansen, K., & Burman I. (in press). Relaxation through massage is associated with decreased distress and increased serotonin levels. *International Journal of Neuroscience*.

Kuhn, C., Schanberg, S., Field, T., Symanski, R., Zimmerman, E., Scafidi, F., & Roberts, J. (1991). Tactile kinesthetic stimulation effects on sympathetic and adrenocortical function in preterm infants. *Journal of Pediatrics, 119*, 434–440.

Older, J. (1982). *Touching is healing*. New York: Stein & Day.

Scafidi, F., & Field, T. (1995). *Massage therapy improves behavior in neonates born to HIV-positive mothers*. Manuscript submitted for publication.

Scafidi, F., Field, T., Schanberg, S., Bauer, C., Tucci, K., Roberts, J., Morrow, C., & Kuhn, C. M. (1990). Massage stimulates growth in preterm infants: A replication. *Infant Behavior and Development, 13*, 167–188.

Sunshine, W., Field, T., Quintino, O., Fierro, K., Kuhn, C., Burman, I., & Schanberg, S. (in press). Fibromyalgia benefits from massage therapy and transcutaneous electrical stimulation. *Journal of Clinical Rheumatology*.

Wheeden, A., Scafidi, F. A., Field, T., Ironson, G., Bandstra, E., Schanberg S., & Valdeon, C. (1993). Massage effects on cocaine-exposed preterm neonates. *Journal of Developmental and Behavioral Pediatrics, 14*, 318–322.

21

TREATMENT ADHERENCE AND CLINICAL OUTCOME: CAN WE MAKE A DIFFERENCE?

JACQUELINE DUNBAR-JACOB and ELIZABETH A. SCHLENK

The costs of nonadherence to pharmacological therapies have been estimated to be as high as $100 billion annually (Grahl, 1994). A significant portion of those costs is attributed to the management of untoward clinical outcomes and to lost productivity. If, in addition to pharmacological treatment, one also considers nonpharmacological interventions, the costs of nonadherence is even higher, although it is unclear by how much. Nevertheless, evidence linking lifestyle behaviors to an excess prevalence of chronic disorders and to premature mortality (Belloc, 1973; Breslow & Enstrom, 1980; Matarazzo, 1984; U.S. Public Health Service, 1991) suggests the costs of nonadherence to behavioral therapies would also be high.

Although nonadherence has been identified as a problem at least since the time of Plato, attention to the role of adherence in moderating treatment effects has been much more recent. Indeed, it has just been over the past 2 decades that the Food and Drug Administration began to require the monitoring of adherence in drug-efficacy trials. Even today, no such standard is universally applied to nonpharmacological interventions.

Not surprisingly then, little is known about the degree of adherence necessary to effect a therapeutic outcome for known therapies. Only a limited number of studies have addressed a minimum adherence level necessary to effect a clinically meaningful outcome (e.g., De Geest, 1996; Haynes et al., 1976). The *Physicians' Desk Reference* (1996) notes the degree of clinical impact seen at varying levels of adherence to a standard prescription only for one drug, cholestyramine. The relationship between adherence to behavioral therapies and clinical outcomes is even less well known.

In the next sections, we review the limited existing knowledge about the relationship between adherence and clinical outcomes. Several therapies are reviewed: (a) prescribed medication, (b) therapeutic exercise, (c) therapeutic diets, (d) homework, (e) appointment keeping, and (f) multicomponent regimen. Six clinical outcomes across these therapeutic modalities were considered: (a) mortality; (b) hospitalization; (c) morbidity, including complications; (d) relapse; (e) symptom relief; and (f) health status. To identify studies for this review, a MEDLINE search was initiated for English-language, empirical studies, reporting an adherence–outcome relationship, published between 1977 and 1994. The search yielded 116 articles. We chose only those articles that examined differences in clinical outcomes between adhering and nonadhering groups. Interestingly, these articles rarely addressed overlapping therapies and outcomes. Thus, the majority of findings are based on single studies.

THE EFFECT OF ADHERENCE TO MEDICATION ON CLINICAL OUTCOMES

The treatment modality for which the effect of nonadherence on outcomes has been studied the most is drug treatment. Adherence in these studies generally was assessed by means of discontinuing medication, urine assays, serum drug levels, self-report, pill counts, physician or nurse ratings, or pharmacy refills. These methods each tend to overestimate adherence. Three studies used electronic monitors to assess adherence (Cheung et al., 1988; Cramer, Mattson, Prevey, Scheyer, & Ouellette, 1989; Granstrom, 1985). The electronic monitors record each medication-taking event onto a microprocessor chip, permitting an assessment of adherence over time as well as patterns of medication taking. Numerous studies did not identify the assessment method.

Prevention of Relapse

Good adherence to prescribed medication regimen was significantly associated with prevention of relapse in several chronic disorders. Most particularly, adherence prevented relapse in the treatment of tuberculosis (Dupon & Ragnaud, 1992); epilepsy (Cramer et al., 1989; Reynolds, 1987); childhood leukemia (Klopovich & Trueworthy, 1985); schizophrenia (Leff et al., 1989; Mantonakis, Jemos, Christodoulou, & Lykouras, 1982); and alcoholism (Fawcett et al., 1984, 1987; Pisani, Fawcett, Clark, & McQuire, 1993). Good adherence was also associated with prevention of symptomatic, but not asymptomatic, relapse in duodenal ulcer disease (Boyd, Wilson, & Wormsley, 1983). Adherence to antibiotics, as assessed by urine antibiotic assay, was not associated with a reduction in recurrence of otitis media in 295 patients treated for the infection (Reed, Lutz, Zazove, & Ratcliffe, 1984).

Symptom Relief

Symptom relief also was found to be significantly associated with adherence in a number of conditions. Adherence was associated with reductions in inflammation in peptic esophageal stenosis (Starlinger, Appel, Schemper, & Schiessel, 1985); symptoms of schizophrenia (Verghese et al., 1989); depressed mood among manic–depressed patients (Connelly, Davenport, & Nurnberger, 1982); and pain among chronic-pain patients (Berndt, Maier, & Schutz, 1993). Although hypertension is asymptomatic, good blood pressure control was associated with good adherence to medication regimen (e.g., Fletcher, Deliakis, Schoch, & Shapiro, 1979; Haynes, Gibson, Taylor, Bernholz, & Sackett, 1982; McKenney, Munroe, & Wright, 1992). This observation also was made for patients when hypertension is comorbid with diabetes (Kravitz et al., 1993).

Good adherence is not, however, always associated with improvement of symptoms. For example, although pulmonary symptoms were alleviated with adherence to medication for patients with chronic bronchitis, they were not alleviated for those with asthma (Dompeling et al., 1992). Surprisingly, progression of visual-field defect also was not affected by adherence among persons with open-angle glaucoma (Granstrom, 1985). In this latter study, adherence was examined by means of an electronic medication monitor and defined as the proportion of time that dose intervals exceeded 8 hours during two 3-week periods.

Health Status

Adherence with prescribed medications has also been examined for its effect on health status, but in few disorders. For patients with hypertension, clinical health status and perceived health status were both associated with adherence to medical regimen, although functional status was not (Given, Given, & Simoni, 1979). Additionally, in the area of rheumatoid arthritis, adherence with treatment, as measured by self-report, was not associated with health status or functional class (Taal, Rasker, Seydel, & Wiegman, 1993), although adherence was associated with pain relief in at least one study (Dunbar-Jacob, Kwoh, et al., 1996). However, self-report generally overestimates adherence. Thus, it is not clear whether a relationship was absent or whether the ability to detect a relationship was compromised by an inaccurate measure of adherence, self-report.

Morbidity

Morbidity was found to be associated with adherence to medication in a number of conditions. Cures for urinary-tract infections among the elderly were associated with adherence to antibiotics in a study in which electronic medication monitors were used to assess adherence (Cheung et al., 1988). Both number of dosing events and dosage intervals, targeting 12 hours between doses, were considered. In chronic conditions, morbidity has also been associated with adherence. For example, poorer adherence was associated with bronchial responsiveness and functional expiratory volume (FEV_1) among patients with chronic bronchitis (Dompeling et al., 1992).

Even with life-threatening conditions, nonadherence not only has been observed, but has been found to lead to poorer outcomes. For example, nonadherent transplant patients have a poorer clinical course. Greater proportions of persons with kidney transplants who adhere poorly return to dialysis (Kalil, Heim-Duthoy, & Kasiske, 1992); develop renal impairment in pregnancy (O'Donnell et al., 1985); and reject their transplanted organs (Rovelli et al., 1989; Schweizer et al., 1990). Just small deviations from prescribed immunosuppressive therapy were linked to late rejection and other untoward events (De Geest, 1996). Poorer outcomes related to poor adherence are also seen among psychiatric disorders. Depressed elderly (Cole, 1985) and manic–depressive patients (Connelly et al., 1982) who were nonadherent were shown to have a poorer course of illness than compliant patients.

Nonadherence to medications taken prophylactically or to manage risk factors has also been associated with increases in morbidity. Hypertensive patients who were nonadherent demonstrated a greater risk of incurring coronary heart disease events (Psaty, Koepsell, Wagner, LoGerfo, & Inui, 1990). Nonadherence to prophylactic medications for infectious disease has also resulted in greater disease occurrence. For example, significantly more cases of tuberculosis were seen among nonadherent persons on prophylactic medication regimen in a study of Southeast Asian refugees (Nolan, Aitken, Elarth, Anderson, & Miller, 1986). Similarly, a greater incidence of malaria was seen in poor adherers to prophylactic drugs among Dutch travelers to Africa (Wetsteyn & de Geus, 1993).

Thus, nonadherence to medication has been associated with significant and costly morbidity in the few studies where it has been examined. The excess morbidity crosses the range of acute, chronic, preventive, and life-threatening conditions.

Hospitalization

Excess hospitalization rates may be a consequence of poor adherence with a number of conditions. First are the major mental health disorders. These include manic–depressive disorder treated with lithium (Connelly et al., 1982) and schizophrenia (Gaebel & Pietzcker, 1985). Hospitalization rates have also been higher among poor adherers attending general medical clinics, including excess rates of drug-related hospitalizations, that is, when too much or too little medication is taken (Cowen, Jim, Boyd, & Gee, 1981). Not only were hospitalization rates higher in this population but the length of hospitalization also was greater, with an average of 7 days for poor adherers, compared with 4 days for adherent controls. Rehospitalization rates were higher for poor adherers with alcoholism (Fawcett et al., 1987) and with hypertension (Maronde et al., 1989).

Mortality

Death itself has been associated with poor adherence. Among 1,000 patients with epilepsy, 25% of cases of sudden death were associated with low adherence (Lip & Brodie, 1992). Mortality also was associated with poor adherence to asthma regimen (Robertson, Rubinfeld, & Bowes, 1992) and posttransplant medications (Lanza, Cooper, Boyd, & Barnard, 1984; Schweizer et al., 1990). Furthermore, among patients with hemotologic malignancies, adherence was associated with survival (Richardson, Shelton, Krailo, & Levine, 1990).

Thus, the weight of the evidence indicates that good adherence to medication therapies will prevent relapse, alleviate symptoms, reduce morbidity, reduce hospitalizations, and reduce mortality. Efforts to enhance adherence to medications among various populations is likely to have significant clinical as well as economic impact. However, the evidence for this effort remains to be gathered.

THE EFFECT OF ADHERENCE TO THERAPEUTIC DIETS ON CLINICAL OUTCOMES

Very few studies have examined the extent of adherence to therapeutic diets and its relationship to clinical outcomes. The studies that were identified in this review addressed patients with diabetes (Fishbein, 1985; Mulrow, Bailey, Sonksen, & Slavin, 1987; White, Kolman, Wexler, Polin, & Winter, 1984); multiple sclerosis (Swank & Dugan, 1990); phenylketonuria (Peat, 1993); and myocardial infarction (Singh, Niaz, Ghosh, Singh, & Rastogi, 1993). Dietary adherence was typically measured by self-report, although physician ratings (Fishbein, 1985) and serum phenylalanine levels (Peat, 1993) were also used in one study each.

Nonadherence to low-fat diets was associated with mortality for both patients with myocardial infarction (Singh et al., 1993) and multiple sclerosis (Swank & Dugan, 1990). It was further associated with other cardiac endpoints in the cardiac patients and with deterioration among the multiple sclerosis patients. Nonadherence to diabetic diets was associated with diabetic ketoacidosis (Mulrow et al., 1987; White et al., 1984) and an excess of hospital admissions (Fishbein, 1985; White et al., 1984) and emergency room visits (White et al., 1984), but adherence was not associated with glycosylated hemoglobin or weight loss in the lone study that examined these clinical parameters (Mulrow et al., 1987). Finally, among pregnant women with phenylketonuria, poor perinatal outcomes were associated with poor dietary adherence, including low birth weight and microencephalophy (Peat, 1993).

THE EFFECT OF ADHERENCE TO THERAPEUTIC EXERCISE ON CLINICAL OUTCOMES

Few studies exist also that examine the relationship of adherence to therapeutic exercise and clinical outcomes. Five studies were identified, addressing sway in elderly women (Lichtenstein, Shields, Shiavi, & Burger, 1989); incontinence (Bishop, Dougherty, Mooney, Gimotty, & Williams, 1992); and postoperative rehabilitation for orthopedic conditions (R. B. Hawkins, 1989; R. J. Hawkins & Switlyk, 1993; Rives, Gelberman, Smith, & Carney, 1992). Overall, poor adherence to therapeutic exercise regimen was associated with negative outcomes. Postsurgically, poorly adhering patients demonstrated poorer range of motion (R. J. Hawkins & Switlyk, 1993); less joint extension (Rives et al., 1992); poorer functional ability (R. J. Hawkins & Switlyk, 1993); and greater recurrence of the presurgical condition (R. B. Hawkins, 1989), when contrasted with adhering patients. Thus, these studies support the value of adherence to postsurgical exercise in the reduction of symptoms and the incidence of relapse. Adherence to group exercise improved change in sway among elderly women also (Lichtenstein et al., 1989). Interestingly, however, adherence to a pelvic muscle exercise program was not related to maximum intravaginal pressures in a sample of parous, continent women (Bishop et al., 1992). Thus, overall, the literature suggests that adherence to exercise is related to improved clinical outcomes when symptoms and relapse prevention are considered.

THE EFFECT OF ADHERENCE TO PRESCRIBED HOMEWORK ON CLINICAL OUTCOMES

Homework is typically prescribed in the behavioral therapies for medical conditions, as a means of promoting skill and generalization, as well as a means of directly managing selected conditions. Conditions in which homework is routinely prescribed, where studies on the impact of adherence were undertaken, include agoraphobia (Edelman & Chambless, 1993); anxiety disorder (Nelson & Borkovec, 1989); obsessive–compulsive disorder (O'Sullivan, Noshirvani, Marks, Monteiro, & Lelliott, 1991); marital therapy (Holtzworth-Munroe, Jacobson, DeKlyen, & Whisman, 1989); substance abuse (Ingram & Salzberg, 1990); incontinence associated with spina bifida (King, Currie, & Wright, 1994); chronic constipation and soiling (Loening-Baucke, 1989); encopresis (Rappaport, Landman, Fenton, & Levine, 1986); defecation disorders (Taitz, Wales, Urwin, & Molnar, 1986); urinary incontinence (Oldenburg & Millard, 1986); hand function in cerebral palsy (Law & King, 1993); and amblyopia (Lithander & Sjöstrand, 1991). As can be seen, the studies examining adherence to homework and clinical outcomes primarily lie in domains of the anxiety disorders and elimination disorders.

Although adherence to homework was associated with reduction in self-reported rituals among patients with obsessive–compulsive disorder (O'Sullivan et al., 1991) and with a reduction in fear among agoraphobic patients (Edelman & Chambless, 1993), adherence to homework was not associated with positive results in other studies. For example, avoidance was not reduced among persons with agoraphobia (Edelman & Chambless, 1993), and therapist- and self-reports did not reflect a reduction of anxiety among persons with generalized anxiety disorder (Nelson & Borkovec, 1989).

Still within the mental health realm are marital therapy and treatment of substance abuse. Adherence to homework was associated with posttherapy marital satisfaction (Holtzworth-Munroe et al., 1989). However, adherence was not associated with the development of assertive behavior among residents of a substance abuse treatment center (Ingram & Salzberg, 1990).

The impact of adherence to homework was more clear among patients with elimination disorders. Improvements in soiling were associated with adherence in all studies (King et al., 1994; Loening-Baucke, 1989; Rappaport et al., 1986; Taitz et al., 1986). However, children with chronic constipation and soiling, while reducing soiling frequency with adherence to the homework, did not show differences in bowel movements per week when compared with the nonadherers (Loening-Baucke, 1989). Success was also associated with adherence to homework among women with urge incontinence who were treated with bladder retraining with and without biofeedback (Oldenburg & Millard, 1986). Thus, adherence to homework associated with programs designed for elimination disorders apparently plays a significant role in the outcome of treatment, at least when symptoms are considered. Data are not available on other outcomes, such as relapse, morbidity, or hospitalization.

Adherence to homework, measured by parental report, was associated with cure rates in children with amblyopia (Lithander & Sjöstrand, 1991). The limited data available also suggest that adherence to a home program for children with cerebral palsy was associated with hand function when adherence was measured by parental ratings, but not by therapist ratings (Law & King, 1993). This may suggest that parent ratings of adherence are more accurate that clinician estimates, which the data on medication adherence would suggest (e.g. Caron & Roth 1968). Thus, measurement method may be an important factor in the ability to detect an effect of adherence on clinical outcome, when examining how extensively patients carry out homework assignments.

The weight of the evidence suggests that adherence to homework may be important in symptom reduction. However, the relationships are not consistent across disorders or measurement methods. Thus, more work is needed to evaluate the effect of adherence to homework in terms of clinical outcomes. It would be particularly important to determine the level of adherence necessary to obtain desired outcomes as well, to avoid burdening patients with unnecessary activity. There are no data at present on the level of adherence to homework assignments necessary to promote optimal outcomes.

THE EFFECT OF ADHERENCE TO APPOINTMENTS ON CLINICAL OUTCOMES

The relationship of appointment keeping to clinical outcomes has been examined in a number of studies. Unkept appointments were associated with mortality among transplant patients (Schweizer et al., 1990);

among patients receiving sclerotherapy for variceal bleeding (Nakamura et al., 1991); as well as patients with hematologic malignancies (Richardson et al., 1990). Nonadherence to appointments was also associated with organ rejection (Schweizer et al., 1990) and return to dialysis (Kalil et al., 1992), among transplant recipients, as well as relapse among patients with schizophrenia (Leff et al., 1989).

Appointment keeping has shown mixed results on symptom reduction in selected psychiatric disorders. Patients with anorexia who attended visits and completed treatment were more likely to have improved functioning (Steiner, Mazer, & Litt, 1990). Session attendance was associated with mood, social adjustment, and problem improvement among suicidal patients but was not associated with physician ratings of progress, suicidal ideation, or repeat overdose (Hawton et al., 1981). Indeed, in one study of psychiatric patients, adherence to appointment keeping was negatively associated with reductions in psychopathology (Bowden, Schoenfeld, & Adams, 1980). Clearly the relationship between therapy-session attendance and outcomes is uncertain at best and may be related to the type of patient or the specific outcome being evaluated.

Appointment keeping in behavioral treatment was related to cure among children with defecation disorders (Taitz et al., 1986) and to hand function among children with cerebral palsy (Law & King, 1993). On the other hand, adherence to appointments when the treatment is focused on medical therapies is less clearly important. Visit attendance was not related to weight loss or glycosylated hemoglobin among patients with non-insulin-dependent diabetes mellitus (Mulrow et al., 1987), nor was it related to the number of days until otitis media was cleared (Reed et al., 1984). Furthermore, appointment keeping was positively associated with FEV_1 among children with cystic fibrosis (Patterson, Budd, Goetz, & Warwick, 1993).

Of interest is the finding of negative associations between appointment keeping adherence and clinical outcomes in the Mulrow et al. (1987) and Reed et al. (1984) studies. One possible explanation could be that patients with fewer symptoms are less likely to feel the need for clinical contacts than patients who are feeling less well. Thus, it would be the more distressed patients who maintain their clinical visits. This finding needs further examination, particularly in the light of whether follow-up of missed visits is important to the patient's outcome.

THE EFFECT OF ADHERENCE TO MULTICOMPONENT REGIMEN ON CLINICAL OUTCOMES

Many patients within the health care system find themselves on multicomponent regimens. Persons with multiple disorders will be treated for each concurrently. Many of the chronic disorders have multiple components to their treatment regimen. Most commonly, these consist of medication, diet, exercise, and regular clinic visits. The question is whether adherence to the regimen as a whole is related to outcome.

Five studies examined adherence to the regimen among persons with diabetes. The findings were mixed. Adherence was related to glycosylated hemoglobin in studies with children (Auslander, Anderson, Bubb, Jung, & Santiago, 1990); adolescents (Hanson, Henggeler, & Burghen, 1987); and adults (Kravitz et al., 1993). On the other hand, two studies with children and adolescents found that adherence to the regimen was not related to glycosylated hemoglobin (Johnson, Freund, Silverstein, Hansen, & Malone, 1990; Johnson et al., 1992). Differing methods of assessing adherence were used between the studies; in some cases, the method was not specified. The exact nature of the regimen also was not specified. It is possible, then, that these differences in findings were due to different measurement methods for adherence or to differences in treatment efficacy.

Nonadherence to the diabetic regimen also was associated with diabetic ketoacidosis among pregnant diabetic women (Montoro et al., 1993). Nonadherence to more general prenatal recommendations was found to be related to perinatal mortality (Moawad, Lee, Fisher, Ferguson, & Phillippe, 1990). Indeed approximately one third of avoidable infant deaths were attributable to maternal nonadherence in this study.

Two studies examined adherence to multicomponent regimen for cystic fibrosis among children and disease-specific clinical outcomes (Patterson et al., 1993; Sanders, Gravestock, Wanstall, & Dunn 1991). No effect of adherence was found when physician rating of clinical status was examined. However, a positive association was found for appointment keeping and FEV_1. Once again, adherence appears to be related to differing parameters of a given disorder.

It is interesting that throughout these studies, little attention has been given to outcomes beyond those biological outcomes specific to the disease or to symptoms, with the exception of studies on medication adherence. Little attention has been given to such important and costly outcomes as relapse, preventable morbidity, hospitalization, or general health status. No data to date exist on the effect of improving adherence on clinical outcomes. Multiple studies examaining the adherence–outcome relationship for specific regimen within and between disorders are necessary. Clearly, much research is needed before one can determine the effect of adherence or of improving adherence to medical and behavioral regimen on disease outcomes or before acceptable levels of adherence can be set for specific regimen in specific disorders.

ADHERENCE AS AN INDEPENDENT FACTOR IN CLINICAL OUTCOMES

As interest has grown in the role of levels of adherence as a moderator of clinical outcomes, so too has interest been generated on the effect of adherence behaviors directly on outcomes. This interest was sparked by findings in the Coronary Drug Project (CDP)—a multicenter, randomized, double-blind clinical trial examining the efficacy of cholesterol lowering in post-myocardial infarction patients (Coronary Drug Project Research Group, 1980). The data suggested that cardiac mortality was associated with adherence regardless of whether the patient was on active drug or placebo. These findings sparked an examination of the direct effect of adherence, that is adherence independent of prescribed treatment, in a number of the multicenter studies thereafter. A review of those findings follows.

Before examining the studies directly, it is important to consider dimensions of the studies that could confound an interpretation of the adherence–outcome relationship. Of particular importance is the design of the study. First, a study of the direct effect of adherence on outcome calls for a placebo-controlled trial. A direct effect of adherence can be identified only if it is found when a nonactive or placebo treatment is examined. Second, the trial should be double-blind to reduce the likelihood of bias in the assessment or ascertainment of outcomes. A double-blind trial would reduce also the likelihood of placebo-treated participants obtaining additional intervention, which could act on the main outcome, outside the domain of the study. Such intervention could be participant initiated or could be primary care physician initiated. It would be most likely if the perception was that the participant was unlikely to receive benefit from the trial. And last, the assessment of adherence should be accurate and blinded from the investigator who was assessing clinical endpoints. This would also reduce bias in evaluating the relationship of the two variables.

In this discussion, then, only double-blind, placebo-controlled studies with blinded ascertainment of outcomes were reviewed. Five trials that evaluated the adherence–outcome relationship were identified. Three addressed cardiovascular disease or risk: the CDP (Coronary Drug Project Research Group, 1980); the Lipid Research Clinics Coronary Primary Prevention Trial, (LRC-CPPT, Lipid Research Clinics Program, 1984); and the Beta-Blocker Heart Attack Trial (BHAT; Gallagher, Viscoll, & Horwitz, 1993; Horwitz et al., 1990).

One addressed granulocytopenia (Pizzo et al., 1983), and one addressed alcoholism (Fuller, Roth, & Long, 1983). The outcome in each of the cardiovascular studies was mortality. For the granulocytopenia study, reduction in fever or infection was the outcome of interest, whereas abstinence was the outcome of interest for the alcoholism trial.

Clearly, the hardest endpoint would be mortality. For two of the three cardiovascular trials, an association was found between death and adherence, regardless of treatment assignment. That is, even in the placebo group, participants who adhered were more likely to survive than participants who did not adhere. The LRC-CPPT study found no effect on either morbidity or mortality (cardiovascular events) of adhering to placebo, although the active drug reduced events. Each of these studies used a pill count in some form. The LRC-CPPT and the BHAT both used blinded packet or pill counts. Still, reliance was on the participant to return unused packets or pills, to ascertain the number that had been consumed between appointment intervals. Pill counts have not been strongly related to event-monitored assessment of medication adherence and have been shown to overestimate adherence when compared with event monitoring (Hamilton, 1996). Thus, a question could be raised about the sensitivity with which adherence was assessed in both trials.

More problematic was the assessment of adherence in the CDP. The design paper of the trial indicates that adherence was assessed by clinician report (Coronary Drug Project Research Group, 1973). Using her or his own estimate, the clinician was advised to place the patient in one of three adherence categories: 80%–100%, 20%–80%, or less than 20%. If the clinician was unable to make an estimate, a pill count was performed. Adherence for the groups was then calculated, using the midpoint of the category. Thus, the estimate of adherence could very well be confounded by the clinician's estimate of the patient's clinical status, with patients who were doing well more likely to be seen as adhering.

Measurement method may also have been a factor in the assessment of an adherence–outcome relationship in the granulocytopenia study and the alcohol study. Pizzo et al. (1983) found a relationship between adherence to antibiotics and reduction in fever or infection. In this case, adherence was assessed by means of self-report. One might question whether patients who developed a fever, an infection, or a potentially salient symptom or who experienced a morbid event would have been more likely to acknowledge poor adherence, regardless of treatment assignment, than those who had no untoward events. As noted, self-reported adherence has been very poorly associated with the more sensitive event monitoring of adherence, with the bias in the direction of overestimation of adherence through self-report (Dunbar-Jacob, Berg, et al., 1996).

The alcoholism study used two measures of adherence: a riboflavin marker in anabuse and placebo and appointment-keeping rates. Appoint-

ment-keeping rates were associated with adherence, regardless of assignment to anabuse or placebo. But adherence assessed through the riboflavin marker was not associated with outcome. Again, one has to examine the sensitivity of the marker. Riboflavin has a very short half-life. Thus, adherence assessed through this method would only address the period immediately preceding the clinic visit, not the interval between visits (Rudd, Ahmed, Zachary, Barton, & Bonduelle, 1990). Research using event monitoring has suggested that patients are more likely to adhere just before and just after a clinic visit. Thus, the marker would bias the ascertainment of adherence toward an overestimate of actual behavior.

Thus, three studies reported a relationship between adherence and outcome, regardless of treatment assignment, suggesting a direct effect of adherence. Two studies had negative findings, suggesting that adherence does not have a direct effect on clinical outcome. Although each of the studies was double-blind and placebo controlled, adherence measurement varied between studies, with, however, each study using assessment techniques that themselves introduce bias. There are sufficient, yet conflicting, data to make this an important issue for further study. If such a direct effect is found, then efforts to promote adherence would assume central importance in the management of clinical disorders. If it is not found to exist, then it is more important to define levels of adherence necessary for desirable outcomes for specific regimens and disorders and to promote adherence to those levels. Further studies, however, require the use of sensitive and accurate assessment strategies.

DISCUSSION

It is interesting that so little work has been carried out on the relationship of adherence to clinical outcome. Numerous studies also have been devoted to identifying factors that contribute to adherence and, to a lesser extent, to identifying strategies that promote or remediate adherence. One assumes that improvements in adherence will lead to improvements in outcomes. Yet, there are little data available to indicate how clinically effective these efforts are. What data are available, however, support adherence–outcome relationships and suggest that efforts to enhance adherence should lead to improvements in clinical outcomes.

Clearly, more research needs to be conducted on the adherence–outcome relationship. The studies reported here suggest that low levels of adherence have a significant and costly impact on the patient's health, medical care utilization, and at times mortality. Yet there are limited data for any particular disease.

Studies on the direct effects of adherence, though interesting, are conflicting and few in number. The existing studies used assessment methods that confound the interpretation of their findings. The examination of a direct effect of adherence on outcome requires a study in the context of a double-blind, placebo-controlled trial. Design strategies need to minimize investigator and participant bias in the assessment of outcomes, as well as the assessment of adherence.

One of the difficulties in examining the role of adherence in clinical outcomes has been the assessment of adherence itself. Biological assays tend to address behavior over a limited period of time and are insensitive to individual variations in adherence patterns. Clinical estimates have been shown to be no better than chance (Caron & Roth, 1968; Mushlin & Appel, 1977; Roth, Caron, & Hsi, 1971). Patient self-reports overestimate compliance, often quite significantly (Dunbar-Jacob, Berg, et al., 1996). Daily diaries or records are dependent on the patients' willingness to report deviations from the prescription and willingness to complete the diary itself. Furthermore, diaries themselves have been shown to promote behavior change through their increased emphasis on self-monitoring. Newer methods of assessment include electronic pill monitors, activity monitors, diaries, and other devices that record on microchips the date and time of the event of interest. Though not error free, these devices represent a leap forward in the assessment of adherence to prescribed therapies. It is through these newer assessment techniques that a clearer picture of the relationship between both overall adherence, as well as patterns of adherence, and clinical outcomes will emerge.

Data on the effects of adherence to treatment regimen on clinical outcomes are promising, though not easily found. Few studies have been carried out with any particular disorder. New studies are needed that address the impact as well as the degree of adherence necessary to influence clinical outcome. Data supporting the direct effect of adherence on outcomes, although interesting, are inconsistent and have been limited to studies of mortality. Further research that takes into account the design flaws of earlier studies is needed to elucidate this potentially clinically important relationship.

REFERENCES

Auslander, W. F., Anderson, B. J., Bubb, J., Jung, K. C., & Santiago, J. V. (1990). Risk factors to health in diabetic children: A prospective study from diagnosis. *Health and Social Work, 15,* 133–142.

Belloc, N. B. (1973). Relationship of health practices and mortality. *Preventive Medicine, 2,* 67–81.

Berndt, S., Maier, C., & Schutz, H. W. (1993). Polymedication and medication compliance in patients with chronic non-malignant pain. *Pain*, *52*, 331–339.

Bishop, K. R., Dougherty, M., Mooney, R., Gimotty, P., & Williams, B. (1992). Effects of age, parity, and adherence on pelvic muscle response to exercise. *Journal of Obstetric, Gynecologic, and Neonatal Nursing*, *21*, 401–406.

Bowden, C. L., Schoenfeld, L. S., & Adams, R. L. (1980). A correlation between dropout status and improvement in a psychiatric clinic. *Hospital and Community Psychiatry*, *31*, 192–195.

Boyd, E. J. S., Wilson, J. A., & Wormsley, K. G. (1983). Effects of treatment compliance and overnight gastric secretion on outcome of maintenance therapy of duodenal ulcer with ranitidine. *Scandinavian Journal of Gastroenterology*, *18*, 193–200.

Breslow, L., & Enstrom, J. E. (1980). Persistence of health habits and their relationship to mortality. *Preventive Medicine*, *9*, 469–483.

Caron, H. S., & Roth, H. P. (1968). Patients' cooperation with a medical regimen: Difficulties in identifying the noncooperator. *Journal of the American Medical Association*, *203*, 922–926.

Cheung, R., Sullens, C. M., Seal, D., Dickins, J., Nicholson, P. W., Deshmukh, A. A., Denham, M. J., & Dobbs, S. M. (1988). The paradox of using a 7 day antibacterial course to treat urinary tract infections in the community. *British Journal of Clinical Pharmacology*, *26*, 391–398.

Cole, M. G. (1985). The course of elderly depressed out-patients. *Canadian Journal of Psychiatry*, *30*, 217–220.

Connelly, C. E., Davenport, Y. B., & Nurnberger, J. I., Jr. (1982). Adherence to treatment regimen in a lithium carbonate clinic. *Archives of General Psychiatry*, *39*, 585–588.

Coronary Drug Project Research Group. (1973). The Coronary Drug Project: Design, methods, and baseline results. *Circulation*, *47*(Suppl. 3), 1–50.

Coronary Drug Project Research Group. (1980). Influence of adherence to treatment and response of cholesterol on mortality in the Coronary Drug Project. *New England Journal of Medicine*, *303*, 1038–1041.

Cowen, M. E., Jim, L. K., Boyd, E. L., & Gee, J. P. (1981). Some possible effects of patient noncompliance. *Journal of the American Medical Association*, *245*, 1121.

Cramer, J. A., Mattson, R. H., Prevey, M. L., Scheyer, R. D., & Ouellette, V. L. (1989). How often is medication taken as prescribed? A novel assessment technique. *Journal of the American Medical Association*, *261*, 3273–3277.

De Geest, S. (1996, March). Assessment of adherence in heart transplant recipients. In J. Dunbar-Jacob (chair), *Adherence in chronic disease*. Seminar conducted at the Fourth International Congress of Behavioral Medicine. Washington, DC.

Dompeling, E., Van Grunsven, P. M., Van Schayck, C. P., Folgering, H., Molema, J., & Van Weel, C. (1992). Treatment with inhaled steroids in asthma and chronic bronchitis: Long-term compliance and inhaler technique. *Family Practice, 9,* 161–166.

Dunbar-Jacob, J., Berg, J., Boehm, S., DeGeest, S., & Hamilton, G. (1996, March). In J. Dunbar-Jacob (chair), *Adherence in chronic disease.* Seminar presented at the Fourth International Congress of Behavioral Medicine, Washington, DC.

Dunbar-Jacob, J., Kwoh, C. K., Rohay, J., Burke, L., Sereika, S., & Starz, R. (1996, March). *Adherence and functional outcomes in rheumatoid arthritis.* Paper presented at the Fourth International Congress of Behavioral Medicine, Washington, DC.

Dupon, M., & Ragnaud, J. M. (1992). Tuberculosis in patients infected with Human Immunodeficiency Virus 1: A retrospective multicentre study of 123 cases in France. *Quarterly Journal of Medicine, 85,* 719–730.

Edelman, R. E., & Chambless, D. L. (1993). Compliance during sessions and homework in exposure-based treatment of agoraphobia. *Behaviour Research and Therapy, 31,* 767–773.

Fawcett, J., Clark, D. C., Aagesen, C. A., Pisani, V. D., Tilkin, J. M., Sellers, D., McQuire, M., & Gibbons, R. D. (1987). A double-blind, placebo-controlled trial of lithium carbonate therapy for alcoholism. *Archives of General Psychiatry, 44,* 248–256.

Fawcett, J., Clark, D. C., Gibbons, R. D., Aagesen, C. A., Pisani, V. D., Tilkin, J. M., Sellers, D., & Stutzman, D. (1984). Evaluation of lithium therapy for alcoholism. *Journal of Clinical Psychiatry, 45,* 494–499.

Fishbein, H. A. (1985). Precipitants of hospitalization in insulin-dependent diabetes mellitus (IDDM): A statewide perspective. *Diabetes Care, 8*(Suppl. 1), 61–64.

Fletcher, S. W., Deliakis, J., Schoch, W. A., & Shapiro, S. H. (1979). Predicting blood pressure control in hypertensive patients: An approach to quality-of-care assessment. *Medical Care, 17,* 285–292.

Fuller, R., Roth, H., & Long, S. (1983). Compliance with disulfiram treatment of alcoholism. *Journal of Chronic Diseases, 36,* 161–170.

Gaebel, W., & Pietzcker, A. (1985). One-year outcome of schizophrenic patients: The interaction of chronicity and neuroleptic treatment. *Pharmacopsychiatry, 18,* 235–239.

Gallagher, E. J., Viscoli, C. M., & Horwitz, R. I. (1993). The relationship of treatment adherence to the risk of death after myocardial infarction in women. *Journal of the American Medical Association, 270,* 742–744.

Given, B., Given, C. W., & Simoni, L. E. (1979). Relationships of processes of care to patient outcomes. *Nursing Research, 28,* 85–93.

Grahl, C. (1994). Improving compliance: Solving a $100 billion problem. *Managed Health Care,* S11–S13.

Granstrom, P. A. (1985). Progression of visual field defects in glaucoma: Relation to compliance with pilocarpine therapy. *Archives of Ophthalmology, 103,* 529–531.

Hamilton, G. (1996, March). Event monitoring of adherence in a hypertension trial. In J. Dunbar-Jacob (Chair), *Adherence in chronic disease*. Seminar conducted at the Fourth International Congress of Behavioral Medicine, Washington, DC.

Hanson, C. L., Henggeler, S. W., & Burghen, G. A. (1987). Model of associations between psychosocial variables and health-outcome measures of adolescents with IDDM. *Diabetes Care, 10*, 752–758.

Hawkins, R. B. (1989). Arthroscopic stapling repair for shoulder instability: A retrospective study of 50 cases. *Arthroscopy: The Journal of Arthroscopic and Related Surgery, 5*, 122–128.

Hawkins, R. J., & Switlyk, P. (1993). Acute prosthetic replacement for severe fractures of the proximal humerus. *Clinical Orthopaedics and Related Research, 289*, 156–160.

Hawton, K., Bancroft, J., Catalan, J., Kingston, B., Stedeford, A., & Welch, N. (1981). Domiciliary and out-patient treatment of self-poisoning patients by medical and non-medical staff. *Psychological Medicine, 11*, 169–177.

Haynes, R. B., Gibson, E. S., Taylor, D. W., Bernholz, C. D., & Sackett, D. L. (1982). Process versus outcome in hypertension: A positive result. *Circulation, 65*, 28–33.

Haynes, R. B., Sackett, D. L., Gibson, E. S., Taylor, D. W., Hackett, B. C., Roberts, R. S., & Johnson, A. L. (1976). Improvement of medication compliance in uncontrolled hypertension. *Lancet, 1*, 1265–1268.

Holtzworth-Munroe, A., Jacobson, N. S., DeKlyen, M., & Whisman, M. A. (1989). Relationship between behavioral marital therapy outcome and process variables. *Journal of Consulting and Clinical Psychology, 57*, 658–662.

Horwitz, R. I., Viscoli, C. M., Berkman, L., Donaldson, R. M., Horwitz, S. M., Murray, C. J., Ransohoff, D. F., & Sindelar, J. (1990). Treatment adherence and risk of death after a myocardial infarction. *Lancet, 336*, 542–545.

Ingram, J. A., & Salzberg, H. C. (1990). Effects of *in vivo* behavioral rehearsal on the learning of assertive behaviors with a substance abusing population. *Addictive Behaviors, 15*, 189–194.

Johnson, S. B., Freund, A., Silverstein, J., Hansen, C. A., & Malone, J. (1990). Adherence–health status relationships in childhood diabetes. *Health Psychology, 9*, 606–631.

Johnson, S. B., Kelly, M., Henretta, J. C., Cunningham, W. R., Tomer, A., & Silverstein, J. H. (1992). A longitudinal analysis of adherence and health status in childhood diabetes. *Journal of Pediatric Psychology, 17*, 537–553.

Kalil, R. S. N., Heim-Duthoy, K. L., & Kasiske, B. L. (1992). Patients with a low income have reduced renal allograft survival. *American Journal of Kidney Diseases, 20*, 63–69.

King, J. C., Currie, D. M., & Wright, E. (1994). Bowel training in spina bifida: Importance of education, patient compliance, age, and anal reflexes. *Archives of Physical Medicine and Rehabilitation, 75*, 243–247.

Klopovich, P. M., & Trueworthy, R. C. (1985). Adherence to chemotherapy regimens among children with cancer. *Topics in Clinical Nursing, 7*, 19–25.

Kravitz, R. L., Hays, R. D., Sherbourne, C. D., DiMatteo, M. R., Rogers, W. H., Ordway, L., & Greenfield, S. (1993). Recall of recommendations and adherence to advice among patients with chronic medical conditions. *Archives of Internal Medicine, 153*, 1869–1878.

Lanza, R. P., Cooper, D. K. C., Boyd, S. T., & Barnard, C. N. (1984). Comparison of patients with ischemic, myopathic, and rheumatic heart diseases as cardiac transplant recipients. *American Heart Journal, 107*, 8–12.

Law, M., & King, G. (1993). Parent compliance with therapeutic interventions for children with cerebral palsy. *Developmental Medicine and Child Neurology, 35*, 983–990.

Leff, J., Berkowitz, R., Shavit, N., Strachan, A., Glass, I., & Vaughn, C. (1989). A trial of family therapy v. a relatives group for schizophrenia. *British Journal of Psychiatry, 154*, 58–66.

Lichtenstein, M. J., Shields, S. L., Shiavi, R. G., & Burger C. (1989). Exercise and balance in aged women: A pilot controlled clinical trial. *Archives of Physical Medicine and Rehabilitation, 70*, 138–143.

Lip, G. Y. H., & Brodie, M. J. (1992). Sudden death in epilepsy: An avoidable outcome? *Journal of the Royal Society of Medicine, 85*, 609–611.

Lipid Research Clinics Program. (1984). The Lipid Research Clinics Coronary Primary Prevention Trial results: II. The relationship of reduction in incidence of coronary heart disease to cholesterol lowering. *Journal of the American Medical Association, 251*, 365–374.

Lithander, J., & Sjöstrand, J. (1991). Anisometropic and strabismic amblyopia in the age group 2 years and above: A prospective study of results of treatment. *British Journal of Ophthalmology, 75*, 111–116.

Loening-Baucke, V. (1989). Factors determining outcome in children with chronic constipation and faecal soiling. *Gut, 30*, 999–1006.

Mantonakis, J. E., Jemos, J. J., Christodoulou, G. N., & Lykouras, E. P. (1982). Short-term social prognosis of schizophrenia. *Acta Psychiatrica Scandinavica, 66*, 306–310.

Maronde, R. F., Chan, L. S., Larsen, F. J., Strandberg, L. R., Laventurier, M. F., & Sullivan S. R. (1989). Underutilization of antihypertensive drugs and associated hospitalization. *Medical Care, 27*, 1159–1166.

Matarazzo, J. D. (1984). Behavioral health: A 1990 challenge for the health sciences professions. In J. D. Matarazzo, S. M. Weiss, J. A. Herd, N. E. Miller, & S. M. Weiss (Eds.), *Behavioral health: A handbook of health enhancement and disease prevention* (pp. 3–40). New York: Wiley.

McKenney, J. M., Munroe, W. P., & Wright, J. T., Jr. (1992). Impact of an electronic medication compliance aid on long-term blood pressure control. *Journal of Clinical Pharmacology, 32*, 277–283.

Moawad, A. H., Lee, K. S., Fisher, D. E., Ferguson, R., & Phillippe, M. (1990). A model for the prospective analysis of perinatal deaths in a perinatal network. *American Journal of Obstetrics and Gynecology, 162,* 15–22.

Montoro, M. N., Myers, V. P., Mestman, J. H., Xu, Y., Anderson, B. G., & Golde, S. H. (1993). Outcome of pregnancy in diabetic ketoacidosis. *American Journal of Perinatology, 10,* 17–20.

Mulrow, C., Bailey, S., Sonksen, P. H., & Slavin, B. (1987). Evaluation of an Audiovisual Diabetes Education Program: Negative results of a randomized trial of patients with non-insulin-dependent diabetes mellitus. *Journal of General Internal Medicine, 2,* 215–219.

Murphy, G., Tzamaloukas, A. H., Quintana, B. J., Gibel, L. J., & Avasthi, P. S. (1989). Clinical significance of hemodialysis performed during the course of continuous ambulatory peritoneal dialysis. *International Journal of Artificial Organs, 12,* 303–306.

Mushlin, A. I., & Appel, F. A. (1977). Diagnosing potential noncompliance: Physicians' ability in a behavioral dimension of medical care. *Archives of Internal Medicine, 137,* 318–321.

Nakamura, R., Bucci, L. A., Sugawa, C., Lucas, C. E., Gutta, K., Sugimura, Y., & Sferra, C. (1991). Sclerotherapy of bleeding esophageal varices using a thrombogenic cocktail. *American Surgeon, 57,* 226–230.

Nelson, R. A., & Borkovec, T. D. (1989). Relationship of client participation to psychotherapy. *Journal of Behavior Therapy and Experimental Psychiatry, 20,* 155–162.

Nolan, C. M., Aitken, M. L., Elarth, A. M., Anderson, K. M., & Miller, W. T. (1986). Active tuberculosis after isoniazid chemoprophylaxis of Southeast Asian refugees. *American Review of Respiratory Disease, 133,* 431–436.

O'Donnell, D., Sevitz, H., Seggie, J. L., Meyers, A. M., Botha, J. R., & Myburgh, J. A. (1985). Pregnancy after renal transplantation. *Australian and New Zealand Journal of Medicine, 15,* 320–325.

Oldenburg, B., & Millard, R. J. (1986). Predictors of long term outcome following a bladder re-training programme. *Journal of Psychosomatic Research, 30,* 691–698.

O'Sullivan, G., Noshirvani, H., Marks, I., Monteiro, W., & Lelliott, P. (1991). Six-year follow-up after exposure and clomipramine therapy for obsessive compulsive disorder. *Journal of Clinical Psychiatry, 52,* 150–155.

Patterson, J. M., Budd, J., Goetz, D., & Warwick, W. J. (1993). Family correlates of a 10-year pulmonary health trend in cystic fibrosis. *Pediatrics, 91,* 383 389.

Peat, B. (1993). Pregnancy complicated by maternal phenylketonuria. *Australian and New Zealand Journal of Obstetrics and Gynaecology, 33,* 163–165.

Physicians' desk reference. (50th ed.). (1996). Oradell, NJ: Medical Economics.

Pisani, V. D., Fawcett, J., Clark, D. C., & McQuire, M. (1993). The relative contributions of medication adherence and AA meeting attendance to abstinent outcome for chronic alcoholics. *Journal of Studies on Alcohol, 54,* 115–119.

Pizzo, P. A., Robichaud, K. J., Edwards, B. K., Schumaker, C., Kramer, B. S., & Johnson, A. (1983). Oral antibiotic prophylaxis in patients with cancer: A double-blind randomized placebo-controlled trial. *Journal of Pediatrics, 102,* 125–133.

Psaty, B. M., Koepsell, T. D., Wagner, E. H., LoGerfo, J. P., & Inui, T. S. (1990). The relative risk of incident coronary heart disease associated with recently stopping the use of beta-blockers. *Journal of the American Medical Association, 263,* 1653–1657.

Rappaport, L., Landman, G., Fenton, T., & Levine, M. D. (1986). Locus of control as predictor of compliance and outcome in treatment of encopresis. *Journal of Pediatrics, 109,* 1061–1064.

Reed, B. D., Lutz, L. J., Zazove, P., & Ratcliffe, S. D. (1984). Compliance with acute otitis media treatment. *Journal of Family Practice, 19,* 627–632.

Reynolds, E. H. (1987). Early treatment and prognosis of epilepsy. *Epilepsia, 28,* 97–106.

Richardson, J. L., Shelton, D. R., Krailo, M., & Levine, A. M. (1990). The effect of compliance with treatment on survival among patients with hematologic malignancies. *Journal of Clinical Oncology, 8,* 356–364.

Rives, K., Gelberman, R., Smith, B., & Carney, K. (1992). Severe contractures of the proximal interphalangeal joint in Dupuytren's disease: Results of a prospective trial of operative correction and dynamic extension splinting. *Journal of Hand Surgery, 17,* 1153–1159.

Robertson, C. F., Rubinfeld, A. R., & Bowes, G. (1992). Pediatric asthma deaths in Victoria: The mild are at risk. *Pediatric Pulmonology, 13,* 95–100.

Roth, H. P., Caron, H. S., & Hsi, B. P. (1971). Estimating a patient's cooperation with his regimen. *American Journal of Medical Sciences, 262,* 269–273.

Rovelli, M., Palmeri, D., Vossler, E., Bartus, S., Hull, D., & Schweizer, R. (1989). Noncompliance in organ transplant recipients. *Transplantation Proceedings, 21,* 833–834.

Rudd, P., Ahmed, S., Zachary, V., Barton, C., & Bonduelle, D. (1990). Improved compliance measures: Applications in an ambulatory hypertensive drug trial. *Clinical Pharmacology and Therapeutics, 48,* 676–685.

Sanders, M. R., Gravestock, F. M., Wanstall, K., & Dunne, M. (1991). The relationship between children's treatment-related behaviour problems, age and clinical status in cystic fibrosis. *Journal of Paediatrics and Child Health, 27,* 290–294.

Schweizer, R. T., Rovelli, M., Palmeri, D., Vossler, E., Hull, D., & Bartus, S. (1990). Noncompliance in organ transplant recipients. *Transplantation, 49,* 374–377.

Singh, R. B., Niaz, M. A., Ghosh, S., Singh, R., & Rastogi, S. S. (1993). Effect on mortality and reinfarction of adding fruits and vegetables to a prudent diet in the Indian experiment of infarct survival (IEIS). *Journal of the American College of Nutrition, 12,* 255–261.

Starlinger, M., Appel, W. H., Schemper, M., & Schiessel, R. (1985). Long-term treatment of peptic esophageal stenosis with dilatation and cimetidine: Factors influencing clinical result. *European Surgical Research, 17,* 207–214.

Steiner, H., Mazer, C., & Litt, I. F. (1990). Compliance and outcome in anorexia nervosa. *Western Journal of Medicine, 153,* 133–139.

Swank, R. L., & Dugan, B. B. (1990). Effect of low saturated fat diet in early and late cases of multiple sclerosis. *Lancet, 336,* 37–39.

Taal, E., Rasker, J. J., Seydel, E. R., & Wiegman, O. (1993). Health status, adherence with health recommendations, self-efficacy and social support in patients with rheumatoid arthritis. *Patient Education and Counseling, 20*(2–3), 63–76.

Taitz, L. S., Wales, J. K. H., Urwin, O. M., & Molnar, D. (1986). Factors associated with outcome in management of defecation disorders. *Archives of Disease in Childhood, 61,* 472–477.

U.S. Public Health Service. (1991). *Healthy People 2000: National health promotion and disease prevention objectives* (Full report). Washington, DC: Author.

Verghese, A., John, J. K., Rajkumar, S., Richard, J., Sethi, B. B., & Trivedi, J. K. (1989). Factors associated with the course and outcome of schizophrenia in India: Results of a two-year multicentre follow-up study. *British Journal of Psychiatry, 154,* 499–503.

Wetsteyn, J. C. F. M., & de Geus, A. (1993). Comparison of three regimens for malaria prophylaxis in travellers to east, central, and southern Africa. *British Medical Journal, 307,* 1041–1043.

White, K., Kolman, M. L., Wexler, P., Polin, G., & Winter, R. J. (1984). Unstable diabetes and unstable families: A psychosocial evaluation of diabetic children with recurrent ketoacidosis. *Pediatrics, 73,* 749–755.

IV

PSYCHOLOGISTS IN DISEASE PREVENTION AND HEALTH PROMOTION

INTRODUCTION

The major cause of wellness is behavior that guarantees a healthy lifestyle. On the other hand, those choices or actions that put one in physical jeopardy or increase the chances of becoming ill, usually in the future, can be seen as contributors to some diseases or the major cause of others. The common factor, whether looking at health promotion or disease prevention, is behavior. Whether behavior is defined as doing something (e.g., lighting up a cigarette) or making a choice (e.g., to engage in unsafe sexual practices, even just once), no other profession is more qualified to speak to wellness than psychology; the profession that studies and treats behavior and thoughts. In this section, we look at four of the many topics areas in which psychologists help in the prevention of disease and the promotion of health.

In chapter 22, "African American Women, Their Families, and HIV/AIDS," Debra Greenwood and colleagues use a case-study approach to highlight the importance of a family-therapy-oriented approach to the emotional and social problems faced by women and their families. Greenwood et al. detail the staggering incidence statistics and emotional toll of HIV/AIDS on the African American family. The family's role in adaptation to environmental stress and in the development of effective coping strategies is presented, along with a structural-ecosystems-therapy approach that is designed to foster a sense of empowerment within the family.

In chapter 23, "Revolution in Health Promotion: Smoking Cessation as a Case Study," James O. Prochaska begins by documenting the costs of cigarette smoking—costs that include human suffering and the financial burden of illness and premature death. Prochaska describes a stage paradigm for change and then applies it to a smoking cessation program. The outcome of a large-scale, clinical trial comparing several treatment methods is presented, and the results for smoking cessation are offered as a model for health-promotion programs, to impact entire populations by preventing chronic diseases and premature death.

G. Alan Marlatt's chapter 24, "Reducing College Student Binge Drinking: A Harm-Reduction Approach," discusses a health problem that finds a significant percent of undergraduate students engaged in the episodic drinking of five or more drinks on a single occasion. Marlatt presents the research results of his alcohol-harm-reduction approach, designed to move those with harmful drinking problems along the behavioral continuum toward abstinence. This approach is based on the belief that any movement toward less harmful behavior is in the right direction, even if abstinence is not met. Other unrelated prevention programs are discussed under the umbrella of harm reduction.

The last chapter in the Disease Prevention and Health Promotion section, chapter 25, "Strategies to Reduce the Risk of HIV Infection, Sexually Transmitted Diseases, and Pregnancy Among African American Adolescents," by John B. and Loretta Sweet Jemmott, reviews a research program on various interventions for those high-health-risk behaviors. This chapter on community interventions exemplifies the kinds of innovative community programs that can be designed by combining research with practice. The authors review programs targeted at male African American adolescents to reduce sexually transmitted diseases and pregnancy among teenagers. They describe a series of innovative programs and outline research methodologies aimed at finding out which elements of these programs are particularly salient. In addition to outlining effective interventions for practitioners, this chapter shows how research can be used to help craft effective community programs.

22

AFRICAN AMERICAN WOMEN, THEIR FAMILIES, AND HIV/AIDS

DEBRA GREENWOOD, JOSÉ SZAPOCZNIK, SCOTT MCINTOSH,
MICHAEL ANTONI, GAIL IRONSON, MANUEL TEJEDA,
LAVONDA CLARINGTON, DEANNE SAMUELS, and
LINDA SORHAINDO

The rate of AIDS among African American women is 15 times that of White women (Centers for Disease Control and Prevention, 1995). In Dade County, Florida, alone, there are approximately 5,000 African American women and girls over the age of 12 with AIDS (Department of Health and Rehabilitative Services, 1995). These figures primarily represent inner-city women who have been devastated for decades by poverty, drug addiction, and the sequelae of crime and family disruption—historical problems in certain segments of the African American community.

Much like other catastrophic illnesses, HIV/AIDS does not only affect the infected woman. The impact of the infection reverberates to her social network, particularly her family.

This work was supported by National Institute of Mental Health Grant 1 R01 MH51402 to José Szapocznik and Debra Greenwood, coprincipal investigators.

The impact of HIV/AIDS on the family is of particular importance (Boyd-Franklin et al., 1995; Landau-Stanton, Clements, & Stanton, 1993; Shelton, Greenwood, & Szapocznik, in press; Walker, 1991). Indeed, family researchers and therapists identify the family as the unit of care, in that the family is the unit to receive and give care. In HIV, as in all other matters that affect an African American woman, to more fully understand the individual, one must understand her family, culture, and environmental context (cf. Szapocznik & Kurtines, 1993). For people affected by HIV/AIDS, the family plays a particularly crucial role (cf. Szapocznik, 1995). Given that in times of illness or distress, the family unit is typically called on to support its member in need, the added stress of HIV may tax the ability of African American families to effectively cope with these additional demands, particularly because many are already living under very stressful conditions.

Although it is well known that discrete, traumatic events (e.g., natural disasters) can negatively impact psychosocial adaptation, some researchers have argued that chronic stressful life conditions may more negatively impact psychosocial adaptation than discrete life events (Krause, 1986; McLanahan, 1983; Sherbourne, 1988). Several studies have identified being poor, African American, female, and a single parent as sources of chronic life stress (G. W. Brown, Craig, & Harris, 1985; Smith, 1985). Another source of stress for African American families is the marginalization that they experience because the preferences, needs, and special circumstances of African American families are peripheral to the concerns of most Americans (Smith, 1985). Pierce (1975) characterized the societal stress that African Americans face as living in an environment where racism and subtle oppression are ubiquitous rather than an occasional misfortune. Although racism is a constant, salient stressor in the lives of African Americans (Boyd-Franklin, 1989; Smith, 1985), other social problems, such as lack of education, low incomes, and unsafe neighborhoods co-occur. In this chapter, we review the environmental stresses on these women and how African American families tend to respond to these stresses. We also present a therapeutic model, adapted for the special characteristics of the African American family. Throughout, we provide a sense of the real-life challenges they face and how their families respond.

ENVIRONMENTAL CHALLENGES

In our work with low-income, African American, postpartum women, we have found that lack of financial resources is a problem that is frequently reported as troubling to their life. One of the manifestations of their poverty is the unsafe neighborhoods in which many of the women live. One of our HIV-seropositive women, Belinda, a recovering crack cocaine addict, told of how she felt victimized in her neighborhood. She told us that she had tried to reach out to her neighbors who had few, if any, food stamps by sharing her own food with them. She was disappointed and angered to learn that those to whom she had been kind were also stealing food from her kitchen: "It really hurt me that some of the very same people I helped when they didn't have nothin' [sic] are now stealing from me." This experience embittered her and fostered a sense of mistrust of her neighbors, heightening her sense of isolation.

Our women also frequently report that one of their greatest fears with regard to HIV is the unsanctioned disclosure of their HIV status within their neighborhoods. Our women have spoken to us about the negative, disparaging remarks their neighbors and family members have made about known seropositives in their community. Another of our women, Ruth, observed, "My sister is real nice to my cousin who is HIV-positive—to his face. But when he leaves, she throws the glass away that he drunk [sic] from. I don't want her treating me like that. That's why I don't tell her about me." And from Tasha, "You don't know what's it like to hear them talk about 'those people' who got that HIV thang [sic] like they's [sic] dogs. They ain't never gonna talk about me like that!" Clearly, for many of our women, the environment poses yet another set of stressors, in that in addition to the unsafe neighborhoods and poverty with which the women must contend, ignorance about HIV in their social context translates into fear of stigmatization and isolation, should their HIV status become known.

However, there are families that remain supportive of their HIV-affected member, despite difficult circumstances. Lynn Collins is a 23-year-old African American woman with three children. The older two children reside with her grandmother in Texas. Lynn and her youngest child live with Lynn's parents (mother and stepfather) and her younger siblings. Although Lynn and her mother have had disagreements about some of the choices Lynn has made in her life (e.g., three unplanned pregnancies), Lynn's mother, Donna, has been supportive of Lynn since becoming aware of Lynn's HIV diagnosis. Lynn works part-time, rears her child, and contributes financially to the household. The family lives in a modest home in the inner city.

THE FAMILY'S ROLE IN ADAPTATION TO ENVIRONMENTAL STRESS

What may be critical to families is their ability to respond and adapt to chronic and acute stress. For the family, this necessitates an appraisal of the stressful event(s), what Lazarus and Folkman (1984) called "primary appraisal" (pp. 31–32), their perception of other, competing stresses and strains and their perception of family resources. The perception of the family's capacity to manage the stress is a "secondary appraisal" (Lazarus, 1966, p. 23). Other elements that affect the family's capacity to manage stress include an assessment of resources, the duration of the stressor, and the disruptiveness of the stressor. In the Collins family, Donna's primary appraisal of Lynn's HIV status competed with the family's struggle to make ends meet and Donna's desire to launch Lynn's siblings into adolescence in such a way that they do not make the same kinds of mistakes Lynn did, that is, unmarried, teenage pregnancy. Donna and her husband monitor their younger children closely, even though they both work long hours to support the family. The ability of the Collins family to juggle competing stressors is illustrative of competence in coping with their reality.

African American families have demonstrated a unique ability to survive and overcome adverse societal conditions such as racism and discrimination (Billingsley, 1968; Hines & Boyd-Franklin, 1982). Much of this success can be attributed to the strength of African American families, that is, their flexibility and resilience and their cultural values (Hill, 1977; cf. Ogbu, 1981). The reliance on an extended network of family and friends allows for more effective sharing of scarce resources (Chatters, Taylor, & Jackson, 1985; R. J. Taylor, 1985). Caregiving burdens are frequently shared by several related or nonrelated "fictive," or "play," kin, thus relieving an individual from assuming an overwhelming responsibility. For example, in the Collins family, the Texas grandmother provides assistance to the family by caring for Lynn's two older children. By caring for the children, the grandmother makes a de facto financial contribution by relieving the family of some of its financial stress. Moreover, in this case, the grandmother's caring for the children is experienced by Donna and the family as compassionate emotional support. The reliance on extended family or nonrelated kin is an example of a family successfully making a secondary appraisal of its resources and galvanizing them to solve acute or chronic family-related problems.

A strong religious ethos is also cited as an important coping resource for African American families (Boyd-Franklin, 1989; D. R. Brown & Gary, 1987; Griffith, Young, & Smith, 1984). African American families often rely on prayer, their clergy, and their church congregation to provide not only a means of support from others but also a sense of meaningfulness and a refuge from the material world (R. J. Taylor & Chatters, 1986). Prayer is a very important part of life for the Collins family. Donna and her husband see to it that the family attends church regularly.

It is clear that the African American family has developed several effective mechanisms for coping with the stress faced in the extreme environmental conditions to which African Americans are often forced to adapt. As we have suggested above, one of these is the kinship network. In our work with African American families, to access the necessary family support on behalf of our clients, we carefully identify the complex web that can potentially provide social support or be a source of stress.

THE IMPORTANCE OF CORRECTLY IDENTIFYING THE AFRICAN AMERICAN FAMILY

Note that for African American families, the concept of family is often fluid, which suggests that our traditional definition of family needs to be expanded to reflect the reality of many African Americans, who do not limit their "family" to biological kin. For many African Americans, the family may include one's biological family (including extended family), significant others, and close friends. These close friends, or fictive kin, that is, people who are identified as relatives but who are not part of the biological family, are typically very important to one or more members of the family. Fictive kin relationships can be intergenerational. Thus, the daughter of one's play aunt may be referred to as one's *play cousin*.

To deliver care to the family or to appropriately identify family resources, it is important to accurately identify the family constellation. Without a clear, accurate picture of the members of the family, important, powerful, family figures may be overlooked, thus distorting the clinician's assessment of the family and its typical pattern of interactions.

In African American families, it is not unusual for many different types of family constellations to occur in the community. A friend or relative may temporarily live with a family for days, weeks, or even years, for a variety of reasons. The family may take in a boarder (who may or may not be a relative) to earn extra money. For example, in the case of Belinda, her ex-husband lived in the home with her, paid rent as if a boarder, yet functioned as an integral part of the family, in that he participated in child rearing and household decisions. Moreover, fictive kin may play an important role in a family, although they need not necessarily reside in the home. This cultural practice of broadening one's definition of family has important implications for researchers and clinicians who assess family composition or family functioning. Traditional methods of family identification, with their overemphasis on biological ties and neglect of function as an indication of family constellation, are often inappropriate for African American families.

Clinical Issues

Our clinical model is structural and strategic. It is concerned with identifying and changing maladaptive family interactions and promoting adaptive interactions within the family, as well as between the family and their social context. The model focuses on process rather than content. Whether the content is which football game to watch or who will take in Aunt Susie's youngest child, the model focuses on the nature of the interactions and not on their content.

If the family constellation is incomplete, the clinician may see incomplete or inaccurate interactions, especially in African American families, in which there is often a reluctance to involve family members with whom there are conflictive relationships. Therefore, it is important to ensure that all key people who contribute to the interactions are involved in both the assessment and intervention.

Research Issues

There is also a need for accurate assessment of the family for research purposes. Clinical and policy decisions are often based on research findings. Inaccurate assessment of the family constellation misrepresents the true nature of the family. There are also implications for generalizability. It is likely that certain interventions work better with certain kinds of family constellations than others. For that reason, it is important to accurately characterize the family constellation(s) within each study.

SOCIAL SUPPORT AND AFRICAN AMERICAN FAMILIES

As noted earlier, the African American family (such as the case of the Collins family) is often able to draw on the support of nuclear, extended, and nonbiological kin to assist in coping with stressful conditions. Several studies have documented the effectiveness of kin and non-kin support networks in African American families. For example, Lewis (1988) found that African American mothers of minor-aged children who frequently used extended kin networks or who had a supportive partner were less likely to report parental role strain than mothers without these supports.

D. R. Brown and Gary (1987) found that African American women with low perceived social support tended to have greater emotional distress irrespective of their stressful life events. In fact, the number of relatives who lived nearby was significantly related to a reduced level of emotional distress.

R. D. Taylor, Casten, and Flickinger (1993) found a positive association of kinship support with adolescent adjustment and more adequate parenting experiences in a sample of 125 African American adolescents from one- and two-parent homes. Single-parented adolescents reported that with more kinship support, their parents were more warm and accepting and more active in monitoring their behavior. These findings underscore the importance of social support in coping with a stressful life condition, the unique way women use support, and the importance of the family as a source of support.

FAMILY HASSLES AND FAMILY CONFLICT

Intense and intimate as are family relationships, they can be a source of support as well as a source of conflict. Among our HIV-seropositive mothers, we found that increased family hassles were related to an inappropriate family developmental level, in that families that were not adequately addressing the demands of their unique developmental stage also tended to report many family-related hassles.[1] Not surprisingly, families in which independent raters observed a high number of conflicts reported a high number of family hassles. Moreover, in families with poor conflict-resolution skills, seropositive mothers were less satisfied with their social support. This suggests that HIV-seropositive women may be cut off from an important source of support in their life, that is, their family, if the families are developmentally inadequate, have a high number of conflicts, report family-related hassles, or have difficulty resolving conflict in adaptive ways. In the Collins family, although Donna is supportive of Lynn, there have been reports of conflict over Donna's tendency to "overcontrol" Lynn's behavior at times. Lynn sometimes feels infantilized by Donna's overinvolvement in her life. Further research should explore if these variables—developmental level, number of conflicts, conflict-resolution skills, and reported hassles—covary in ways that suggest a syndrome of family problem behaviors in some families.

Clearly, African American women with HIV face many personal, family, and environmental challenges. Some of the problems they report, for example, lack of financial resources, family hassles, and a nonsupportive environment, may be amenable to treatment. Given the multidimensionality of their problems, however, an intervention that addresses the environmental, familial, and intrapersonal contexts of the women is indicated.

---

[1]By *development level* (see Szapocznik et al., 1991), we mean the appropriateness of the behaviors of each family member given their role and age (e.g., a parentified child who has too much responsibility, or a parent who fails to guide and assumes too little responsibility).

STRUCTURAL ECOSYSTEMS THERAPY

Structural ecosystems therapy (SET) is based on a systems approach pioneered by Szapocznik and colleagues in work with inner-city families (Kurtines & Szapocznik, 1996; Szapocznik, 1995; Szapocznik et al., in press). Structural-ecosystems-therapy targets interactions at the interface between the intrapersonal, familial, and environmental dimensions. It is designed to foster a sense of empowerment in the family as they learn to better negotiate their environment and to increase positive, supportive interactions among the woman and her family.

HIV-seropositive women and their families face numerous challenges: the HIV infection of the woman (about which the family may or may not be aware), environmental stresses and strains, family hassles, and problems in resolving family conflicts, among others. At the same time, many of these women and their families have important strengths: the flexible definition of family, which can serve to broaden the family's base of support, and a strong religious ethos. Based on our many years of experience with African American families at the Center for Family Studies, we believe that the necessary ingredients for an intervention to be successful with this population must address the challenges these women and their families face on many different levels.

The socioecological model on which SET is built is essentially an empowerment model. The therapist who works with the woman and her family seeks to teach them how to better negotiate their environment and how to better communicate and interact with each other. From our systems perspective, we believe that an ecological, structural model, which focuses on strengthening interactions, will result in improvements not only in family functioning but in intrapersonal functioning as well.

The goals of SET are as follows: (a) to identify patterns of interactions, (b) to strengthen supportive interactions, (c) to correct problematic interactions, and (d) to support the family in learning to better negotiate its environment. Just as we found problems in all three areas of context of the women—intrapersonal, (e.g., distress); familial (e.g., family conflicts and hassles); and environmental (e.g., financial need and poor neighborhoods)—SET addresses all three, in particular, the interface among them. The SET therapist identifies both supportive and problematic interactions in the family. Using a systems perspective, the therapist assesses how these interactions impact the family system in positive or negative ways. The therapist is very directive, yet diplomatic and strategic, in reinforcing supportive interactions and restructuring problematic interactions. For example, in the case of Donna's overinvolvement in Lynn's life, the SET therapist might reframe Donna's actions as expressions of her love and concern, thereby creating the opportunity for Donna to "express her love" in other ways. She might also recharacterize

Lynn's frustration as her desire to prove to her mother how well she has learned from her, thereby creating the opportunity for Lynn to explore, within a very positive frame, the possibility that Donna might step aside and allow Lynn to parent without interference.

In addition to identifying, supporting, and correcting family interactions, the SET therapist also identifies environmental stresses that negatively impact the family, as well as environmental supports that may serve to buffer some of the stress of the family. The therapist will help clarify the needs and aspirations of the family in improving their ability to cope with their environment. For example, Lynn has expressed a desire to enroll in school. The SET therapist might work alongside Lynn in identifying a potential area of study, identifying an appropriate school, and assisting in the enrollment process, as needed. The level of assistance will vary from individual to individual and family to family. Some people may require little more than information and supportive advice, whereas others may require assistance with filling out applications, making telephone calls, applying for financial aid, and so on. The SET therapist does whatever it takes to help the family to achieve its goals of improved family interaction and improved environmental negotiation.

CONCLUSION

The well-being of the woman with HIV or AIDS and her surviving children is often intimately tied to the well-being of her family. Families that are supportive and nurturing can provide both the woman and her children an atmosphere of acceptance that facilitates the personal growth and development of its members. We believe the SET approach to addressing the multifaceted context of African American, HIV-seropositive women and their families can offer viable alternatives to the environmental and familial stress that is far too common. It is our belief that interventions that are ecological and family based (e.g., SET) can help provide better family and environmental circumstances for HIV-affected women and children.

REFERENCES

Billingsley, A. (1968). *Black families in White America*. Englewood Cliffs, NJ: Prentice Hall.

Boyd-Franklin, N. (1989). *Black families in therapy: A multisystems approach*. New York: Guilford Press.

Boyd-Franklin, N., Aleman, J., Jean-Gilles, M., & Lewis, S. (1995). Cultural competency model: African American, Latino and Haitian families with pediatric HIV/AIDS. In N. Boyd-Franklin, G. Steiner, & M. Boland (Eds.), Children, families and AIDS/HIV: Psychosocial and psychotherapeutic issues (pp. 53–77). New York: Guilford Press.

Brown, D. R., & Gary, L. E. (1987, Winter). Stressful life events, social support networks, and the physical and mental health of urban Black adults. Journal of Human Stress, 165–174.

Brown, G. W., Craig, T. K., & Harris, T. O. (1985). Depression: Distress or disease? Some epidemiological considerations. British Journal of Psychiatry, 147, 612–622.

Centers for Disease Control and Prevention. (1995). HIV/AIDS Surveillance Report, 7(1), p. 18.

Chatters, L. M., Taylor, R. J., & Jackson, J. S. (1985). Size and composition of the informal helper networks of elderly Blacks. Journal of Gerontology, 40, 605–614.

Department of Health and Rehabilitative Services. (1995). HIV–AIDS reporting systems (HARS). State of Florida, Dade County Department of Public Health. HRS State Health Office, 1317 Winewood Blvd., Tallahassee, FL 32399-0700.

Griffith, E. E., Young, J. L., & Smith, D. L. (1984). An analysis of the therapeutic elements in a Black church service. Hospital and Community Psychiatry, 35, 464–469.

Hill, R. (1977). Informal adoption among Black families. Washington, DC: National Urban League Research Department.

Hines, P. M., & Boyd-Franklin, N. (1982). Black families. In M. McGoldrick, J. K. Pearce, & J. Giordano (Eds.), Ethnicity and family therapy (pp. 84–107). New York: Guilford Press.

Krause, N. (1986). Life stress as a correlate of depression among older adults. Psychiatry Research, 18, 227–237.

Kurtines, W. M., & Szapocznik, J. (1996). Structural family therapy in contexts of cultural diversity. In E. Hibbs & R. Jensen (Eds.), Psychosocial treatment research with children and adolescents. Washington, DC: American Psychological Association.

Landau-Stanton, J., Clements, C. D, & Stanton, M. D. (1993). Psychotherapeutic intervention: From individual through group to extended network. In J. Landau-Stanton & C. D. Clements (Eds.), AIDS, health, and mental health (pp. 214–266). New York: Brunner/Mazel.

Lazarus, R. S., & Folkman, S. (1984). Stress, appraisal, and coping. New York: Springer.

Lewis, E. (1988). Role strengths and gender role attitude among teenage mothers. Adolescence, 25, 709–716.

McLanahan, S. S. (1983). Family structure and stress: A longitudinal comparison of two-parent and female-headed families. Journal of Marriage and the Family, 45, 347–357.

Ogbu, J. U. (1981). Origins of human competence: A cultural–ecological perspective. *Child Development, 52,* 413–429.

Pierce, C. B. (1974). *All our kin: Strategies for Survival in a Black Community.* New York: Harper & Row.

Shelton, D., Greenwood, D., & Szapocznik, J. (in press). Family systems therapy with African American families coping with HIV/AIDS. In E. H. Johnson, H. Amaro, M. Antoni, J. Jemmott, & J. Szapocznik (Eds.), *AIDS in African Americans and Hispanics: The role of behavioral and psychosocial factors.* New York: Praeger.

Sherbourne, C. D. (1988). The role of social support and life stress events in the use of mental health services. *Social Science and Medicine, 27,* 1393–1400.

Smith, E. M. (1985). Ethnic minorities: Life stress, social support, and mental health issues. *Counseling Psychologist, 13,* 537–579.

Szapocznik, J. (1995). Research on disclosure of HIV status: Cultural evolution finds an ally in science. *Health Psychology, 14*(1), 4–5.

Szapocznik, J. (Ed.). (1996). *Structural ecosystems: Theory and practice.* Manuscript in preparation, University of Miami, Miami, FL.

Szapocznik, J., & Kurtines, W. M. (1993). Family psychology and cultural diversity: Opportunities for theory, research, and application. *American Psychologist, 48,* 400–407.

Szapocznik, J., Kurtines, W., Santisteban, D. A., Pantin, H., Scopetta, M., Mancilla, Y., Aisenberg, S., McIntosh, S., & Coatsworth, J. D. (in press). The evolution of a multisystemic structural approach for working with Hispanic families in culturally pluralistic contexts. In J. Garcia & M. C. Zea (Eds.), *Handbook of Latino psychology.* Needham Heights, MA: Allyn & Bacon.

Szapocznik, J., Rio, A. T., Hervis, O. E., Mitrani, V. B., Kurtines, W., & Faraci, A. M. (1991). Assessing change in family functioning as a result of treatment: The Structural Family Systems Rating Scale (SFSR). *Journal of Marital and Family Therapy, 17,* 295–310.

Taylor, R. D., Casten, R., & Flickinger, S. (1993). Influence of kinship social support on the parenting experiences and psychosocial adjustment of African-American adolescents. *Developmental Psychology, 29,* 382–388.

Taylor, R. J. (1985). The extended family as a source of support to elderly Blacks. *The Gerontologist, 25,* 488–495.

Taylor, R. J., & Chatters, L. M. (1986). Church-based informal support among elderly Blacks. *The Gerontologist, 26,* 637–642.

Walker, G. (1991). *In the midst of winter.* New York: Norton.

23

REVOLUTION IN HEALTH PROMOTION: SMOKING CESSATION AS A CASE STUDY

JAMES O. PROCHASKA

Health care costs in the United States total $1 trillion. Pharmaceuticals account for 7% of that total. Behavior accounts for 60%. With the way behavioral health is currently practiced, however, it impacts on only a small percentage of those costs. So there are huge unmet needs and great opportunities, but only if psychologists revolutionize the way they do science and the way they apply our science.

Smoking is an excellent case study, because it is so costly to individual smokers and to society. In the United States, approximately 47 million Americans continue to smoke. Over 400,000 preventable deaths per year are attributable to smoking (U.S. Department of Health and Human Services, 1990). Globally, the problem promises to be catastrophic. Of the people alive in the world today, 500 million are expected to die from

The research cited in this article was supported by National Cancer Institute Grants CA 27821, CA 50087, and CA 63745.

this single behavior, losing approximately 5 billion years of life to tobacco use (Peto & Lopez, 1990). If even modest gains could be made in behavioral science and the practice of smoking cessation, millions of premature deaths could be prevented, and billions of years of life could be preserved. Unfortunately, most smoking cessation programs have had little impact in reducing overall levels of smokers. This failure may be due to these programs' focus on achieving a specific outcome without reference to the larger process of how people come to stop a harmful, but engrained, behavior. This chapter describes a stage paradigm of smoking cessation and outlines how it can be integrated into sucessful interventions.

THE EFFICACY OF SMOKING CESSATION PROGRAMS

Currently, smoking cessation clinics have little impact. When offered for free by health maintenance organizations in the United States, such clinics recruit only about 1% of subscribers who smoke (Lichtenstein & Hollis, 1992). Such behavioral health services simply cannot make much difference if they treat such a small percentage of the problem.

Startled by such statistics, behavioral scientists took health-promotion programs into communities and work sites. The results are now being reported, and in the largest trials ever attempted, the outcomes are discouraging. In the Minnesota Heart Health project, for example, $40 million was spent with 5 years of intervention in four communities totaling 400,000 people. However, there were no significant differences between treatment and control communities on smoking, diet, cholesterol, weight, blood pressure, and overall risks for cardiovascular disease (Luepker et al., 1994).

What went wrong? The investigators speculate that they may have diluted their programs by targeting multiple behaviors. But the Community Intervention Trial for Smoking Cessation (COMMIT Research Group, 1995) had no effects with its primary target of heavy smokers and only a small effect with light smokers. Similarly, the largest work site cessation program produced no significant effects (Glasgow, Terborg, Hollis, Severson, & Boles, 1995).

A closer look at participation rates can probably account for the dismal results. In the Minnesota study, nearly 90% of smokers in both the treatment and control communities had processed media information about smoking in the past year (Lando et al., 1995). However, only about 10% had physicians intervene, and only about 3% participated in the most powerful behavioral programs, such as individualized and interactive clinics, classes, and contests. Behavioral scientists cannot have much impact on the health of our communities if they interact only with a small percentage of populations at high risk for disease and early death.

A NEW VISION FOR INTERVENTION STRATEGIES

There is an old interventionist rule that reads, if we don't like how our clients or our communities are acting, we need to change our behavior. Behavioral scientists cannot continue to offer only action-oriented cessation programs and expect the results to be better. A shift needs to be made, from an *action* paradigm to a *stage* paradigm, if psychologists are to interact with a much higher percentage of populations at risk. An action paradigm focuses on achieving a specific behavioral change, such as smoking cessation. The stage paradigm, however, construes behavior change as a process involving progress through six stages: precontemplation, contemplation, preparation, action, maintenance, and termination. Action is seen as one of the six stages, and it becomes integrated as part of the process of individual, community, or population change.

Precontemplation is the stage in which people are not intending to take action in the foreseeable future, usually measured as the next 6 months. People in this stage are often defensive and resistant, particularly against programs and persuasions designed to have them take action. They can also be demoralized by previous failures, and as a result, they tend to avoid reading, viewing, listening, or talking about their unhealthy habits. They certainly are not ready to enroll in action-oriented programs. Historically, psychologists labeled such individuals as *unmotivated, resistant,* or *not ready for therapy*. The reality is that psychologists were not ready for them, and were not motivated to match their needs. Without planned interventions, people in precontemplation can remain stuck in this stage for years.

In the contemplation stage, individuals are intending to take action in the next 6 months. They are more aware of the benefits of changing, but they are also acutely aware that change costs. The profound ambivalence they often experience can keep them contemplating for years. Chronic contemplators tend to substitute thinking for acting. In one sample, we found that less than 50% quit smoking for 24 hours over 12 months, even though all had initially intended to quit smoking for good in the next 6 months (Prochaska, DiClemente, Velicer & Rossi, 1993).

In the preparation stage, people are ready to participate in action-oriented interventions, because they are intending to take action in the next month and have taken some action in the past 12 months. They are more convinced that the pros outweigh the cons of quitting smoking, for example. These are the more motivated members of a population, though psychologists prefer the concept of preparation over motivation.

TABLE 1
Distribution of Smokers by Stage Across Four Different Samples

Sample	n	Stage		
		Precontemplation	Contemplation	Preparation
Random digit dial	4,144	42.1%	40.3%	17.6%
4 US work sites	4,785	41.1%	38.7%	20.1%
California	9,534	37.3%	46.7%	16.0%
RI high schools	208	43.8%	38.0%	18.3%

Note. RI = Rhode Island.

People often perceive motivation as something that happens to them, like hitting bottom, whereas preparation is perceived as more under personal control.

Action involves overt behavioral modification, such as stopping smoking, and is one of the reasons that change has been equated with action. Action is the stage in which people work the hardest, applying the most processes of change most frequently. In our research, we found that people have to work hard for about 6 months before they can ease up (Prochaska & DiClemente, 1983). One problem is that the public expects the worst to be over in a few weeks or a few months and ease their efforts too quickly. Such poor preparation is one of the reasons so many people relapse so quickly.

After about 6 months of concentrated action, people enter the maintenance stage. They continue to apply particular processes of change, but they do not have to work nearly as hard to prevent relapse. During maintenance, the most common risks for relapse are times of emotional distress, such as anger, anxiety, boredom, depression, and stress. People need to be adequately prepared to cope with such distress without resorting back to their unhealthy habits.

How long does the maintenance stage last? For some, it is a lifetime of maintenance. Others can totally terminate their unhealthy habits and experience zero temptations across all high-risk situations, with 100% confidence that they will never again resort back to their unhealthy habits.

INTEGRATING THE STAGE PARADIGM INTO PLANNED INTERVENTIONS

Let us examine how this stage paradigm can be applied to five of the most important phases of planned interventions.

Recruitment

Recall that action oriented cessation programs fail in this first phase of intervention. Table 1 reports results that can help explain such failures.

Across four different samples, it can be seen that 20% or less of smokers are in the preparation stage (Velicer et al., 1995). When action-oriented programs are advertised or announced, they explicitly or implicitly target less than 20% of a population. The other 80% plus are left on their own.

In one of the Minnesota Heart Health studies, smokers were randomly assigned to one of three recruitment methods for home-based cessation programs (Schmid, Jeffrey, & Hellerstedt, 1989). These announcements generated 1% to 5% participation rates, with a personalized letter doing the best.

In two home-based programs, with 5,000 smokers in each study, we reached out, either by telephone alone or by personal letters followed by telephone calls if needed, and recruited smokers to stage-matched interventions. Using these proactive recruitment methods and stage-matched interventions, we were able to generate participation rates of 82% to 85%, respectively (Prochaska, Velicer, Fava, & Laforge, 1995; Prochaska, Velicer, Fava, & Rossi, 1995). Such quantum increases in participation rates provide the potential to generate unprecedented impacts with entire populations of smokers.

Impact equals participation rate times efficacy or action. If a program produced 30% efficacy (such as long-term abstinence), historically it was judged to be better than a program that produced 25% abstinence. But a program that generates 30% efficacy but only 5% participation has an impact of only 1.5% (30% × 5%). A program that produces only 25% efficacy but 60% participation has an impact of 15%. With health-promotion programs, this would be a 1,000% greater impact on a high-risk population.

The stage paradigm would have us shift our outcomes from efficacy to impacts. To achieve such high impacts, psychologists need to shift from reactive recruitment, in which they advertise or announce their programs and react when people reach them, to proactive recruitments, in which they reach out to interact with all potential participants.

Proactive recruitment alone will not work. In the most intensive recruitment protocol to date, Lichtenstein and Hollis (1992) had physicians spend up to 5 minutes with each smoker, just to get them to sign up for an action-oriented cessation clinic. If that did not work, a nurse spent 10 minutes to persuade each smoker to sign up, followed by 12 minutes with a videotape and health educator and even a proactive counselor call, if necessary. The base rate was 1% participation. This proactive protocol resulted in 35% of smokers in precontemplation signing up. But only 3% showed up, and 2% finished up, and 0 ended up better off. With a combination of smokers in contemplation and preparation, 65% signed up, 15% showed up, 11% finished up, and some percentage ended up better off. To optimize impacts, behavioral scientists

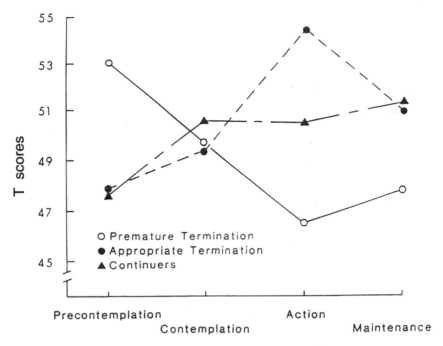

Figure 1. Pretherapy stage profiles for premature terminators, appropriate terminators, and continuers.

need to use proactive protocols to recruit participants to programs that match their stage.

RETENTION

One of the skeletons in the closet of psychotherapy and behavioral change interventions is their relatively poor retention rates. Across 125 studies, the average retention rate was only about 50% (Wierzbicki & Pekarik, 1993). Furthermore, this meta-analysis found few consistent predictors of which participants would drop out prematurely and which would continue in therapy. In studies on smoking, weight control, substance abuse, and a mixture of disorders (as listed in the *Diagnostic and Statistical Manual of Mental Disorders*; American Psychiatric Association, 1994) stage-of-change measures proved to be the best predictors of premature termination. Figure 1 contains the stage profile of three groups of psychotherapy participants: the pre-treatment-stage profile of the entire 40% who dropped out prematurely, as judged by their therapists, was that of patients in precontemplation. The 20% who terminated quickly but appropriately had a profile of patients in action. Using pre-treatment-stage-related measures, we were able to correctly classify 93% of the three groups (Medeiros & Prochaska, 1995).

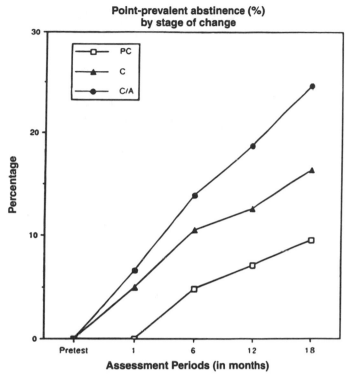

Point-prevalent abstinence (%) by stage of change

Figure 2. Percentage abstinent over 18 months for smokers in precontemplation (PC), contemplation (C), and preparation (C/A) stages before treatment (*N* = 570).

We simply cannot treat people with a precontemplation profile as if they were ready for action interventions and expect them to stay with us. Relapse-prevention strategies would be indicated with addicted clients who are taking action. But those in precontemplation are likely to need drop out-prevention strategies.

The best strategy we have found to promote retention is matching our interventions to stage of change. In four smoking cessation studies using such matching strategies, we found we were able to retain smokers in the precontemplation stage at the same high levels as those who started in precontemplation (Prochaska, 1994a).

Progress

The amount of progress participants make following health-promotion programs is directly related to the stage they were in at the start of the interventions. This *stage effect* is illustrated in Figure 2, where smokers initially in precontemplation show the smallest amount of abstinence over 18 months and those in preparation progress the most (Prochaska, DiClemente, & Norcross, 1992). Across 66 different predictions of progress, we found that smokers starting in contemplation were about two thirds more successful than those in precontemplation at 6-, 12-, and 18-month follow-ups. Similarly, those in preparation were about two thirds more successful then those in contemplation at the same follow-ups (Prochaska, Velicer, Fava, Rossi, & Laforge, 1995).

These results can be used clinically. A reasonable goal for each therapeutic intervention with smokers is to help them progress one stage. If over the course of brief therapy, they progress two stages, they will be about 2 2/3 times more successful at longer term follow-ups.

This strategy is being taught to nurses and physicians' assistants in Britain's National Health Care System. One of the first reports is a marked improvement in the morale of such health promoters intervening with all patients who smoke, abuse substances, and have unhealthy diets (Burton, L., personal communication, February 1996). These professionals now have strategies that match the needs of all of their patients, not just the minority prepared to take action. Furthermore, these professionals can see the majority progressing, where previously they saw most failing, when action was the only measure of movement.

Process

To help populations progress through the stages, we need to understand the processes and principles of change. One of the fundamental principles for progress is that different processes of change need to be applied at different stages of change. Classic conditioning processes, such as counterconditioning, stimulus control, and contingency control, can be highly successful for participants taking action but can produce resistance with individuals in precontemplation. With these individuals, more experiential processes, such as consciousness raising and dramatic relief, can move people cognitively and affectively and help them shift to contemplation (Prochaska, Norcross, & DiClemente, 1994).

We have reported in detail which processes are best matched to each stage (Prochaska, Norcross, & DiClemente, 1994). Space limitations will permit only a couple of examples of progress principles. Figure 3 contains the pros and cons of changing, across the stages of change, for 12 different behaviors from 10 different populations (Prochaska, Velicer, et al., 1994).

There are some remarkable consistencies across 12 diverse behaviors. With all 12, the cons of changing are evaluated as greater than the pros, by people in precontemplation. No wonder they are not intending to change. But this is not necessarily a rational or conscious process. With smokers in precontemplation, for example, their raw scores on the pros of quitting will usually be higher than their cons. It is only when we transform raw scores into standardized scores (as we do on the Minnesota

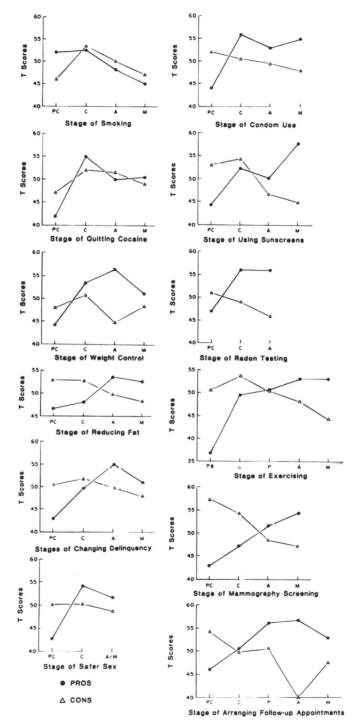

Figure 3. The pros and cons (in T scores) by stages of change for each of 12 problem behaviors. PC = precontemplation; C = contemplation; P = preparation; A = action; M = maintenance.

Multiphasic Personality Inventory or Wechsler Adult Intelligence Scale) that we see the clear pattern of cons greater than pros. Compared with smokers in other stages, those in precontemplation are underestimating the pros of quitting, overestimating the cons, and probably are not conscious of the process. No wonder we need to apply consciousness-raising techniques, such as feedback, to help them progress.

With all 12 problems, the pros are higher in contemplation than precontemplation, but there is no consistent pattern with the cons. With some behaviors, the cons of change increase as people begin to seriously think about taking action. So, one principle of progress is that the pros of changing must increase for people to move from precontemplation to contemplation.

With all 12 problems, the cons are lower in action than in contemplation. A second principle of progress, then, is that the cons of changing must decline as people move from contemplation to action.

We can be even more mathematical. Across all 12 behaviors, we discovered a strong principle of progress:

$$PC \rightarrow A \cong 1\ SD \uparrow Pros.$$

To progress from precontemplation to action, the pros of changing increase approximately 1 standard deviation (Prochaska, 1994b).

We also discovered a weak principle:

$$PC \rightarrow A \cong 0.5\ SD \downarrow Cons.$$

To progress from precontemplation to action, the cons of changing must decrease 0.5 standard deviation. One application of these principles would be to place twice as much emphasis on increasing the appreciation of the pros of changing than on decreasing the cons.

After 15 years of research, we have identified 14 variables that we intervene with, to accelerate progress across the first five stages of change (Prochaska, Norcross, & DiClemente, 1994). At any particular stage, we need to intervene with only a maximum of six variables. To help guide individuals at each stage of change, we have developed computer-based expert systems that can deliver individualized and interactive interventions to entire populations. These computer programs can be used alone or in conjunction with counselors.

Outcomes

In our first large-scale clinical trial, we compared four treatments: (a) one of the best home-based action-oriented cessation programs (standardized), (b) stage-matched manuals (individualized), (c) expert-system computer reports plus manuals (interactive), and (d) personalized counselors plus computers and manuals (personalized).

We randomly assigned by stage 756 smokers to one of the four treatments (Prochaska, DiClemente, Velicer, & Rossi, 1993). Note that we did not test our new treatments against placebo or no treatment controls. In our research, we test our hypotheses against the riskiest tests we can devise. That way, if our new treatments outperform one of the best tests available, then we can be more confident that we have something worth writing about, than if we outperform placebos or controls.

In the computer condition, participants completed, by mail or telephone, 40 questions, which were entered in our central computers and which generated feedback reports. These reports informed participants about their stage of change, their pros and cons of changing, and their use of change processes appropriate to their stages. At baseline, participants were given positive feedback on what they were doing correctly and guidance on which principles and processes they needed to apply more, to progress. In two progress reports, delivered over the next 6 months, participants also received positive feedback on any improvement they made on any of the variables relevant to progressing. Thus, demoralized and defensive smokers could begin progressing without having to quit and without having to work hard. Smokers in the contemplation stage could begin taking small steps, such as delaying their first cigarette in the morning for an extra 30 minutes. They could choose small steps that would increase their self-efficacy and help them become better prepared for quitting.

In the personalized condition, smokers received four proactive counselor calls over the 6-month intervention period. Three of the calls were based on the computer reports. Counselors reported much more difficulty in interacting with participants without any progress data. Without scientific assessments, it was much harder for both clients and counselors to tell whether any significant progress had occurred since their last interaction.

Figure 4 contains point-prevalence abstinence rates for each of the four treatment groups over 18 months, with treatment ending at 6 months (Prochaska et al., 1993). The two self-help-manual conditions paralleled each other for 12 months. At 18 months, the stage-matched-manual participants moved ahead. This is an example of a *delayed-action effect*, which we often observe with stage-matched programs. It takes time for participants in early stages to progress all the way to action. Therefore, some treatment effects, as measured by action, will be observed only after considerable delay. Nonetheless, it is encouraging to find treatments producing therapeutic effects even months and years after termination.

The computer-alone and personalized counselor conditions paralleled each other for 12 months. Then, the effects of the personalized

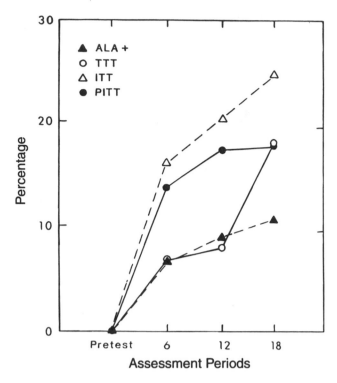

Figure 4. Point-prevalence abstinence (%) for four treatment groups at pretest and at 6, 12, and 18 months. ALA + = standardized manuals; TTT = individualized stage-matched manuals; ITT = interactive computer reports; PITT = personalized counselor calls.

counselor condition flattened out while the interactive computer condition effects continued to increase. We can only speculate as to the delayed differences between these two conditions. Participants in the personalized condition may have become somewhat dependent on the social support and social control of the counselor calling. The last call was after the 6-month assessment, and benefits would be observed at 12 months. Termination of the counselors could result in no further progress because of the loss of social support and control. The classic pattern in smoking cessation clinics is rapid relapse beginning as soon as the treatment is terminated. Some of this rapid relapse could well be due to the sudden loss of social support or social control provided by the counselors and other participants in the clinic.

In this clinical trial, smokers were recruited reactively. They called us in response to advertisements, announcements, and articles. How would their results compare with the smokers that we called to proactively recruit to our programs? Most people would predict that smokers who called us for help would succeed more than smokers who we called to help.

Figure 5 shows the remarkable results of comparing smokers in a study who called us (reactive; Prochaska et al., 1993) to those in a study

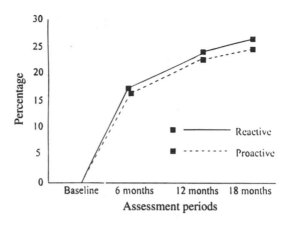

Figure 5. Point-prevalence abstinence rates for smokers recruitment by reactive versus proactive strategies and treated by stage-matched, home-based, expert-system computer reports.

that we called (proactive; Prochaska, Velicer, Fava, & Laforge, 1995). Both groups received the same home-based expert-system computer reports delivered over a 6-month period. Although the reactively recruited participants were slightly more successful at each follow-up, what is striking is how similar are the results.

CONCLUSION

If these results continue to be replicated, health-promotion programs will be able to produce unprecedented impacts on entire populations. We believe that such unprecedented impacts require scientific and professional shifts: (a) from an action paradigm to a stage paradigm, (b) from reactive to proactive recruitment, (c) from expecting participants to match the needs of our programs to having our programs match their needs, and (d) from clinic-based to community-based behavioral health programs that still apply the field's most powerful individualized and interactive intervention strategies.

With this type of revolution in health promotion, psychology and other health sciences and professions will be able to respond to the huge, unmet needs and the great opportunities related to the prevention of chronic diseases and premature death.

REFERENCES

American Psychiatric Association. (1994). *Diagnostic and statistical manual of mental disorders* (4th ed.). Washington, DC: Author.

COMMIT Research Group. (1995). Community Intervention Trial for Smoking Cessation (COMMIT): I. Cohort results from a four-year community intervention. *American Journal of Public Health, 85,* 183–192.

Glasgow, R. E., Terborg, J. R., Hollis, J. F., Severson, H. H., & Boles, S. M. (1995). Take heart: Results from the initial phase of a work-site wellness program. *American Journal of Public Health, 85,* 209–216.

Lando, H. A., Pechacek, T. F., Pirie, P. L., Murray, D. M., Mittelmark, M. B., Lichtenstein, E., Nothwehyr, F., & Gray, C. (1995). Changes in adult cigarette smoking in the Minnesota Heart Health Program. *American Journal of Public Health, 85,* 201–208.

Lichtenstein, E., & Hollis, J. (1992). Patient referral to smoking cessation programs: Who follows through? *The Journal of Family Practice, 34,* 739–744.

Luepker, R. V., Murray, D. M., Jacobs, D. R., Jr., Mittelmark, M. B., Bracht, N., Carlaw, R., Crow, R., Elmer, P., Finnegan, J., Folsom, A. R., Grimm, R., Hannan, P. J., Jeffrey, R., Lando, H., McGovern, P., Mullis, R., Perry, C. L., Pechacek, T., Pirie, P., Sprafka, J. M., Weisbrod, R., & Blackburn, H. (1994). Community education for cardiovascular disease prevention: Risk factor changes in the Minnesota Heart Health Program. *American Journal of Public Health, 84,* 1383–1393.

Medeiros, M. E., & Prochaska, J. O. (1995). *Predicting termination and continuation status in psychotherapy using the transtheoretical model.* Manuscript submitted for publication.

Peto, R., & Lopez, A. (1990). World-wide mortality from current smoking patterns. In B. Durstone & K. Jamrogik (Eds.), *The global war: Proceedings of the Seventh World Conference on Tobacco and Health* (pp. 62–68). East Perth, Western Australia: Organizing Committee of Seventh World Conference on Tobacco and Health.

Prochaska, J. O. (1994a, April). *Staging: A revolution.* Master science lecture presented at the annual meeting of the *Society for Behavioral Medicine,* Boston.

Prochaska, J. O. (1994b). Strong and weak principles for progressing from precontemplation to action based on twelve problem behaviors. *Health Psychology, 13,* 47–51.

Prochaska, J. O., & DiClemente, C. C. (1983). Stages and processes of self-change of smoking: Toward an integrative model of change. *Journal of Consulting and Clinical Psychology, 51,* 390–395.

Prochaska, J. O., DiClemente, C. C., & Norcross, J. C. (1992). In search of how people change: Applications to the addictive behaviors. *American Psychologist, 47,* 1102–1114.

Prochaska, J. O., DiClemente, C. C., Velicer, W. F., & Rossi, J. S. (1993). Standardized, individualized, interactive, and personalized self-help programs for smoking cessation. *Health Psychology, 12,* 399–405.

Prochaska, J. O., Norcross, J. C., & DiClemente, C. C. (1994). *Changing for good.* New York: Morrow.

Prochaska, J. O., Velicer, W. F., Fava, J., & Laforge, R. (1995). *Toward disease-state management for smoking: Stage-matched expert systems for a total managed care population of smokers.* Manuscript submitted for publication.

Prochaska, J. O., Velicer, W. F., Fava, J., & Rossi, J. (1995). *A stage-matched expert-system intervention with a total population of smokers.* Manuscript submitted for publication.

Prochaska, J. O., Velicer, W. F., Fava, J., Rossi, J., & Laforge, R. (1995). *Stage, interactive, dose-response, counseling, and stimulus-control computer effects in a total managed care population of smokers.* Manuscript submitted for publication.

Prochaska, J. O., Velicer, W. F., Rossi, J. S., Goldstein, M. G., Marcus, B. H., Rakowski, W., Fiore, C., Harlow, L., Redding, C. A., Rosenbloom, D., & Rossi, S. R. (1994). Stages of change and decisional balance for twelve problem behaviors. *Health Psychology, 13,* 39–46.

Schmid, T. L., Jeffrey, R. W., & Hellerstedt, W. L. (1989). Direct mail recruitment to house-based smoking and weight control programs: A comparison of strengths. *Preventive Medicine, 18,* 503–517.

U.S. Department of Health and Human Services. (1990). *The health benefits of smoking cessation: A report of the surgeon general* (DHHS Publication No. CDC 90–8416). Washington, DC: U.S. Government Printing Office.

Velicer, W. F., Fava, J. L., Prochaska, J. O., Abrams, D. B., Emmons, K. M., & Pierce, J. (1995). Distribution of smokers by stage in three representative samples. *Preventive Medicine, 24,* 401–411.

Wierzbicki, M., & Pekarik, G. (1993). A meta-analysis of psychotherapy dropout. *Professional Psychology: Research and Practice, 29,* 190–195.

24

REDUCING COLLEGE STUDENT BINGE DRINKING: A HARM-REDUCTION APPROACH

G. ALAN MARLATT

How many college students drink, and what are the problems they experience with alcohol? A recent random survey conducted with 1,595 students at the University of Washington (Lowell, 1993) provides illustrative data from a large public West Coast university with a total population of over 35,000 students. More than half the students were light drinkers or nondrinkers, but undergraduates tended to be more extreme in their drinking patterns than graduate students. Although there were more abstainers (28.6%) among undergraduates than graduate students (19.0%), among undergraduates there was a higher proportion (31%) of *binge drinkers* (defined as drinking five or more drinks on a single occasion) than among graduate students (17%). A significant minority of undergraduate students (11.4%) reported drinking more than eight drinks on a single occasion.

This research was supported in part by a Research Scientist Award AA00113 and MERIT Award AA05591.

Binge-drinking rates among undergraduate students may be even higher on other campuses. In one survey of drinking practices among freshman-class students at 14 colleges in Massachusetts, Wechsler and Issac (1992) found that over half the men (56%) and a third of women (35%) reported binge drinking. Over a third of the male and one quarter of the female binge drinkers reported engaging in unplanned sexual activity, compared with only 10% of non-binge drinkers. Binge drinkers were six times as likely to drive after consuming large quantities of alcohol and were twice as likely as non-binge drinkers to ride with an intoxicated driver (Wechsler & Issac, 1992).

National surveys reveal that American college students have a slightly higher annual prevalence of any alcohol use (88%) compared with their age peers who do not attend college (85%), 43% of college students report at least one episode of binge drinking in the past 2 weeks, compared with 34% of their age peers (Johnston, O'Malley, & Bachman, 1992). Other surveys indicate that heavy alcohol use is associated with a wide range of harmful consequences for college students, including school failure, relationship difficulties, vandalism, aggression, and date rape (Berkowitz & Perkins, 1986; Engs & Hanson, 1985). Alcohol-related accidents and injuries are the leading cause of death in this age group (National Institute on Alcohol Abuse and Alcoholism, 1984).

Adolescent drinking patterns change over time (Grant, Harford, & Grigson, 1988). Although drinking rates show a significant increase in the transition from high school to the college freshman year (Baer, Kivlahan, & Marlatt, 1994), heavy drinking declines as students get older and assume increased adult responsibilities (Fillmore, 1988; Jessor, Donovan, & Costa, 1991; Zucker, in press). Although the majority of young adults show this "maturing out" pattern over time, longitudinal studies have shown a continuity of drinking problems for a subset (approximately 30%) of heavy drinkers (Fillmore, 1988; Zucker, in press). Among identified risk factors for continued alcohol problems in this age population, environmental factors, such as residence (Larimer, 1992) and "party" settings (Geller & Kalsher, 1990; Geller, Russ, & Altomari, 1986), along with personal dispositional factors, such as family history of alcoholism (Sher, 1991) and history of conduct disorder (Jessor, 1984), have all been identified in the literature. Our prevention efforts, described below, are designed with these two goals in mind: (a) to reduce the harm of alcohol abuse in adolescents who show a pattern of binge drinking and (b) to prevent the development of alcohol dependence among high-risk drinkers.

BACKGROUND RESEARCH AND PRELIMINARY STUDIES

We developed our first alcohol-harm-reduction programs based on past research conducted in our laboratory on determinants of college student drinking (Marlatt, Baer, & Larimer, 1995). With our background and theoretical orientation in behavioral psychology and social cognitive theory, we were initially interested in psychosocial and environmental influences on drinking in this young population. Over the past 2 decades, our laboratory group conducted a series of studies in which college students consumed alcohol under controlled experimental conditions (Caudill & Marlatt, 1975; Collins & Marlatt, 1981; Collins, Parks, & Marlatt, 1985; Higgins & Marlatt, 1975; Marlatt, 1978; Marlatt, Kosturn, & Lang, 1975).

From these background research studies described above, we developed a cognitive–behavioral harm-reduction program for college student drinkers called the Alcohol Skills-Training Program (ASTP). We then conducted a controlled clinical trial to evaluate the impact of ASTP, presented in the form of an 8-week class (Kivlahan, Marlatt, Fromme, Coppel, & Williams, 1990). The design of this study called for random assignment of student drinkers ($N = 43$) to one of three conditions: the ASTP experimental group, a comparison group called the *Alcohol Information School,* or an assessment-only control group. Students were followed for a period of 1 year; a brief description of the study and the results follows.

Student volunteers were recruited to participate in the study by flyers, campus newspaper advertisements, and class announcements asking for participants who wanted to better understand or to change their drinking patterns. Participants who qualified were paid for their time and effort for participation. To qualify, participants needed to be heavy social drinkers, who reported at least one negative consequence of drinking and who indicated no more than mild physical dependence on the Alcohol Dependence Scale (Skinner & Horn, 1984). The sample of students who completed the study were 58% men and 42% women and averaged 23 years of age. On average, baseline drinking averaged 15 drinks per week, and participants reported, for the prior year, an average of 7.5 occasions of driving after consuming 4 or more drinks.

Students assigned to ASTP completed an 8-week course (each weekly class was 2 hours long). Groups of 8 students were led by male and female co-leaders. Each weekly session focused on a specific topic: (a) models of addiction and effects of drinking, (b) estimation of blood alcohol levels and setting drinking limits, (c) relaxation training and lifestyle balance, (d) nutritional information and aerobic exercise, (e) coping with high-risk drinking situations, (f) assertiveness training and drink-refusal skills, (g) an expectancy challenge, in which students consumed placebo beverages in Behavioral Alcohol Research Laboratory (BARLAB), and (h) relapse-prevention strategies for maintaining drinking-behavior changes. In each class, a cognitive–behavioral psychoeducational model was adopted, with didactic presentations and small-group discussions.

In the Alcohol Information School control condition, students received an 8-week course required by the State of Washington for those convicted of underage possession of alcohol or driving under the influence of alcohol. The program content was purely informational, and no new coping skills were taught. Lecture topics included physical and behavioral effects of alcohol, dispelling myths about alcohol, alcoholism problems, and legal aspects of alcoholism. In the assessment-only control group, students participated in all assessment and follow-up measures but received no prevention program until after the completion of the 1-year follow-up period. This control group provided data to assess the effects of completing the assessment forms and self-monitoring drinking.

The impact of the prevention programs was assessed by student evaluations, self-monitored drinking rates, and estimates of weekly drinking rates. Self-monitored drinking (daily drinking diaries) were scored by computer, to yield standard drinks per week and the peak (maximum) blood alcohol level reached each week. At baseline, before program entry, students reported an average of 15 drinks per week and a peak weekly blood alcohol level of 0.13% (0.10% or above defines legal intoxication in most states). At the 1-year follow-up, ASTP participants reported 6.6 drinks per week and a maximum blood alcohol level of 0.07%, compared with 12.7 drinks per week and a maximum blood alcohol level of 0.09%, for students in the Alcohol Information School and 16.8 drinks per week and 0.11% blood alcohol maximum for assessment-only controls. Measures of self-perceived drinking patterns (in which participants reported their drinking over a 90-day period) showed students in the ASTP to have reduced their drinking significantly more than the other two groups when assessed at the 1-year follow-up.

The results of this preliminary harm-reduction study were encouraging. Students involved in the research project reported that they significantly reduced their drinking, and participants in our ASTP condition showed the greatest changes at each follow-up period. Limitations included the small sample size, the use of only volunteer participants, and the lack of collateral reports to validate self-report measures of drinking (the issue of the validity of self-report and the use of collaterals is discussed further below). In addition, participant recruitment was difficult; as expected, students failed to respond to an invitation to participate in an "alcohol program." Once engaged, however, the evaluation feedback indicated that the ASTP was perceived as just as helpful as typical alcohol-education programs.

The second trial of our alcohol-harm-reduction approach was designed to evaluate the effectiveness of the ASTP program presented in different formats (Baer et al., 1992). Students ($N = 134$) were randomly assigned to one of three conditions: a classroom program (a replication of the ASTP program but reduced to six sessions from the original eight), a "correspondence course" (the ASTP program content presented in a written six-lesson format), and a single session of "professional advice," consisting of individual feedback and advice presented to the student. Although this third condition could be considered a minimal-contact control group, other studies indicated that even a single session of advice or motivational enhancement can have a significant impact on subsequent drinking behavior, even for those with serious alcohol problems (Edwards et al., 1977; Miller & Rollnick, 1991).

Student volunteers were again recruited from the campus population through flyers and newspaper ads, offering participation in a skills-training program to learn more about or change personal drinking patterns. As in the first study, participants were offered monetary compensation for the time and effort involved in participating in a research program with multiple assessment periods. To qualify, students needed to report at least one significant alcohol problem and at least 2 days of drinking on an average week with blood alcohol levels approaching 0.10% or above.

The sample of 134 students who enrolled in the program was slightly younger (average age = 21) than those in the first study. Over half of the sample consisted of women. Drinking patterns included an average of six drinking problems as assessed by the RAPI (Rutgers Alcohol Problem Inventory; White & La Bauvie, 1989); students reported drinking an average of 20 drinks per week spread over four drinking occasions (average drinks per occasion = 5, the lower cutoff for binge-level drinking). Estimated peak blood alcohol levels for weekly drinking averaged 0.14%. Students assigned to the correspondence-course format were least likely to complete the assignment; less than half completed all six assignments. Dropouts were less likely in the classroom-group condition, perhaps because of the peer support available in this format. The classroom condition was rated highest in the evaluation forms.

As in the first study, all students significantly reduced their alcohol consumption during the course of the intervention program. Average drinks per week declined overall from 12.5 to 8.5, and peak blood alcohol levels dropped from 0.14% to 0.10%. Reported reductions in drinking levels were maintained significantly over the 2-year follow-up period. At each assessment, participants in the classroom condition drank the least, although differences between the conditions only approached statistical significance. Note that the single session of professional advice showed results comparable to that of the more extensive prevention programs. On the basis of this finding, we decided to begin with a single session of advice as the first of a series of "stepped-care" options. Our major study investigating the effectiveness of a stepped-care prevention model is described next.

OVERVIEW OF THE LIFESTYLES '94 PROJECT

Rational for Stepped Care and Study Design

The Lifestyles '94 project was designed to replicate and extend our earlier studies of brief, harm-reduction programs with college student heavy drinkers. The Lifestyles '94 study differed in several ways from our earlier studies. First, we did not wish to bias the sample by advertising for volunteers for a research program but rather to apply this prevention to a cross-section of heavy drinkers in the college population. As a result, we screened all students in an entering college class and directly invited the heavier drinkers into a longitudinal study. Second, because we wished to test our interventions in a more preventive context, when students are younger and before problems develop, we focused on the 1st year in college (average age = 19) as the time for intervention (our previous samples were 3–4 years older, on average). Third, we wished to test if our brief, 1-hour feedback interview could be used as the first step in a graded program of interventions.

Our previous success with brief interventions suggested that motivational interventions such as feedback and advice may be sufficient to reduce harm associated with drinking among the college population. However, for those who did not respond, more intensive treatments were available. What is not clear is how to move students into more intensive and focused services. We felt that a brief, nonconfrontational feedback session might be the best first step in gaining rapport and access to students, hence facilitating the use of other, more intensive treatments as needed. Finally, the Lifestyles '94 study included specific research-design improvements (from our earlier studies), including a much larger sample size, longer term (4-year) follow-up, the use of collateral reporters to confirm self-reports of alcohol consumption, and the assessment and analysis of individual differences that might explain differential response to treatment. These individual-difference measures included gender, family history of alcoholism, history of conduct-disordered behavior, and type of student residence.

Procedure

Screening and Recruitment

In the spring of 1990, we mailed a questionnaire to all students who were accepted and had indicated an intention to enroll at the

University of Washington the next autumn term (by sending in $50 deposit), who were matriculating from high school, and who were not over 19 years of age. Each student was offered $5 and entrance into a drawing for prizes, for return of the questionnaires. Of 4,000 questionnaires sent, 2,179 completed forms were returned. Of these 2,179, 2,041 students provided usable questionnaires and indicated a willingness to be contacted for future research.

From the screening pool, a high-risk sample was selected. Students were considered high risk if they reported drinking at least monthly and consuming 5–6 drinks on one drinking occasion in the past month, or if they reported the experience of three alcohol-related problems on three to five occasions in the past 3 years, on the Rutgers Alcohol Problem Inventory (RAPI; White & Labouvie, 1989). These criteria identified approximately 25% of the screening sample ($n = 508$). An additional control sample was randomly selected from the pool of 2,041 responders, to provide a normative comparison group ($n = 151$). Because this sample was selected to represent normative practices, it was not restricted to those not previously screened as high risk. As a result, 33 individuals were selected both as high risk and as representing a normative comparison.

When they arrived on campus, students selected for the study were invited into a 4-year longitudinal study of alcohol use and other lifestyle issues, through a letter. Phone calls were used to ensure the receipt of the letter and to respond to questions. Students were asked to agree to be interviewed for approximately 45 minutes and to fill out questionnaires, for a $25 payment during the autumn academic term. Students in the high-risk group agreed also to be randomly assigned to receive or not receive individualized feedback the next academic quarter. All participants agreed to additional questionnaire assessments annually for payment. Of the 508 high-risk students invited, 366 were successfully recruited for the current study; 115 of 151 randomly selected participants were similarly recruited (26 students were in both groups). Comparisons on screening measures between those participants successfully recruited for the project and those not recruited revealed no significant differences in drinking rates (quantity and frequency), alcohol-related problems (RAPI scores), or gender.

Baseline and Follow-Up Assessments

The initial, or baseline, assessment was used to guide individual feedback sessions for those in the experimental group. The interview protocol was based on three standardized interviews: the Brief Drinker Profile (Miller & Marlatt, 1984); the Family Tree Questionnaire (Mann, Sobell, Sobell, & Pavan, 1985); and the Diagnostic Interview Schedule—

Child, or DIS–C (Helzer & Robins, 1988). From these protocols, we assessed typical drinking quantity and frequency, alcohol-related life problems, history of conduct disorder, *Diagnostic and Statistical Manual of Mental Disorders* (American Psychiatric Association, 1987) alcohol-dependency criteria, and family history of drinking problems and other psychopathology. Interviewers were trained members of our research staff. In addition, students completed questionnaires at baseline that included indexes of the type of living situation; alcohol expectancies; perceived risks; psychiatric symptomatology (assessed by the Brief Symptoms Inventory; Derogatis & Spencer, 1982); perceived norms for alcohol consumption; and sexual behavior.

Students completed follow-up assessments through mailed questionnaires in the spring of the 1st year in college and every autumn thereafter throughout college. At the time of this writing (March 1994), we have analyzed data from the junior-year assessment, 2 years after baseline assessment. Note that the 2-year assessment took place in the junior year for those students who pursued their college education continuously (all participants were followed regardless of enrollment or academic status). At each follow-up assessment, students reported their typical drinking patterns, drinking problems, and alcohol dependency, in addition to measures of alcohol expectancies, life events, and psychiatric symptomatology. Details of these assessments are described below.

Measures

Drinking rates. At all assessments, students used 6-point scales to report their typical drinking quantity, frequency, and the single greatest amount of alcohol consumption (peak consumption) over the past month. A second measure of drinking quantity and frequency was obtained at each follow-up assessment, by means of the Daily Drinking Questionnaire (Collins et al., 1985).

Alcohol-related problems and dependence. Alcohol-related problems were assessed with two different methodologies at each assessment. As a measure of harmful consequences, students completed the RAPI, rating the frequency of occurrence of 23 items reflecting alcohol's impact on social and health functioning over the past 6 months. Sample items include "Not able to do homework or study for a test," "Caused shame or embarrassment," and "Was told by friend or neighbor to stop or cut down drinking." The scale is reliable and accurately discriminates between clinical and normal samples (White & Labouvie, 1989). Students also completed the Alcohol Dependence Scale (ADS; Skinner & Horn, 1984), a widely used assessment of severity of dependence symptoms.

Other risk factors. Students were classified as family-history-positive if they reported either natural parent or a sibling as being an alcoholic or problem drinker and reported at least two identifiable problem-drinking symptoms for that individual. History of conduct problems was assessed from 14 items on the DIS–C that reflect common adolescent conduct problems, excluding alcohol or drug use (i.e., truancy, fighting, stealing, and school misconduct). These were coded as present or absent before age 18 and summed to form a scale. College residence was coded as living off campus, in the dormitory system, or in a fraternity or sorority (Greek) house.

Participants

The samples' drinking during high school and the transition into college have been described elsewhere (Baer et al., 1994). Of the 366 high-risk students recruited, 11 were removed from randomization because of extreme levels of drinking and drinking-related problems. These individuals were given our clinical intervention (described below) and referred for additional treatment. In addition, 7 participants returned questionnaires too late for the randomization. The final sample of 348 participants were randomly assigned to receive or not receive intervention. At baseline, before randomization, 63% of the sample of high-risk drinkers (188 women and 160 men) reported drinking at least "1–2 times a week"; 52.2% reported drinking as many as "three to four drinks" on a typical weekend evening of drinking; 61.4% reported binge drinking at least "five to six drinks" on a single drinking occasion during the previous month. On the RAPI, the sample reported an average of 7.5 ($SD = 5.86$) alcohol-related harmful consequences as having occurred at least once over the 6 months before the 1st-year autumn assessment; these students reported an average of 2.2 ($SD = 2.83$) problems occurring at least 3 to 5 times over this same period. Students reported an average of 2.5 ($SD = 1.94$) conduct incidents during childhood, although the distribution was predictably skewed. Most high-risk participants reported between 0 and 3 previous conduct incidents (72.1%). Fifty-three participants (12.9% of the sample) reported significant drinking problems in a first-degree relative (parent or sibling).

Motivational Interviewing

The motivational intervention provided in the winter of the 1st year of college was based on prior research with brief interventions among the college students described above (see also Baer et al., 1992) and motivational interviewing more generally (Miller & Rollnick, 1991).

Students assigned to receive an intervention were contacted first by phone and subsequently by mail to schedule a feedback interview (based on the data obtained the previous autumn term). Students were provided with alcohol-consumption-monitoring cards and asked to track their drinking for 2 weeks before their scheduled interview.

In the feedback interview, a professional staff member met individually with the student, reviewed their self-monitoring, and gave them concrete feedback about their drinking patterns, risks, and beliefs about alcohol effects. Drinking rates were compared with college averages, and risks for current and future problems (grades, blackouts, and accidents) were identified. Beliefs about real and imagined alcohol effects were addressed through discussions of placebo effects and the nonspecifics of the effects of alcohol on social behavior. Biphasic effects of alcohol were described, and the students were encouraged to question if "more alcohol is better." Suggestions for risk reduction were outlined.

The style of the interview was based on techniques of motivational interviewing. Confrontational communications, such as, "You have a problem, and you are in denial" are thought to create a defensive response in the client and were specifically avoided. Instead, we simply placed the available evidence to the client and sidestepped arguments. We sought to allow the student to evaluate their situation and begin to contemplate the possibility of change. "What do you make of this?" and "Are you surprised?" were common questions raised to students, to facilitate conversations about risk and the possibility of behavior change. The technique is quite flexible. Issues of setting (life in a fraternity), peer use, prior conduct difficulties, and family history were addressed only if applicable.

From a motivational interviewing perspective (Miller & Rollnick, 1991), students are assumed to be in a natural state of ambivalence and must come to their own conclusion regarding the need to change behavior and reduce risks. Thus, the goals of subsequent behavior changes were left to the student and not outlined or demanded by the interviewer. This style leaves responsibility with the client and, hence, treats all clients as thoughtful adults. Each student left the interview with a personalized feedback sheet, which compared their responses with college norms and listed reported problems, and a "tips" page, which described biphasic responses to alcohol and placebo effects and provided suggestions for reducing the risks of drinking. Each student was encouraged to contact the Lifestyles '94 project if they had any further questions or were interested in any additional services throughout college.

Results to Date

Early results of this brief intervention with college freshmen have been reported previously (Baer, 1993). In summary, those receiving the feedback interview reported less drinking than those in the control group at the 3-month follow-up. Longer term outcomes are described briefly here; a more thorough report of 2- and 3-year outcomes is currently being prepared. We have been generally successful in retaining the sample of students, with over 88% providing data at the 2-year follow-up assessment.

Multivariate analyses completed on 1- and 2-year postbaseline follow-up points revealed that although all students, on average, reported reduced drinking over time, significantly greater reductions were continually reported by those given the brief advice intervention. Furthermore, two different measures of alcohol-related problems (RAPI and ADS) revealed statistically significant differences between treatment and control groups, with results favoring the treatment group. Despite a general developmental trend of reporting fewer problems over time, examination of mean RAPI scores indicates that those given the brief intervention in the freshman year reported on average 3.3 harmful consequences from alcohol use by the junior year, compared with 4.7 for the high-risk control group. Our random group, which serves as a normative comparison for high-risk students, reported on average 2.4 problems at the junior-year assessment. Thus, these differences, if reliable, reflect meaningful harm reduction among those receiving the motivational intervention.

Analyses of individual differences that might relate to treatment response are complex: There are simply too many factors to analyze simultaneously and retain power to test all possible interactions. Therefore, a series of multivariate repeated-measures analyses of variance was completed, to evaluate each individual-difference factor (i.e., family history of alcoholism, conduct problem history, and type of university residence) as a main effect and in interaction with gender and treatment in the prediction of drinking trends. Both alcohol use rates and alcohol-related problems were evaluated as dependent measures. Analyses completed to date can be summarized by describing a few consistent trends in the data, pertaining to the report of alcohol-related problems. None of the individual-difference factors studied consistently interacted with treatment response: Our treatment seems effective for all students regardless of risk status. However, several trends in our data suggested that not all students are equally at risk, and therefore, treatment may be more important for certain individuals.

First, a family history of alcohol problems did not relate in any consistent fashion to changes to the self-report of drinking problems (no main effects or interactions). However, those with a history of conduct problems or delinquent behaviors reported more alcohol-related problems at all points in time (main effect). In addition, men living in fraternities reported more alcohol-related problems than women or those living elsewhere at all points in time (Sex × Residence interaction). Finally, compared with men, women reported greater decreases in problems over the 2-year follow-up time period (Sex × Time interaction).

The treatment effects described above and the individual differences in developmental trends sum or compile to create a risky picture for certain individuals, in particular, men with conduct histories living in the Greek system. For women, our prevention program appeared to enhance a downward developmental trend for drinking problems, regardless of residence. For men, a different and more troubling picture emerged. Men living in the Greek system reported more problems on average, and all men reported more consistent problems over time. Furthermore, all of these trends were exacerbated by a history of conduct difficulties, and roughly two thirds of those reporting conduct histories were men. As a result, individuals with multiple-risk profiles (men living in fraternities who also have a history of conduct problems) showed the most severe pattern of harmful drinking over time and the least decline. These individuals, therefore, may benefit the most from our preventive programming. For example, in this study, men in the Greek system who did not receive treatment represented our only subgroup in which alcohol-dependence scores actually increased during the first 2 years of college.

Our studies of college student drinking, described above, naturally are limited by the self-report nature of the data pertaining to alcohol use and estimates of blood alcohol levels. Although often criticized, self-reports of drinking behavior often show considerable reliability and validity under conditions of confidentiality and safety (Babor, Stephens, & Marlatt, 1987). We emphasize repeatedly to participants the confidential and nonevaluative nature of our data. Nevertheless, we cannot control completely for possible increases in the social desirability of reporting drinking reductions among those receiving treatment (and developing relationships with program staff), compared with those in the control condition. As a result of this concern, we have spent considerable effort in our latest study collecting confirmatory data from collateral reporters. Collateral data serves two general purposes. First, the procedure communicates to the participant an emphasis on accuracy and a check on self-report. A long history of research on "bogus pipeline" effects in social psychology suggests that this procedure should promote accurate reporting by subjects (Jones & Sigall, 1971). Second, collateral reports constitute a separate data source. With collateral reports, we can check if others perceive changes in our participants' drinking.

In our current longitudinal study, collateral data have provided support for our self-report data. We asked collaterals to rate fairly specific aspects of participants' drinking and the presence of low-level problems. Follow-up assessments resulted in reliable collateral assessments (both within collaterals and between participants and collaterals); reliability for some responses are above .70. Furthermore, these reports begin to confirm some behavioral differences based on self-report between treatment and control groups. In particular, collaterals perceive those in the treatment group as drinking less frequently and drinking to intoxication less often, compared with those in the control condition. These trends appear most evident when collaterals report on female participants, and less so with male participants. Treatment-group participants are also more likely to be seen as having decreased their drinking than are control participants. These data offer one important source of confirmatory evidence that our brief preventive intervention resulted in decreased drinking behavior.

HARM REDUCTION AND THE PREVENTION OF ALCOHOL ABUSE

Our work on the prevention of alcohol problems with college students is best conceptualized as a harm-reduction approach (Marlatt, Larimer, Baer, & Quigley, 1993). We believe that harm reduction provides a conceptual umbrella that covers a variety of previously unrelated programs and techniques in the addictive-behaviors field, including needle-exchange programs for injection-drug users, methadone maintenance for opiate users, nicotine replacement methods for smokers, weight management and eating-behavior-change programs for the obese, and safe-sex programs (e.g., condom distribution in high schools) to reduce the risk of HIV infection and AIDS (Marlatt & Tapert, 1993). Our work in the prevention of alcohol abuse in college students fits well within this domain.

Habits can be placed along a continuum of harmful consequences. The goal of harm reduction is to move the person with alcohol problems along this continuum: To begin to take "steps in the right direction" to reduce harmful consequences. It is important that the harm-reduction model accepts abstinence as the ideal or ultimate risk-reduction goal. But the harm-reduction model promotes any movement in the right direction along this continuum as progress, even if total abstinence is not attained.

Clearly, the excessive use of alcohol is associated with increasingly harmful consequences as consumption increases. Harm reduction is based on the assumption that by reducing the level of drinking, the risk of harm will drop in a corresponding manner. By this logic, total abstinence from alcohol would seem to be associated with the lowest level of harmful consequences. In some areas, however, the benefits of moderate drinking may outweigh the harm-reduction advantages offered by abstinence.

Moderate drinking can have both harmful and helpful consequences. Moderate-to-heavy drinking is reported to increase the risk associated with motor vehicle crashes, birth defects, and harmful interactions with certain medications; yet, it is also associated with reduced risk of cardiovascular disease (National Institute on Alcohol Abuse and Alcoholism, 1992). Given the mixed risks associated with moderate drinking, arguments have been presented on both sides concerning whether abstinence or moderation should be recommended to the public concerning the use of alcohol (Peele, 1993; Shaper, 1993).

Harm-reduction approaches are not limited to the type of individual clinical approaches or self-management training programs described in this chapter. Changes in the physical and social environment can also be implemented, along with public policy changes designed to minimize harm (e.g., legalization of needle-exchange programs). The best results occur when all three methods are combined. For example, to reduce the harm associated with automobile accidents, it is possible to develop better driver-training programs (individual self-management, or autoregulation); to construct safer automobiles and highways (changing the environment); and to introduce safety-enhancing public policies (e.g., reduced speed limit or enhanced enforcement programs). To reduce the harm of drunk driving, it is again possible to combine these three elements: programs mandated for the drunk driver (e.g., programs designed to modify drinking and avoid intoxicated driving); physical and social environmental changes (e.g., use of car ignition systems that are designed to foil the intoxicated driver and designated driver selection); and policy changes (e.g., reducing the blood alcohol minimum for legal intoxication while driving).

As documented in the present review, harm reduction can be applied to the secondary prevention of alcohol problems with moderation as the goal. In sharp contrast to the disease model and Twelve-Step programs that insist on abstinence as the First Step in dealing with any alcohol problem, harm reduction encourages a gradual "step-down" approach to reduce the harmful consequences of alcohol or other drug use. By stepping down the harm incrementally, drinkers can be encouraged to pursue proximal subgoals along the way to either moderation or abstinence.

REFERENCES

American Psychiatric Association. (1987). *Diagnostic and statistical manual of mental disorders* (3rd ed., rev). Washington, DC: Author.

Babor, T. F., Stephens, R. S., & Marlatt, G. A. (1987). Verbal report methods in clinical research on alcoholism: Response bias and its minimization. *Journal of Studies on Alcohol, 48,* 410–424.

Baer, J. S. (1993). Etiology and secondary prevention of alcohol problems with young adults. In J. S. Baer, G. A. Marlatt, & R. J. McMahon (Eds.), *Addictive behaviors across the lifespan* (pp. 111–137). Newbury Park, CA: Sage.

Baer, J. S., Kivlahan, D. R., & Marlatt, G. A. (1995). *High-risk drinking across the transition from high school to college. Alcoholism: Clinical and Experimental Research, 19*(1), 54–61.

Baer, J. S., Marlatt, G. A., Kivlahan, D., Fromme, K., Larimer, M., & Williams, E. (1992). An experimental test of three methods of alcohol risk reduction with young adults. *Journal of Consulting and Clinical Psychology, 60*, 974–979.

Berkowitz, A. D., & Perkins, H. W. (1986). Problem drinking among college students: A review of recent research. *Journal of American College Health, 35*, 1–28.

Caudill, B. D., & Marlatt, G. A. (1975). Modeling influences in social drinking: An experimental analogue. *Journal of Consulting and Clinical Psychology, 43*, 405–415.

Collins, R. L., & Marlatt, G. A. (1981). Social modeling as a determinant of drinking behavior: Implications for prevention and treatment. *Addictive Behaviors, 6*, 233–240.

Collins, R. L., Parks, G. A., & Marlatt, G. A. (1985). Social determinants of alcohol consumption: The effects of social interaction and model status on the self-administration of alcohol. *Journal of Consulting and Clinical Psychology, 53*, 189–200.

Derogatis, L. R., & Spencer, P. M. (1982). *The Brief Symptom Inventory (BSI): Administration, scoring, procedures manual—I*. Baltimore, MD: Johns Hopkins University of Medicine.

Edwards, G., Orford, J., Egert, S., Guthrie, S., Hawker, A., Hensman, C., Mitcheson, M., Oppenheimer, E., & Taylor, C. (1977). Alcoholism: A controlled trial of "treatment" and "advice." *Journal of Studies on Alcohol, 38*, 1004–1031.

Engs, R. C., & Hanson, D. J. (1985). The drinking-patterns and problems of college students: 1983. *Journal of Alcohol and Drug Education, 31*, 65–82.

Fillmore, K. M. (1988). *Alcohol use across the life course*. Toronto, Ontario, Canada: Alcoholism and Drug Addiction Research Foundation.

Geller, E. S., & Kalsher, M. J. (1990). Environmental determinants of party drinking: Bartenders vs. self-service. *Environment and Behavior, 22*(1), 74–90.

Geller, E. S., Russ, N. W., & Altomari, M. G. (1986). Naturalistic observations of beer drinking among college students. *Journal of Applied Behavior Analysis, 19*, 391–396.

Grant, B. F., Harford, T. C., & Grigson, M. B. (1988). Stability of alcohol consumption among youth: A national longitudinal study. *Journal of Studies on Alcohol, 49*, 253–260.

Helzer, J. E., & Robins, L. N. (1988). The Diagnostic Interview Schedule: Its development, evolution, and use. *Social Psychiatry and Psychiatric Epidemiology, 23*(6), 6–16.

Higgins, R. L., & Marlatt, G. A. (1975). Fear of interpersonal evaluation as a determinant of alcohol consumption in male social drinkers. *Journal of Abnormal Psychology, 84,* 644–651.

Jessor, R. (1984). Adolescent development and behavior health. In J. D. Matarazzo, S. M. Weiss, J. A. Herd, N. E. Miller, & S. M. Weiss (Eds.), *Behavior health: A handbook of health enhancement and disease prevention* (pp. 69–90). New York: Wiley.

Jessor, R., Donovan, J. E., & Costa, F. M. (1991). *Beyond adolescence: Problem behavior and young adult development.* New York: Cambridge University Press.

Johnston, L. D., O'Malley, P. M., & Bachman, J. G. (1992). *Smoking, drinking, and illicit drug use among American secondary school students, college students, and young adults, 1975–1991.* Washington, DC: National Institute on Drug Abuse.

Jones, E. E., & Sigall, H. (1971). The bogus pipeline: A new paradigm for measuring affect and attitude. *Psychological Bulletin, 76,* 349–364.

Kivlahan, D. R., Marlatt, G. A., Fromme, K., Coppel, D. B., & Williams, E. (1990). Secondary prevention with college drinkers: Evaluation of an alcohol skills training program. *Journal of Consulting and Clinical Psychology, 58,* 805–810.

Larimer, M. E. (1992). *Alcohol abuse and the Greek system: An exploration of fraternity and sorority drinking.* Unpublished doctoral dissertation, University of Washington, Seattle.

Lowell, N. (1993, December). *University life and substance abuse: 1993 survey* (Report No. 93-4) Seattle: University of Washington, Office of Educational Assessment.

Mann, R. E., Sobell, L. C., Sobell, M. B., & Pavan, D. (1985). Reliability of a family tree questionnaire for assessing family history of alcohol problems. *Drug and Alcohol Dependence, 15,* 61–67.

Marlatt, G. A. (1978). Behavioral assessment of social drinking and alcoholism. In G. A. Marlatt & P. E. Nathan (Eds.), *Behavioral approaches to alcoholism* (pp 35–37). New Brunswick, NJ: Rutgers Center of Alcohol Studies.

Marlatt, G. A., Baer, J. S., & Larimer, M. E. (1995). Preventing alcohol abuse in college students: A harm-reduction approach. In G. M. Boyd, J. Howard, & R. A. Zucker (Eds.), *Alcohol problems among adolescents: Current directions in prevention research* (pp. 147–172). Northvale, NJ: Erlbaum.

Marlatt, G. A., Kosturn, C. F., & Lang, A. R. (1975). Provocation to anger and opportunity for retaliation as determinants of alcohol consumption in social drinkers. *Journal of Abnormal Psychology, 84,* 652–659.

Marlatt, G. A., Larimer, M. E., Baer, J. S., & Quigley, L. A. (1993). Harm reduction for alcohol problems: Moving beyond the controlled drinking controversy. *Behavior Therapy, 24,* 461–504.

Marlatt, G. A., & Tapert, S. F. (1993). Harm reduction: Reducing the risks of addictive behaviors. In J. S. Baer, G. A. Marlatt, & R. J. McMahon (Eds.), *Addictive behaviors across the lifespan: Prevention, treatment, and policy issues* (pp. 243–273). Newbury Park, CA: Sage.

Miller, W. R., & Marlatt, G. A. (1984). *The Brief Drinker Profile*. Odessa, FL: Psychological Assessment Resources.

Miller, W. R., & Rollnick, S. (1991). *Motivational interviewing: Preparing people for change*. New York: Guilford Press.

National Institute on Alcohol Abuse and Alcoholism. (1984). *Report of the 1983 Prevention Planning Panel*. Rockville, MD: Author.

National Institute on Alcohol Abuse and Alcoholism. (1992). *Alcohol alert*. Rockville, MD: Author.

Peele, S. (1993). The conflict between public health goals and the temperance mentality. *American Journal of Public Health, 83*, 805–810.

Shaper, A. G. (1993). Editorial: Alcohol, the heart, and health. *American Journal of Public Health, 83*, 799–800.

Sher, K. J. (1991). *Children of alcoholics: A critical appraisal of theory and research*. Chicago: University of Chicago Press.

Skinner, H. A., & Horn, J. L. (1984). *Alcohol Dependence Scale* (ADS). Toronto, Ontario, Canada: Addiction Research Foundation.

Wechsler, H., & Issac, N. (1992). "Binge" drinkers at Massachusetts colleges. *Journal of the American Medical Association, 267*, 292–293.

White, H. R., & Labouvie, E. W. (1989). Towards the assessment of adolescent problem drinking. *Journal of Studies on Alcohol, 50*, 30–37.

Zucker, R. A. (in press). Alcohol involvement over the life span: A developmental perspective on theory and course. In I. S. Gaines & P. H. Brooks (Eds.), *Alcohol studies: A lifespan perspective*. New York: Springer.

25

STRATEGIES TO REDUCE THE RISK OF HIV INFECTION, SEXUALLY TRANSMITTED DISEASES, AND PREGNANCY AMONG AFRICAN AMERICAN ADOLESCENTS

JOHN B. JEMMOTT III and LORETTA SWEET JEMMOTT

Adolescence is a time of experimentation, as young people strive to develop their identity in preparation for adulthood. For many young people, it is a time of sexual experimentation. Unfortunately, the consequences of such experimentation far too often include increased risk of pregnancy and sexually transmitted disease (STD), including infection

Preparation of this manuscript was supported in part by National Institute of Mental Health Grants R01-MH45668 and R01-MH52035 and National Institute of Child Health and Human Development Grant U01-HD30145.

with human immunodeficiency virus (HIV), the virus that causes acquired immunodeficiency syndrome (AIDS). In this chapter, we discuss the incidence of pregnancy, STD, and HIV among adolescents and research on strategies to prevent these problems.

PREGNANCY, SEXUALLY TRANSMITTED DISEASE, AND HIV INFECTION AMONG ADOLESCENTS

Pregnancy

More than three fourths of American adolescents have had sexual intercourse by the time they are 19 years of age (Centers for Disease Control [CDC], 1991; Hatcher et al., 1994; Sonenstein, Pleck, & Leighton, 1989). Much of this sexual activity occurs without protection against pregnancy and STDs, and lack of protection is especially likely among adolescents who are sexually active during early adolescence (Pratt, Mosher, Backrach, & Horn, 1984; Taylor, Kagay, & Leichenko, 1986; Zelnik, Kantner, & Ford, 1981). One in eight women age 15 to 19 years in the United States becomes pregnant each year, a figure that has changed little since the late 1970s (Hatcher et al., 1994). In 1991, about 1.1 million pregnancies occurred among those age 15 to 19 years, and another 57,000 pregnancies occurred among women age 14 years or younger. Roughly 85% of teenage pregnancies are unintended (Jones et al., 1986; Pratt et al., 1984; Zelnik et al., 1981). Pregnancy is particularly likely during adolescents' initial sexual intercourse experiences, when contraceptive use is especially unlikely (Jones et al., 1986; Pratt et al., 1984; Taylor et al., 1986; Zelnik & Kantner, 1980). One half of all initial adolescent premarital pregnancies occur within the first 6 months after initiation of coitus; 20% occur in the 1st month alone (Zabin, Kantner, & Zelnik, 1979).

Sexually Transmitted Diseases

The problem of pregnancy among adolescents has much in common with the problem of STDs. Obviously, the two problems share a common pathway: They are both caused by sexual behavior. The structural variables that predict pregnancy also predict STDs. Just as there is concern about adolescent pregnancy, there is concern about STDs among adolescents. Although the use of latex condoms can reduce substantially the risk of STD (CDC, 1988; Stone, Grimes, & Magder, 1986), most sexually active adolescents do not use condoms consistently (Hingson, Strunin, Berlin, & Heeren, 1990; L.S. Jemmott & Jemmott, 1990; Keller et al., 1991; Sonenstein et al., 1989). Rates of syphilis, gonorrhea, and hospitalization for pelvic inflammatory disease have been highest among adolescents and decline exponentially with age (Bell & Holmes, 1984). About two thirds of all STDs occur among persons who are 24 years of age or younger (CDC, 1995b).

There are important consequences of STDs. The immediate consequences of STDs can be physical discomfort and embarrassment. However, STDs are often asymptomatic, particularly in women: The adolescent may not know she is infected. Sexually transmitted diseases are sexist. The consequences for women are more substantial than those for men. These more long-term consequences include pelvic inflammatory disease, infertility, cervical cancer, ectopic pregnancy, chronic pelvic pain, and infections passed on to newborns (CDC, 1995b).

Human Immunodeficiency Virus

The STD that is now of greatest concern is HIV, which causes AIDS. A diagnosis of AIDS is accompanied by a truly dismal prognosis. As of June 1995, over 295,000 deaths had been attributed to AIDS (CDC, 1995a). But this represents only part of the problem, for an estimated 1 million people in the United States have been infected by HIV (CDC, 1990), and these people will also develop AIDS. Human immunodeficiency virus infection is transmitted by exposure to infected blood, semen, and vaginal secretions, usually through sexual activities or the sharing of hypodermic needles and other drug paraphernalia by injection-drug users. Human immunodeficiency virus can also spread from infected mothers to their newborns in the womb or during birth, but for the most part, it is the behavior of individuals that creates their risk of HIV infection. To be sure, adolescents represent less than 1% of all reported AIDS cases in the United States (CDC, 1995a). But this statistic may underestimate the potential for HIV infection among adolescents. Young adults in their twenties constitute 18% of all AIDS cases, and because several years typically elapse between the time a person is infected with HIV and the appearance of clinical signs sufficient to warrant a diagnosis of AIDS, many of these young adults were infected during adolescence. The consequences of HIV and AIDS are disability and death.

Inner-City African American Adolescents

The risks associated with unprotected sexual activity are especially great among inner-city African American adolescents. Whether one considers self-reported sexual activities, unintended pregnancy rates, or

STD rates, the statistics on these youths are especially grim. Studies have indicated that African American adolescents, compared with White adolescents, are younger at first coitus (Taylor et al., 1986; Zelnik et al., 1981). Inasmuch as younger adolescents who are having sex for the first time are particularly unlikely to use any contraception (Zelnik et al., 1981), it is not surprising that African Americans are less likely than are Whites to use any contraception at first coitus.

The adolescent pregnancy rate is more than twice as high among African Americans as among Whites. For example, in 1988, 25% of African American female adolescents 15 to 19 years of age and 11% of their White counterparts became pregnant (Henshaw, 1992). In part, the higher rates among African Americans are explained by socioeconomic status (SES) differences. Low SES is associated with increased pregnancy rate, and African Americans are more likely to be of lower SES. Sexually transmitted diseases are substantially more common among African Americans than among Whites. For instance, in 1994, the gonorrhea rates among African American male and female adolescents 15 to 19 years of age were, on average, more than 28-fold higher than those in White adolescents 15 to 19 years old (CDC, 1995b). There are no known biologic reasons to explain why racial or ethnic factors alone would affect risk for STDs. Rather, race and ethnicity are risk makers that correlate with other more fundamental determinants of health status, including poverty, access to quality health care, health-care-seeking behavior, illicit drug use, and living in communities with high prevalence of STDs (Cates, 1987; CDC, 1995b; Hatcher et al., 1994).

The issue becomes even more pressing when it is considered that African American adolescents, particularly those who reside in inner-city areas, would also be at risk for infection with HIV. Although in the United States, the largest number of reported AIDS cases have involved White men who engaged in same-gender sexual activities, AIDS has levied a heavy toll on African Americans (CDC, 1995a). Seroprevalence surveys of civilian applicants for military service, women's health clinics, and Job Corps entrants (CDC, 1990) have indicated higher rates of HIV infection among African Americans as compared with Whites. African Americans are also overrepresented among reported AIDS cases. About 34% of AIDS cases in the United States have involved African Americans (CDC, 1995a), who constitute only 12% of the United States population (U.S. Bureau of Census, 1989). The disparity in reported AIDS cases is particularly great among women and children. As of June 1995, African American women accounted for 55% of adult female AIDS cases, whereas White women accounted for only 24%. More than one half of children under 13 years of age who have AIDS are African American. Compared with White pediatric AIDS cases, African American cases are more likely to have a mother who was exposed due to injection-drug use or heterosexual contact (CDC, 1995a). The prevalence of injection-drug use in the inner city also heightens the risk of HIV infection for African American adolescent residents. Although the adolescents themselves may not use injection drugs—indeed, some data (Turner, Miller, & Moses, 1989) indicate that injection drug use among adolescents is rare—they may have sexual relationships with injection-drug users or with individuals who have had sex with such potentially infected persons. The elevated adolescent pregnancy and STD rates, the potential for sexual involvement with injection drug users, and the potential for perinatally transmitted HIV infection all suggest the urgent risks among African American adolescents.

THEORETICAL FRAMEWORK

A common feature of pregnancy and STD, including HIV, is that they are tied to personal behavior, which suggests the possibility that through the use of behavioral interventions it may be possible to curb these risks. Our research has attempted to develop culture-sensitive, developmentally appropriate, theory-based interventions to curb these risks among inner-city adolescents. A solid theoretical framework is important to intervention research. Theory can be used in the development of intervention activities. Theory can be used to direct attention to the modifiable psychological determinants of risk behavior. By measuring the putative theory-based mediators of intervention-induced behavior change, a better conceptual understanding of risk behavior will emerge. While maintaining an emphasis on a theory-based approach to risk reduction, our research has also focused on practical questions regarding the most effective way to intervene to reduce risk of HIV infection.

As an organizing conceptual framework, our research has drawn on the *theory of planned behavior* (Ajzen, 1991; Madden, Ellen, & Ajzen, 1992), which is an extension of the more widely known *theory of reasoned action* (Ajzen & Fishbein, 1980; Fishbein & Ajzen, 1975; Fishbein, Middlestadt, & Hitchcock, 1994). The theory of reasoned action has been used successfully to predict and explain a broad range of health-related behaviors, including breast self-examination (Temko, 1987); smoking cessation (Fishbein, 1982); weight control (Schifter & Ajzen, 1985); infant feeding (Manstead, Profitt, & Smart, 1983); and contraceptive use (Davidson & Jaccard, 1979). According to the theory, behavior is the result of a specific intention to perform that behavior. A *behavioral intention* is seen as determined by attitude toward the specific behavior, the person's overall positive or negative feeling toward performing the behavior, and by subjective norm regarding the behavior, the person's perception of whether significant others would approve or disapprove of him or her performing the behavior. Thus, people intend to perform a behavior when they evaluate that behavior positively and when they believe significant others think they should perform it. A valuable feature of the theory is that it directs attention to why people hold certain attitudes and subjective norms. *Attitude* toward behavior is seen as reflecting behavioral beliefs, salient beliefs about the consequences of performing the act, and the person's negative or positive evaluation of those consequences. *Subjective norms* are seen as the product of salient beliefs about what specific reference persons or groups think should be done regarding the behavior and the person's motivation to comply with these referents.

According to the theory of reasoned action, attitudes and subjective norms are the sole direct determinants of intentions. Although other variables may affect intentions, these effects are indirect, mediated by the effects of the variables on the attitudinal component, the normative component, or both. However, Ajzen (1985, 1991; Ajzen & Madden, 1986; Madden et al., 1992; Schifter & Ajzen, 1985) recently argued for an exception to the general rule that all variables external to the theory of reasoned action have their effects on intentions and behavior by influencing the attitudinal and normative components. A fundamental assumption of the theory of reasoned action is that its predictive power is greatest for behaviors that are fully under the volitional control of individuals. Ajzen proposed the theory of planned behavior to account for behaviors that are subject to forces that are beyond individuals' control. For instance, performance of the behavior might depend on another person's actions, or the behavior might be performed in the context of strong emotions. Under such circumstances, Ajzen reasoned, prediction of intentions might be enhanced by considering not only attitudes and subjective norms, but *perceived behavioral control*. Defined as the perceived ease or difficulty of performing the behavior, perceived behavioral control reflects past experience as well as anticipated impediments, obstacles, resources, and opportunities.

Perceived behavioral control has affinity with the social–cognitive theory construct of *perceived self-efficacy*, or individuals' conviction that they can perform a specific behavior (Bandura, 1986, 1989, 1994; O'Leary, 1985). In fact, much of what is known about perceived behavioral control comes from research on perceived self-efficacy by Bandura and associates. What the theory of planned behavior does is to place the construct of perceived self-efficacy or perceived behavioral control within a more general framework of the relations among beliefs, attitudes, intentions, and behavior (Ajzen, 1991). Perceived behavioral control is determined by *control beliefs*—beliefs about factors that facilitate or inhibit perfor-

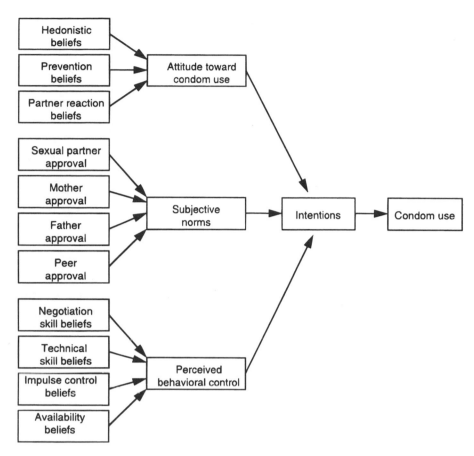

Figure 1. The theory of planned behavior as applied to condom use.

mance of the behavior. We hypothesized that the theory of planned behavior would be valuable to an understanding of sexual risk behavior. Sexual behaviors are performed in the context of strong emotions, and safer sex practices are not always under the individual's direct control because they may require a sexual partner's cooperation. In this view, in addition to inducing positive attitudes and supportive subjective norms, it might be useful to increase perceived behavioral control to implement safer sex practices.

As illustrated in Figure 1, we have applied the theory of planned behavior to HIV-risk-associated sexual behavior. As shown in the figure, the behavior, in this case, condom use, is a function of the intention to use condoms. Consistent with the theory of planned behavior, condom-use intention is determined by attitude toward condoms, subjective norms regarding condoms, and perceived behavioral control over condom use. This reflects our hypothesis that people intend to use condoms when they evaluate condom use positively, when they believe significant others think they should use condoms, and when they feel confident in their ability to implement condom use.

Attitudes and Behavioral Beliefs

Several behavioral beliefs may affect attitude toward condoms. Elicitation surveys conducted with inner-city African American adolescents suggest the importance of three behavioral beliefs in particular. The most obvious perhaps is *prevention beliefs*, or beliefs about whether the use of condoms will prevent pregnancy, STD, and HIV infection. *Hedonistic beliefs*, or beliefs about the effects of condoms on sexual enjoyment, are also likely to be important to condom-use attitude. Thus, to the extent that adolescents believe that using a condom ruins sexual enjoyment, their attitude toward using a condom should be negative. Several studies have tied such beliefs to condom use or intentions to use condoms (Catania et al., 1989; Hingson et al., 1990; L. S. Jemmott & Jemmott, 1992; Valdiserri, Arena, Proctor, & Bonati, 1989). The third type of behavioral belief is *partner-reaction beliefs*, or beliefs about how sexual partners will react to condom use.

Subjective Norms and Normative Beliefs

Subjective norms are determined by *normative beliefs*, which are beliefs about whether salient reference persons or groups would approve or disapprove of the person's engaging in the behavior. People may modulate their risk-associated behavior as a function of their beliefs about how significant others would view it (Fishbein & Middlestadt, 1989). Quite apart from the person's beliefs about other consequences of the behavior—as might be reflected in hedonistic beliefs, for example—if significant others disapprove of a risk behavior, the person may be less likely to engage in that behavior than if they approve of the behavior. The key referents that emerged in elicitation surveys include sexual partner, mother, father, other family members, and peers or friends. It is often argued that sexual partners are more important for women than for men and that they are singularly important in the case of ethnic minority women. Women's relative power in the relationship and their dependency on it (Guttentag & Secord, 1983; Milan & Kilmann, 1987) are likely to affect sexual risk behavior. Studying an African American female adolescent clinic sample, Ager, Shea, and Agronow (1982) found that partner opposition to, or reluctance to use, birth control was a factor in respondents' nonuse of contraception, a common finding in adolescent samples (Thompson & Spanier, 1978; Zabin & Clark, 1981). Studies have also indicated that friends or peers, parents, and other family members may affect adolescents' sexual risk behavior (Fox & Inazu, 1980; Furstenberg, 1971; Handelman, Cabral, & Weisfeld, 1987; Hofferth & Hayes, 1987; Milan & Kilmann, 1987; Morrison, 1985; Nathanson & Becker, 1986).

Perceived Behavioral Control, Self-Efficacy, and Control Beliefs

We have distinguished among four types of control beliefs, which are hypothesized to influence perceived behavioral control. *Negotiation-skill beliefs* concern adolescents' confidence that they can convince a sexual partner to use condoms. Thus, inducing more positive attitudes toward condoms among some African American adolescent women might not increase their intentions to use condoms because of their negotiation-skill beliefs—their perceptions that they may not be able to convince their sexual partner to use a condom. In this connection, it might be important to increase the adolescent's skill at convincing her partner to use a condom. This might result in greater perceived behavioral control or self-efficacy regarding condom use. In fact, there is evidence that behavioral programs that enhance adolescents' interpersonal skills (which should increase their self-efficacy) have produced significant changes in patterns of contraceptive use and unintended pregnancy (Schinke, Gilchrist, & Small, 1979). An intervention that increased assertiveness also increased use of condoms during anal intercourse among White gay men (Kelly et al., 1989). Another study found that a skill-building intervention increased condom use during insertive anal intercourse among White gay men (Valdiserri, Lyter, et al., 1989).

Availability beliefs concern whether adolescents feel confident that they can have condoms available for use when they need them. This would include their beliefs about the financial cost of condoms and beliefs about the appropriateness of carrying condoms. *Impulse-control*, or *self-control*, *beliefs* concern adolescents' confidence that they can control themselves in the midst of a sexual encounter to use condoms. *Technical-skill beliefs* concern adolescents' confidence that they can use condoms with facility, that is, without fumbling or ruining the mood. The focus here is on adolescents' confidence about their abilities, not on their actual abilities. Presumably, confidence and actual skill are correlated, but we are focusing on the belief. To the extent that people believe that they have the requisite skills and resources to use condoms, they should perceive greater control over performance of that behavior.

Variables External to the Theory

The theory of planned behavior does not include many variables that traditionally have been studied in attempts to understand preventive health behavior. Attitudes, subjective norms, and perceived behavioral control are viewed as the sole determinants of intentions and behaviors. The effects on intentions and behaviors of other variables are seen as mediated by their effects on the attitudinal component, the normative component, the perceived-control component, or all three. Thus, for instance, low socioeconomic background, low parental education, belonging to a nonintact or female-headed household, and residing in households with a larger number of children have been linked to heightened sexual activity, lower contraceptive use, and lack of condom use among adolescents (Brown, 1985; Fox & Inazu, 1980; Hofferth & Hayes, 1987; Hogan, Astone, Kitagawa, 1985; Hogan & Kitagawa, 1985; Zelnik et al., 1981). The theory of planned behavior holds that these variables that are external to the model would affect specific behavioral intentions and behaviors by influencing attitudes toward those behaviors, subjective norms regarding them, and perceptions of control over them. In this way, the theory can accommodate variables that are external to it (Ajzen, 1991; Fishbein & Middlestadt, 1989). Behavioral interventions, too, would constitute external variables. Hence, their effects on sexual risk behaviors and intentions would depend on their impact on the attitudinal component, the normative component, the perceived-control component, or all three. Accordingly, our interventions are designed to affect these components.

INTERVENING WITH INNER-CITY AFRICAN AMERICAN ADOLESCENTS

In this section, we discuss studies that are illustrative of our approach to sexual behavior intervention research. This research has emphasized risk of HIV infection, but it is also relevant to pregnancy prevention and STD prevention more broadly. The first study focused on inner-city African American male adolescents (J. B. Jemmott, Jemmott, & Fong, 1992). We were interested in this population for several reasons. First, inner-city African American male adolescents are considered difficult to reach and difficult to maintain in intervention trials. No HIV-risk-reduction intervention studies had been focused on them. In addition, as alluded to earlier, they are at high risk of contracting and spreading STDs, including HIV. For the most part, research on adolescents' sexual behavior has focused on female adolescents. Male adolescents, especially African American male adolescents, typically have been left out of the picture. This is especially troublesome because, aside from abstinence, the most advocated means of protecting against sexually transmitted HIV infection is the male's use of a condom.

The study was designed to test the effectiveness of an intervention on sexual risk behavior and theory-based putative mediators of such behavior among inner-city African American male adolescents. We were also interested in a practical question regarding how HIV-risk-reduction interventions should be implemented with African American male adolescents, namely, whether the gender of the educational facilitator or health educator would moderate effectiveness of the intervention. It is often reasoned that it is important to match the race and gender of participants and facilitators, to maximize the effectiveness of an intervention with ethnic minority individuals. The facilitator of a similar race and gender might have greater credibility, might be able to establish rapport more rapidly, and may have a deeper understanding of pertinent aspects of the participants' lives. According to this line of reasoning, African American male adolescents may be more receptive to behavior-change recommendations if they come from African American male facilitators, as compared with African American female facilitators. We tested that hypothesis.

The participants were 157 inner-city African American male adolescents from Philadelphia who were recruited from a local medical center, community-based organizations, and a local high school. They volunteered for a risk-reduction project, designed to understand African American male youths' behaviors that may create risks such as unemployment, truancy, teenage pregnancy, and STDs, especially AIDS, and to find ways to teach African American male youth how to reduce these risks. The overwhelming majority of the participants (97%) were currently enrolled in school, and their median grade in school was between 9th and 10th grade. Their chief risk was from heterosexual activities, particularly failure to use condoms. Although the mean age of the sample was only 14.6 years, about 83% of the participants reporting having had coitus at least once. About 21% of respondents who had coitus in the past 3 months reported that they never used condoms during those experiences, and only 30% reported always using condoms. Few (less than 5%) participants reported ever engaging in same-gender sexual behavior or injection drug use.

The adolescents were assigned randomly to an HIV-risk-reduction condition or a control condition on career opportunities and to a small group of about 6 boys led by a specially trained male or female African American facilitator. The adolescents in the HIV-risk-reduction condition received an intensive 5-hour intervention. The intervention included videotapes, games, and exercises designed to influence AIDS-related knowledge, behavioral beliefs, attitudes, and perceived behavioral control supportive of safer sex practices. The intervention materials and activities were selected not only to influence the putative theoretical mediators, but also to be interactive and enjoyable. For example, participants played AIDS Basketball, a game in which the adolescents were divided into two teams that earned points by correctly answering factual questions about AIDS. In this game, which adolescents find especially entertaining, there are two-point questions, three-point bonus questions, and one-point foul shot questions. One video, *The Subject Is AIDS*, presented factual information about AIDS. It was narrated by an African American woman and had a multiethnic cast. Another video, *Condom Sense*, addressed negative attitudes toward the use of condoms and hedonistic beliefs. It attacked the idea that sex is substantially less pleasurable when a condom is used. A major character is an African American man who tries to convince a basketball buddy that his girlfriend's request that they use condoms during sex is reasonable. The intervention also addressed perceived behavioral control. A condom exercise focused on familiarity with condoms and the steps involved in the correct use of them. Participants engaged in role-playing situations depicting potential problems in trying to implement safer sex practices, including abstinence.

To control for Hawthorne effects, to reduce the likelihood that effects of the HIV-risk-reduction intervention could be attributed to nonspecific features, including group interaction and special attention, adolescents randomly assigned to the control condition also received a 5-hour intervention. Structurally similar to the HIV-risk-reduction intervention, the control condition involved culturally and developmentally appropriate videotapes, exercises, and games regarding career opportunities. For example, the participants played Career Basketball, in which teams earned points for correctly answering questions about careers and job hunting. This control intervention was designed to be both enjoyable and valuable. Although career-opportunity participants did not learn about AIDS, given the high unemployment among inner-city African American male adolescents, the goal was to provide information that would be valuable to them as they plan their future.

Adolescents in both conditions completed questionnaires before, immediately after, and 3 months after the intervention. These questionnaires were administered not by the facilitators who implemented the interventions, but by project assistants. The project assistants, who were trained African American community residents, emphasized the importance of being honest. The participants signed an agreement, pledging to answer the questions as honestly as possible—a procedure that has been shown to yield more valid responses on sensitive issues. The project assistants told the participants that their responses would be used to create programs for other African American adolescents like themselves and that the programs would be effective only if they answered the questions honestly. In this way, we sought to pit the social responsibility motive against the social desirability motive. In addition, the Marlowe–Crowne Social Desirability Scale (Crowne & Marlowe, 1964) was used to measure the tendency of participants to describe themselves in favorable, socially desirable terms. Analyses of covariance (ANCOVAs), controlling for preintervention measures, revealed that adolescents who received the HIV-risk-reduction intervention subsequently had greater AIDS knowledge, less favorable attitudes toward HIV-risk-associated sexual behaviors, and reduced intentions for such behaviors, compared with adolescents in the control condition. In addition, they expressed more favorable hedonistic beliefs and stronger perceived behavioral control regarding condom use than did their counterparts in the control condition. In summary, these analyses on postintervention data made clear that we achieved changes on theoretically relevant variables thought to mediate behavior change immediately after the intervention. The next question was whether the intervention resulted in less sexual-risk behavior. A 3-month follow-up assessment was designed to address this question.

An important threat to the validity of studies like ours, involving several data-collection points, is the possibility of participant attrition, particularly differential attrition from conditions. Attrition reduces generalizability, and differential attrition from conditions clouds causal interpretation of treatment effects. We allocated participant reimbursement so as to increase the likelihood that participants would return for follow-up. The participants could have received a total of $40. They received $15 at the end of the intervention session, which involved an 8-hour time commitment, and they received $25 at the 3-month follow-up, which involved a 2-hour commitment. Questions are sometimes raised about paying participants in HIV-intervention studies. However, we believe that an important advantage of paying the participants is that it increases the diversity of the sample. If participants are not paid, then only those highly interested in risk reduction are likely to volunteer. By reimbursing participants, we recruit not only the highly interested, but also those who are volunteering just for the money; hence, a broader population.

Of the original participants, 150 completed follow-up questionnaires 3 months after the intervention, a return rate of 95.5%. ANCOVA, controlling for preintervention sexual behavior, indicated that adolescents in the HIV-risk-reduction condition reported less HIV-risk-associated sexual behavior in the 3 months postintervention than did those in the control condition. This analysis was done on a composite risky sexual behavior score, which combined responses to several sexual behav-

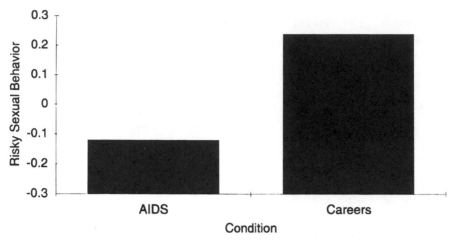

Figure 2. Mean adjusted 3-month follow-up risky sexual behavior among African American male adolescents by condition.

ior questions. Because the behaviors had different means and standard deviations, the responses were standardized to z scores. The composite score was the mean z score. The adjusted means are shown in Figure 2.

Additional ANCOVAs were performed on the specific behaviors that comprised the composite risky sexual behavior score. As shown in Table 1, the participants in the HIV-risk-reduction condition, compared with those in the control condition, reported having coitus less frequently and with fewer women, they reported using condoms more consistently during coitus, and fewer of them reported engaging in heterosexual anal intercourse. In addition, the HIV-risk-reduction-intervention partici-

TABLE 1
Adjusted Means for Specific Sexual Behaviors, by
Experimental Condition

	Condition	
Sexual behavior	HIV-risk-reduction	Career opportunities
Coitus	0.5	0.6
Days had coitus	2.2**	5.5
Coital partners	0.9***	1.8
Rated condom-use frequency	4.4*	3.5
Days did not use condom during coitus	0.6***	2.4
Heterosexual anal sex	0.1*	0.3

Note. For each variable, the preintervention measure was partialed out of the 3-month follow-up measure. Coitus and heterosexual anal sex were coded 0 = did not engage in the behavior in the past 3 months and 1 = did engage in the behavior in the past 3 months. The number of self-reported days on which the participants had coitus ranged from 0 to 50. The number of self-reported coital partners ranged from 0 to 9. Condom-use frequency was rated on 5-point scale from *never* (1) to *always* (5). The number of self-reported days on which the participants had coitus without using a condom ranged from 0 to 19.

*$p < .02$. **$p < .008$. ***$p < .003$.

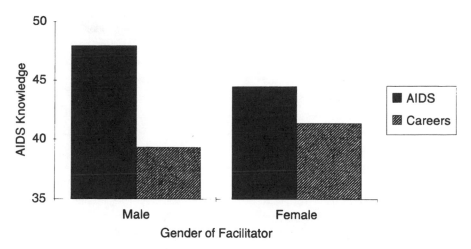

Figure 3. Mean adjusted postintervention AIDS knowledge among African American male adolescents by condition and facilitator gender.

pants still had greater AIDS knowledge and weaker intentions for sexual risk behavior in the next 3 months than did the other participants. Marlowe-Crowne Social Desirability Scale scores were unrelated to preintervention, 3-month follow-up, or amount of change in self-reports of risky sexual behavior. In addition, scores were unrelated to pre, post, or follow-up intentions and attitudes or to changes in these variables.

We had expected Condition × Gender of Facilitator interactions such that the effects of the HIV-risk-reduction intervention would be enhanced with African American male facilitators. Surprisingly, we did not find consistent support for this hypothesis. Consonant with the hypothesis, analyses on the postintervention questionnaire revealed a Condition × Gender of Facilitator interaction such that the HIV-risk-reduction intervention caused a greater increase in AIDS knowledge among participants who had a male facilitator than among those who had a female facilitator (see Figure 3). On the other hand, this interaction was not evident on postintervention measures of hedonistic beliefs, attitudes, perceived behavioral control, or intentions or on 3-month follow-up AIDS knowledge. In addition, the effects of the HIV-risk-reduction intervention on attitudes and sexual behavior measured at the 3-month follow-up were significantly *stronger* with female facilitators than with male facilitators, which was opposite to the predicted result (see Figure 4).

This study indicates that a relatively brief intervention can have impact on theory-based mediators of behavior change and self-reported sexual risk behavior among African American adolescents. Since this initial study, our research has proceeded in two directions. The study raised the question of whether particular conceptual variables are particularly important to achieving behavior change. Thus, one line of work seeks to identify the particular conceptual variables that are most important to achieving intervention-induced sexual risk behavior change. The lack of consistent effects of facilitator gender and the fact that the study included only male adolescents leave unanswered some practical questions about the best way to intervene with inner-city African American adolescents to reduce their sexual risk behavior. A second line of research seeks to elucidate whether the effectiveness of HIV-risk-reduction behavioral interventions is moderated by characteristics of facilitators, such as gender and race.

J. B. Jemmott, Jemmott, Spears, Hewitt, and Cruz-Collins (1992) conducted a study that focused more directly on the conceptual variables that mediate African American female adolescents' intentions to use condoms. J. B. Jemmott, Jemmott, Spears, et al. compared the effects on condom-use intentions of three interventions: (a) a social–cognitive intervention designed to increase hedonistic beliefs and perceived behavioral control regarding condoms, (b) an information-alone intervention designed to increase general AIDS knowledge and specific prevention beliefs, and (c) a general health-promotion intervention designed to provide information about health problems other than AIDS. The subjects were 19 sexually active African American adolescent women from an inner-city family planning clinic. As in the J. B. Jemmott, Jemmott, and Fong (1992) study, all interventions lasted the same amount of time and involved the use of videos and small-group exercises and games.

Analysis of covariance ANCOVA revealed that although participants in both the social–cognitive condition and the information-alone condition scored significantly higher in AIDS knowledge and prevention beliefs than did those in the health-promotion condition, participants in the social–cognitive condition registered significantly greater intentions to use condoms than did those in the other two conditions. In

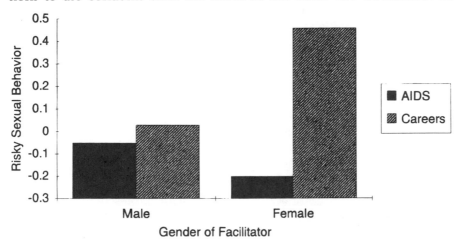

Figure 4. Mean adjusted 3-month follow-up risky sexual behavior among African American male adolescents by condition and facilitator gender.

addition, participants in the social–cognitive condition, as compared with the other conditions, reported significantly greater perceived self-efficacy and behavioral control and more favorable hedonistic beliefs— the two hypothesized mediators of the effects on condom-use intentions of the intervention. Thus, the study indicates that intervention-induced increases in AIDS knowledge and prevention beliefs do not portend changes in plans for sexual risk behavior. In addition, it highlights the importance of self-efficacy and hedonistic expectancies. The sample size was small, thus, it might be argued that the implications are limited. However, significance tests take sample size into account. In this sense, the fact that the intervention had significant effects on intentions and other theoretically relevant variables is impressive.

In another study bearing on conceptual variables, L. S. Jemmott and Jemmott (1992) evaluated an HIV-risk-reduction program for inner-city adolescent women, implemented by a community-based organization, the Urban League of Metropolitan Trenton. The three-session, 5-hour HIV-risk-reduction program drew on the studies by J. B. Jemmott, Jemmott, and Fong (1992) and J. B. Jemmott, Jemmott, Spears, et al. (1992) and used many of the same activities. The intervention, implemented by an African American female facilitator, addressed perceived behavioral control, hedonistic beliefs, and prevention beliefs. The 109 adolescent women who participated in the program scored higher in AIDS knowledge, registered more favorable prevention beliefs and hedonistic beliefs, expressed greater self-efficacy and perceived behavioral control, and scored higher in intentions to use condoms after the program, as compared with before it. Additional analyses indicated that increases in perceived self-efficacy, behavioral control, and hedonistic beliefs predicted increases in intentions to use condoms, whereas increases in general AIDS knowledge and specific prevention beliefs did not. One weakness of the study is that the changes in intentions might not reflect intervention effects, but history. L. S. Jemmott and Jemmott (1992) reasoned that history was an unlikely explanation, because the women participated in intervention groups that were run sequentially over a 6-month period. In this view, it is unlikely that events besides the intervention activities could have occurred between preintervention and postintervention and increased scores for these multiple-intervention groups. Although history cannot account for the differential predictive power of perceived self-efficacy and hedonistic beliefs, as compared with AIDS knowledge and prevention beliefs, the fact that the study did not include a control group that did not receive HIV-risk-reduction interventions limits the ability to draw causal inferences about intervention effects.

J. B. Jemmott, Jemmott, and Hacker (1992) tested the theory of planned behavior as a model of intentions to use condoms among 179

African American (72%) and Latino (19%) inner-city adolescents who attended a minority youth health conference organized by the Urban League of Metropolitan Trenton. Participants completed a confidential preconference questionnaire. Hierarchical multiple regression analysis was used to test the theory of planned behavior. In the first step, condom-use intentions were regressed on attitudes and subjective norms. The squared multiple correlation (.31) was statistically significant, as were the regression coefficients for attitudes and subjective norms. According to the theory of reasoned action, only attitude and subjective norm have direct effects on intentions. Thus, perceived behavioral control should not be significantly related to intentions if attitudes and subject norm are in the regression equation. However, in keeping consistent with the theory of planned behavior, in Step 2 of the hierarchical regression analysis, perceived behavioral control contributed a significant increment (.19) to the squared multiple correlation. Behavioral beliefs about the effects of condoms on sexual enjoyment, normative beliefs regarding sexual partners' and mothers' approval, and control beliefs regarding technical skill at using condoms were associated with condom-use intentions. These results suggest the utility of the theory of planned behavior for understanding condom-use decisions among inner-city African American adolescents.

Group Demographics

The second line of research focused on practical questions about the best way to intervene with inner-city African American adolescents. We were interested in pursuing further the issue of gender of facilitator. Gender of facilitator did not have consistent effects in the J. B. Jemmott, Jemmott, and Fong (1992) study, a result that may have occurred because the study included only male adolescents. Perhaps gender of facilitator is more important if the intervention participants are female adolescents. The literature on disclosure of personal information would suggest that men and women prefer to discuss personal or embarrassing information with a woman rather than a man and that this preference for female confidantes is particularly strong among women (Bennett & Dickinson, 1980; Noller & Callan, 1990). A second issue of interest was the race of the facilitator. We tested the hypothesis that an intervention with African American adolescents would be more effective if the facilitator were African American, as compared with White. Another issue the study addressed was the gender composition of the group. Interventions dealing with sexual behavior of adolescents may be more effective if implemented in single-sex groups. The advantage of single-sex groups may be particularly great for female adolescents. Thus, we tested whether the effectiveness of the intervention would vary depending on whether the group contained participants of only one gender or both male and female adolescents.

The participants were 506 seventh- and eighth-grade African American adolescents recruited from the public junior high schools and elementary schools of Trenton, New Jersey (J. B. Jemmott, Jemmott, & Fong, 1995). They volunteered for a health-promotion project, designed to reduce the chances that teenagers will develop devastating health problems, including cardiovascular diseases, cancers, and AIDS. Although the mean age of the participants was only 13.1 years, about 55% of respondents reported having experienced coitus at least once, and about 31% of all respondents reported having coitus in the past 3 months. About 25% of those reporting coitus in the past 3 months indicated that they never used condoms during those experiences, whereas 30% indicated that they always used condoms during those experiences.

The adolescents were assigned randomly to either an HIV-risk-reduction condition or the control condition and to a small group that was either homogeneous or heterogeneous in gender and that was led by a specially trained male or female facilitator who was African American or White. Adolescents in the HIV-risk-reduction condition received a 5-hour intervention designed to influence variables theoretically important to behavior change and to be meaningful and culturally and developmentally appropriate for young, inner-city African American adolescents. From a theoretical perspective, the intervention was designed (a) to increase perceived self-efficacy/behavioral control regarding the ability to implement condom use, including confidence that they could get their partner to use one; (b) to address hedonistic beliefs to allay participants' fears regarding adverse consequences of condoms on sexual enjoyment; and (c) to increase general knowledge of AIDS and STDs and specific beliefs regarding the use of condoms to prevent sexually transmitted HIV infection. As in our previous intervention studies, videotapes, games, and exercises were used to facilitate learning and active participation.

Participants in the control condition received an intervention targeting behaviors (e.g., dietary and exercise habits and cigarette smoking) that affect the risk of certain health problems other than AIDS. These health problems, including cardiovascular disease, hypertension, and certain cancers, are leading causes of morbidity and mortality among African Americans (Gillum, 1982; Ibrahim, Chobanian, Horan, & Roccella, 1985; Page & Asire, 1985). Structurally similar to the HIV-risk-reduction intervention, the general health-promotion intervention also lasted 5 hours and used culturally and developmentally appropriate videotapes, exercises, and games to reinforce learning and to encourage active participation.

Before, immediately after, 3 months after, and 6 months after the intervention the participants completed questionnaires of intentions, hedonistic beliefs, prevention beliefs, perceived self-efficacy to use condoms, and AIDS knowledge. The Marlowe–Crowne Social Desirability Scale, included in the preintervention questionnaire, was used to measure the tendency of participants to describe themselves in favorable, socially desirable terms. Adolescents in the HIV-risk-reduction condition subsequently expressed stronger intentions to use condoms; had more favorable beliefs about the effects of condoms on sexual enjoyment and about the ability of condoms to prevent pregnancy, STD, and AIDS; had greater perceived self-efficacy to use condoms; and had greater knowledge about AIDS than did those in the control condition, controlling for preintervention measures of the particular dependent measure. Of the original participants, 489 (97%) took part in the 3-month follow-up, and 469 (93%) took part in the 6-month follow-up. The effects of the HIV-risk-reduction intervention on the conceptual variables were sustained over the 6-month time interval. At both follow-ups, participants in the HIV-risk-reduction intervention scored higher on intentions to use condoms, AIDS knowledge, hedonistic beliefs, and perceived self-efficacy to use condoms than did the participants in the health-promotion condition. Although there were no significant effects of the HIV-risk-reduction intervention on self-reports of unprotected coitus at the 3-month follow-up, there was a significant effect at the 6-month follow-up: Adolescents who had received the HIV-risk-reduction intervention reported fewer days on which they had coitus without using a condom in the past 3 months than did those who had received the health-promotion intervention, controlling for preintervention self-reports.

Pearson product–moment correlations and multiple regression analyses revealed that scores on the Marlowe–Crowne Social Desirability Scale were unrelated to self-reports of condom use preintervention, at the 3-month follow-up, or at the 6-month follow-up or to changes in self-reports of condom use from preintervention to the 3-month or 6-month follow-up. Marlowe–Crowne Social Desirability scores were also unrelated to preintervention, postintervention, 3-month follow-up, or 6-month follow-up intentions to use condoms or to changes in intentions. Moreover, hierarchical multiple regression analyses revealed that the scores did not interact with experimental condition to affect self-reported condom use or intentions at postintervention, 3-month follow-up, or 6-month follow-up. The scores were also unrelated to self-reported condom use, intentions, or changes in these variables in the subsample of adolescents in the AIDS condition.

Analyses also examined whether effects of the intervention varied as a function of race of the facilitator, gender of the facilitator, gender of the participants, and gender composition of the intervention groups. We tested these interactions on four classes of variables: (a) the participants' perceptions of the intervention—how much they liked it, how much they talked, and how much they felt they learned; (b) the facilitators' perceptions of how much the participants liked it, talked, and learned from the intervention; (c) AIDS knowledge test, prevention beliefs, hedonistic beliefs, intentions, and perceived behavioral control; and (d) self-reported unprotected sexual intercourse. Results revealed that none of the interactions were statistically significant. Race of the facilitator, the gender of the facilitator, the gender of the participants, and the gender composition of the intervention group did not moderate facilitators' reports of how the participants reacted to the intervention or participants' own reports of their reactions to the interventions: How much they liked it, how much they talked, and how much they felt they had learned. In addition, these factors did not moderate effects of the intervention on AIDS knowledge, prevention beliefs, hedonistic beliefs, perceived self-efficacy, intentions, or self-reports of unprotected coitus. The effects of the HIV-risk-reduction intervention were about the same, irrespective of the race of the facilitator, the gender of the facilitator, the gender of the participants, and the gender composition of the intervention group.

CONCLUSION

First, these studies suggest that intensive 1-day interventions can influence theory-based motivational determinants of sexual risk behavior among inner-city African American adolescents, including African American male adolescents. Second, the studies suggest that it is possible to influence self-reports of unprotected coitus among inner-city African American adolescents, including African American male adolescents. Third, the present results suggest that the influence of the race and gender of facilitators or health educators may be more complex than previously assumed.

The lack of effects of race of facilitator is particularly surprising. In theory, African American facilitators should have a better grasp of the language, values, and experiences of African American adolescents, they should be better able to adapt prevention strategies to suit the adolescents, they should be less likely to offend the adolescents by using inaccurate and pernicious group stereotypes, and they should be able to establish rapport more readily and rapidly. This should presumably translate into better intervention outcomes. Yet, we found that race matching did not enhance intervention effects.

Although one possible explanation for this is that race matching is less important than previously assumed, a number of additional explanations should also be considered. First, perhaps the race matching did not matter because the intervention itself was culturally sensitive. All of the intervention materials had been selected to be culturally appropriate. Second, the activities were highly structured and engaging, which would have minimized the importance of individual facilitators. Third, all facilitators trained together, which may have served to calibrate their behavior. The training of the facilitators emphasized the importance of implementing the interventions according to the protocol, which might have further minimized any differences among facilitators with different characteristics. Thus, the culturally sensitive nature of the intervention and the strict nature of the facilitator-training protocol may have attenuated any effects of facilitator race. In the absence of such training, if culturally inappropriate materials had been used, and if the intervention had been less highly structured, differences in facilitator behavior by race might have emerged. Under such circumstances, results might have been different from those observed in the present study. This, of course, is an empirical question.

The significant effects of the interventions studies cannot be explained as a simple result of special attention received by the adolescents in the HIV-risk-reduction-intervention conditions. Participants in the control conditions (whether career opportunities or general health promotion) received the same amount of attention as those in the HIV-risk-reduction condition. Participants in the HIV-risk-reduction and control interventions went through similar activities that lasted the same amount of time.

By its very nature, sexual risk behavior is private behavior and, consequently, must be assessed with indirect measures. Thus, in our studies, *self-reports* of sexual risk behaviors, not sexual risk behaviors, were examined. Interpretations of findings should include consideration of the possibility that the participants' reports of their sexual practices might have been to some degree unintentionally or intentionally inaccurate. On several grounds, however, confidence about the accuracy of the responses in the present experiment is warranted. The fact that participants were asked to recall sexual risk behavior over a relatively brief period of time (i.e., 3 months) would facilitate their ability to recall their behavior. In addition, we used a number of techniques to make it less likely that participants in the present study would minimize or exaggerate reports of their sexual experiences, (a) code numbers rather than names were used on the questionnaires, (b) facilitators were not involved in any way in the administration of questionnaires, (c) the importance of responding honestly was emphasized, and (d) participants were assured that their responses would be kept confidential, and they signed an agreement to respond honestly. In addition, if concern about how they would be viewed by others influenced respondents' reports of their sexual behavior, the adolescents who were higher in the need for social approval might have differed from the other adolescents in self-reported sexual risk behavior or in the change in their reports after the HIV-risk-reduction intervention. However, analyses in the J. B. Jemmott, Jemmott, and Fong (1992) study and the J. B. Jemmott, Jemmott, and Fong (1995) study revealed that preintervention and follow-up self-reports of sexual risk behavior and the change in reported behavior were unrelated to social desirability response bias. Nevertheless, interpretations of our findings should include consideration of the possibility that the participants' self-reports might have been inaccurate.

In future research, it would be valuable to include other measures of sexual risk behavior. Another approach to assessing sexual risk behavior would be to measure physiological proxy variables that are indicative of unprotected sexual intercourse. For example, clinically documented STDs (e.g., chlamydia, gonorrhea, and syphilis) would provide valuable information. Still, note that even STD testing is not a perfect measure of unprotected sexual intercourse because it underestimates the actual frequency of unprotected sexual intercourse. Although a positive STD test establishes that unprotected sexual intercourse has occurred, a negative test result does not rule out the possibility that unprotected sexual intercourse has occurred. The test could be negative, not because of the practice of safer sex or abstinence, but because of unprotected sex with a partner who was not infected.

One common argument against HIV-risk-reduction education programs for adolescents and children has been that exposing them to information about sex will encourage them to engage in sexual activity. Our data, however, provide some evidence that the opposite may be true. Adolescents who received the HIV-risk-reduction intervention were less likely to engage in sexual activity, and those who did were more likely to engage in safe sexual activity. Thus, the fear that providing adolescents with information about AIDS will result in greater sexual activity is perhaps simply a fear.

Given the widely recognized potential risk of pregnancy and STD, including HIV, among inner-city African American adolescents, the results of these studies are encouraging. They suggest that relatively brief but intensive intervention can have significant impact on sexual risk behavior and theory-based mediators of such behavior among African American inner-city adolescents. We are optimistic that continued work along these lines will increase understanding of the social psychology of sexual risk behavior and will reduce the problems of pregnancy and STD, including HIV, among African American adolescents.

REFERENCES

Ager, J., Shea, F., & Agronow, S. (1982). Method discontinuance in teenage women. In I. Stuart & C. Wells (Eds.), *Pregnancy in adolescence* (pp. 236–263). New York: Van Nostrand Reinhold.

Ajzen, I. (1985). From intentions to actions: A theory of planned behavior. In J. Kuhl and J. Beckmann (Eds.), *Action-control: From cognition to behavior*, (pp. 11–39). Heidelberg: Springer.

Ajzen, I. (1991). The theory of planned behavior. *Organizational Behavior and Human Decision Processes, 50*, 179–211.

Ajzen, I., & Fishbein, M. (1980). *Understanding attitudes and predicting social behavior.* Englewood Cliffs, NJ: Prentice Hall.

Ajzen, I., & Madden, T. (1986). Prediction of goal-directed behavior: Attitudes, intentions, and perceived behavioral control. *Journal of Experimental Social Psychology, 22*, 453–474.

Bandura, A. (1986). *Social foundations of thought and action: A social cognitive theory.* Englewood Cliffs, NJ: Prentice Hall.

Bandura, A. (1989). Perceived self-efficacy. In V. M. Mays, G. W. Albee, & S. F. Schneider (Eds.), *Primary prevention of AIDS: Psychological approaches* (pp. 128–141). Newbury Park, CA: Sage.

Bandura, A. (1994). Social cognitive theory and exercise of control over HIV infection. In R. DiClemente & J. Peterson (Eds.), *Preventing AIDS: Theory and practice of behavioral interventions* (pp. 25–60). New York: Plenum.

Bell, T. A., & Holmes, K. K. (1984). Age-specific risks of syphilis, gonorrhea, and hospitalized pelvic inflammatory disease in sexually experienced U.S. women. *Sexually Transmitted Diseases, 7*, 291.

Bennett, S. M., & Dickinson, W. B. (1980). Student–parent rapport and parent involvement in sex, birth control, and venereal disease education. *Journal of Sex Research, 16*, 114–130.

Brown, S. V. (1985). Premarital sexual permissiveness among Black adolescent females. *Social Psychology Quarterly, 48*, 381–387.

Catania, J. A., Dolcini, M. M., Coates, T. J., Kegeles, S. M., Greenblatt, R. M., Puckett, S., Corman, M., & Miller, J. (1989). Predictors of condom use and multiple partnered sex among sexually-active adolescent women: Implications for AIDS-related health interventions. *Journal of Sex Research, 26*, 514–524.

Cates, W., Jr. (1987). Epidemiology and control of sexually transmitted diseases: Strategic evolution. *Infectious Disease Clinics of North America, 1*, 1–23.

Centers for Disease Control. (1988). Condoms for the prevention of sexually transmitted diseases. *Morbidity and Mortality Weekly Report, 37,* 133–137.

Centers for Disease Control. (1990). *National HIV seroprevalence surveys: Summary of results. Data from serosurveillance activities through 1989.* Atlanta, GA: Author.

Centers for Disease Control. (1991). Premarital sexual experience among adolescent women—United States, 1970–1988. *Morbidity and Mortality Weekly Report, 39,* 929–932.

Centers for Disease Control and Prevention (CDC). (1995a). *HIV/AIDS Surveillance Report, 7*(1), 1–34.

Centers for Disease Control and Prevention (CDC). (1995b). *Sexually transmitted disease surveillance, 1994,* Atlanta, GA: Author.

Chu, S., Buehler, J., & Berkelman, R. (1990). Impact of the human immunodeficiency virus epidemic on mortality in women of reproductive age. *Journal of the American Medical Association, 264,* 225–229.

Crowne, D., & Marlowe, D. (1964). *The approval motive.* New York: Wiley.

Davidson, A. R., & Jaccard, J. J. (1979). Variables that moderate the attitude-behavior relation: Results of a longitudinal survey. *Journal of Personality and Social Psychology, 37,* 1364–1376.

Fishbein, M. (1982). Social psychological analysis of smoking behavior. In J. R. Eiser (Ed.), *Social psychology and behavioral medicine* (pp. 179–197). New York: Wiley.

Fishbein, M., & Ajzen, I. (1975). *Belief, attitude, intention and behavior.* Boston: Addison-Wesley.

Fishbein, M., & Middlestadt, S. (1989). Using the theory of reasoned action as a framework for understanding and changing AIDS-related behaviors. In V. Mays, G. Albee, & S. Schneider (Eds.), *Primary prevention of AIDS: Psychological approaches* (pp. 93–110). Newbury Park, CA: Sage.

Fishbein, M., Middlestadt, S., & Hitchcock, P. J. (1994). Using information to change sexually transmitted disease-related behaviors: An analysis based on the theory of reasoned action. In R. DiClemente & J. Peterson (Eds.), *Preventing AIDS: Theory and practice of behavioral interventions* (pp. 61–78). New York: Plenum.

Fox, G. L., & Inazu, J. K. (1980). Patterns and outcomes of mother-daughter communication about sexuality. *Journal of Social Issues, 36,* 7–29.

Furstenberg, F. F. (1971). Birth control experience among pregnant adolescents: The process of unplanned parenthood. *Social Problems, 19,* 192–203.

Gillum, R. F. (1982). Coronary heart disease in Black populations: I. Mortality and morbidity. *American Heart Journal, 104,* 839–843.

Guttentag, M., & Secord, P. F. (1983). *Too many women?* Beverly Hills, CA: Sage.

Handelman, C. D., Cabral, R. J., & Weisfeld, G. E. (1987). Sources of information and adolescent sexual knowledge and behavior. *Journal of Adolescent Research, 2,* 455–463.

Hatcher, R. A., Trussell, J., Stewart, F., Stewart, G. K., Kowal, D., Guest, F., Cates, W., Jr., & Policar, M. S. (1994). *Contraceptive technology* (16th ed., rev.). New York: Irvington.

Henshaw, S. K. (1992). *U.S. teenage pregnancy statistics*. New York: Alan Guttmacher Institute.

Hingson, R. W., Strunin, L., Berlin, B., & Heeren, T. (1990). Beliefs about AIDS, use of alcohol and drugs, and unprotected sex among Massachusetts adolescents. *American Journal of Public Health, 80*, 295–299.

Hofferth, S., & Hayes, C. (1987). *Risking the future (Vol. 2)*. Washington, DC: National Academy Press.

Hogan, D. P., Astone, N. M., & Kitagawa, E. M. (1985). Social and environmental factors influencing contraceptive use among Black adolescents. *Family Planning Perspectives, 17*, 165–169.

Hogan, D. P., & Kitagawa, E. M. (1985). The impact of social status, family structure, and neighborhood on the fertility of Black adolescents. *American Journal of Sociology, 90*, 825–855.

Ibrahim, M., Chobanian, A. V., Horan, M., & Roccella, E. J. (1985). Hypertension prevalence and the status of awareness, treatment, and control in the United States: Final report of the Subcommittee on Definition and Prevalence of the 1984 Joint National Committee on Detection, Evaluation, and Treatment of High Blood Pressure. *Hypertension, 7*, 453–468.

Jemmott, J. B. III, Jemmott, L. S., & Fong, G. T. (1992). Reductions in HIV-risk-associated sexual behaviors among Black male adolescents: Effects of an AIDS prevention intervention. *American Journal of Public Health, 82*, 372–377.

Jemmott, J. B. III, Jemmott, L. S., & Fong, G. T. (1995). *Reducing the risk of AIDS in Black adolescents: Evidence for the generality of intervention effects*. Unpublished manuscript, Princeton University, Princeton, NJ.

Jemmott, J. B. III, Jemmott, L. S., & Hacker, C. I. (1992). Predicting intentions to use condoms among African American adolescents: The theory of planned behavior as a model of HIV risk associated behavior. *Journal of Ethnicity and Disease, 2*, 371–380.

Jemmott, J. B. III, Jemmott, L. S., Spears, H., Hewitt, N., & Cruz-Collins, M. (1992). Self-efficacy, hedonistic expectancies, and condom-use intentions among inner-city Black adolescent women: A social cognitive approach to AIDS risk behavior. *Journal of Adolescent Health, 13*, 512–519.

Jemmott, J. B. III, & Miller, S. M. (in press). Women's reproductive decisions in the context of HIV infection. In A. O'Leary & L. S. Jemmott (Eds.), *Women and AIDS: Issues in coping and caring*. New York: Plenum.

Jemmott, L. S., & Jemmott, J. B. III. (1990). Sexual knowledge, attitudes, and risky sexual behavior among inner-city Black male adolescents. *Journal of Adolescent Research, 5*, 346–369.

Jemmott, L. S., & Jemmott, J. B. III. (1992). Increasing condom-use intentions among sexually active inner-city Black adolescent women: Effects of an AIDS prevention program. *Nursing Research, 41*, 273–279.

Jones, E. F., Forrest, J. D., Goldman, N., Henshaw, S. Lincoln, R., Rosoff, J. I., Westoff, C. F., & Wulf, D. (1986). *Teenage pregnancy in industrialized countries*. New Haven, CT: Yale University Press.

Keller, S. E., Barlett, J. A., Schleifer, S. J., Johnson, R. L., Pinner, E., & Delaney, B. (1991). HIV-relevant sexual behavior among a healthy inner-city heterosexual adolescent population in an endemic area of HIV. *Journal of Adolescent Health, 12*, 44–48.

Kelly, J. A., Lawrence, J. S., Hood, H. V., & Brasfield, T. L. (1989). Behavioral intervention to reduce AIDS risk activities. *Journal of Consulting and Clinical Psychology, 57*, 60–67.

Madden, T. J., Ellen, P. S., & Ajzen, I. (1992). A comparison of the theory of planned behavior and the theory of reasoned action. *Personality and Social Psychology Bulletin, 18*, 3–9.

Manstead, A. S. R., Profitt, C., & Smart, J. L. (1983). Predicting and understanding mothers' infant-feeding intentions and behaviors. *Journal of Personality and Social Psychology, 44*, 657–671.

Milan, R. J., & Kilmann, P. R. (1987). Interpersonal factors in premarital contraception. *Journal of Sex Research, 23*, 289–321.

Morrison, D. (1985). Adolescent contraceptive behavior: A review. *Psychological Bulletin, 98*, 538–568.

Nathanson, C. A., & Becker, M. H. (1986). Family and peer influence on obtaining a method of contraception. *Journal of Marriage and the Family, 48*, 513–526.

Noller, P., & Callan, V. J. (1990). Adolescents' perceptions of the nature of their communication with parents. *Journal of Youth and Adolescence, 19*, 349–362.

O'Leary, A. (1985). Self-efficacy and health. *Behavioral Research and Therapy, 23*, 437–451.

Page, H. S., & Asire, A. J. (1985). *Cancer rates and risks* (NIH Publication No. 85-691, 3rd ed.). Bethesda, MD: National Institutes of Health.

Pratt, W., Mosher, W., Bachrach, C., & Horn, M. (1984). Understanding U. S. fertility: Findings from the National Survey of Family Growth, Cycle III. *Population Bulletin, 39*, 1–42.

Schifter, D. E., & Ajzen, I. (1985). Intention, perceived control, and weight loss: An application of the theory of planned behavior. *Journal of Personality and Social Psychology, 49*, 843–851.

Schinke, S. P., Gilchrist, L. D., & Small, R. W. (1979). Preventing unwanted adolescent pregnancy: A cognitive behavioral approach. *American Journal of Orthopsychiatry, 49*, 81–88.

Sonenstein, F. L., Pleck, J. H., & Leighton, C. K. (1989). Sexual activity, condom use and AIDS awareness among adolescent males. *Family Planning Perspectives, 21*, 152–158.

Stone, K. M., Grimes, D. A., & Magdeer, L. S. (1986). Personal protection against sexually transmitted diseases. *American Journal of Obstetrics and Gynecology, 155*, 180–188.

Taylor, H., Kagay, M., & Leichenko, S. (1986). *American teens speak: Sex myths, TV, and birth control*. New York: Planned Parenthood Federation of America.

Temko, C. (1987). Seeking medical care for a breast cancer symptom: Determinants of intentions to engage in prompt or delay behavior. *Health Psychology, 6*, 305–328.

Thompson, L., & Spanier, G. (1978). Influence of parents, peers and partners on the contraceptive use of college men and women. *Journal of Marriage and the Family, 40*, 481–492.

Turner, C., Miller, H., & Moses, L. (1989). *AIDS: Sexual behavior and intravenous drug use*. Washington, DC: National Academy Press.

U.S. Bureau of the Census. (1989). Projects of the population of the United States, by age, sex, and race: 1988–2080. *Current population reports* (Series P-25, No. 1018). Washington, DC: U.S. Government Printing Office.

Valdiserri, R. O., Arena, V. C., Proctor, D., & Bonati, F. A. (1989). The relationship between women's attitudes about condoms and their use: Implications for condom promotion programs. *American Journal of Public Health, 79*, 499–503.

Valdiserri, R. O., Lyter, D. W., Leviton, L. C., Callahan, C. M., Kingsley, L. A., & Rinaldo, C. R. (1989). AIDS prevention in homosexual and bisexual men: Results of a randomized trial evaluating two risk reduction interventions. *AIDS, 3*, 21–26.

Zabin, L., & Clark, S. D., Jr. (1981). Why they delay: A study of teenage family planning clinic patients. *Family Planning Perspectives, 13*, 205–217.

Zabin, L., Kantner, J., & Zelnik, M. (1979). The risk of adolescent pregnancy in the first months of intercourse. *Family Planning Perspectives, 11*, 215–226.

Zelnik, M., Kantner, J. F., & Ford, K. (1981). *Sex and pregnancy in adolescence*. Beverly Hills, CA: Sage.

V

PSYCHOLOGISTS AS HEALTH CARE PROVIDERS

INTRODUCTION

The last chapter in the book, chapter 26, "Expanding Roles in the Twenty-First Century," is written by six psychologists whose experiences and expertise provide both an overview of issues confronting the science and practice of psychology and a vision of the profession's future. Patrick H. DeLeon et al. strongly suggest that the profession is in need of individuals who understand the "big picture" of health care from a public policy vantage point. By taking steps to place psychology in the public eye and assuring that we take into account the societal and political forces that shape health care, research, and educational funding, only then can our relatively young profession hope to prosper. The chapter presents the various perspectives from the various authors' uniques perspectives from which to view psychologists' role as health care providers.

From a scientific perspective, DeLeon et al. challenge the field to address and mend the schism between scientists and practitioners. Issues are discussed that if not attended to, will impede even the best trained scientific psychologist from finding meaningful employment or that will interfere with the important contributions the field can make to society at large.

From a practice perspective, the chapter looks at the effects of congressional action (or inaction) and the corporatization of health care through various managed care paradigms to encourage the field to continue its evolution. DeLeon et al. believe that sticking to the field's identity as only a mental health field would go against the current of today's health care changes.

A section next reviews the educational and training issues that will influence the very survival of the field. DeLeon et al. point to the uniqueness of the scientist/practitioner tradition in the education of clinical psychologists and how psychologists provide not only health care but also new knowledge to the understanding of illness. The chapter discusses advocacy to ensure continued funding for the training of psychologists and for public information about the role of psychology, to guarantee our inclusion in the twenty-first century's health care system.

Looking at psychology's goals in the public interest, the chapter next highlights several projects of the American Psychological Association. Conferences on psychosocial and behavioral factors in women's health, projects on violence—both youth violence and male violence against women—and the Public Interest Directorate's involvement in occupational safety and workplace stress are reviewed.

Next, the chapter discusses the importance of psychology's expanding its scope of practice to include the authority to prescribe medication. The reasons for this expanded role are outlined, and levels of training are suggested to prepare psychologists for this new role.

The chapter, and the book, ends with a timely reflection on the rapid maturation of the relatively young field of psychology. By proactively addressing society's needs, psychology can not only improve the human condition but also make for itself, and our colleagues in the field, unlimited opportunities.

26

EXPANDING ROLES IN THE TWENTY-FIRST CENTURY

PATRICK H. DELEON, WILLIAM C. HOWELL,
RUSS NEWMAN, ANITA B. BROWN,
GWENDOLYN PURYEAR KEITA, and JOHN L. SEXTON

I (Patrick DeLeon) have had the opportunity to serve on Capitol Hill for slightly more than 2 decades, and without question, it has been a very satisfying and stimulating experience. For those of us who work in a public sphere, we know, however, that at some point we will leave. The experience is a constant reminder of how personal and how "temporary" the political/public policy process is. In each case, it seems not long ago that some other very impressive individual served in an important capacity, whether this be for the Appropriations, Finance, or Labor and Human Resources Committee. Although I am a chief of staff, I am unaware of who served in that capacity for the previous chairpersons.

This represents a fundamentally different way of looking at the world, or at one's professional identity, than many of our colleagues

The views expressed do not necessarily reflect those of the U.S. Army, Navy, or Department of Defense.

typically do. Working within the political process, the philosophy of doing what can be done to improve society and, in all candor, not really worrying very much about that which can not be influenced was adopted. The public policy/political process is truly evolutionary in nature. Over the years, it has become evident that it cannot be controlled by any one individual or special interest group. Furthermore, when one leaves Capitol Hill, one has truly left!

BARRIERS

Over the past 2 decades, it has become very clear that although our colleagues in psychology—whether they be clinicians, researchers, or educators—are extraordinarily intelligent and professionally competent individuals, at the same time, they are surprisingly narrow in their perspective. If one seeks a researcher in a given area, it is true that a nationally renowned psychologist, with the appropriate expertise, who will truly do an outstanding job, can readily be found. But if one asks that individual about an important public policy issue in an area that is not directly relevant to his or her expertise, as a 12-year-old might say, "They do not have a clue."

Consider an image of a raft, with seven or eight distinguished psychologists on it, going down the Amazon River. Our colleagues know a considerable amount about their individual areas of expertise. And yet, none of them have ever been on a raft before, let alone on the Amazon River, where there are poisonous snakes, crocodiles, and many other creatures that, simply described, are not the type that one wants to put one's hands near. So this raft, with all of them on it—for none of them can get off—eventually will come to a waterfall. Some of our colleagues will vigorously expound as to why the raft should go right over the waterfall. They will argue, very forcefully, that they know, in their heart of hearts, from their personal experiences, that rafts go over waterfalls. That they should just proceed and see what happens. In this case, however, not only will the raft go over that waterfall, it will go down about 2,000 feet—straight down. Our colleagues are correct. The raft will go down. But none of the occupants will remain on the raft. They will become dinner for this crocodile or perhaps be hung up on a rock waiting for the birds to come. But because this has not been their personal experience, our traveling companions really do not believe the inevitable will happen. They really do not.

Psychology, as a profession, at this point in its evolution (for all of us are on that raft), is in need of individuals who possess the "bigger picture"—specifically, individuals with a public policy perspective. Perhaps they will not be quite as skilled as some of our colleagues about a particular research design, or as knowledgeable about how to conduct specific types of clinical therapies, but they will know something about rafts and waterfalls. We need to listen to individuals who appreciate the notion of "fording rivers," rather than blindly going over the waterfall and then wondering why eventually one hits bottom rather forcefully. Our collective lack of a public policy perspective is what may well be our profession's most significant weakness (DeLeon, 1988).

It is particularly unfortunate that many of us simply do not understand that we need this type of companion. We need colleagues who appreciate the specific place and societal context in which we find ourselves today. We do not need "friends" proclaiming, "Right, I have heard about 'fording.' We all 'hop off' right here and swim. Let the raft go first, and then we will just follow right behind." Or "Let us sit near those crocodiles, they are sound asleep. We'll just sit there for a while and rest." This is the image of our profession we should carry with us as we think about the evolving health care arena. Without question, we are maturing; however, this still is the image that comes to mind. We do not believe that most of our colleagues possess the big picture. Psychologists do not truly appreciate the societal or political context in which they live today.

Our profession is still very young. We are just beginning to mature. Our membership is maturing in both age and numbers. We are maturing in clinical techniques, research methodologies, and administrative responsibilities. Perhaps most significantly, we are finally beginning to mature in the public's eye (Resnick, DeLeon, & VandenBos, in press).

Approximately 2 decades ago, in 1977, the last state in the nation licensed psychologists as independent practitioners—in the terminology of today, as *health care providers*. That was not that long ago. As a youthful and evolving profession, we do not appreciate that it was not that long ago that most other professionals did not know that we existed. They could not, because until we became licensed, we did not exist as a "profession." The notion of having our own "scope of practice" and the concept of being one of the "educated professions"—these simply did not exist for us not that long ago.

Another fundamental concept, the significance of which many of us do not seem to understand, is that as individuals, we are extraordinarily fortunate. Our average income is $68,000; in contrast, our nation's median household income is less than $31,000. Realistically, this means that most of us live in families that possess at least two times the resources of the average American family. Educationally, we have no peer. As psychologists, we possess advanced degrees, with the doctorate taking, on average, more than 7 years to obtain. By comparison, nearly 80% of our nation's adult population possess less than a baccalaureate degree

(79.7%). Other studies suggest that nearly 20% of U.S. adults cannot read; they are functionally illiterate. Psychologists really represent society's elite. And yet, most of us do not realize how truly fortunate we are. Psychology has a major, not a tangential, responsibility to use its education in a manner that directly benefits society. We can no longer passively sit back and expect someone else to fulfill our responsibilities. As individuals, we often act as though we are paraprofessionals, not professionals. We act as though we have no control over our own destiny. Perhaps we view ourselves as an isolated professor in a small department, within a major university. The chair of a psychology department may complain that she or he does not possess the authority to make programmatic decisions. Yet, many psychology departments actually possess greater faculty resources than comparable law schools. Psychology chairs have greater resources than many deans. We often do not act as if we have the resources or the authority. We do not act as though we are an integral component of the university system or, more important, of society.

Even the American Psychological Association (APA) Board of Directors does not seem to appreciate the significance of having psychologists serve in high-level administrative positions, such as president of a university. In those positions, one establishes policy. The former APA treasurer, Judith Albino, was the president of the University of Colorado. At that policy level, she helped establish the priorities for the university and for each of its campuses. She would discuss with us the responsibility and challenges of providing high-quality education to citizens throughout the state, including rural Colorado. She conceptualized using the most up-to-date technology to deliver quality education and quality health care to those who traditionally would not have access. That is the type of dialogue that we should be having at the level of the APA board of directors and at APA's annual conventions. Unfortunately, however, this is quite rare. A defining element of a profession is an appreciation for how fast the world is evolving. By definition, professionals grasp the bigger picture and their societal responsibilities.

Within health care, skilled dermatologists, located at the Tripler Army Medical Center in Hawaii, can today perform quality consultations for patients on Guam. The visual resolution is that clear. The technology exists that allows health care providers and patients to effectively interact even though separated by thousands of miles. We suggest that this technology revolution, and that is what it is, demands a quantitatively different way of conceptualizing how to provide quality health care. It represents both a challenge and an exciting opportunity. Unfortunately, psychology does not appreciate the magnitude of required change, or more concretely, is not capitalizing on the advances in technology in a proactive fashion. There is no limit to how we can evolve as a profession.

However, we must seize the opportunity to develop our own substantive agenda (DeLeon, Sammons, & Sexton, 1995).

The most significant barrier facing psychology today is the profession's collective lack of vision. At times, psychologists can be so verbally assertive that they do not allow others to show us how little they (the psychologists) know. They do not appreciate that psychologists do not see the bigger picture. They simply do not listen to what society is saying. For example, teenage pregnancy has become a major problem in the United States. Of any industrialized nation in the world the United States has the highest incidence of teenage pregnancy. The American Medical Association understands this. The American Academy of Pediatrics understands this. The popular media vividly portrays a major role for the physician in addressing teenage pregnancy. However, teenage pregnancy is a behavioral phenomenon. It is the behavioral scientists who are, and who should be, on the cutting edge of developing prevention programs that work. Psychology should not continue to allow the medical profession to take credit for its accomplishments. The same situation is true for teenage violence and smoking cessation—both represent major public health hazards facing our nation today.

Another fundamental concept, which one serving on Capitol Hill quickly learns to appreciate, is the allocation of economic resources. Psychologist Debra Dunivin, a former APA congressional science fellow, investigated the amount of support provided by Medicare for training physicians. The reports varied considerably, ranging from $9 billion to $26 billion annually. By comparison, over each of the past several years, there has only been $2.5 million appropriated for mental health clinical training. Consider, $2.5 million to be shared by the five core mental health disciplines, contrasted with perhaps as much as $26 billion targeted for medical (and other health provider) training. Not surprisingly, psychology has historically not sought training support from Medicare. A Harvard medical school scholar and expert on stress physiology recently reported that 60% to 80% of visits to physicians involve stress-related problems that patients can help cure with self-care. Where is psychology in this emerging field of stress management? Surely, it has as much, or more to offer than medicine does (DeLeon, Frank, & Wedding, 1995).

The APA Practice and Education directorates are now beginning to address psychology's potential eligibility for Medicare's Graduate Medical Education initiative. However, at the same time, our professional training institutions remain blissfully unaware of what they are missing and what modifications they might ultimately have to make in their training programs to establish eligibility. Our educational institutions simply do not understand the bigger picture. They are not asking for their "fair share" of these substantial training resources. Health psychology, in particular, could be very responsive to Medicare's fundamental mission of providing high-quality health care to the elderly. Yet, as a profession, psychologists continue to be blissfully unaware of what potential training and service delivery resources they are missing.

The National Institutes of Health (NIH) develop an agenda from personal interaction between and among senior staff, and what emerges over the years is a picture of their personal pragmatic priorities. Personal involvement is the key. Our NIH colleague, Norman Anderson, is a perfect example. His behavioral science background will significantly influence how he ultimately recommends that funding be allocated. He may decide to focus on historically underserved populations, or he may not. However, until psychologists pay attention to what senior staff and institute directors believe should be the priorities of their individual institutes at the programmatic policy level, their profession (psychology) will never understand how the NIH is evolving. They will constantly react; they will not be proactive. They must become personally involved with policymakers. Unfortunately, they do not seem to conceptually understanding this.

To cite another concrete example, for the past decade, witnesses on behalf of the National Institute of Dental Research (NIDR) have consistently raised issues that many would consider to be within the domain of psychology. They discussed problems such as getting patients to see a dentist, problems with compliance, and emotional issues surrounding treating children. For NIDR, these are "dental issues"; for psychologists, they represent "behavioral health." Psychology has much to offer to the mission of NIDR. But psychologists must learn to listen to the institute's leadership rather than continuing to ignore this potential source of significant support. The same is also true for each of the other institutes, for example, the National Institute of Child Health and Human Development, the National Cancer Institute, and the National Institute of Nursing Research. The same underlying policy message exists.

Let us now focus on a related evolution occurring within health care: Psychology does not conceptually understand the significance of the fact that today 25% of doctoral level nursing faculty possess their degree in psychology. Over the next decade, there will be an increasing number of advanced-practice nurses, trained by these behavioral scientists, functioning throughout the health care arena in a wide variety of roles. Many aspects of advanced-practice nursing are, by definition, health psychology. But at the conceptual level, psychologists are not thinking about where the health care system is going. Psychologists do not understand that "they are we." We do not routinely have the type of interdisciplinary discussions that we should have. Once again, the only barrier preventing psychology from participating in these crucial interdisciplinary discussions is ourselves. We talk to ourselves excessively, but not about what is evolving in the real world. We do not systematically address society's needs, and we do not personally interact with those who set health care policy.

In many ways, psychologists seem to professionally agree that the American Medical Association should claim teenage pregnancy and teenage violence as their exclusive domain. They do not publicly proclaim the importance of the psychosocial aspects of working with families with diabetes. We psychologists do not insist that because more than half of the visits to primary health care providers are for psychosocial reasons, our practitioners should be actively involved. We do not argue in the public domain that a very high percentage of emergency room visits are primarily for psychological reasons or have psychological underpinnings. Perhaps we simply do not know how to assert our clinical value. We do not seem to even try. We often do not act like professionals, willing to accept clinical responsibilities. Yet we are starting to learn. Conceptually, we are beginning to think of ourselves as one of the health professions and as possessing a societal responsibility. This represents real progress. Over the years, psychologists have begun to understand that this nation's elected officials will be responsive to the needs of those who truly address society's problems—if and when they can see the contributions being made.

SOLUTIONS

Psychologists must become more personally involved in the public policy/political process. They must understand that their societal responsibilities include becoming intimately involved with those who establish public policy, including health care policy. From a policy perspective, mental health care is but a very small component of health care. Health care represents approximately one third of our nation's economy, and providers per se are only a subset of the total industry (Prospective Payment Assessment Commission, 1996; Samuelson, 1995).

We recently reviewed a report from the Library of Congress (1995) describing the composition of the 104th Congress (1995–1996). We were interested in learning how many members of Congress actually possessed a health care background. In the Senate, there is one physician and one social worker; 2% of the Senate have any firsthand experience as health care providers. In contrast, 54% of the Senate possess law degrees. If one has taught or taken a course in law school, it becomes readily evident that lawyers do not think the way psychologists think. The legislative process, in particular, expects the active participation of those with opposing views. It can be quite adversarial. Personal involvement is critical. In the Senate, those who establish health care policies definitely do not have any personal experience in providing mental health care. And unless they took a course in psychology at the undergraduate level or read about our research in the popular media, they may not be familiar with psychology.

In the House of Representatives, a very similar picture exists. The House has 4 physicians (1 of whom is a psychiatrist), 1 nurse, 2 dentists, 2 veterinarians, 1 pharmacist, and several social workers. During the last Congress, there was a psychologist, who hopefully will soon return. Of the 435 members in the House of Representatives, less than 15 have a health care background—approximately 3%. Simply stated, we should not expect our nation's elected officials to appreciate the nuances of providing mental health care or the potential broad clinical contribution of psychologists.

We think that one potential long-term solution is the APA Congressional Science Fellowship program. Over the past 2 decades, APA has been able to provide nearly 50 psychologists with the experience of working on Capitol Hill. This is a very positive approach. Not only have members of Congress and their staff been exposed to our colleagues' psychological expertise, a significant segment of the psychology profession has gained a firsthand glimpse of the political/public policy process. After their year of experience, the Fellows return to their universities and other employment settings, able to educate other psychologists about the all-important public policy process.

It has been our observation, however, that many of our colleagues often do not fully capitalize on the potential inherent in working on Capitol Hill. Over the years, there have been a number of psychologists working on Capitol Hill, on the personal staff, committee staff, and even as committee staff directors. Most of them refuse to identify themselves as psychologists and become quite defensive if the issue is raised.

We really do not understand this phenomena and sincerely hope that the APA Congressional Science Fellowship program will ultimately change this over time. Our training institutions must begin to systematically address the public policy process in a way that institutionally develops pride in public service. As psychologists, we should be proud of our profession and of what we can contribute to society. Unfortunately, too often we do not act proud. We do not regularly talk to elected officials or to policymakers in this program.

OPPORTUNITIES

Over the years, it has been extraordinarily difficult for psychology to convince the leadership of the NIH of the importance of the behavioral sciences to their fundamental mission. This is a very important objective, however, both for psychology and for our nation. Historically, almost all of the NIH directors have been physicians. Today there is a nurse, a dentist, and finally a psychologist. We must continue to collectively work to educate the NIH and those elected officials with oversight responsibilities regarding the importance of our behavioral science expertise. We can learn from professional nursing, now with its own National Institute of Nursing Research.

We must also learn to work collaboratively with those administrative psychologists who, for example, serve as directors of state mental health systems. Today a psychologist is the head of the state of California's mental health system. That governor understands the importance of psychology. Governors do not appoint individuals to their cabinet that they do not respect. Across the nation, there are a number of psychologists who serve in high-level administrative policy-setting positions. In all candor, however, we do not know very many of them. They frequently do not hold themselves out as psychologists, and equally important, we do not give them visibility within the profession.

By contrast, when a psychiatrist or other medical specialist is appointed to these important policy positions, they act as if they value their own profession. A physician was the director of the federal Office of Health Promotion and Disease Prevention. His strictly medical orientation was always evident. Behavioral health, however, was another matter. Psychologists must learn from the physicians. They must stop putting themselves down and, instead, learn to value their own expertise.

As an example, medicine can always find a position for their younger colleagues and actively mentors them for future leadership positions. Psychology does not do this. We do not find positions for new psychology graduates; we do not provide them with the experience of being deputy director of a community mental health center or health department.

We were very pleased, and in all candor quite surprised, that at the Opening Ceremony of the 1995 APA convention, a psychologist represented the mayor of New York. She had an impressive presence. What other psychologists are in potentially high visibility leadership positions? As a profession, psychologists must learn to value administrative expertise and to hold themselves out as possessing such. The clinical application of psychological knowledge is extraordinarily important. We must ensure that our nation's health care systems readily use our expertise.

Sometimes personal experiences speak volumes. Emergency rooms, to cite but one graphic example, are a place where the psychosocial aspects of health care are extraordinarily important. A decade ago, it became necessary for Patrick H. DeLeon's daughter to use an emergency room. At first, they said that she would be dead by morning, then that she would be brain-damaged for life. She is fine today, but the experience will never be forgotten. That is not the way anyone should be treated in an emergency room. Parents do not know how to deal with those blunt messages. No doubt there were well-intentioned professionals in that emergency room; however, they definitely did not know how to handle the psychosocial aspects of dealing with parents, especially those who had to explain to a sibling what might happen to his baby sister. Psychology has much to offer to families, and they must ensure that their expertise is utilized. There are many opportunities throughout the generic health care arena—far more than many of us appreciate.

One of the aspects of Robert J. Resnick's APA presidency that we have particularly come to admire has been his willingness to use the office on behalf of all of psychology. He has been willing to reach out and meet with people. From the very beginning, he has been particularly sensitive to the needs of our colleagues within the Department of Defense, perhaps because his son was on active duty. He has said to our military colleagues, "Tell me how you can use me!" That unusual message has been well received, and Dr. Resnick was recently awarded the U.S. Army's highest civilian recognition. Earlier APA presidents, such as Jack Wiggins, have also been willing to reach out and use the prestige of the office. President-Elect Dorothy Cantor will undoubtedly continue this tradition, particularly in addressing women's issues and inner-city needs. Although we do not really know how to most effectively use the office of our presidency, we are learning. Our association's leadership is actively attempting to have a real impact on society and on our nation's decision makers. We suggest that the availability of health care in our nation will continue to be a major agenda for the administration and for both nationally and locally elected officials in the years to come—an excellent forum for meaningful input.

The larger societal context is that in spite of managed care trends, our nation's health care costs continue to escalate faster than almost any other segment of the economy. The most recent figures suggest that in 1995, health spending exceeded $1 trillion for the first time in history (Prospective Payment Assessment Commission, 1996; Samuelson, 1995). Something has to be done. We are currently in the midst of major changes, and accordingly, we really cannot know with any sense of certainty how our health delivery system will ultimately evolve.

From the beginning of his administration, President Clinton made the enactment of comprehensive national health care reform legislation his highest priority. He has not yet succeeded, but in each of his State of the Union addresses, he continues to stress the importance of this issue. The Republican majority have made it clear that in time, they will have their own major health care legislation. Yet, it is too early to predict specifically how curtailing health care costs and increasing health care access will ultimately relate to reducing the national deficit. However, health care costs cannot continue to escalate. Radical changes are upon us.

Hopefully, we will soon see an era of systematically using objective data to make clinical decisions and to establish programmatic priorities. However, psychologists must not ignore our profession's history of aggressively fighting to retain the status quo. How dare someone try to tell our practitioners that what they have been doing for 40 years will not be reimbursed in the future? Listen to the intensity of our internal debates, particularly those surrounding managed care. Many of our practitioners simply refuse to understand that the world is moving forward. We refuse to understand the significance of clinical guidelines being required of the various medical specialties, including surgery. What has been happening throughout the generic health care arena is now just beginning to be experienced in mental health. Accountability is coming. Unfortunately, a sizable proportion of our practitioners simply refuse to believe the inevitable.

One of the important policy concepts that psychology is beginning to understand is that governmental entities will pay for services rendered by those health professionals whose training they have supported. The current buzzword is *primary health care provider*. Where are the training dollars for the next generation of primary health care providers? How will federal research activities relate to their practices? We are beginning to look at those federal statutes that address primary care to find out where, in fact, training resources exist. We are finally asking how we might obtain our fair share of these resources: Title VII of the health professions legislation and Medicare.

Over the years, we have been quite successful in having psychology statutorily recognized under an increasing number of health professions initiatives. This is very important. Few of us have ever read the federal health statutes or sought to obtain a comprehensive understanding of the Public Health Service Act. But as we have moved forward on new initiatives, two areas of caution have surfaced. First, we have not been careful in addressing how Congress actually defines our services. During the recent revisions of the health professions legislation, we were defined as being almost exclusively involved in mental health practice, expressly on par with social work and marriage and family therapists. In our judgment, this potentially very narrow definition is one that at the policy level, represents a distinct step backwards. A second concern is the apparent lack of interest in pursuing health professions initiatives that has been demonstrated by our professional training institutions.

To cite another graphic example, all of us are aware of the tremendous need for quality psychological care within our nation's nursing homes. Over the years, the administration, the Senate Special Committee on Aging, and the Institute of Medicine have released impressive reports noting the high incidence of residents with mental disorders; the importance of effectively addressing behavioral and environmental issues, including resident perception of social isolation; and, specifically, the relevance of biofeedback treatment for those being considered for admission. Similarly, numerous scientific studies have raised serious questions regarding the appropriateness of psychotropic medication usage (DeLeon & Wiggins, 1996).

Our nation's medical and nursing schools have come forth with proposals for "model teaching nursing homes," which would incorporate the most up-to-date clinical and research knowledge into patient care. At their suggestion, federal (and private foundation) funds have been made available to test out these models. But what psychology programs have been willing to get involved? Which of our schools have proposed a model psychology-based teaching nursing home? If our training institutions would get involved with this societal need, they would find the necessary resources, not only to provide the clinical care that is necessary but also to provide stipends for psychology interns and postdoctoral fellows (residents). When physical or dental care becomes necessary, one would expect the project managers to hire the necessary clinical expertise, not to provide it themselves. But historically, we have not thought this way.

By focusing on society's needs, we will learn that society will take care of us. In the health care arena, there is a tremendous range of possibilities, opportunities, and needs. Throughout the 1995 APA convention, speaker after speaker touched on some of the possibilities; it was fascinating. Our colleagues addressed the psychological needs of those with diabetes, those who require kidney dialysis, those who had premature births, and many other medical problems. However, there was a component missing: the involvement of our training programs. We did not hear our training institutions suggesting that with sufficient resources, they would provide the nation with the next generation of skilled clinicians who could competently care for our sons, daughters, or other loved ones.

Within the federal establishment, there is a programmatic entity entitled "centers of excellence." These represent a vehicle for ensuring a comprehensive, and often interdisciplinary, focus by training institutions on identified problems (or special populations). For example, there are centers of excellence focusing on the elderly, HIV patients, workplace violence, and teenage pregnancy. These represent a visual and tangible component of the federal government's programmatic planning and budgetary process. The Centers for Disease Control and Prevention (CDC) have been particularly adept in using this approach to explore their programmatic priorities. They allow the Department of Health and

Human Services to invest resources in targeted priorities and to promote interest among academic health centers and others in their priorities.

In Hawaii, we are currently interested in having a center of excellence designated to address public health issues surrounding volcanic emissions. Statistics suggest that on one of the Hawaiian islands, when the winds shift, there is a 15% increase in the use of emergency rooms, particularly by children—primarily for respiratory distress. Such a center would be an excellent example of the effectiveness of the public policy/political process in influencing NIH or CDC programmatic priorities. Psychology should similarly be actively involved in developing relevant public policy and public health priorities. Psychologists must learn to systematically focus on society's needs and use their unique expertise. They must learn to conceptualize in a manner that *visibly* allows others to appreciate their potential contributions. And most important, they must become involved in establishing their own agenda, highlighting what psychology has to contribute and sustaining that agenda at the local and national level for a prolonged period of time. By controlling the agenda, psychologists will ultimately serve themselves and society admirably.

For many psychologists, the prescription privilege agenda represents, above all else, a timely social policy agenda (DeLeon, Fox, & Graham, 1991). Psychologists are convinced that to significantly improve the quality of life for individuals either who require psychotropic medication or, perhaps more important, for whom psychotropic medication has been inappropriately prescribed, behavioral scientists must become intimately involved in this clinical decision-making process. The power to prescribe is equally the power not to prescribe or the power to ensure that medications are appropriately used. There is considerable data indicating that, for example, children, the elderly, women, people of color, and those residing in nursing homes, rural America, and inner-city ghettos are often inappropriately medicated.

Those of us supporting the prescription agenda are convinced that psychology's clinical and diagnostic skills can contribute significantly to ensuring that medications are appropriately used when necessary. Support within the profession for this policy agenda has been gradually building over the past decade, and at the 1995 APA Convention, our Council of Representatives, under Dr. Resnick's leadership, formally went on record overwhelmingly supporting prescription authority for appropriately trained psychologists. Five years earlier, at the 1990 Convention, the Council voted to establish an exploratory task force.

One must wonder, however, why so many of our colleagues felt that it was necessary, or appropriate, for the Council to even address this matter. As a profession, we have never adopted a formal Council policy expressing endorsement of biofeedback care, the use of projective techniques, or group therapy, for example. We have always taken the policy position that individual psychologists should not exceed their scope of competence and that our clinicians should be properly trained before engaging in specific clinical interventions. But for many, the pursuit of prescription privileges apparently represents a quantitative shift in psychology's fundamental self-image.

Rather then viewing the movement toward obtaining this particular clinical competence as opening up entirely new marketplaces or as allowing our clinicians to more comprehensively provide quality care, a number of our colleagues have expressed fears of medicalizing psychology and of deserting our fundamental behavioral science heritage. We suggest, in the alternative, that these colleagues have not been really thinking about what would be best for individual patients and, further, that they do not truly appreciate the extent to which our clinicians are currently very broadly involved in the generic health care arena. They really do not understand that as one of the health professions, psychology must be concerned with the patients' whole health picture.

As our practitioners obtain this new clinical responsibility, we will evolve into entirely new arenas, including providing care in nursing homes and ensuring that women have appropriate access to medications. We will undoubtedly develop new psychology specialties. No longer will we be able to ignore the clinical reality that less than 20% of psychotropic medications are provided by practitioners with substantial mental health training. We will instead possess the legal standing to address one of society's pressing needs. This is our responsibility, because we are among the leaders of society. This underlying concept is what we keep forgetting.

To those psychologists who seek to hold us back from obtaining prescription privileges and, thus, from expanding our clinical responsibilities, we would also point out that our profession must be very careful that mental health care per se is not deemed to be merely a very expensive specialty service that, in fact, can be competently provided by a wide range of professionals. Currently, we have considerable difficulty in convincing ourselves, not to mention policymakers, that there really is a qualitative difference between doctoral level providers and those with less training. In an era of constricting costs and finite budgets, why should those who "pay the bills" favor psychologists? More expensive care must be justified. We are facing very stiff competition from both extremes: from psychiatry, which considers us to be "public health hazards," and from lesser trained therapists, who stress how much more expensive we are.

Psychology must become more actively involved in policy-setting positions, thus determining how our expertise can most appropriately be used. Reimbursement-policy decisions will continue to be made, and we must strive to see psychologists actively involved in the decision-making process. Psychologists should seek to testify before the Senate Special Committee on Aging regarding the psychosocial expertise our profession could offer to the elderly. We should expect psychology-training programs to testify about their newest programs designed to improve the quality of life for the elderly. This is where psychology and APA must evolve, into the public policy arena. We must particularly get more active with the popular media, which has always had a major impact on our nation's expectations and priorities.

We have no doubt that our nation's health professions will rise to the occasion. Hopefully, psychology will be among them. Two decades ago, we started working closely with professional nursing. At that time, there were approximately 1,800 certified nurse midwives and several thousand nurse practitioners. Today, it is estimated that there are 50,000–75,000 advanced-practice nurses. Studies from the Office of Technology Assessment clearly indicate that the quality of care provided by advanced-practice nurses is excellent, comparable to that provided by physicians. We would challenge psychology to provide similar data. If psychology does not get actively involved in addressing society's health care needs, others will, and they will do very well. If we do not get involved, in all candor, we doubt that we will be missed. Our nation's health care system will continue to evolve, with or without us. The final choice is ultimately ours.

COMPLEMENTARY THOUGHTS

A Psychological Science Perspective

The questions of what is preventing psychology from being a more significant player in the nation's evolving health care system and what should be done about it have distinct parallels in the world of basic and applied science. Just as our health care providers bemoan the adverse impact of "outside forces" such as insurers, managed care companies, physicians, and politicians on their practice, researchers and academics wring their collective hands over the way psychological science is treated by the media, other disciplines, and the policymakers who control federal research dollars.

The failure of psychologists to grasp the big picture and to project ourselves into it; our lack of full appreciation for what we have to offer society; and our reluctance to get personally involved in the nasty business of advocating in the public arena—self-imposed barriers that limit psychology as *practice*—apply equally to psychological science.

To this list let us add just one more barrier: the culture gap that separates our scientists from our practitioners. Psychological practice should be informed on a continuing basis by psychological science, and vice versa, but we each seem to prefer sticking within our own communities and talking mostly to ourselves. Unless we can find better ways to share our respective knowledge and perspectives on human behavior, and to adopt a problem-solving rather than adversarial approach to controversial issues such as recovered/implanted memories and the criteria for treatment efficacy, we could wind up destroying the credibility of our discipline as both a practice and a science.

Returning to the original list, however, we would like to offer a few examples of barriers as they function outside the health care environment. Medical and nursing schools are not the only places where professional psychologists lose their identity (and we might well have included psychological researchers in epidemiology, neurology, and pediatrics departments among the medical illustrations). Engineering and computer science programs depend heavily on our cognitive and engineering psychologists for expertise in human factors; business schools use industrial/organizational, social, and quantitative psychologists to teach courses in management, organizational behavior, research design, and marketing; and psychologists are central to a host of hybrid programs such as neuroscience, cognitive science, educational technology, and occupational health. Clearly, therefore, other academic disciplines value what psychologists have to offer. One might expect this cross-fertilization to breed greater respect for the discipline than it does. The reason it does not is that our colleagues tend to adapt so completely to their environment that they no longer see themselves as psychologists.

Much the same thing happens in nonacademic settings where some of our scientists find work. They become principal engineers, human–computer interaction specialists, product development managers, or whatever the job title says, which is rarely *Psychologist*. Many even try to obscure the fact that they were trained in psychology, fearing stigmatization! So the opportunity to change psychology's image in the workplace and overcome the health care stereotype is lost because psychologists choose to become something else.

Of course, that same stereotype serves to keep many research psychologists out of these jobs in the first place. The high-tech industries, the communications and transportation fields, service industries, and the burgeoning world of technical training are but a few of the places where psychological expertise is sorely needed but largely unrecognized.

The stereotype barrier is just part of the problem. Another is our limited self-image. Why is not the field (most notably the graduate programs that train psychological scientists) doing more to prepare students for the kinds of applied opportunities that exist in the real world and will grow in the future rather than continuing to produce only traditional academicians for a shrinking market? Why are not faculties doing more to educate themselves and potential employers about these worlds of opportunity? Why are not our science professors building relationships with employing organizations, like the chemists, biologists, and physicists do? Why are we not training graduate students to appreciate the causal relationship between federal science policy and their future prospects as researchers or other career professionals?

The answer is a combination of resistance to change and a lack of vision. Like our health care provider counterparts, psychological scientists tend to adopt a myopic perspective on who they are, which prevents them from conceptualizing what they might be. In a world that is changing as rapidly as ours is, that could be fatal.

To this point, only barriers have been discussed, and no solutions offered. That is because the remedy becomes pretty obvious once one accepts the diagnosis. In a word, psychology needs to get out of some self-imposed ruts and broaden its horizons. As psychologists, we know this sort of change in mindset is a lot easier said than done. But it is high time we got started, and the place to begin is in our graduate schools. The APA Science Directorate has mounted one initiative toward this end, but it is far too early to tell what kind of reception it will receive there. Psychology's role in the twenty-first century, in science as in health care, can be pretty much whatever we choose to make it. If we ever wake up to that fact, our future can be bright indeed. If we do not, we have no one but ourselves to blame. And the clock is ticking.

A Practice Perspective

If we are on the metaphorical raft, the first thing we need to do is determine which way the current is moving. Although this may seem self-evident, we are aware of too many instances in which psychologists paddle upstream against the current. By contrast, if the profession is headed into new directions, we ought to know which way the current is flowing, to take best advantage of it. In other words, moving in the direction of the current and steering the raft to the profession's advantage seems entirely more reasonable than trying to paddle against the current.

In this context, we argue that sticking with a mental health focus for the profession would be akin to paddling against the current. This is not to say that psychology's past mental health focus has been an unimportant one. In fact, it has played a critical role in the profession's development. As a nascent profession, psychology's advocacy work to expand its activities in the mental health arena took advantage of a door that was already slightly open. It made perfect sense to move forward by pushing on that door rather than doors that were completely shut. And we have done quite well by becoming independent mental health providers in all the major publicly funded programs, such as Medicare, CHAMPUS, and Medicaid. The problem, however, is that we too often accept inclusion in the mental health world as our end goal rather than as an interim step on the way to an even more expansive future.

It is time to focus on that next step, a step that will be considerably aided if we are clear in which direction the water's current is flowing. To know that, we must first look at the big picture influencing health care. Despite the failure of Congress to enact a comprehensive health care reform plan, the very creation of the proposal begins to articulate the bigger picture. What is often overlooked is that legislation is only partly intended to stimulate change; it is in larger part intended to codify changes that have already taken place. The bigger picture, then, includes the fact that health care reform has been occurring for at least the past 15–20 years.

Among the significant changes that have been occurring in health care for some time now is the increasing integration and consolidation of the health care system. In other words, previously separate and fragmented pieces of the system are being joined together in the service of economic efficiency. This integration has been fueled over the years by a number of developments. First was the corporatization of health care. This was initially most evident in the for-profit hospital industry, which witnessed previously separate hospitals begin to chain together under one corporate umbrella.

Soon to follow was the rise of one particular form of health care corporate entity: the managed care company. One result of this development has been that previously separate and independent providers have been integrated together in panels or networks. Integration in health care was further facilitated by a period of mergers and acquisitions by health care corporate entities of all types. As one corporation joined with another and then another, greater consolidation in the industry resulted. Finally, we have witnessed legislative efforts at health care reform, which would have codified this integration but which also actually increased integration by virtue of the discussions and activities stimulated by the proposal themselves.

Two major trends of particular relevance to psychology have resulted from this integration. One is a transition from an emphasis on hospitals to a focus on health systems. These health systems, often comprising multiple hospitals as well as group practices, are equipped to provide the entire range of services: outpatient, partial hospitalization, residential treatment, inpatient treatment, after-care services, and even home health care. Because these systems and the services they provide are still usually "gated" by a medical staff organization and credentialing process, psychologists' membership on the medical staff and ability to be credentialed continue as important advocacy goals for the profession. In fact, this is even more important, because without medical staff membership and privileges in a health system format, psychologists stand to be excluded from the entire continuum of care rather than just prevented from providing inpatient treatment.

The other major trend that has resulted from increasing integration of the health care system, and the one that needs emphasizing, is the transition from an emphasis on specialty care to a focus on primary care. This is a particularly relevant direction of the current that psychology's raft must recognize to avoid paddling upstream. Because *primary care* has become somewhat of a buzzword, with multiple meanings, our own operational definition is provided here. For psychology's future directions, *primary care* is characterized broadly as prevention-oriented health care that integrates psychological and physical treatment. It is, without a doubt, much broader than mental health treatment, although it includes such treatment as a component part.

For psychology, we believe the emphasis on primary care is a significant and useful development. By virtue of our training and diverse capabilities, we are, or at least have the capacity to be, primary care providers. Yet those outside of our profession do not always see us as we see ourselves. The rude awakening we received on this point stems from efforts 2 years ago to have psychology included in a program sponsored by the U.S. Public Health Service called Putting Prevention Into Practice. It was a program intended to bring together prevention-oriented health professions in the context of a demonstration project. A letter was written to the PHS making psychology's best case for why we should be included in the program. Although the response to the letter recognized the valuable contribution of psychologists to health care, the PHS indicated that psychology did not meet the designated criteria for inclusion in the program. In particular, health professions who were to be included had to be able to provide immunization services and, according to the PHS, psychology did not. This conclusion seems especially ridiculous considering that 60% of visits to primary care physicians are actually for symptoms created by behavioral and psychological factors! Yet, in the context of the medical model in which health care remains entrenched, immunization equates with an inoculation. In reality, we have much work to do to change this unfortunate stereotype.

While we are affecting policy change, we must be emphasizing the actual primary care work psychologists do. We must continue to perform primary care activities. We must increase our work in primary care settings. And we must increase our collaboration with primary care providers. Only then will we begin to be seen by others as we see ourselves.

The last point we want to make has to do with one other obstacle to psychologists being recognized as true health care providers rather than as just mental health providers: The long-standing separation of physical health from behavioral and mental health, particularly for reimbursement purposes. Despite a generation of research that supports a decrease in health care costs as a result of psychological interventions, as long as behavioral and mental health care are carved-out of health care, the medical-cost offset can never be realized. Our ability to have an impact on health care in this way is also hampered by an insurance industry that views the financial bottom line on an annual or even quarterly basis. As a result, the industry sees little benefit to integrating psychological services with physical health services if the immediate costs go up and only create savings over time. Even Congress makes budget decisions from annual "scorable savings." In other words, unless savings are realized in the same budget as money is appropriated, cost savings cannot be accounted for.

Part of psychology's work, then, needs to target the decision makers, who must be persuaded of the overall and long-term benefit of including psychological services as a central part of health care services. The Practice Directorate of APA is presently initiating a demonstration project with Blue Cross and Blue Shield of Massachusetts to show the health and cost benefit of integrating psychological services within the traditional medical services for the treatment of breast cancer patients. Not only do we expect better overall health outcomes to result from the integration of services, but the actuarial model on which the project is based predicts a savings of $5 in health care costs for each $1 spent on psychological services. Armed with data such as we hope this project yields, we believe we can steer psychology's raft in a beneficial direction, aided, rather than impeded, by the current.

An Educational Perspective

From the barriers that can be identified as limiting the roles that psychologists should rightfully assume in the future of health care provision, three separate yet related problems immediately come to mind. First, there is poor recognition of the myriad of roles we currently fulfill and the amount of education and training that we represent. Whether we are delivering services, conducting research, teaching, consulting, or involved in administration, we bring to bear access to a whole body of psychological literature on human behavior and the knowledge that flows from that vast amount of information. Furthermore, training in clinical psychology is unique in its combination of practitioner as well as scientist skills, meaning that not only can we deliver services according to a variety of treatment models but also we are experienced in the theoretical development of these models, their empirical validation, and in training others to use them.

Psychology provides extensive training for many of the health care providers from other disciplines who are receiving funding for their training under legislation from which we are excluded. This illustrates the dangerous and defeating ways in which a lack of recognition of our skills and limited information about our position as the only doctoral trained mental health provider limit our roles. These factors contribute, in no small way, to significant decreases in the level of funding for psychology training, which is a second important barrier. Shutting down the pipeline of new psychologist providers and researchers further restricts the potential for continued contributions to health care that have historically been made by members of our field.

A third barrier is that of the conflicts between various players in the health care arena that divert energy and resources away from expanded and improved delivery of services. Interorganizational conflicts between national groups representing psychology often arise from historical events having little to do with common goals of enhancing the provision of psychological services, supporting the development and application of psychological science, and facilitating the production of well-trained psychologists. Intraorganizational struggles, among scientist, practitioner, and educator, to gain adequate resources for accomplishing our mission can result in a disconcerting lack of coordination of effort on issues of advocacy, public education, and membership participation. Finally, interdisciplinary conflicts between providers of health care, and especially between those disciplines traditionally involved in the delivery of mental health care, are rooted in historical differences in philosophy and training and in more recent financial restraints imposed on payment for services. These dividing issues cause us to fail to unite effectively in seeking a common goal, that is, increased access and funding for services and the removal of limitations to the delivery of care.

Solutions to these barriers include the provision of information to the public and to our nation's policymakers about psychology and its many contributions to health care. Advocacy aimed at increasing funding for training of psychologists and psychological research and seeking inclusion of psychologists as service providers is crucial. Links between organizations and individuals who share common ground in the provision of health care services, and common goals in the advancement of health care delivery to keep pace with the demands of the next century, must be developed and sustained. Continued leadership by our national governance in the development of a targeted and coordinated agenda is our most powerful weapon against further erosions in psychology's full participation in twenty-first century health care.

The issue of prescription privileges for psychologists is illustrative of how these barriers and solutions occur. As suggested earlier, arguments against prescription privileges are fueled by a lack of information about how psychotropic medications are currently being prescribed (i.e., mostly by general practice physicians with little mental health background or training); about the shortage of psychiatrically trained physicians, especially for underserved populations; and about the nature and extent of proposed training programs for psychologists. Furthermore, providing information to dispel some of the myths about prescription privileges leads to attitude change about the issue. Conflicts on all fronts have been probably the most consistent aspect of this endeavor. However, advocacy has successfully kept the issue alive and evolving and has given those of us involved with the experience a chance to demonstrate that the training of psychologists to prescribe is a feasible goal. Important links with those involved in a similar goal should be more fully explored. Clearly, this new role for psychologists offers an opportunity to expand the way in which health care is delivered.

A Public Interest Perspective

The American Psychological Association's Public Interest Directorate has been involved in several projects that attempt to show directly the importance of psychology in health. For example, at the request of the Committee on Women in Psychology, the Women's Programs Office convened a conference on Psychosocial and Behavioral Factors in Women's Health in May 1994. They are planning the second conference, a follow-up to the first, for September 1996. The September 1996 conference is titled "Psychosocial and Behavioral Factors in Women's Health: Research, Prevention, Treatment, and Service Delivery in Clinical and Community Settings." One of the major goals of these interdisciplinary conferences is to highlight the importance of psychosocial and behavioral factors in all aspects of women's health, including etiology, prevention, treatment, and rehabilitation. Although the specific focus is women's health, the points made are relevant to health in general.

In keeping with the conference goals, the Women's Programs Office is trying to broaden the definition of health to include psychosocial and behavioral factors. According to the U.S. Public Health Service, 7 of the 10 leading causes of death in the United States could be substantially reduced if people would change their behavior, namely adhere to medical regimens, eat proper diets, stop smoking, exercise, and stop abusing alcohol and other drugs. Psychology is the field that addresses behavior and behavior change and compliance with medical regimens. Moreover, research is beginning to show the importance of psychological well-being for recovery from major illnesses, including cardiovascular disease. Additionally, an accumulating body of research suggests that immune-related disease processes and immunological functioning are affected by psychological stress. Relatedly, psychological interventions have been shown to be effective in treating immune-related disease. These accumulating scientific data clearly indicate the importance of psychology in the treatment of, and recovery from, disease.

Another important area of women's health that is often overlooked is women's victimization in intimate relationships. A large number of women who report to emergency rooms are there because of intimate violence, yet health care providers continue to fail to ask about violence, even when there are clear indicators. Therefore, this issue is included in the women's health conference.

Violence in the United States, whether domestic violence, youth violence, or other types of violence, cannot be solved by legal and criminal interventions. The Public Interest Directorate has been involved in addressing broader issues of violence. Psychosocial factors and interventions are also critical and must be addressed. The Male Violence Against Women Task Force and the Youth Violence Commission were organized to address these issues. Reports that shed light on these issues are available from both groups.

The Public Interest Directorate also has been very involved in the issue of workplace, or occupational, stress. Over the past 6 or more years, they have been working with the National Institute of Occupational Safety and Health in a series of conferences on occupational stress, to increase the involvement of psychologists and to clearly show the importance of psychological stress in workplace issues. This focus has included highlighting the work, stress, and health connection. Again, the our goal is to showcase the importance of psychology to critical aspects of health and well-being. The message is not only for psychologists and other professionals, but for the media, government personnel, legislators, and the lay public.

A Prescribing Psychologist's Perspective

The authority to prescribe elevates a psychologist to the status of a full-service mental health provider capable not only of providing the traditional roles of psychological assessment and mental health counseling but also of providing the full spectrum of care for patients with mental disorders. This "one-stop mental health provider" not only makes good economic sense but also simplifies access problems and enhances the continuity of care for our patients. However, even given the obvious benefit to patients, the public sector, and the health care industry, significant barriers to prescriptive authority for psychologists remain.

One of the greatest potential benefits of psychologists prescribing is increased access for a number of underserved populations in the United States. In spite of the nearly $1 trillion spent on health care each year in this country, there continues to be large populations whose mental health needs are underserved. One of the largest of these populations is in rural America. In 90% of rural hospitals, where psychiatry is not present, who does the prescribing of psychotropics? Surveys (DeLeon, Sammons, & Sexton, 1995) show that it is probably someone who has not had sufficient training to accurately diagnose a mental disorder, and who knows relatively little about psychotropics for specific mental disorders. Even when the proper medication is prescribed, appropriate dosing is seldom attained. Additionally, 66% of the counties in the United States have no psychiatrists. In the state of Wyoming, one child psychiatrist might travel several hundred miles for consultations concerning pharmacologic intervention for children with mental disorders.

Another underserved group is the chronically mentally ill, a large contingent of our homeless population. In their 1990 report, the National Alliance of the Mentally Ill and the Public Citizen Health Research Group recommended that because psychiatrists have abandoned the public sector, psychologists, nurse practitioners, and physician assistants should be given special training and allowed to prescribe. The National Alliance of the Mentally Ill, with nationally recognized experts on the needs of the chronically mentally ill, continues to recommend that psychologists move aggressively to fill this significant health care void.

In contrast to our underserved populations, the United States also has overserved, or at least overmedicated, populations. For example, the use of Ritalin for "diagnosed" attention deficit disorder has reached an alarming rate, with as many as 15% (DeLeon, Sammons, & Sexton, 1995) of children in some elementary schools on this medication. This rate is in stark contrast to the 3% to 5% that the *Diagnostic and Statistical Manual of Mental Disorders* (American Psychiatric Association, 1994) suggests is the actual prevalence of ADD in our youth. Consider the value of prescribing psychologists who could accurately diagnose, use appropriate behavioral interventions, and also provide adjunctive pharmacologic therapy, including discontinuing drugs for incorrectly diagnosed children.

The elderly present a different type of challenge—sometimes underserved and sometimes overserved. Elderly individuals constitute 12% of our population but consume 40% of all psychotropics, primarily sedatives (DeLeon, Sammons, & Sexton, 1995). In our nursing homes, for example, a staggering 40% of the patients receive psychotropics

(DeLeon, Sammons, & Sexton, 1995). It is truly difficult to believe that the rate of mental illness among the elderly is that much greater than in the general population. In fact, the problem of overmedication for our elderly population has been addressed in the literature for years, with little apparent improvement. If one considers that by 2020, the number of licensed drivers over the age of 75 will double and that a significant percentage of these drivers are likely to be on some type of sedating medication, the roads will indeed be a hazardous place.

Solving the problem of unmet mental health care needs in our country will not be easy. Only one in three patients with a major depressive disorder seeks treatment. In the primary care setting, where these patients are most often seen, the diagnosis of depression is missed in about 55% of the cases (DeLeon, Sammons, & Sexton, 1995). These patients often present with chronic headaches, back pain, or gastrointestinal disturbances. And because their depression is often not diagnosed, it is often not treated. Thus, prescribing psychologists collaborating as mental health consultants would be an invaluable addition to the primary care team.

All indications are that these disparities in mental health care will only get worse if current trends continue. As the number of psychiatric patients increases, there are fewer psychiatrists to treat them. In the past 10 years, the medical profession has seen a significant decline, from 10% to 4%, in the number of medical school graduates that have chosen psychiatry as their specialty. With the "graying of America," the increased use of psychotropics, and the attrition of psychiatrists, the need for competent, comprehensive mental health care providers will only become greater.

What can psychologists do? The American Psychological Association's Ad Hoc Task Force on Psychopharmacology recommends that all psychologists receive one of three levels of training in psychopharmacology. The lowest level of training could best be completed in graduate school, with approximately 50 classroom hours.

The second level, possibly termed *collaborative practice*, would require more in-depth training and would prepare the psychologist to assist physicians, particularly primary care providers, in developing and monitoring medication-care plans for patients in need of psychotropic therapy. The third level would require considerably more classroom and practicum training and would prepare a psychologist for prescriptive privileges.

The opportunities are growing. Today, many physicians call on psychologists' knowledge to help them in selecting and managing the use of psychotropic agents. Managed health care will likely expand this already common practice. Because greater than 60% of all mental health patients are pharmacologically treated by nonpsychiatrists, the opportunity for collaborative-practice psychologists is great.

Across the country, psychologists are making progress in overcoming some of the barriers to obtaining prescriptive privileges. Programs to train psychologists to prescribe are already in the development process. Furthermore, a number of states have already completed or are working toward legislative action to license psychologists to prescribe. Those few psychologists who have earned prescriptive privileges know well the barriers but have successfully navigated around them. The needs are obvious and the opportunities abundant—it is now up to psychology to make them happen!

REFLECTIONS

Although a relatively young profession, psychology is rapidly maturing in numbers and breadth (i.e., scope) of practice. The next step is for the field to appreciate the importance of developing a broad vision, one that includes affirmatively addressing society's pressing needs. This is true for all aspects of psychology, including science, practice, education, and public interest. Our field possesses unlimited opportunities; the barriers are internal and self-imposed. Society is undergoing major and rapid changes; the challenge for psychology is to become a proactive participant in these developments. The future for psychology will be what we make it, no more and no less.

REFERENCES

American Psychiatric Association. (1994). *Diagnostic and statistical manual of mental disorders* (4th ed.). Washington, DC: Author.

DeLeon, P. H. (1988). Public policy and public service: Our professional duty. *American Psychologist, 43,* 309–315.

DeLeon, P. H., Fox, R. E., & Graham, S. R. (1991). Prescription privileges: Psychology's next frontier?

DeLeon, P. H., Frank, R. G., & Wedding, D. (1995). Health psychology and public policy: The political process. *Health Psychology, 14,* 493–499.

DeLeon, P. H., Sammons, M. T., & Sexton, J. L. (1995). Focusing on society's real needs: Responsibility and prescription privileges? *American Psychologist, 50,* 1022–1032.

DeLeon, P. H., & Wiggins, J. G. (1996). Prescription privileges for psychologists. *American Psychologist 51*(3), 225–229.

Library of Congress. (1995, May). CRS *report for Congress—Membership of the 104th Congress: A profile* (95-205 GOV). Washington, DC: Author.

Prospective Payment Assessment Commission. (1996, June). *Medicare and the American health care system*. (Report to Congress). Washington, DC: U.S. Government Printing Office.

Resnick, R. J., DeLeon, P. H., & VandenBos, G. R. (in press). Evolution of professional issues in psychology: Training standards, legislative recognition, and boundaries of practice. In J. R. Matthews & C. E. Walker (Eds.), *Beginning skills and professional issues in clinical psychology*. Needham Heights, MA: Allyn & Bacon.

Samuelson, R. J. (1995, October 25). Managed-care revolution. *The Washington Post*, p. A19.

INDEX

ABOUT THE EDITORS

Robert J. Resnick, PhD, is Professor Emeritus of Psychiatry and Pediatrics and former Chair, Division of Clinical Psychology, Health Sciences Center, Virginia Commonwealth University. He is presently Professor of Psychology at Randolph-Macon College and maintains a pediatric health psychology practice. Dr. Resnick has been the recipient of the American Psychological Association's (APA) Division of Clinical Psychology Award for Distinguished Contributions to Clinical Psychology, the Society of Pediatric Psychology's Lee Salk Distinguished Service Award, the Department of the Army's Outstanding Civilian Service Medal, and the APA Award for Contributions to Applied Psychology as a Professional Practice. He is a Diplomate in Clinical Psychology and a Distinguished Practitioner in the National Academy of Practice. Dr. Resnick has held numerous elected offices in the APA, including the 1995–1996 presidency. He serves on the editorial boards of several journals and has published and presented widely in the areas of attention deficits and health policy.

Ronald H. Rozensky, PhD, is the Associate Chairperson of Psychiatry and Chief Psychologist at the Evanston Hospital. He is a Professor of Psychiatry and Behavioral Sciences and Adjunct Associate Professor of Psychology at Northwestern University and Medical School. Dr. Rozensky is a Diplomate in Clinical Psychology and a Distinguished Practitioner in the National Academy of Practice. He is founding editor of the *Journal of Clinical Psychology in Medical Settings* (Plenum) and coeditor of the *Handbook of Clinical Psychology in Medical Settings*. Dr. Rozensky is a past president of the Illinois Psychological Association and is a member of the APA's Council of Representatives. He received a 1995 APA Heiser Presidential Award in behalf of Professional Psychology. He serves as the APA's representative to the Joint Commission on Accreditation of Healthcare Organizations. Dr. Rozensky has published numerous chapters and articles on such topics as professional issues, credentialing, trauma, and health psychology.